The Politics of Postal Transformation
Modernizing Postal Systems in the Electronic and Global World

The postal sector is a multi-billion dollar set of activities that touches billions of lives daily and continues to be one of the world's largest employers. Until recently all Posts were monopolies owned by governments in order to maintain a universal postal service. However, in response to technological and international competition as well as public disenchantment with postal subsidies and inefficiencies, governments have embraced a range of new strategies.

In *The Politics of Postal Transformation* Robert Campbell investigates and analyses the most important policy innovations in recent years as countries struggle to create a postal regime that matches domestic political expectations with international and technological realities. Through extensive interviews with numerous key government, regulatory, postal, and union officials in North America, Europe, and Australasia, he identifies four models or strategies, each reflecting particular national characteristics and ambitions: from privatization (Netherlands, Germany) and deregulation (Finland, Sweden, New Zealand) to increased national support (France) and mixed strategies (UK, Australia).

Campbell's comparative analysis provides a backdrop for a set of recommendations for policy makers and lays the foundation for informed speculation about future international postal developments and the possible domination of the system by a select group of postal behemoths.

ROBERT M. CAMPBELL is dean of arts and professor of political science at Wilfrid Laurier University.

The Politics of Postal Transformation

*Modernizing Postal Systems
in the Electronic and Global World*

ROBERT M. CAMPBELL

McGill-Queen's University Press
Montreal & Kingston · London · Ithaca

© McGill-Queen's University Press 2002
ISBN 0-7735-2284-0 (cloth)
ISBN 0-7735-2368-5 (paper)

Legal deposit first quarter 2002
Bibliothèque nationale du Québec

Printed in Canada on acid-free paper

This book has been published with the help of grants
from the Office of the Dean of Research and Graduate
Studies at Wilfrid Laurier University, The Donner
Canadian Foundation and McGill-Queen's University
Press.

McGill-Queen's University Press acknowledges the
support of the Canada Council for the Arts for its
publishing program. It also acknowledges the financial
support of the Government of Canada through the
Book Publishing Industry Development Program
(BPIDP).

**National Library of Canada Cataloguing
in Publication Data**

Campbell, Robert M. (Robert Malcolm), 1950–
   The politics of postal transformation: modernizing
   postal systems in the electronic and global world.
   Includes bibliographical references and index.
   ISBN 0-7735-2284-0 (bnd)
   ISBN 0-7735-2368-5 (pbk)
   1. Postal service – Government policy. I. Title.
   HE6071.C34 2002   383′.4   C2001-902794-X

Typeset in New Baskerville 10/12
by Caractéra inc., Quebec City

Contents

Preface

When I completed my book *The Politics of the Post: Canada's Postal Service from Public Service to Privatization* in 1994, I would not have dreamed that I would write another book on postal matters in this lifetime. *The Politics of the Post* was the culmination of six years of research and writing on the Canadian postal system. The book was reasonably well received by postal authorities, analysts, and academics as a comprehensive analysis of the evolution of the Canadian postal system. I felt that I had written what I had to offer about postal matters and should move on to other matters.

Three years later, I was beginning a sabbatical stay in Montreal when I began to receive telephone calls from the media asking me to comment on the looming postal strike. I had not followed postal matters in the intervening years to any great extent, and I needed to get updates on developments if I were to offer informed responses to the media. I travelled to Ottawa to be updated by my contacts at Canada Post Corporation (CPC) and the Canadian Union of Postal Workers (CUPW). I was struck by a number of issues during these briefings, which stimulated the writing of this book.

First, Canada Post continued to operate in an odd, quasi-regulatory environment that had not changed or developed from the late 1980s. Its features were clearly dysfunctional for Canada Post's managers, the shareholder (the government), and postal customers. Canada Post's responsibilities and authority had become increasingly opaque and inappropriate as evolutions in markets and technology changed its working and business environment. This unsatisfactory regulatory context seemed to me to be exacerbating Canada Post's uncertain existence in the increasingly competitive and high-tech communications market, and had made business and labour-management issues fraught and uncertain. The negotiations crisis of 1997 looked all too predictable as a result.

Second, after its election in 1993, the Liberal government had initiated a process to review Canada Post's mandate. A one-person mandate review, chaired by George Radwanski, held public hearings, received submissions, carried out research, and submitted a report in which it made numerous recommendations to the government. The review process had some limited salutary effects. Overall, though, it created more problems than it solved. When I arrived in Ottawa in the fall of 1997, the government's response to the mandate review remained partial and incomplete – and closure did not arrive until late 1998. I was struck by the degree to which Canada Post's evolution seemed to have stalled during this extended process and how the postal scene lacked coherence or a sense of purpose.

Third, in the process of being updated, I became aware of a number of postal developments that were taking place abroad in the 1990s – developments that seemed to be genuinely progressive and creative and that seemed to be leaving Canada Post behind in the competitive and evolutionary race. These international developments were sketched out in a number of consultants' reports as well as in a book produced by Coopers and Lybrand entitled *Postal Performance: The Transformation of a Global Industry*, edited by John Dowson, Edward Horgan, and T.W. Parker. Few postal observers or actors on the Canadian scene seemed to be aware of these developments.

Fourth, I was impressed by the extent to which Canada Post had transformed itself – in reasonably successful terms – into a business organization that was trying hard to serve its clients. Notwithstanding Cassandra-like anticipation of the death of the letter in the electronic age, Canada Post had become an important communications partner for thousands and thousands of both large and small firms and organizations. It provided them with relatively inexpensive, high-quality, and technologically sophisticated communications products and services. This was confirmed as the strike loomed in November 1997. On the other hand, I was struck by how postal matters continued to be pitched by policy makers in relatively traditional terms – unlike, say, in Australia, New Zealand, or Scandinavia, where the Post was conceptualized within the competitiveness framework as a potential contributor to an economy's comparative advantage.

By the time I felt comfortable answering the media's questions about the impending strike, I had been begun thinking about postal matters in a different way than in the early 1990s. Moreover, I had been seduced into considering a new postal project – in comparative terms and within the competitiveness framework. The broad contours of the project would comprise a comparative examination of the regulatory and governance environments of a number of the most successful postal regimes, by way of providing concrete analysis and advice about the Canadian postal situation. Given what I had learned in the fall of 1997, I was reasonably certain that there was a correlation between the character of a postal regime's political-regulatory environment and its corporate and social performance. I was also certain that a country's postal performance remained a substantial contributor to its economic efficiency and competitiveness and the fabric of its social life. The project would thus have a number of dimensions. First, it would seek to move postal discussions into a different conceptual space by considering postal activity in the competitiveness context. Second, by way of seeking alternatives to Canadian postal arrangements, it would comprise a comparative examination of the accomplishments of the most successful postal regimes. Third, it would address the lacunae and drift in the Canadian postal policy scene by examining their causes and by providing alternative approaches.

This project began from a dead start in late 1997 and it would not have got off the ground without the advice and support of a number of kind and generous individuals. I will list below the various people around the world who have helped me in my work over the last three years. But at the origins of the project, a number of people played a special role. One of the first persons I called at Canada Post was a past student of mine, Greg Crevier. Greg directed me to the comparative studies, reports, and books about postal developments in other countries, and this opened up a myriad of avenues for me to explore. Second, Geoff Bickerton and Kathie Steinhoff at CUPW introduced me to a number of people on the international scene, including Jim Sauber at the National Association of Letter Carriers in the United States; Jim had a wealth of international information and contacts, which he generously shared with me. Third, three people at Canada Post contributed crucially to the momentum and progress of the project at its origin and their genuine excitement and enthusiasm helped to get the research ball rolling. Doug Long in the Communications Office was assigned to help me navigate my way through the corporation and to introduce me to its personnel. In the process, he worked miracles in ensuring that I rediscovered who was who and where, and he worked very hard and with purpose to get my schedule in shape. Hank Klassen was completing his career at Canada Post when I met him in the fall of 1997. He provided me with access to the experience, wisdom, and knowledge that he had gained through the evolution of the entire modern postal era, from Post Office Department through corporatization and modernization. More than any single individual, he convinced me to take my research into the comparative and international domains. Gordon Ferguson, strategic thinker par excellence and now also corporate secretary, became an intellectual mentor and guru for me and, at the start of the project, introduced me to a number of postal people abroad. Finally, the project could not have been attempted without financial support. The process of researching and writing this book was supported financially by two organizations, the Social Sciences and Humanities Research Council and the Donner Foundation. The first has given me much assistance over the years, assistance that enabled my research into *The Politics of the Post* and that makes possible my ongoing work on the Canadian scene. The Donner Canadian Foundation gave me the generous funding I required to travel widely for research and interview purposes and thus pursue the comparative dimension of the project. I am particularly grateful to Sonia Arrison, who was then at the Donner Foundation. She encouraged me to apply for a grant and was very helpful through the application process.

My research on the Canadian postal scene has been assisted and encouraged by numerous individuals at Canada Post. I would like first to express my appreciation to Georges Clermont, who was then president of CPC. His early, enthusiastic, and uninhibited support for the project gave me valuable credibility within, and open access to, the CPC organization, and he offered frank insights and observations in an extended interview. I also interviewed the Honourable André Ouellet, who was, at the time, the chair of the board and acting president, and he has offered considerable support to the project as well. As mentioned above, Hank Klassen, a former senior vice-president of CPC, was tremendously supportive and encouraged and advised me when this project was only a vague idea. Gordon Ferguson spent many hours discussing postal matters with me, giving me insights and advice about postal developments in Canada and abroad. Bill Price (director, Economic Strategy and Regulatory Affairs) has been another wise and generous intellectual mentor. Doug Long in the communications office had the thankless task of organizing and scheduling meetings. His efforts and enthusiasm for the project are much appreciated. Two former students of mine have gone on to successful careers at CPC. Greg Crevier helped me to keep up with postal matters when my own work was focused elsewhere, and he directed me to the interesting international postal developments. Jeremy Cotton, counsel, Legal Affairs, led me through the intricacies of the mandate-review process. I also interviewed a number of Canada Post executives and personnel, including Stuart Bacon (senior vice-president, Marketing and Sales), André Villeneuve (who was then the head of Human Resources), Phillipe Lemay (senior vice-president, Electronic Products and Services), Peter Melanson (vice-president, Electronic Products and Services), Gary Billyard (then at Executive Services), David Eagles (Communications Business, Finance, Planning, and Strategy), Tim Burke (Government Relations), and Bob Labelle (who was then secretary of the board).

I was also fortunate to have discussions with CPC's "shareholder," the government of Canada. I had an interesting meeting with the minister responsible for Canada Post – the Honourable Alfonso Gagliano. I had discussions on a number of occasions with CPC's administrative support – the Corporate Implentation Group (CIG), Public Works and Government Services Canada. Many thanks to April Nakatsu, Marla Israel, and Jane Billings; the last has left CIG and will be sorely missed. I interviewed Terry Dunn, who worked as the postal analyst at Treasury Board from 1992 to 1997, and with Pierre Laflamme at the Treasury Board.

CUPW helped my research in many ways, as it had done in the past. Its research director, Geoff Bickerton, was generous with his time and insights and kindly placed me on his electronic-mailing list – which kept me in touch with countless developments and events. I had discussions with Deborah Bourque, Kathie Steinhoff, and others. A number of Canada Post's major customers were generous in providing documentation and offering insights. I would like to offer particular thanks to Doug Moffat, executive director of the Canadian Couriers Association, and John Gustafson, president and chief executive officer of the Canadian Direct Marketing Association.

As noted above, my Donner Foundation grant allowed me to travel to the countries analysed in this study. Postal, government, regulatory, union, and user-group officials and representatives in a number of countries have been incredibly generous and supportive. They have sent me documents and reports, connected me to their web sites, communicated with me electronically and through the post, helped me make contacts within their countries and with officials in other countries, and offered their insights and experiences in open-ended interviews. I remain in contact with many of them, and they keep me abreast of the latest developments in their countries.

Maurice Castro engineered the organization and execution of my research trip to Australia. He was then group manager, Strategic Planning, and will be greatly missed after his retirement. He organized a terrific schedule for me at Australia Post, which included meetings with Linda Bardo Nicholls (chairman of the board), Gerry Ryan (secretary to the board), Robert Gray (group manager, Business Analysis), David Barker (group manager, Human Resources), and John Power (group manager, Letters). I gained insights into the labour situation from Paul Watson, national president of the Communications Electrical Plumbing Union, Brian Baulk (who was then a communications divisional secretary in the national office), and Jim Claven, industrial research officer. The Australian postal situation has been subjected to critical analysis from the competitiveness perspective over the last decade. The National Competition Council (NCC) carried out an extensive, excellent study, and I met with its deputy executive director, Deborah Cope. Geraldine Anthony at the NCC has subsequently been equally helpful. I also met with Margaret Arblaster and Anne Plympton at the Australian Competition and Consumer Commission. In Canberra, I had discussions with shareholder and regulatory officials – John Neil at the Department of Communications and the Arts, Jim Livermore and Adam McKissack at the Treasury, David Ingham at the Department of Finance, and Genevieve Bessell, assistant to the minister of finance. I also met with Senator the Honorable Chris Schact, the then shadow minister for communications. Many in Australia have communicated with me subsequently.

In Denmark, Troels Thomsen, head of International Relations, was a gracious and knowledgeable host at Post Danmark. Jan Svendsen and Lars Lynsge – president and general secretary of the National Union of Postal Workers (Dansk Postforbund) – were generous and extremely hospitable in introducing me to the intricacies of the postal labour scene, as was Mutty Rotenberg at the Special Workers Union of Denmark. I gained insights about the shareholder perspective from Carsten Marckstrøm Olesen and Carl Thaarup-Hansen at the Ministry of Transport when I was in Copenhagen and, subsequently, we have been in written communication on the same subject.

All countries were supportive and encouraging, but I must make a special note about my reception in Finland, where I was treated with exceptional care, warmth, and conscientiousness. For this, I would like to offer my appreciation to Virpi Palo formerly at Finland Post, who organized my visit with incredible care and comprehensiveness. At the Post, I had discussions with Tero Alen (Public Affairs), Pekka Leskinen (chief legal counsel), and Hannu Tuminen (director, Network and Development). The Post organized a seminar on public policy, public administration, and the Post with two of Finland's leading public administration specialists – Markku Temmes of the University of Helsinki and Pertti Ahonen of the University of Tampere. I was briefed on the shareholder perspective at the Ministry of Transport and Communications by Liisa Ero (director, the Mass Media Unit) and Samuli

Haapasalo (director, Ownership and Privatization Policy Unit). Asta Virtaniemi has since provided valuable support. The Telecommunications Administration Centre regulates the Post, and I met with its director, Jorma Koivunmaa, and its legal counsel, Matti Linnoskivi. The competition agenda has high policy resonance in Finland, and I interviewed Riita Ryhanen, deputy director, and Anne Petajaniemi-Bjorklund, senior research officer at the Finnish Competition Authority. At the Finnish Consumers Association, I met with its secretary general, Sinikka Turunen, and Martii Luukko and Tero Leino. I met with representatives of the two postal unions – Antti Palkinen, president, and Heli Maki, information manager, of the Union of Post Office Employees, and Matti Nissinen of the Finnish Post Workers' Union. Sakari Virtanen, managing director of the Finnish Direct Marketing Association, gave me insights into the customer perspective. Lasse Autio, managing director of Suomen Suoramainonta, guided me through the incredible tale of the rise and fall of postal competition in Finland through the eyes of the Post's potential competitor.

In France, M. Edouard Dayan, director of European and International Affairs, La Poste, gave me an incredibly thorough interview about French postal matters. Marie-José Varloot (secretary general) and Maric-Claude Brun (head of the secretariat) hosted a meeting with a number of members of the Commission Superieure du Service Public des Postes et Télécommunications. I had a roundtable discussion about postal matters with a number of representatives of the French postal union, Force Ouvrière des Travailleurs des Postes et des Télécommunications, including Jacky Arches and Michel Pesnel.

Sabine Muller of Deutsche Post AG did a superb job organizing my visit to Germany. I had sessions at the Post with Andrea van Arkel (head, Brussels Liaison Office), Dr Jurgen Lohmeyer (Strategic Department), my good friend Thomas Baldry (then director, New Business Fields, now with International Relations), and Eugen Pink, assistant director, Regulation and European Competitive Strategy) – with whom I have had telephone conversations since. At the Federal Ministry of Economics (the shareholder ministry), I had a good discussion with Gerold Reichle and Axel Kirmess of the postal policy section of the Federal Ministry of Economics. Dr Hans Engelke joined us for this discussion; he is with the Regulatory Authority for Telecommunications and Posts (Reg TP), where he is director of the bureau that issues postal licences. Cara Schwarz-Schilling at Reg TP has been helpful as well.

In the Netherlands, I had discussions with Mark Zellenrath and Hansje Huson of Public Affairs at the TNT Postal Group; Jeanette van der Hooft has also been helpful. Meindert van den Berg at the postal union ABVAKABO FNV explained the postal union and labour-management situation. Petra De Roover of the Policy Affairs Directorate, Telecommunications and Post Department, Ministry of Transport, Public Works and Water Management, offered the shareholder perspective. I discussed regulatory affairs with Hetty Joosten (who has since departed) and Elles van Geest at OPTA (the post and telecommunications authority), and subsequently with Fui Moy Chan.

Tracy O'Neale in the Letters Group made arrangements for my visit to New Zealand Post, for which I am greatly appreciative. At the Post, I had sessions with Ross Armstrong (chairman of the board), Louise Affleck (company secretary), Garry Whale (executive assistant to the CEO), John Allen (group leader, Letters), Suzanne Morton (research manager), and Robert Lake (operations leader). I also had the opportunity to have an extended discussion with Elmar Toime, president of New Zealand Post. New Zealand has what might be considered the best public postal-oversight system, and I was grateful to meet most of the players within this system. At the Ministry of Commerce, I met with David Galt, manager, Resources and Networks Branch, and Greg Harford, advisor, Communications Policy. Both David and Greg have moved on to other postings, and I now communicate with Phillip Toye. I had discussions with Jean-Pierre André, Justus Haucap, and David Taylor at the Treasury. At the Crown Company Monitoring Advisory Unit (CCMAU), I met with John Cooper, principal adviser, State Owned Enterprises, and John Wardrop, senior adviser. The former has left CCMAU and I have communicated with Mervyn English. Rex Jones, national secretary of the Engineers Union, introduced me to labour-management issues. I have subsequently been in correspondence with Sarah McCrae.

Goran Olsson at the Union of Service and Communication Employees orchestrated my trip to Sweden. I was welcomed at Sweden Post by Borje Sprong (group controller) and Sture Wallander (director, International Division), and Desiree Veschetti Holmgren at the International Relations Secretariat has provided useful feedback. I discussed the shareholders' perspective with Anna Rygaard and Jonas Iversen at the Ministry of Industry, Employment and Communications. Anna introduced me to Hakan Ohlsson, deputy managing director of City Mail. Sten Selander, deputy director of General Postal affairs at the National Post and Telecom Agency, guided me through the evolution and practice of postal regulation in Sweden.

Claire Prater organized my visit to the United Kingdom, and I am extremely grateful for her fine efforts. At the Post Office, I interviewed Richard Adams (secretary to the board, recently retired) and Ian Reay (head, Competition and Regulation Policy). I have continued to communicate with Ian regularly, and he has been of particular help in keeping me informed of British postal developments. I have also had the opportunity to have discussions with John Dolling (Business Strategy), Tim Walsh (International Affairs), Catherine Churchard (Legal Services), and Frank Rodriguez (head, Economics). I had an extended session at the Department of Trade and Industry with some members of the postal-review team, Mike Whitehead and Nigel Leese. The Communication Workers Union (cwu) has been generous in providing me with documents and reports, and I had a productive session with Roger Dollington, Derek Bright, and Marcus Rubin. I interviewed Alan Johnson, MP, the former head of the cwu who is now a cabinet minister with responsibility for the Post. I also met with Martin O'Neill, MP, who chaired the parliamentary committee that reviewed the Post Office in the 1990s. I interviewed John Hackney, then chairman (now retired), and George Brown, assistant secretary (now returned to the Department of Trade and Industry), at the Post Office Users' National Council. I have subsequently had discussions with Marc Seale, director of strategy at the newly formed Postal Services Commission.

Sheila Daout kindly organized my visit to the United States Postal Service. I met with Deborah Willhite, vice-president, Government Relations, and members of her team for an extended discussion. I also met with Charles McBride (manager, Strategic Planning Analysis) and Jim Van Loozen (manager, Corporate Messaging). I was guided through the intricacies of postal politics and Bill HR-22 by Robert Taub, staff director, Subcommittee on the Postal Service, House of Representatives Committee on Government Reform and Oversight. I met with Jim Sauber, research director of the National Association of Letter Carriers, who also provided me with an extensive list of contacts.

The international dimensions of the postal world are centred in Switzerland and Belgium. Jim Gunderson kindly invited me to the headquarters of the Universal Postal Union (upu) in Berne, where I met with director general Thomas Leavey and Luiz Pinheiro, senior counsellor, director general's Chef de Cabinet. Jim has kept me abreast of upu developments. In Geneva, I met with Phillip Bower, general secretary of Communications International (formerly PTTI), the international organization of postal and telecommunications unions. I visited Directorate-General XIII of the European Commission in Brussels, where I met with Fernando Toledano, head of division, and Alexander Willan. The International Post Corporation is headquartered in Brussels as well, and I interviewed its president and CEO, Yves Cousquer (who has since moved on to oversee the Paris airports). M. Cousquer was helpful in introducing me to numerous postal and government officials, and I am extremely grateful for his assistance and support of this project.

There is a lively international postal-research community, centred in universities, international agencies, and the consulting sector. I met many of the individuals mentioned above and others through the annual Conference on Postal and Delivery Economics, organized by the Center for Research in Regulated Industries, Rutgers University. I attended the sixth, seventh, eighth, and ninth conferences in Montreux, Switzerland, Sintra, Portugal, Vancouver, Canada, and Sorrento, Italy, respectively. The conferences are co-chaired by Paul Kleindorfer (Wharton School, University of Pennsylvania) and Michael Crewe (director, Centre for Research in Regulated Industries, Rutgers University). They deserve a tremendous amount of credit for their efforts and imagination in building up the postal-policy community and postal knowledge and intelligence. Michael Crewe has been particularly supportive, for which I would like to offer appreciation. Jim Campbell, an attorney and adviser to express companies, is a formidable and knowledgeable observer of the postal scene and creator of the Rowland's postal web site. I met Jim at Montreux, and he has since been especially helpful and encouraging. I have had discussions in Canada and in England with John Dowson of PriceWaterhouseCoopers (pwc), who is one of the best-known and experienced consultants on the postal scene. I have also had discussions with Cathy Rogerson at pwc. The staff at the National Economic Research Associates (London) has been generous in providing studies and documentation. I met Kumar Ranganthan (World Bank) at a cpc conference in Toronto and he has provided me with documents and reports. Peter Hanley, former director, Institute for the Future, Monika Plum, former head of postal research group at Wissenschaftliches Institut fur Kommunikationsdientse GmbH, and William Kovacic, professor of law at the National Law Center, have all been helpful.

All of the individuals mentioned above – and others whom I cannot cite here – have been generous, open, and frank in their discussions with me. They have provided documentation, insights, and contacts, and contributed to the development of my analysis and understanding of postal developments. It goes without saying that any errors or omissions are exclusively my responsibility. But I wish to make it abundantly clear that I could not have executed this research plan and written this book without their support.

I have also received tremendous support from McGill-Queen's University Press, particularly its executive editor, Philip Cercone, as well as Joan McGilvray, Brenda Prince, and Filomena Falocco. Curtis Fahey was a superbly thorough and professional copy editor and I enjoyed working with him. Tammy McNamee prepared the index.

Finally, I would like to dedicate this book to my family – my wife, Christl Verduyn, and our children, Malcolm, Lachlan, Colin, and Frances. They have indulged me in what must seem to them to be a strange if not perverse interest in postal affairs. They have accepted my extended research absences with good grace, listened to my postal stories with tolerance, and never wavered in giving me their support.

May 2001

Abbrevations

ACCC   Australian Competition and Consumer Commission
ACTU   Australian Council of Trade Unions
AEI   Air Express International
AP   Australia Post
APC   Australian Postal Commission
ATM   Automatic Teller Machine
CCA   Canadian Couriers Association
CCD   Crown Corporations Directorate (Canada)
CCMAU   Crown Company Monitoring Advisory Unit (NZ)
CCPS   Consumer Council for Postal Services (UK)
CDMA   Canadian Direct Marketing Association
CEP   Courier, Express, Parcel
CEPU   Communications, Electrical, Plumbing Union (Australia)
CEWU   Communications and Electrical Workers Union (NZ)
CIG   Corporate Implementation Group (Canada)
COAG   Council of Australian Governments
CPA   Competition Principles Agreement (Australia)
CSAU   Commonwealth Shareholder Advisory Unit (Australia)
CSO   Community Service Obligation
CPC   Canada Post Corporation
CSSPpt Commission Supérieure du Service Public des Postes et Télécommunications (France)
CUPW   Canadian Union of Postal Workers
CWU   Communication Workers Union (UK)
DCITA   Department of Communications, Information Technology and the Arts (Australia)

DGPT Directorate General of Posts and Telecommunications
      (France)
DOCA Department of Communications and the Arts (Australia)
DOFA Department of Finance (Australia)
DOU   Deed of Understanding (NZ)
DTI   Department of Trade and Industry (UK)
DPAG Deutsche Post AG
DPWN Deutsche Post World Net
EBA   Enterprise Bargaining Agreement (Australia)
EBIT Earnings before Interest and Taxes
EC   European Commission
ECA   Employment Contracts Act (NZ)
EFL   External Financing Limit (UK)
EU   European Union
FAA   Financial Administration Act (Canada)
FO   Force Ouvrière des Travaileurs des Postes et
      Télécommunications (France)
GAO   General Accounting Office (US)
GATS General Agreement on Tariffs and Services
GBE   Government Business Enterprise (Australia)
IPC   International Postal Corporation
KPN   Koninklijke PTT Nederland NV
LCUC Letter Carriers Union of Canada
MIEC Ministry of Industry, Employment and Communications
      (Sweden)
MOTC Ministry of Transportation and Communications (Finland)
MMC   Monopolies and Mergers Commission (UK)
MMU   Major Mail Users
NAFTA North American Free Trade Agreement
NALC National Association of Letter Carriers (US)
NAMMU National Association of Major Mail Users (Canada)
NCC   National Competition Council (Australia)
NERA National Economic Research Associates (UK)
OPTA Onafhankelijke Post en Telecommunicatie Autoriteit
      (postal regulator – Netherlands)
PMO   Prime Minister's Office (Canada)
POD   Post Office Department
POUNC Post Office Users' National Council (UK)
PSA   Postal Services Act (Sweden)
PSC   Postal Services Commission (UK)
PTS   National Post and Telecom Agency (Poch och Telestyrelsen
      – Sweden)
PTT   Posts, Telephones and Telecommunications

PWC   PriceWaterhouseCoopers
PWGSC   Public Works and Government Services Canada (PWGSC)
Reg TP   Regulatory Authority for Telecommunications and Posts (Germany)
REIMS   Remuneration of the Exchange of International Mails
ROE   Return on Equity
SAPO   South African Post Office
SCI   Statement of Corporate Intent (NZ)
SEKO   Union of Service and Communication Employees (Sweden)
SID   Specialarbejderforbundent I Danmark (Special Workers Union – Denmark)
SOE   State Owned Enterprise
SSM   Suormionta Oy (Finland)
TAC   Telecommunications Administration Centre (Finland)
TISC   Trade and Industry Select Committee (UK)
TNT   Thomas Nationwide Transport
TPG   TNT Postal Group (Netherlands)
UPS   United Postal Service
USO   Universal Service Obligation
UPU   Universal Postal Union
USPS   United States Postal Service
VAT   Value Added Tax
WIK   Wissenschaftliches Institut fur Kommunikationsdientse GmbH (Germany)
WTO   World Trade Organization

The Politics of Postal Transformation
Modernizing Postal Systems in the Electronic and Global World

Introduction

This is a book about postal policy in the modern world. It seeks to explain and understand how recent developments – particularly technological, international, and ideological changes – have altered the range of policy possibilities in the postal area. Public postal regimes in general – and its quintessential product, the "letter," in particular – exist tenuously in an increasingly competitive and hostile market of cellphones, fax machines, electronic-document transfers, ATMs, and e-mail. The Posts[1] also compete against large multinational express companies (like FedEx and UPS) as well as in each other's markets. Prodded by economic deregulation and liberalization at home and abroad, a number of national Posts have developed an international reach, taking over private-sector shipping and express companies and entering into partnership or "alliance" arrangements with private and public competitors abroad. These technological and international changes have unfolded within the successful execution of the neoconservative agenda, which encouraged and facilitated these developments. The neoconservative agenda appears to have run its course, however, now that governments have eliminated their deficits and met much of the neoconservative challenge. Within the context of an unfolding debate on what shape post-neoconservatism will take,[2] postal policy appears to be on the cusp of a new era.

This book will track and evaluate the Canadian postal scene in the 1990s against the backdrop of these technological, international, and ideological developments. It will draw conclusions about, and make recommendations for, Canadian postal policy. At the same time, it is a study in comparative-policy analysis, which comprises much of the book. The Canadian analysis and recommendations will be informed by developments in a number of postal regimes around the world, where progressive[3] postal corporatization, liberalization, deregulation, and sometimes privatization have taken place. Readers with little or no background or only a modest interest in the Canadian postal scene can thus read and, it is to be hoped, benefit from this book.

This study is written from the perspective of public policy makers and is based on two premises: that the Post still matters and that politics matters. Notwithstanding technological developments, a national postal system continues to be important both for its economic contributions (to competitiveness and to a country's comparative economic advantage) and for social reasons (as a large employer and provider of a universal public service). There are signs of postal-policy convergence in response to technology and globalization. But national politics and historical factors generate postal-policy differences as much as policy choices. The aim of this study is to demonstrate that a country's successful postal performance is related to the construction of a postal regulatory and governance environment that adequately reflects technological change and global developments, within the political constraints and opportunities offered by its particular national context.

This study maintains that there is no "optimal" or universal model for the Posts that is ready to be discovered, constructed, and applied to the postal scene. Countries have particular cultures, histories, and traditions that play out in different postal realities, and their place in the world economy also offers constraints on and opportunities for postal development. As Christopher Pollitt and his associates discovered in their analysis of national policy adjustment to global pressures: "Trajectories were parallel in the sense that specific reforms ... have been taken up in each country, but have been used to very different degrees, in different combinations and with considerable adaptations to suit the specifics of the national and political administrative system ... each country has borrowed from an international stock of ideas, but has used these ideas selectively, often modifying them considerably, in the pursuit of different trajectories."[4] National differences range from administrative arrangements to contrasting geography, from the symbolic role of the Posts to differing retailing and banking traditions. Some have been high-price and high-protection countries with elaborate postal services. Others have been low-price and low-protection ones with modest services. These factors temper policy comparisons and constrain developing a "one-size-fits-all" regulatory model.

One can discern and aggregate a number of tendencies or models that have emerged across the postal world. These will be used to structure the presentation of material as well as for analytical purposes. Also, the origins, strategic logic, and policy possibilities of these models will be utilized to situate the Canadian case, delineate policy options, and make policy recommendations.

As a broad introductory generalization, most countries that have reformed their Posts have felt the need to liberalize their postal markets to some degree, as a way of realigning their Posts to technological change and globalization. Yet, regardless of the particular national degree of liberalization, deregulation, or even privatization, there has also been a subsequent trend to "re-regulate" the reformed postal regime for a number of social, legal, and political reasons. There has been a discernible movement from the postal deregulation of the neoconservative period to the postal re-regulation of the emerging post-neoconservative era. This interpretation is consistent with the findings of the most recent cross-sectoral and comparative work on regulation, by Bruce Doern and his associates. They have found that, at the end of the neoconservative era, states have been reasserting their political authority through the regulatory instrument (which is more or less costless to them).[5]

This study emanates from a postal intellectual community that is emerging internationally. One of its major axes is the annual conference organized by the Center for the Study of Regulated Industries at Rutgers University, whose conference papers are published regularly.[6] Another axis is the public and private postal intelligence created through international public agencies (such as the Universal Postal Union [UPU] and the World Bank)[7] and private consultancy firms (PriceWaterhouseCoopers in particular).[8] James I. Campbell, Jr, an attorney for a number of express companies in the United States, has played a critical lead role in the creation of postal intelligence, through his writings, participation at conferences, and construction of a postal website (which comprises a repository of documents, papers, articles, and references on postal matters around the world[9]). Domestically, the Posts, regulatory bodies, and postal unions in many countries have developed a research capacity and postal intelligence that can be accessed.[10] For a number of reasons, Canada has not made a substantial contribution to this postal intellectual and policy community.[11] This study is a modest contribution to that end.

This book has three methodological dimensions. In the first instance, it proceeds within a political-economy framework, delineating the ways in which politics and economics are intersecting in liberal-capitalist societies at a period of intense internationalization and rapid technological change. Second, the book uses a public-policy framework, focusing on how postal policy is formulated in the interaction between the state and the major players in the postal-policy community. The analysis concentrates particularly on the state's assessment of how to react to forces emanating from technology and the international area, as these are mediated by the major players in the postal-policy community: postal management and boards, unions, big and small competitors, big and small users, postal bureaucrats and regulators. Third, the book adopts a comparative-policy perspective, examining and contrasting the actions of a number of countries that have been characterized as having a progressive or modern postal character.

WHY THE POSTS MATTER

Given the rapid and far-reaching changes in the communications world (to be detailed below), why study the Posts as a policy subject at the beginning of the twenty-first century? This is a fair question, particularly given that the Posts are not a high priority on many governments' policy agendas. The latter tendency reflects a range of political factors that will be presented throughout this study. On the one hand, the Posts' performance has improved remarkably over the last decade, with the result that they do not draw the degree of critical attention that they used to. Their recruitment of good managers has made them increasingly well run. Government interference in their day-to-day operations has declined, allowing Posts the space and opportunity to develop to a commercial rather than a political agenda. To this extent, government neglect has had some benign and positive consequences. Service has improved, customers are reasonably satisfied, and most progressive Posts are not losing money. Indeed, many of the better ones pay huge amounts of taxes and dividends. On the other hand, governments tend to be ignorant of the continuing importance of the postal market and focus their attention to a greater degree on the glamorous high-tech communications areas. Governments tend to become anxious when contemplating the political consequences of initiating postal change. The adage "if it ain't broke don't fix it" has come to be applied to the postal sector in many countries. Governments also remain uncertain and sometimes perplexed about precisely what to do with its high-value, labour-intensive postal corporation in a complex and constantly changing communications environment. Some experts trumpet the end of traditional mail and the advent of the electronic-communications revolution. Others insist that hard-copy communication will remain important for reasons of security, accessibility, and familiarity. In any event, as one of the largest employers

Table 1
Distribution of mail worldwide

	1995	2005
Business to Household	40.9%	45.8%
Household to Business	7.5%	8.6%
Business-Business	31.5%	31.5%
Household-Household	19.8%	14.1%

Source: Universal Postal Union, *POST 2005: Core Business Scenarios*
(Berne: April 1997), 6.

of labour, the Post's future resonates with possible crises and upset. So the tendency is for governments to ignore their Posts, set up studies or task forces, and put off and delay policy decisions.

The reality is that the Posts remain an important policy area that should command governments' attention, for a number of substantial reasons. First, postal activity comprises a large, indeed enormous, part of the market economy. Admittedly, postal growth has not kept pace with the extraordinary expansion of the communications market. Nonetheless, its scale and scope remain impressive, its growth prospects are moderately reasonable, and the postal market comprises some of the largest companies and employers in the world. According to the UPU,[12] 413 billion letters are posted annually – about 1.1 billion letters a day. In the industrialized countries, an average person sends more than 400 letters a year. The United States has one of the most highly developed postal markets in the world. It has an amazing degree of postal traffic – 188 billion units a year, about 700 letters per person per year (Canada Post carries 11 billion messages a year.) The European Commission (EC) reports that operators in the European Union (EU) (including private ones) handle 135 billion items per year, which generates US$74.6 billion turnover – about 1.4 per cent of GDP. Over and above letters, 3.4 billion parcels are sent through the mail each year – around 10 million a day. These letters and parcels find their way through three million street letter boxes and 770,000 permanent post-office outlets around the world, making the Post Office one of the world's most extensive networks – both domestically and internationally. International mail has been the fastest growing postal sector; about 24 million letters cross national borders every day (8.6 billion letters a year). Generally speaking, by far the largest proportion of mail is business mail, and this is growing, as indicated in Table 1. Over 80 per cent of mail is business mail. This figure is closer to 90 per cent in most high-income countries. As will be seen presently, this poses a possible problem. But it demonstrates the extent to which postal activity is integrally related to market activity, in traditional areas and in new areas that are emerging and expanding (for example, ad mail, fund-raising, financial reporting, small-business marketing, e-commerce, and so on). Most postal observers see economic growth as the single most important determinant of postal growth (with an elasticity to economic growth in the 0.8–1.0 per cent range). A moderate assessment of mail growth over the next five to seven years anticipates annual growth of around 2.5 per cent.[13] In the developed world, mail or the letter looks to be a fairly mature market, although most countries have not come close to the postal development that has been generated in the United States. The market in the developing countries is likely to expand over time; currently, the average varies in these countries between five and thirty-three letters sent per person per year.

The Posts' activities intersect with all aspects of the economy and represent 2 per cent of GDP in industrialized countries. The major Posts represent some of the largest corporations in the world. The United States Postal Service (USPS) is America's ninth largest corporation, with 34,000 postal facilities. It ranks in the world's top thirty in revenue generated (around US$60 billion).[14] The German Post – Deutsche Post World Net (DPWN) – anticipates revenues of US$30 billion in 2000–01. Canada Post is in the top thirty firms in Canada, generating over $5 billion in revenues and serving 900,000 business clients. Its network of 20,000 retail points is larger than the network of all of the banks combined.

The Posts have enjoyed a symbiotic relationship with technological change, both encouraging its development and being one of its biggest consumers. For example, the Posts have been central to the development of air transportation, logistics, sorting machinery and barcode technology, electronic-document transfer, electronic retail counters, track and trace technology, funds transfers, and electronic mail. The trade fairs associated with postal conferences are enormous. Post Expo '99 (Hamburg, 5–7 1999) – the world's largest postal-technology conference and exhibition – brought together representatives from over 100 countries and 120 international exhibitors, from Pitney Bowes and Siemens to Lockheed Martin, IBM, and Mannesmann Dematic.[15] CPC hosts an equivalent biannual conference, which is attended by dozens and dozens of companies, demonstrating CPC's connection to the business world as both a provider of postal services and a consumer of postal and communication products and services. The Posts are among the largest consumers of transportation services – land, air, and sea. Over a half a million motor vehicles are used to deliver the world's mail – the world's largest civilian vehicle fleet.

As will be seen in the country studies, the Posts are involved in a number of complementary activities. Indeed, the benchmark objective for the most ambitious Posts is that no more than 50 per cent of their turnover should be generated from the traditional postal sectors. The postal banking sector in some countries is enormous. Indeed, Euro-Giro is the world's largest branch network (it is owned by twenty-two postal and Giro banks), comprising eighty million accounts and fifty thousand offices.[16] The Posts' retail networks are typically amongst the largest in their countries, providing a range of products and services beyond postal ones from insurance and travel tickets to licences and currency exchange. Through direct marketing and ad mail – a briskly developing postal market – the Posts are intimately tied into the worlds of marketing and promotion for all sectors of the economy. E-commerce is generating an enormous expansion of parcel delivery. As businesses adopt "just-in-time" production and selling strategies, the Posts have played an increasingly important role in warehousing, logistics, and supply-chain management. Throughout these developments, the private postal-consultancy business has become enormous. For example, PriceWaterhouseCoopers has a worldwide network of 400 persons who are engaged in postal consultancy.[17] The Posts in industrial countries have set up subsidiary companies to give advice to, and manage the modernization processes of, Posts in the rest of the world.

Given the quantity of business and the range of activities, the Posts remain one of the world economy's largest civilian employers, and employment is a politically sensitive issue. There are around six million postal employees worldwide (there are likely another 1.5 million in the private sector). The European postal workforce alone comprises 1.7 million people. The USPS has the largest national postal workforce – 859,000 employees. The DPWN group has grown to 300,000 employees. Canada Post is Canada's fourth-largest employer

Despite the emergence of competitive technological communications and products (described below), the Posts remain a critical, vital, and competitive component of the communications market. If properly managed, Posts can offer efficiency and productivity benefits to individual firms and to the economy as a whole, since they provide numerous important transportation and communications services. This is demonstrated in the EU's recent efforts to make the postal sector more competitive and efficient. The Post has confronted technological competition in the past (telephone, telegraph, fax, and so on) and has survived each revolution, albeit emerging in a slightly different form and with different purposes. This is partially because the new technological products often compete against each other and not against the Post (for example, e-mail versus fax, fax versus telephone calls, and so on). Moreover, the Posts offer a number of comparative communications advantages. First, the Post's system of universal access is a strategic asset. Posts connect on a daily basis to millions of customers, at each address within an economy. This is an unrivalled communications advantage and a daunting challenge to competitors, for the Posts' scale, complexity, and connectedness are unrivalled. Second, unlike the new electronic communications, the Posts can communicate on both a one-to-one and a one-to-many basis. Third, Posts have developed close, long-term relationships with business and customers. They enjoy a certain degree of brand equity and loyalty, particularly with respect to reliability, security, and costs. Fourth, the Posts have the capacity to fuse old and new technologies and delivery modes into new and competitive products and services, such as targeted direct mail and fulfillment and support systems for electronic commerce.[18] Fifth, the Posts offer a seamless and integrated connectedness for customers, from national to international distribution and from electronic origins to hard copy and product delivery. Within certain of these streams, they enjoy the trust of customers that their privacy will be protected. Postal and telecommunications products and services are not perfect substitutes for each other. A recent Organization for Economic Co-operation and Development (OECD) study delineated a number of advantages that the Post has over telecommunications. Postal products can be produced on paper that can be read anywhere. It is easy to scan large volumes of mail and more difficult to ignore it. There are low barriers to access the postal system and it is inexpensive to start up and to get connected to it. There is no need to "log on" and the Posts offer reasonable reliability against fraud and impersonation. Overall, their sense of familiarity and reliability is a huge attraction and advantage.[19]

A few examples may clarify the point that the Posts remain vital in the modern communications world. The information revolution has allowed advertisers to direct their marketing in a focused, "niche" manner to particular consumers. Print remains the medium of direct-mail choice. The three largest generators of bulk ad mail – consumer products, financial services, and utilities – spend two-thirds of their advertising dollars on print media. The electronic growth that is anticipated in this area is likely to be at the expense of newspaper and magazine advertising, not the Post. Mailed direct marketing enjoys a number of advantages over electronic forms, including its flexibility, use of shape and colour, tactile qualities, adaptable responses, and focused selectivity. It is anticipated that direct advertising as a share of business spending on advertising will increase, given its proven success and cost-effectiveness. The United States is the leader in this area, where direct marketing is a $350-billion business. The growth potential in Canada and elsewhere remains enormous.[20]

There are other opportunities that the information revolution offers to the Post. Security is emerging as the key concern in the area of the electronic transmission of documents. Postal services are in the fore-front of developing international protocols for electronic-document transfer, to offer high security for sender and receiver. Canada Post has developed a system and arrangement with La Poste in France and the USPS. Posts can also offer central electronic directories, to allow businesses to send bills directly to a central directory of addressees, which mail them forward either electronically, by fax, or by hard copy – depending on customer choice. Hybrid products – combining electronic and hard-copy possibilities – offer the Post considerable market possibilities. All Posts are developing electronic (e-post) options which are attractive both to large-volume customers and to consumers. As e-commerce expands, the products purchased will have to be delivered; there is an enormous potential market for the Posts in fulfillment and support systems for electronic commerce.[21] Globalization has increased international transactions in an exponential way. For example, the express market is a huge, multi-billion dollar market that appears to be doubling in size every five years or so. Historically, the Posts' presence in this market has been marginal and the biggest players have been private firms – DHL, TNT, (Thomas Nationwide Transport), FedEx, and UPS. But DPWN has taken a substantial share of DHL and the Dutch Post has purchased TNT, so that the express market has increasingly become part of the Posts' domain.

As an operating premise, then, one can proceed from the view that the Posts will continue to be a major and important participant in the market economy, a communications player that touches all sectors. This in itself would make the Posts an object of policy interest – particularly since they are ubiquitous and such huge employers. This leads to a related dimension of their ongoing policy importance – their social and national significance and their public-service role. The Posts have played an historic nation-building role, particularly in "new" settler nations (for example, Australia, New Zealand, Canada, the United States) and in nations outside the economic centre and/or with low-population density (for example, Scandinavia). The Posts played an enormous infrastructural role in building up, extending, and connecting markets and communities. Their national presence in thousands of cities, towns, villages, and rural communities served an integrating national function. Posts typically subsidized transportation and communication costs, particularly in the distribution of newspapers, books, and information. As a relatively cheap and accessible means of mass communication, the Posts played an integral democratic role in the development of modern societies. Over time, the idea of a universal postal service – with regular delivery to all addresses at one, low price, and easy access to a universal network – has gained tremendous popular resonance as a kind of "public good." Overall, the Posts enjoy a distinct symbolic or psychic national status, somewhat similar to a country's military. Indeed, their importance for social and economic development has been recognized by the World Bank, which has used its lending program to sponsor postal development and improvement projects with the UPU.[22]

Thus, there has been at most only modest movement towards privatization of the Posts, even after they have been modernized and "corporatized." On one level, this is surprising, given the extent of privatization of state enterprises in the late 1980s and 1990s across the industrial world. This ranged from the privatization of national rail and airlines through water, electricity, and telephone companies. For example, in Canada, the government sold off more than twenty crown corporations between 1984 and 1991, from Air Canada and Canadian National to Teleglobe and PetroCanada. This privatization process is unfolding even in Scandinavia, where only recently Sweden partially privatized Telia (its telecommunications company) and Finland abandoned the air-transportation area.[23] On the postal front, though, there has been little privatization, notwithstanding an intense corporatization and deregulation of the sector. The Dutch Post was partially privatized in 1994, but the Dutch government retains 45 per cent of shares including the "golden share" (a kind of veto power over decisions of national consequence). The Germans sold 30 per cent of the Post's shares in 2000. Both of these actions reflect a particular postal-policy strategy, which will be examined below. Argentina decided to organize its postal system on private lines, but its public system had collapsed and almost disappeared. There are signs that postal privatization is likely to take place in some Eastern European countries (Romania, Albania), in Africa (Namibia), and elsewhere (Malta, Philippines, Brazil). By and large, though, most national Posts remain firmly within the public domain. Neither Margaret Thatcher nor Ronald Reagan seriously considered the privatization of Royal Mail or the USPS.

Governments' aversion to postal privatization reflects a number of factors, many of which will be rehearsed more fully later in the book. Generally speaking, it does not appear to be in most governments' interests to give serious consideration to postal privatization. To begin with, the idea of the universal postal service at a universal price has enormous popular and business support. Despite the fact that most private citizens mail letters only infrequently, the idea of an inexpensive universal service has tremendous popular hold. This is particularly the case in rural or outlying areas, where the prospect of postal privatization is nothing short of apocalyptic. For business, too, the universal system remains attractive. Numerous national studies and surveys suggest that business is not keen to see privatization of the postal system, since this might lead to the fragmentation of what is a highly effective – and cheap – universal delivery system. This is particularly the case for firms that do mass universal distribution, or for small and mid-sized firms that cannot afford the use of expensive modern technologies.[24] As Posts have become more efficient and customer-oriented, their business customers have become increasingly supportive of them. Governments are sensitive to the popularity of the universal postal system. Notwithstanding periodic postal strikes or complaints about inefficiencies (both declining), governments are risk-averse in this particular area. Moreover, as was seen above, the Posts are huge employers. Governments are not keen to experiment or initiate radical public policy if the employment consequences appear to be substantial. Postal trade unions are among the best-organized unions, and they ensure the visibility of employment on the policy agenda. Finally, there are logistical problems in and constraints on privatization. Any potential purchaser is aware of the requirement to maintain the universal service in some form, to honour labour contracts and pension plans, to ensure post-privatization deregulation, and so on. These factors either scare off potential buyers or lower the share or sale price. Ironically, to the extent that governments deregulate and liberalize the Posts (and eliminate the postal monopoly – see below), the sale proceeds of privatization are also likely to fall, making the sell-off less fiscally attractive to governments.[25]

Governments have their own interests in keeping the Posts in the public domain. In many countries, the Post has been a "cash cow" that has produced a steady revenue stream to the state (for example, the United Kingdom). As the Posts have increased their efficiency and productivity, most of them have become profitable and provide a reliable source of fiscal resources to the state. To the extent to which they act to maintain the Post as a universal service provider, governments thus have the best of both worlds. They can be the champions of social equity in one of the last remaining public services. And they can do so at no cost to their budgets. Indeed, they can continue to gain revenues from the provision of this public service. Governments generally see the Posts as an emblem of the nation state and of national prestige; at bottom, Posts remain an intensely national issue even in the face of globalization.[26] Countries like Germany and the Netherlands have seen the economic and mercantile potential of the Post in the modern global economy and have, in effect, made them "national champions." In other countries, the issue of a governmental presence in cities, towns, and villages remains a matter of prime importance. In Canada, the Post projects a national image of the Canadian state, national unity, and the government's presence in all towns and villages across the country. The French government conceptualizes La Poste as an instrument of national social solidarity, particularly in economically deprived areas. For the foreseeable future, then, most national Posts will remain in the public domain and hence be the ongoing object of public policy.

CHANGING CONTEXT

The postal world remains a substantial one, with an important and public future. That said, the postal world is also a rapidly changing one, which has been buffeted recently by intense and dramatic pressures and change. Three interrelated forces have been especially influential – technological change, globalization, and the ideological shift to neoconservatism. These forces have intersected in a manner that has increased market competition for the Posts and has undermined their legal monopoly over mail service.

Technology

Historically, the Posts have been assigned a monopoly over letter mail (called the "exclusive privilege" or the reserved area), which has given it a guaranteed market in delivering mail (up to a certain weight that has varied from country to country but typically was in the 500-gram range). The rationale for this monopoly was to allow the Posts to generate sufficient revenue to maintain a universal and accessible service at a universal and accessible price. Letters would be picked up from any locale and delivered to any address at the same, low price – regardless of cost, which would often be far above the price of a stamp. The mail monopoly thus allowed a universal system, financed by an internal cross-subsidy of expensive mail by inexpensive mail. The mail monopoly typically did not extend to other categories of mail, such as newspapers and periodicals, ad mail, or parcels (although some countries did offer protection in some of these markets). Typically, only about 50 per cent of the Posts' revenues have been generated in the protected mail market; the rest has been generated in competitive markets.

Posts have always faced product and technological development, starting with the telegraph and telephone and including as well as land and air-shipping and courier services, each of which slowed the pace of postal volume growth. The more recent examples of technological

Table 2
Shares of world communications market

	1995	2005
Physical Mail	20%	15%
Fax and Telephone Calls	75%	75%
E-mail	5%	11%
Hybrid Mail		1%

Source: Universal Postal Union, *POST 2005*, 35.

development – fax, e-mail, ATMs, electronic-document transfer – have more or less neutralized the impact of the exclusive privilege and mocked the postal monopoly. We will see presently that deregulation has also resulted in a lessening of the range of the exclusive privilege. But even without this change, technology has generated alternate modes of communication, whose features and price compete effectively with the Post, thereby undermining its "protection." The monopoly may have simply become irrelevant.[27]

As James I. Campbell, Jr has declared, "a wave of technological advances has brought into question the long term viability of the core functions of national post offices."[28] From electronic transmission of documents through improved physical delivery systems, from modern telecommunications to improved and accessible air transportation, the world's public Posts face a competitive, hostile, and uncertain world. The communications market – of which the post is a significant part – has been growing recently at a remarkable pace, far above the growth of GDP. But as Table 2 indicates, the postal sector has not kept pace with this growth. For example, during the 1970s and 1980s, the Canadian communications market grew almost three times as fast as the postal market. By the early 1980s, there were more long-distance calls made than first-class letters mailed. By 1992, there were over two billion fax transmissions compared to 4.5 billion letters mailed. Over the last decade, international telecommunications traffic has grown by 15.4 per cent a year – while letters grew by only 6 per cent in total. Within the mail world, any real growth was generated by ad mail, which comprised 50 per cent of Canada Post's volumes by 1993 (letter mail's share fell from 63 per cent in the 1970s to 45 per cent in 1993). Overall, it is estimated that letters' share of the communications market will decline from 20 per cent in 1995 to 15 per cent in 2005. E-mail's share will double from 5 per cent to 11 per cent, with fax and telephone calls holding their own at around 75 per cent. In the United States, electronic messaging is growing at 17 per cent a year and unit costs for these messages are declining by 4 per cent a year.[29] The USPS has lost about one-third of its business to electronic mail over the last part of the decade.[30] A recent General Accounting Office (GAO) report to Congress declared that "the Postal Service may be nearing the end of an era." It predicted that USPS first-class letter mail growth would peak in 2002 and begin to decline thereafter; ad mail growth will mitigate this, but the GAO anticipates that total mail volume will peak in 2006.[31] The Posts' expected 2–3 per cent annual growth through 2005 or so, as noted above, looks modest and potentially optimistic indeed.

Technology and competition threaten what is left of the postal market itself. The competitive impact of postal deregulation will be discussed below. But, for now, it is important to note that the Posts command only a certain percentage of the mail sector – about 56 per cent. This is because the Posts have not been terribly successful in the competitive markets like express and parcels, where their monopoly (exclusive privilege) does not reach. Thirty-five per cent of the mail market is express mail and private players have dominated this market. Internationally, the Posts' market share is 82 per cent of the mail, 16 per cent of packages, and 11 per cent of the express market.[32] Much of the change in communications centres on business's use of communications technology. This is critical for the Posts, since 80–90 per cent of their volumes comprise business mail, the bulk of which now has its origins in an electronic form. Indeed, the UPU estimates that household-to-household mail will fall from 20 per cent of mail volumes in 1995 to 14 per cent in 2005.[33] Moreover, a relatively small percentage of customers – around 10 per cent – generates about 80 per cent of the mail.[34] This makes the mail particularly sensitive to technological developments, since business items like bills and payments – postal mainstays – are susceptible to technological use. A Canadian metaphor for this possibility was the case of Canada Post's own Ministry – Public Works and Government Services Canada (PWGSC) – shifting to a direct-deposit system. This cost CPC $6–7 million annually. A substantial number of consumers are now paying bills electronically, at ATMs or via their home computers.[35]

Internationalization

A second factor that has increased competition and changed the postal world has been the internationalization of economic life. Generally speaking, international mail is growing faster than domestic mail, in response to globalization and to liberalization of domestic markets. Much of this has occurred in the express and parcel markets, which literally created FedEx and UPS. The Posts have not had any monopoly control over this sector. For example, in Europe, the Posts hold only 30 per cent of the parcels market and 7 per cent of the express market.

In the first instance, then, an increasingly international communications market sees the Posts confronting huge private corporate giants like FedEx and UPS, which compete with the Posts in both domestic and international markets for the 50 per cent or more of the Posts' revenue that is generated competitively. FedEx and UPS are substantial and able companies with an increasingly international outlook. The former is a dominant player in parcels while the latter is a force in letters and small packages. They generated $25 billion and $17 billion in revenues respectively in 1998, dominating the deferred-package delivery and overnight markets respectively. UPS issued its own public-share offering in November 2000, raising US$5 billion, some of which provides a nest egg to counter the German Post. It has purchased Challenge Air – an all-cargo airlines – and ordered sixty Airbus Industries jets for $6 billion. FedEx paid $1.2 billion for American Freightways, after purchasing RPS. It has also entered into a $7.2 billion, seven-year alliance with the USPS, in order to take on UPS, and has partnered with the parcel arm of La Poste.[36] The FedEx/USPS deal will see FedEx placing drop boxes in 10,000 post offices. This initiative has been countered by UPS, which purchased Mail Box Etc. and in so doing provided itself with a national retail network.

Some of the national Posts have confronted this competitive reality in the manner that a private-sector corporation would. They have either entered into partnership arrangements with their private competitors and public counterparts or they have gone out and purchased the competition. For example, Canada Post intensified its participation in the express-courier market by purchasing Purolator. The German Post Office purchased 20 per cent (later increased to over 50 per cent) of one of the global giants, DHL, which has perhaps the best network in the world for express mail, documents, and parcels; its market penetration in Europe ranges from 40 to 70 per cent and it has partnered with the USPS to deliver international parcels. Deutsche Post World Net (DPWN) has also recently purchased AEI to extend its global reach into the Americas. The Dutch post office bought the world's largest shipping company, TNT, which operates in most countries of the world.

These initiatives will be examined in the country studies. For now, it is worth noting simply the competitive origins and effects that this has had. On the one hand, customers in effect forced postal mergers and takeovers, because they demanded global service not simply domestic service in the international economy. This required national Posts to develop overseas external-market strategies to ensure that they could deliver quality service outside their own markets. On the other hand, this resulted in the national Posts increasingly competing against each other in each other's markets. Royal Mail has communication offices in many countries in order to market its international services. It is a shareholder in Sweden's City Mail, which competes directly with Sweden Post in the deregulated Swedish market. Royal Mail recently purchased the largest private carriers in Germany and so competes directly with Deutsche Post – and La Poste – in the lucrative German market. Great Britain is the largest generator of international mail, with nearly a billion letters leaving its borders annually. The Dutch Post has been pursuing an international strategy for a number of years. It acts as a hub for much international mail in Europe and is a major player in the phenomenon known as "remail" – in which mail is posted through a third country to the second, to take advantage of differences in postal rates. At the same time, it is building up a business presence in all of the major postal markets of the world. The general strategy of the major postal players is to become the "number two" postal presence in national markets outside its home one. This has led to a kind of panic buying of shipping, transportation, delivery, and logistics companies around the world, since national Posts do not want to be left behind with no direct presence in any particular market. Indeed, of the big four global giants – TNT, DHL, FedEx, and UPS – only the latter two remain private. Many of the intermediate-sized transportation and mailing firms are falling into the Posts' hands, along with logistics and related companies.

A further dimension to this international competition is the consultancy work done by the Posts in the "developing" postal markets. For example, Canada Post International Limited, a subsidiary of CPC, has carried out over eighty projects in thirty-five countries over the last six years. It is currently organizing the postal systems of Guatemala and Lebanon. New Zealand Post recently won substantial contracts to help modernize the South African postal system and to prepare the Nigerian Post for privatization. Both Royal Mail and Deutsche Post are presently helping competitors in Argentina. This public-consultancy network parallels the private network, which includes an international firm like PriceWaterhouseCoopers with its network of 400 consultants around the world. There is also a strengthening of international postal cooperation, through the UPU, the EU, the International Postal Corporation (IPC), and the World Bank that will be examined in the concluding chapter. A World Bank study of fifty non-developed countries suggests that many of these countries will likely "skip over" the pure public stage of state-run post offices. They will enter private-public partnerships and initiate new, non-monopoly ways of proceeding in order to attract needed capital and technology. This will create opportunities for the mature Posts and pitch competition up to another level.[37]

An odd twist to the internationalization of the postal market is the fact that the United States is not a player. Given the Americans' role in trade liberalization and its general ideological orientation, this appears to be odd. The USPS is one of the thirty largest companies in the world and carries 40 per cent of the world's mail. This reflects the predominance of the American economy in the world as well as the advanced stage of development of its own postal market. However, the USPS is tightly regulated and limited to core postal activities by its legislation and its regulator, the Prices Review Commission. A reform bill championed by New York congressman John McHugh aimed to modernize the postal scene, but the legislation faced too many political constraints and obstacles to succeed. As a result, the USPS has been a passive factor in this area (and it will not be a major case study in this book as a result). Its recent partnership deal with FedEx will help stave off – but only for a time – what will likely be a serious business crisis in the next few years. The USPS entered a deficit position in 2000–01, with an anticipated deficit between US$2 and 3 billion. It is simply not well positioned to adjust to rapid international and technological changes.

The internationalization of the postal world has resulted in increased competition between public Posts and private operators and among the public Posts themselves. This reflects the market reality that there is no longer such a thing as a national network. Posts have to have international networks, because their customers – mainly business – have increasingly international aspirations and needs. If a national Post cannot provide the international service that a customer requires, then that customer has alternatives and options to choose from, on both the public and private sides of the postal fence. This can have enormous competitive consequences for Posts in all areas of their business operations, from pick-up and sorting to delivery. Competition in general, and international competitive pressures in particular, have forced Posts to be far more "customer-oriented" than in the past. The Posts have far less command over their traditional markets than they did earlier. They have a diminished capacity to dictate to their traditional customers. The focused and intense attention to the customer has been one of the most profound changes in the postal environment in the last two decades. This in turn has reflected a third sea change in the postal universe – the ideological tilt away from Keynesianism to neoconservatism.

Neoconservatism

In the post-war era, the Posts enjoyed a kind of benign existence, insulated from competition and change by the Keynesian social-welfare agenda, which emphasized stability, security, social goals, and high if not full employment. In Canada, for example, the Keynesian period saw the unionization of postal employees and improvements in their wages and working conditions; the use of the Post Office as an employment "shock absorber"; the extension of the postal network into most towns and rural areas; the maintenance of low postal prices; the persistence of subsidies to newspaper and periodical distribution; the extension of services and products; and the absorption of large and regular postal deficits in governments' operating budgets. In short, these developments reflected the classic Keynesian paradigm of high employment, mass consumption, low prices, extensive and inexpensive social services, and the raising and lowering of public expenditures in response to swings of the business cycle.

With the end of the post-war boom, the Keynesian paradigm was slowly but surely replaced by the neoconservative approach. The latter blamed Keynesianism for economic decline, because it had constrained private initiative, undermined efficiency, inhibited economic growth, and created a bloated public sector with an enormous deficit. To redress this situation, the neoconservative approach called for the regeneration of private enterprise and the market and the rolling back of government involvement in the economy. The policy priorities of this era included deficit reduction, cuts in government expenditure, and incentives to economic initiative and efficiency – such as tax reform, deregulation, and privatization.

This ideological shift had a number of "life-changing" consequences for the Posts. The most important was the broad political strategy of decoupling the Posts from direct management by government and their re-creation as autonomous state enterprises or crown corporations. Posts were transformed from administrative, departmental units of the state bureaucracy into free-standing business units. This happened first in the Anglo-American democracies (the United Kingdom 1969, the United States in 1971, Canada in 1980, and New Zealand and Australia later in the 1980s), where the neoconservative agenda originated. Similar developments in Europe followed in the 1990s. A number of factors pushed along the postal agenda within the neoconservative paradigm. First, states confronted a fiscal problem, to which the Posts contributed substantially via their perpetual deficits (for example, postal deficits in Canada totalled $3 billion in the 1970s). Governments tried to redress this situation by establishing the Posts as self-financing autonomous business units which would no longer drain public resources. Indeed, governments went even farther and set up financial frameworks for the Posts, which were now expected or mandated to contribute to the state budget by making profits not deficits. Second, within the broad competitiveness agenda of neoconservatism, the Posts' poor performance was seen as a drag on national economic efficiency and productivity, one that harmed economic growth. Thus, the new autonomous postal units were set up as quasi-corporations, which were expected to think and perform efficiently like private-sector firms and to maintain targeted levels of economic performance comparable to private-sector expectations and results. This had been encouraged as well by the major mail users, who themselves were facing increased global, competitive pressures. They demanded either more efficient postal services or a rolling back of the postal monopoly to allow an opportunity for private participation in the postal market. Third, as in other areas of the economy, governments feared the prospect of competitive decline, brought on by technological, market, and product competition. If postal volumes and revenues declined, the Posts would be unable to invest to remain competitive, with the result that they would lose all business save for the expensive tasks associated with the universal service obligation. As an operator of last resort, the Posts would then have to charge high prices and diminish the quality and limit the extent of their services, or look for postal subsidies from the state. All of these scenarios would put governments on the political spot. Hence, there was a compelling need from the state's perspective to ensure that the Posts acted like corporations, became competitive, and grew in size and profitability.

The advent of neoconservatism was an ideological reflection of the technological and global changes that were unfolding at the time. This changed political paradigm produced a series of postal-policy initiatives that will be examined in this study. To point out but two here – governments distanced themselves from Posts to have them act like corporations, and they liberalized and deregulated the postal market to spur the Posts to efficiency and competitiveness. With respect to deregulation, governments rolled back the amount of monopoly protection given to the Posts – in some cases eliminating the monopoly altogether to create a completely deregulated postal environment (for example, Finland, Sweden, and New Zealand). Domestic deregulation and liberalization not only increased domestic competition but also pushed the political agenda internationally, which resulted in increased international competition, as noted above. With respect to corporatization, some states have encouraged their Posts to become international champions. The Dutch and German Posts are international postal behemoths, which compete intensely with every national Post and private-sector postal player across the world.

CHARACTER OF THE "CORPORATIZED" POST

Technological change, globalization, and neoconservatism changed the postal scene dramatically and affected national posts in different ways. These differences reflected the choices that were made by governments, which in turn reflected domestic political pressures, the national economy's place in the world economy, and the ambitions and skills of postal management – among other factors. These differences will be seen in the country studies. Generally, though, the changed political paradigm produced a postal-policy convergence in a number of "progressive" or reformed Posts around four developments: corporatization, liberalization, deregulation, and re-regulation.

Corporatization

To begin with, the progressive postal regimes have been removed from the direct machinery of government. The most successful Posts seem to be the ones that have simultaneously distanced themselves from their governments while remaining "in sync" with the government's postal vision. Previously, the Posts were part of a department of government, typically a unit comprising posts, telephones, and telecommunications (PTT). There are few industrial nations where the Posts remain part of the machinery of government (Japan and Russia are exceptions). Rather, the progressive Posts have been given some sort of corporate form, often with a legal status no different from that of a private corporation. The major difference, of course, is that there happens to be only one shareholder, the government. The Netherlands is an exception, where 55 per cent of the shares in what is now called TPG (TNT Postal Group) are held privately; the company is listed on four stock exchanges, including New York. Yet even in the Netherlands, as already noted, the government holds the "golden share" – an ultimate veto in matters of national significance.

Typically, for progressive postal regimes around the world, the shareholder's relationship to the postal corporation is set out in legislation and executed through one or two units of government. One unit of government (say the Department of Finance or Economics) pursues the shareholder's interest in maintaining and increasing shareholder value. Another unit (say the Department of Communications or an independent third-party regulator) looks after regulatory and social issues. This is the situation in New Zealand and Australia. In some countries, like Finland and Sweden, both functions exist within one department of government – albeit with a third-party regulator. But the trend – mandated by the European Union – is to separate these functions institutionally. Broadly put, the purpose of the corporate form is to distance the Post from the day-to-day control of government and political interference, and to allow the Posts to develop a corporate culture and way of thinking.

The corporatized Posts are directed by the shareholder to attain a certain level of financial performance. This has obliged them to act in a business-like fashion, to be efficient and productive, and to contribute to the competitiveness of the economy. The shareholder's financial expectations have been communicated in a number of ways. Typically, the Post is directed to attain a level of performance consistent with private firms in that sector. A series of financial ratios are then established (return on investment, return on sales, and so on). In some countries, this is done in a formal way, perhaps as part of a corporate plan, an agreement, or a declaration. In other countries, a soft target may be established at the annual shareholder meeting. In either case, the shareholder expects the Post to pay taxes and to provide profits and dividends. This has obvious benefits for the government. But this is also designed to ensure that the Post's capital and resources are being used effectively and that shareholder value is maximized. In this way, the rate of return is a kind of "test." In order to attain this rate of return, the Post will have to behave like a private corporation – thinking of its clients as customers, emphasizing quality and service, innovating and growing, and recruiting managers with proper business skills. This approach also ensures that the Posts operate on an equal footing with private operators in the market, with regard to paying taxes and dividends and being self-financing. Many of the Posts have shown a remarkable financial performance. The Australian and British Posts generate enormous revenues for their shareholders and the German and Dutch Posts are hugely profitable.

Liberalization

A country's postal legislation also indicates the degree of monopoly protection or exclusive privilege that the Post will enjoy. This varies from country to country at the moment, but an inexorable process of liberalization is unfolding. National levels of exclusive privilege are converging over time – and will likely be eliminated eventually. On the one hand, there are countries that have already eliminated all monopoly protection as a spur to increase the competitiveness of their postal sectors. This has been the case in Sweden, Finland, and, most recently, New Zealand, where there has been active encouragement of market competition. On the other hand, most countries still struggle with the issue of "proportionality" in this regard. That is, they try to balance two considerations: How much protection does a Post require to ensure the maintenance of the universal service? And how much liberalization is required to get the Posts to act in an efficient and competitive way? If a Post is given "too much" protection, then it can realize its universal-service obligations too easily, at low levels of efficiency and productivity. On the other hand, if a Post has insufficient financial capacity, it may have to decrease the universal service or the quality of its activities. Australia has studied the issue thoroughly and has struggled the most with this issue. The protection now assigned to its Post represents about 15 per cent of the market. This debate revolves around the actual cost of the universal service, which is difficult to quantify with any precision (or agreement).[38] Many observers feel that a Post's dominant position in the market gives it competitive advantages that suffice to pay for the cost of the universal-service obligations. This was the rationale for eliminating the exclusive privilege in Sweden. As noted, there has been a narrowing of the area of protection, partially brought on by the European postal directive, which obliged EU members to decrease price protection and the protected area to 350 grams. The European Commission has recently proposed a further (and controversial) reduction to 50 grams, although this is likely to generate discussion and a compromise in the 100–150 gram area. There is little evidence that a monopoly threshold below 100 grams is enforceable.[39] Most progressive regimes have lowered their protected areas to below 350 grams, and 100 grams is now not untypical. But there is concern that, if a country lowers the protected area faster than others, its market becomes open to competitors whose markets remain protected. All of this has become increasingly academic, however, as inflation and technology have undermined and weakened the impact of the exclusive privilege.

Deregulation

Liberalization has narrowed the monopoly area in the corporatized postal world. In turn, deregulation has widened the range of commercial autonomy open to the Posts. This speaks to a number of strategic principles and realities. First, increased commercial freedom has been a kind of quid pro quo for the diminishing of the area of exclusive privilege. If the public Posts are to maintain a universal service, they need sufficient revenues to do so. The extension of commercial autonomy is designed to allow the Posts to make up for revenues lost because of liberalization and the weakening or loss of the exclusive privilege. Second, if the Posts are to act like corporations, they should be allowed to make strategic commercial decisions, expand their market, and to develop new products and services – so long as these initiatives are not cross-subsidized from the protected areas. Since being corporatized, the Posts have been led by boards and senior management recruited typically and increasingly from the private sector. They often have little connection with the bureaucracy or public-sector experience. They bring with them commercial experiences, values, and objectives. They in turn look for more freedom and autonomy for their Posts in order to expend their business and maximize market share and shareholder value. They are far more aware of competitive and commercial realities than governments. In conjunction with customer expectations, it is this new postal leadership that will drive the postal agenda in the twenty-first century. The boards and CEOs of the large mercantile Posts in Germany and the Netherlands are extremely powerful and read like a who's who of the corporate elite. For example, the board of TPG comprises executives and board members from ABN-Amro, Phillips, KLM, Unilever, and Heineken. The new presidents of the Post in Finland and Sweden were recruited from the senior ranks of the private telecommunications sector.

Third, the policy of deregulation and resulting commercial autonomy reflects the reality that the absolute and relative importance of the traditional letter-mail market will decline over time. This makes the exploitation of new markets a critical matter if Posts are to generate revenue sufficient to maintain the universal system. As will be seen in the country studies, the Posts have expanded into an incredible array of areas. The Dutch Post has purchased the two largest bookstore chains in the Netherlands, and New Zealand Post is also partnering with a bookstore chain. The German Post has moved deeply into logistics and warehousing, carrying out these functions for the pharmaceutical, car, and even fashion industry. A typical British postal outlet offers dozens and dozens of non-postal services, from travel bookings and licences to insurance and currency exchange. Australia Post is the leader in bill payments. The major Posts are partnering and making acquisitions in complementary areas of the market. The larger Posts are transforming themselves into integrated logistics firms.

As a corollary to increased commercial freedom, most corporatized Posts have been given increased authority to make borrowing, capital, and investment decisions – even in the area of joint partnerships and the purchase of other firms. Typically, there are some limits to this –

whether in the form of a maximum-investment cap or a government veto where the Post is moving into a new field or affecting national policy in other areas. Yet, if the corporate plan is well constructed and understood, most postal investment decisions should be automatic under the agreed framework. Lately, Posts have been more or less encouraged to enter into joint partnerships, seek business alliances abroad, and expand their strategic and commercial reach as a way of strengthening their financial capacity and future in an increasingly hostile environment. A number of corporatized Posts are setting up subsidiary companies to pursue these strategic initiatives. As mentioned earlier, there is a corporate-buying spree taking place, with the Germans in the lead and the Dutch and the British in pursuit. La Poste has subsidiaries in express mail, banking, insurance, freight, and so on.

Re-regulation

The relationship between the corporatized Post and its shareholder has developed into a far more elaborate, formal, and specific relationship as time has passed. Ironically, the processes of liberalization and deregulation may end up in a more "regulated" postal environment than previously. The Posts have been obliged to become more transparent and accountable recently, for a number of reasons. First, they are being called on to justify their existence as one of the last remaining state enterprises. Second, they have to demonstrate that they are using their remaining exclusive privilege fairly and to effect. Third, they have to prove to their shareholders that they are performing efficiently. The shareholders' expectation of performance has increasingly been formalized and signed off in a public accord, pact, or contract, which forms the backdrop against which the performance of the Post is evaluated. Dealing with price levels, profits, service performance, and community-service obligations (social responsibilities), these agreements have become quite precise, specific, and quantified – from the number of deliveries a week to addresses served, retails outlets opened, prices charged, and so on. The most striking example is in New Zealand, where a Deed of Understanding (DOU) specifies price and service objectives, while a Statement of Corporate Intent (SCI) specifies the nature and scope of activities to be performed, performance targets and measures, dividend policy, and other specific understandings and objectives. Both the DOU and the SCI are presented to the public and are widely distributed and advertised as accountability documents. The idea is to articulate clearly the economic and social obligations of the Post in advance, to avoid ad hoc judgment and political interference when the Post is carrying out its day-to-day responsibilities. The Post in turn is held accountable for performing to the set objectives and understandings. The community-service obligations are increasingly being costed out very precisely, as the basis for a contractual relationship between governments and the Posts. In some situations, this has seen the government "pay" for the performance of community-service obligations, either in a direct subsidy or as the basis for the allocation of some protection in the market. On the price front, most countries have adopted some sort of price-cap formula, again to avoid political interference and ad hoc decisions.

Generally, most countries have tried to ease the regulatory and governance environment in which their corporatized Posts operate, in order to encourage innovation, risk-taking, productivity improvement, a commercial orientation, and the development of a corporate culture. The experience has varied from country to country. A number of countries rely heavily on their competition laws to regulate the Posts, particularly in the area of prices and fair competition (for example, New Zealand, Sweden). However, there is some recent pressure to re-regulate the Posts, particularly given the postal directive from the EC to the effect that the regulation function be divorced from the shareholder function. Third-party regulation exists in Finland, Sweden, Denmark, the Netherlands, Germany, the United Kingdom, and the United States. Licensing arrangements exist in Finland, New Zealand, Denmark, Sweden, Germany, and United Kingdom. The separation of postal administration from postal regulation produces three distinct postal players within the postal regime: the Post itself, the shareholding ministry, and the regulator. This has required the development of subtle, nuanced regulation, lest it interfere with efficiency and competitiveness and the capacity of the Posts to maintain the universal service. Indeed, there is an emerging notion of "light-handed" or "passive" regulation as the appropriate mode for this sector. Governments have been flexing their political muscles recently as the post-neoconservative era unfolds, and regulation is an inexpensive way of asserting their authority.[40]

NEW AND ENDURING THEMES

The above snapshot of the corporatized Posts should not be seen as evidence that postal reform has been carried out without controversy and/or that postal uncertainty has been eliminated. On the contrary, the ongoing and uncompleted processes of corporatization have generated considerable political controversy and uncertainty in a variety of traditional and new postal areas. The central policy challenge has been this. What is the best approach and set of conditions to ensure that the Posts have sufficient revenues to continue to deliver a universal and accessible service at low and universal prices? And how is this to be done while the Posts modernize and invest to remain efficient and competitive and contribute to the health of the national economy?

Political discussions about this issue have actually raised the question of the idea of the universal service itself. What does this mean in the age of cellphones and fax machines? Indeed, some postal officials themselves query the notion of postal universality in a world where wire and satellite are providing the universality of communications and access. The costs associated with the universal service are, perhaps, not as high as was once thought. Nonetheless, policy makers must ask the question of how much the universal postal service is worth. How much does a country want to invest in its postal system? What degree of quality and service does it expect? If a country wants a "world-class" or "Cadillac version" of the postal system, it may need to provide monopoly protection and wide commercial latitude. Alternatively, a country may accept that a modest or "Lada version" will suffice, in the context of numerous communications possibilities. It might not feel the obligation to protect and feed the Post to ensure sufficient revenues to maintain a first-class system. The perceived importance of the universal postal service varies enormously across regions, classes, and users, and this generates political as well as economic considerations of the issue.

A related issue is the degree of monopoly protection or exclusive privilege that a Post should enjoy in order that it has revenues sufficient to maintain the universal service. Here, policy makers face intense cross-pressures. On the one hand, they want their Posts to act in a competitive and efficient manner and to produce a fiscal return. On the other hand, this produces pressures on Posts to cut costs and services to remain competitive and produce a positive bottom line. Governments want good service and good returns, which can be competitive goals. Moreover, the *idea* of a postal monopoly is anathema at the turn of the century. Its elimination would have other postal-policy consequences, which governments have to consider. What should the Posts be allowed to do to make up for lost (monopoly) revenues and to ensure adequate resources to pursue the universal service and to invest sufficiently to stay competitive?

What are the ingredients that make up the universal service in the twenty-first century? Traditionally, this has comprised a price element, a geographic dimension, and a principle of regularity. Each of these has fiscal consequences for the Posts – particularly in an environment where competitors do not face these obligations. Traditionally, the price of a letter was set at a level (low) that would allow mass access.

Changing postal prices was a highly charged event, and tinkering with the universal price was unthinkable. This state of affairs has been addressed recently in two ways. First, most Posts now establish prices in the reserved area according to some sort of formula, which makes the process apolitical. They are allowed price flexibility in their competitive markets. Second, Posts have introduced an element of price differentiation for products and services that "add on" advantages and services over and above the basic letter service (for example, speed of delivery, security, and so on). Similarly, prices have been discounted to large users to the extent that they absorb a degree of sorting costs themselves (for example, bulk discounts for pre-sorted mail). This has fed into the geographic principle – the idea that the price of a letter would be the same regardless of the distance travelled. This principle, which has been at the heart of the idea of the universal postal system, has not been an enormous burden to bear recently, as the proportion of costs attributed to travel has declined to an almost trivial amount in total. For example, John Haldi and John Schmidt report that the transportation costs for a letter sent 2,500 miles is 2.7 cents, while for 5,000 miles it is 4.1 cents.[41] Nonetheless, "the ability of an incumbent postal operator to maintain geographically uniform prices after liberalization remains largely untested."[42] Posts have also adjusted the time sensitivity of letter delivery to accommodate differentiated costs, distinguishing between time-sensitive mail (which is charged a premium) and normal mail (which has modest time ambitions and a modest price). Finally, the principle of regularity has been maintained, albeit with some variation by product and in rural areas. Indeed, the rural and small-town dimension of the postal market presents an ongoing challenge to the Posts and to the idea of universal service, generating tension between service/equity and economic/efficiency goals. This tension plays itself out as well in concerns over job losses, contracting out of functions, and quasi-privatization of parts of the postal business when Posts try to cut costs and increase productivity. Alternatives to the universal service have been mooted. The state could offer direct subsidies to the Post (or private operators) to provide services in areas that do not pay for themselves. Subsidy options are controversial, however, and looked upon sceptically by groups that fear that subsidies will become easy targets for budget cuts.

As noted earlier, the Posts have been given a quid pro quo for the liberalization of markets (and loss of monopoly revenue for cross-subsidization). Deregulation has allowed the Posts more commercial autonomy to participate in competitive postal markets and in markets that are only indirectly related to their postal mission. For example, the Posts have been allowed to lever or expand their networks, that is, to deliver advertising as they deliver letters, to sell insurance and lottery tickets as they sell stamps, or to drive goods and materials to businesses and factories on their delivery routes. This has generated varying degrees of controversy in different countries, depending on the Posts' historical participation or non-participation in these various economic activities. Generally, the question is whether a publicly owned company should be participating in markets where there are already private-sector players. This is a particularly compelling question if there is a chance for unfair competition (via a cross-subsidization of the competitive activity from monopoly revenues). The latter concern has been assuaged, to the extent that the exclusive privilege has been reduced or eliminated. But as a dominant market player, with enormous resources, infrastructure, contacts, and brand equity, the Posts have an intrinsic advantage even in a completely competitive environment. There is also the issue of whether the Posts should be involved in non-postal activity, potentially crowding out private players and buying out competitors with their enormous resources. This is an issue that has led to court challenges in Europe by their competitors, whenever a national Post makes a significant acquisition.

At bottom, the public Posts live an intensely political existence within an unavoidable political context. Governments ultimately determine the degree of exclusive privilege, the character of shareholder regulation, the acceptable level of service and performance, and the extent of liberalization and deregulation. At the international level, as we will see, this is being played out in a political process at international institutions, like the UPU (an agency of the United Nations) and the EU (whose postal directives have the force of law). Posts have been allowed to engage in foreign takeovers and mergers, which demonstrates the extent to which governments still conceptualize the Posts as instruments of national identity and purpose. Domestically, states feel intense political cross-pressures from a variety of political constituencies, which can be characterized as a kind of policy community. Postal unions urge the kinds of policies and approaches that maintain employment and postal growth, and they typically respond vehemently against moves towards liberalization and privatization. The private-sector competitors to the Posts – from behemoths like FedEx and UPS to trucking and courier associations and small-town retail and transport businesses – constantly alert the government to the Posts' anti-competitive or unfair behaviour and look for the increased economic opportunities that could result from changes in postal policy. For example, UPS is challenging Canada's postal regime under the terms of the North American Free Trade Agreement (NAFTA) and (along with La Poste and Royal Mail) has been challenging German postal policy under the EU agreements. The Posts' largest customers (typically organized in an "MMU" – major mail user association) present a formidable political presence in policy discussions. Some countries have organized postal users' councils or groups, which also act as a political pressure group. Rural and small-town constituencies are incredibly vocal in insisting on the maintenance of the universal service. Postal management has its own agenda, as do the boards of Posts, for the construction and pursuit of a certain kind of postal strategy. Finally, the state itself has its own postal interests and agenda; indeed, it has an intrinsically ambivalent perspective on Posts. This may be characterized as the tension between the shareholder and the regulatory dimensions of its responsibilities. On the one hand, the state would like to pursue a postal strategy that maximizes shareholder value, profits, and, perhaps, share value in the event of privatization. On the other hand, it has responsibilities for ensuring the quality of service, equity, and social goals, as well as the maintenance of the universal service. These are, at bottom, contradictory goals that need political resolution.

The recent ideological transition and ongoing policy uncertainty has manifested itself in a kind of policy "pause" on the postal front. After a spurt of reforms in the late 1980s and early 1990s, an element of caution has crept into governments' consideration of postal matters. Almost all major nations have initiated some sort of postal study recently, although little political initiative or substantive results have ensued. For example, the Australian government initiated an elaborate process of study surrounding the competitiveness agenda, but it has backed away from the recommendations made by the National Competition Council (NCC). A reform agenda was articulated in the United States Congress for a number of years, but congressman John McHugh's reform package was stillborn. It took the better part of a decade for the EC to produce its Green Paper on the postal sector and its postal directive – and it is likely to be a lengthy procedure to push the European postal-reform agenda. In most cases, the cause of delay has been the uncertainty and political anxiety about potential policy fallout.

The momentum or motive for change has shifted from governments to the Posts. The postal-reform process was at first driven by governments, who were concerned about postal losses, their own deficits, and complaints about poor service. The reform impulse was resisted initially by the old Posts and their bureaucratic managers, who were subsequently forced to change in the face of the corporatization and liberalization imposed by governments. The corporatized postal agenda has now been taken over by the Posts themselves. They are led by professional managers, boards, and CEOs – typically recruited from the private sector – whose outward and forward-looking perspective demands more liberalization so their business can expand and take on the competition. Governments, in contrast, have become timid, since they are worried about employment, domestic political pressures, and the future of the universal service.

PATTERNS OF REGULATION

Governments' responses to technological, international, and ideological pressures have not played out randomly nor have they elicited consistent responses from country to country. There has been a postal-policy convergence among states. This reflects the fact that nations have had to respond to the same pressures – from technological changes to legal decisions by international bodies. Yet even the most cursory glance at the postal world indicates that there are real differences in how individual countries have chosen to adapt to these pressures. These differences reflect political choices. Governments adopt particular institutional arrangements that channel and process information, expectations, pressures, and necessities in particular ways. On the one hand, they establish particular governance arrangements that set out the legal and operational relationship between the state and the Posts. On the other hand, they establish regulatory arrangements and processes that create postal policies and decisions and give access and life to the postal-policy community. The purpose of this study is to present, examine, and evaluate the governance and regulatory arrangements that have developed in the so-called "progressive" postal regimes over the last decades. The objective of this process is to establish the extent to which the character of these governance and regulatory arrangements affects postal performance, by way of analysing the Canadian scene and making recommendations for Canadian policy initiatives.

Domestic political traditions and actions have intersected with the universal experience of technological, international, and ideological changes to produce a cluster of policy tendencies or "models." Political responses to the Posts' situation can be characterized as adhering to five models: mercantile, market, national, hybrid, and transnational. These models are approximations that simplify complex realities in order to organize and illustrate broad themes and explanations. While they overlap to a degree, each has an essential strategic logic and set of implications. They also demonstrate the character of postal-policy options that are available in the twenty-first century. These models reflect the postal experiences of a number of the so-called progressive

Posts as well as the internationalization of the postal environment. In addition to Canada, the countries to be examined include Australia, Denmark, France, Finland, Germany, the Netherlands, New Zealand, Sweden, and the United Kingdom. The United States was originally chosen to be a case study. But, as noted earlier, the failure of its postal-reform agenda disqualifies it from becoming a "progressive" post and one from which useful comparisons to Canada can be drawn. As a result, the American postal system will simply comprise part of the general postal environment.[43]

The book will present and illustrate these models through a series of national case studies. It concludes with a set of observations about recent postal developments and presents a set of recommendations for the Canadian situation.

Mercantilist Model

The first model is the *mercantilist* model, in which states pursue an aggressive "national champion" strategy. They provide policy support and advantages to expand the Post nationally and internationally, across postal and non-postal sectors, and make it a world communications leader. Technology and globalization framed the postal issue and established its national economic importance. Governments concluded that "what was good for the Posts was also good for the national economy." Postal strategy aimed neither to protect Posts from competition and change nor to remove protection to force Posts to adjust to competition. Postal strategy encouraged and helped the Posts to control technological and international circumstances so as to become a dominant force for the benefit of the entire national economy. Growth is the essence of the mercantile strategy, and without it the postal future is seen to be highly uncertain.

The Dutch Post – TPG – is assertive and growth-oriented. Its character has been highlighted by dramatic initiatives such as the purchase of TNT, its global alliance with the British and Singapore Posts, its intense diversification across postal and non-postal lines (for example, logistics), its aggressive internationalization, and its partial privatization in 1994–95. The last was part of the state's growth and competition agenda. But it was not complemented by liberalization. The state maintained the Post's large exclusive privilege (500 grams) until quite recently (when it was reduced to 100 grams). This maintained a substantial revenue stream to allow the Post to expand commercially and internationally. Germany's Deutsche Post AG – now re-named Deutsche Post World Net (DPWN), the largest Post in Europe – has been on a worldwide shopping spree, purchasing parts or all of a number of major shippers and transportation companies, including AEI and majority shares of DHL. No country has levered its postal network more than the Germans. Postal reform unfolded slowly in the 1990s, when DPAG pursued an aggressive diversification, modernization, and growth strategy. Its revenue base has grown to US$30 billion. Its strategy of internationalization, diversification, and growth prepared it for a successful share issue, which compried 30 per cent of the shares of the company. Both the Dutch and German Posts pursue an integrated strategy of world-brand leadership, entering partnerships and alliances in a manner similar to the airline industry's alliance approach.

As we will see, domestic governance and regulatory arrangements sanctioned, if not encouraged, this strategic approach. Both countries assigned substantial autonomy and independence to their postal boards of directors, both of which comprise high-powered chief executives and directors from the major sectors of the Dutch and German economies. Posts are legislatively mandated to act in a businesslike fashion and to pursue an assertive growth and market-expanding approach. Ministerial oversight is formal and unobtrusive. Partial privatization further limits state involvement in postal affairs in the Netherlands and will do so in Germany. Both countries have formal third-party regulators, reflecting the principle of separation of ownership and regulatory functions. Third-party regulation was pursued for different reasons: to supervise the ongoing monopoly in the Dutch case and to create an orderly transition to German postal competition. The Dutch regulator – OPTA – oversees a highly formal regulation that is all but invisible in the postal-policy process. Regulation is passive, mechanical, and benign, the Post's performance evaluated against a backdrop of quantitative standards. Regulation of the Post's performance is not very restrictive. Dutch domestic regulation reflects a number of particular factors, including a modest public-service tradition in the postal area, a high degree of sensitivity to international competitiveness (complemented by a low sensitivity to domestic competitiveness), small geographic size, a tolerance of monopoly protection and diversification, and a tradition of integrated, consensual decision making in which organized labour is potentially less disruptive.

The Germans liberalized to a degree before they privatized the Post, so they required and have adopted a traditional and more complex model, via a third-party regulator, the Regulatory Authority for Telecommunications and Posts, or Reg TP. Given a larger national market, and the objective to have domestic competition, the Germans have adopted a complex licensing system and a more nuanced regulatory model that aim to maintain the universal system in a liberalized market. As in the Dutch case, accountability is based on a passive application of quantitative standards; the accountability regime is thin and underdeveloped relative to that of countries in the market model. Regulation does not inhibit the high degree of autonomy that the Post enjoys. This model reflects a number of historical inheritances, as in the Dutch case.

Market Model

Each postal regime examined has demonstrated some reliance on market forces to drive postal development. What distinguishes the market approach is the elimination of the postal monopoly from the policy mix, characterized by some as the "Big Bang" approach.[44] The strategy is premised on the benefits of forcing competitive adaptation. Posts will best be able to meet international and technological challenges if they are obliged to act like any corporation that is facing similar pressures, without any help from the government. Posts will have to innovate, become competitive, provide good-quality service, keep their customers happy, and make a profit – if they are to survive. To protect competition and to ensure the universal service, some re-regulation of these competitive markets persists.

The Posts in Finland, Sweden, and New Zealand do not enjoy any monopoly protection. These countries liberalized their markets in similar circumstances. Each is relatively small and isolated, with liberal traditions and consensual political approaches (save for New Zealand). Postal reform was initiated by Labour governments as part of two large and interrelated agendas: the competitiveness agenda and the state-enterprise reform agenda. The latter produced a legislative framework for all state enterprises. These agendas shaped reform, whose subsequent growing pains centred less on social than on economic issues. This result also reflected the adoption of specific, public, and quantified community-service obligations and standards – some etched in legislative stone – which neutralized the backlash against marketization. These countries' experiences demonstrate how liberalization can co-exist with a high-quality universal postal system.

The Finnish postal market was the first to be deregulated (1991) and the Swedes followed thereafter (1993). The Posts have no exclusive privilege or protected area. Each separated ownership from regulation and created a third-party regulator (the Telecommunications Administration Centre, or TAC, and the National Post and Telecom Agency, or PTS, respectively.) The Post in Finland is a limited-liability company with a considerable degree of autonomy. Ministerial postal resources and oversight are modest. The board of directors of the Post has a wide degree of space in which to manoeuvre. The Finnish regulatory model is pragmatic and simple: a limited array of performance expectations are clearly articulated, within a licensing system in which participants are bound by these standards, to be overseen by a regulatory structure (the TAC) that monitors performance against these standards. The Post experiences little inhibitions from the TAC. The Finns' licensing system has been difficult to operate. As in the Swedish case, liberalizing a postal market does not guarantee that postal competition will develop. The Post's stature, size, and familiarity are formidable barriers to entry. The SSM case (Suorminonta Oy) led the state to introduce a licensing fee to neutralize possible cream-skimming (that is, an operator pursuing the least cost-expensive and most lucrative part of the market without having to bear the fiscal or other responsibilities of maintaining the universal system). This case demonstrates what happens, politically, if postal competition undermines the Post's financial capacity to maintain the universal service.

The Post in Sweden is a limited-liability company. Ministerial oversight of the Post is modest. The government has the legal responsibility to maintain the universal service, and it licenses the Post to this end. This agreement sets quantified and ambitious commercial targets for the Post, which mimic private performance. The government has encouraged postal competition, and it has bent over backwards to ensure it. The Post has one major competitor (City Mail, in the bulk-mail market) and a series of small, local competitors. The regulatory environment is as simple and straightforward as the Finnish one. Third-party re-regulation has emerged in areas like pricing and access agreements, because of the reality of competition. PTS – the regulator – is politically autonomous, with a small postal sector that exercises a light touch. It has no authority in areas like investment, diversification, and so on. The growing pains of liberalization and competition have generated considerable regulatory trial and error and "interference." Once the transitional dust settles, regulation will likely become a matter of routine.

A third version of the market approach is New Zealand, which has the best-articulated postal regulatory and governance environment in the world. The Post is a limited-liability company, directed by an active and assertive board of directors, which is mandated to pursue the best interests of the Post. It enjoys considerable autonomy against the accountability backdrop of two well-defined public declarations. A jointly produced Statement of Corporate Intent specifies the owner's objectives and expectations of financial and business performance. A jointly produced Deed of Understanding lays out the owners' expectation of service and quality performance. The postal market was liberalized gradually and became fully open in 1999. Postal competition has begun to develop, and numerous postal licences have been issued. New Zealand does not have third-party regulation. Rather, it separated the ownership and regulation functions and assigned them to two departments of government (Treasury and Commerce respectively) in a checks-and-balance process. The Crown Company Monitoring and Advisory Unit (CCMAU) supports the ownership-accountability function with complimentary advice and private-sector experience. The regulatory function is exercised in an informal and light-handed way, given the competitive environment and the existence of the DOU. There has been one significant case where the Post appeared to have been inhibited by the government (the Freightways purchase, which was denied by the government); this occurred before liberalization.

The market model comprises a mix of policy instruments, including both liberalization of the postal market and its re-regulation to ensure competition and the universal service. This approach remains in its infancy, making it difficult to offer judgments as to its success. Moreover, the model will be "tested" only after real competition develops, at which time the Posts' weakened capacity to maintain the universal service will put governments on the spot. This may also test these states' unwillingness to allow diversification, which has been modest to this point.

National Model

The third model is the national – or public – model, which is characterized by the predominance of social and political considerations over economic ones in formulating postal policy. Traditionally, the Post's social and economic dimensions co-existed in an uneasy balance. The policy discourse and practice of countries in the market model have seen the predominance of economic objectives and the downplaying of social objectives and/or their articulation through economic arrangements and accomplishments. Governments within the national or public model have tended to maintain social objectives while bearing and tolerating the economic costs of this choice. These governments have not ignored the technological and international realities of the postal world, but they have asserted that the best way for a country to meet them is to control and manage them to national purposes. In contrast, the market approach accepts the logic of these changes and liberalizes the market to force postal operators to build the capacity to meet the challenges involved. The mercantile approach confronts the logic of these challenges by privatizing or corporatizing the monopoly Post so as to make it a stronger, dominant player in the new postal world. The national or public approach neither liberalizes nor privatizes, although it contains elements of both in an eclectic policy mix. This approach seeks to control or neutralize the challenges confronting the Post in order to ensure the maintenance of traditional postal objectives and political control over the postal agenda.

The countries within this model have reformed their postal systems to a degree. Posts have been corporatized to an extent and are motivated considerably by commercial values and logic; markets have been partially liberalized and reserved areas have been narrowed; regulatory and operational matters have sometimes been separated to limit government's involvement in daily postal life. However, these reform processes stop before total liberalization and/or complete corporatization and/or serious deregulation. The Posts continue to enjoy some exclusive privilege, which perpetuates political obligations, dependency, and scrutiny. State ownership limits the process of corporatization. Governance and regulatory arrangements have been designed to perpetuate government influence and authority.

This model casts postal policy across a national political backdrop. Employment, national unity, rural development, nation building, social solidarity, and other public considerations – from financing pension plans to helping the state to balance its budget – determine many postal-policy choices. While often corporatized, Posts enjoy less commercial and market freedom, recruit less personnel with private-sector backgrounds, confront a constrained set of policy options, see more public and bureaucratic figures on their boards, and remain under greater public, parliamentary, and media scrutiny. The Posts are not pushed as hard by governments to be financially and commercially successful, because wider political goals drive postal policy. For example, the French government continues to conceptualize La Poste within its employment and social-equity agendas more than it does within a technological or international-economy framework. An intriguing and innovative tactic is the separation of market from traditional postal activities – the former being played out through subsidiaries (*fililization.*) The Danish government remains ambivalent about whether to follow a market strategy. It constrains the Post from following a mercantile strategy (or at least waits for an acceptable one to take shape) and remains heavily involved in the Post. After a period of liberalization and corporatization, the Liberal government of Canada repositioned Canada Post into a more political framework during the 1990s. It accepted a policy status quo rather than pushing the Post to improve its performance and to build up its capacity to confront international and technological challenges.

These countries have elaborate and dense institutional arrangements that reproduce the state's objectives and keep the state at the heart of the postal-policy process. For example, the French postal regime has multiple policy layers: Conseil National des Postes et télécoms, Commission Supérieure du personnel et des affaires sociales, Commission Supérieure du Service Public des postes et télécoms (CSSPPt), the DGPT (Directorate General of Post and Telecommunications), Ministry of Finance and Ministry of the Budget, and the Conseil d'Administration. The state retains a substantial presence on La Poste's board, via representatives from seven different ministries as well as by an economic and financial adviser (*contrôle économique et financier d'état*) and a regulatory presence (*commissaire du gouvernement*). In Canada, the board is comprised of political appointees, named to ensure regional, gender, and other non-postal criteria. These nations have less clear-cut regulatory and governance environments than the other models. The lines of accountability are fuzzy, particularly in the absence of well-articulated and well-publicized objectives, standards, and goals. For example, the regulatory agency in France is the CSSPPt, which combines parliamentary representatives, ministerial representatives, and experts, but has only an advisory role (French law does not allow the delegation of regulatory powers). Canada does not have a formal third-party regular. Regulatory and ownership functions overlap in Public Works and Government Services Canada and the lines of authority and accountability are unclear. The Ministry of Transport remains central to postal policy in Denmark, with both regulatory and ownership functions housed there, and representatives of the ministries of Transport and Finance are members of the board. These countries maintain a reserved area for their Posts.

Hybrid Model

The fourth model is the hybrid or transitional model. It comprises countries whose evolution could proceed in any number of directions to settle within one of the other models or to remain as a kind of mixed or hybrid model. These countries have pursued corporatization, liberalization, and deregulation initiatives, but they have not resolved competing objectives and/or determined their ultimate policy paths. The United Kingdom and Australia were two of the first countries to adopt a "progressive" approach. They have recently studied and scrutinized postal matters extensively. Both countries have postal legislative measures waiting to be implemented. Their extended reform processes may unfold indefinitely, in which case they will remain in a kind of mixed or hybrid state.

Australia corporatized and commercialized its Post, which enjoys a high degree of business autonomy. A substantial, active, and assertive board directs its affairs and is dedicated to increasing the Post's growth and stature. The Post enjoys a considerable amount of market freedom, particularly in levering or diversifying the use of its retail network to become a serious player in the financial and bill-paying sectors. The Post has been highly successful financially and has generated hundreds of millions of dollars in dividends and taxes for the government. Its service record is good. The postal regime has separated the ownership and regulatory function, albeit without third-party regulation. Australia has recently adopted the New Zealand model of dual administrative oversight (Finance for ownership, and DCITA – Communications, Information Technology, and the Arts – for regulation). A five-year plan, community-service obligations, a code of practice, and a service charter provide accountability processes and mechanisms that are highly quantified, elaborate, and perhaps more public than those of any other postal regime. The regulatory process has been light-handed, reflecting an emphasis on increased competitiveness as the best regulatory tool.

In Australia, the Post has been studied and evaluated within the competitiveness and deregulation framework. The National Competition Council made recommendations that would have seen complete liberalization save for householder mail. The government was politically uneasy with this suggestion. The rural and "bush" areas, as well as organized labour, expressed serious concern about the impact of this approach on the future of the universal service. The government offered a compromise, proposing to cut the Post's protection to about 12 per cent of the market (50 grams and 45 cents, or one times the price of a first-class stamp). This compromise was almost two years in the making, and in the end it was dropped when the government proved unable to build up a political consensus in its favour. Australia thus rests on the cusp of a development. If the government pursues this and other initiatives, Australia may eventually enter the market model. If political concerns continue to inhibit change, then Australia may enter the national or public model. If Australia were to adopt the market model, this would provide a serious test to the model – given that the country's size and population makes maintaining the universal service a complex business.

The United Kingdom was the first country to transform its Post from administrative into corporate form. Its subsequent performance generated billions of pounds for the government even as it maintained a quality universal service. This performance, however, obscured the fact that the postal governance and regulatory environment was poorly defined, informal in practice, and basically inhibited the Post's operations and developments. Its board had limited autonomy while the government retained considerable authority that allowed it to remain central to the Post's decision making. It controlled the Post's financial existence, the infamous EFL targets – external financing limit – draining resources from the Post. It also controlled the Post's strategic existence, retaining key decision-making authority. The Post could not adjust to new international and technological circumstances, since it did not have the financial capacity or authority to take the required strategic decisions.

After extended study, the Blair government adopted a new Postal Services Bill. This initiative authorized the Post to make strategic decisions as a public limited company (plc) under the Companies Act. Financial targets will now be based on a formula (dividends set at 40 per cent of profits) and the Post will have increased investment and strategic autonomy (albeit to a borrowing and investment limit). Third-party regulation has been introduced. The first task of the Postal Services Commission (PSC) – generically called Postcomm – will be to evaluate the political hot potato that the government chose to avoid: further liberalization of the domestic market.[45] This issue was a metaphor for "reform" – it was dominated by political as much as by economic considerations. The union continued to insist that the Post remain as a public corporation, and the public expressed concern with the quality of service. This postal reform represents what was euphemistically termed a "politically balanced package." The state will retain considerable postal authority, to service public and union expectations. The proposal will not push the Post into much deeper corporatized waters, since the government will retain investment and strategic authority. Nor will it push the Post into deeper liberalized waters, for some or all of its exclusive privilege will remain. The reform initiative expressed mercantile, liberal, and national political concerns and sensibilities. There is some government determination to allow the Post to develop into an international behemoth like DPWN or TPG. But there are also real limits on how far the Post can go on its own in this regard. Some liberalization is proposed as a possibility – but it reflects a "liberalization if necessary but not necessarily liberalization" tactic and certainly not a "big bang" approach. The British model will continue to be a hybrid one, with mercantile, market, and national features.

Transnational Model

Each of the previous models intersects with the transnational model. An increasing number of postal-policy actions and initiatives are led or shaped by international agencies or groups, such as the European Union, the Universal Postal Union, the World Bank, and the

International Postal Corporation. As the internationalization of the postal environment continues, a pressing postal issue is this: will Posts cooperate with or compete against each other?

While there is evidence of postal bilateralism and multilateralism, this is unlikely to be a substantial or predominant strategy in the future. On the multilateral front, there have been a number of developments through the UPU and the World Bank, particularly in the less developed world. These bodies have initiated international postal reforms, encouraged liberalization and corporatization, and helped particular postal regimes via special projects. Nevertheless, the UPU and the World Bank are awkward and unwieldy organizations with limited authority and clout. Moreover, they are not seen by the major postal players as a place to pursue their economic interests. It is the location where governments play out primarily their political interests. The recent UPU congress in Beijing set up a reform process to make the UPU's institutional framework reflect the modern postal reality – but this is a process that is still unfolding.[46] The EU has pushed the postal-reform agenda in Europe in a coherent, albeit painstaking way. However, there are divisions of national interest within the EU, basically between the northern "liberalized" Posts and the southern "national" posts. The plan to reduce the exclusive privilege to 50 grams was scuttled and the compromise move to 150 grams may not be adopted as a result of internal divisions.

There is a tremendous amount of international institutional interaction in the postal world, but it is unlikely that a cooperative international postal model will develop. National political interests continue to predominate, particularly with respect to employment, profits, growth, and prestige. A Darwinian model is more likely to emerge than a cooperative one, particularly as liberalization and deregulation processes unfold. When the reform process is introduced, Posts tend first to move to protect their own markets then move on to diversification, regionalization, and internationalization perspectives. There will likely be intense and growing competition among national Posts. At some point, mergers and alliances will be the rational strategy; there is evidence of this stage having been reached already. Some firms and companies will go under or be taken over, even national ones. Given competition and customer demands for "seamless" international service across sectors, an alliance model of sorts is likely to develop – possibly organized around the "Big Four" (TPG, DPWN, Royal Mail, and La Poste) or around an even smaller grouping. Generally speaking, there does not appear to be a postal or political vision or consensus about how increasingly large, commercial, and growth-oriented Posts are going to deal with each other. What is most likely to emerge is a dual postal market dominated by the Big Four and a few major regional players. The remaining Posts and governments will be left either to pursue the more expensive features of their domestic universal service or to sell off their markets to and/or partner with the major Posts. Market, customer, and technological pressures will drive this process, and the Posts themselves will try actively to manage it. Governments – at the national and international levels – are more likely to respond to these initiatives rather than manage them, and to have only a moderate influence on the ultimate result.

In pursuing the comparative analysis, we will be sensitive to the fact that postal-policy differences reflect national historical and cultural differences as much as they reflect actual policy choices. As Christopher Pollitt and his associates have demonstrated, the postal-reform agenda has been generated by "global economic pressures for restraining public expenditure and increasing the competitiveness of national economies ... However the specific *trajectories* taken by these reforms in individual countries appears to have been decisively shaped by the main features of the politico-administrative system in each country rather than directly by economic forces ... it would be mistaken to suppose that a programme of reform that had been successfully carried out within one politico-administrative system could be translated to another."[47]

The politico-administrative differences are but one in a series of comparative differences that must be considered in making comparisons. For example, the geography of countries differs enormously, with the result that the density of the postal market varies tremendously. Canada's population density is 10 per cent that of the United States and 1 per cent that of the United Kingdom. As a result, there are 12 times more points of call per square kilometre in the United States and 120 times more in the United Kingdom. This has an impact both on costs and potential service targets, but also on the political culture and expectations surrounding the Posts. Indeed, the political or symbolic role of the Posts looms larger in continental countries (with vast expanses to build up and develop) and isolated countries than in more developed and settled areas. The range of postal services and traditions – and expectations – varies historically across countries. For example, the retail and banking traditions of the Posts have a stronger history in Europe and the Antipodes than in North America, where there has been a stronger private-sector presence and tradition. The expectation of six versus five-day delivery, and delivery to the lot line or the door (or the lobby or the apartment door), separates postal systems internationally. Some countries have traditionally been high-price and high-protection societies (for example, Germany, the Netherlands) while others have been low-price and low-protection ones (North America and the Antipodes). Some Posts have been cross-subsidized historically by the telephone-telecommunications side. All of these and others factors have had an enormous impact on numerous aspects of postal life, from revenue flows and postal expectations to postal legitimacy and authority in various markets. All of these factors temper the degree to which policy comparisons can be executed in a fair and meaningful way. And these factors constrain the possibility of developing a "one-size-fits-all" governance and regulatory model.

PART ONE

The Mercantile Model

As suggested in the Introduction, political responses to the Posts' situation can be divided into five strategies or models: mercantile, market, national, hybrid, and international. These models are approximations and simplify complex realities in order to organize and illustrate broad themes. Moreover, the models and strategies overlap each other to a degree. Nonetheless, there is an essential strategic logic and set of implications for each of these approaches.

We begin with the mercantile model. By this, we mean a policy approach that commits the state to the strengthening and growth of the postal sector, in order that that sector make the maximum possible contribution to the national economy as a whole. The German and Dutch cases reflect political decisions to turn the domestic Posts into national leaders in the world communications market. That is, the states pursued an aggressive "national champion" strategy. They provided policy support and advantages to transform their Posts nationally and internationally, across postal and non-postal sectors, into world communications leaders. Both governments perceived the importance of technological change and globalization to their respective economies, and they were concerned about the increasing competitive challenges that this would generate. They did not try to protect their Posts from the competition that these developments produced, as was traditionally the case in the national or political model. Nor did they strip protection away and force their Posts to adjust to the new competitive realities, as in the market model. Rather, given the importance of the new technology and growing internationalization, they accepted the importance of the postal sector for the overall health of their national economies. They concluded that "what was good for the Posts was also good for the national economy." As a result, they encouraged and helped the Posts to gain control over their technological and international circumstances, so that the Posts could act as a dominant force for the benefit of the domestic economies as a whole.

Recent highlights of these mercantile Posts include their aggressive growth and diversification initiatives. The Dutch Post – TPG (TNT Postal Group) – is partially privatized. It has purchased TNT, entered a global alliance with the British and Singapore Posts, made an enormous investment and expansion in transportation and logistics, and pursued an intense internationalization of its activities. The German Post – DPWN (Deutsche Post World Net) – is also partially privatized and is the largest Post in Europe. It has been on a worldwide shopping spree, purchasing parts or all of a number of major shippers and transportation companies, including AEI and DHL. It has pursued an assertive strategy of diversification, internationalization, and growth. Both countries pursue an integrated strategy of world-brand leadership, entering partnerships and alliances in a manner similar to the airline industry's alliance approach.[1]

As will be seen below, domestic governance and regulatory arrangements sanctioned, if not encouraged, this strategic approach. The mercantile approach comprises a policy mix of instruments that includes deregulation and regulation, liberalization and continued monopoly control, passive and active initiatives, and market and statist initiatives. At bottom, though, all of these initiatives are directed to making the Posts world leaders.

1 The Netherlands

Jim Campbell calls the Dutch Post "the most business-like" of Posts.[1] Indeed, it is one of the world's most profitable Posts – in contrast to its modest economic performance in the 1980s, when profits were rare and losses typical.[2] Campbell's characterization is also appropriate given the businesslike way in which the Dutch political authorities adjusted their postal system to the realities of technological competition and globalization. The Dutch Post is perhaps best known for its being the first Post in an industrial nation to be (partially) privatized. At bottom, though, Dutch postal policy has been as political as it has been economic in its rationale and goals. In fact, the Dutch case is the example par excellence of the political and postal authorities proceeding in unison and acting on the same wavelength.

The origins of the transformation of the Dutch postal system lie in the early 1980s.[3] Like most industrial economies, the Dutch post-war economy flourished in the Keynesian social-welfare environment that was sustained by strong international economic expansion. The Dutch pursued their economic goals via a unique approach to policy making, organized around consultation and consensus. The result was one of the world's largest public sectors and welfare systems and an ongoing political commitment to full employment. In the aftermath of the energy shocks of the 1970s, economic growth slowed in the 1980s, budget deficits grew (the national debt rising to over 70 per cent of national income), and unemployment rose to the unheard of level of 17 per cent in 1983 and 1984. A Christian Democrat/Liberal coalition (under Prime Minister Rudd Lubbers) was formed in 1982, with a mandate to pursue a "no nonsense" policy of reducing the role of the state in the economy. This program included cuts and alterations in government spending, reducing the size of the public sector, wage adjustments, deregulating many tasks to the private sector, and privatization of state enterprises.

These forces and policy developments swept along the Dutch postal system and created the conditions and momentum for its reform. This is one of the most striking contrasts between the Dutch postal experience and that in Canada and elsewhere – the extent to which the postal-policy agenda in the Netherlands was a "passive" ingredient in a larger policy agenda. Dutch policy initiatives in the mid-1980s included a substantial amount of privatization. This privatization was motivated less by ideological considerations than by a quest for administrative efficiency and budget reduction.[4] As a result, there was insubstantial opposition and criticism, even from the "left" parties and the unions. Indeed, a complementary policy initiative saw wages reduced by 3 per cent in 1982 (albeit after a long and unresolved strike) in exchange for the shortening of the work week. While the unions made some public declarations against wage cuts, deregulation, and privatization, they essentially accepted these developments as inevitable. They then worked effectively to make the best possible deal in the new environment, such as attaining a no-layoffs commitment.[5] Postal reform – and the repositioning of labour and wages within that reform – did not play out in isolation as "postal policy." Rather, it was pulled along in "business-like" fashion by the pragmatic policy agenda engineered by the coalition government in the mid-1980s. This allowed postal policy to avoid the intense scrutiny that it received in countries like Canada.

There was a second pragmatic dimension to the Dutch authorities' initiation of postal reform. Political and policy leaders were aware of the likely long-term and qualitative impact of the computer revolution and information technology on Dutch economic development. This was demonstrated forcefully in the government's response to the Steenbergen Committee report (on the future of the Post). As a small and open trading economy with an enormous reliance on world markets, the government declared that the Netherlands could not hide from these developments. Indeed, authorities recognized that the Dutch economy would have to absorb technological developments fully into their economic infrastructure, if it were to continue to have a comparative advantage in new and traditional markets. The Posts and telecommunications were seen by the government to be critical ingredients in the economic infrastructure, and hence of critical importance for the future competitive position of Dutch trade and industry.[6] The government's response to technological change, and its relationship to external national competitiveness, was at the heart of the Dutch authorities' initiation of postal reform. So, too, was the sense that the best – indeed only – solution for the Post in this context was a "growth" strategy. This was because the new technology would provide enormous payoffs for economies of scale, which the Dutch market alone would be too small to produce.[7]

A third feature of the reform of the Dutch postal system was the extent to which there was an identity of interest and purpose between political and postal authorities. Following the post-war consultative model, the government was careful to build up a set of common understandings and viewpoints between it and the Post before embracing and pursuing the reform agenda.[8] After examining the postal situation, the government concluded that its direct involvement with the Post impeded postal development and the Post's possible reaction to changed economic circumstances. So it moved to give the Post more freedom and independence – not for ideological but for pragmatic economic and national reasons. Once adopted, postal policy has been pursued vigorously and coherently without much public or private aggravation or tension. There has been a political and postal identity of interest over the last decade. Currently, there is a bit more debate, but mainly over the pace of change.[9]

In sum, the reform of the Post in the Netherlands was part of a larger policy agenda, in which Dutch policy makers pragmatically adjusted the economy and economic policy to changed circumstances. Dutch postal policy per se focused on technological change, the importance of the Post for national competitiveness, and the growth requirement for survival in the international economy. A decade later, the following statement in 1996 by the Post was a perfect reflection of the postal strategy that was subsequently pursued by political and postal authorities: "PTT Post foresees that after 2000 a small number of companies will provide Europe's postal services. It is PTT Post's ambition to be one of those companies. A precondition of this ambition is fast growth, both autonomously and through acquisitions."[10]

HISTORY

Until the creation of the Statenpost in 1751, the cities controlled the postal system. The remainder of the eighteenth century saw a centralization of the postal system, culminating in the 1799 reorganization of a strong national Post, based on the French model. The first Postal Act (1807) made it part of the Ministry of Finance, and uniform pricing was introduced at this time. The Post was expected to contribute revenues to the Treasury, and the public saw it as much a tax-raising body as a public service. Its perspective shifted somewhat to the latter in the 1850s, and modernization was carried out in the 1870s. There were three postal rounds daily, but this was reduced to two in the 1930s (to cut costs) and to one round in the 1970s. After the Second World War, the Post operated persistently at a loss, which led to studies, reports, and attempts to control costs (for example, the closing of smaller post offices). The postal system grew substantially in the 1960s and 1970s, when mechanization of sorting was introduced, as was the postal code (in 1977). This set the stage for the Dutch policy-reform process, which has unfolded in five stages.

Stage One – De-nationalization

The Dutch government studied the issue of the future of the postal system throughout the 1980s, against the backdrop of the end of the post-war boom and the advent of technological change and the information age. In 1981 the Swarttouw Committee was set up to advise the minister of transport and public works regarding the role Posts, Telephones, and Telecommunications would play in the information age (the post office and telecommunications were, and remained, part of the same organization until 1997). It reported in March 1982. The government presented its reaction to this report to Parliament in June 1984. Among other things, it recommended that an external (private) management team study the future status and supervision of PTT. Making use of an earlier study by the McKinsey company, the Steenbergen Committee was established and reported in 1985 ("Signals for the Future"). It recommended that PTT be "de-nationalized" – that is, that it be removed and distanced from government administration and re-established as a limited-liability company. At the same time, it recommended that the Post retain its monopoly feature and continue to carry out its traditional universal-service tasks. Broadly speaking, the government responded favourably to the Steenbergen report in 1986 and established a transitional board (of three non-civil servants) which implemented the recommendations by 1989.

The government decided to transform PTT from a state enterprise to a Naamloze Vennootschal (NV) – a private-law company. The new company would be a holding company, with two subsidiaries – post and telecommunications – and one shareholder. The company was commonly referred to as KPN – Koninklijke PTT Nederland NV. PTT Post BV was the name of the Dutch postal service, a wholly owned subsidiary of KPN. The government decided that the new postal company should be given the same operational independence as any private company. For example:

- it would conduct its own policy with regard to raising funds on the capital market, acquiring its own capital, participating in other companies, and entering into joint ventures;
- it would face no limits on the range of products and services that the Post could provide in open competition;
- it would conduct an independent employment policy in conformity with the market, negotiating a separate collective agreement with its employees, who would no longer be civil servants;
- it would install its own management team, which would be obliged to pursue sound business practices;
- its shareholder – the government – would expect it to make a profit or rate of return on invested capital in line with the private-sector expectations (the rate of interest in the capital market in the long term supplemented by a sum for contingency purposes); and
- it would establish a set of prices in accordance with shareholder expectation of receiving income, which should be roughly the existing level.[11]

The Post retained its existing monopoly and was expected to carry out its traditional postal obligations. As a result, the government was be obliged to supervise it. This regulation would be of a very general character, however, and would be directed to the fulfillment of postal objectives, as laid out in a clearly detailed concession or list of rights and obligations (see below).

Stage Two – Privatization

In the Netherlands, stage one is termed "privatization" – since PTT was organized as a private-law, limited-liability company. The government retained full ownership, however, and so it is perhaps more accurate to describe that stage as de-nationalization or corporatization. After 1989, the Post reorganized itself into a more businesslike operation, decentralizing into seven business units. It separated postal retail outlets into a different operation, gave far more attention to the parcels business, and made a substantial initiative in the courier and international areas. In short, it began to behave like a modern corporation in the market place.

The corporatization process was extended further in 1994, when the Netherlands was the first industrial country to privatize its Post (which was still part of the holding company KPN, which in turn controlled telecommunications as well). The government's motivation in this regard was consistent with that demonstrated in the late 1980s. Privatization reflected the view that the Post should be given business space and independence from the government. It should be encouraged to act as far as possible like a typical corporation in responding to market signals in the high-tech, globalized environment of the 1990s.[12] Privatization would both generate needed capital (see below) and inject increased private-sector values and considerations into the operation of the Post.

The privatization was a partial one, which took place in two steps. KPN sold 30 per cent of its ownership in 1994 and another 25 per cent in 1995. The first sale raised almost Dfl.7 billion and the second sale another Dfl.6 billion. Of the 188,500 shareholder purchasers, 31,000 were KPN employees. Foreign institutions took 65 per cent of the shares. Privatization thus internationalized the Dutch Post even further. The privatization was popular in the market: the share issues were oversubscribed threefold.[13] As will be seen below, private shares are valued highly because of the Post's strong market position and solid cash flow. The company is listed on stock exchanges in Amsterdam, London, Frankfurt, and New York.

The government retained 45 per cent of the shares and indicated that it intended to reduce this to below one-third by 2004. As will be seen presently, it continued its supervisory relationship to KPN. Moreover, it retained the "golden share," which gives the state special privileges. It is designed to be used in circumstances where a takeover, sale, or initiative is considered to change the company fundamentally or to be against the general interest.[14]

Stage Three – Expansion

Privatization allowed PTT Post to pursue an aggressive and innovative commercial strategy, because it gave the Post increased freedom and the capital required for rapid modernization and expansion.[15] The study will review a multitude of Post activities and initiatives below. For now, one development should be given special notice. In 1996 the Post startled the postal and business world by purchasing TNT, the world's largest transportation and shipping company. TNT was an Australian company, founded by Ken Thomas in 1946 (hence the name, Thomas Nationwide Transport).

During the 1980s, the major developed Posts tried to jump-start their share of the lucrative and expanding express market, where they had only a modest presence. As will be seen in the concluding chapter, they formed the International Postal Corporation to this end. But the member companies could not work together for a common purpose to compete with the international express companies. As a result, a number of them (France, Germany, Sweden, Canada, and the Netherlands) grouped together (as GD Express Worldwide) to buy a 50 per cent share of the worldwide express business of TNT. In June 1996 the Dutch bought out the 50 per cent share of their postal partners. And, in a friendly takeover in August 1996, it bought out the remaining 50 per cent. This initiative was given the state's approval. The result of the initiative was that the Dutch Post instantaneously became a world market player. It became a direct owner-operator in 47 countries and could offer its services in 200 more.[16] A large number of the world's Posts – Canada's included – use TNT as their international express courier. The TNT acquisition was an early step in the Post's broad-based strategy of international mergers and acquisitions, which will be addressed below.

Stage Four – De-merger

From 1989 to 1997, the Post and Telecommunications existed within the holding company umbrella of KPN. The two units operated quite separately. But it made increasing sense to have separate boards and supervisory responsibilities. To this end, in June 1997 the board recommended to its shareholders that the company be de-merged into two stand-alone companies. The government in turn accepted the recommendation and set the wheels in motion for the creation of two separate companies. On the Post side, KPN disappeared to become TNT Post Group, or TPG. This new entity combines a national Post with a global express company (the old TNT) in a formidable union. It comprises a holding company structure, with subsidiaries focusing on different parts of the market.

Stage Five – Liberalization

De-nationalization, privatization, and de-merger did not comprise a strategy of postal liberalization – in contrast, say, to the postal strategies pursued in Scandinavia or the Antipodes. Unlike any other country, the Netherlands privatized first and liberalized after. Indeed, the postal monopoly (and postal responsibilities) remained as they had been before 1989 (indeed, since the turn of the century). The postal concession granted the Dutch Post a monopoly on mail items up to 500 grams (or a price level of Dfl.11.90). This monopoly protection had a limited impact on certain parts of the postal market and was undermined to a great extent by product and technological substitution as well as by inflation. Nonetheless, the exclusive privilege guaranteed the Post a healthy revenue flow, which in turn financed a number of the commercial and mechanization initiatives that will be detailed below. This in turn made the shares in the Post attractive to investors.

The 500-gram level of protection was not sustainable over the long run, although it was useful in establishing the Dutch Post as a world leader in the transition period of the 1990s. Once the European Commission determined to modernize the European postal market (see concluding chapter), the European liberalization process would initiate a legal imperative to reduce the level of the exclusive privilege to 350 grams.

Both the Dutch Post and the government favoured liberalization, provided that neighboring countries reduced their protection at the same time (or else the postal monopolies in other countries would be given an unfair advantage in the Dutch postal market). The Postal Act directed the government to review the postal situation every four years, which it did in 1993 and 1997 (to modest effect). It carried out a much larger review in 1998, in response to the European Postal Directive. It devised a series of changes (to be detailed below), including a reduction in the exclusive privilege to 100 grams and three times the price of a first-class stamp (2.4 guilders) and the removal of outbound international letters from the reserved area. This proposal was approved by Parliament and became effective in June 2000.

The liberalization of the Dutch postal market came later than in many other countries, notwithstanding the Dutch tradition of being outward looking and not particularly protectionist. However, because the Netherlands was situated in the geographic heartland of Europe – unlike, say, Scandinavia – there was considerable concern that being a "leader" on liberalization would be too costly and potentially dangerous. This would particularly be the case if neighboring countries chose not to liberalize. Today, the Dutch position remains pro-liberalization, but only to the extent that the Dutch market does not get overly exposed to competitors (especially the German Post, whose turnover is twice the size of the Dutch).[17]

STATUTORY AND REGULATORY ENVIRONMENT

The broad changes that were presented above have been engineered by the Dutch government within a particular statutory and regulatory environment that it created. The Post retained some monopoly powers and the state remained a shareholder, so the government was obliged to remain in a supervisory relationship with the Post, notwithstanding the partial privatization. The statutory tasks of the state Post were transferred to a ministry with responsibility for the postal sector. A new regulatory body was formed and a process of regulatory supervision and control was constructed. However, given the state's and the Post's shared interests and vision of a corporatized international Post, the regulatory environment that was created has been a relatively benign and passive one. This has allowed the Post a considerable amount of room to manoeuvre.

The Post's regulatory environment is constructed from three legislative documents: the Postal Act of 1988 (and subsequent amendments), the General Directive for Postal Service (1988 and amendments), and the Order Concerning Minimum Rates for Courier Service.

The Postal Act outlines the broad contours of the new postal world and postal policy, the details of which are fleshed out in the other two documents. The ambition of the act is clear: it is informed by the objective of "granting ... greater autonomy to the postal service."[18] The act grants a postal concession to the Post – to the exclusion of all others – in order to guarantee a high-quality universal postal service and a national postal network. The Post maintained its existing exclusive privilege over mail delivery, collection from boxes, and sale of stamps for letters, now up to 100 grams (see changes below). Exceptions to the exclusive privilege are specified (Section 12), particularly with respect to express mail.[19] Unaddressed direct mail, magazines, and parcels had already been liberalized outside monopoly protection. The act assigns the concessionaire the obligation to deliver mail up to a weight and dimensions specified by the minister in a General Directive (10 kilos), which determines and defines the principles of good service, delivery, the extent of the retail network, quality targets, and so on. Access to the network is allowed on a commercial basis. Section 5(5) declares that the directive should be constructed "with due regard to the need for the concessionaire to operate in a way appropriate to normal business practice." Section 5 outlines the Post's reporting relationship to the ministry, and subsection (4) establishes the contours of the regulatory relationship between the state and the Post: "The directives shall contain only obligations with regard to the results to be achieved by the concessionaire and not the method of management to be pursued in order to obtain said results." In other words, the state would not interfere in the management of the Post, as long as the Post delivered the results expected and provided the ministry with adequate information to make the case. The directive was to be re-evaluated every five years by the ministry.

The General Directive specified the postal outputs or service results that were expected by the state, in return for which the Post was granted the postal concession. These included formulae for the number of post-office outlets and boxes (and criteria for their closure on "reasonable grounds"), delivery standards (six-day delivery; next-day delivery), and a formula for postal-rate increases (a price-cap system, tied to an index of private-sector wage rates). The directive basically maintained the principle of a universal service at a universal price, for all materials up to 10 kilos to be delivered six days a week. But it introduced some criteria for differentiated services at different rates. The directive elaborated how the Post might alter the national network or change features of the universal service. It also maintained any existing compensation arrangements between the state and the Post for "unprofitable" activities associated with its universal-service obligations, and established the principle that any new "unprofitable" activities required by the state would require public compensation. Section 7 detailed the range of information that the ministry required to evaluate whether the Post was meeting the expectations laid out in the directive. This included summaries of postal activities and developments (delivery performance, numbers of outlets, boxes and delivery points, and so on), a long-term plan, and details of financial performance. Nothing in the act or the directive circumscribed or limited the Post's actions in entering into different markets or the introduction of new products. But Section 6(6) insisted that the Post not cross-subsidize other competitive or market-based activities by the returns from its monopoly-protected activities. The directive also created a consultative body of management and user groups to meet at least twice a year.

The Order Concerning Minimum Rates for Courier Service established the ground rules for private express couriers to participate in the time-sensitive postal market. It established the principle of eligibility, on the basis of extra speed and different or added service. It laid out the minimum rates that would have to be charged. The order presented an extremely elaborate rationale, including an explanation of how these rates reflect the costs borne by the Post in equivalent activity.

Generally speaking, the legislative framework created a considerable amount of space for the Post to function and act in a corporatized manner. The regulatory environment emphasized transparency, specification and clarification of objectives, and a quantitative approach to evaluation of performance. The state's regulatory role would not be activist and interventionist but rather passive and evaluative – reacting to the Post's performance against a set of clear and transparent criteria. The regulatory process itself comprised three major players and some minor ones: the ministry, the regulatory body, and the Post.

The Ministry

Statutory and policy responsibility for the Post was given to the Ministry of Transport, Public Works and Water Management. It supervises the implementation of the postal legislation and its rules and regulations. It also safeguards the state's general interests as a shareholder and names representatives to the board of the Post. These directors are independent once appointed to the board and do not offer ministerial opinion. Originally, the ministry had the responsibility of evaluating the performance of the Post's universal-service obligations. But the regulatory and shareholder interests clashed with each other and put the ministry in a kind of conflict-of-interest situation. As is the trend in Europe – and more or less demanded by the EC postal directive – regulatory responsibilities have been transferred to a new agency that is independent of the ministry (see below). The ministry has two directors and five sections, and the Post is assigned to one of these sections (the Market Development Branch). Postal resources within the ministry are modest. There are three people in this branch, plus one other person with responsibility for the ministry's international and UPU obligations.

The Regulator

OPTA – a Dutch acronym for the independent posts and telecommunications authority – was established in 1997 as an independent supervisor of the Post.[20] It was created by legislation, which split regulatory activities away from the ministry. This ended the conflict of interest between the ministry's shareholder and regulatory functions. OPTA's budget is shared between the market players and the ministry, but it is independent of both. Its independence makes it difficult for the ministry to overturn any rulings that it makes. OPTA is led by a three-person central group, all named by the ministry, and a director (who came over from the ministry). It has three departments, including Retail Markets, which houses the Post and telecommunications sectors. Its operation is also modest, comprising three people with legal and economics background (one of whom came from the ministry). About half their time is spent on the Post. While the personnel know the telecom file well, they have no special background on the Post. For independent postal intelligence, OPTA relies on information provided by the Post's competitors and customers, consultants, the academic and professional literature, and common sense.[21] Its lack of extensive postal intelligence and understanding is aggravated by staff turnover.

OPTA evaluates the extent to which the Post is meeting its universal-service obligations and realizing the objectives that are set out in law, in areas like tariffs, financial statements, the post-office network, and fair competition. With respect to tariffs, the price-cap formula has mitigated the politics of price change in the monopoly or protected area. In any event, the Post has more or less frozen prices for the indeterminate future. However, OPTA plays a regulatory role in looking at various market-based prices, such as discount pricing to large customers. If customers feel that the discounts are not sufficiently cost-oriented, the law allows OPTA to ask the Post for information to allow a confidential evaluation to be made. With respect to the network, there has not been much controversy about post-office closures since the early 1990s. OPTA has intervened in areas dealing with exceptions to the mail monopoly, particularly in the area of non-commercial mail being delivered by the employees of local governments. Its most elaborate responsibility relates to the evaluation of the Post's financial statements, with regard to the issue of cross-subsidization. This is a technical issue, inasmuch as it is based on an evaluation of accounts. The ministry developed an accounting system in 1997, which required the Post to separate universal-service activity from its market activity (this accounting system will, in the future, be approved by OPTA). OPTA analyses the data submitted by the Post from the perspective of this agreed-upon accounting system. It checks whether the bookkeeping is "correct" and gets a second opinion from another auditor. OPTA submits an annual report to the ministry comprising a list of activities, a statement about postal-market developments, reports on service and quality, and an evaluation of the cross-subsidy issue. It does not comment on the introduction of new products and services, or corporate takeovers or alliances, except if there is a cross-subsidy issue.

The Post

The third player in the regulatory triangle is the Post itself. At the top of the corporation is the Supervisory Board, which oversees the work of the Board of Management. This Supervisory Board has seven members, three of whom are named by the ministry. An internal process appoints the rest. A board member "profile" was established by its Corporate Governance Committee, which includes the following criteria: management experience in the private sector and an understanding of one of the Post's priority issues at the time of appointment; ability to act independently of the Board of Management; a grasp of the social and political situations in countries of great importance to TPG; the need for a high proportion of board members to have positions of relevance to TPG internationally; and people who are "widely esteemed."[22]

Not surprisingly, the board created to such standards is composed of exceptionally able and powerful individuals, with enormous international experience. In 1998 the board included:

· J. Cochrane, executive director of Glaxo Wellcome (British);

- W. Dik, former secretary of state for foreign trade; former chair of Unilever;
- V. Halberstadt, chair of Supervisory Board of Xerox (Netherlands);
- J. Hommen, vice-president and chief financial officer of Philips;
- A. Maas, on supervisory board of Heineken, KLM, and other large corporations;
- C. Oort, chair of BCE, chair of KLM, board member Northern Telecom International and Royal Phillips;
- R. Stromberg, past managing director of BP and CEO of BP International (German); and
- M. Tabaksblat, chair of Board of Unilever.

In 1999, two new members were added: Robert Abrahamsen, chief financial officer of KLM, and Franco Bernabe, former CEO of Telecom Italia SpA and ENI.

These individuals comprise a formidable board that has set an assertive and ambitious corporate and international agenda for the Post. Its experience and expertise give it authority and provide the government with confidence that its postal asset is in good hands.

The Public Affairs Department at the Post works to ensure positive relations with the government and stakeholders. It is located within the Business Unit of the Post, in order to keep the business operation politically sensitive and to make clear within the Post what is occurring politically. It works to provide information and postal intelligence to the board as well as to the ministry, which has few people working on the postal area.

Others

The NMa – National Competition Authority – has broad responsibilities to maintain competition in the Dutch market. On occasion, it has acted in the postal marketplace. For example, it has been asked to rule on issues such as the tariffs charged by the Post for the use of its postal boxes. As liberalization is extended, it likely will play a stronger regulatory role than OPTA.

The Postal Act of 1998 required the creation of a consultative process. There are two such bodies: OOP (Overlegorgaan Post), which is organized by the Post, and OPT (Overlegorgaan Post), which is organized by the ministry secretariat. These bodies are comprised of postal users, unions, larger clients, and other interested parties such as consumer organizations. They meet twice a year to discuss issues, provide feedback to the Post, and ensure that the Post is meeting its obligations to the community. Within this group, the Post's competitors are the largest players. They pressure the government to accelerate the liberalization process and create market room for themselves, and they criticize any monopoly privileges as creating cross-subsidies and unfair competition. In contrast to the situation in other countries, the competitors have not made a large impact on the postal-policy process.

Postal workers are unionized through ABVAKABO FNV, which was originally a government-sector union and now represents public servants, institutions dependent on government support, and enterprises that used to be state-run but are now autonomous. In the latter category there is a separate unit for post and telecom workers. There is no compulsory union membership in the Netherlands, and only about 40 per cent of the Post is unionized (only 25 per cent ABVAKABO). This low union density reflects the extent to which the government in general, and particular state institutions in particular, accommodated workers' needs and interests in the Dutch consensus-building system. Through the periods of de-nationalization, deregulation, and privatization, the postal unions were consulted and took negative positions on these developments. By and large, though, there was no ensuing political fight. The union leadership informed their members that "history could not be stopped" and worked with the government to limit any damage that these developments might have on postal workers.[23] Then and subsequently, the unions' participation in the postal-policy process has been marked by a quiet and effective pragmatism.

The general public's response to Dutch postal changes has been fairly quiet. The changes have not generated political headlines, political drama, or a struggle over symbolic issues. This reflects the absence of the strong sense of *service publique* in the postal service that prevails in other parts of Europe. A culture of "reasonableness" and pragmatism surrounds policy in general and postal policy in particular. Thus the public, like the unions, accepted the basic argument that postal reform was directed to improving efficiency and the quality of service and that most mail was basically business mail. The public has also responded positively to the internationalization of the Post, which is in tune with the external and trade-orientation of the Dutch. The Post has not been a large or compelling dossier for Members of Parliament.[24]

Regulatory Process

The impression may have been gained by now that the regulatory process surrounding the Post in the Netherlands is relatively passive, a bit mechanical, and not very restrictive on the Post's performance. What is interesting is the emergence of OPTA as the critical and independent third-party regulator, a classic case of the emergence of re-regulation after a period of deregulation. But this development is in its early stages and it is premature to draw conclusions about how far-reaching OPTA's influence and impact will be.

The government's participation in the regulatory process, via the ministry, is episodic and passive. Ministry officials meet regularly with TPG; there is a custom that the head director meets with the minister once a month for an hour or so. At lower levels, there is ongoing information exchange. The modus operandi is the building of consensus. The ministry plays an active role in policy development and when the content of the General Directive is being reconsidered every five years (see below on the most recent case). With respect to the former, the Post and the ministry have seen eye-to-eye for years on liberalization, privatization, and regulation, so there is little policy tension in this regard.[25] Once the directive is in place, the ministry's role fades into the background. It has ongoing responsibilities to maintain shareholder value, but the state is now a minority shareholder. Issues like rates of return, dividend policy, and so on are more the purview of the CEO, CFO, and board of the Post than they are of the ministry. At most it has an indirect involvement, via the reports that all companies are obliged to make to their shareholders. In this way, the traditional tension between the state's shareholder responsibilities and its regulatory responsibilities has, to a great extent, been neutralized by the partial privatization. Moreover, the application of the directive in action is now carried out by OPTA, which is taking on increasing responsibilities for developing the accounting framework for evaluating the actions of the Post. Complaints from competitors and customers – and related price issues – are dealt with at OPTA as well, and postal pricing on the universal-service side is formula-driven. As will be seen below, other politically sensitive issues like postal closings and restructuring have not required political intervention. On the one hand, this reflects the fact that the *service publique* tradition in the Dutch postal area is not strong, in contrast to southern Europe, where postal issues are heavily and politically symbolic.[26] On the other hand, the Post was given the opportunity to deal with these issues directly in the early 1990s, and it did so to great effect. The result was that the government was not put on the political spot for employment issues, postal closings, and so on.[27] Lastly, the ministry is modestly staffed on the postal front and has limited sources of postal intelligence, so it relies on others, particularly the Post itself, for this.

On the Post's side, it is not required to go through an elaborate planning process culminating in ministerial review and approval. Rather, it provides the ministry with an annual plan of action, which is simply teased out of the corporation's business plan (which is not a public document). More problematic for the Post is the evaluation of separate accounts, to determine allowed rates of return on activities in the protected and market areas. Initially, there was some tension between the public authorities and the Post in developing an agreed-upon set of accounting principles. These have now been established, which has made the process a rather mechanical exercise of applying the system and formulae to the data. These figures are checked by an independent auditor and reviewed by OPTA.[28]

The relationship between the Post and OPTA is in the early stages of development (OPTA was created only in 1997). There is no set calendar of events, just as there is no formal planning process that requires approval. OPTA reviews tariff proposals in the fall and reviews the financial statements (after they have been issued). There have been no disagreements between TPG and OPTA on the accounts as yet. From the Post's perspective, the only real irritant has been the issue of the agreed-upon allocation of costs, but this is a universal problem experienced in all regulatory environments. The Post is habituated to working in an environment framed by business practices and cost-allocation systems, so the accounting and evaluation system used by OPTA and the elaborate quantification exercises are something that the Post can live with. The process has required the Post to provide more information, a typical cost of a formal regulatory process. Basically, though, the Post accepts this process given its universal-service obligations and ongoing exclusive privileges.[29]

OPTA's relationship with the ministry is fairly formal and increasingly distant, to ensure independence. When the ministry is engaged in reviewing the General Directive, OPTA is obliged to make a submission or commentary, which goes on record after the process is completed. The minister is not obliged to follow OPTA's advice. The ministry is obliged, though, to talk with OPTA about new policy developments. OPTA in turn is obliged to comment on new developments in the market.

1999–2000 Regulation Change

The last remaining ministerial role rests predominantly on the question of future liberalization. While OPTA has the more active role, the ministry still sets standards and makes regulations. The government now sees its role as basically guiding the market and the process towards liberalization. The ministry carried out its periodic review of the General Directive in 1998, but it pushed this review into deeper waters in response to the EC directive to which it was obliged to respond. It consulted widely and asked market participants about their postal experiences over the last five years. OPTA was asked for its input, particularly to comment about draft proposals (to see if they were workable). A postal-policy paper was developed within the ministry, which was then sent to cabinet for approval. After approval it was recast into legal and legislative form for submission to Parliament. A revised Postal Act worked its way through the administrative and parliamentary systems in 1999–2000 and came into effect in June 2000. The essential ingredients included:[30]

- cutting the exclusive privilege to 100 grams (the EC directive set the standard at 350 grams) and three times the price of a standard letter;
- maintaining the freeze on basic prices until the new EC system is in place (there will be an eventual move to a cost-based pricing system);
- ending special tariffs on items like periodicals; all universal-service obligations are to be financed from the remaining monopoly (save for materials for the blind, for which there are international legal obligations); no compensation fund will exist;
- increasing the quality of international service, by formally liberalizing outward international mail;
- providing competitive access to post-office boxes;
- unpacking the accounts into three categories: the monopoly category (0–100 grams); the remaining concession category (100 grams–10 kilos); and the market (non-monopoly) sector;
- redefining the universal-service obligation so as to have it comprise the provision of postal services at a uniform price on items up to 10 kilograms;
- reducing the monopoly or protected area to items below 100 grams and three times the basic tariff; and
- applying the uniform tariff only to single or individual items, not to bulk items.

The purpose of the last three items is to remove business mail from the universal-service obligation and thereby follow the imposition of the value-added tax (VAT) on bulk materials where discounts are offered and where the absence of the tax provides unfair competition.

The Dutch regulatory process over the last decade has been a relatively benign one, absent of tension or political controversy. This reflects the fact that the Post and the state have seen eye-to-eye on postal matters, particularly the two-step process of corporatization/privatization followed by liberalization. The regulatory system is a relatively formal one, with participants' respective roles clearly established and expectations made concrete and specific. Regulatory authority has shifted away from the ministry to an independent third party. But the regulator plays a passive rather than an active role. It applies clear quantitative criteria in a mechanical process, according to guidelines set by the ministry. In this way, it responds to the Post's performance rather than attempting to shape it. The Post in turn accepts this quantitative, passive regulatory environment with equanimity, and gets on with the job of modernization and expansion, led by a high-powered board which has a considerable degree of autonomy from the state.

PERFORMANCE

The strategy of the Dutch Post in the 1990s has been clear, focused, and ambitious: to grow rapidly and become the dominant market player in the world. The Dutch government has encouraged this "imperial" strategy. It gave the Post autonomy and corporate direction, established a regulatory framework that did not inhibit this strategy, established a high-powered board to pursue it, and allowed the Post to pursue a diversified and international corporate strategy. This strategy has been carried out in an aggressive if not ruthless manner. Its orientation has been informed by an understanding of the Darwinian consequences of technological and international changes that has given its actions a hard-edged sense of urgency: "In a few years time, only a handful of major global players will remain: TPG and the other global integrators will be among them."[31] The other national Posts might not survive – and the aggressive policies of the Dutch will accelerate this scenario.

The Dutch postal strategy is essentially a growth strategy. This strategy emerged from the Post's understanding of three complementary developments. The first was its understanding that the domestic Dutch postal market was saturated (a "mature" industry). The 6–7 per cent of mail-volume growth of the 1980s had fallen to 1–2 per cent, despite the 10 per cent annual growth in the communications market. The Post's bread-and-butter markets – like financial mail, bills, and so on – were at the end of their life cycle. Over half of the Post's business was in competitive markets like parcels and express. Second, this saturation was partially the result of traditional mail being replaced by electronic competition, as well as the competition created by domestic deregulation, the market entry of remailers and couriers, and the acceleration of global liberalization. Substitution pressures could not be mitigated by pricing, since the prices of new technological products were also low. Third, costs were the key factor to survival. On the one hand, traditional mail confronted rising unit costs, the results of increasingly far-flung networks (addresses rising by 90,000 a year); this made mail less competitive. On the other hand, alternative communication technologies and international expansion required strong economies of scale to become competitive and sustainable over the long run. The upshot of this was that the Post would have to grow rapidly. Growth was vital to create the economies of scale in markets such as mail and express which are scale-driven. And growth was required to generate the capital required to increase network capacity, acquire new networks, diversify, and add new value-added products. Growth required deregulation and liberalization of domestic and world markets, so the Dutch have not been against postal liberalization – which was taking place almost automatically without a change in the regulatory environment in any event. The greater anxiety has been technological competition, which has spurred the growth orientation. Liberalization and growth was seen as the best strategy to deal with this threat.[32]

The TPG mission statement is clear: "to achieve a recognized world leadership position in three business areas – mail, express and logistics – based on a strong market position in Europe."[33] This statement demonstrates a number of features of the Post's orientation. First, it has a basically international posture or orientation. Second, Europe is considered to be the "domestic" market, not the Netherlands. Third, mail is a part – and only a part – of the Post's world, which focuses increasingly on competitive markets such as express and logistics (see below). Fourth, the Post's aim is to be the world leader.

Competition Strategy – The Mail Market

The growth strategy has a symbiotic relationship with TPG's competition strategy. Growth produces economies of scale, which keeps costs down. A lower cost structure increases competitiveness, thereby generating growth. TPG's competition strategy comprises three elements: pricing, quality, and efficiency.

The pricing of postal products and services has traditionally been a highly politicized issue for Posts. The Dutch regulatory environment neutralized this problem by embracing a price-cap system and a market-oriented pricing approach for competitive products. TPG has tried to keep prices stable, changes infrequent, and increases within the rate of inflation. As Table 1 indicates, the result has been postal prices among the lowest in Europe. The low-price level reflects a combination of high volumes and efficiency. The Briefpost 2000 program was launched in 1992, with the aim of increasing the proportion of mail sorted mechanically from 25 per cent in 1990 to 98 per cent in the next century (it reached 56 per cent by 1998 and 74 per cent

Table 1
EU-tariffs, first-class mail, 1999
(corrected for purchasing power, in guilders)

Spain	0.55
Netherlands	0.80
Greece	0.80
United Kingdom	0.80
Ireland	0.88
Denmark	0.90
Finland	0.93
Belgium	0.93
France	0.95
Italy	1.05
Sweden	1.06
Germany	1.15
Portugal	1.18

Source: TPK, *Annual Report*, 1999.

by 1999). Over 1 billion guilders were invested to this end, and twelve sorting plants were reduced to six mail-sorting centres and four parcel-sorting centres. Mechanization in turn aided the attainment of a higher level of quality of service, which in turn maintained and encouraged business growth. The rate of next-day (twenty-four-hour) delivery rose through the 1990s from 90 per cent to 96 per cent, with a 99.8 per cent accuracy rate (to the correct address). The Dutch Post was the first in the world to obtain ISO 9002 certification (an international standard of quality and efficiency) for its production processes and it won the Dutch quality prize in 1997. There have been some difficulties extending mechanization, partially as a result of higher than expected volumes, which had some impact on quality in 1999.[34]

Despite prognoses that letter mail is dead, the mail sector continues to be a strong component of TPG's activities and still generated 40 per cent of its business in 2000. Domestic mail volumes grew from 6.1 billion in 1994 to 7 billion in 1998 – an increase of 16 per cent. The number of postal items per address rose from 898 to 974 in that period as well. Mail revenues grew 23 per cent from 1993 to 1996 and 7 per cent again in each of 1997 and 1998.[35] But the letter market was flat in 1999 and 2000, with only marginal growth. Direct mail remains a good growth generator. Despite competition, the Post retains 95 per cent of this market.

Express

Express post is seen by TPG as one of the critical growth markets for the future. It expects sustained growth in this market, particularly as international business and communications increases as a result of globalization. Indeed, express revenues grew by 27 per cent in the first half of 2000. It anticipates that a single European express market will emerge, by the year 2006, which will be bigger than the U.S. market. Express presently represents 41 per cent of the business (1999), mainly as the result of the purchase of TNT. In 1996, express generated 381 million guilders in revenue – compared to 6.5 billion in 1998. Revenues from express increased by 25 per cent between 1996 and 1998, including 9 per cent in the highly competitive European market in 1998. Express revenue grew by another 20 per cent in 1999. The Post is investing considerably in TNT as a brand – to gain and regain customers – and it launched a new corporate or brand identity in 1998. The organization of express service is undergoing a dramatic change. A new European express centre has been established in Liege (Belgium), as a high-tech nucleus capable of handling a thousand tons of freight a night. A new international road hub and national depot was established in Duiven (Netherlands). TPG plans to acquire fourteen Airbus A300B4 freighters to increase its capacity by 60 per cent. At present, the TNT brand holds 28 per cent of the European market. In March 2001 TNT launched a new product in the United States, a one-rate, no-weight-restriction express service in major metropolitan areas.

Logistics

Logistics involves an integrated approach to business across the supply chain to ensure that the right goods get to the right place at the right time. This includes: database and response management, storage and warehousing, addressing and packaging, transporting small and large goods and express deliveries, and billing and collection. TPG develops tailor-made logistics services for its business clients, as they contract out non-core activities to specialized providers and shift increasingly to "just-in-time" production and retail (a method developed by the Japanese, who mastered the flow of production in their auto plants such that they had just enough parts on hand to build only those cars for which they had orders, thereby lowering inventory costs and minimizing the need for expensive warehouses). Logistics represents the strongest growth area of the business, where TPG has the opportunity to lever its express network. This sector has experienced 15 per cent annual growth over the last five years, and it grew by 44 per cent in 1999 and 40 per cent in the first half of 2000. Whereas logistics comprised less than 1 per cent of the business in 1995, it now represents around 20 per cent of revenues. The number of contracts gained has increased by an average of 24 per cent a year over the last three years and TPG's range of warehouses grew from 85 to 137 in 1998 and 248 in 1999. TPG's 1999 report indicates that only an insufficiency of trained and skilled personnel limits growth in this market.

This segment of the business is centred at its expertise centre in Maarsten. Under the TNT brand, the Post provides logistical support for a wide array of clients in a bewildering array of activities. For example, it operates the spare-parts warehouses for car manufacturers and distributes accessories and parts to dealerships, in partnerships with Fiat, Renault, Volkswagen, and Toyota in various countries and with Shanghai Automotive in China. TNT's logistics division has become a partner in Renault's transportation and logistics subsidiary, CAT (Companie d'affrètement et de transport). It carries out warehousing and archiving contracts for banks, warehouse and distribution support to telecommunications and electronic-products firms like Telstra, and logistical support to pharmaceutical, paint, computer, motorcycle, heavy-machinery, metal-production, and soft-drink companies on every continent. Through TNT Logistics, it will support Benetton's e-commerce initiatives in Europe. It took over ownership of Holland Districare, which provides logistical support for the medical and pharmaceutical markets, storing and distributing medicines and medical supplies. It recently was awarded a contract to distribute soap and detergents in China and it is the largest carrier in the United Kingdom (where, among other things, it distributes telephone directories). It provides logistical services to Xerox in the United Kingdom and to Black and Decker in Europe. It helps publishers by doing the billing and collection of subscription fees. Through InterPost, it distributes magazines and direct mail worldwide.

It has consolidated its European presence through the logistics part of Jet Services and Tecnologistica, both of which were purchased in 1999.

Diversification and Alternate Products

The Post's growth strategy has also included initiatives in product development and breaking into new markets. The purpose of these initiatives has been to decrease the company's reliance on letter mail, to expand into products and services with higher value-added, and to retain customer loyalty. For example, the Post has initiated a number of hybrid mail products. FAX-POST allows customers to fax a letter to any post office (by 9:30 PM) and a hard copy of that letter will be delivered the next day. In the broad "print and mail" area, the Post handled over 100 million documents this way in 1997, including the phone bills of KPN, and recently acquired a five-year contract to handle billing and notices for a major bank. The Post has a Vacation Service, providing for the temporary forwarding of mail to the vacation address. In the parcel area, customers are offered tracking and tracing services, electronic payment at the receiver's door, and the opportunity to submit shipping orders electronically. The Post offers direct-mail advice as well as a professional service to help companies design and manage their mail rooms. TPG developed a mail-order service called Telekado and delivers prescription drugs by mail. It has recently made a major initiative in the e-commerce area, particularly with regard to managing the demand chain. In March 2001 it purchased Lason UK Group, which specializes in database services.[36]

Retail

TPG has the largest retail-distribution network in the Netherlands. Postkantoren is owned jointly in equal parts by the Post and Postbank and operates as an independent company. It has around 2,600 sales outlets in the Netherlands, over half of which are franchises (many bought by postal workers). The Post purchased Bruna and De Boekelier, two bookstore chains comprising over 500 sites, in order to expand its retail presence. As is the case elsewhere, the number of postal transactions taking place in post offices has declined, so TPG has expanded into other areas. Postkantoren performs services for insurance and temporary employment companies, and added a ticket-purchasing service in 1997. It invested 340 million guilders between 1993 and 1997 to modernize its retail outlets. There was some rationalization of the network in the early 1990s, but this occurred quickly and with little political disruption. There were no forced dismissals. If a worker did not want to buy a franchise, (s)he was transferred or retired at 80 per cent salary.

Mergers and Alliances

The shareholders have given TPG a clear commercial mandate, which has allowed an aggressive market strategy. The company has substantial commercial freedom, including the freedom to enter into partnerships and to raise private capital. Much of the postal growth strategy has taken place through mergers and takeovers as well as via alliances. This strategy was directed to increasing the Post's presence in geographic areas and selected market areas, where it had little or no presence before, and at a modest cost (relative to starting from square one). The company distinguishes its strategy from the more "generic" takeover strategy of other Posts, declaring that it does takeovers at strategic spots in the supply chain. It has also been directed to create interconnections and to increase end-to-end quality.

With respect to mergers and takeovers, the most significant initiative was the purchase of TNT. This instantaneously made the Dutch Post a major player in the express market. The Post has made numerous acquisitions since 1991, including:

- The Rinaldi Group – an Italian mail-provider and distribution group;
- Pony Express – a city courier in Italy;
- Technologistica – a logistics company in Italy;
- GMA Verwaltungsgesellschaft mbH (GMA) – a direct-mail and magazine-delivery company in Germany;
- Jet Services – the joint market leader in domestic express in France;
- Bross-Fouya – a parcel company operating primarily in the Paris area;
- Net Nachtexpress Terminidienst GMBTT – a German/Austria overnight transport firm;
- Europa DTS Express APS – a Danish express company;
- Dentex and Colande – to gain 50 per cent of the courier market in Holland and 30 per cent in Belgium;
- Belgische Distributiedienst – a Belgian distribution company, with strength in unaddressed mail;
- Datatransbeheer – a Dutch computer company;
- Great Glen – a hanging-garment distributor in Ireland;
- Independent Distributors BV – a distribution company that operates in St Petersburg and Moscow;
- Speedimac – a company that transports and instals electronic equipment;
- IVA-DES – a Dutch data-entry firm;
- VSP – a 55 per cent share in this direct-mail firm;
- Tesselaar Marketing Service – direct marketing and direct-mail response;
- Holland Districare – a company that provides logistics services for medical and pharmaceutical markets;
- Inter Post – a 75 per cent share in this group of companies that distributes magazines and direct mail worldwide;
- E-Post 2000 – hybrid mail;
- Ansett Air Freight, an Australian firm;
- Schrader, a German logistics firm;
- Taylor Barnard, the largest privately owned logistics firm in the United Kingdom;
- Barlatier S.A., the French logistics company, and Mendy Developpement S.A.; and

• CTI Logistix, merging it with TNT Logistics to form the seventh largest logistics company in North America. This $US650-million puchase was its largest since partial privatization.

The Post has also entered into strategic alliances with other national posts. For example, it signed a Memorandum of Understanding with China State Post in September 1999. This will see TPG doing international express delivery for the Chinese. TPG will also study the domestic postal market for the Chinese, do consultancy work, and provide training courses. Another example is the recent strategic alliance with Swiss Post, announced in November 1999 and confirmed in June 2000. In a joint venture, TPG will get access to Swiss Post's post offices and technology, while Swiss Post will connect to TNT/TPG in mail, express, and logistics. PTG established a joint venture with Luxembourg Post in November 2000. In March 2001 it signed a letter of intent with CTT Correies – the Portuguese Post – to explore the possibility of a long-term strategic alliance in express services. The Dutch have been in a strategic alliance with Singapore Post as well. TPG carries business mail as bulk cargo from North America to Singapore, where it is processed into individual postal items and distributed by Singapore Post in Asia. This alliance has recently expanded into a joint venture among TPG (51 per cent), the British Post Office (24.5 per cent) and Singapore Post (24.5 per cent). Officially signed in July 2000, this joint-venture agreement will create the world's largest business-mailing partnership, directed to cross-border mail. European anti-trust regulators recommended blocking this joint venture, leading TPG to offer to sell part of its international mail business as a remedy. The Dutch have also constructed strategic alliances and joint ventures with private-sector operators in other countries, such as the Turkish group Koc.

Employment

The Dutch have not experienced a postal-employment problem or crisis, because the Post handled the situation with the union very well at the beginning of the privatization and deregulation process.[37] The union negotiated quietly with the company to ensure that there would be no forced dismissals.[38] It was anticipated that there would be 5,000 job losses in the early 1990s, particularly as a result of mechanization and the decline in the number of sorting plants from twelve to six. However, the growth strategy increased postal traffic to neutralize a large portion of the threatened decline. Any job losses were modest and eased by early retirement packages. The overall level of employment was around 100,000 people in 1989 and total employment remains around that level in the late 1990s and is growing slightly, partially as a result of acquisitions. The only significant change was a shift in the part-time to full-time ratio, whereby a few thousand full-time jobs have been converted to part-time. Finally, given mass unionization in the Netherlands, the Post did not have much incentive to contract out. Transportation services have been contracted out, but the workers in that sector are unionized.

The Competition

The flip side to TPG's growth strategy in the liberalized world is the growth of domestic competition. TPG faces direct competition in the Netherlands in direct-mail services and parcels (which were open markets already) and in courier and logistics from both private operators and national Posts. TPG claims that it generates 86 per cent of its revenue in competitive markets. Its stiffest competition comes from firms with lower wage costs that focus on delivery efficiency and simplicity (without universal-service obligations). Despite this, the Post remains the market leader in direct mail, magazine distribution, the parcel market, and national express and courier.[39]

In the courier area, the Post faces competition from the large express firms (UPS, DHL, FedEx) as well as local Dutch companies. There are over 2,000 active express companies, 1,600 of which perform in local areas. In the parcels area, the Post continues to dominate the customer-customer market. However, in the business-customer market, it faces a formidable competitor in the form of Selektvracht – a subsidiary of Nedlloyd, which is now owned by the German Post. In the business-business market, there are three significant competitors: Correct Express, Nederlandse Pakketdienst, and the German-owned Van Gend and Loos. Newspapers in the Netherlands are typically delivered by the newspaper companies themselves, although the Post delivers a number of small national newspapers. With respect to magazines and periodicals, there is a parallel national-distribution network that does not connect to the Post's network. This is the closed network of private VNU publishers, one of the major publishing companies in the Netherlands. The network is called Medianet, and it is a serious competitor. It delivers magazines in large-subscription volumes twice a week.[40]

Results

One of the most pronounced results in recent years has been the increasing importance of international markets for TPG's turnover. There are TPG-owned operations in 60 countries, and TPG operates

Table 2
TPG financial results (millions of euros)

	1999	1998	1997	1996	1996	1995
REVENUES	8,536	7,409	6,928	6,143	3,045	2,759
Mail	3,651	3,523	3,281	3,071	2,901	2,678
Express	3,538	2,953	2,824	2,364	173	104
Logistics	1,522	1,058	894	785	25	19
NET INCOME	419	372	315	264	289	245
RETURN ON CAPITAL (%)	12.9	13.1	12.3		11.9	15.1

Source: TPG, *Annual Reports*, assorted years.

in over 200 countries. With globalization, one can expect to see even more movement away from domestic markets and the creation of international alliances and takeovers. In 1998 the Post delivered two billion units internationally – about 20 per cent of its volumes. By 2000, 65 per cent of TPG's revenues were generated internationally (compared to 11 per cent in 1997). As internationalization increases, the importance of traditional mail activity has declined – from 94 per cent of revenues in 1997 to 40 per cent in 2000.[41] For world Posts, 50 per cent has become a benchmark: they seek to reduce their dependence on mail revenues to below 50 per cent in the face of technological and product change.

As Table 2 indicates, TPG's revenues have grown steadily, by 39 per cent from 1996 to 1999.[42] Its recent profit performance has been extremely positive. It has made a 12–13 per cent return on capital in this period. Thirto to thirty-five per cent of profits are returned to shareholders as dividends. From the first day of its listing, TPG has outperformed the Amsterdam Stock Exchange by 22 per cent. In the second half of 1998, it created around five billion guilders of share-holder value.[43] More recently, first-half results in 2000 showed net-income growth of 25 per cent (17 per cent net of sales of non-core business). Operating revenues increased by 20 per cent and earnings before interest and taxes (EBIT) by 18 per cent. The company antic-ipates net income growth of 12–18 per cent in the next few years.[44]

HIGHLIGHTS OF THE DUTCH CASE

What can one learn from the Dutch case and what interest does its experience hold for policy makers?

First, postal reform in the Netherlands was not scrutinized and attacked on its own grounds. It was enveloped in a larger competitive-ness agenda, which brought the stakeholders into a common position in supporting reforms to make the Post technologically and internationally competitive. This neutralized a series of possible political roadblocks and constraints.

Second, the reform process unfolded in an uninterrupted way and at an accelerated pace, because of the Post's and the state's shared understanding and vision. This gained the Post a large degree of autonomy and an unrestrained commercial mandate, which allowed it to perform aggressively in the market.

Third, the regulatory environment synthesized freedom with accountability in an obliging combination for the Post. On the one hand, the state slowly but surely faded into the background. Its role as shareholder became a minority one as a result of partial privatization, and a high-powered board took the lead shareholder hand. An independent regulator – who was given a passive, mechanical mandate – supplanted the government's regulatory role. On the other hand, the Post's mandate, expectations, and obligations were set in a clear and quantitative way which allowed accountability without great inhibition.

Fourth, there are specific national features to the Dutch case that would be difficult to emulate. The weak public-service tradition in the postal area, the consensus processes surrounding labour-management relations, the geographically small and easy-to-service domestic market, the nation's intense historical tradition of having an outward-looking trade orientation, and the tolerance of monopoly protection to generate growth and strength for global competition, are all factors that have contributed to the Post's success in the Netherlands – and its seeming ease of success.

Notwithstanding the last point, TPG's success has also reflected an aggressive, daring, and active commercial policy which has made it a world leader and arch-competitor to national Posts around the world. Its growth strategy has positioned it to generate sufficient revenues to expand, invest, and maintain its universal-service obligations. It has also positioned itself to be a leader of an eventual international alliance of national Posts and major private-sector players. None of this could have been accomplished without the positive, indeed friendly, regulatory environment and policy support provided by the state.

2 Germany

The German Post – Deutsche Post World Net – is the largest postal provider in Europe. Relative to other Posts, DPWN has a particularly large domestic market and enjoys substantial postal volumes. Even in the absence of any postal reform or strategic initiatives, the Germans would be a major player in the world postal market and their plans and initiatives would constitute an important variable for Posts in Europe and abroad. The global importance of the German Post has intensified throughout the 1990s, as its postal-reform process has led to an aggressive postal strategy of growth, diversification, and internationalization. This has seen it develop into one of the predominant postal and communications players in the world, with ambitions to be *the* predominant postal actor in the world. This may turn out to be a not unreasonable or unattainable ambition.

In Germany, the postal-reform process evolved quickly into the mercantile model, following the same logic and similar pressures as in the Netherlands. However, the process has had some differences and it began at a later date in Germany than in the Netherlands. It has also taken longer to execute. This reflects a number of factors, including differences in size and geography between the two countries and the fact that the Netherlands is a maritime, outward-looking trading nation while Germany is a self-contained, continental one. The Netherlands proved to be lighter on its feet in making fast decisions and initiating bold developments, while the Germans have pursued an extended reform process in a more deliberate fashion. The two countries were also affected differently by the economic downturn of the early 1980s, which caused far greater anxiety and policy change in the Netherlands than in Germany. However, each national postal-reform process was based on a similar evaluation of circumstances, which led to the development of similar mercantile strategies and generated comparable results. This suggests the extent to which technological and international forces can result in a kind of postal-policy convergence, when the Posts' backgrounds are similar. Nonetheless, there have been variations within this mercantile theme. The most pronounced variation is with respect to the postal-regulatory environment. Jim Campbell describes the German experience as "arguably the most sophisticated postal reform in the world," which has resulted in "the most flexible, deregulatory postal law among the major developed countries."[1] One might take issue with Campbell's ranking. But it is certainly the case that the evolving German postal-regulatory environment is different from and more nuanced than the Dutch system. This reflects a number of factors that will be reviewed below.

A number of key factors or considerations underlie the German postal-reform process. First, the process was a dependent one. It was driven largely by the telecommunications initiatives of governments, as well as by the European postal-reform agenda. Because there was far more attention paid to the telecommunications agenda, the postal agenda was insulated from the intense political scrutiny that informed the postal-reform experience in Canada and elsewhere. There was no nationwide public movement against corporatization and privatization; public opinion has been basically passive in this context. Given that the Post was not the focus of attention, the political and policy dynamic was an interesting mix of ingredients. On the one hand, there was an opportunity for initiative and experimentation, since few outside the postal world were watching developments there critically. On the other hand, there was scepticism and resistance within the postal community, mainly because there was not the same degree of economic anxiety as had enveloped the Dutch experience. As a result, the civil-service and union environment of the Post has been a bigger factor in Germany than in the Netherlands. Once the Post was split from telecommunications, the corporatization of the Post was all but inevitable. This was because it lost the financial infrastructure and security provided by its more fiscally solvent telecommunications partner. It was assumed politically that the Christian Democratic government's broad privatization agenda would then extend to the Post, particularly since its coalition partner – the Liberal Party – was pushing the liberalization agenda very hard. But there was considerable resistance from government employees and unions at the Post. This explains partially why the reform agenda has unfolded more slowly in

Germany than in the Netherlands. The postal unions were against the reform process at the start, but they have come to accept its rationale. Deutsche Post has been able to negotiate arrangements with the postal unions and adjust the size of its workforce to a corporatized strategy.[2]

Second, like the Dutch, the Germans understood how the new technology and postal changes have internationalized the postal environment and made growth a prerequisite for survival. The two key objectives in recent German postal strategy have been to develop new products and services and to internationalize the business. With respect to the former, the German view is that without growth there is no postal future.[3] A key strategic factor has been the Post's effort to neutralize the notion that the postal sector is a sunset industry. No Post has levered its network more than the Germans, in order to diversify into new product and service lines – particularly in the fast-growing area of logistics but also in retail, finance, consulting, and retail trade. While the "letter" remains a vital component of business, it is no longer a predominant feature of Deutsche Post's image and a less important contributor to its bottom line than in the past. As in the Netherlands, the Post has set a 50 per cent benchmark for the division between mail and non-mail sources of revenue – the goal is to see the former fall below 50 per cent. DPWN describes itself as a "diversified provider in the communications, transport and logistics markets"[4] – hardly a phrase that evokes the image of a Post Office. A second component of the postal-growth strategy is the Post's international orientation. Like the Dutch, the Germans see Europe as their home market and they aim to dominate it. But they also look to dominate the international market. They have executed this ambition through an extensive array of acquisitions and alliances – again, to a far greater degree than other Posts. Two highlights can be noted here. DPWN made a partial purchase of DHL, the world market leader in international courier and express (it now owns 51 per cent of DHL). This placed Deutsche Post into 227 countries and signalled to the postal and communications market that the Germans planned to participate as a global actor. DPWN also purchased the parcel and logistics business of Royal Nedlloyd in conjunction with the DM1-billion takeover of Danzas. This made DPWN an important international logistics force.

Third, this process unfolded against the backdrop of the planned privatization of Deutsche Post. "The company has been consistently preparing itself for its admission to official listing and privatization since Postal Reform I (in 1989 – RMC)."[5] In particular, internationalization has been seen by the Post as a prerequisite to a successful stock option.[6] This is because Deutsche Post had to prove to the market that it is competitive with the Dutch TPG – already privatized and listed – if its shares were to be floated successfully.[7] In November 2000, 29 per cent of its share capital was sold for US$5.6 billion. One of the big differences between the German and the Dutch experience has been the fact that the Dutch corporatized and privatized first and the Germans have had to react to, and in a sense catch up with, the Dutch initiative. This has led to a reverse pattern of development. The Germans have corporatized and (partially) liberalized first, in anticipation of privatization, whereas the Dutch privatized before they liberalized. The upshot of this is that the German government has had to be more concerned about regulating its Post than has the Dutch government.

Fourth, these postal-policy developments have been developed by the German state, in close cooperation with the board and senior management of the Post. The state has provided an encouraging market and regulatory environment that supported DPWN's growth and internationalization. It created a strong board and gave it autonomy and market direction. The preparation for postal reform and the resulting liberalization of domestic markets took place in a slow and deliberate fashion, most recently demonstrated by the government's decision to extend the Post's letter monopoly by five years, until 2007. This allowed the Post time to improve its finances and to strengthen its market position, in order to build up its resources and to modernize its postal operations. The state has approved and supported the Post's diversification and acquisition initiatives, which was assisted by the liquidation of unused or underutilized assets to finance modernization and acquisitions. The latter in turn were approved by the state. Notwithstanding the enormous modernization effort, the expansion into new product and service areas, and the frenetic pace of acquisitions, Deutsche Post approached privatization in a remarkably debt-free situation.[8] The German Department of Finance thus stands to do quite well in a share option, although a substantial part of the proceeds may have to be used to cover unfunded pension obligations.[9]

In sum, there has been an identity of interests between German postal and governmental authorities on the postal-policy agenda. Together, the Post and the government have redirected the Post to a growth strategy via diversification and internationalization. This process unfolded in a slow and deliberate but coherent and uncontroversial fashion during the 1990s, as did the deliberate process of liberalization. State policy allowed the Post to develop in two distinct stages. First, the Post modernized and reconstructed itself into a profitable corporation, which dominated the domestic and regional market. Second, the Post was then poised to head into international waters, to diversify and expand its business and prepare itself for privatization.[10]

While this has been an uncontroversial and relatively smooth process domestically, it has generated international controversy. As will be seen below, the German strategy has been challenged legally by private-sector competitors and other national posts – demonstrating the extent to which the postal world has been internationalized.

HISTORY

Like most postal systems in Europe, the German Post was organized within a PTT organization along with the telephone and telegraph. Over the post-war period, the profits from the latter were used to subsidize the operations of the former. The German Post was a classic state-bureaucratic organization, with a huge workforce and a civil-service orientation to its responsibilities. The postal losses that it incurred were justified politically as the price to pay to finance the costs associated with the Post's social obligations. These losses totalled in the billions; the deficit in 1990 alone was DM624 million. Postal-policy initiatives from Brussels intersected with the telecommunications revolution of the 1980s to lead the German government to initiate a postal-reform agenda in the late 1980s. This process has taken over a decade to unfold. It is unclear where the process will settle eventually. The recent election of a Social Democratic government may lead to the reopening of some policy issues and to the extension of the time-frame of postal liberalization.

Postereform I (1989)

The first stage of postal reform involved the separation of postal services from the postal banking, telecommunications, and regulatory functions of the old PTT organization. A new postal entity was created – Deutsche Bundespost Postdienst. This was a hybrid organization, inasmuch as the Post remained part of the Ministry of Posts and Telecommunications. It did, though, have a separate Board of Directors, with members recruited from the private sector to inject market sensibilities and values into its postal deliberations. The board quickly recruited a new corporate-management team, and to great effect. Dr Klaus Zumwinkel was recruited as CEO, a position he has held to the present. Most of the senior-management team recruited at that time also stayed with the Post over the course of the 1990s, providing policy continuity and heightened postal intelligence. Management quickly introduced corporate practices, reorganized the Post into sections (letters, cargo, post offices, and new business), simplified postal services, reorganized the network, and diversified the retail operation.

Despite the managerial revolution that had taken place, there still remained a high degree of government involvement and contact with postal management at this time. This required a second stage in the postal-reform process.

Postereform II *(1994)*

Five years after *Postreform I*, the German government passed a new postal law: the Law Concerning the Reorganization of Posts and Tele-communications. This was an extremely important development, since the law made the Post an "Aktiengesellschaft," or "AG." An "AG" is a joint-stock company, which is operated and managed under private law. This government initiative transformed Deutsche Bundespost Postdienst into Deutsche Post A.G. – DPAG – a public corporation with all of its shares owned by the government. The AG status required both the government and the Post to accept the requirements of the law under the corporations' acts. For example, the board now had the ultimate responsibility for the business health of the Post. This insulated the Post from the government, which had reduced opportunities to interfere in postal operations. At the same time, the postal law amended the constitution to guarantee the provision of an "appropriate and adequate" universal service. This became the ultimate responsibility of the state rather than the Post (Article 87,f).

This stage in the reform process was designed to prepare the Post for eventual privatization. Subsequent to the law being passed, the government introduced a number of regulatory changes that were designed to liberalize the market. For example, the Post's monopoly over advertising and bulk mail was opened to competition in 1995, and the weight limit for direct mail was lowered in 1997.

Postereform III *(1997)*

Immediately after *Postreform II* was passed, the next stage in the postal-reform process began. The minister presented a draft policy in June 1995 which proposed further liberalization of the postal market. A draft law in May 1996 and public hearings in September 1996 soon followed. The government proposed to extend the liberalization process at a pace somewhat faster than deemed appropriate by the Post itself and by the postal unions. The upshot of these developments was that a new postal law was passed in December 1997.[11]

The objective of the new law was to increase liberalization and postal competition in the market while maintaining the universal postal service. The law provided for the abolition of the postal monopoly and total liberalization of the postal sector at the end of the year 2002. In the interim five-year period, the law reduced DPAG's monopoly protection. While the European postal directive required a reduction in the reserved area to 350 grams, the German government lowered the exclusive privilege for letter mail to 200 grams or five times the price of a first-class stamp (DM5.50). It also opened up the direct (ad mail) market to competition on bundles of items (minimum 50) weighing more than 50 grams a unit. Thus the law created a new "competitive area" out of part of the old monopoly area, for unaddressed mail over 50 grams and letter mail between 200 grams and 2 kilograms. This segment of the market would be open for competition and would be regulated in a new licensing system. All other areas – including publications, courier, document exchange – would not be regulated. However, as explained below, DPAG would continue to have universal-service obligations and to be obliged to deliver all items up to 20 kilograms.

After 2002, all weight groups and categories would be open to competition. The universal system would then be financed by contributions from licence-holders through a compensation scheme (see below for a more detailed discussion). The new law further distanced politics from postal markets by abolishing the Ministry for Posts and Telecommunications. It created a new, independent Regulatory Authority for Telecommunications and Post (Reg TP), which would oversee and regulate the postal market and manage the licensing system. Reg TP would be separate from and independent of the Ministry of Economics. The ministry would have functional responsibility for postal policy but would have far less direct involvement in postal matters than previously.

The history of German postal reform thus differs in one important respect from the Dutch experience. In the latter case, privatization predated liberalization by a considerable period of time. Indeed, a largely privatized TPG enjoyed a 500-gram monopoly protection until 2000. In the German case, monopoly protection declined to 200 grams well before privatization – which will likely take place early in the new century. Indeed, the 200-gram exclusive privilege is below that which was dictated by the European postal directive (350 grams).

The Post has been anxious that this market exposure is out of step with market conditions in, for example, the Netherlands and France. This anxiety is exacerbated by the concern that DPAG's private competitors within Germany enjoy greater price flexibility and do not have to bear the universal-service burden – called infrastructure-service mandate (*infrastrukturauftrag*).[12] On the other hand, the Post welcomed the policy certainty created by the act as well as the price and product flexibility that enjoyed in the five-year transition.[13] As noted, the German government has recently extended the Post's monopoly protection past 2002 until 2007, concluding that liberalization in Europe will unfold more slowly than it had anticipated.

The most recent stage in postal evolution was the November 2000 partial privatization of the Post – now called Deutsche Post World Net – to identify itself better in world markets. There was some trepidation about how the share offering would unfold, given the fact that the German market had cooled on the earlier share sale of Deutsche Telekom. Notwithstanding these fears, the share offering was a clear success in privatizing 29 per cent of the company. The offer was eight times subscribed and raised US5.6 billion.[14] In March 2001 DPWN entered the DAX (German stock exchange) as part of its thirty-member blue-chip index.

STATUTORY AND REGULATORY ENVIRONMENT

As noted above, the German postal-reform process has a degree of sophistication and complexity in its thinking and rationale that sets it apart from other postal regimes. This is not stated to suggest that the German system is "better" than others. Rather, it is stated to anticipate the complexities and subtleties of the discussion that will follow. Three broad observations should be noted before a detailed presentation is made. First, the postal-regulatory regime is still a work in progress. There are a number of basic issues that remain to be settled, including the setting of licensing fees, prices, and regulations. Second, the evolving postal-regulatory regime is breaking new ground in legal, economic, and political terms. This has opened up possibilities for creativity but also gives the process a degree of uncertainty and "ad hocery." Third, the idiosyncrasies of the regime reflect a key fact – the government wished to create both a strong Deutsche Post (mercantile model) as well as a liberalized postal sector (market model). The compelling, if not contradictory, reality is that once the postal market is liberalized in 2003, Deutsche Post will be a postal behemoth capable of dominating the domestic market. Thus, the policy ambition for a liberalized postal market will of necessity require a substantial degree of regulation – to the extent of monitoring Deutsche Post to allow opportunities for new players and for the development of a real postal market. This explains the German government's reduction of the exclusive privilege to 200 grams, far below the EU maximum of 350 grams.[15] The German case provides another example of the phenomenon of the re-regulation of a deregulated market – albeit for reasons particular to the German regime.

The postal-regulatory regime in Germany follows the modern postal practice of separating policy, ownership, regulatory, and operational responsibilities. The Ministry of Economics determines overall postal and regulatory policy. A different ministry has ownership responsibility – the Ministry of Finance. A separate agency has been created – Reg TP – to implement the policy and regulatory guidelines established by the Ministry of Economics. Finally, operational matters are the strict responsibility of the Post, which is headed by a board that is appointed by, and reports to, the ownership ministry, the Ministry of Finance. Each of these functions and organizations will be discussed below.

The objective of the regulatory regime is to extend liberalization of the postal market while ensuring the persistence of a nationwide universal postal service, at a certain degree of quality and with universal and reasonable prices.[16] The regulatory regime is sector-specific. That is, the regulatory process focuses on one market (in this case posts and telecoms). Unlike other sector-specific regimes, the German regulatory process covers the whole of the industry, including both the public Post and private players. This is necessary because the system has opened up competition to licensed participants in the competitive segment of the postal market. But, in practice, the regulatory regime pays particular attention to the dominant provider and attempts to ensure the existence of competition. The regulatory authority is separate from the government, in order to insulate the postal realm from politics and to ensure independent regulation of the market.

The Government Role

There are two government roles in this postal-regulatory regime. First, the government has the responsibility for setting postal policy and guidelines, particularly in conjunction with the international obligations set by the UPU and the EC. The Ministry of Economics, which has a unit of five persons that works on postal matters directly, carries out this responsibility. This includes the setting of the Post's universal-service obligations. Technically speaking, this is the government's responsibility, as set out in the constitution after *Postreform II*. The Post is assigned these obligations, in return for retaining some monopoly protection. The universal-service obligations will change after 2002, as discussed below. The ministry's postal-policy guidelines are translated into law by a decree or ordinance that specifies postal-policy objectives and obligations like quality targets, network specifications, prices, delivery time, and service standards. These then become the legal guidelines against which the regulatory authority assigns and specifies licences and evaluates performance. The regulatory authority makes a report to Parliament every two years about how the postal market is developing and makes recommendations including proposed changes to the universal-service obligations. The government is obliged to issue a public reponse to this report.

For a time, there was a kind of regulatory vacuum, because the government had not passed a new postal ordinance since *Postreform III.* The regulatory guidelines were those that existed in the pre-1997 law. Deutsche Post promised to maintain these pre-1997 standards.[17] The ministry prepared a draft ordinance, which made the rounds of discussion and consultation over most of 1999 and was adopted in December 1999 (to take effect from January 1998[18]). The ordinance outlines the universal-service obligation to:

- deliver letters up to 2 kilograms and parcels up to 20 kilograms six days a week;
- maintain 12,000 postal outlets (5,000 of them the Post's own outlets[19]);
- provide a minimum number of post boxes and outlets, according to a formula;
- deliver at least 80 per cent of letters the next working day and 95 per cent by the second working day, and a minimum one delivery per working day; and
- set a uniform tariff for items within the exclusive privilege.

The setting of the postal ordinance became a modest political football. Some players wanted high and specific standards in the ordinance (for example, the Social Democrats, the unions, the Ministry of Economics) while others prefered a looser set of guidelines to corporatize the post (for example, the Liberals) or to ensure maximum profits for the Post (for example, the Ministry of Finance, Deutsche Post). Now that the ordinance is passed, though, its application is removed from the political arena.

Even with partial privatization, the government remains the predominant, majority shareholder of the Post. This is the government's second role, to carry out certain ownership responsibilities. The Ministry of Finance has this responsibility, which is organized around a post and telecommunications unit of four to six people. The ministry names members to the board. Once appointed, these members have autonomy from the government and, indeed, are legally obliged to act in the best interests of the corporation. The ministry has set-piece meetings with the Post quarterly, at which time it is briefed on business and investment plans and results. While the government continues to play some role in the setting of the business plan, there is no formal requirement that it accept or approve the Post's business plans. Management creates plans that are approved by the board – which contains one or two representatives of the government (see below). Profit targets are not set formally, the expectation being that the Post produce returns at a private-sector level of performance. While the Post has a great degree of space for investment and acquisition decisions, and there is no formal mechanism for government approval, major decisions continue to be rehearsed at the ministerial level.

The ministerial split between ownership and regulatory responsibilities creates a natural and healthy tension. The Ministry of Economics aims to liberalize markets, ensure an efficient postal system, and increase the standards associated with the universal-service obligation. The Ministry of Finance wants the Post to maximize shareholder value and so is not as enthusiastic about liberalization and an ambitious universal-service obligation. The two ministries talk to each other to come to accommodations, but there is no formal or public mechanism to this end. There was some anticipation that the election of the Social Democrats would see the pendulum of influence swing away from the latter to the former. However, since entering office, the new government has become very interested in the dividends paid by the Post.

Reg TP

The Regulatory Authority for Telecommunications and Post (Reg TP) is a regulatory authority, with responsibility for both the postal and telecommunications sectors. It has the highest possible degree of independence. Since January 1998, it has been a federal authority within the scope of business of the Ministry of Economics. It has taken over the functions previously carried out by ministries responsible for Post and Telecommunications. Reg TP reports every two years to Parliament, which provides its budget. It comprises about 300 people, 20–30 of whom work on the postal sector. Reg TP carries out policies and applies principles established by the Ministry of Economics but is substantially independent of it. Indeed, the unit was deliberately separated from the ministry and is physically located quite a distance from it. However, a certain degree of "overlap" in personnel exists, which was likely inevitable. For example, its director, Dr Hans Engelke, worked in the Ministry of Economics before his appointment at Reg TP.

The postal-regulatory regime was created to extend market liberalization while maintaining the universal postal system. These are the major objectives and responsibilities of Reg TP – to ensure fair competition, promote the development of the market, and ensure adequate postal service. While the Ministry of Economics sets policy and guidelines, Reg TP has information and investigative rights to allow it to carry out its responsibilities.[20] Moreover, it has authority for imposing sanctions against inappropriate behaviour. Most important, though, its decisions cannot be overturned by the ministry or overruled by ministerial decisions (although the ministry can give advice). Its rulings can be challenged only in the administrative courts. Reg TP's processes are public, via special proceedings, in order to ensure transparency. Its activities include: monitoring the quality of service against standards set by the Ministry; approving rates and service conditions in monopoly areas; acting as an arbiter in market and operational disputes; and issuing postal licences, which will be discussed presently. Its discretion is limited to the extent that the postal ordinances and ministerial directives are made detailed. If licensees do not meet its standards and guidelines, Reg TP can make public these poor performance results, ask and perhaps tell participants to improve their performance, report these results to the ministry and, ultimately, remove the licence.

The biggest innovation in the German regulatory regime is the licensing system that has been adopted. There are two features or rationales to this system. One is to ensure and provide for competition. The other is to maintain the universal system. Each issue will be discussed in turn.

Postreform III segmented the postal markets into a number of categories:

- an unregulated, free area for items greater than 2 kilograms;
- a monopoly area for the Post, for letters up to 200 grams (and five times the letter-mail price) and ad mail up to 50 grams (minimum 50 units); and
- a competitive or licensed area for addressed articles between 200 grams and 2 kilograms and unaddressed mail over 50 grams.

Postal firms that wish to enter the competitive, licensed segment of the market are obliged to apply to Reg TP for a licence.[21] The regulatory authority checks the application for competence and capacity to comply with the licence, including maintaining public safety and providing adequate working conditions.[22] Firms can apply for one or more licences to participate in local, provincial, regional, or national markets. Reg TP issued a significant number of licences in the first year, perhaps as high as 300.[23] A licence defines the licensed area that has been granted. Reg TP also approves rates for services that are provided by those with a dominant position in the market being served.[24] These are typically cost-based and vary according to a formula reflecting overall price changes. The costs determined by Reg TP aim to avoid anti-competitive results. Those with dominant market position in their area must provide unbundled services and post-office services to others at cost-based rates. Reg TP had anticipated that the ministry would pass an ordinance on the regulation of prices, without which its pricing action had taken on an ad hoc quality. In the event, while preparing a price-cap regime, it maintained prices at the current rates. In March 2000 the minister of economics directed Reg TP to extend the 1998 price regime through to 2002 (at the end of the period of Deutsche Post's licence and exclusive privilege).[25]

The postal act gave the Post a transitional "licence" that extended its exclusive privilege to 2002. The licence also had a universal and exclusive character to it, for mail below 200 grams.[26] This was granted because Deutsche Post was then the only firm that had the capacity to guarantee the universal system. The exclusive privilege represented a transitional step until the anticipated elimination of the Post's monopoly in 2002. As we have seen, however, the government has recently decided to extend the exclusive privilege until 2007, at which time a different system will be introduced.

The government does not interfere in the licensing process, which is managed exclusively by Reg TP. Any firm with a "dominant market position" is not permitted to cross-subsidize competitive products and services from non-competitive ones. It must provide Reg TP with a separate accounting system for its different activities, in order to guarantee transparency. Reg TP may prescribe an accounting system to this end, but there is no such system yet in place, in contrast to the Netherlands.[27] Deutsche Post's performance and actions are scrutinized against the backdrop of universal-service expectations. But this scrutiny is exercised only on the macro level. For example, there would be no question of Reg TP evaluating the closing of a particular post office unless this threatened to lower the total number of postal outlets to a level below that agreed upon.

The second feature of the licensing system is the manner in which it is directed to maintaining the universal system. As noted above, Deutsche Post was granted an exclusive licence for letters less than 200 grams in order to ensure that the universal system was maintained. The government planned to eliminate the Post's exclusive privilege in 2002, but monopoly protection has now been extended until 2007. After 2007, this protected market will become part of the competitive market, open to applicants for a licence (the fee for which has not yet been set). The plan proposed in this ultimate stage of the regulatory regime is an extremely bold one. The plan is to provide a universal service without a cross-subsidy from the protected or monopoly areas. The system will work as follows. All firms doing deliveries up to one kilogram will be required to apply for and purchase a licence, the fees going into a central fund. The regulatory system assumes, in the first instance, that the sum total of applicants for licences will cover the entire market, such that the array of licence holders will provide a universal postal service locally, regionally, and nationally. No licence holder will be obliged to provide the universal service on its own. If the actions of all the licence holders generate a universal system, as set out in the ordinance, then no more action is required. However, if there are no firms providing the universal service in a particular area, then Reg TP will require a particular licensed operator(s) to provide this service. If this service proves to be uneconomical for the provider(s), it would then be compensated for this activity from a compensation fund created by contributions from all licensed operators in proportion to their turnover.[28]

One can evaluate this proposal only in the abstract, since it will not come into being until after 2007. As noted, the plan is a bold one, for it anticipates the maintenance of a universal postal system without a monopoly or cross-subsidy provision to the national provider or an obligation for the Post or any other particular actor to provide it. The model anticipates that, during the transition period, an extensive array of postal operators will appear in all segments and areas of the market, thereby creating a universal system much like Adam Smith's invisible hand. If there are market "imperfections," then these will be repaired by the visible hand of Reg TP, which will purchase services to fill in any gaps. In the abstract, this plan looks complicated and open to some start-up chaos, since Reg TP will have to react to market imperfections only after the fact. Moreover, the licensing system itself looks complex and intimidating.

The Board

Deutsche Post has a Supervisory Board of twenty members. Ten of these are employee representatives, within the context of the German system of "co-determination." The other ten members are shareholder representatives, who are put forward by the Ministry of Finance. The law dictates that the board must act in the best interests of the enterprise. This principle has not yet tested. The government's aims in the 1990s were to deregulate and liberalize the postal market, and its appointments to the board were "pro-market." The board has autonomy from the government but basically has seen eye-to-eye with it. The shareholder representatives tend to be well-known figures from large German firms. For example, the first chair of the board –

Dr Helmut Sihler – was from Henkel KC AA, and the present chair –
Josef Hattig – is managing director of Brauerei Beck GmbH. Other
board members include directors or board members from Axel
Springer Verlag AG, Bayerische Landesbank Girozentrale, the Gerling
Group, and Linde AG. There are typically two shareholder representatives from the Ministry of Finance. The postal union's influence on
policy is likely to increase with the election of the Social Democrats.

The Management Board reports to the Supervisory Board. It is
chaired by Klaus Zumwinkel, the Post's CEO. He has been in this
position since 1990 and has provided valuable continuity (as have four
of the eight members of the senior-management team who were
recruited the same year). Zumwinkel is a metaphor for the new managerial orientation and competence of the Post. A graduate of the
Wharton school of business, he worked previously for Europe's largest
mail-order catalogue company as well as for McKinsey as a management consultant.

The board has been a very business-oriented and market-savvy
group, whose corporate and business orientation will only intensify as
a result of the partial privatization and increasing pressure to create
shareholder value.

The Public

The regulatory-reform process has not generated much public controversy or scrutiny, and there is not a significant participatory dimension to the system. Reg TP's hearings are public and open, to ensure
transparency. There is a popular dimension to the composition of
the board, but this relates to co-determination between owner and
workers and does not extend to postal users. There is a subnational
level of postal scrutiny through a Regulatory Council, which comprises one representative from each state. The council looks at issues
like new licences, mandatory services, consumer protection, and
cross-subsidization. Its objective is to ensure that there is a nationwide
postal infrastructure. But it provides only advice and has no authority
to make decisions.

Relations among the Players

The objective of the reform program was to depoliticize the postal
world to allow the postal market to develop in a competitive and
efficient manner. The regulatory regime was designed to separate the
functional players from each other, with each player to carry out
different tasks. In particular, the system was designed to give the Post

independence from the government and to separate regulation from ownership functions. Before this, there was a considerable degree of government involvement (interference) in the Post.

As noted above, one way to ensure this was to split the regulatory authority from the ministry and literally place it physically in an area far removed from the ministry. The interaction between the ministry and Reg TP appears to be irregular and episodic, although the personnel are quite familiar with each other – having worked together before 1998. As elsewhere, there is a tendency for the same personnel to switch "hats." For example, the head of the Regulation Department for Deutsche Post (Michael Els) used to be at the Ministry of Economics. Moreover, while Reg TP is independent, its authority vis-à-vis the Ministry of Economics will not really be demonstrated until after 2007, since many regulatory arrangements are currently circumscribed or ad hoc.

There continues to be considerable contact between the government and senior management and the board. The head of the board was a close associate of the former chancellor. The relations between the ministry and the board continue to be close. This was inevitable, given the acquisition and internationalization agendas and the European postal directive. However, there are no examples of major Deutsche Post decisions being overturned by the government. Indeed, the Post enjoys a great deal of strategic autonomy, which should increase as a result of the partial privatization.

OBSERVATIONS

The regulatory system is still very much in an early stage of development. Not surprisingly, it has generated some controversy. For example, Deutsche Post feels that it is being unfairly treated. It has to bear the burden of the universal-service obligation (including deliveries in all parts of Germany of materials up to 20 kilograms, six days a week, maintaining 12,000 postal outlets, and so on), which is actually greater than that set out in the EU postal directive. Moreover, as a dominant provider, it receives more price and cost scrutiny than competitors who participate only in the unregulated areas. Finally, it feels that the regulator has misinterpreted the licensing legislation, to allow courier services to cream-skim the market. Courier services are not subject to licensing, if they are determined to be offering services greater than a higher-quality service, by virtue of some special features. This is a grey area in the legislation. Deutsche Post has taken the issue to the Court of Justice, where it lost its case. It is contemplating taking the issue to a higher court of appeal.[29] Moreover, the regulator ordered Deutsche

Post to open part of its delivery network to UPS, to accept partly sorted bulk-mail items heavier than 200 grams from UPS, and to forward them at a discount to their destination. The effect is to have Deutsche Post forward mail at a price cheaper than its own rates.[30]

Generally speaking, the Post has had some mixed feelings about the new regulatory system, which has actually increased the degree of regulation that it experiences. However, it accepts this re-regulation as a necessary step in creating a liberalized postal market and prefers the certainties of the new act to the uncertainties of the absence of a regulatory framework.[31]

The regulatory system looks complicated, with many players, processes, and practices. There are two ministries directly involved, not to mention ministries dealing with competition and international matters as well as an independent regulatory body and a regulatory council. Part of its admitted complexity reflects the existence of a transition phase to market liberalization. This stage is somewhat messy. The German authorities' view is that the complexity is a necessity if market development and liberalization is to be realized. The Germans have watched the Swedish and Finnish cases, where a total and quick market deregulation did not spontaneously create a competitive postal market. The regulatory complexities are designed to make a free market work where there is a dominant market player like DPWN.[32] However, the hard fact is that while 19 per cent of the market has been opened up to competition (in the licensed sector), Deutsche Post retains a 99 per cent share.

The European legal environment could act as a further and substantial regulatory constraint on the evolution of Deutsche Post. The EC is investigating a number of legal challenges made against Deutsche Post. Its private-sector competitors have accused the German government of giving it illegal state aid (which the competitors argue has been used to finance Deutsche Post's diversification and business purchases). The commission is also investigating whether Deutsche Post disobeys EU competition rules in the manner in which it handles cross-border mail. In a lawsuit initiated by UPS, the Post was held to be using its exclusive privilege to subsidize shipments and out-price its competitors in the business-parcels sector. It was fined EURO24 million and required to set up a separate parcels division, insulated from the monopoly letters division.

PERFORMANCE

Until the time of the postal-reform process, the performance of the Post had not been particularly impressive.[33] Postal prices were high and quality was low. There were weak operational and control systems, an overly complicated and extensive product line, no transparency or understanding of costs, and complex restrictions on the use of personnel. The Post did not have a market, service, or customer orientation but rather functioned in an environment dominated by bureaucratic norms and values. The overall result was low postal quality and consistent losses. Indeed, at the beginning of the 1990s, losses rose to over DM600 million.

The corporate strategy through the 1990s was far more market- and growth-oriented, with internationalization, diversification, and value-added products as the key strategic ingredients. New corporate management transformed a bureaucratic orientation to a market one, emphasizing the need to grow in order to survive. This strategy was supported by the state, which allowed and encouraged the Post to expand internationally, diversify into new product and service areas, enlarge its products base, and specialize in points of comparative advantage in the supply chain. This strategy was, like the Dutch one, informed by a number of understandings, particularly the need to grow in order to survive. Growth could be attained only if postal products were competitive, which required substantial improvement in the control of costs and in the quality of service. Finally, growth required the corporation to expand into new products and into international markets. As CEO Zumwinkel put it: "The corporate strategy is based on the three pillars of internationalization, expansion of the product base and value-added logistics."[34] The German strategy has been less sensitive to, but not unaware of, technological competition compared to the Netherlands (and, as will be seen, Scandinavia). This is due substantially to the enormous size of the German postal market, which is three times larger than that in the Netherlands and more or less guarantees high volumes. The goals of Deutsche Post comprise market-leadership domestically, opening of foreign markets, boosting sales and income, and increasing quality to an international standard. All of this is directed to preparing the company for privatization early in the new century.

Overall, the growth, diversification, and internationalization strategies have been remarkably successful. Revenues have increased to over DM65 million. The letter-mail market generates but 34 per cent of total revenue and 29 per cent of revenue is derived from foreign sources.

Growth (I): Mechanization, Labour Reduction, and Quality

Improved quality and efficiency were the key objectives in the Post's consolidation and growth strategy in the 1990s. In an increasingly competitive European market, the Post would have to improve control over costs and the quality of service if it were to compete effectively and maintain and build up postal volumes. This was a particular challenge for the German postal system, which comprised a huge labour force that enjoyed comfortable civil-service salaries and conditions of work and that was not particularly focused on quality. To meet its goals, Deutsche Post pursued a two-pronged strategy, both parts of which were supported explicitly or implicitly by the state: reduction of the size of the labour force (see below) and postal mechanization. With respect to the latter, the BRIEF 2000 (Letter Mail 2000) strategy was devised. The objective of this policy was to increase the proportion of mail sorted mechanically from 24 per cent in the late 1980s to over 85 per cent, in order to reduce unit costs and improve speed and efficiency.[35] The complementary service objective was to raise the proportion of mail delivered in one day to 95 per cent. The Post invested an enormous amount of capital in the mechanization process in the 1990s. The 1997 annual report noted that the Post invested DM16 billion in western and eastern Germany in the 1990s. This included a DM8-billion investment in 83 major letter-processing centres across the country. These centres have sorting equipment that sort mail down to the house number. The last of the centres was opened in 1998, one year ahead of schedule. Further, a new hub for international mail was opened in Frankfurt in September 1997, with a capacity to process up to 5 million letters and 50,000 parcels daily to 140 countries. Complementing the letter-mail stream, there has also been a comprehensively redesigned and relocated parcel-distribution network of thirty-three new freight centres.

The challenge for Deutsche Post will be to generate the postal volumes needed to keep these high-tech systems operating at peak efficiency. The Post likely has the capacity to generate a sufficient volume of letters in Germany, given the size of its domestic market. While the package and freight side of the business remains an open question, since this is a highly competitive market,[36] Deutsche Post has proven to be very competitive to this point. For example, it managed to hold off the UPS initiative in Europe because of its remarkable array of mechanized plants and a conscious strategy of lowering prices to increase volumes.[37]

The degree of capital investment in the German postal system has been especially striking and very high comparable to other Posts. But this has not been without controversy. The ongoing, recent capital expenditures continue to be large – DM1.9 billion in 1996, DM1.93 billion in 1997, and DM1.8 billion in 1998. What is particularly striking is that this has been generated from internally generated cash flow –

including the selling off of fixed assets not required for operations (fixed assets fell by DM1 billion in 1998). The overall result of the investment has been the creation of an extended, high-technology operational network which has made Deutsche Post a top-performing and dominant market player.

These initiatives have generated some controversy and uncertainty, in the form of a state-aid case being made against the German government at the EC. There have been complaints made by private competitors like UPS to the EU since the mid-1990s to the effect that Deutsche Post's international parcel expansion has been financed from the monopoly side of the postal operation. The Post's position is that this expansion has been financed appropriately by barter in assets, namely, the sale of unused real estate, production buildings, and staff accommodation.[38] The timing of this case was unfortunate for the Post, given the impending stock flotation in the summer of 2000.

The second arm of the cost-reduction dimension of the growth strategy was the reduction in labour costs. This objective was not pursued with any great vigour in the early part of the 1990s. The civil-service ethos, culture, and tradition, as well as the strength of the postal unions, kept the employment objective central on the postal-policy agenda – particularly during the years when the state was still involved in postal matters. Since *Postreform II and III*, Deutsche Post has quietly gone about reducing the total number of workers employed. There have been no forced redundancies. Instead, attrition, early retirements, and part-time employment have been the tactics used to reduce the labour components of total costs. Since 1995, the average number of employed has fallen from 315,000 to 267,000. This has had a substantial impact on the Post's bottom line. For example, the proportion of total costs represented by personnel costs fell by 1.5 per cent (to 66 per cent) in 1998. Deutsche Post reported that this was the source of increased profits in that year.[39] The focus on reducing labour costs has also resulted in initiatives in the area of work practices. In the 1997 collective agreement, for example, the Post promised that there would be no dismissals for operational reasons before 31 December 2000. In return, the unions agreed to a number of cost-cutting initiatives, including shorter breaks, relinquishing one free day, and the elimination of hardship pay. It is also looking to introduce a greater degree of performance-based compensation to increase overall competitiveness (management remuneration has already moved in that direction).[40]

The overall impact of the cost-control measures on the quality of service has been considerable. By 1996, 91 per cent of letters received next-day delivery, a level that climbed consistently to 95 per cent in

1998 (and 99 per cent delivered within two days). The average delivery time for parcels fell to 1.1 days in 1998. These are quality standards that have increased Deutsche Post's capacity to compete effectively in the increasingly competitive German and European markets.

Growth (II): Expanding Markets

The second dimension of the growth strategy has been the maintenance of postal volumes and markets and the creation of new ones. This has featured some striking initiatives, particularly in the area of internationalization and the intervention into related – indeed "non-postal" – areas like logistics. Indeed, over 30 per cent of the Post's revenue was generated internationally in 2000 and the target is 40 per cent in 2001.[41] In some countries, diversification and internationalization have been controversial and politically divisive initiatives. In Germany, these developments have had the backing of the German state either directly or indirectly (the latter through the creation of a more deregulated postal environment).

Mail In the first instance, the Post has worked to maintain mail volumes and revenues in the face of increasing product and technological competition. There has been greater than 25 per cent growth in letter volumes since 1991, and the total volume is now over 21 billion units annually (65 million units a day). Deutsche Post is the largest mail player in Europe, comprising 24 per cent of the 80-billion-unit market (followed by La Poste at 22 per cent, Royal Mail at 14 per cent, and the Netherlands Post at 8 per cent). Its turnover has increased recently by over DM1 billion to reach DM20 billion. Mail revenue represents a declining proportion of total revenues, falling from 73 per cent in 1997 to 34 per cent in 2000, partially as a result of diversification. As elsewhere, the growth of the traditional letter market has been steady yet modest and the volume of magazines and publications has decreased, but advertising mail has increased substantially – 5.4 per cent in 1997, for example, to 4.6 billion units. The mail strategy has recently been twofold. On the one hand, the Post has reoriented itself to key accounts: large volume, mail order, public organizations, insurance companies, brand-name companies, and so on. The idea here is to maintain and grow major accounts as far as possible. Generally, this reflects again the extent to which postal activity focuses on business mail. On the other hand, the ad-mail market is seen as an underdeveloped one with huge potential. The Post has gone on the offensive in this market, which is not a protected one. It has opened over thirty direct-marketing centres, targeting small- and medium-sized companies. It also continues to be the major player in publications mail.

Courier, Express, Parcels   The courier, express, and parcel (CEP) market is an important one for the future. Its European value is around twenty-three billion Euros, and this is expected to double by the year 2010. Express itself is expected to have double-digit annual growth into the indeterminate future.[42] The CEP market is less susceptible to techno-logical and electronic substitution than letters, because bulk products cannot be transported electronically. Indeed, the Internet revolution will likely increase business for the Post, particularly in the area of business-home and business-business deliveries. This presents a tremen-dous growth opportunity – but a real challenge. The CEP market is an open and competitive one, comprising large public and private players as well as a vast number of small private ones. Of the DM55-billion market, DPAG has 12.7 per cent, DHL (now partially owned by DPAG) has 6.7 per cent, La Poste has 10.2 per cent, TPG has 6.4 per cent, UPS has 6.2 per cent and Royal Mail has 3.6 per cent.[43]

Historically, Posts in general and the German Post in particular have not been particularly successful in the freight or parcels market. Indeed, this feature of Deutsche Post's business operates in the red and volumes have stabilized only recently (at around DM3 billion). The Post plans to be on a positive financial footing in the parcels area early in the twenty-first century. It has developed a state-of-the-art array of 33 freight centres and lowered the average delivery time for a parcel in Germany to 1.1 days. The aim is to build up a European market for parcels (and direct mail), since consumers are demanding a Euro-pean service. As will be seen presently, this European expansion has been carried out mainly through acquisitions. The Germans anticipate that the European market will settle down into a Big Five: the Posts of Germany, the Netherlands, France, and Britain, plus UPS. The last player is an interesting case to note here. UPS invested over US$1 billion and built up a fleet of 10,000 trucks in an effort to penetrate the European market. However, it lost almost US$1.5 billion internationally in the 1990s, mainly in Europe. Deutsche Post resisted this initiative by building up its network and then cutting prices and offering discounts to build up business. UPS then charged the German government with providing unfair assistance before the European court. "Our objective," declares CEO Zumwinkel, "is to build a yellow machine for Europe, as UPS has done with a brown machine for the United States."[44] By 1998, it was selling its parcel-mail products directly in ten European countries.

The issue of "brand" competition is emerging in this area in Europe. Deutsche Post is emphasizing its yellow colour and the traditional looped horn icon as an international brand. Indeed, DPWN has recently introduced a universal brand for its express services in Europe, called Euro Express. The objective is to create a pan-European distribution network with all of its European partners, under the umbrella of Deutsche Post Euro Express (the acquisitions and alliances of these partners is discussed below). This strategy is being carried out in two stages. In the first stage, the Post's European partners – like Ducros in France, Securicor in the United Kingdom, and so on – will operate under their own names, jointly designated with Euro Express. The objective is to build Euro Express as an independent label in the national market. In the second stage, there will be a total transformation to the uniform brand name.

Diversification and Retail Strategy   Deutsche Post's growth strategy has seen it expand into new product areas and rationalize and refigure its retail operation. The purpose of these initiatives has been to decrease the corporation's reliance on mail volumes and revenues, expand the business into new product lines, and build up customer loyalties.

A major effort has been made to connect to different points on the supply chain, to go beyond simple distribution into the various forms of communication from direct marketing through to order fulfillment.[45] This effort has been orchestrated through a "new business sector" division, which has made overtures in the communications, transportation and logistics, and advertising areas. A number of new businesses have been developed jointly with other firms or by the Post itself, particularly in the electronic-communications area. EPost is a hybrid service whereby firms submit electronic files that can be printed and delivered locally. Eighty-four million units were delivered in this manner in 1997. DPWN has created a number of subsidiaries in areas such as data-base management, software, in-house sorting, printing, and logistics. Some specific examples include:

Inhaus Post (In-house Service)
A firm that provides internal mail service for large-volume customers that want to outsource this activity. It currently has more than 100 clients and annual revenues of DM45 million

Post Address
In a joint venture with Bertelsmann (the large German publisher), this firm adapts notification of change-of-address information for

other purposes. Security of private addresses is a significant issue in Germany and this company has been set up as a hands-off subsidiary, for security purposes.

Post Direct
This state-of-the-art firm is 100 per cent owned by DPNW. It provides full-service support for its customers' direct-advertising initiatives, as well as the high-quality, accurate information that underpins these efforts.

Post Com
This company provides hybrid services, including printing data streams to linked sorting centres; electronic-communication services; a clearing centre for secure, signed electronic-document exchange; and scanning of incoming mail for internal distribution.

Clip Multimedia
Provides learning software for training.

MCC System
DPAG purchased 70 per cent of this firm for software development (it is a partner of Lotus Notes). It supports the Post's communications system.

Merkur
This is a full-service agency for direct mail, from addresses to storage, from call-centre services to order fulfillment.

Deutsche Post has also made important initiatives in the world of web-based business. A twenty-two-person-design team developed EVITA, an Internet marketplace.[46] EVITA provides a kind of electronic shopping mall and business information. It has developed alliances with a number of businesses in the areas of health and fitness, travel and dining, and family services. The service does not make money for the Post directly. Rather, it is designed to get transportation business and expand the Post's core business. It has set up a separate holding company for this purpose – eBusiness GmbH. This has been a remarkably successful initiative. The Post is Germany's leading on-line carrier, accounting for 64 per cent of all on-line business and delivering 46 per cent of total volume. It made thirty million deliveries in 2000, generating US$1 billion in revenues.

Like the Dutch, the Germans are making a concentrated initiative in the area of logistics, providing advice and getting involved in supply-chain management, including warehousing, order fulfillment, billing, and receiving and delivery. This has been pursued in an industry-specific way. For example, it has become involved in fashion and textiles logistics, moving material and products to and from design shows and from manufacturers and warehouses to retail outlets. Typically, it has expanded into this area through acquisitions (for example, Munich ITG Group, ITG Internationale Spedition GmbH). Another sectoral example is PostMed, a logistics initiative that sees the Post providing a seamless transport and information system for the pharmaceutical industry.

Like other Posts around the world, Deutsche Post has tried to adjust its retail operation to a world in which people carry out fewer postal transactions at the post office. There has been a stable level of transactions in the postal branches (not quite DM300 million in each of 1996 and 1997). Part of this effort has involved a rationalization of the network, including the closing of traditional post offices and the opening of postal agencies in grocery stores, petrol stations, and stationary shops – with longer hours, convenient locations, and so on. First opened in 1993, there were over 4,000 agencies by 1996. In the interim, post-office branches were being closed – 1,800 in 1996 and 1,190 in the first eight months of 1997. However, there is a limit to this tactic, since maintaining a universal network is part of the Post's universal-service obligation, although it aims to reduce its network to about 10,000 outlets early in the twenty-first century. The broader strategy has been to generate more and different economic activity through a reconfigured retail network, which now totals about 15,000 outlets and is the largest sales network in Germany. This strategy has involved three ingredients.

First, the retail network has become one of Deutsche Post's key investment foci, now that the mechanization process has been completed. The 1998 report declares that investment in the retail network will be a key priority, particularly in the application of new information technology and the internationalization of the network. All outlets are being modernized with computer technology and electronic point-of-sales systems (EPOS), so that 98.5 per cent of all transactions will be made via information technology systems. This will involve a capital expenditure of about DM1 billion over four years.[47]

Second, new styles and kinds of retail outlets have been designed or utilized as a way of improving service and maintaining and increasing business. A new kind of "open plan," customer-friendly post office has been designed called "Centre Outlets." These are designed to be more like a shop or store than a barricaded postal outlet. There are already about sixty of such centres open, in locations with the greatest customer demand. There will be 300 by the end of 1999 and the target is to have 750 across the country, serving half of the Post's customers in this manner. Putting outlets in existing retail outlets has also increased the postal retail presence. "Shop-in-Shop" branches are outlets in retail stores where there is high-volume business. The first was opened in 1996. Postal outlets were placed in gas stations and department stores. One experiment in this regard was the placing of postal products in the McPaper stationary store chain. The experiment was so successful that the Post bought the entire chain in 1998 and operates it as a subsidiary. The plan is to open 500 joint Post-McPaper stores in the next five years.

A third initiative has been to expand the range of products sold in outlets to postal -related and non-postal products. Immediately upon the adoption of *Postreform I*, post offices started offering a wider range of products, including postcards, envelopes, writing and packing material, bus and tram tickets, and even clothes for the dry cleaner in rural areas. In one pilot project, 500 postal agencies opened grocery shops and gas stations. A pilot project called PostPlus saw 191 test outlets provide convenience items like newspapers, snacks, tobacco, and writing and office supplies. The product-diversification program has been utilized particularly in rural areas.

A final element in the diversification and product-growth strategy is financial services. It will be recalled that *Postreform I* split the Post away from telecommunications and postal banking, each of which was organized separately. This development has more or less been undone. In 1997 Deutsch Post bought 18 per cent of the Postbank and concluded an extensive and close cooperation agreement with it. It then partnered with the Wutenrot savings-and-loan association and the HDI insurance company, in which it has a 50 per cent stake. It purchased the remaining stock in the bank in the next year. The objective is to increase the competitiveness of the Postbank and make full use of the Post's retail-network capacity. Financial services are now offered in the postal retail outlets and involve one-stop shopping – including savings, property and life insurance, and consumer loans and funds products. Insurance is provided by PB Versicherung. The Postbank purchased 81 per cent of DSL Holding AG, which had come about from the partial privatization of the DSL Bank. Financial services now comprise about one-third of the business generated in the retail outlets. The Postbank has also become a contact for logistics financing and offers its customers direct brokerage. The objective is to become "The Basic Banking Service Bank" for private customers and their choice of financial-service provider. In an environment with few regulatory inhibitions, the German postal bank has become Germany's largest retail bank and provides one-quarter of the Post's total business sales.[48]

Acquisitions and the International Strategy As noted earlier, German postal strategy has evolved in two stages. The first stage involved turning the company into a modern organization, through domestic reorganization and consolidation, with respect to the corporate management and organizational structure as well as to the modernization of operations in the sorting, delivery, business, and retail areas. The second stage has accelerated the overall growth objective into the international area and involved a considerable number of mergers and acquisitions and a redirection into areas like financial services, logistics, and value-added services. According to Deutsche Post's figures, about 5 per cent of its revenues were derived internationally in 1990. In 1998 this figure was 8 per cent and in 2000 it was 29 per cent (DM60 billion).[49] Before *Postreform III*, the international area was not a priority. It is now included as an ingredient in all company declarations on plans and objectives. The international area currently has its own director, who sits on the board.

By and large, this process has been customer-driven, since business in particular has demanded a European, indeed international, service. Postal customers tend to want one contact for all their mailing activities. The Post could have simply moved to increase cooperation with the public Posts in other countries. In some cases, this type of inter-Post cooperation exists. For example, Deutsche Post has a cooperation agreement with Luxembourg Post and an agreement with Russia for the delivery of mail-order goods. In a country like Argentina, which has no public Post, Deutsche Post has entered into a cooperation agreement with the large private postal company Organizacion Cordinadora Argentina (OCA). In other countries, it has built up a provider from scratch – such as Quickstep in the Czech Republic. However, in order to guarantee the quality of service and to increase revenues, Deutsche Post has set up its own operation in a number of countries, its goal being to become the number-two operator in other domestic markets. In the process, it has created its own integrated parcel, express, and logistics network across Europe and, to a lesser extent, across the world. It has its own transport networks in business-business parcel conveyance from the Baltic and the Iberian peninsula through the Mediterranean into Eastern Europe. It participates in parcel companies in ten countries across Europe, such as Austria, Belgium, Switzerland, and the United Kingdom. Deutsche Post now competes directly with other public Posts in their domestic markets as well as with international Posts across all markets. Indeed the Germans are competing with the Dutch and the French to purchase a part of the Greek Post. DPWN sees the Dutch Post as a major competitor, with a particularly aggressive style (a view shared by most other public Posts in Europe). Notwithstanding its own acquisitive march through Europe, Deutsche Post claims not to share TPG's highly competitive approach. Nonetheless, Royal Mail and a number of other public operators are presently suing it for over-protecting its domestic market.[50]

What follows below is a list of its acquisitions and mergers in the last few years, beginning with those comprising the creation of the European network (1–12) followed by those in North America (13–15).

1   DHL

This has been perhaps Deutsch Post's most dramatic and important purchase. DPAG bought 25 per cent of DHL in 1998 and raised its stake to 51 per cent in 2001. An American company that pioneered international express service, DHL is the world market leader for international courier and express. It is the top provider in the European and Asian express markets and second in the United States after FedEx. In purchasing DHL, Deutsche Post became an immediate participant in 277 countries and linked to the world's strongest express product. As seen earlier, the German Post is now poised to create the dominant brand name for express in Europe. The operations of DHL and Deutsche Post are integrated, and the chair of DHL International (Uwe Dörken) is on the Board of Management of DPWN. The USPS recently contracted with DHL to deliver its international parcels.

2   Royal Nedlloyd and Danzas

Deutsche Post purchased the parcel and logistics business of Royal Nedlloyd, which has a substantial presence in the Benelux parcel market and in logistics in Europe. This purchase was made in conjunction with the DM 1-billion takeover of Danzas. This long-established Swiss company was the third-largest transport, international forwarding, and logistics group in the world. The EC approved this acquisition in March 1999. The parcel business of Royal Nedlloyd will be integrated into Deutsche Post while the logistics business will be merged with Danzas, which will continue to operate as an independent business.

3   Belgian Parcel Distrubution

Deutsche Post purchased a majority share in this Belgian firm.

4   Trans-o-flex Schnell-Lieferdienst AG

Deutsche Post bought a 25 per cent stake in this DM1-billion firm in 1997 through a holding company. In tandem with participation in the pan-European Eurodis Network (in which it has an equity interest), this contributed to the creation of a top-quality European network. In Germany, Trans-o-flex is the leading express-delivery service, with specific industry orientation and expertise. It operates as well in six other European countries through its subsidiaries.

5   Securicor Distributions

Deutsche Post purchased 50 per cent of this United Kingdom parcel carrier, which is the market leader for express and parcel deliveries in the U.K. and Ireland. The EC approved this purchase in February 1999.

6   Ducros Services Rapides

Deutsche Post purchased 68 per cent of this French delivery company.

7   Qualipac AG

This purchase consolidated Deutsche Post's status as the number-two parcel-service provider in Switzerland. It had already taken over GP Paketlogistik AG in December 1997, renaming it Quickstep Parcel Service. Qualipac was the third-largest parcel company in Switzerland.

8   MIT and SAV S.P.A.

Deutsche Post purchased a 90 per cent stake in MIT, an Italian express and parcel company in January 1999. In July 2000 it purchased SAV S.P.A. which, in conjunction with its other Italian holdings, has established an integrated parcel-and-distribution network in Italy.

9   Ipp Paketbeforderung

Deutsche Post purchased 100 per cent of this Austrian parcel and express delivery company.

10   Servisco

Deutsche Post purchased 60 per cent of this Polish parcel and logistics firm.

11   ASG – Scandinavia

ASG was purchased by Danzas, a subsidiary of Deutsche Post, and will be fully integrated into Danzas. ASG is one of the leading forwarding, air-freight, and logistic companies in northern Europe and the Baltic areas, with full mail, truck, and parcel lines. It is an enormous company, with 5,700 employees and DM2.64 billion in revenues. Its purchase was controversial in Sweden, inasmuch it appeared that Sweden Post (or the government) fumbled the opportunity to purchase it.

12   Guipuzcoana

Deutsche Post purchased 49 per cent of this Spanish parcel carrier in July 1999. It is the market leader in day-certain business-business delivery in Spain and has a comprehensive network in Portugal as well. It became the Iberian partner for delivering all network parcels to the area, while Deutsche Post will transport parcels from the area to the rest of Europe.

13   Air Express International (AEI)

AEI is the oldest and largest American-based international freight forwarder and the world leader in integrated logistics. It has over 700 locations in more than 135 countries, with gross revenues of US$1.5 billion. Its top clients include Intel and Caterpillar. This US$1.1-billion purchase made Deutsche Post an immediate and serious rival to FedEx and UPS in the global-freight and air-express business generally and in the American market specifically. It plans to integrate AEI into Danzas, which will then become the leading air-freight forwarder worldwide. The purchase raised eyebrows for the market strength that it gave Deutsche Post. Royal Mail characterized the purchase as "unfortunate ... a move which will raise concerns over continued high profile consolidation in the industry."[51]

14   Global Mail

In 1998 DPWN purchased 100 per cent of Global Mail, a major U.S. exporter of international remail and a significant player in the direct-advertising market.

15   Yellowstone International Corportation

In May 1999 DPWN purchased YellowStone, the largest privately held international-publications distribution company in the United States. It is the leading provider of international-distribution services for business, trade, and financial publications, delivering more than 650 American magazine titles overseas (for example, the *Wall Street Journal*).

The upshot of all of these acquisitions – totalling over US$5 billion – is that Deutsche Post has become an international postal behemoth, with its own networks in industrialized markets across Europe, North America, and much of the world. The revenue from foreign sources has grown from 2 per cent in 1998 to 29 per cent in 2000. DPWN's turnover rose to over DM60 billion in 2000. These purchases have been made basically with internally generated funds, leaving the company remarkably debt-free and in terrific shape for privatization. This state of affairs is an important reflection of the character of the German regulatory regime, which did not inhibit or constrain Deutsche Post's diversification and internationalization. Indeed, the regulatory regime established by the government was suited to the mercantile strategy constructed by governments and the Post in the 1990s.

PERFORMANCE RESULTS

The German Post became a substantial and profitable operation over the course of the 1990s. In the early 1990s, it produced losses as high as DM600 million on revenues of DM18 billion (the deficit from the East pushed this to over DM1 billion). Until 1993, these losses were covered by profits from the telecommunications organization and justified by the government as required to cover the burdens of the past. There has been no direct subsidy or cross-transfer since that time. From 1990 to 1998, postal revenues increased by 54 per cent to DM28.7 billion. Extensive acquisitions, expanded international operations, and market growth have seen DPWN; revenues grow to over DM65 billion in 2000. What is particularly striking is the international character of this growth. In the nine months ending September 1999, Deutsche Post generated only 30 per cent of its revenues from Europe but 40 per cent from North America, 21 per cent from Asia, and 9 per cent from rest of the world. Overall, as already noted, 29 per cent of its revenue in 2000 was international in origin. It continued to post losses through to the mid-1990s. But, as indicated in the table below, it has made profits consistently since and in an upward trajectory to over DM1 billion in 1998.

The increase in revenue has had three sources: price increases (40 per cent), volume increases (40 per cent), and new business (20 per cent).[52] The volume increase in particular reflects a degree of customer satisfaction. The improved profit picture reflects the payoffs from system rationalization, reduction in the labour force, and substantial investment in mechanization and modernization. As indicated in Table 1, the return on equity has been reasonable, at about the level experienced in the German transportation industry. Dividends were paid to the government for the first time in 1997 (DM103 million) and this level tripled in 1998 (DM300 million). Its net income in 2000 was DM3 billion.

Table 1
Results (millions of DM)

	1995	1996	1997	1998
Revenue	26,680	26,702	27,136	28,100
Profit	364	576	752	1,276
Equity Ratio (%)	26.8	26.6		
Equity Return (%)	1.2	6.9	8.5	6.8
Employees (000s)	315	307	284	266
Personnel (% costs)	70.6	67.2	67.9	66.2

NOTE: DM28.7 billion = US$15.6 billion or Can$24 billion, at about 1.8 marks to the US dollar
and 1.2 marks to the Canadian dollar.
Source: Annual Reports, assorted years.

HIGHLIGHTS OF THE GERMAN CASE

What can one learn from the German case and what interest does its experience hold for policy makers? In what ways does it differ from the Dutch case?

First, as in the Netherlands, the postal-reform process in Germany was marked by a high degree of consensus among the major players. The reform process was not scrutinized politically nearly as intensely as in Canada, mainly because of the Post being carried along by the telecommunications agenda. Government appointments of top corporate officials to the board, and the board's recruitment of private-sector management, saw the development of a consistency of views across the postal-policy community. The postal unions did play a larger role in Germany than in the Netherlands, inasmuch as their influence was not neutralized by the economic downturn of the 1980s to the same extent as in the Netherlands. Nonetheless, the co-determination approach, combined with rapidly expanding postal activity and growth, ensured that labour adjustments were carried out in a non-conflictual way. The key factor here has been the extent to which postal and government authorities have consistently seen eye-to-eye on the basic elements of the reform agenda. A regulatory system was constructed and evolved which reflected this shared thinking. It did not inhibit subsequent postal development.

Second, the postal-reform agenda unfolded less rapidly in Germany case than in the Netherlands, although this did not pose serious problems for the Post. The slower pace reflected a number of factors including Deutsche Post's enormous size and the inhibiting weight of a large bureaucratic organization. The extended reform process created some uncertainty for the Post, but nothing resembling the uncertainty generated by the long policy pauses that marked the Canadian case. This did not lead to the process getting derailed in Germany, although the impact of the election of the Social Democratic government remains to be seen. The advantage of this protracted process was that it gave the Post an opportunity to reconstruct itself and to build up its market strength over the course of the 1990s, when price and market liberalization unfolded far slower than it might have.

Third, like the Dutch, the German government made policy decisions with the objective of maximizing the growth of the Post, to make it a dominant player in Germany, Europe, and the world. This involved the use of a mixed set of tools, combining regulation and deregulation, liberalization, and protection. The sequence of steps has been the reverse of the Dutch case, with early liberalization preceding privatization, whereas the Dutch privatized first and liberalized after. Both approaches had the result of quickly building up market share and market value.

Fourth, the German government wanted to have its cake and eat it too. That is, it aimed to have a strong Deutsche Post within a liberalized postal environment. As a result of encouraging the maximization of growth before privatization, the German government was required to re-regulate the postal market – lest it never develop into a competitive one and remain totally dominated by Deutsche Post. Because the Post is such a large and dominant force, liberalization and the development of market competition will require regulatory assistance and indeed even protection for competitors. The situation is different in the Netherlands, where the Dutch government seems less concerned about the domestic impact of TPG's size and predominance. The fact is that the Dutch market is much smaller than the German one and there is not much room for a multitude of postal players of significance. On the other hand, there is likely room for a variety of competitors in the German market, which is at least three times as large as that of the Netherlands.

Fifth, as a result of the previous considerations, the German Post confronts a mixed postal environment of autonomy and constraints. On the one hand, it has been granted space from the government to develop as a typical modern corporation – which it has done in a remarkable and successful fashion. The regulatory regime has distanced the government from the Post. The regulatory authority plays no role in investment decisions, capital or business plans, strategic diversification initiatives, and so on. The Post was given a reasonably large, albeit diminishing, exclusive privilege to maintain revenues for its mixed public and corporate objectives. On the other hand, it exists within a re-regulated environment, in which much of its activity is in competition with non-regulated players and in which it is being scrutinized on various price and performance fronts by the regulatory authority. Overall, though, this combination of autonomy and regulation can likely become a balanced and effective mix if handled successfully by regulators. Admittedly, the Post's delicate balancing act could go awry if the regulatory authority layers too much complexity into the system. The accountability regime for universal-service obligations at the moment is a bit thin. Yet, in the last analysis, the greater part of DPWN's business and earnings will be outside the regulatory area and outside Germany as well. But there it will face the regulatory inhibitions of the EU.

Sixth, the German regulatory model is likely the most bureaucratized and complex that this study will examine. This reflects, to a degree, the political-cultural history of the country and its social-market economy. German regulators seem unfazed at the likely complexities that they will have to deal with. Reg TP has a far more elaborate and less mechanical task than OPTA in the Netherlands. Nonetheless, the untested state of the licensing system, the segmentation and possibly elaborate fragmentation of markets that liberalization will produce, the likelihood that substantial parts of the market may not be serviced automatically, and the use of the compensation fund to guarantee the universal system – all of these issues and factors add up to a great deal of uncertainty about how regulation will work in a completely liberalized market. Indeed, the jury remains out on whether this system will actually work.

Finally, there are local and national characteristics of the German case that are close to the Canadian case, including the geographic and continental scale of the postal operation and the mixed public/private style regime that reform has created. Yet there are issues that would be hard to replicate in or export to Canada. These include the co-determination model between management and labour at the board level, the public tolerance for the intentional growth of a dominant market player, and the government willingness to allow extended diversification and internationalization beyond the (domestic) postal market. These factors have contributed enormously to the German postal-policy dynamic and to the remarkable turnaround and success of Deutsche Post.

The German Post is likely to emerge as one of a small handful of world players in the international postal market. It has been an aggressive market player, although perhaps not as ruthless as the Dutch have been. Each finds itself in court battles against both public and private competitors. DPWN's growth strategy has been successful, such that it has secured a revenue base for carrying the universal-service obligation, reinvesting in new technologies, and expanding into new and related markets. It has also positioned itself to be an alliance leader, in conjunction with public and private postal partners. None of this could have been accomplished without the supportive, non-inhibiting postal-regulatory environment created by the German government.

PART TWO

The Market Model

Each of the postal regimes examined in this book have demonstrated an increasing reliance on market forces to drive postal development. Indeed, even the most national or mercantile regimes have opened their Posts to increasing competition and have used market forces as a way of stimulating postal development. What distinguishes the market model from other models is the elimination of the postal monopoly or protected area from the policy mix. In a sense, the market model is the most "radical" of the postal-policy approaches.

Historically, it was argued that providing a universal postal service incurred extraordinary costs that could be borne by a postal authority only if it were guaranteed sufficient revenues to carry out its responsibilities. Thus, an "exclusive privilege" or reserved area was assigned to the Post by the state. The monopoly earnings in this area could be used to cross-subsidize the uneconomic dimensions of the universal service and perpetuate reasonable postal prices across the nation. In this paradigm, political authorities would calculate how much monopoly protection would be required to generate the requisite revenue to guarantee the universal service. This was a balancing act that juggled a number of variables. First, political authorities had to calculate the appropriate size of the reserved area, to make sure that there would not be a revenue shortfall (resulting in a deficit that they might have to pick up). But if the reserved area chosen were too large, the Post would be able to provide the universal service and balance its books too easily and effortlessly, in an inefficient and unproductive manner. There was thus a perpetual tension between political and postal authorities over the appropriate size of the reserve area. Moreover, political authorities have had to be clear about what the universal service actually comprised – that is, what the reserve area was actually delivering. How high or low should postal prices be? How fast should postal delivery be? How often should the mail be delivered? How many post offices should there be? A "Cadillac" postal service with low prices, frequent and fast deliveries, and an extensive network might require a very large protected area to finance it. A "Lada" service with high prices, infrequent and moderate delivery, and a modest network might require a very small protected area, if any. Finally, in the context of globalization and technological change, political authorities had to determine what reserved area would be needed to ensure the perpetuation of the universal service, while at the same time ensuring that the Post confront the long-term realities and implications of globalization and technological change.

Like the Dutch and German governments, political authorities in countries in the market model – Finland, Sweden, and New Zealand – were deeply aware of the consequences of globalization and technological change for their economies in general and their Posts in particular. Their responses, though, were tactically quite different and involved what has (somewhat inaccurately) been characterized as a "big bang" approach.[1] The governments of Finland, Sweden, and New Zealand withdrew their reserved postal areas and eliminated any monopoly protection for their Posts – in order for the Posts to adjust quickly and forcefully to the new economic realities. These face their postal and communication markets with no protection and no subsidy from their governments. Yet, at the same time, the expectation of a universal postal service remains and has not been diminished to any significant extent. Indeed, the move to total liberalization of postal markets has forced the political authorities in these countries to define and specify concretely and clearly the precise character of their universal postal systems.

The policy rationale for this market approach is that these Posts will best be able to meet international and technological challenges if they are obliged to act like any other private corporation that is facing similar pressures. That is, if they are to survive over the long term, the Posts will have to innovate, become competitive, provide good-quality service, keep their customers happy, and make a profit. From the market perspective, the most effective way to attain these objectives is to oblige the Posts to adjust to new economic realities without any protection or help from the government.

The Scandinavian countries (and New Zealand to a lesser extent) were well known for their elaborate social-welfare systems and commitments to social-democratic principles and organizations. It may appear ironic, then, that such a radical, Thatcher-like market approach has been pursued in these countries. There is, however, some historical rationale for this approach, particularly in Scandinavia, given the degree of liberalization that existed in the postal market historically (see below). There is also a geographic rationale. The relative isolation, long distances, and small size of the postal markets in these countries means that the absence of domestic monopoly protection is not as consequential as it might be in more centrally located and economically attractive postal markets. Nonetheless, their experiences reflect a well-considered policy decision to confront technological and global realities, improve public services, and strengthen the Post directly via a market strategy. This policy approach remains, relatively speaking, in its infancy. Therefore, as will be seen below, firm judgments on its record are, at the present time, impossible. What is clear is that, as in the mercantile model, the market model comprises a mix of policy instruments, including both liberalization and deregulation of the postal market and its re-regulation to ensure competition and the maintenance of the universal service

3 Finland

Finland is one of the most technologically sophisticated countries in the world. It has more cellphones per capita than any other country and boasts a brand leader in the production of cellphones (Nokia). It also has more Internet sites per capita than any other country. In this context, it should be no surprise that in 1991 Finland was the first country to liberalize its postal market. The Finns are as sensitive to the new technological environment for the Post as anybody in the world.

The history of the Finnish Post is intimately related to Finland's history as part of larger nations' empires. The country's existence dates to 1638, when it was part of Sweden. In 1809 it became an autonomous duchy of Russia, and the Post was organized and managed by a Postal Council (1811–1917). Finland became an independent republic in 1917 and in 1927 the Post and Telegraph were combined in one organizational unit. Finland was one of the first countries in the world to start regular telephone traffic. This was carried out in a decentralized and competitive way, organized around fifty local phone companies. The origins of the liberalization of the Finnish postal market are deep-rooted and reflect the experience in the telephone area. Even before the 1980s, the Post was not regulated or managed tightly by governments, and there has long been competition in the business-mail and parcels markets. Governments did supervise prices, set postal budgets as part of the state budget, and make senior postal appointments. Beyond this, though, the Post had a considerable degree of autonomy. Compared to other parts of Europe, Finland is not fond of rules and there is a policy taste for simple, pragmatic, and straightforward approaches.[1] As in a number of other countries, the liberalization of the postal sector was carried along by the momentum of changes in the telecommunications sector. The decentralized, competitive telephone sector adapted easily and successfully to the new technological environment. The telecommunication industry's success domestically and internationally in turn created momentum for deregulation and partial privatization of this sector, in order to attract investment from abroad. This example encouraged the idea that postal liberalization and deregulation could also be attained.[2]

The economic recessions of the 1980s and early 1990s contributed to the liberalization of the postal market. As in the Netherlands, the recession had serious consequences for the state's budget and for the performance of the wide array of state enterprises that existed in Finland. Governments faced a crisis in financing, a crisis in service (the latter having deteriorated in the less propitious economic conditions of the day), and a crisis and loss of confidence in public administration. Politicians and parties became keen to liberalize the railroads, airline, PTT, and so on, and they joined together in large coalitions across the political centre to pursue these changes.[3] The reform of the state sector unfolds to the present, where there is ongoing movement towards privatization of key state activities. For example, 22 per cent of the telecommunications company Sonera has been privatized, IVO and Neste (energy) have also been privatized, and the state's share has been lowered in Rautaruukki (steel), Esno (forest products), and Kemijoki (hydropower). The government has articulated openly the possibility of selling Finnair.[4] But the major policy impulse coming out of the recession was the creation of a pragmatic process of modernizing and improving the organization of the public sector, to increase the efficiency, quality, competitiveness, and value of state enterprises.[5] At the same, the economic recession neutralized the strength of the postal unions in any possible reaction against liberalization and corporatization. The postal unions were relatively weak and uncertain, and they concluded that the existence and perpetuation of a strong Post was in their best long-term interests. Given the cross-party coalition at the time, and given postal management's own interest in reform and liberalization, postal and government authorities could persuade the unions to go along with postal-policy reform.[6]

As noted above, the Finns have been sensitive to technological change and deeply aware of the threat that technological change poses to the future of the postal service. Postal volumes decreased in each of the last two recessions. More important, there was an awareness that the traditional letters market was a mature and saturated one. Studies showed that 30–40 per cent of all letters had been replaced by electronic messaging.[7] This awareness also contributed to the policy-reform process. Moreover, the authorities were aware that the bulk of their remaining volumes comprised business mail, where the 6,000 largest accounts generated 80 per cent of the Post's turnover.[8] Technological substitution in these accounts would be easy – and devastating. In order to deal with this reality, a more customer-oriented policy would be required to maintain business and customer loyalty. This also encouraged postal-policy reform.

There was, therefore, a political and administrative consensus in Finland in the 1980s and early 1990s that postal-policy reform was required, given the broad economic and technological changes of the time. There was an identity of understanding and vision among postal and political authorities and, to a certain extent, the postal unions. Political leadership from the ministry and the bureaucracy was strong and consistent; the reforms were defended vigorously in Parliament and negotiated effectively with the unions.[9] The resulting policy-reform process was pragmatic and incremental and built on an existing policy base. The pragmatic character of this reform will become evident in the historical review below. The process unfolded in a step-by-step fashion, with no clear sense of where it would end. Indeed, there has been a sense of surprise at how far the process has evolved, since each stage was considered more or less self-contained.[10] Authorities have also been aware of the increasingly global character of the postal world, but this has not loomed as large in policy discussions and developments, mainly because of Finland's size and relative isolation. The flavour of the Post's annual reports is far more domestic-centred and less internationally oriented than recent reports of the other Posts in this study.[11]

HISTORY

As was typical of most European countries, the Post Office in Finland was organized within a PTT framework. It had banking facilities in some its offices, but its activities centred on postal activities. In the late 1920s, there was a General Directorate of the Post and Telegraph, whose authority changed into Posts and Telecom of Finland in 1981. It was regulated as a monopoly under a statute passed in 1980. Until 1990, it functioned as a department of government and its financial existence was tied up in the state's budget. The postal-reform process did not begin in a formal way until the 1990s, but the government demonstrated throughout the 1980s that it wanted the Post to be a service-oriented and corporate-style operation. It gave the Post a fair amount of autonomy. The deregulation of the telecommunications and the banking sectors began in the mid-1980s, at which time there was an increasingly relaxed, capitalist atmosphere. State controls were loosened in a variety of areas. The postal monopoly – which was never particularly strong or extensive – was also loosened. The Post did not try to impose its monopoly when competition developed in the late 1980s, at which time the Finnish monopoly laws were abandoned. The Post functioned in a policy vacuum for a year or two. Within the Post, there was also a series of leadership changes from which sprang the impulse for postal liberalization.[12]

The postal-reform process in Finland comprises four key ingredients: the Post's transformation into a state enterprise (1990); the liberalization of the postal market (1991); the Post's transformation into a limited liability company (1994); and "de-merger" from Telecom (1999).

Stage One – Deregulation and a New Form of Public Enterprise

Postal-policy reform was part of a larger process of modernizing and reforming the state sector in Finland in the late 1980s. This was an important ingredient in the political coalition's master plan at the time, which was made concrete in the form of framework legislation for much of the state-enterprise sector. The Law of State Enterprises was passed in 1988 and came into effect in 1989. Its purpose was to improve the efficiency and competitiveness of public enterprises, to encourage them to improve the quality of their service, to increase their managerial capacity and speed of decision making, and to improve their economic performance and independence of action.[13] The law comprised an umbrella or framework approach that created a new model of public enterprise. Parliament and the Council of State would flesh out this framework out by passing specific laws in particular areas. The legislation determined the sectors to which it would be applied – six in all, comprising 14-billion marks (FIM) and 64,000 employees (including the railroads, finance, and aviation). The legislation was applied to the Post and Telecom, which became a state enterprise in 1990.

This renewed state-enterprise form involved a new and experimental type of organization, combining features of both public enterprise and a limited-liability company. Any new state enterprise would remain 100 per cent government-owned. But it would enjoy a considerable amount of independence, since the government would impose only a modest number of expectations and constraints of a general sort. Parliament would set the objectives for the sector, including quality standards, and note the amounts of capital investment available and its objectives. The Council of State would target the results (income and yield requirements) that were expected. But the state enterprise's budget would be set outside the state budget, and it would have access to profits for investment. It would be free to set its own prices, to invest, to manage its personnel, and to make all decisions not specified by Parliament.

The Post operated in an almost fully competitive and corporate setting between 1990 and 1993. In July 1991 Finland became the first country in the world to liberalize its postal market fully when the government eliminated the postal-reserve area. There had already been open competition in publications, parcels, bulk direct mail, and banking services, so this was not a particularly controversial decision. The Post had been profitable for a number of years and it was confident of maintaining its profitability in the liberalized market setting. The major unions were not opposed to liberalization and were part of the negotiations leading up to it. Both postal management and the government saw this as a necessary step to ensure the Post's competitiveness and to improve its management.[14]

The Post itself underwent a substantial reorganization in this environment, changing from a regional to a sectoral structure of organization. There was considerable shuffling of management personnel, albeit with little recruitment from the external business environment. The existing postal director (Tarjanne) was very much from the old administrative culture and was replaced by Pekka Vennamo, who pushed the postal-reform process aggressively. Vennamo had been the minister of communication and the chair of one of Finland's populist parties (rural and pro-capitalist). He was well placed politically to build up the political alliances and consensus required for change. A colourful and visionary populist, he had made a dramatic impact in the 1986 election, and his appointment was somewhat controversial at the time. He pushed reorganization, liberalization, and postal reform energetically, particularly (and ironically) in the area of post-office closings. His liberal views were very much in concert with those of the government, and he was skilful in lobbying politicians and in working with opponents to get them on side.[15]

Stage Two – Corporatization and the New Postal Act

There was no long-term game plan beyond transforming the Post into a state enterprise. So it was a considerable surprise when, just four years later, the Post was transformed into a limited-liability company and the postal market was liberalized. At bottom, it was pressure from the state enterprises themselves that pushed the government into extending the corporatization process.[16]

This stage followed a wide-ranging review by government of how public services were delivered. It also followed a period in which the Post's change in delivery methods (from inside to outside boxes) and the closing of a number of post offices had generated some political backlash to liberalization. There was a resurgence of parliamentary interest in postal matters – particularly with regard to how to guarantee the universal postal service in a liberalized environment.[17] The fact was that the state-enterprise model was an unstable one. On the one hand, it maintained a sufficient amount of political authority in the postal area to threaten the limited corporate autonomy that had been granted to the Post. On the other hand, it generated sufficient corporate autonomy and limited political authority to make uncertain the perpetuation of the universal postal system. The old ways of regulating the Post would not work under this new model. A new law was required, to ensure that political goals could co-exist with sufficient room for the Post to develop.[18]

In 1994, then, the Post and Telecom was granted corporate company status under the new Act on Postal Services. It became a limited-liability company, 100 per cent owned by the state. But the sort of control exercised by the state became far closer to that exercised by majority shareholders in a private company. At the same time, a new regulatory and competitive environment was created, which comprised three key ingredients that would work to maintain the universal postal system. First, there was a formal separation of postal regulation from postal administration. The latter would become an exclusive matter for the Post, while a third-party regulator – the Telecommunications Administration Centre – would monitor its activities. Second, the public or political expectations of the Post regarding the universal postal service were formalized and articulated in the Act on Postal Services and the corresponding Decree on Postal Services. TAC was directed to regulate the Post to ensure compliance with these political expectations. A Supervisory Board was formed to create political consensus and to offer parallel "political" advice. Third, the act created a postal licensing system, under which the liberalized competitive postal market would function. Each of these ingredients will be examined in detail below.

The new postal legislation offered a subtle balance between economic goals (for postal efficiency and competitiveness) and political goals (for the maintenance of the universal postal system). The new system aimed to maintain the universal system within a competitive and liberalized postal environment. It addressed the political fears that a competitive postal market would undermine the universal system, while ensuring that politics would not interfere with the evolution of the competitive postal market.

Stage Three – De-merger and Beyond

Through the 1990s, Finland Post was a subsidiary of Finland PT – which also comprised Telecom Finland and PT Automotive Services. Beginning in July 1998, Finland PT was restructured and eventually ceased to operate. The Post and Telecom were separated and became autonomous companies. The Telecom part was renamed Sonera, and Parliament authorized its partial privatization. The earlier deregulation of the telecommunications sector generated a faster move towards privatization, since the sector had become technologically advanced and competitive internationally. Some senior executives at the Post felt that the Post should also have been privatized at this time. A disadvantage of the de-merger for the Post was that it lost the information-technology (IT) part of Finland PT. TT Tieto Oy, the biggest IT operation in Scandinavia, was assigned to Sonera.

The Act on Postal Services was amended in 1999 to comply with the European Union's postal directive. Because Finland Post has no reserved area, no substantial changes were required to implement the directive. The earlier 1994 decree was amended to specify quality targets (of 85 per cent next-day delivery, 95 per cent two-day delivery) and an annual report to the ministry on the topic would now be required. The amendment also provided a definition of universal-service obligations (daily delivery of items up to two kilograms, requirement to service items up to ten kilograms). It insisted that prices should reflect costs and required the Post to develop an accounting system that would be transparent and non-discriminatory (it separated accounts into universal, basic, and other services).

To sum up, postal reform in Finland has been a fairly straightforward and consistent process, focused essentially on liberalization of the postal market and corporatization of the Post. A broader process of reform of the state sector, and a wide-ranging political consensus that reform of the Post was required, carried along this process. Starting from a reasonably liberal basis in the late 1980s, the Finnish postal market has become a completely open one, in which the Post has no monopoly or reserved services and potentially faces competition in all segments of the postal market. The Post is a limited-liability company, which has a considerable degree of formal autonomy from the government. The Post makes all of its own investment decisions, determines its postal rates, and decides personnel matters on its own.

It is free to raise capital from the financial market and to enter new markets. In all dimensions, it has the same authority as a private-sector company. As will be seen presently, it has a licence from the government to provide a universal postal service, in a market regulated by an independent agency whose mandate it is to ensure that the universal system is maintained.

STATUTORY AND REGULATORY ENVIRONMENT

The Finnish statutory and regulatory model is reasonably simple and straightforward. This reflects the pragmatic character of Finnish policy in general and the political and policy response to the postal situation in particular. There was no model of a liberalized postal market in the world at the time the Finns liberalized their market. Moreover, the European Commission did not offer much guidance as to how to operate a regulatory regime in a liberalized and corporatized postal environment. Thus, the Finnish authorities decided to keep the statutory and regulatory model simple when they liberalized the postal market and made the Post a limited-liability company.[19] The Act on Postal Services is less than ten pages of typescript and the Decree on Postal Services is less than three pages.

The Act on Postal Services (29 October 1993) sets out the broad parameters of the postal system, while the Decree on Postal Services (22 December 1993) spells out concrete details about licensing and the universal postal system. The overall political and policy ambition is to maintain the universal postal system. The objective of the act "is to ensure that post can be sent and received under equal conditions throughout the country." The act specifies this further by stating that "the availability of the postal service and the fairness of costs must be ensured for sparsely populated regions" (Section 1). The statutory arrangements comprise three sets of players in a system of licensing businesses to provide postal services. First, ultimate responsibility for the universal system is assigned to the Ministry of Transportation and Communication (MOTC), which determines the actual substance or goals of the universal system (Section 15). Second, regulatory responsibility was assigned to TAC, which was to administer and monitor the application of the act, to ensure compliance with it, and to deal with complaints (Section 15). TAC is financed by fees from licence holders (Section 15). It has the right to obtain the information required to carry out its duties (Section 17) and acts as a dispute settlement agency (Section 22) with powers of enforcement (Section 18). Third, licensed postal operators – such as the Post – carry out the actual business or operation of the postal system. Postal operators apply to the Council of State for a licence to provide postal services (Section 3). Licences are granted to operators that are "well-established and evidently capable of regularly providing postal services."

The act thus separated postal business from postal administration. It assigned responsibility to an agency (TAC) outside the shareholder (the government) to regulate the postal market, in a licensing system in which any respectable company could enter the postal business. The act allowed postal operators to set their own prices, as long as the prices were "fair and in reasonable proportion to the average costs incurred" (Section 4). Delivery standards and other objectives and criteria would be spelled out by the ministry in a postal decree (Section 4), but, at a minimum, delivery every working day would be required (Section 7).

The Decree on Postal Services sets out the details of the postal regime. The decree establishes the boundary between the licensed area and the totally free market area. There are no licensing restrictions on a variety of areas, including newspapers, organizations' internal mail, express, and courier. Indeed, the decree specifies that the act does not apply to "operations which are carried out pursuant to separate agreements concluded with individual clients and founded on the speed or security of transportation, or other corresponding customized agreements" (Section 1). There was some pressure at the time from the newspaper companies to include newspapers as part of the licensed area, but it would have been difficult politically to move a previously non-regulated item into the regulated area.[20] The act applies only to "postal items," which are defined narrowly as items up to a maximum weight (two kilograms) and size ($25 \times 40 \times 3$ centimetres) (Section 2). The decree details how operators were to apply for a licence to provide postal services (see below). An amendment to the decree (29 January 1999) responded to the EU Postal Directive. It established specific delivery standards: 85 per cent next-day delivery of first-class items and 95 per cent within two days (Section 2a). The new decree also declared that the cost-accounting system of any postal operator should be transparent and non-discriminatory (Section 2b). This was fleshed out further in a decision by the ministry (4 February 1999) which detailed the cost-accounting system (Section 7) and defined the universal service as postal items up to ten kilograms (Section 4).

Licensing System

The licensing system is the heart of the liberalized postal market in Finland. It simultaneously provides the means to ensure the provision of the universal system while encouraging a competitive and lively postal market. However, the licensing system in Finland has had substantial birth pains. It has been the subject of political and judicial controversy and, at present, functions in an incomplete way.

As noted above, the Act on Postal Services requires potential postal operators to apply to the Council of State for a licence. In principle, a licence will be granted to any established and capable operator. Applicants must provide proof of their being capable and established businesses, and they must submit a detailed two-year financial and operational plan. The act allowed the government to provide a licence "until further notice to postal operators providing unrestricted postal services" – that is, to the Post. Any licence granted for less than universal service – for example, to a specific geographic area or for a type of service – would be for a maximum of three years.

The Council of State issued a licence to Finland Post in February 1994 to provide unrestricted domestic and international postal services, a licence that was reissued in January 1999. This is the mechanism by which the government aims to maintain the universal postal system. Finland Post's licence assigns it responsibility "for ensuring the basic availability of postal services in the whole country"(Section 2). The Post is obliged to clear, sort, transport, and deliver items up to 10 kilograms and to transport and deliver items up to twenty kilograms (Section 6). The Post must also provide a service network for the whole country, including sparsely populated areas (Section 7). The licence offers no state compensation to these ends (Section 11). Indeed, the subsidy granted to the Post for delivering newspapers to sparsely populated areas has ended.[21]

There was also a restricted licence granted to a company called Suomen Suorminonta Oy (SSM) in March 1997. This licence has never been used and has been the subject of an extended and messy controversy. The case illustrates the limits to and a potential fatal flaw of the Finnish licensing system. It reflects, as well, the extent to which the system was not thought through sufficiently before it was adopted. The SSM is part of a well-established media group in Finland that specializes in delivering non-addressed items and newspapers door-to-door.[22] It is an organization of sixty independent partners and distributions companies, which acts much like a franchise system. By 1997, it had been operating for twenty-five years. When the opportunity arose under the act to apply for a licence, it discussed the possibility with its clients who responded positively. While recognizing that the Post was efficient, the SSM felt that it could compete and so applied for a licence. However, it applied for a specific or narrowly defined licence – to deliver second-class mail in the Helsinki area. This was a natural strategy for the company to pursue, since it owned production plants in Helsinki and could reduce its fixed costs by focusing on this market, by concentrating on business (as opposed to personal) mail, and by pursuing high volumes. It anticipated a turnover of FIM8.5 million in 1997–98, 15 million in 1998–99, and 30 million in 1999–2000.

The SSM applied for this licence in April 1995. It was granted the licence almost two years later – in March 1997. In the intervening period, political pressures mounted to deny the application, which was seen by many to threaten the national postal infrastructure.[23] This included pressure from the postal unions (who insisted that all licences be for the whole country) and a petition from seventy Members of Parliament to change the law so as to limit competition. The state authorities agonized over what to do, since they were committed to postal competition and to the system of licensing. Indeed, the ministry recognized the extent to which it was difficult to create competition in a market with a dominant player such as the Post.[24] But the SSM's application looked like a classic case of "cream-skimming."

An MOTC working group studied the way in which opening up competition would affect the universal postal system. It produced a report in 1996, recommending the reintroduction of a reserved area or the imposition of a tax on postal operators.[25] The state responded by passing the Act on the Fee Collected for Securing the Provision of Postal Services in Sparsely Populated Areas. This was, in effect, a tax on postal operators whose licence did not comprise delivery in all parts of the country. Its purpose was "to secure postal services on sparsely populated areas" (Article 1). Article 4 defined a formula that established a sliding tax which varied according to the population density of the area serviced by the licence holder. If the licence holder serviced an area with a low-population density – as low as 250 people per square kilometre or less – then the tax would be zero. If the licence holder serviced an area exclusively limited to a high-density area, the tax would be as high as 20 per cent. The rationale of the act was that cream-skimmers would pay a 20 per cent tax on their "easy" revenues. This tax revenue could be transferred to postal operators – such as the Post – who lost revenue to cream-skimmers, revenue that had been used to cross-subsidize postal services in sparsely populated areas.

When the SSM was granted its licence, it was also notified that it would be required to pay a 20 per cent tax. From its perspective, the tax would kill the SSM's chances of making a profit, since it would undermine any price advantage that it might have had relative to the Post. It responded by expanding its bid to include areas outside Helsinki, so as to increase its coverage from 450,000 households to 650,000 households. This had the effect of lowering the tax to zero.[26]

The Council of State rejected the new application, an action that has had political and judicial consequences. On the political level, Parliament and the Council of State continued to oppose granting the licence to the SSM in the absence of a "deterrent tax." On the judicial level, the SSM complained to the courts, which have subsequently been critical of the Finnish government's actions. The Finnish Administrative Supreme Court ruled in February 1999 that the government had not given sufficient reasons or principles for rejecting the SSM application. The Social Democrats prepared a list of principles (on the eve of an election) to try and justify their decision, but the court ruled against the government again in the fall of 1999. The SSM has also complained to the EC Competition Authority. The government reissued the licence to SSM in June 2000 for a three-year period. The licence, which covers twenty cities and towns in southern Finland, does not contain any tax provisions, but the government has not repealed the legislation that establishes fees to safeguard services in sparsely populated areas. The SSM has yet to provide any postal services.

Throughout this case, the government has given the impression of not knowing what to do. The case has been marked by a certain political naivety about how the licencing system would work and the kind of competition that liberalization would generate. It is almost inexplicable that the government did not anticipate this situation, for which it appeared to be totally unprepared. The court challenges and political machinations betrayed a kind of panic and misunderstanding. The liberalization and licensing model would turn out to be flawed or even useless if it did not allow real competition to develop. The state itself has been internally divided over the issue. As the ultimate regulator of the postal sector, the MOTC supported the licence application, since it wants and encourages postal competition. However, the shareholding side of the MOTC and the minister of finance tend to focus more on shareholder value. From their perspectives, competition from the SSM would lower the value of the Post. The government finally issued a three-year licence in June 2000, but SSM is not happy with its terms. Currently, the government is preparing a new law on postal services, which may address this issue more effectively.

For its part, the Post appears to be sanguine about the prospects of having a private company competing against it in a lucrative market segment. It may very well be able to resist the SSM's intervention in this urban, business market. Indeed, if it were able to compete successfully with the SSM, this might benefit the Post in proving to its customers and others how efficient an operation it is.[27] From its perspective, the SSM feels wiser now about politics and government processes. But it is upset that its application was used to many groups' advantage. For example, some companies appear to have been able to use the threat of SSM competition to extract lower rates from the Post. The Post itself can point to the prospects of SSM competition as a way of dampening union expectations.[28]

The Ministry

The MOTC is responsible for about 60 per cent of Finland's state enterprises. It has ultimate political authority over and responsibility for the postal market. As in most modern postal regimes – and as required by the EC – postal operations are separate from postal regulation, and the MOTC has no direct involvement in the operations of the Post.

The two public postal functions of the state – regulation and ownership – are housed in the same ministry. This is similar to the state of affairs in other sectors, including telecommunications. As a result, the ministry is in the awkward position of regulating a market in which it is an owner, a contradictory position that has been exposed in the SSM case. For good or bad, this housing of both functions within one ministry appears to be a tradition in Finland, which EC and competition requirements may oblige Finland to change.[29] The two functions are housed in separate units of the ministry, with separate personnel and strict and clear rules about the interaction of the two areas. The two roles meet in the person of the minister or the government as a whole.[30] There appears to be widespread awareness that this state of affairs is not acceptable. At the same time, it is seen to be less a practical problem than a formal one.[31] The wider administrative reform process in Finland is still unfolding and the ministry is looking at this question. Why have the functions not been placed in two separate ministries? Part of the answer lies in the size of the country. To have specialized ministries look after particular activities would generate prohibitive costs. There is also some concern that this would increase the political authority of the Ministry of Finance and make its financial objectives paramount. Finally, there is anxiety that an already limited pool of knowledge would be fragmented and diffused.[32]

The postal-regulation dimension of the MOTC comprises but two people, who have responsibility for television and radio as well. This experienced section is charged with ensuring that postal operators meet universal-service standards. It meets with different people in the Post for different purposes. It oversees issues like quality of service, the adequacy of the network, fairness of prices, and the meeting of the universal-service obligations. There have been few matters of controversy or tension in these areas, save for the closing of post offices, and the overall view is that the Post has performed well.

The shareholder's unit of the MOTC comprises four people. It is concerned about the efficient operation of the postal market and its modernization. It makes appointments to the Board of Directors of the Post, and the minister chooses the chair. This part of the ministry has its own representative on the board, currently the head of the Transportation Economics Department. The shareholder's division of the ministry has become more active recently, with a particular focus on increasing the value of the Post. This has taken the Post by surprise, particularly with respect to the ministry's expectations about dividends. The ministry has adopted a policy for all of its state-owned enterprises, which are expected to make a profit sufficient to renew themselves and to provide a return to the shareholder. It expects the Post to make a profit of about FIM500–600 million on revenues of FIM6 billion – to be divided equally among taxes, dividends, and retained earnings. The ministry needs to build up its postal-policy knowledge and capacity, if it is to become more active with respect to dividend policy, growth, management direction, and so on. The representatives of the share-holding division typically meet twice a month with the Post, to receive information regarding postal business and financial flows. The ministry has its own program to analyse the information reports it receives from all state enterprises, so as to have an independent basis for evaluation. It leaves questions like the capital and business plan, and major investment decisions, to the board. There is nothing in the act to inhibit the diversification of the Post, which has the freedom to make business decisions. But if a large investment in a totally new area were proposed, this question would come to the ministry and perhaps to the economic committee of the government.[33]

The ministerial oversight of the postal market is an awkward mix of regulation and shareholder activity, which puts the ministry in a kind of conflict of interest whereby it regulates a market in which it is a player. There is a modest degree of postal intelligence within the ministry, which depends to an extent on the Post and on outside sources and consultants for information and expertise. The shareholding side of the ministry seems poised to increase its involvement in, and expectations of, all state enterprises, including the Post. Much of this ambition remains on the wish list – since the ministry has a crowded policy agenda at the moment. It is proceeding as if the government were planning to privatize the Post, and hence it has a distinct interest in increasing the Post's share value. Overall, the ministry has been happy with the performance of the Post, for its quality of service has been high and its pricing policy moderate.

The tension between the state's shareholding interest and broader public-policy issues is also exemplified in the relationship between the MOTC and the Ministry of Finance. The latter owns Leonia, which is the modern version of the Post Bank that was carved out of the old PTT. It has exclusive rights to provide pension and social services. Finance is likely to sell Leonia at some time, so it is interested in maximizing its share value. As will be seen below, Leonia has had a presence in a number of postal outlets, for which it paid a fee. The compensation terms have become a matter of dispute between the Post and Leonia, pitting the shareholding interests of two ministries against each other. An arbitration process did not resolve the dispute, and the existing arrangements were extended for a year, albeit with less compensation for the Post and a directive that the Post not rationalize its network for a year until a permanent solution is found.[34]

The Regulator

Regulation of the postal market on an ongoing and day-to-day basis is the responsibility of the Telecommunications Administration Centre. The TAC is an independent agency under the MOTC, which names the head of the agency. It has the responsibility of monitoring compliance with the act and the decree, and it reports to the ministry twice annually to this end. It functions to control and supervise the postal service and to ensure good service, affordable prices, and the confidentiality of the mail. It has the authority to review complaints and to issue administrative decisions to secure users' rights. TAC can fine a postal operator or suspend its licence if it violates the law.[35]

It originated in 1988 with the liberalization of the telecommunications sector, and it moved into the postal scene in 1994. The postal dimension of its operation is relatively small – only about four people of the overall staff of two hundred. Its FIM5-million budget is financed by the licences that it grants (on a scale relative to turnover). Its monitoring of the postal market in general and the Post in particular is relatively passive and benign. The Post experiences few inhibitions or constraints from TAC, mainly because the law sets up a postal framework more than regulatory law.[36] It receives a small number of complaints each year, mainly focusing on failed delivery, and they are usually settled through conciliation. When a citizen makes a formal complaint, TAC may act as an administrative court, but there were only four such cases in 1999.[37] There were thousands of complaints when the Post moved a number of delivery points from inside to outside delivery, but this issue has been sorted out and has settled down.[38] It was one of the first "tests" of having the ministry *not* involved in postal policy or controversy. In any event, the delivery of newspapers is not a matter under the postal act. Indeed, there are numerous and important areas of the postal field where the regulator has not become involved. The Post-Leonia case was handled exclusively at the ministerial level. Similarly, the regulator has not been involved in the licensing controversy with the SSM. Post-office closings are seen as a business matter, where TAC has no authority because the postal act makes no reference to the network.

Postal operators are free to set their own prices. But the act and the decree insist that prices should reflect costs, and TAC has the responsibility to monitor this. Its role is limited, however, since the Post is given wide discretion. TAC has had little to do in this regard to date, mainly because the Post's price changes have been so moderate.[39] It has the right to demand information from the Post and postal operators that will allow it to do its job. Yet it has little to no independent source of information. For example, it relies on the Post's own surveys to establish the extent to which the Post is delivering a quality service.[40] It will likely have to develop an independent source of postal intelligence in order to meet EC standards and expectations. The 1999 amendment to the decree requires postal operators to provide different accounts for different parts and activities of the postal market (that is, those dealing with universal-service obligations, those that are pure market activities, and so on). The accounting system must be transparent and non-discriminatory, and this should go to some considerable extent in ensuring that the Post does not cross-subsidize its operations.

TAC interacts with the Committee for Postal Affairs. This is a consensual body comprised of two representatives from each of four parties – consumers, companies, postal operators, and government authorities. The director of postal administration chairs it. TAC sets up the committee once a year, on the basis of recommendations from the ministry, postal operators, and the Chamber of Commerce. The committee is designed as an advisory body (to TAC), to safeguard the interests of postal users. The strategy is to allow users a role in setting targets and objectives and in the development of postal services.

The Board of Directors and the Supervisory Board

There are two organizational "hinges" between the political realm and the Post. The formal connection of the Post to its shareholder is via the Board of Directors. There is also an informal link between politics and the Post via the Supervisory Board.

The Board of Directors is appointed by the MOTC and comprises eight members. There are two representatives from the postal unions. There is also one representative from the ministry. Of the five other members, one is an economist and private consultant (with a background in the mail-order business) and the others have business backgrounds at the managing director or CEO level of medical-wholesaling, finance, forest-industry, and catering firms. This is a relatively new board, which was reconstructed after the de-merger of the Post and Telecom. It is fairly business-oriented, but is in the early stages of its learning curve. The chairman – Matti Elovaara – is a no-nonsense sort and gives the impression of being a supporter of the Post.

The board has responsibilities typical of the board of a limited-liability company. It is obliged to look after the financial health and performance of the Post. The board sets the financial objectives and targets of the Post and decides how to use the Post's profits. The board has the authority to appoint the president or CEO and informs the ministry of its decision. Board appointments are made at the annual general meeting, with input and advice from both the Post and the ministry and its secretary general – which indicates what kind of board is needed. Formally, there is little to no political interaction between the board and the ministry. The more obvious political issues surrounding postal life are discussed at the Supervisory Board (see below). However, the informal links persist and, formally, the ministry does assign one of its representatives to the board. This seems to be an anomaly in a liberalized-market framework, with a licensing system and a third-party regulatory system. Currently, there is political discussion about whether this practice should be continued. The situation is rationalized within the ministry as simply a case of the shareholder having direct access to the board for information and understanding, with the representative having no special authority or vote and no authority or interest to get involved in regulatory or broader issues. In the last analysis, all board members are seen to represent the owner, although this ignores the point of the board's responsibility in a limited-liability company that is operating in a wider market context.

The Supervisory Board is a recent innovation. This is a consensual body, designed to give advice to the Post and to build up policy awareness and understanding. The Supervisory Board comprises twenty members, all of whom are appointed by the ministry. One-third of the members are from the business world, the remainder from administration and politics. There are nine Members of Parliament, two of whom co-chair the board. There is one bureaucrat, three local authority representatives, six business people (including two CEOs and one board chair), and one farmer. It meets six times a year. The Supervisory Board is purely a political body, which was designed to assuage parliamentary and political concerns that liberalization and corporatization would undermine the universal postal system. The board has no formal decision making role. It acts as a kind of weather-vane for the ministry and the Post, and it brings possible postal critics into the policy process. It is a negotiating body, which builds up policy consensus and understanding and gets people "on side" for policy innovations and developments, to avoid political controversy and division. The Supervisory Board has had a short history and it has not yet had to address any serious or divisive issues.

The Post and the Government

The Post itself has not undergone the sort of dramatic changes that made Finland's postal market the most liberalized in the industrial world. While it has reorganized itself in line with modern business principles, its corporate ethos has not changed dramatically.

There was a major reorganization in 1990, when the Post restructured its operations from regional to sectoral lines. It was separated into a number of operating segments, including Letters, Goods Transport, Publications Services, Direct Market, Banking, and Insurance. It was later reorganized into Products, Counter Services, Major Accounts, and Production Groups. There are separate companies for activities like counters, messaging, logistics, and so on. It was given the ministerial mandate to make a profit, and this became the focus of the company.

Unlike other Posts that we have examined, there has been only a modest recruitment of management from outside the Post. Some corporate changes have been implemented, but the impression is that the Post still functions in a 1970s public-administration culture. While there have been some retirements, the management has emphasized using experienced Post people.[41] Some private-sector recruiting was done to help with deregulation, but the management group has been recruited mainly from within the Post. The immediate past-president was from the government side; he worked for the Ministry of Finance and was its representative on the board of directors of the Post. He was expected to remain in the position until 2004. However, Jukka Alho was named president of the Post in the spring of 2000. He was previously the vice-President of Finland's largest private-owned telecommunications, and he has initiated a number of organizational and strategic changes.

The Post interacts with the government on a number of levels. It has a political unit that deals with Members of Parliament, to keep them informed and reasonably happy. There does not appear to be much on the political agenda on this level at the moment.[42] The board, in principle, makes the big policy decisions that are executed by management. The government sets a profit target in the state budget, which is set formally at a shareholder meeting. But the practice is that the minister sets profit targets. Indeed, there is a widespread sense that strategic decisions are still being made at the ministry. The recent Leonia controversy over the state bank's presence in the postal network demonstrated some limits to the Post's autonomy to make its own policy and decisions. The deal was imposed on the Post by the government, and its effect was to require the Post to make extraordinary profits to meet its targets in the context of the new banking constraint.

The state's relationship to the Post is shaped by the Post's performance. If the Post performs well, the government is happy and does not get involved. Since the Post's performance has generally been good, this model has not yet been tested. That is, it is unclear what would happen if the Post performed poorly or in a way that the government found unacceptable.[43]

Others

As in many European countries, unions are members of the postal regime. There are two major unions: the Union of Post-Office Employees represents the counters workers, and the Postal Workers' Union represents inside workers and letter carriers. Both are represented on the Board of Directors, and both are consulted extensively about postal policy and developments.

The postal unions have, broadly speaking, supported the postal-reform process in Finland through the consensus-building processes. There were, at various stages, protests, demonstrations, and so on, but at the end of the day the unions did nothing that constrained or undermined the reform process. In general, the Post in particular has been extremely able and clever in devising consensus arrangements with the unions. The general union attitude has been that a strong Post is good for union members. The major union protest was against making the Post a limited-liability company, which seemed an uncertain strategy from the unions' perspective. Overall, the unions have been willing and able to cut the best possible deal for their members.

This approach has benefited the Postal Workers' Union to a greater extent than the Union of Post-Office Employees. The latter's willingness to make a deal with the Post resulted in huge job losses when the Post rationalized its network. The inside workers and letter carriers have done better. While the counters' workers had a sympathetic hearing in Parliament and at the board level for their plight, their case was ignored when the Post really wanted to do something. The Postal Workers' Union appears to focus its lobbying efforts more on the ministry and the state representatives on the boards than on the Post. This suggests that, notwithstanding formal divisions, the ministry plays an ongoing strategic policy role in Finland.[44] Issues like wages and working conditions, though, are pursued through the collaborative processes within the Post.

The Competition Authority has played an increasingly important role in Finland since liberalization. Working out of the Ministry of Trade and Industry, the sixty-person staff at the Competition Authority has had a role in tracking the behaviour of the "dominant player" in the market. It has initiated a number of formal investigations of complaints, including charges of cross-subsidization, denial of access to the network, and requirements that customers purchase a bundle of services in order to qualify for discounts. In most cases, the Post has been exonerated or a change in practice has been negotiated before formal charges were laid. The Competition Authority has provided reasonable scrutiny of the Post. However, its feels that its authority and effectiveness are limited by the government's perpetuation and rationalization of the dominance of the market by the Post. This ties the hands of the Competition Authority, which does not have the option of suing the government.[45]

PERFORMANCE

As noted earlier, it is difficult to evaluate the performance of Finland Post in the context of liberalization – for the licensing system has not yet produced any new postal competitors in the previously reserved areas. Of course, the Post faces ongoing competition from other technological products and from the non-letter areas that are not part of the formal letter market – newspapers, unaddressed mail, parcels, express, and courier. The fact remains, though, that it is the only operator with a postal licence and it is still the dominant operator in most postal markets. It has lost some market share to technological and product competition, but in 1996 it retained 85 per cent of all letter traffic, 60 per cent of newspaper deliveries, 90 per cent of periodicals, and 90 per cent of addressed and 50 per cent of unaddressed direct-mail items. Notwithstanding technological competition, letter volumes continue to grow. The total number of postal items delivered by the Post has increased by over a third between 1994 and 1998. Factoring in fax and e-mail, it is estimated that the Post retains a 45 per cent market share in the communications market.

There is increasingly strong competition from international players, but Finland's relative isolation and small market has allowed the Post to focus primarily on the maintenance and nurturing of the domestic market. It has made substantial investments to increase quality and service, to moderate prices, and to remain competitive. It has acted to control its costs, particularly through rationalizing the network and

Table 1
Key figures

	1993	1994	1995	1996	1997	1998	% increase
POSTAL ITEMS (MILLIONS)	1,925	1,924	2,386	2,374	2,553	2,597	35
1st class	418	415	423	438	462	484	17
2nd class	388	405	407	418	396	394	
addressed ad mail	225	232	248	267	305	311	34
unaddressed ad mail	208	396	597	548	625	619	198
newspapers	366	352	359	358	415	431	18
periodicals	322	321	327	317	323	332	
parcels	23	24	25	27	27	26	
Net Turnover (MFIM*)	4,526	4,851	4,984	5,213	5,667	5,957	32
Operating Profit (MFIM)	205	356	420	491	508	331	
as % turnover	7.3	8.4	9.4	8.96	5.5		

* Millions of Finishmarks.

Source: Finland Post, Annual Report, assorted years, and PT Finland Group, Statistics, 1994 and 1997.

by mechanizing mail sorting. Foreign excursions and diversification have been modest. The Post has performed sufficiently well domestically to allow it to carry out its universal-service obligations while performing above the financial break-even point.

Overall Performance

As Table 1 indicates, the Post experienced a steady if not spectacular growth through the 1990s. Postal volumes grew by 35 per cent between 1993 and 1998, although this reflected a rebound from a 10.5 per cent decline between 1990 and 1993.[46] Overall volume growth between 1990 and 1998 was 20 per cent. Recent volume growth has been higher than expected. First-class mail volumes held their own throughout this period and grew in every year after 1994. This was an improvement over the early 1990s, when first-class volumes fell from 440 million units to 378 million (−2.6 per cent). As in other postal markets, postal volumes have been driven substantially by the expansion of direct or ad mail, which grew by 115 per cent, from 433 million units in 1993 to 930 million in 1998. Finns take their newspapers very seriously, and the Post's volumes in this area have increased from 366 million to 431 million, notwithstanding the controversy surrounding the Post's decision to shift delivery from inside to outside boxes.[47] The parcel and periodical markets – open to competition – remain fairly static. The reasonably buoyant volume increases – in the context of fairly stable prices – have resulted in a

Table 2
Price of a first-class stamp (purchasing power parity in FIM)

Netherlands	2.33
U.K.	2.39
Finland	2.46 + VAT = 3.00
Sweden	2.51 + VAT = 3.14
Norway	2.55
Ireland	2.61
Denmark	2.70
France	2.78
Germany	3.31

Source: Finland Post, *Annual Report,* 1998.

32 per cent increase in turnover in this period.[48] This result also reflects the Post's efforts to control costs (see below). The profit picture has been fairly positive, too, but the Post has been making a profit since 1980. The Post is expected to make a profit, and the government specifies a profit target of about FIM400 million in the state budget. Starting from a profit of FIM205 million in 1993, the Post's profits rose steadily until 1998, at which time they declined to FIM331 million. This decline was seen to be the result of a 9 per cent rise in costs, driven by staff expenses, pension expenditures, and a 19 per cent rise in depreciation charges to FIM310 million.[49] The Post pays taxes and dividends out of these profits.

Prices

The Post has been free to set its own prices since 1992. However, the regulators' expectation is that prices reflect costs, and there have not been complaints about this issue. The Post has to be price-sensitive to retain customers and market share. As Table 2 indicates, postal prices in Finland are among the lowest in Europe – net of the value-added-tax. The decision in 1994 to impose the VAT on postal services is consistent with the policy objective of making the Post function in a competitive and efficient manner, as other communication services are also taxed. This makes postal prices neutral in the market. The Consumers Association was unhappy with this policy decision.[50] First-class prices have been stable at around FIM2.5 in the 1990s. The price of a stamp has risen at a rate below the rise in the cost of living. The pre-tax price of a stamp declined by 2.6 per cent in real terms between 1990 and 1997. This follows the earlier trend of a fall in real prices, which declined by almost 10 per cent in the 1980s.

Investment and Mechanization

The Post is free to set its capital budget and to determine the allocation of its investments. It has pursued a persistently high level of investment in the 1990s, particularly in the area of logistics, mechanization, and information technology. This has been motivated by its objectives of increasing the quality of its service and the range of its capacities, in order to remain competitive. An investment level of FIM 100 million in the early 1990s and FIM 200–250 million in the mid-1990s jumped to over FIM 300 million in 1997 and FIM 665 million in 1998. This has had obvious short-term implications for profits but also offers long-term possibilities for productivity and growth. The mechanization of mail processing has increased to over 60 per cent of the mail, which takes place in seven sorting centres. The most recent investment was in the parcel centre in Vantaa on Helsinki's Ring Road II near the airport. Constructed at the cost of FIM 230 million, it has the capacity to process up to 20,000 parcels an hour.

These investments have paid off in a top-rate quality of service. Ninety-four per cent of first-class mail is delivered the next working day, and 94 per cent of second-class mail is delivered within three working days. Over 80 per cent of consumers and over 90 per cent of businesses received their mail before noon. Customer satisfaction is extremely high – 80 per cent of private customers and 85 per cent of corporate customers rated the Post's service as good or excellent.[51]

The Network

The most dramatic change in the Finnish postal system has been the rationalization of the postal network. Much of this change preceded liberalization and corporatization. Until the late 1970s, there were over 4,000 post offices in Finland, with a high of around 4,800 in the late 1960s. There was a plan in the 1980s, in cooperation with the postal banks, to eliminate about 2,000 outlets. Only about half this target was reached, which reflected an inadequate level of management courage more than any particular government inhibition (although there were frequent elections in the 1980s). There were just over 3,000 outlets by the time the postal-reform process began in 1990, a number that had been halved to just over 1,500 by 2000. There is a sense that the ministry has drawn a line in the sand at this number, although it has not been formalized and, in any event, neither the Postal Act nor the Decrees make a reference to the network. Only 567 of these outlets are Post-owned, the remainder being part of stores or private businesses. Nonetheless, this still provides the most comprehensive network in Finland.

The decline in the number and character of post offices reflected a number of strategic considerations. First, the Post extended its network of home delivery, in response to urbanization and suburbanization. This had the effect of decreasing the need for mail pick-up at local post offices. Second, the Post determined to change the character of the remaining postal outlets, also in response to the changing lifestyles of a more urban country. For economic and service reasons, the Post partnered with local retail businesses, as a way of improving service, extending business hours, and exploiting opportunities created by the decline in other networks. The Post has attempted to change the character of the outlets, to give them more of a self-service character and to make them more technologically sophisticated. There has been some political criticism of the diminution of the network, which was a partial cause of the creation of the Supervisory Board. However, the political reaction has had little thrust or impact. For example, the Consumers Association has been critical of the closing of local offices and the associated job losses. But it has been supportive and positive about the accompanying increase in quality and service.[52] There has been little public complaint about franchising.

The retail network has struggled financially, like retail networks in other countries, and the Post looks to lever its network to generate increasing revenues. About 60 per cent of the Post's counter revenue consists of commissions derived from various activities that it carries out on behalf of its business partners. The 1998 report notes a 12 per cent reduction in income in 1998 to FIM569 million, although much of this decline was related to reduced income from banking services (which will be outlined presently). The Post is looking to the sale of insurance services to be the third major component of its counter sales, after postal and banking products and services. The counters have started to offer products from the Financial Insurance Company (U.K.) under the Post's brand name, "Onni." These insurance policies are available in 550 outlets in cities and densely populated areas. The Post now offers the most extensive network for private insurance policies in Finland.

The banking situation remains uncertain and a bit of a mess.[53] The Post and Leonia – the state bank – have had an access agreement since 1995, whereby Leonia provides banking services in 485 postal outlets in return for a fixed fee. The fee was set for the first three years but was not finalized for the last two years of the arrangement. Despite efforts to finalize a fee, no agreement was reached. In the interim,

Leonia looked to rationalize its involvement and to limit its presence to only the most lucrative outlets. If it reduced its presence substantially, this would have had devastating consequences for the Post's networks and likely required the closure of another 200 outlets at a loss of a significant number of jobs. There was an arbitrated interim settlement of the dispute, to get the issue out of the spotlight before an election. The issue pitted the interests of the MOTC against the Ministry of Finance. The interim settlement saw the existing agreement extended for another year, albeit at a reduction in the fee of FIM 130 million. Moreover, the Post has been constrained from rationalizing the network until after this issue is settled.

Diversification and Internationalization

Of the Posts that are considered in this study, Finland Post is one of the least diversified. This reflects not any recent policy or government inhibitions (as in Canada), but rather a combination of Finland Post's historical position in the market and the company's recent strategy of focusing on its core competencies. The Post has not had a strong or diversified retail tradition, and the postal bank was teased out of its operation at a relatively early stage. This explains, in part, the weakness of the retail network that was noted above. Moreover, Finland's relatively small size and isolation do not encourage a growth strategy through product diversification and economies of scale, as in the Netherlands and Germany. The result has been that Finland Post's diversification initiatives have been modest and have not comprised an important strategic component of its market strategy. A business development unit was organized, but its activities were suspended through the de-meger talks and decision. Correspondingly, the Post's international initiatives have been modest as well. There is a political and policy sense that the Post will have to become more internationally oriented. The international scene is developing at a pace that appears to be outstripping the authorities' capacity to understand it or to develop a strategic response.

Like other Posts, Finland Post has made considerable efforts to expand its electronic services.[54] One initiative is ePOST, a hybrid product that allows companies to send items to the Post electronically, which then prints and distributes them in electronic and/or hard copy form. One in ten companies use ePOST and forty million units were sent in 1998, a fourfold increase since 1994.[55] The Post is also making a big initiative in the area of electronic-data transfer. Related to ePOST is the Post's activity in printing. In a joint venture with Tieto Corporation, the Post owns 51 per cent of Nordic Printmail Oy, the largest provider of print services in the Nordic countries. Its net turnover in May-December 1998 was FIM 123 million.

The Post is active in a number of complementary activities, with which it has had an historical association. PT Automotive Services is a subsidiary operation, which provides workshop and leasing services for vehicles. The company owns the vehicles, which it leases to the Post. It has the same relationship with Sonera (telecom) and a number of other companies. Similarly, it has a subsidiary bus company called Golds Line, which focuses on transportation in northern Finland and in charters.

The Post is attempting to make a push into the logistics area, under the name Post Transport. Its turnover increased by 3 per cent in 1998 to over FIM 1 billion. This is an increasingly competitive market, particularly as a result of the presence of international companies. But the Post retains 60 per cent of the parcels market. The Vantaa parcel centre is part of this strategic initiative. The Post was voted the logistics company of the year in 1998. It owns 70 per cent of LP Logistics Services in the warehousing area. It also owns Logistics Mail STP, which provides courier services to Russia.

Perhaps the most dramatic initiative in this regard is the pan-Nordic parcel initiative. The four Nordic companies have grouped together to form Pan Nordic Logistics AB, an international parcel company, in an effort to protect their markets and their presence in the Baltic area. The initiative was being tested and due to start in January 1999, but there were logistical delays and political uncertainty. Moreover, Sweden paused as a result of the ASG development there (see chapter 4). The initiative, however, has now come on stream. This case will test the capacity of the public Posts to cooperate among themselves. There have been a number of other joint ventures in Latvia and Estonia. These have included media distribution with local city companies, mail-order and catalogue sales, and logistics activity with transport companies.

Employment

Despite mechanization and the rationalization of the retail network, the Post remains the third-largest employer in Finland. The level of employment was nearly 30,000 in the early 1990s and this fell to around 25–26,000 at the end of the decade. About 30 per cent of postal employment is part-time. The decline in employment cannot be attributed in any great degree to liberalization. Rather, it reflects ongoing changes in demand coupled with mechanization, rationalization, and control of costs. Employment at the postal retail outlets has declined substantially, particularly as the number of Post-owned outlets declines. The de-merger of the Post and Telecom also affected staffing levels, as a smaller support staff was required.

HIGHLIGHTS OF THE FINNISH CASE

What can one learn from the Finnish case? What interest does its experience and a market approach hold for policy makers?

As a preliminary general observation, the Finnish experience is a compelling one that illustrates how a liberalized postal market can co-exist with the maintenance of a universal postal service – with no reserved area, no political subsidies, and no special treatment of a Post. The standards of the universal service in Finland are more or less of the same character as they were pre-liberalization and pre-corporatization: daily delivery of postal items across the entire address network at one, relatively low price. Moreover, the standards are now specified and defined. Unlike the pre-liberalization and pre-corporatization period, service standards are also etched in (legislative) stone and met, and the Post functions at a profit as well.

The Finnish regulatory model is an economical and elegant one, which combines simplicity with a grasp of the essentials. It combines three straightforward but critical ingredients:

- a clear articulation of a limited array of public expectations and standards for the universal system, as laid out in the Postal Services Act and the associated decrees;
- a licensing system that allows participation in postal activity on condition of the pursuit of the expectations and standards that are articulated in the act and the decrees; and
- a non-aggressive or passive regulatory structure that monitors postal participants' performance against the broad standards articulated in legislation and in the licence.

The implementation of this model, however, has unfolded alongside some fortuitous circumstances, most notably the willingness and capacity of the Post to provide a service to the entire nation. This has avoided the problem that the German licensing system is likely to confront: the absence of a universal service in certain segments of the market. The Finnish legislation anticipated, in Section 3 of the Postal Act, that the Post would be licensed in the manner it has been. This has not happened spontaneously.

On the other hand, the Finnish legislation did not seem to anticipate or think through the participation of postal operators in limited geographic areas of the market and the impact that this might have. The Finnish approach is built on postal liberalization, but it does not guarantee it or help it come into being. As will also be seen in the Swedish case, a liberalized market cannot be assumed to be able to come into existence automatically. The Finnish postal regime has no reserved area and, in theory, any reasonable, competent operator can get into the postal-services business. But a competitive postal market has not developed in the area of traditional postal business and letters. This reflects both market and political realities in Finland. With respect to the former, the hard reality is that Finland Post continues to control the commanding heights of the postal market. This includes 45 per cent of all communications, 85 per cent of the letters market, 60 per cent of newspaper deliveries, 90 per cent of addressed and 50 per cent of unaddressed direct-mail items, and 60 per cent of the parcel-transport market. The Post is a formidable, dominant presence in the Finnish market, and it is difficult to see – given the limited size of this market – how a competitive postal market might evolve. With respect to politics, notwithstanding the formal separation of the shareholder from the operation of the postal market, the Finnish political authorities seem unwilling to release or eliminate their influence in the postal market. The ssm case illustrates the extent to which the authorities have not thought through the implications of the liberalized market approach. The state finds itself in a conflict of interest over the ssm case. It is committed to market liberalization, but it is unwilling to allow the Post to confront competition in its traditional markets. On the one hand, it lacks confidence that the Post could withstand this competition; the consequence of competitive failure would be the undermining of the Post's capacity to maintain the universal postal system. On the other hand, the state does not want to lose share value if the Post falters financially in a competitive battle. The ssm case has created uncertainty. But it appears to be on the brink of resolution. The new president of the Post supports issuing the competitive licence. This issue will be the test of the Finnish state's real or imaginary commitment to a liberalized-market approach – and a test of the viability of the Finnish model.

Critical observers might point to the limited significance of the Finnish model, given the unique national features specific to the Finnish case. Some features would be difficult to emulate in Canada or other countries, while others might appear to be unattractive. With respect to the former, these conditions begin with the relative isolation and limited size of the Finnish market. The nature of the Finnish market makes the opening up or liberalization of the postal market less consequential than elsewhere. This is especially the case with respect to the way in which the Finns liberalized the postal market as a way of confronting technological change. With respect to the latter issue, the Finnish postal regime looks "cluttered" from an outside perspective. The consensual approaches and institutional processes surrounding policy making and labour-management relations in Finland are dense if not overwhelming. From the Committee on Postal Affairs to the Supervisory Board, from union representation on the Board of Directors to TAC, from the Competition Authority to the ambivalent if not schizophrenic presence of the MOTC – the Post functions in a dense web of institutional arrangements and processes. Of course, these arrangements contribute to the consensual processes that produce agreement over postal reform or legitimize the tough decisions that have been made in Finland. These are not arrangements or processes that could be willed into existence in countries that lack these traditions, but reflect the political cultural inheritance of the Finnish experience. Overall, the liberalization and corporatization process evolved rapidly and thoroughly because of the consensus around it, particularly the shared vision and commitment of the senior officials at the ministry and in the Post.

Ironically, this institutional web has evolved parallel to a basically liberal postal inheritance, which has in effect set boundaries to postal policy options and possibilities. This liberal inheritance has been an advantage to the Finnish postal scene in many ways, and it certainly encouraged the postal route taken in the 1990s. At the same time, the institutional web has not discouraged the ongoing involvement of state authorities in postal matters at key policy moments and at critical times. This may seem surprising, given the nature of the model, but it is not truly surprising when one grasps the pragmatic character of policy making in Finland. The state has removed itself from postal matters in a wide array of areas, most noticeably pricing and investment decisions and performance evaluation. But the state has been at the heart of key issues like the SSM case. The Finnish experience illustrates how difficult it is to separate politics from postal policy and activity, even in a liberalized and corporatized environment, when the state remains the shareholder of the Post.

There are two last features of the Finnish case to point out that have considerable significance for the Canadian scene and elsewhere. First, as in the Netherlands, the postal-reform process did not take place in isolation from other administrative reforms, in a way that would allow it to be scrutinized and attacked on its own grounds. This has been the Canadian experience. Rather, Finnish postal reform was enveloped in a larger reform of the state-enterprise sector. Indeed, the Post's reform was first carried along by umbrella legislation that applied to an array of state enterprises. This legislation was applied to the Post no differently than to other sectors, with the result that the reform had an apolitical, even-handed character that neutralized any possible political backlash. The wider reform process within the realm of public administration then took on a momentum of its own. It was not "planned" to any great extent. Rather, the accomplishments of one stage then generated the movement towards the next reform stage – such as the unanticipated transformation of the Post into a limited-liability company. In general, the strategy has been to make all state enterprises more commercially viable, and this drove the liberalization of the postal market.

Second, one element of the Finnish postal regime is consistent with a pattern that is emerging in the reformed or progressive postal regimes across the world – the creation or reintroduction of third-party regulation of the postal market. The EC postal directive more or less insists on this, as a way of guaranteeing the separation of ownership from operations. The specific national reasons for adopting or re-adopting third-party regulation reflect the specific conditions in any particular country. In Finland, a third-party regulatory approach was not adopted, as it was elsewhere, to regulate a postal monopoly; after all, there is no reserved area in Finland and the Post does not have any special market privileges. Rather, a broad but relatively benign regulation was adopted to ensure that the universal postal service could be maintained. The licensing system was an intelligent strategy whereby a third-party regulator could require that certain features of the universal system be maintained, in exchange for a licence to be issued. This required that the political objectives of the authorities – their idea of the precise nature and character of the universal postal system – be articulated, specified, and etched in stone in legislation. This would set the standard against which postal activity could be assessed. The goals of the universal system could thus be pursued in a hands-off yet businesslike way. The Finnish regulatory model – in the abstract – is simple, compelling, and elegant.

4 Sweden

Sweden abolished its postal monopoly on 1 January 1993, and a competitive postal market came into legal effect in March 1994. The subsequent postal story is one of trying to make postal competition work in real terms. The Post has become a limited-liability company under Swedish corporate law (Sweden Post AB), and it remains the dominant postal player in the market – retaining around 95 per cent of all postal business. The Swedish state has the legal responsibility to maintain the universal postal service, and it pursues this through a licensing arrangement with the Post, which has the operational duty of maintaining the system. The Swedish approach, then, is characterized by liberalization *without* privatization and has the universal service maintained effectively on a commercial basis, even in the absence of a postal monopoly.[1] Two particular and interrelated features have marked the liberalization of the postal market in Sweden, making it comparable to the Finland case. On the one hand, there have been growing pains in establishing a functioning postal market, since competition has developed neither automatically nor smoothly. On the other hand, there has been a re-regulation of the postal market, partially in response to the growing pains of the competitive market. More competition has developed in Sweden than in Finland. This competition has not had a negative effect on service to any extent, but it has placed stress on the tradition of a universal pricing system

It may seem ironic that it was a Social Democratic government that ended the postal monopoly in Sweden. The fact is, though, that the Social Democrats confronted a context and momentum for postal reform that they could not possibly stop. This momentum had a myriad of sources.

First, as elsewhere in northern Europe, the welfare state and the public sector in Sweden were experiencing the stresses and strains associated with economic recessions, which exposed some flaws in the welfare state and encouraged a change in popular attitudes towards it. There was a general political movement towards deregulation and even privatization in the 1980s and 1990s. Even the Social Democrats admitted the need for reform of the public sector. This reform process continues to unfold and includes a process of privatization. For example, the state has adopted the principle that it will not own a bank and has sold off a large portion of Nordbanken. It has also sold its remaining stake in Pharmacia and Upjohn. An initial purchase offer has seen the state sell 20 per cent of its shares in Telia, the state telecommunications company. Other state enterprises remain on the privatization and reform agenda. The state commissioned a study to discuss the restructuring of their profit targets, dividend policies, and reorganization in a new governmental unit.[2] A related factor was the market example provided by the telecommunications sector. The Post had been part of a typical PTT. Telecom's success in adapting to technological change and world markets through deregulation was very compelling to policy makers.[3]

Second, Swedish postal authorities were as intensely aware of the threat posed to the Post by technological change as any other postal authority in the world.[4] Ninety per cent of Swedish mail is business mail. The Post had documented the impact that the fax machine had had in slowing down the growth of letter-mail volumes in the late 1980s and early 1990s. Over time, the Post saw that what little monopoly protection it had was either worthless or a business and practical liability. The unions, government, and media imposed political demands and expectations on it as a public monopoly, and these expectations acted as a business constraint. Similarly, its monopoly status projected a bad business image to its customers and the market.[5] When Ulf Dahlsten arrived at the Post in 1988, he brought the view that the Post needed to reorient itself to its customers and adapt quickly to the competitive environment. It was his view that a liberalized postal environment would help the Post to do this, since commercial and business flexibility was required to adapt to the changing market.

Third, the Post had enjoyed but a limited postal monopoly in a fairly liberal postal market tradition in Sweden. This monopoly centred on *letters* in particular (personal handwritten correspondence), not a defined postal area in general.[6] Given the decline in the market importance of letters in the late twentieth century, this monopoly became almost meaningless. The Post did not insist on maintaining its monopoly when competitive market challenges arose in the late 1980s and early 1990s. The last remnants of the monopoly were challenged in the early 1990s by the advent of City Mail, a private-sector company that specialized in the delivery of computer-generated business mail such as catalogues and bills. The arrival of City Mail forced the political decision over liberalization. No government wanted to be embarrassed by quashing City Mail when it was trumpeting the benefits of deregulation. And the Post saw City Mail's arrival as confirmation and validation of its argument in support of a more commercial and liberalized postal market. So the postal monopoly was eliminated quickly and fairly easily, as will be seen below, before a new postal regime was put into place.

Public opinion was well on the side of postal deregulation, by the early 1990s, particularly with respect to the promise of better service and low prices. These promises effectively neutralized the postal union's well-articulated fears that this liberalization would undermine the universal system. Indeed, there was widespread support for the idea of separating the Post from the government.[7] This public support bolstered postal management's position that the Post had to prepare itself for not only technological competition but for the international competition that would develop once the EC postal directive came into effect.[8] This identity of vision between the Post and the public gave confidence to the government that it could de-monopolize the Post without enormous political consequences.

The Social Democrats could not halt the momentum for postal reform. Indeed, postal management convinced the government of the merits of postal reform and liberalization, and there was a unity of vision and purpose from that point on.[9] While the postal union, the Union of Service and Commications Employees, (SEKO), had historically supported management's accelerated push for change, it was not as enthusiastic about the decision to end the postal monopoly. It saw this as premature (when others in Europe had not done so) and potentially damaging (in a ratcheting down of wages and conditions to market levels). At the same time, though, SEKO's leadership saw the German and the Dutch Posts looming on the horizon, considered that their members' best interests were served in a healthy Post, and accepted the need for the Post to adjust to the new competitive reality.[10] So while protests were made, the postal union did not stop liberalization. SEKO was able to articulate its concerns and defend its interests effectively through its representation on the board of the Post.

The government decision to abolish the postal monopoly confirmed the reality that the postal market had withered away. Postal management, which understood the nature of the challenges it faced (technological and international) and felt that the monopoly had become an economic and political burden, had long lobbied for such a decision. The government, for its part, did not want to be embarrassed politically in dealing with City Mail in a heavy-handed way. It was publicly in support of liberalization and deregulation, and the population favoured this orientation. Once the government was convinced of the merits of postal management's case, it determined to end the postal monopoly. It devised a liberal-market approach to the construction of a competitive postal market combined with the maintenance of the universal postal system.

HISTORY

The Swedish Post Office administration was founded in 1636. Its traditional letters services expanded to include parcels in the nineteenth century, at which time the Post took on banking and payments services that continue to the present. Unlike typical European Posts, the Posts and Telecom were never combined in the same administration. The Post did not enjoy the invisible cross-subsidy from the Telecom side that propped up postal regimes in many other countries.

Prior to liberalization, the Post had actually functioned much like a private company in a liberal market for about a quarter of a century. On the one hand, there was a long tradition of competition in the postal market. The Post's reserve area – last defined in legislation in 1947 – was extremely narrow and excluded parcels, direct mail, and courier and express mail. The Post did not impose its monopoly rigorously in these areas for image (market) reasons.[11] On the other hand, the Post Office was transformed into a state-owned utility (*affarsverk*) in the late 1970s. While the Post remained owned by the state and accountable to it, it was given more extensive authority than a typical public administrative unit.[12] State-owned enterprises were allowed to apply their current income to operating expenses, with only the surplus paid into the state's budget. The Post's autonomy evolved substantially over the next two decades. For example, it attained its own Board of Directors in 1985, when it changed to a customer-oriented organization. It bought its assets from the state in the mid-1980s, at which time it was given the authority to decide upon and finance all of its investments.[13] Eventually, it retained both its revenues and its profits, not as equity but as a buffer against market developments. It was allowed to make investments up to a certain level (beyond which it needed the government's approval). It was obliged to finance its investments from its own resources and could not borrow money. It did not have the benefits of Telecom revenues but it did enjoy the liquidity and cash flow associated with the payments received by the postal giro bank.[14] It even had a degree of price autonomy within a price-cap system.

Given this "pre-history," it was not surprising that the Post lobbied for more autonomy in a liberalized market environment. The Post had tasted a high degree of corporate autonomy, which it wanted to expand and utilize to adapt the Post to a changing market. On the other hand, the Post's postal monopoly was no longer of substantial value – it did only about 30 per cent of its business in the monopoly sector.[15] Moreover, the monopoly exposed it to government, union, business, media, and popular scrutiny and expectations. The government commissioned the Post to undertake an internal review of the postal situation at this time. The study concluded that, because of its strong market position, the Post no longer needed the legal monopoly to survive. Indeed, the report concluded that its scale and scope would allow the Post to maintain the universal postal system without the benefits of a reserved area or compensation from the state. This analysis underpinned the decision to end the postal monopoly and to construct a new postal-policy regime.[16]

Four major decisions created the new Swedish postal regime: the abolition of the mail monopoly, the transformation of the Post into a limited-liability company, the creation of a new legal framework and regulatory regime, and the government's negotiation of an agreement with the Post to maintain the universal system. Each of these is outlined briefly below and will be examined in greater detail in the next section (on regulation).

Abolition of Mail Monopoly

The Riksdag (Swedish Parliament), as noted, abolished the mail monopoly, effective 1 January 1993. This created a liberalized postal market, in which there is free and open competition for postal products and services. The last legislative statement of the Post's exclusive privilege had been in 1947, and product and technological change had made this legislation outdated and irrelevant. This was demonstrated by the City Mail case in the early 1990s. City Mail claimed that its computer-generated mail (bank statements, catalogues, magazines, and so on) was not covered under the 1947 law. The courts never decided on the merits of the claim, since the Post's monopoly was abolished before the court made a decision on the legal challenge.[17] At the same time, the Post's internal review demonstrated that any extra costs imposed on the Post in carrying out its universal-service obligations were at least covered by the economic benefits that it enjoyed as the dominant player in the market.[18] The government then decided to abolish the reserved area.

Corporatization

The Swedish Post Office was transformed into Posten AB – Sweden Post Limited – and the Postal Services Act came into force on 1 March 1994. The Post became a limited-liability company under Swedish law, bound by the same business law as all other limited-liability companies. It is a normal stock company, but the state owns all of its shares and appoints the board, as any shareholder in a limited-liability company would. The board in turn names the president and CEO. This made the Post an independent and self-sustaining financial operation. Its prime but not exclusive objective is to make a profit. Its licensing agreement with the state, as will be seen presently, creates other targets and objectives, including the universal-service objectives. In all other respects – pensions, labour contracts, business development, market alliances, and so on – the Post is no different from any private company.

The corporatization of the Post was the culmination of a long process that began in the 1980s. This final step was required if the Post were to have the same legal structure as its competitors and function on an equal footing in the new competitive postal market. That is, corporatization created a level playing field in the market for the Post and any other postal operators. Complementing this change was the decision in March 1994 to impose the VAT on postal products and services. This created policy consistency and competitive fairness, since other postal and communications operators were paying the VAT as well. Similarly, any privileges that the Postal Giro enjoyed were removed in 1994, with respect to government payments, transfers, pension and tax distribution, and so on, and a competitive system was created.

While there was little public reaction to the VAT decision, the corporatization of the Post passed Parliament by only a slender margin. There had been some political and public backlash to job losses at the Post and post-office closings. But the government held firm in seeing through this element of the postal-reform process.[19]

New Postal Regime

There had been no general postal law in Sweden prior to liberalization of the postal market. Thus, the decision to abolish the postal monopoly required the state to pass a general framework law for the functioning of the postal market, which would apply to all postal operators. Ironically, then, the Swedish postal market moved from being a non-regulated to a regulated one, as a result of liberalization.

The Postal Services Act of 1994 is short (four pages), in keeping with what appears to be the Nordic tradition (the act is complemented by Ordinances that are issued from time to time and that provide further details). The act created a new legal framework for postal services for all postal players, including private ones. It is designed to ensure the maintenance of the universal postal system and defines the elements of the universal service. It states that there will be a nationwide postal delivery and counter service, at uniform and reasonable prices. Maintaining the universal system is the state's responsibility. The act does not specify how this will be achieved, but the government can contract with any company to provide postal service. The act creates a licensing system, in which any potential postal player can enter the market. These licences may be issued subject to certain conditions, such as providing the universal service. The act separated the ownership and regulatory functions of the state into two divisions, albeit within the same department – the Ministry of Transportation and Communications, later to become the Ministry of Industry, Employment and Communications (MIEC). The ministry would have broad responsibility for the ownership function. An independent regulatory authority – the National Post and Telecom Agency (Poch och Telestyrelsen) – would have responsibility for the regulatory function. Sweden Post is the only operator that has conditions imposed on it.

The act was updated in 1997–98 in response to the EC postal directive and to changing conditions. This reflected changes in form rather than in substance. The amendments detailed the functioning of the licensing system, increased the duties of the regulator, and specified the definition of the universal system.

The State's Agreement with the Post

The government pursued its responsibility for the universal service by negotiating a contract – called the "Agreement" – with the Post to provide the universal service for a three-year period (1 March 1994 to 31 December 1996). Subsequent agreements have fine-tuned arrangements. The government really had no other option than to contract out to the Post the universal-service obligation. Only the Post had the capability at this time of providing the universal service.

The major ingredients of the first Agreement included:

- a direction that the Post should operate commercially and make a return on equity comparable to the private sector (11–13 per cent return on capital, after tax);
- an equity: asset ratio of 15 per cent;
- a price cap-approach, whereby the Post could alter prices by no more than the average net change in the net-price index over a three-year period;
- an annual productivity-improvement rate of 2 per cent;

- a 95 per cent overnight-delivery target; and
- a range of regional and social responsibilities, including the maintenance of a network of at least 2,000 outlets (the state provided some compensation for these responsibilities).

More recent agreements included:

- a provision for daily and basic counter service;
- a requirement that any change in the scope of the universal service is to be implemented with care; and
- a provision that the Post has a duty to consult other parties before deciding on changes in the postal code system.

The latest Agreement was to have ended on 31 December 1999 but was prolonged to 30 June 2000. The corporatization decision created an awkward debt: equity ratio for the Post, since it had been obliged by the state to take on responsibility for historical and current pension commitments. The government decided to waive any dividend expectations until this ratio reached a normal level.

In sum, the postal-reform process in Sweden resulted in the liberalization of the Swedish postal market and the corporatization of the Post. The formal transformation of the postal regime took place from 1993 to 1995, but this represented a last qualitative step after a long period of growing postal autonomy and market deregulation. The Swedish postal regime comprises an open, competitive market; a corporatized Post that is now a limited-liability company; and a regulatory regime in which a third-party administrator issues postal licences and monitors the market to ensure the maintenance of the universal postal system whose existence is guaranteed in legislation and whose specific features are spelled out in agreements and in the licence. The Post has the same authority as a private-sector company and makes its own investment, pricing, personnel, and financial decisions. It has no special privileges or reserved areas and is assigned the responsibility of maintaining the universal system through a licensing agreement with the state. This formal liberalization of the postal sector was, in reality, only the first step in the subsequent effort to create a competitive postal sector.

STATUTORY AND REGULATORY ENVIRONMENT

The Swedish statutory and regulatory model is straightforward and simple, as reflects the Nordic style in policy making. The regulation and operation of postal activities are separated legislatively and in practice as well.[20] The regulatory and policy environment is sketched out legislatively in simple, broad-brush strokes. Yet, its simplicity notwithstanding, the regime has had growing pains and remains in an early stage of development. For good or bad, the specification of many policy issues has had to be sorted out or determined by the courts. The courts' involvement has focused not on universal-service issues (on the public-service side) but rather on price issues (on the competitive market side). This illustrates two points. First, the universal system can be maintained in a liberalized market environment. But, second, it appears unlikely, if not impossible, for a competitive system to come about spontaneously or automatically. In this section, the main features of the statutory and regulatory environment will be presented, along with a description of the main players in the postal regime. A presentation of the system "in action" will be presented in the following section, which will highlight a number of key cases.

The Postal Services Act sets out the broad parameters and objectives of the postal system, while the Postal Services Ordinance lays out the concrete details and expectations about how the postal regime will work and how the act will be applied. An Agreement between the state and the Post and a postal licence sets out the state's responsibilities for the universal service. The overall ambition of the legislation is to maintain a universal postal system within a competitive postal environment.

The Postal Services Act, as noted, was passed in 1993 and amended on three occasions, most recently in 1999. The act declares that there will be both a nationwide mail service and a nationwide counter (payments) service, accessible at uniform and reasonable prices (Section 1). The Swedes consider the network as part of the universal system, reflecting the fact that the Post has long offered financial services through its network of offices and rural postmen. However, while the Act established the principle of the network's existence, there is no specification of how this principle is to be realized. The government itself – or an authority appointed by it – is assigned the ultimate responsibility to provide the universal system (Section 2). Thus, it is the state – not the Post – that is accountable ultimately for maintaining the universal system. The act outlines abstractly how this will work out in practice. On the one hand, the act establishes a licensing system in which postal operators will be licensed to participate in the postal market, as long as they are capable and reliable (Section 4.5). Until 1997, the act allowed any operator to go into the postal business, provided it gave notification to the authorities. This has been replaced by a more formal application and licensing system, reflecting the increased (and unanticipated) level of competitive activity in the postal market, at least with respect to the overall number of participants. Thus, the act anticipates an open market, one where the Post will have no special privileges. It applies to the whole of the postal market and to all postal operators. On the other hand, the state delegates to a regulatory authority the duty to issue licences and monitor postal developments against the backdrop of the act (Section 4a.15). This establishes one primary element in the separation between postal ownership and regulation, in a system of third-party regulation. The regulator is assigned adequate powers to pursue its duties (Section 16.17). The act also lays out basic definitions of postal activity, letters, and so on. The act was later amended to reflect the EC postal directive, and it now includes statements on how postal prices are to be geared to costs, how the regulatory authority will make annual public reports on postal activities (including complaints), and other requirements. The act now considers the universal service to include all addressed postal items up to twenty kilograms, so parcels are part of the universal-service obligation. Newspapers and periodicals are considered to be letters.

The Postal Services Ordinance (1993, amended 1994, 1996, and 1998) fleshes out the broad principles of the act. The latest versions of the ordinance reflect policy adjustments made in response to the requirements of the EC postal directive. The ordinance specifies that it is the National Post and Telecom Agency that will act as the licensing authority under the act, with all the powers required to carry out its duties (Section 2.5). The PTS is required to report on postal performance and development and monitor the attainment of the universal-service obligations (Section 7). The ordinance indicates the means by which the competitive licensing system will maintain the universal postal system: "The National Post and Telecom Agency shall for one or more licence holders link the licence to conduct postal operations with conditions concerning the obligation to provide universal postal services" (Section 7). The ordinance establishes the state's expectations of how the universal postal system will function. These expectations now include daily service (five days) and 85 per cent next-day delivery (97 per cent within three days) (Section 8). These "expectations" reflect EC guidelines, and the performance of the Post is far beyond this formal expectation. The ordinance also lays out a price-cap formula, in which prices (on items weighing less than 500 grams) cannot be increased beyond a rolling three-year average increase in the consumer-price index.

Finally, the act and the ordinance are put into motion through an agreement between the state and the Post. As will be seen presently, the licensing system allows any capable and reliable company to participate in postal activity. However, it was obvious that the Post was the only possible operator with the capability to deliver the universal postal system. Thus, the state entered into a contract or agreement with the Post, whereby the Post would provide the basic mail and counter services required by the act. This agreement was required, according to the government, "to ensure that in a transitional period certain political objectives for postal operations are fulfilled" (Section 1). The first agreement was for the period 1 March 1994 to 31 December 1996. The agreement has subsequently been renewed, with minor changes. The most recent agreement was between the Post and the PTS. This licensing arrangement has increased the degree of formality in the state's expectations of the Post. The authority of the regulator has increased in conjunction with the EC postal directive.

The Agreement (and later the licence) is essentially the articulation of the state's universal-service obligations, as assigned to the Post in the contract. This mechanism for pursuing the universal-service obligation required a clearer and more specific statement of the components of the universal service than had existed previously. These sections of the regulations are laid out within the Postal Service Ordinance. First, the Agreement required the Post to maintain daily mail services for products up to two kilograms across the country, with a "high degree of reliability," "high quality," and "reasonable and uniform" rates (this was increased to twenty kilograms in the latest Agreement). The Post would receive no remuneration from the state for this service (Section 3.2) The government expected the Post to attain this universal-service objective out of its profits. Changes in the character of the mail service in sparsely populated areas could be initiated by the Post but "should be implemented with sensitivity" (Section 3.3).

Second, the Agreement required the Post to maintain a basic counter service across the nation at uniform prices on a daily basis. The Post would receive remuneration for this activity "where alternatives are lacking and it is not commercially justifiable to operate such services" (Section 4.2). The compensation level was established at SEK300 million in 1993 and 1994, an amount that dropped to 200 million in 1996 and 1997. The latest Agreement requires the Post to seek approval from the PTS, if it plans to close an access or distribution point. The Post would also receive compensation for its role in assisting the state in preparing emergency measures (Section 8) and in providing services to the functionally disadvantaged (Section 9).

The latest Agreement reflects the EC postal directive and requires the Post to achieve 85 per cent next-day delivery for first-class letters (97 per cent within three days). With respect to mail and counter service, it was estimated that around 1,800 households lacked daily service at the time of the Agreement being signed. The Agreement required that this number should not increase.

Third, the Agreement established a price-cap mechanism. The Post could increase prices on private, individual letters up to 500 kilograms within a range determined by a formula. The price cap was set at the three-year average change in the net-price index (Section 5.1.1). By implication, this suggested that the Post was free to set its own prices for other postal services and products on a commercial basis. However, the Agreement required that uniform prices be set in each weight scale. The latest Agreement enshrines the EC principle that prices be based on costs.

Fourth, the Agreement required the Post to report on its activities to the government or its delegate (PTS), with sufficient information and adequate explanation of the accounting system used (Section 10). The last version of the Agreement – reflecting the EC directive – requires the Post to devise a transparent and objective accounting system. This includes the providing of different accounts for different segments of its activity, in order to allow the regulator to evaluate whether prices of products and services reflect actual and reasonable costs.

The Agreement between the state and the Post comprises a commercial approach for the delivery of a universal postal system. The agreement quantifies a number of service objectives and specifies a number of political objectives, such as regional and social responsibilities. Only one part of the community-service obligation receives compensation. This approach reflects an assessment of the actual costs of providing the universal service. Sweden is one of the few countries to have undertaken a rigorous cost analysis of its regional and social responsibilities, which was carried out for the Post by an independent consulting firm. The study assessed the Post's social (blind, handicapped) and regional responsibilities in the letter service and its regional responsibilities in the payments service. It found that there was some cause for transitional assistance with respect to the first item. But, overall, the Post's scale, scope, and profitability were considered to be adequate to cover the first two responsibilities. On the other hand, the study concluded that partial compensation was called for with respect to the last responsibility.[21]

Licensing System

At the beginning of the liberalization process, any postal operator could participate in the postal market. Its only legal requirement was to inform the regulator. The number of postal operators forthcoming was much larger than had been anticipated. This raised concerns about quality, privacy, and consumer protection. A more formal approach to licensing was introduced in the 1997 amendment to the act and the regulator was given more formal authority in scrutinizing and accepting/rejecting applications for a postal licence. The regulator bases its decision whether to grant a licence upon its estimation of the applicant's dependability and integrity. Terms and agreements are set, which are imposed and regulated. A licence can be revoked if the terms are not followed.

The Ministry

The Ministry of Industry, Employment and Communications – better known as the Ministry of Industry – has ultimate responsibility for the entire postal sector as well as for the Post. A merger of a number of ministerial functions has created this rather large conglomerate of a ministry. It houses both the postal ownership and regulatory function, albeit in different units.

The ownership function is situated in the Division of State-Owned Enterprises, which reports to a minister (presently Bjorn Rosengren). Sweden retains a large state-enterprise sector, comprising sixty enterprises, of which the Post is the fourth-largest (largest in terms of employment). This division has responsibility for overseeing twenty-six government-owned enterprises in Sweden, including the Post. The policy of the government and the ministry is that these companies "generate the highest possible long-term returns on their owners' capital … [and] operate with the lowest possible costs in terms of the benefits they provide."[22] The division makes appointments to the board (including a representative of the shareholder). It deals with the Post on strategic issues and sets performance and financial targets. It is a small and lean operation, comprising about twelve employees, headed by a director who is a permanent civil servant. The main responsibility for the management of the Post is assigned to one particular employee, who has responsibility for three or four other enterprises. The unit builds up policy intelligence by having regular contact with consultants, investment bankers, and so on. Prior to 1994, almost all postal intelligence rested with the Post.

The regulatory function is housed in the Division for Information Technology, Research and Development (IT, R&D), which reports to a different minister (currently Mona Sahlin). The PTS – the regulatory agency – is independent but is accountable to this division. This division employs around twenty-five people, one of whom is assigned main responsibility for postal-regulatory matters. This division has the duty to ensure that the postal sector and the Post function in conformity with the objectives of the Postal Services Act and other postal rules and regulations.

There is only a modest sense among authorities that housing the regulatory and shareholding functions within the same ministry might be inappropriate. There is some isolated opinion that the ownership function should likely rest with a separate ministry, like Finance. But the housing of the two functions within one ministry is defended with the argument that the ministry is a large one and ownership and regulatory discussions take place within different ministerial processes. For example, the Division of State-Owned Enterprises does not interact with the PTS, since this would be inappropriate. These intradivisional discussions could generate conflicts of opinion and perspective, which would have to be resolved at the political level. There has been no such experience as yet.[23]

The Regulator

The National Post and Telecom Agency carries out the regulatory function of the postal system. The PTS is responsible to the IT, R&D division of MIEC, whose minister appoints the director general of the PTS. The director general in turn makes all other appointments. A board oversees the agency, although it is not clear what the board actually does other than oversee the budget; it has no day-to-day involvement with the regulatory process. The board comprises ten people with substantial public- and private-sector backgrounds, including two Members of Parliament.

The origins of the PTS lie in the corporatization of the telecommunication sector, at which time it was created to regulate this sector. After the Postal Services Act was passed, its mandate expanded to include the postal sector. The licence holders finance its operations, so that 94 per cent of the costs of postal regulation are borne by the Post. The agency houses 165 people, with eight having postal responsibilities. This suggests that the postal regulatory touch is a fairly light one. The PTS is a legally autonomous body, whose leadership and members are independent of changes in government. Indeed, Sweden's constitution forbids ministries and ministers from interfering with or handling individual matters dealt with by agencies. Thus, it has de jure autonomy. It does not receive individual orders from a particular minister but rather general orders from the government (as set out in legislation).[24] All impressions and opinion suggest that it is genuinely independent of government.[25] Its decisions are appealable, first to the District Administrative Court of Stockholm then to the Appeal Court for Administrative and Legal Issues. Few appeals go that route – they tend to be resolved at the political level instead.

As noted above, the Postal Services Act (Sections 15–17) grants the agency the authority to get the information required to do its job and gives it the authority to impose and enforce rulings. Responding to the EC postal directive, the state has increased PTS's authority in recent years. Generally speaking, it has four functions and responsibilities. First, it is charged with monitoring the postal market, to ensure the existence of efficient postal services and to guard against some postal operators having unfair competitive advantages over others. The Competition Authority plays the substantial and formal role in the area of ensuring competition. Second, it assigns licences to applicants who wish to carry out services and activities in the postal market. Third, it monitors the performance of the Post, to ensure that it meets the terms of the Agreement with the government. This last includes monitoring the Post's universal-service obligations and price changes. Fourth, PTS has a number of technical responsibilities for overseeing redirection of mail, shared use of the postal infrastructure, dealing with undeliverable mail, and resolving postal disputes. Fifth, it performs a number of duties on behalf of the government in international settings such as the UPU and European postal agencies.

There are a number of areas where the regulator has no responsibility. For example, it does not implement competition law, which is the responsibility of the Competition Bureau. The Post's financial performance is set and monitored by the minister and the board, not by the PTS. Similarly, the Post's business decisions – such as investment, partnerships, and diversification – are outside the regulator's orbit. There have been complaints from its competitors about the Post's diversification initiatives. But the regulator's view is that there are no rules against this.[26] There are general rules and targets in the Agreement dealing with the network and with delivery. Much of the rationalization in this area had already been carried out before 1994, so this has not been a major issue on the PTS agenda. When the Post has made moves in this area, the PTS has accepted the Post's business case and has been sympathetic to the Post's position. The PTS has not inhibited these actions, even when there was public controversy or criticism about postal closings or changes in postal delivery.[27] It has played a substantial role in the pricing area, postal infrastructural and access matters, government purchase of services in rural areas, and bulk-mail issues – which will be examined below.

The ministry gives the PTS its broad instructions and the PTS reports regularly to the ministry. There is regular, albeit infrequent, contact between the PTS and ministry representatives, in which reports are made and information is exchanged. Other than that, there is little contact. Once a year, the ministry issues its instructions and, from time to time, asks for an investigation or study.

The Post

As noted earlier, Posten AB – Sweden Post – is a limited-liability company under private corporate law, whose shares are owned by the state. Liberalization and the Postal Services Act did not change the Post very much, in the sense that it had experienced a considerable degree of corporate autonomy since the late 1970s. This autonomy had included the areas of pricing and investment. The Post purchased its assets from the state in the mid-1980s, at which time it began to make and finance its investments. It adopted a commercial orientation in 1984, when it adopted a basic business orientation and created business and profit centres. From this time on, the Post transformed itself from being basically a "production-led" government department to a "customer and profit-led" business operation. It introduced a systematic business plan in 1989, with a focus on profits and the satisfaction of its customers and personnel. Later, it acquired a private-sector information technology company and two leading electronic mail-order companies in order to increase its market competitiveness.[28]

The transformation from a public enterprise to a limited-liability company in 1993–94, then, was the culmination of a corporatization process which eventually placed the Post on a "technically" level playing field in a competitive market. It remains, of course, the dominant market player, but it is organized, motivated, directed, and operated just like a private-sector company. The Post has undergone a number of internal restructurings into various operating units. It broke out into a number of separate operations for a time – Counter Sales, Postgirot Banking, Letters, Logistics, Parcels, International – each with full sales, operational, and profit responsibilities. This reflected an organizational trend to decentralization, to get operations closer to the customer. More recently, it has moved to reintegrate the organization into one unit. The Post can determine the scope of its services, as long as its contract with the government is satisfied.

The transformation from the late 1980s through the mid-1990s was led by Ulf Dahlsten, who came to the Post in 1988–89. Dahlsten had been a secretary of state in Olof Palme's government, which gave him a special authority or aura within the company and in its relations with the government. This ensured that the Post was on solid ground in its transitional dealings with government. Dahlsten was keen to ready the Post for competition and to adapt to the new technologies. He was an effective leader in the run-up to liberalization in 1994. But his leadership of the Post after 1994 was a bit heavy-handed politically, as exemplified in what appears to be the mishandling of the City Mail challenge, as well as in the stealth-like price increase of 1997. Dahlsten was replaced by Lennart Grabe, from the electronics firm Ericsson. Grabe had previously been head of the Swedish Confederation of Industry, and his private-sector experience makes him a more appropriate and business-oriented CEO in the liberalized postal environment. The management of the Post until 1994 was derived primarily from the government side of the Post's experience, and there was not a great amount of recruitment from the private sector. While the composition of the Board of Management has changed recently, there remained a considerable number of fifteen- to twenty-five-year veterans on the Board of Management as recently as 1998.

Postal management reports to a Corporate Supervisory Board, which has also experienced a changing composition. When the Social Democrats returned to power, they recognized that postal deregulation and liberalization were inevitable. The result has been that their appointments have made it a much more business-oriented and substantial board. The board comprises ten members named by the government. This includes three union representatives (there has been labour representation on the board since the mid-1980s) as well government officials (currently, one each from the Ministry of Finance – because of its interests in the Post Girot – and MIEC). The other members have private-sector business backgrounds as chairs and chief operating officers and directors of firms, ranging from forestry and industry through communications and finance. The chair is a well-connected former cabinet member who is a governor of one of the regions.

The board has the same sorts of responsibilities as any private-sector board – save for the particular obligations that are associated with the Agreement with the government and the general rules associated with state-owned enterprises. The state – as shareholder of the Post – has laid out broad guidelines and goals within the Postal Services Act and in the Agreement with the Post. The state requires a long-term return on its equity in line with normal expected market performance – around 10 per cent. The profits earned are used for normal payment of company tax and for self-financing of investments. In principle, the Post is expected to pay dividends to the shareholder. However, because the Post took on unfunded pension liabilities representing a considerable amount of debt, the government will not ask for dividends until the Post's debt: equity ratio approaches a normal level. Within this framework, the board proceeds like any private-sector board in working with management in the pursuit of profits and business expansion. The government seems poised to reorganize its state enterprises into new units, with a new corporate-governance regime, changed profit targets, and so on. A private-sector consultant was commissioned by the government to explore possibilities in this regard.[29]

At this point, it is unclear how the government would protest to the Post if it were unhappy with its performance. There would likely be intense discussions and the board could be replaced. This scenario has not arisen. The board approves management's business plan, not the state, which stays out of this area. The board accepts or rejects management's strategy with respect to purchasing of companies, investments in plant and equipment, diversification into related fields, selling of buildings and assets, and so on. Within the broad guidelines set by the state in the Postal Services Act and the Agreement, the Post has day-to-day business autonomy. If the Post proposes an initiative that takes it outside of the agreed-upon framework – for example, diversification into an area that does not seem to support the postal function or would have a substantial impact on profits – then shareholder approval would be required.[30] Changes in the universal service would have to be discussed with the IT, R&D division and the PTS.

The postal regime in action will be examined below. As a generalization, at the highest levels of policy and decision making, there remains a fairly intimate relationship between the Post and the government – between the board chair and/or CEO and the minister. However, there is no hard evidence of government interference in the operation of the Post.[31] For good or bad, past CEO Dahlsten was able to get the government on side for two controversial cases – the 30 per cent price increase and the bulk-mail pricing decision. Both decisions reflected the close relationship between the CEO and people at the ministry, many of whom were from the Post. And both decisions could be characterized as unfortunate ones, with negative consequences for the Post (and for CEO Dahlsten). There has been a subsequent increased formalization of the respective roles of the ministry and the Post, and the impression now is that the relationship between the government and the Post will settle into the more formal, hands-off relationship that the Swedish model had anticipated originally.

One case that has tested the model was the ASG affair. ASG is the logistics company that was the trucking arm of the state railroad. The Post had been planning to buy this company for some years, and it owned 20 per cent of the share capital and 27.1 per cent of the voting rights in ASG in July 1999. However, the German Post Office purchased it, almost from under its nose, in a messy case that involved the courts. This was a case where ministry approval was required before the Post could proceed with the purchase. At the moment when the Post had to move quickly, the issue rested within the ministry. There were criticisms that the ministry moved too slowly on the issue, with the result that the Post lost a competitive market opportunity to a foreign competitor. The view from the ministry side, though, is different. It maintains that, because the purchase of ASG was not part of the Post's core activity or mandate, there was a need for substantial study and background information and a proper and convincing presentation of the Post's case. In its view, that case was not convincing.[32]

Others

There are two other direct "players" in the Swedish postal community that are worth noting. First, the Swedish Competition Authority has been drawn into the formulation of Swedish postal policy. This was the logical, if unintended, consequence of liberalizing the postal market. Given the asymmetry among postal participants (that is, the Post as dominant player), a number of competition cases have been brought to the authority by the Post's competitors, some of which have gone on to the courts. As will be seen below, "making" competition work in the postal market has required significant regulatory and judicial effort.

Second, SEKO – the postal union – has played an important role in the Swedish postal regime. SEKO has been represented since the mid-1980s on the Board of the Post, where it participates in the construction and operation of the Post's business plan. This consensual feature of Swedish political life has worked to considerable effect in the postal regime. At the same time, SEKO represents postal workers "on the ground," and has participated with postal management in numerous initiatives, including the most recent developments of deep decentralization down to the local level. Ironically, SEKO also represents the workers at the Post's main rival, City Mail. SEKO has a sophisticated understanding of postal realities and a pragmatic view of postal policy, and it has been effective in defending its members' interests.

THE STATUTORY AND REGULATORY SYSTEM IN ACTION

The liberalization of the Swedish postal market has had a number of economic and policy consequences for the postal sector in general and the Post in particular. Many of the "performance" dimensions will be examined in the next section. In general, it appears that competition has increased but not in a manner that has threatened the Post's market dominance. The increased competition in turn has not had serious consequences either for the universal postal service or for the health of Sweden Post, which continues to be profitable. "Does the new situation with competition in some segments of the postal market constitute a threat to Sweden Post's ability to maintain universal services? As far as the National Post and Telecom Agency is concerned there is no evidence that this should be the case."[33] Liberalization has led, ironically, to a re-regulation of the postal market, as the next step in making a competitive market. It has also generated a number of regulatory and court cases to sort out legal disputes, as competition has evolved into conflicts and disagreements. This experience has been seen by policy authorities to be a necessary transition stage, required in order to make the postal market work.[34] This re-regulation has been a source of considerable concern for the Post, since it feels that it has lost considerable price and competitive flexibility in the new environment.[35] Generally, liberalization has generated more problems associated with competition than with the maintenance of the universal service.[36] There have been some developments, though, that raise questions about the future of the universal system – including the development of differentiated pricing and musings on whether the Post will eventually require compensation for it to be able to carry out its community-service obligations. Each of these issues will be examined below.

The Rise of Competition and City Mail

When the postal market was first liberalized in 1994, any company could participate in the postal market, as long as it notified the PTS. There was no application or licence required. There were, however, a far greater number of postal participants than had been anticipated – in the area of one hundred or so. This raised a number of concerns, including ones associated with security, reliability, and consumer protection.[37] When the Postal Services Act was amended in 1997, a licensing system was introduced, whereby postal operators applied to the PTS for a licence. Neither the system nor the application is particularly elaborate, although the legislation increased PTS's authority to scrutinize and reject applications (reflecting as well as the EC postal directive to formalize the powers of the postal regulator). The applicant must demonstrate to the regulator that it has the integrity and capacity to perform postal activities in a reliable and secure way. The regulator is indifferent to the applicant's competitive viability.[38] There are no limitations on foreign operators participating in the Swedish postal market and, indeed, Royal Mail owns 11 per cent of City Mail, which it uses as a local partner in distributing international mail.

Table 1
Distribution of postal volumes (millions)

	1995	1997	1998	1999	% share (1999)
Sweden Post	3,370	3,311	3,275	3,247	94.8
City Mail	33	123.7	151.5	163.4	4.8
Other	5	11.1	18.6	14.5	0.4

Source: Sweden Post, *Annual Report,* assorted years, and Andersson and Bladh.

The vast majority of the hundred or so competitors are small companies that provide local mail collection and delivery, using their own stamps and letter boxes.[39] Their numbers rise and fall. Their start-up costs are small and the barriers to entry are low. But their operations are small as well (150–1,500 items a day), so they are prone to failure. The PTS reports that there were eighty licences issued as of February 1999. About sixty of these firms appear to be stable.[40] There are some larger operators, such as City Mail (computer mail), Swedish Direct Mail (SDR – unaddressed printed mail), and City and Financial (document exchange). There are also niche operators like Novydux HB, Georgsson Mail Inv., Fraktkonsult Lokalpost City, and Financial Sweden AB. The overall degree of competition remains marginal. As Table 1 indicates, competition represents about 5 per cent of total volumes. City Mail, though, covers about 30 per cent of households in Stockholm and Malmo with its pre-sorted computer-generated mail (about 10 per cent of the bulk-mail market).[41] The Post estimates that, in the urban, computer-generated, pre-sort segment of the market (minimum 500 units and no time sensitivity), it has lost 20 per cent of the market. The increase in the number of small, local competitors in the postal market reflects a number of factors, including Sweden Post's decision to increase the price of first class letters by 30 per cent in 1996. This created a market opportunity for small competitors, who found increased market space to offer competitive postal services at a price just below just below the increased price. But this segment of the market is limited: local mail comprises but 15 per cent of the Swedish postal market. There is no indication that the small local operators will or could coalesce into an alternative national network.

The most dramatic illustration of the rise of competition in the Swedish postal market is City Mail, the self-proclaimed first private postal provider to operate in direct competition with the traditional postal monopoly. The brainchild of Bror Anders Mansson, City Mail entered the postal market in 1991 and forced the government to decide on the liberalization of the postal market, which it did at the end of 1992. City Mail concentrates on business or industrial mail that is computer-generated, addressed, and sorted, thereby eliminating the need for expensive sorting machinery. Focusing on dense urban markets like Stockholm and central Goteborg and Malmo, City Mail offers twice-weekly delivery of catalogues, bills, financial statements, and so on via its own large-scale postal-distribution operation.[42]

City Mail has experienced the normal growing pains of any new business, and has had a number of reincarnations. But its ongoing competition and legal battles with Sweden Post have exacerbated this. The Post had charged before 1992 that City Mail was breaking its monopoly and, even after liberalization, the legal challenges between City Mail and the Post continued in a new and uncertain competitive market. Swedish competition law was not particularly well designed to deal with a situation in which there was a dominant provider. The Post's and City Mail's legal challenges took an extended period of time to resolve.[43] Yet they were eventually resolved by the courts, as well as by a strengthened competition law. In effect, these court cases formed the new rules of the competitive postal market. But the transition to competition was difficult for City Mail, since the extended period of court cases was both expensive and uncertain for its business. It went bankrupt and was actually taken over (75 per cent) at one time by Postbolagen AB – Sweden Post's holding company. It was placed in receivership at the end of 1995, at which time its assets were sold to the original owners, who re-entered the market with new financial support.[44]

Since then, City Mail's market share has grown but its viability remains shaky. The regulatory agency appears ready to bend over backward to try and ensure City Mail's survival. Its new board chair is Jan Freese, who is the former director general of the Swedish National Post and Telecom Agency. It employs close to 1,000 people, had revenues of SEK319 million in 1998, and is approaching but has not yet attained profitability. It is listed on the Stockholm stock exchange. Its partnership with Royal Mail (which has a representative on its board) has been extended recently. City Mail has decided to outsource its core business, and Royal Mail has purchased directly the Malmo and Gothenberg operations. City Mail has also entered into a joint venture with ASG to distribute parcels from the Internet. It claims to enjoy 8 per cent of the computer-addressed mail segment, equalling 4–5 per cent of the overall postal market.[45]

Pricing

Nowhere have the competitive stresses and strains of the new liberalized postal market been more evident than in the area of pricing of postal products. Strategic price adjustments have always been an integral feature of competitive-market positioning. There was no reason to anticipate that this would be any different in the liberalized postal market. On the one hand, competitors to the Post would, in most cases, try to enter the market by undercutting the prices charged by the Post. They had competitive advantages in this regard, since they enjoyed lower wages and overhead. The Post, in turn, would naturally attempt to protect its market position by making price adjustments to these competitive threats. This has been the case particularly with respect to lucrative business and bulk mail.

It was unclear how this would play out. This sort of competitive-pricing process had never occurred previously in the postal market, where there were traditional pricing principles like a universal and accessible price. Generally speaking, the new postal regime gave autonomy to postal operators. Under its Agreement with the state, the Post was limited to a price cap for its letter-mail products of less than 500 grams. The Post was subject to the competition laws, like all other corporations, for its pricing actions in all product areas. What happened eventually was that the regulatory and competition authorities set pricing policy and the rules of the game in this area, via the resolution of a series of challenges and complaints.

James Campbell reports that "As competition intensified, Sweden Post sought to maintain its customers with an aggressive campaign of exclusivity clauses, tie-in arrangements ('bundling' services to make then eligible for discounts), discriminatory discounts, and other pricing strategies."[46] According to its competitors, many observers and the courts, the Post attempted to use its dominant position to fight competition. As a general strategy, the Post offered incentive mail prices for customers who used the Post exclusively, to the benefit mainly of the Post's large customers. The Post also lowered its prices in specific areas, in order to meet competition locally. These initiatives by the Post generated policy and legal controversy, which was predictable given the uncertainty that existed at the time with the advent of a new Competition Act. More than a hundred cases were heard under the Competition Act after July 1993, many of which were brought forward by the Post itself in an attempt to clarify the situation. In the event, the Swedish Competition Authority condemned most of these actions as predatory and designed in particular to eliminate City Mail. The court's rulings forced the Post to end its exclusivity and tie-in contracts. They also clarified the extent to which the Post would be allowed to differentiate prices on a geographic basis. The Post is now obliged to offer the lower local price across the whole system.[47]

With respect to the latter point, a competitive pricing strategy ran into the principle of universal pricing, when the Post cut its prices locally in response to local competition. The Post justified this on cost grounds, arguing that its local costs justified the lower local price. This is a delicate and nuanced issue, since the allocation of costs on specific or precise activities is difficult and requires judgment if not assumptions about where particular costs are allocated. In the event, this issue has played out through the courts, which have pronounced on this. In March 1997 the Stockholm District Court overruled the Competition Authority's decision to ban geographical price differentiation. The courts have allowed the Post to differentiate prices for services where there is a "differentiated cost profile." That is, if the Post can deliver a local letter at a lower cost, it can charge a lower price. However, it can do this only if the similar service is offered at a similar price throughout Sweden. As the regulator has put it: "To avoid any discrimination these offers have to be general and not selective, meaning that all customers who can comply with the conditions for the discount are entitled to have it. For that reason, these conditions have to be made publicly known e.g. by being published in schedules of standard discounts. In practice this means that the incumbent shall not be allowed to undercut and selectively offer these customers special discounts."[48] The competitive-market uncertainty also reflected a grey area that needed sharper focusing. On the one hand, the rules for single or individual letters are quite clear: uniform pricing is required. On the other hand, competition rules apply in the area of bulk mail. Where a problem arose was in the transition or grey area between the two, around 500 pre-sorted units and even less. This has been a difficult area to sort out. While PTS is not involved on the competitive side, it has responsibility for the proper accounting of prices, to make sure that they are geared to costs. This has required it to get substantial information from the Post, and it has run into confidentiality issues. This issue has created some friction between the regulator and the Post.[49]

In sum, the courts and the competition authority have set the rules for the new competitive market system. This has been a mixed blessing, inasmuch as the Competition Authority does not have a particular competence or understanding of the postal industry. It may make sense to increase the responsibilities of the regulator in this regard, since it has the merit of having built up some postal expertise. The Post, in effect, played a game of trial and error, to see where the competitive boundaries existed and to explore the amount of flexibility that it enjoyed under the new postal regime. The Post has had to prove that it is not underpricing, and this has involved a lot of back and forth with the courts, particularly in documenting and explaining accounting and costing systems. These cases have, to a certain extent, clarified the situation and made it more predictable. However, the Post is likely to be the dominant player for the foreseeable future and its competition always has the option of testing the "court market," so to speak. This is likely to continue for some time. The Post's view, however, is that this re-regulation of the market has put considerable constraints on its freedom of action. It feels caught between the competition authority (which limits its price cuts) and the regulator (which limits its price increases). It feels that its prices are being kept high in profitable markets, where it could discount prices to increase competitiveness and maintain profits. On the other hands, it feels that it is forced to keep its prices low in unprofitable markets, which in turn harms its profits.[50]

There is another ironic dimension to this competitive situation and its fallout for the Post. The extent of competition in Sweden has been related to the overall pricing policy pursued by the Post. As noted earlier, the Post "manipulated," if not abused, the price-cap formula to increase the price of letter mail by 30 per cent in 1996. This initiative reflected the fact that the Post's profits had declined in 1995 and 1996. The Post managed to increase the price by this amount by introducing a "blended" price change. It cut the price of discount stamps (which it can offer to customers under the Postal Services Act) by 3 per cent, but assigned 90 per cent of the overall price cut under the formula to this change. This allowed it to offer a 30 per cent increase in letter-mail charges, which netted out to an acceptable number under the price-cap formula.[51] The result was a considerable political outcry in Parliament and at higher levels, which may have contributed to Dahlsten's departure as CEO of the Post.

The regulation of prices in the Swedish regime poses considerable dilemmas for the regulator. On the one hand, a competitive market should have the effect of keeping postal prices low, which benefits consumers. On the other hand, if postal prices fall too low, there will likely be few participants in the postal market. Similarly, the regulator must ensure that the Post has sufficient room to adjust to international pressures and developments.

Infrastructure Policy

A second competitive strain in the new liberalized postal market has been the issue of access to postal infrastructure. By postal infrastructure is meant a series of operating components of the postal system, including post-office boxes, redirection of mail, change of address, postal-code system, codes to doors in apartment buildings, and so on. It was the intention of the Postal Services Act to create a liberalized postal environment, in which all licensed operators would have access to the infrastructure on an equal basis. Postal legislation assigned to PTS the responsibility to oversee negotiations among the operators to get an agreement to infrastructure access that would work. If it could not sort out disagreements, the issue would go to the Competition Authority.

With respect to the redirection of mail, this issue was resolved in a creative and market-oriented way. The Post and City Mail created a joint company – Svensk Adressandring AB – to oversee the system. Postal customers inform this company when they change address, and the company coordinates this to ensure smooth transitions for customers. The system appears to have worked well.[52]

A similar resolution was not so easily forthcoming with respect to access to post office boxes. The Post has built up the system of post-office boxes over time, and it has insisted on charging its competitors "market prices" for access to the boxes. In effect, it considered the post office boxes to be its own. Its competitors, like City Mail, lodged complaints, arguing that manipulation or denying access to boxes and code systems gave the Post a competitive advantage. For competitors, the boxes were considered part of the essential infrastructure in the postal market to which it should be granted equal access.[53] The issue went to the Competition Authority. Indeed, the issue has been sufficiently problematic to require a change to the Postal Services Act, which occurred in June 1999. The act assigns responsibility to the Post for the postal-code system. The act also declares that all postal operators shall have the same access to mail boxes, change of address system, and postal codes. Sweden Post and City Mail have reconciled their dispute over the postal-box issue. The terms of the agreement are confidential, but City Mail will pay for access to the boxes and the Post will pay compensation damages to City Mail for past behaviour.[54]

Community-Service Obligation

The postal experience to date has not raised concerns that liberalization of the Swedish postal market has undermined the principles of the universal postal system. As will be seen below, the quality of postal service remains high, an extensive postal network continues to function, and the Post generates sufficient profits to carry the obligations for which it receives no compensation.

However, the Swedish government has expressed concern about this issue, particularly at moments (like 1995 and 1996) when falling profits appeared to weaken the Post's capacity to maintain the universal system. The government has studied this issue, and on two occasions it considered the creation of a compensation fund, to be financed by the turnover of all operators. The government was stimulated to consider this approach by the EC postal directive, which floated the idea of a compensation fund for this purpose. On both occasions, though, all members of the postal community – including the Post – expressed their disagreement with the idea. So the government has not pursued the approach.[55] The Post sees it as a competitive marketing advantage for it to declare that it can offer this universal service. And it believes that its capacity to provide the service will be maintained if it can enjoy sufficient price flexibility to remain competitive and profitable.[56]

The future of the postal retail network is under serious scrutiny. This would likely have developed as a problem even in the absence of liberalization. As will be seen below, the network is a financially losing proposition. This was anticipated in the Agreement, which grants the Post SEK200 million to maintain uneconomical regional and local services. However, this level of compensation is dwindling relative to the real costs for the Post, which are now over SEK400 million. There is no obvious "solution" to this matter. Its resolution lies with the government, which has formal responsibility for the universal service. As the expiry of the Agreement with the Post approached (31 December 1999), the government initiated a study on the issue. Numerous ideas have been floated. A controversial one is to limit counter and bill-paying services in rural areas to a limited number of days per month, in order to save labour costs. The government has also considered withdrawing its responsibility for providing financial services via the counters network altogether, since this is something that the market can do. If it took this approach, it could withdraw responsibility (and compensation) for the existence of a network. In the event, the issue has not been resolved, and the Agreement with the Post has been prolonged. This is a highly charged political issue.[57]

In sum, the liberalized postal regime in Sweden remains in a state of transition and development. Some issues like pricing in particular markets and access to infrastructure have been resolved. Other issues remain to be sorted out by regulatory and legal trial and error. Competition has developed, but to an extent limited by the reality of the Post's market dominance and its market performance. The universal postal system remains intact. The postal system has been re-regulated, in ways that appear problematic for the Post. This will likely be a transitory phenomenon, however, since the regulatory regime is a reasonably soft and non-intrusive one. But, as Peter Andersson and

Mats Bladh have argued, liberalization of the market was only the first step in a process of creating a competitive postal market.

PERFORMANCE

Sweden Post's market performance and results have not been affected negatively by liberalization. Its competitors have attained perhaps 4–5 per cent of the market, and its profits dropped for a period after liberalization as it adjusted to the new competitive reality. Nonetheless, the Post is profitable, its quality of service remains high, and it is still capable of carrying out its universal postal responsibilities. The retail and bill-paying sector remains problematic, as in most other countries. But this is a problem that the government has responsibility over and that it will have to sort out.

The General Picture

A number of factors threatened the growth of the Post's volumes in Sweden over the last decade. These included the increased presence of international operators, technological competition in the form of faxes, e-mails, ATMs, and so on, liberalization and deregulation, and certain growing pains from the introduction of its new letter network.[58] The letter market stagnated after the early 1990s, with faxes taking up to 25 per cent of domestic mail and 50 per cent of the international market. Competitors like City Mail took away business volumes particularly in the larger urban markets, where they were very price-competitive. Nonetheless, a buoyant economy and the broad expansion of the communications market have sustained the postal market. As Table 2 indicates, postal volumes have continued to grow even in an uncertain postal market. Indeed, volumes grew faster in the five years after liberalization (23 per cent) than in the five years previous to it (16 per cent). This was driven considerably by the expansion in the non-letters areas. The revenue picture was not quite as flush, partially owing to a change in the mix of volumes (with a greater proportion of non-letter volumes) and the price sensitivity that came with increased competition. Revenues grew by over 40 per cent from 1988 to 1993 but by only 13 per cent in 1993–98. Revenue growth was flat in 1994–96 but has rebounded somewhat recently – substantially because of the large price increase in 1996.

The profit picture reflected this situation on the revenue side. The Post was always a profitable operation as a crown corporation, and neither corporatization nor liberalization has changed this. However, profits declined seriously in 1995 and 1996, after the liberalization

Table 2
Post performance

	1987	1988	1993	1994	1995	1996	1997	1998
Revenues (billions SEK)	13.0	15.4	21.6	21.6	22.3	22.7	23.4	24.4
Profit (millions of SEK)	594	954	1363	1401	831	570	1,055	1,075
After-tax	594	945	1367	1043	454	363	726	752
Profit Margin (%)	4.6	6.2	6.3	6.5	3.7	2.5	4.5	4.4
ROE (%)	21.7	30.1	13.4	46.0	20.7	12.6	21.0	16.9
ROC (%)	22.6	27.9	11.6	15.6	11.1	7.9	11.1	14.7
Personnel (000s – average)	54	54.8	50.2	46.9	46.1	45.1	42.9	42.1
% full-time				79	72	72	72	71
Capital Investment (MSEK*)	972	673	917	978	1,683	1,707	1,186	971
Productivity (% change)	3.6	1.2	3.0	7.0	–1.2	–1.2	2.4	0.5
Mail Items (billions)	3.68	3.96	4.53	4.89	5.01	5.4	5.16	5.57
On-time Delivery (%)		92	96				97.1	97.3
Post Offices	2,128	2,110	1,473	1,341	1,289	1,177	1,075	1,019
Service Points		94	419	537	564	640	720	781

* Millions of Swedish crowns.

Source: Sweden Post, *Annual Reports*, assorted years. Derived from their annuel ten-year reviews.

process took hold. This decline also reflected the pension payments that increased in the wake of a decrease in staff numbers. Profits fell to SEK570 million in 1996 (SEK363 million after tax). The Post's profit margin was a tiny 2.5 per cent and the return on capital employed fell to 7.9 per cent. Given the revenue levels, the state was expecting a level of profits in the SEK1-billion area at least. The profit picture has subsequently bounced back. Competition and price-cutting were mitigated by system rationalization and employment cuts. Profits rose back over the SEK1 billion, and the Post attributed this improvement to its rationalization efforts over the decade.[59] The Post's letter division remains its profit centre – where it attains an 8 per cent return. This reflects the large price increase of 1996. The GIRO and counters sectors have declined and parcels – while improving substantially – remain at a negative rate of return.

Prices

One of liberalization's greatest impacts has been on postal pricing. There have been three interesting developments. The first was the introduction of the VAT (12 per cent in 1994 and 25 per cent in 1995), which created a level playing field. The second was the creation of pricing flexibility for Post letters, within a rate cap. Third, the Post has attempted to meet competition through differential pricing. Generally speaking, liberalization has resulted in a greater degree of price differentiation, with prices rising in some areas (such as household letters) and falling in others (such as bulk mail). This has shaken although not destroyed the traditional universal pricing system.

The Post's first impulse in meeting competition was to set prices strategically to meet the competition's price challenge (the Post had and maintains a distinct quality advantage). It restructured its prices and offered bulk discounting, and it introduced differential prices to adjust local prices to costs. This twin strategy met the Post's major competition in computer-generated business mail and competition at the local level. However, it was challenged by the Post's competitors. As seen earlier, the regulator and the courts established certain principles and policy rules in resolving these challenges. The Market Court has allowed the Post to differentiate prices under certain conditions. Generally, the principle has been established that prices must reflect costs. The Post cannot use discounts, predatory pricing, and cross-subsidization to eliminate competition. And any price differentiation in a particular market has to be based on an open agreement and its terms and conditions offered to all other equivalent markets.

While bulk- and second-class mail prices have fallen, the price for standard letters has increased. Notwithstanding the price cap, the price of a twenty-gram letter rose from SEK2,90 in 1993 to 3,70 in 1995, 3,85 in 1996, and 5,00 in March 1997. The 30 per cent rise in 1997 was extremely controversial. The state had constructed the price-cap formula in a way that allowed the Post to raise the letter-mail rate substantially while remaining within the price cap. It did this by offsetting or balancing the rise in letter-mail rates by a 3 per cent cut in the rate offered on discount stamps and by assigning 90 per cent of the value of the price increases to the latter initiative. It thus managed to introduce a total package that was within that allowed by the price-cap formula. To outside observers, the policy appeared to involve a manipulation of the price-cap formula that undermined the spirit of the approach if not its letter. But it was allowed under the law. The state moved quickly after this incident to reconstruct the price-cap formula to disallow this sort of result in the future.

The Post's view has been that all of these changes have been revenue-neutral. Customers who do bulk and pre-sort mailing receive lower prices. Prices have risen for longer distances and more expensive mail. The Post's competitors are free to set their tariffs without any restrictions, and the Post has sought price flexibility in its own terms as well. This seems to defy the principle of universal pricing, although it should be recalled that the practice predated liberalization and exists in many postal systems around the world. Generally, the new Swedish system has seen the principle of cost-based pricing pushed further along than in most systems in the world. This is a principle that the EC postal directive has encouraged if not demanded. The relationship between cost-based pricing and the traditional idea of universal pricing remains to be resolved.

Rationalization

The Post attributes its recent profit success to system rationalization and employment cuts. It has made a consistently high level of capital investment in the 1990s – over SEK6 billion in the period 1994–98. This has increased mechanization, raised the presence of information technology, and allowed for system rationalization. A new letter network is now in place – at the cost of SEK1.8 billion. The productivity improvement record has been spotty but has improved recently – as indicated in the table above.

The average level of employment at Sweden Post has been cut by 13,000 over the last decade, which represents about 24 per cent of the workforce. The greater part of this occurred after liberalization (over 60 per cent), during which time the proportion of full-time employment fell to 72 per cent. This decline also reflects the overall decline in the economy, the effort to reduce the government debt, and the general falling off of transactions at postal counters. But the fact is that reduction of employment levels has been part and parcel of the Post's competitive strategy in dealing with deregulation, liberalization, and internationalization. The postal union, SEKO, has not been totally positive about the loss of jobs but has accepted it mainly because of the broad popular or public support given to these changes. Moreover, employment decline has been the broad picture in most sectors of the economy, including the postal sector. SEKO estimates that one-third of those who lost their postal jobs took early retirement pensions, another one third found new jobs, and a final one-third were left empty-handed.[60]

Quality

One of the most profound results of liberalization of the Swedish postal market has been its impact on the quality of service. It had been widely feared in postal circles that a competitive postal market would see postal operators cutting corners to remain competitive, even to the extent of undermining the universal service.

There is general agreement, though, that the quality of service offered by the Post has never been so high and is one of the best in Europe.[61] As the table above indicates, the rate of on-time (next day) delivery of first-class letters has climbed to above 97 per cent. With respect to the delivery of business parcels, 91 per cent are delivered the next business day. IPC surveys suggest that Sweden ranks first in Europe with regard to both inward- and outward-bound delivery of letters.[62]

The Post has devised an index to measure the satisfaction of its customers. This index measures reliability, speed of service, attitude and service mindedness, handling of grievances and complaints, and so on. This index has rated customer satisfaction reasonably high and rising – although it dipped for a time around the introduction of the new letters network.[63]

The Network and Banking

Like many postal regimes around the world, the Post's retail network has struggled over the last decades. This struggle pre dates liberalization although the latter has placed the problem under increased scrutiny. The Postal Services Act declares that the postal-service network is part of the universal postal system, although it is silent on how this objective is to be met. This reflects the historical importance of the Post's role in the payments network, particularly in rural areas. Ultimately, then, this is a government responsibility and the problem will require a government solution.

Neither the Postal Services Act nor the Agreement requires the Post to maintain a certain fixed number of service outlets of either a public or private character. There has been a rebalancing of the mix between traditional post offices and alternate retail points in stores and franchises. This issue generated political controversy at its start. But this has passed, with the public adapting to and enjoying the flexibility in hours and access provided by the mixed system. As the table above indicates, the number of post offices was cut in half between 1987 and 1998, from over 2,000 to just over 1,000 post offices. The greater part of this decline predates liberalization. The number of alternate-service points has grown from below 100 in 1988 to almost 800 in 1998. There has been a modest decline of 100 total outlets in the period from 1993 to 1998 (5 per cent).

Post offices have traditionally offered both postal and financial services but have added insurance, stationary, office supplies, and gift items as a way of maintaining revenues. This has not been sufficient to stem the tide of the decline in counter transactions. Swedes have been switching their bill-paying habits to automatic deductions. With respect to financial payments, there has been a 75 per cent decline in transactions since 1979. A further 20 per cent decline in counter services is anticipated in the next few years.[64]

The net result of these developments is that the counters network runs at a substantial loss – over SEK1 billion in 1997–98. The Agreement with the state provides the Post with SEK200 million to maintain this part of the system. However, a MIEC study suggests that it costs the Post over SEK400 million to maintain the system in its present form.[65] A government study of this situation is currently being circulated among the postal players, and a number of ideas are being mooted. These include merging the system with a bank on the one end, cutting rural-payment services from daily to a few times a month on the other, and getting out of financial services altogether. The latter would represent a substantial and possibly controversial move, since the Post has traditionally provided a payment service in all areas – including a mobile counter service by rural postmen.

The future of the Post Girot was up in the air for a long time, since it was not making sufficient money. There were developments in this area, including the Post's collaboration with Nordbanken in 1996 to create a Post Office Savings Bank. But the Post felt that it was not obtaining full coverage for the costs of its undertakings on behalf of Nordbanken.[66] The Post Girot is the leader in the Swedish payment market, accounting for almost half of the transactions. But the trend to paperless transactions has undermined the value of this market position. The Future of Post Girot was discussed in a recent budget bill, where the authority to decide on its future was delegated to the government. There were three options considered: making it into a bank, selling it, and selling some part of it. In the event, the government has decided to sell it. This makes the future of the counters network even more uncertain, since the Post seems anxious to get out of banking and financial activities altogether.

Diversification and Internationalization

The Postal Services Act and the Agreement give the Post a considerable amount of flexibility to diversify and to partner, in order to increase revenues and profits sufficiently to allow it to maintain the universal service. On the regulation side, there is little in the Postal Services Act or the Agreement to inhibit the Post. On the shareholder side, the state can limit the Post's activity with respect to non-core activities, if that is its wish. The case of the DPAG takeover of ASG – the trucking arm of the Swedish state railroad – is a modest case in point.

As noted earlier, there has been some diversification of activity at the retail level, but this has been fairly modest. The Post's major diversification activity has been in the parcels and logistics area. The Post segmented the parcels operation into a separate division, and its performance moved into the black and attained a higher level of quality. Sweden Post Logistics is one of the three biggest goods carriers in Sweden and Sweden Post Transport is the biggest haulage operator. Logistics is seen by the Post to be its main growth area, particularly tied to e-commerce and warehousing.[67]

This initiative has had an international character, particularly since the Post has concluded that "with the advance of deregulation and the intensification of competition, particularly in Sweden, Sweden Post appears too small for its long term survival on its own."[68] On the one hand, the Post has made cautious forays into the Baltics, Poland, and northwest Russia.[69] It purchased In Time, an Estonian transportation company situated in Tallin. It owns 91 per cent of the Polish company Masterlink Express z.o.o, a national door-to-door delivery company. It has entered into a joint venture with Latvia Post to develop Bizpak-service (an express service of small parcels and packages to the business community). At the same time, it has entered into a joint business venture with the other Nordic Posts to protect and expand their parcels markets collectively. This development was a long time in the making, a delay caused in part by the need for Sweden Post to work through the consequences of the DPAG takeover of ASG. However, the collaborative partnership came on stream in 2000.[70] Sweden Post has recently entered into a cooperative regional arrangement with Post Danmark to offer one-step service to business clients on either side of the Oresund Bridge.

Finally, Sweden Post has been aggressive in the electronic area, which it sees as its biggest long-term threat. It has assigned an e-mail address to all the citizens of Sweden and created one of the most visited electronic market sites in Europe – Torget. Sweden Post has partnered with NET delivery, EDS, and Checkfree to develop Scandinavia's first online postal service for e-business – including electronic-document exchange and bill payment.[71]

HIGHLIGHTS OF THE SWEDISH CASE

What can one learn from the Swedish case? What interest does its experience and market approach hold for policy makers?

Perhaps the most compelling conclusion that can be drawn from this case is that it appears to be possible to maintain a universal postal system of reasonably high quality in a liberalized, competitive postal environment. There is no reserved area assigned to the Swedish postal operator that has this responsibility. Indeed, formally speaking, it is the Swedish state itself that has ultimate, formal authority for the universal system. There is a good case to be made for this approach. The maintenance of the universal system is a public policy matter – not one that is haphazardly assigned to a traditional service provider. The Swedish case makes this point clearly. The state can determine how it chooses to see through its universal-service responsibility although, admittedly, it does not have many options. Nonetheless, by contracting out this goal in its Agreement with the Post, the state is forced to make clear what are the objectives that comprise the universal system and what are the terms it is willing to "pay" to guarantee the attainment of these objectives.

This point is well illustrated in the case of the counters or payments network. Unlike most other postal regimes, the postal legislation declares that this network is part of the universal postal system – making explicit what is left implicit in most other postal regimes. At the start, the state contracted to have the Post provide the counter service, with compensation for particular uneconomic areas. This compensation package was formulated on the basis of a quantitative assessment of the real costs of the counters system. This was an unusual if not unique step, but also a vitally important one, which allowed the state to devise a rational policy. A few years later, this feature of the agreement has come under strain, for the counters network is losing considerable amounts of money. What is critical is that it is the state that is now on the spot – not the Post or any postal operator. The state will have to determine – after consultation, analysis, and discussion – what kind of counters service Sweden can expect, and at what cost to the Swedish taxpayer.

This case should not be taken as a sign that the universal service in Sweden has foundered under liberalization. Swedish postal standards are more or less of the same character as they were pre-liberalization and pre-corporatization. Prices remain reasonably low by European standards, the quality of the service is higher than ever, and the main features of the universal service remain in place. These standards and expectations are now specified and a regulatory process oversees their maintenance.

The maintenance of the universal system reflects the fact that Sweden Post – assigned the universal-service obligation by the state – continues to be profitable and have the capacity to maintain the universal system. This is the contingent factor in the model. It cannot be assumed that Sweden Post (or another operators(s)) will have this capacity forever. The Post remains the dominant player in the competitive market and, notwithstanding the rise of City Mail and others, its market share remains high. If the Post's economic performance should founder, then the model would be placed under strain. What would the state do if no postal operator were sufficiently healthy to carry the universal-service obligation? This is what led the state to consider compensation agreements, as mooted by the EC. It is quite interesting that there is little to no support for the idea of a compensation fund propping up the Post's capacity to deliver the universal service. Indeed, the Post itself is not favourable to the idea. There is general agreement that the best way to maintain the Post's (or another's) capacity is to allow it (or others) to develop into healthy economic organizations in the market. The Post has a symbiotic relationship with the universal-service issue in this regard. On the one hand, the Post's success is intimately related to the quality of its service. On the other hand, its ability to promise a universal service at low cost is an integral part of its quality standard or promises.

This raises two points: the competition issue and the pricing issue. The Swedish experience demonstrates, as in Finland, that liberalization does not necessarily or automatically result in the creation of a competitive market. This is especially the case in the Swedish postal market, where there is a historically dominant player with a de facto monopoly and financial and technological superiority in functioning in a relatively small market. The liberalization regime, ironically, has required significant regulatory and legal input into the creation of a competitive market. Competition in turn put the Post on the spot, and it responded to competition with an aggressive pricing strategy. This, too, required considerable regulatory and legal intervention to create a fair and fluid postal-pricing system. Neither the competition nor the pricing issues – not to mention infrastructure issues – are totally resolved. What these issues demonstrate is the inevitability of regulatory interventions to make liberalization work.

Thus, Sweden is another example of how the postal-reform process has led to the re-regulation of the postal market. Like its Finnish counterpart, the Swedish regulatory model is simple and straightforward. The objectives of the regime are spelled out in the Postal Services Act and the Ordinance, which are short and clear documents. These are implemented through a licensing system, which is also simple and straightforward and which, through the Agreement with the Post, lays out how the objectives of the regime are to be attained. Finally, a third-party regulatory agency monitors postal performance against these public standards and expectations.

This model has been placed under greater strain than the Finnish one, because of the development of actual competition. The regulatory authorities – along with the competition and legal authorities –

have been far more active than might have been expected in 1994 when the model was mooted. Indeed, at first blush, the degree of intrusions on the Post might even suggest that it had actually enjoyed more freedom and autonomy pre-1994! However, this may simply reflect the growing pains of the transition to this new regime. The authorities predict that, once the rules of the market game have been established, the model will unfold on automatic pilot. If that turns out to be the case, then the "soft" or passive regulatory model that was anticipated may very well come to pass.

A second feature of this strain is the pricing one. After the legal and court dust has settled, there is something that appears to look like a differentiated pricing system in place. To the extent that the pricing model moves increasingly to a cost-based one, then the notion of a universal price system (in letters) may weaken or be undermined. The Swedish domestic market is a relatively small one, such that the postal costs outside urban areas are not particularly high (indeed, it is suggested by some authorities that they are actually lower than in the cities). A cost-based model may have less consequence in Sweden than in other countries.

The regulatory dimension of the Swedish postal regime has been insulated from political intrusion. This reflects the Swedish tradition of creating a clear and broad divide between the two; it is illegal to make political intrusions into regulatory matters. The ownership dimension remains an open question. There has not been any particular shareholder-Post tension to note, although circumstances have not put this relationship under particular pressure. The Post has been making profits and the state is not expecting dividends at this time, given that it assigned to the Post responsibility for both funded and unfunded pension liabilities. Yet the ASG case demonstrated that there are political limits to the Post's commercial freedom and that the state determines public postal policy at the highest level. There has been an ongoing closeness between the Post and the government, as a result of the players involved on each side. The 30 per cent price increase, the Post's strategic response to City Mail, and the bulk-mailing decisions were dubious policy decisions that reflected, perhaps, a too comfortable relationship between the shareholder and senior management. These cases highlighted the ongoing awkwardness of the state owning a particular player in a competitive market. There is a sense that the regulatory and shareholding responsibilities should be placed in different ministries to create some policy tension. The appointment of Lennart Grabe as Post CEO should create a healthier day-to-day distance between the ministry and the Post.

The apparent political ease of postal reform in Sweden reflects a number of economic and political factors that other countries might not enjoy. On the one hand, the relative isolation and size of the Swedish market means that liberalization, in the first instance, will not have the same sort of competitive consequences as in more attractive and central markets. On the other hand, Swedish politics is based on a consensual approach to policy making, in which any group that can create a "roadblock" to change is consulted and is involved in the decision-making process. This minimized the extent to which major postal-policy changes were disruptive or created operational problems for the new postal model. It should not be surprising, then, that the regime's growing pains have not been on the social (universal-service) side but on the economics (competitive) side. The Swedish postal system also had a far greater liberal inheritance – particularly the weak postal monopoly – than many other countries, which accelerated and eased the postal-reform process.

An important unanswered question is whether the Swedish model has any significance, or long-term chance for survival, given the technological and international challenges ahead. Postal authorities recognize the need to partner and to internationalize, as demonstrated in the cross-Nordic postal-parcel initiative. However, this initiative was fairly difficult to get off the ground – demonstrating how challenging it is to create cross-national commercial agreements. More important, though, the entire Nordic market is only twenty million people and a greater degree of internationalization will be required if the Post is to maintain the capacity to provide the universal service in the face of technological, product, and international competition. That said, the Swedish market model is an elegant and intelligent regime that has created the basis for forward- and outward-looking policy making.

5 New Zealand

New Zealand is the latest country to have embraced the market model, having deregulated its postal market in 1998. This was the culmination of a series of steps that had seen a progressive liberalization process over the previous decade. The Scandinavian countries and New Zealand, then, comprise a group of nations that have embraced the market approach to dealing with contemporary postal challenges. But the rationales for adopting this approach have been different in these two cases. The policy authorities in Sweden and Finland were concerned primarily about their Posts' capacity to survive in an increasingly international market that is informed by an increasing degree of technological and product competition. These factors certainly gave pause to policy makers in New Zealand. However, the primary driver of postal deregulation was the condition of its domestic economy and the political ambition to make its Post an efficient and productive contributor to the national economy.

The New Zealand postal case is one of the most interesting and compelling examples of progressive postal policy. New Zealand has been one of the "pioneers" in postal commercialization and progressive change, according to Jim Campbell, "the first country to address the full implications of new technologies for postal policy."[1] New Zealand (or NZ Post, as it is commonly known) is a highly successful and well-run company.[2] It is New Zealand's twenty-ninth largest firm (in terms of turnover) and its fifth-largest employer. It has been assigned numerous honours by the Deloitte/Management magazine, including government enterprise of the year, company of the year, and best corporate-strategy awards.

New Zealand offers an excellent case study of how a well-considered postal regime can balance a competitive and efficient postal market with the maintenance of the universal service – without privatization of the national Post. The Post itself (and, now, its competitors) function within one of the clearest and best-articulated postal regulatory environments in the world. This regime created a momentum for postal deregulation, which saw the construction of a *formalized* balance between the commercialization of the Post and the maintenance of universal postal goals. The prospect of deregulation loomed constantly since the late 1980s, so the Post had prepared itself for the introduction of the deregulation that arrived inevitably in April 1998. For over a decade, the Post developed a greater customer focus, introduced new products and services, improved its network, increased its efficiency, and controlled and reduced its prices. It was thus price, product and service competitive when deregulation arrived. Many of these initiatives were ambitious and required aggressive tactics to implement them. This often "resulted in difficult and unpopular decisions."[3] But the postal regime allowed the Post's commercialization policies to be pursued without oppressive, detailed, or ongoing government inhibition or interference. The Post remains profitable even as it maintains universal-service obligations, confronts considerable letters, parcels, and technological competition, and endures the government's lack of enthusiasm for diversification beyond the postal core. Of all the Posts examined in this study, New Zealand Post remains perhaps the most buoyant and optimistic about the future of the letter, and it displays a real customer focus in its strategic thinking.

The postal-reform experience in New Zealand was driven by domestic considerations more than by fear of technological and international change. This generalization is partially overstated, since New Zealand's place in the world economy was an "international" factor in the many policy changes that took place in New Zealand in the late 1980s. Moreover, New Zealand is – like countries in Scandinavia – intrigued by the marvels of the new technologies and has become a highly wired society. At bottom, though, New Zealand is isolated physically and geographically compared to the other countries in this study, and it comprises a much smaller market. Thus, the presence of, say, a TPG, a DPWN, or a FedEx or alternative products was not as pressing as in European or North American countries. More important, though, the postal-reform experience in New Zealand was driven by a wider policy agenda and executed within a particular political process. This is what has given the new postal regime its particular New Zealand character.

The postal-reform story begins at the end of the Keynesian post-war era, which saw the collapse of the old New Zealand economic model in the early 1980s. This model had combined protection of the domestic market, a highly focused export strategy, and the construction of the welfare state.[4] The protected domestic economy was insufficiently robust to absorb the economic consequences of the weakening of world trade that accompanied the end of the post-war era. In the process, New Zealand fell from fifth to twentieth place in world GDP per capita. Its economy was marked by low growth, high inflation, and increasing unemployment. This translated into an enormous public debt, which – by 1984 – was the largest in New Zealand's history. The state sector in New Zealand was quite substantial – comprising 31 per cent of employment and 40 per cent of GDP.[5] Within the public sector, the state-enterprise sector was formidable, comprising about 12 per cent of GDP and 20 per cent of gross investment. But state enterprises contributed little to nothing financially to the state, and their contribution to the economy was insubstantial. In short, they were part of the problem within the weakening New Zealand economy.[6]

The election of a Labour government in 1984 brought an economic revolution to New Zealand. The previous economic policy orthodoxy was in shambles, both practically and in terms of legitimacy. A new orthodoxy was in the wings, ready to replace it.[7] This economic policy approach had been articulated in a book by the incoming minister of finance, Roger Douglas, "There's Got to be a Better Way." What subsequently became known as "Rogernomics" was formulated and executed by the formidable troika of Roger Douglas, Richard Prebble and David Caygill and their officials in the Treasury. They introduced free trade, deregulated the labour and financial markets, focused monetary policy on price stability, lifted restrictions on foreign investment, and initiated radical reform of the state-enterprise sector.[8] Any state activity with a potentially commercial function was corporatized and many were privatized. From 1986 to 1999, the government sold thirty-four assets worth NZ$19 billion (all currency references in this chapter are in New Zealand dollars) – including NZ Steel, Air New Zealand, the Bank of New Zealand, NZ Rail, and Telecom.

Such was the broad political economic context for postal reform. The momentum of a larger state-enterprise reform agenda carried along postal reform, which in turn was a part of an even wider economic-reform agenda. This eased the political problems associated with postal reform. It removed the Post from the political spotlight or particular scrutiny, since the Post was being treated no differently than a number of other enterprises and sectors. In this way, postal reform has been shaped over the last fifteen years by two broad political agendas that shaped the policy discourse around it. In the late 1980s and early 1990s, the government wanted the state-enterprise sector in general, and the Post in particular, to increase efficiency and productivity and make a contribution to the health of the New Zealand economy. This orientation shaped postal-policy discussion and action for a decade. More recently, the election of the National government shifted the ideological terrain to deregulation, which has swept along postal reform to the present.

The currency crisis in 1984 and the stock market crash of October 1987 produced a sense of economic crisis and urgency that encouraged new policy thinking and the suspension of old beliefs. As suggested above, there was a set of ideas and a policy package ready to use, which filled the void created by the public's loss of faith in the old New Zealand model. There were few effective political constraints on, forces against, or alternatives to the postal-reform agenda for fifteen years. For example, the economic crises of the 1980s placed the unions – traditional opponents of postal reform – in a difficult and weakened position, at a time when public support for unions was waning. The unions had little to no political leverage or room to criticize, for it was a Labour government that had introduced the reform package. Indeed, Labour won a second term in August 1987. It ruled consecutively from 1984 to 1990, during which time the main parameters of the reform agenda were put into place. This agenda was filled in and extended by the National government until the election of the Helen Clark minority government (Labour) in 1999.

These governments were totally committed to the reform approach. They made their objectives clear to all those who would participate in, or be affected by, these changes. There was no doubt about the direction that the state wanted the Post to move. Given this commitment, New Zealand's parliamentary (unitary) system of government allowed fast, forceful action – using what came to be termed a blitzkrieg approach. This allowed far-reaching action to be pulled off more quickly than in cooperative and consensual systems (in real contrast to the situation in Australia).[9] The Post itself quickly came to share the government's orientation. It accepted the government's desire to liberalize and deregulate, because it wanted more autonomy and the opportunity to become a more commercialized operation. While there were often tense moments, the Post and the government were both committed to the broad parameters of postal reform.

In sum, the reform of the Post in New Zealand was part of a larger economic-policy agenda in the late 1980s and early 1990s. This saw the state-enterprise sector commercialized and corporatized, in an effort to improve the efficiency, productivity, and strength of the New Zealand economy. The agenda was sustained politically for a fifteen-year period without serious detours and roadblocks. This scenario was reinforced by New Zealand's relative isolation. The upshot was that, by April 1998, the postal sector was completely deregulated and competition began to emerge in the letters market. New Zealand Post had prepared itself for deregulation, so that by the twenty-first century it was able to remain profitable in a competitive postal market and carry out the universal-service obligations. As the new millennium began, though, there was some evidence that it would be a real challenge for NZ Post to remain profitable in a deregulated environment in which the letters market had become static.

HISTORY

New Zealand's first Post Office was established in Russell in 1840. A Post Office Department was established in 1858, which later merged with the Telegraph Department in 1880 to become a PTT operation. The Post remained part of the government bureaucracy for the next century, responsible to a political postmaster general. It functioned with a highly centralized chain of command, marked by hierarchical decision making within the department. While unionism came to New Zealand in 1938, the Post Office Act recognized the postal union in 1890. The department wanted to deal with only one representative of workers and to have a strike-free environment. The leadership of the postal union was thus central to the decision-making process in most areas, including the appointment of the postmaster general. Political and social concerns and objectives rather than commercial ones dominated the postal world. The retail network was seriously and expensively overextended, in order to create a ubiquitous postal (political) presence. The Post Office was periodically used as an employment agency and shock absorber for changes in the labour market. Post jobs were for life, which created a disincentive for capital expenditure and mechanization. In any case, there was little capital expenditure directed to the Post, since modernization initiatives focused on the telecom side of the operation. As a result, the Post had no modern plants and its operations were archaic. It provided poor service and responded slowly to customer and market needs. Its poor market performance was obscured by the fact that the PTT operation as a whole was in the black. The Telecom in effect cross-subsidized the Post. This hid its weaknesses and undermined the case for price increases, which were politically difficult to execute (there were some

increases in the 1984–87 period prior to corporatization). The fact
was that postal prices would have to have been increased by 30 per
cent in order for the Post to balance its books. When the economy
weakened in the mid-1980s, the Post's financial situation became dire.
It lost $24 million in 1985–86 and $38 million in 1986–87, and it was
forecast to lose $50 million, in 1987–88. Even worse, the government
itself seemed incapable of controlling the Post's unpredictable spending and employment commitments, even as it attempted to control
overall spending in the mid-1980s.[10]

The government addressed the Post's immediate financial situation
in a short-term manner by increasing the price of a stamp from twenty-
five to thirty cents in 1985. In February 1986 this was increased to
40 cents, which included the introduction of a 10 per cent goods and
services tax (GST). The government accepted the political heat that
was generated by the price increases. It initiated a postal review in
September 1985, headed by Roy Mason (CEO of NZ Motor Corporation) and Michael Morris (Chairman of KPMG Peat Marwick). Five
months later, the Mason-Morris report catalogued a series of problems:
the Post's organizational structure was inappropriate, it suffered from
overstaffing and a closed shop, its retail network was three times larger
than that of the biggest bank, its plants were plagued by outdated
equipment, it had only ten accountants but thousands of engineers,
and the organization lacked basic business-management systems. It
recommended that the Post, telecom, and banking be established as
three separate businesses, each with a board of directors comprised
of experienced business people with authority to set prices and determine basic policies.[11] The government received the report and asked
Mason to chair Telecom and Morris to chair the Post.

In the interim, Finance Minister Roger Douglas had made his
famous Economic Statement of 12 December 1985, which outlined
the government's economic-reform program. One of the statement's
most crucial elements related to the state-enterprise sector: "Government trading activities would be corporatized using the existing institutional governance structure provided by the Companies Act and the
Commerce Act ... government companies would become limited liability companies governed by the general laws that apply to all other
companies."[12] This strategic-policy orientation set the framework for
the State-Owned Enterprise (SOE) Act (December 1986), which aimed
to enhance the economic performance of the state's business enterprises while distancing political considerations from management
decisions. The act created nine state-owned corporations, each of
which would be governed by the specific and overarching legal framework for corporatization that was created by the Act. The SOEs would

function under the corporate legal system, meaning that they would function like a typical corporation, within a commercial framework with commercial freedom. The act directed the soes to be run as a business and to be as profitable and efficient as businesses in the private sector. The act also directed the soes to be good employers and to have a sense of community and social responsibility.[13]

While this general framework would govern all the soes, each of them would be obliged to write a Statement of Corporate Intent. The sci outlined the objectives of each soe, the nature and scope of its activities, the financial expectations, targets, and dividends expected by the government, the compensation to be paid for any non-commercial activities that it would be asked to pursue, and a number of other matters. The sci would be negotiated by each soe with the government and would be tabled in Parliament. Each soe would be free to act as it wished, within the general framework set by the act and the specific expectations set by the sci.

The formal separation of the Post from government took place with the Postal Services Act of 1987 (the one-year delay will be explained below). The main features and parameters of the Post were set in the soe Act and the sci. The Post's existence as a limited-liability company was initiated under ordinary company law. The Postal Services Act also established the Post's exclusive privilege or reserve area (500 grams or $1.75 – which was 4.5 times the price of a regular stamp).

The Labour government was re-elected in August 1987, and the reform process continued to unfold. It announced in October 1987 that 432 uneconomic post offices would close. Government officials later recommended that the postal monopoly should be repealed, or that the government should at least initiate a drastic reduction in the Post's monopoly.[14] nz Post opposed deregulation at this time,[15] but the government announced its intention in July 1988 to abolish the Post's monopoly and to privatize the Post. In anticipation of deregulation, the government allowed the Post to close down one-third of its post offices, to increase its annual fee for rural delivery, and to make a huge investment in updating its plant and equipment. This was an important moment symbolically, since it signalled the passing of the Post into the modern age and led to enormous changes in its retail operations.[16] On the other hand a huge public outcry about these changes resulted in the creation of a parliamentary enquiry into the postal situation. This political reaction had two important consequences.

First, the public's concerns that the universal postal system was unravelling resulted in the creation of the Deed of Understanding. This was a social contract between the Post and the government, which formalized the service obligations that the Post accepted in return for being granted a protected area in the postal market. The DOU was thus the political arm of the legal protection that the Post continued to receive – and comprised a veritable *quid pro quo*.[17] The DOU set out the basic ingredients of the Post's universal-service obligations, including six-day delivery, universal letter pricing (under a price-cap system), universal service, and the maintenance of a minimum number of retail outlets. The Post's delivery record would be independently surveyed and the results published in the Post's annual report. The DOU provided postal access to competitors.

Second, the public's reaction to postal modernization led the government to pull back from its earlier decision to privatize the Post. Instead, it introduced a program of staged deregulation. The Postal Services Act of 1990 lowered the exclusive-privilege area from 500 grams to 200 grams, and lowered the price limit in a series of steps: to $1.35 on 30 November 1990, $1 the following year, and to 80 cents thereafter. Given that the price of a first-class system had increased from 40 to 45 cents in 1991, the protection provided to the Post was becoming increasingly slight. The Act also opened the postal market to competition in a number of areas, including outgoing international mail and addressed ad mail above the legal thresholds.

There were on-again, off-again discussions, decisions, delays, and changes in policy regarding full postal deregulation over much of the 1990s. The government initiated another review process in April 1991. Twenty months later the resulting report proposed full deregulation. But a government decision was put off again until after the 1993 election. At this time, the National government pledged that it did not intend to privatize the Post. After the election, it announced its intention to abolish the monopoly. This intention was not pursued until April 1997, by the National/NZ First coalition. Each of the government parties found the political timing to be propitious, and an announcement was made in short order.[18] The Postal Services Bill of 1997 abolished the postal monopoly and established the parameters of a new competitive postal market. A market framework provided competitors with access to the Post's network at fair and reasonable prices. The law also extended rights and obligations to postal operators to maintain the integrity of the postal system. The legislation required the Post to offer access to competitors.

The government renewed the DOU in February 1998, which complemented the new deregulatory regime established by the Postal Services Act. The DOU continued the Post's social obligations regarding the network, the frequency and extent of delivery, and customer and competitor access to the system. In a policy departure, the new DOU established a *maximum* letter pricing approach, as opposed to a universal pricing one. In the DOU, the Post agreed to not raise the standard letter price above 45 cents, and to not impose a surcharge on rural delivery. Indeed, the present price (40 cents) is far below the price cap. In addition, the Postal Services (Information Disclosure) Regulations laid out how competition would be facilitated and developed within the postal-services market. A document entitled "Obligations and Rights of Postal Operators" explains how a deregulated postal market should work.

STATUTORY ENVIRONMENT

The statutory environment in New Zealand for the postal market is exemplary, perhaps the best in the world. New Zealand authorities made tough but excellent and clear-headed decisions at the front end of the reform process. They constructed a policy infrastructure for state enterprises that was thorough and well considered and more or less got all the pieces right. The regulatory regime is well organized and clearly articulated. The state's objectives and public purposes are expressed and articulated through this framework. There is a clean split between ownership and regulation functions. Responsibilities are well specified and assigned concretely to institutions and actors who have sufficient authority and postal intelligence to carry out their responsibilities. This is not to suggest that there are no tensions or contradictions that are generated or arise within the system. As will be seen below, the Post and the government disagree or come into conflict from time to time. The particular character of the regime does not cause these tensions or conflict, unless they arise as a matter of policy difference that requires a political decision or solution. This is how any well-constructed regime should work, if the government owns the Post or enterprise. In this section, we outline the basic parameters and principles of the New Zealand postal regime. The following section presents the major actors in the regime and illustrates how these players interact when the regime is in operation.

As noted in the historical presentation, the basic parameters of the postal regime are established by the SOE Act, which applies to all the state enterprises listed under the act – including the Post.[19] The act separates ownership and regulation clearly and strongly and establishes principles for clarity of objective and accountability for SOE actions.

Ownership

Roger Douglas's Economic Statement of December 1985 laid out a set of principles for SOEs, which were later put into legislative form in the SOE Act. The statement directed the government to tease out the non-commercial objectives from the SOEs' operations, in order to place the SOEs on a corporatized and commercial footing and orientation. The advantages (and disadvantages) of being a state-owned company were to be eliminated. State-enterprise managers would be directed to run the SOEs as a successful business. The enterprises would be restructured and guided by boards, whose members would be recruited from the private sector. The boards would set objectives jointly with the government and would be held accountable for the performance of the enterprises.

The SOE Act distanced the commercial management of state enterprises from the political control of government. The state would continue to own the Post, and would have key authoritative power in naming board members and articulating policy objectives in a number of ways. But Section 4 of the SOE Act placed the SOEs on a commercial footing and established a number of principles for their operation. The primary principle in this context was that the SOE was directed to act like a private-sector firm. It was directed to make a profit, to repay any loans that it had with the government, to fund itself from its own earnings and private-sector borrowings, and to pay taxes and dividends. In fundamental respects, then, the Post was directed to act like a private firm. Indeed, legally, the Post would be treated no differently than a private-sector company, because it was made a limited-liability company under the Companies and the Commerce Act. This was a critical decision. It reduced the possibility of political interference, ensured that the government would not underwrite its performance (or non-performance), and required the Post's board to place the interests of the business first, ahead of the government's interest. For example, this was spelled out with regard to borrowing money. All SOE loans would include a disclaimer indicating that the state would not be liable for this borrowing. Similarly, postal staff was given the same status as employees in the private sector, as labour reform removed them from the public service and made them contract employees (see below).

The Post's ongoing existence as a *state* enterprise was informed by two other principles – that it should be a good employer and that it should behave in a socially responsible way. However, Section 7 of the SOE Act declared that any non-commercial activities required by the state should be spelled and compensation (if necessary) should be specified.

The Economic Statement of December 1985 also proposed the creation of a twin-shareholding model, in order to emulate private-sector practices and pressures. NZ Post was issued an initial share capital of $120 million,[20] to be held by two ministers on behalf of the

Table 1
SCI 1996–2000 Performance targets (%)

	1997	1998	1999
Operating Profit after Tax: Average Shareholders' Funds	31.8	41.8	38
Profit Before Interest and Tax: Total Tangible Assets	19.9	22.7	22.7
Profit Before Interest, Tax, and Depreciation: Turnover	17.7	19.5	19.6

Source: NZ Post, Annual Reports, assorted years.

crown – the minister for state owned enterprises and the minister of finance. This created an interesting business tension within the shareholder's model. On the one hand, the former is interested in the market and commercial developments of the Post. On the other hand, the latter is more interested in receiving an annual and healthy financial return. This tension between long-run and short-term goals mimics the corporate tension between profits and growth.

The company is headed by a board, whose members are appointed by the state through the shareholding ministries. Each year, the board and the government construct a SCI for the current year and two succeeding years. The SCI serves an accountability function, which is required under the SOE Act. The SCI also sets a monitoring framework for the shareholding ministries.[21] The SCI contains general objectives, key corporate aims, and details on the nature and scope of activities including plans for diversification, financial performance and other targets, dividend policy, planned capital expenditures, and accounting policies. The SCI has been rolled over each year since its origins with some incremental changes.[22] The 1996–99 SCI for the Post included some general themes that were to inform postal strategy and action for the following years. These included the objective to be efficient, effective, profitable, and financially prudent; the direction to grow, through a focus on new technologies and new products; to enhance the network and build community support through the fulfillment of the universal-service obligation; to achieve best market practices. The SCI also laid out a number of specific performance and target measures (see Table 1), including a minimum 50 per cent ratio of shareholders' funds to total assets. Dividends were set at 60 per cent of after-tax profit, and a three-year capital-expenditure plan was laid out ($55 million, $40 million, and $40 million).

Regulation

The regulatory function is organized separately from the ownership function. When the Post was set up as an SOE, this function was transferred to the Department of Trade and Industry and later carried out by the Ministry of Commerce (recently renamed the Ministry of Economic Development). There is no formal independent postal regulator, which is a distinguishing feature of the New Zealand postal regime. Instead, a department of government executes the formal regulation, albeit one that is not the shareholding ministry. The regulatory approach in New Zealand can be characterized as a "light handed touch."[23] There is a minimal amount of formal regulation under the Postal Services Act. Regulation is generated in a number of formal and informal ways – via the application of competition law, through information disclosure, and via the mechanism of the competitive market. The two most important features of the regulatory regime are the increasingly liberalized market and the DOU.

The New Zealand postal market underwent a continuous process of deregulation until full deregulation was accomplished in 1998. Previously, the Post enjoyed a certain modest level of monopoly protection in the letters market alone, which funded the universal-service obligation. Throughout this period, the board of the Post has been free to set its own prices – under the normal scrutiny of the Commerce Commission – within a price-cap formula. The Post determined the scope of the services that it provided. It was required to produce three separate sets of accounts to demonstrate that it was not cross-subsidizing competitive products and services from protected ones.

In the now fully deregulated market, these sorts of concerns are less pressing, since the market imposes a certain competitive business discipline on the Post. The government prepared a document to illustrate how the deregulated market will work – "Obligations and Rights of Postal Operators." Any company can carry letters for profit in the postal market, as long as the secretary of commerce registers it as a postal operator. The conditions imposed on postal operators are minimal. Any company applying to the secretary of commerce must demonstrate that its owners and executives do not have a criminal record. Once approved as a postal operator, the company must design and use a postal identifier. All postal operators are bound by basic technical and legal obligations and also enjoy certain rights. These include access to the Post's system, on competitive terms, which is a general obligation under competition law. The DOU also requires Post to provide access on equivalent terms to equivalent customers. As the dominant provider in the market, the Post must make public any access agreement that it enters into with a postal operator and must disclose any arrangements that comprise offering a discount greater than 40 per cent. The threat of competition – and its subsequent development in the letters market after 1998 – provided an ongoing regulatory discipline on the Post.

The DOU stands at the heart of the regulatory regime and allows the regime to be light-handed. The DOU approach was designed after the Post began its corporatization process. A number of developments alarmed many New Zealanders, who felt that the universal system might be undermined in the pursuit of economic rationality and business performance. The DOU was produced as the "social service" counterpart to the SCI. It lays out the government's expectation of the Post with respect to the universal postal system, in the same way that the SCI lays out the government's expectation of the Post's business performance. The DOU is a political agreement between the Post and the minister of communications, serviced by the Ministry of Commerce – not with the shareholding ministries. This demonstrates the principle of the separation of ownership from regulation. The Ministry of Commerce monitors the Post's service performance in accord with the targets and criteria laid out in the DOU. Within this framework, the Post is free to act as it sees fit.

The service levels and the scope of the network that are expected by the government have more or less been rolled over from one DOU to the next. A new DOU was established in 1998 after the postal market was deregulated. It will exist indefinitely but will be reviewed after three years. The 1998 DOU contains ingredients similar to previous ones (save for the relaxation of the requirements on ownership of the retail outlets)[24]:

- six-day-a-week delivery to 95 per cent of the delivery points in New Zealand;
- five- or six-day delivery to 99.8 per cent of delivery points;
- a limit to the number of delivery points that are at counters or community boxes (1.5 per cent);
- price cap to a maximum of 45 cents for a letter;
- no rural delivery fee;
- any change in service levels must be justified by a change in demographics, or an agreement with the community, or another operator providing as good a service;
- the maintenance of a minimum number of retail outlets (880) and a minimum numbers of post offices (240), with a formula to determine conversions from one to the other (up to eight conversions to postal centres for every $2-million reduction in service-contract revenues); and
- provision of network access to competitors.

In sum, the two basic ingredients of the postal regime – the ownership and regulatory functions – are separated, with different arms of the government responsible for each. The statutory ingredients of each function are spelled out clearly, and the government's expectations in each area are specified in two pubic documents – the SCI and the DOU. The Post's performance is set and judged against these public documents, which are themselves the result of negotiations between the Post and the government. The postal market has now been deregulated, and private operators have easy access to the market and fair access to the Post's infrastructure. This provides another competitive discipline to the Post.

THE PLAYERS AND THE POSTAL REGIME
IN ACTION

The major players in the New Zealand postal regime are the two shareholding ministries, the regulatory ministry, and the board and management of the Post. Parliament plays a benign role, monitoring the performance of powers exercised by shareholding ministers. It receives the SCI and annual reports, and a parliamentary select committee reviews the performance of SOEs. This is a relaxed and not oppressive affair.[25] There are a limited number of competitors to the Post, and most of them are small and local operations. The postal union has played a fairly passive and moderate role (it will be examined separately below). All evidence indicates that the major players interact well and that the system works reasonably. There have been a few tense moments, particularly in the late 1980s and early 1990s when the system was taking shape.[26] Currently, the working relationship between the Post and the government is good and far more open and relaxed than in the past, certainly since Elmar Toime's advent as CEO.[27] The Post has a considerable degree of autonomy within the parameters set by the SOE Act, the SCI, and the DOU.

The shareholding and regulatory ministries are quite, indeed sharply, separate. They are located physically in different buildings, have different responsibilities, pursue different agendas, and interact infrequently. The Ministry of Commerce focuses on regulation. Its postal group is a modest operation comprising a few people, who have a good grasp of the postal terrain. In a real sense, Commerce is less concerned about the Post per se than about the entire postal sector or industry. It feels no particular obligation to or responsibility for the Post. This is encouraged by the act and by the regime structure. The ministry interacts with the Post regularly, focusing particularly on the constructing and monitoring of the DOU (which has been merely fine-tuned since 1993). The DOU more or less used the then existing service level as a base line. The Post requires approval of the minister of communications only if it contemplates changing an element of the DOU to reduce some service level.[28] The Post receives no compensation for carrying out the duties associated with the DOU. The government and Post consider that the Post's market position and branding advantages give it sufficient advantages and benefits in the market to finance the DOU activities.[29] This regulatory function will not disappear in the deregulated environment. The ministry will focus and advise on issues like competition, privacy, registration, and the interaction between private operators and the Post. The ministry approves postal operators' applications to participate in the market, but this is a fairly mechanical and automatic task. It also houses the registry of operators and receives the competitor-access arrangements struck between them and the Post.[30]

There are two shareholder players on the government side – the Treasury and the Crown Company Monitoring and Advisory Unit. The Treasury's primary role is to advise the minister of finance, and CCMAU's primary role is to advise the minister for SOE. Prior to CCMAU's establishment in 1993, the minister for SOEs had a small unit of advisers within the minister's office.

The CCMAU is an intriguing and highly effective institution within the New Zealand postal regime. Its origins lie in a small SOE advisory unit of Treasury officials and private-sector advisers, which became the CCMAU in 1993. It was formed because the government felt that there was inadequate parliamentary scrutiny of the SOE Act as well as insufficient SOE accountability in the model as it then existed. The CCMAU was created to provide the minister with complimentary and contestable advice, which would help the shareholder to keep the SOEs accountable to the SCI and to the act. Its ultimate purpose is to help enhance shareholder value. The CCMAU comprises a seven-person unit, many of whom have strong commercial backgrounds.[31] Each adviser carries responsibility for a number of SOE portfolios. The staff is small, and the turnover is in two-year cycles, to ensure that staff members do not get too close to the SOEs, become meddlesome in its affairs, or get "captured" by the SOEs.[32] The CCMAU provides centralized monitoring and oversight of the thirteen SOEs and some other institutions, against the backdrop of their SCI. It is essentially an extension of the minister's office and has a purchase contract with the minister's office. When it was first formed, it helped to construct a business-planning process, which eased the tense and often antagonistic relationship between the SOEs and the ministers. The CCMAU participates in the business-planning process, interacting and exchanging views with the Treasury, and giving advice to the minister. The ministry prefers to have issues resolved and determined at that level. But if there is disagreement between the CCMAU and the Treasury, each makes a submission to their minister, where the issue will be resolved at that level. Once the plan and the SCI are in place, the CCMAU keeps out of the business process and allows the Post to pursue its affairs. The Post's business plan is very good, better than most, according to the CCMAU.[33] CCMAU's influence is considerable, as it evaluates the performance of the boards of the various SOEs. If a board fumbles the ball, or acts outside of the approved plan or its SCI, the CCMAU can recommend its removal (this has actually taken place).

For its part, the Post was concerned at the start of the reform process that the minister of finance would continue to dominate the postal world. This would have been to the Post's disadvantage, given that the minister of finance tends to focus on economic returns and the minimization of risk. The result would have been a high degree of government involvement in internal postal matters. The Treasury itself was not anxious about its loss of influence in the SOE sector. In the event, the board of the Post stood firm and insisted that the integrity of the SOE model be preserved. This helped to establish and maintain the authority of the SOE minister's advisers, and the dual-shareholder model has subsequently worked out in practice.[34]

To date, the dual-shareholders model has worked by having the CCMAU focus on corporate development and business issues while Treasury focuses on financial issues. Their visions and interests are articulated and executed through an annual planning process, as well as in the construction of the SCI. Treasury has less involvement in postal matters on a day-to-day basis, and concerns itself with broad strategic issues. There were some indications that Treasury would became more involved after the election of the National government, but there has been little subsequent evidence of much change.[35] The Treasury's policy orientation is to ensure that the SOEs emulate the kind of financial disciplines that exist in the private sector through corporate takeovers. So it presses hard on them financially, and in the early days it set high dividend targets. The Post recently paid a special dividend to the government, which had the effect of drawing liquidity out of the cash-rich Post. As a consequence, the Post aims to get greater leverage out of its borrowing capacity.[36] This orientation disciplines the Post financially. It also contributes to the realization of a second objective. Treasury is concerned about the problem of incremental creep into new business activities. By limiting the SOEs' cash flow, it aims to keep state enterprises focused on their core activities. The government issued a statement on this topic in 1989. The SOEs were directed to avoid diversification and to stick to their core activities, unless ministers approved new initiatives.[37] Generally speaking, Treasury would like to see state enterprises stick to activities where their expertise is greatest and where new commercial risks can be avoided. This places it in an interesting relationship with the CCMAU, which places a greater emphasis on how to add value to state enterprises.

There is a built-in tension in the relationship between the shareholding ministries and the regulating ministry. The Ministry of Commerce has been a firm supporter of deregulation, which it has seen as having positive implications for market development and for the consumer. For the shareholding ministries, deregulation provides mixed blessings. The reduction of the Post's monopoly has the effect of decreasing shareholder value. Indeed, any government contemplating privatization would not be inclined to deregulate a market, since this would undermine the value of the corporate asset. Treasury has always supported deregulation despite its implications for the value of its asset, because of the broader economic benefits that deregulation brings to the economy as a whole. The coalition team of National and NZ First happened to agree on this issue ideologically. Moreover, the deregulation timing was propitious for each of them politically. The decision to deregulate, then, was a policy and political decision, as it should be, given that the state owns the Post. This was an appropriate way for any policy logjam to be broken.

A fourth player in the postal regime is the Board of Directors of the Post. The board appoints the chief executive, who in turn appoints the senior-management team. It sets prices, approves capital expenditures, manages the capital structure of the business, determines policies and priorities, and approves the overall strategic direction of the enterprise. The board makes these decisions in line with the annual plan and the SCI, which it negotiates with the shareholder.

The non-executive board comprises between five and nine members, who are named by shareholding ministers. The original board had five people from the business sector, one union representative, and two members of the administration. The board appointments are not intended to be political, unlike the more politically driven board-appointment process in Canada. The latter process results in a kind of "coalitionization" of the board, which did not happen in New Zealand. This was an important side effect of the SOE Act. The act had promised that governments would not interfere in the business of the state enterprises, which allowed the government to attract good people to the SOE boards.[38] These appointments have been based on candidates' qualifications and demonstrated competence in the private sector. The most recent appointments have been predominantly hard-driven and entrepreneurial people, who have worked hard and developed enormous loyalty to the Post.[39] The CCMAU plays an advisory role to the minister in this regard. It keeps a data bank of volunteers and their experiences and qualifications, and matches possible appointees with the particular needs of the board at the moment.[40]

The present board is chaired by Ross Armstrong, a person with formidable intellectual credentials (a PHD), political credentials (past president of the Auckland division of the National Party), and business credentials (owner of Far East Export, a fish-exporting business). The other members of the board have solid business credentials and experience: directors or presidents of investment firms, managing directors, individuals with backgrounds in law, finance, utilities, and many other fields. The boards have been strong and focused on the best interests of the Post. While it has contained some people with political backgrounds and affiliations,[41] it has not been a particularly political board. It appreciates, understands, and "works" the political process. But it has been a more business-oriented than political board and has developed good working relationship with management.[42]

Each year the board and the shareholders agree to a SCI for the current and succeeding two years. There is also an annual business-planning process, which basically involves fleshing out the SCI (unlike the SCI, this is a company document that is closed to the public). A three-year plan is produced and updated each year. This process is orchestrated through the office of the CEO, with discussions with Treasury and the CCMAU. The plan addresses three broad areas that interest the government. The *financial* goals of the company (as listed above) have not been a matter of controversy, given the Post's performance. The plan includes a target debt:equity ratio. The plan also addresses the *scope* of the Post's operation, an area where the government has not been keen to have the Post expand from its core activities. The third area deals with particular *initiatives* proposed by the Post. The Post can use its retained earnings or debt-finance to fund initiatives. Significant initiatives require consultation with shareholding ministers, which in turn may be discussed at cabinet depending on their size, strategic importance, and possible impact on other government objectives.[43]

The Post has been reorganized on a number of occasions during the reform process, to better reflect its business activities. It is currently organized into five areas: letters, retail, parcels, international, and electronic. The board brought in top management from the private sector, particularly in the areas of marketing, human resources, planning, and finance. The first CEO was Harvey Parker, a tough-minded Australian with corporatization experience, who favoured both deregulation and privatization.[44] The working relationship between the board and senior management has developed into a solid partnership. The CEOs of all SOEs are given explicit mandates and fixed term contracts tied to success. In turn, the CEOs were promised real authority to get on with the job.[45] Senior managers are paid on a performance basis.[46] The board's relationship to the management team is very positive, but it is also demanding of management. There has been a consistent turnover of senior people as the defined needs of the business change. The present CEO, Elmar Toime, has been extremely successful and a vigorous proponent of a competitive and commercial postal model.[47] Generally, the Post has favoured deregulation as the "price" to pay for increased commercial freedom, and it has been "ahead" of the government on this issue.

The relationship between the board and the shareholder has generally been good and the government has kept its distance from the internal operation of the Post.[48] The SOE Act directs the board to act in the best interests of the Post and not according to the government's interests or a political agenda. The board has worked to increase the commercial autonomy enjoyed by the Post and to keep politics out of postal decision making. The board has a considerable degree of autonomy, partially because of the act, but also because of its past success and the feistiness of its members. This has seen the board stand firm on numerous occasions, holding its position when the shareholder disagreed with its proposals. Its determination goes back to the origins of the Post as an SOE. The negotiations between the Post and the government over the valuation of the Post were tense. The Post was essentially buying itself from the government, and the Treasury pitched the purchase price high. The board nearly resigned over the issue before an appropriate figure was eventually set.[49] Similarly, in the late 1980s and early 1990s, the Post purchased its own airplanes, given that it was getting poor service from what were basically passenger airlines. The shareholder was against this initiative but, after vigorous debate, the Post won the argument.[50] There was enormous political pressure placed on the board when the Post rationalized the retail network and increased rural postal fees, but again the board hung tough.[51] In another case, the board convinced the government that it should be able to sell magazines in its retail outlets, despite protests from newsagents and other shops that the Post was stealing their business. The Post convinced the government that broadening its revenue base was required to maintain the retail operation at its existing level.[52] In other cases, the Post initiated actions that could be seen to be contrary to the interests of the shareholder. For example, the board decided to cut postal prices and also determined that this did not require government approval. Its decision had the short-term effect of hurting the company's bottom line and hence the dividends paid to the government.[53] Notwithstanding Ross Armstrong's past career as an officer of the National Party, the board is less a political manager than a business one.

The major exception to the picture drawn above has been the Freightways case. Freightways was a New Zealand firm that specialized in parcels and express, areas that complemented the Post's strengths. The purchase would not have extended the Post beyond its core areas. After evaluating the business case, the Post's board decided to make an offer to purchase Freightways. Given the scale of the purchase (NZ$120 million) and its potential impact on the market, the board presented the case to the government for its scrutiny and ultimate approval. A number of administrative units evaluated the proposed purchase from different perspectives. Monopoly concerns were assuaged, once the purchase was approved by the Commerce Commission under the Commerce Act. The CCMAU evaluated the business case for the purchase and made a positive recommendation, having concluded that its financial and strategic criteria demonstrated that this would be a good investment. However, at the eleventh hour, the minister of finance objected to the recommendations to cabinet. This decision surprised most observers (including the press). The impact on the morale of the Post was substantial. This was exacerbated by the fact that another SOE – Contact Energy – had made a similar sized investment without informing the ministers. The bitterness of the case was further intensified when Freightways was sold offshore, to an Australian company.[54]

Why did the government turn down a board request to make a purchase in a core business area, a purchase that was supported by a number of players within the postal regime? There is no doubt that the government had the authority to do so, as well as the responsibility to review the case, given the scale of the purchase and its likely impact on the market (the Post would have reportedly ended up with 45 per cent of the courier market). The government did not reject the case on commercial grounds, for the business argument for the purchase was strong. Rather, the decision reflected financial and political reasoning. Financially, the government was less keen on future business success than on receiving its dividends now – dividends that would have been tied up in the purchase. Politically, the government was committed to reducing the scale of its spending and operations and strengthening the private sector. Notwithstanding that it made business sense, the Post's purchase of Freightways would have cut across the government's political agenda.[55]

The Freightways case was untypical, given its size and scale and the ideological temper of the time. The proposed purchase arose before full deregulation; the government may have been more hands-off after deregulation.[56] Nonetheless, the Freightways case demonstrated the ongoing authority of the shareholder, who retains considerable authority in a number of areas – from appointing directors to commenting on and reviewing the planning and SCI process and monitoring the financial and business development of the Post. The government is not interested in seeing the Post expand unless there are compelling reasons. This creates real roadblocks to the Post's efforts to grow.[57] The state's authority will, obviously, continue unless the Post itself is privatized – an issue that is not on the policy agenda at present.[58]

Unions and the Reform Process

The postal union has not been a major player in the postal-reform process. Given the historical role of the unions in New Zealand politics, it is worth giving this point some attention. As noted earlier, the postal unions had played a central role in postal decision making prior to the reform process. This changed in the late 1980s, as a result of a number of government initiatives. This had considerable impact on the postal-reform process.

First, the SOE Act removed the Post from the core public service and from the control of the State Services Commission over its employment relations. The government made it quite clear then – as it does now – that it would stay out of negotiations and industrial relations generally.[59] In effect, SOEs have the equivalent of private-sector control over their workforce. This weakened the previously strong public-sector unions. Second, the Employment Contracts Act (ECA) replaced the old system of national awards and national bargaining with individual employment contracts. The union has had no special privileges, once the process shifted from national to plant awards. Indeed, there is no longer compulsory membership and unions have to sign members up, one by one. Third, the Labor Relations Act forced the unions to rationalize their structures. By the end of Labour's second term, the unions had been seriously affected. These legislative initiatives weakened the power of labour and unions enormously. Many of New Zealand's best-known unions folded or had to merge. Union density fell from 56 per cent of the workforce to 26 per cent. In 1991, there were 603,000 union members. By 1994, this had fallen to 374,000.

With respect to the Post, these initiatives transformed the situation completely and contributed to the lack of substantial union opposition to postal reform.[60] To begin with, the postal union itself fell on hard times and went bankrupt. It joined the CEWU (Communication and Electrical Workers Union), which was a poor organization that soon went bankrupt. The union leadership of the Post recognized that the wider economic-reform agenda was one that could not be rolled back. So it made the tactical decision to cut the best possible deal that they could in the circumstances. The political environment provided few options to the union. The government was Labour, there was nowhere else to turn. The union did reasonably well under the circumstances. It attained a rollover of wages and conditions, a good redundancy deal, a reasonable job loss (less than 1,000), and the inclusion of a good-employer clause in the act.[61]

Some unions embraced the post-ECA environment and tried to make it work for their members. This was particularly the case with respect to the Engineers Union, led by Rex Jones, a professional and progressive unionist who had been President of the Labour Party. The Engineers Union restructured itself into a limited-liability company and amalgamated with unrelated unions. It reorganized the labour force at the Post, which is presently 50–60 per cent unionized (of which the Engineers Union represents 93 per cent.) The 1980s economic crisis had scared the postal workers intensely. The workforce was far less cosmopolitan and radical than, say, the Australians, and the economic threats made them particularly accommodating to the new postal strategy. There is a tendency to look to the Post in general – and Elmar Toime in particular – to fix things and to protect postal workers from a more threatening-looking government. This pragmatic orientation complements the practical, make-things-work attitude of the Engineers Union. It gives a less combative and more cooperative face to the Post. The various legislative initiatives have encouraged, if not forced, cooperation and partnership. There has been but one small strike at the Post during the reform process.[62] The union led a protest against deregulation and criticized the Postal Deregulation Bill, but this was a modest and almost token effort.

The resulting management-union relationship is by no means a cosy one. Each side recognizes its roles and works professionally and reasonably cooperatively to that end.[63] The union has been fairly accommodating to technical change and at least looks at initiatives from the Post to see if they work – without first objecting on principle or trying to veto them immediately. The Post has initiated a number of policies to try and bring its workers to support the reform agenda. This has included "Talk Back," an enormous company-led discussion process. The Post surveys employment morale regularly, which appears to be at a positive 90 per cent level. The Post and the union worked to transform the collective agreement into a "plain English" text. The resulting product is amazing in its simplicity and brevity, only 98 pages long (the Canadian one is almost 500 pages). It is framed by a 10-page introduction, which lays out the purpose of the

Post, its vision, principles, and partnership approach. This is all very humane and personal. In a Memorandum of Understanding, the parties "acknowledge that securing the future requires the building of a new business culture." The parties agreed to explore performance incentives and new frameworks and approaches to ensure competitiveness (this initiative has not yet borne fruit). The 1998–2000 agreement was signed before deregulation arrived and before the expiry of the previous contract. The Post wanted to ensure a period of stable industrial relations through the crucial early period of deregulation. The terms and conditions of the previous contract were rolled over, with a 2 per cent wage increase inducement.

The economic conditions of the mid-late 1980s, the transformation of the legislative environment, and the attitudes of the Post and the union have combined to create a fairly benign labour-relations environment. This allowed the postal-reform process to unfold without crises, strikes, or constraints. It also allowed the board to avoid serious confrontations with the unions. There are some signs, though, of a revival of radicalism in the face of ongoing rationalization and reform.[64] This is particularly the case where the Post has moved to meet competitive pressures (low-cost ad mail) or to reform the retail chain. Both initiatives have implications for wages and jobs, as we will see below. Moreover, the incentive-based bargaining and negotiations that the union wishes to engage in may create negotiation problems in the future.

PERFORMANCE

The Post's first year as an independent SOE can be seen as a metaphor for its subsequent performance. It was faced with an immediate 25 per cent loss in revenue, as the telecom and banking operations were split off from the Post. It initiated a series of "survival" measures, lest its anticipated $40-million deficit spiral completely out of control. These measures included: the rationalization of basic operations (such as moving to once-a-day box clearing), contracting out of non-core activities (such as transportation), reducing labour costs (such as voluntary redundancy, increasing use of part-time labour), system rationalization (such as closing of uneconomic post offices), and pay-as-you-go services (such as charging banking and telecom for doing their business). In conjunction with the price increases introduced in 1985 and 1986, the Post turned a profit in its first year, paid taxes, issued a dividend, and had funds left over for investment and modernization.[65] The Post subsequently operated at a profit in every year but one (1992), notwithstanding the subsequent introduction of price

Table 2
Financial performance (millions of dollars)

	Turnovers (millions)	Earnings before tax	Earnings after tax	Operating margins before tax (%)	Return on equity after tax (%)
1992	526	44.5	−2.2	8.4	−1.0
1993	589	96.6	37.4	16.4	17.7
1994	620	99.7	66.7	16.1	30.1
1995	644	107	72.4	16.6	32.4
1996	658	105	75.2	15.9	35.5
1997	678	65.1	47.7	9.6	24.8
1998	706	29.4	18	4.2	9.9
1999	790	37	23	4.7	12.3
2000	*922	49	30	5.4	15.5

* Reflects purchase of Ansett Express.
Source: NZ Post, Annual Reports, assorted years.

cuts and the increasing competition associated with deregulation. Its after-tax earnings reached a record $75 million in 1996. The Post paid taxes and dividends totalling $700 million between 1987 and 1997, while reinvesting $370 million. Earnings since then have not been quite as high, since the Post invested in preparing itself for deregulation (restructuring, new technology, severance payments, acquisitions). Standard and Poor's issued it a long-term foreign currency corporate credit rating of AA+ and a short term rating of A–1+, the same rating as the government. As the Table 2 indicates, the Post's profit performance has improved steadily since 1998.

The Post's performance turnaround has started at the top, with a strong management hand at the helm backed by an equally strong and committed board. Its first CEO, Harvey Parker, introduced quantitative-management thinking and a scientific approach. This saw the Post increase efficiency, lower costs, introduce new products, and improve service – all with a sharp focus on the bottom line. This was implemented by managers who were recruited from the private sector and personnel who underwent formal training. The market and sales function was strengthened, and the sales force was increased from 10 to 120 personnel. The Post paid increasing attention to its customers, introducing new products and improving services while cutting letter prices and introducing volume discounts.[66] It introduced a free post day that was wildly successful. All of these initiatives increased its volumes, notwithstanding the development of technological and product competition. By the late 1990s, the Post was handling 20 per cent more volume than at the beginning of the 1990s, with 40 per cent less staff and in a vastly improved network configuration.[67]

The Basics: Price, Volumes, and Quality

Of all the Posts examined in this study, NZ Post remains the most optimistic about the future of the letter. This is articulated ceaselessly in annual reports, public documents, and presentations by CEO Elmar Toime. In a speech to the UPU in 1997, Toime declared that "the letter is and will remain a superb tool for businesses to communicate with customers."[68] Per-capita mail volumes in New Zealand are about half the level of the United States and well below the level in Europe. There is also a sense that the ad mail market is underdeveloped. This optimism is striking, given that the NZ Post market has always been fairly competitive. The previous restricted area was not expansive, since unaddressed mail was excluded, as was self-delivery (for example, in the early 1990s, about 25 per cent of mail from local authorities and utilities was self-delivered). Outward-bound international mail was excluded in 1990, and the restricted area diminished in a series of steps in the early 1990s, to 200 grams or eighty cents. The market was totally deregulated in 1998. The Post's optimism has been reasonably borne out in practice. Total letter volumes passed the 1-billion level in 1997, having increased by more than 5 per cent a year throughout much of the 1990s. This pace slipped to 2.4 per cent in 1998 but rose to 3.9 per cent in 1998–99. The 1999–2000 results were the first indication that deregulation (and electronic substitution) might affect the volume of letters, which was static in a slower economy. Total volumes rose to over 1.5 billion items in 1999 and increased again by 5 per cent in 2000, driven mainly by unaddressed admail.

The strength of the letters market has been related to the complementary policies of keeping prices low and quality high. The price dimension has unfolded in two stages. First, the Post was allowed to increase its prices substantially, from 30 to 40 cents in 1986. This decision was highly politically charged and fought out in cabinet. The price hike was introduced to ensure that the Post began its SOE existence reasonably debt free. This allowed it to avoid the situation that officials had viewed in Canada, where Canada Post's early deficits required continuing staff and services cuts and a resulting loss in business.[69] The early price increase allowed the Post to maintain and improve services, products, and volumes, although it should be recalled that all prices included the GST. Pricing was simplified in 1988 by rationalizing the system to three price steps by size (not weight): medium, large, and extra-large. This was a world first devised by Toime. The Post was regulated by a price-cap system, which saw the price of a first-class stamp rise to forty-five cents in 1991. Over the next few years, the price was effectively frozen, in anticipation of deregulation (low prices would act as a barrier to easy competitive entry). Major mail users were given price cuts in 1993. Once its finances were settled, and deregulation loomed large, the Post could then "afford" to lower the price of a letter in 1995 to forty cents. This was an unprecedented initiative that astounded postal observers around the world and was a shrewdly calculated move to maintain the Post's position in the communications market while avoiding the development of an image of itself as a hidden tax-collector. At forty cents, the Post maintains that it offers the lowest letter price in the industrial world. Postal observers also suggest that, in terms of purchasing-power parity, it is likely the cheapest in the world.[70] A further intriguing development was introduced in the 1998 DOU, which replaced the universal price system with a maximum pricing constraint. The Post is free to set its prices as long as the price does not exceed forty-five cents.

The sensitivity to price has contributed to the Post's success in maintaining and growing volumes, as has its service performance. This objective has been driven exclusively by the Post, with the government demonstrating only modest interest.[71] The Post's delivery performance must be presented in its annual reports. The DOU insists that the universal service must be maintained, and the vast proportion of the population (96.8 per cent) receives six-day delivery. The quality of this service increased after 1986. Starting from 88 per cent in 1988, the rate of next-day delivery rose to 96 per cent in 1993.[72] Its level of performance has slipped in recent years to the 94 per cent level, partially attributable to technological change, cutting back on part-time labour, and other system changes.[73] This remains well above European standards of performance, but there is disappointment that the level has not been not higher recently.

Competition

The Post faced considerable competition before deregulation, both directly and indirectly. The Post had functioned in a competitive market with respect to non-protected products, such as parcels, courier and express, unaddressed mail, and so on. Outward-bound international mail was deregulated in 1990. Overseas Posts and private consolidators did not have much of a presence in New Zealand. But TNT (the Australian transport company purchased by the Dutch Post Office) made some interventions into the postal market, such as its offer to mail Christmas cards to any place in the world for seventy-seven cents (with pick-up service for orders of five or more). The Post faced competition in the courier market, where it ranked third behind

NZ Couriers and Post-Haste (both owned by Freightways). There were a number of business-mail services, including New Zealand Document Exchange Limited. A group called DX (document exchange) has a strong presence in the legal, bank, and travel-agency business. It has a private box network that collects material and has it processed through the Post's system.[74]

Since deregulation, a number of private postal operators have registered with the Ministry of Economic Development (formerly Department of Commerce). There have been thirty-four registered companies, but a number have subsequently withdrawn from the market.[75] The Post's pre-deregulation strategy – low prices, good service – appears to have protected it from losing market share to new competition. Its two major competitors have been National Mail and Fastway Post.[76]

National Mail was one of the first private-sector casualties in the deregulated environment. It was started in mid-1999 and floated shares in 2000, raising nearly $13 million. It provided mail services primarily in the Auckland area and began to expend to Wellington and to Christchurch. It specialized primarily in the business-to-home and business-reply market, offering bulk contract, pre-priced mail. It rolled out delivery services in Auckland, purchasing 100 motorcycles and setting up its blue collection boxes near to the Post's boxes. It developed an access agreement with the Post. However, it was not able to attract a sufficient number of high-volume customers to become profitable.

Fastway Post is a franchise operation centred in Napier; it began as Hawke's Bay Courier. It currently comprises around two dozen franchises and is aiming for 100. Fastway comprises franchised store-within-a-store operations, providing pre-paid envelopes that can be dropped off at the franchise office or in red street boxes. These envelopes are delivered via New Zealand Post's network. It had a group turnover of $94 million in 1999–2000, mainly generated from courier and parcel operations.

Pete's Post is a recent competitive development, comprising a set of franchised delivery operations. It appears to be having some success and focuses its business on residential and small-business customers. It operates franchises in 11 cities and delivered about 14 million pieces of mail in 2000.

Product Innovation, Mergers, and Acquisitions

While the Post has confidence in the future of the letter, it has sought out new business activities to buffer it from product and technological competition. As noted, the government has not supported postal diversification away from the postal core, both on ideological grounds (in the case of National) and because it has not been anxious to see the Post expand financially. An exception has been the census, which is orchestrated by the Post. Indeed, the CEO of NZ Post holds the statutory position as chief registrar of electors. The Post has the authority to introduce new products and services within the core postal area. With deregulation, the government inhibition on diversification has weakened. PostPlus was NZ Post's organizational platform for developing new businesses and activities in four areas: direct marketing, stamps, data mail, and new business.

A major opportunity and a major challenge for the Post is the courier market, where there has been considerable competition and the Post had an historic third-place ranking. It introduced FastPost in 1988, an overnight mail-delivery service, and CourierPost was launched. It has captured large accounts like the EDS utilities company and the Bank of New Zealand, which has pushed the Post successfully into first place in the courier market. Smack on Time was introduced as a subsidiary, to create a courier service that had high value-added and technological sophistication. In July 1999 the Post acquired the courier Ansett Express, which expands its distribution capability and builds a multi-brand strategy. Through its ten brands, NZ Post leads the courier and parcels market in New Zealand. NZ Post purchased a 40 per cent share of Communications Arts Limited, through its subsidiary Datamail. Communication Arts is New Zealand's largest independent print-management and logistics company. Establishing subsidiaries and making acquisitions has allowed the Post to compete against low-cost competitors, but at the price of providing lower wages and less permanent conditions to workers. This may have consequences for the Post's relationship with its union.

The Post has also tried to grow in the expanding ad-mail or direct-mail market. It entered into a joint venture with an Australian direct-marketing and mail-production business in 1988. Datamail is a direct marketing venture, which comprises the electronic preparation of letters, their documentation and management, and delivery. The Post was originally a 50 per cent participant but is now the sole owner. Major customers include Inland Revenue and electrical utilities. Over 10 per cent of letters are now generated in this fashion. Kiwimail was launched in 1997–98 to deal with low-cost competition in the addressed and unaddressed mail market. The Post offers a 6 per cent discount on standard delivery rates to allow competitors to access its network.

The Post has also tried to expand the physical side of the business, particularly given the expansion of e-commerce (where products purchased off the Internet have to be delivered physically). This was the logic or rationale behind the doomed Freightways bid. The Post purchased xp Group (nz) in 1998. This is a parcel-delivery company with a network of 163 owner/drivers. It will act as a complement to Courier Post. The Post has also entered the contract-logistics business

The Post has entered the electronic age. It entered an arrangement with CheckFree Corporation, the largest u.s. provider of electronic bill-payment services, to provide e-bills on the Internet. E-bill is New Zealand's first Internet bill delivery and payment service. Its major customers include Bank of New Zealand credit cards, Contact Energy, and Saturn Communications. By the spring of 2000, it had 2,300 customers.[77] In November 1999, the Post purchased 30 per cent of Silent One, a software-development company, following its March purchase of a 50 per cent stake in Electronic Commerce Network. This has strengthened the Post's capabilities in electronic messaging and e-commerce. The Post is also testing the use of electronic kiosks in a number of post offices, which would allow its customers to pay bills, do e-mail searches for information, and purchase products.

Mechanization and Labour

The origins of mechanization and modernization in New Zealand lie in the review of sorting plants and retail operations commissioned by the government in 1990. This study was carried out by a private firm, Proudfoot PLC, since the Post itself did not have the technical capacity to perform such a study (Parker took the cost of the study out of his managers' bonuses). This was a fairly brutal process, both in theory and execution. The consultants proposed and carried out a tough rationalization plan. This included moving away from the old twenty-four-hour sorting cycle to one in which sorting was done only when necessary. This cut working time in half, with obvious implications for staffing levels, the mix of full and part-time sorters, and the increasingly unnecessary dayshift. Staff and costs were reduced by 30 per cent and severance settlements amounted to $32 million. The Proudfoot process introduced quantitative planning and monitoring systems that helped the Post to get its costs under control and to increase its quality of service.[78]

The Post thereafter sunk a considerable amount of money into transforming its operations. It invested $32.4 million through 1996 to automate and modernize its system. Savings made in rationalizing the retail network (see below) financed much of this investment. The first OCR (optical scanning readers) machines were introduced in 1992 at a cost of $20 million. By 1998, it had completed the transformation of its network into a leading-edge processing and mail service, comprising twenty-two mail centres. In 1998 its capital expenditures totalled $53.3 million (the second-highest level on record), money that was spent on introducing new IMP technology and upgrading mail handling. Mechanization had implications for staffing levels, which declined by about 40 per cent between 1987 and 1996. There were around twelve thousand full-time equivalent staff in 1987, which was reduced to eight thousand by 1990 and seven thousand by 1993. Part-time employment has become a central feature of staffing. There has been a modest increase in employment levels since 1996, which reflects real business growth.[79] Contracting out has been a central feature of this process. For example, owner-drivers now do all transport.

Retail Network

The rationalization of the retail network was an early test of the government's commitment to the SOE model and the implications thereof. NZ Post had a network of 1,244 post offices in 1986. Six hundred of them were identified as being uneconomical. Under the terms of the SOE Act, the government was obliged to compensate any SOE for performing uneconomical activities that were requested by the government. The government retained title to these post offices and paid the Post subsidies to maintain them. This expensive and uncomfortable arrangement came under stress and scrutiny when the government began cutting expenditures and services in other sensitive areas as part of its wider economic policy agenda. The upshot was that the compensation arrangement ended; the government removed the subsidy and 432 post offices were closed in a short period in 1987–88. These offices represented 35 per cent of the retail-network business yet generated only 5 per cent of the Post's stamp sales, while costing $20 million to operate. The rationalization of the retail network generated enormous public reaction and protest, legislative debates, and high court actions. When the political dust had settled, the government had stood its ground and insulated the Post. The retail sector now combined both commercial and social considerations, with the former predominant.

The number of post offices – renamed post shops in 1988 – declined from 900 in 1987 to 400 in 1989, 300 in 1990, and 250 in 1993. Parallel to this process was the emergence of franchises and private-sector agencies – called Post Centres – as well as stamp outlets. The upshot of this was that the number of post offices declined but the number of contact points increased. Indeed, the retail network expanded in the late 1990s, as Table 3 below indicates. The DOU establishes a minimum level of outlets – 880 – that must be provided (excluding stamp outlets). The

Table 3
The retail network

	Post Shops	Post Centres	Total
1996	288	683	971
1997	297	705	1,002
1998	308	717	1,025
1999	314	719	1,033

Source: NZ Post, Annual Report, assorted years

DOU also indicates that at least 240 of the 880 must be post shops, which is the social dimension of the arrangement. But the Post is given the authority to decide what kinds of outlets are most appropriate in particular circumstances or situations.

The retail network in New Zealand has not introduced the degree or range of diversified products and services that exist in some other countries, such as the United Kingdom. Magazines were introduced into a number of outlets, and tickets to events are now sold in post shops. There have been a number of technical innovations, such as the Post-Link computer terminals provided in post shops (1992). This program was expanded in 1997 (Post-Link II), which saw computerized point-of-sales systems introduced in 296 post shops. These outlets provide EFTPOS, an electronic funds-transfer system. Such technical innovations allowed the Post to partner with financial-services companies. The Post struck a deal with Ergo Personal Financial services in 1996–97 to accept counter deposits. In September 1999 the Post introduced a number of banking activities and initiatives with ANZ Bank, the Taranaki Savings Bank, and the Westpac Trust (WT), the largest branch network in New Zealand. In March 2001 the Post entered the banking sector with a vengeance and with the government's backing. It created the New Bank, which will operate in NZ Post branches starting in 2002.[80]

The most dramatic retail initiative has been the Post's partnership with Blue Star, a leading books and stationary retailer. Blue Star runs a chain of bookstores – Whitcoulls, Bennetts. and London Bookshops. Blue Star and the Post have a fifty/fifty partnership in a new chain called Books and More, which combines a book and stationary shop with a postal outlet. These stores have been opening regularly across New Zealand and numbered nineteen by March 2000. Typically, an adjacent post shop closes. This initiative has been scrutinized closely and criticized by the postal union, since Post workers become redundant and have either to apply for jobs at Books and More or be redeployed within Post.[81]

Internationalization

The international theme has consumed NZ Post's interest to an increasing extent in recent years.[82] The Post has entered into a number of strategic alliances, particularly in Australia, Great Britain, and the United States. It has contracted with DHL Worldwide Express to deliver its international letter products on its behalf, and vice versa. It has entered into global alliances with Lockheed Martin USA, British Post Consultancy Services, and Deloitte Touche Tohmatsu Global Consultancy. In July 2000 it purchased the Australian courier company Couriers Please, the market leader in cross-town same-day delivery. This will allow it to provide an integrated New Zealand-Australia courier service to its customers without having to rely on third parties in Australia.

Like other Posts, it has sold its postal expertise to a number of Posts abroad. New Zealand Post International – now called Transend Worldwide – is the largest postal consultancy in the world and has undertaken work in forty-three countries. It has carried out modernization programs and has had major operational contracts in a number of countries. In July 1999 it won the largest postal contract ever tendered internationally – a strategic management partnership with SAPO, the South African Post Office. This three-year, multi-million dollar contract will see NZ Post provide personnel to improve SAPO's operational and financial performance, expand South Africa's address network, and upgrade its postal technology. It has contracted Royal Mail, Lockheed Martin, and Deloitte and Touche Consulting for support. Most recently, it has signed a memorandum of understanding with the Nigerian government to modernize its post office department and ready it for privatization.[83]

HIGHLIGHTS OF THE NEW ZEALAND CASE

What can one learn from the New Zealand case? What interest does its experience and market approach hold for policy makers? The most obvious issue that has been demonstrated is that it is possible to have both a deregulated postal market and the maintenance of the universal postal system. The Post has no protection or special privileges or subsidies. Prices are low and service levels are of the same character as pre-1986 – and are now specified and made public. The New Zealand postal market was not an especially protected one throughout the postal-reform process. Nonetheless, the Post quickly became a profitable business and maintained the universal postal service at a reasonably high quality level. Since deregulation in 1998, the Post has continued to maintain a high-quality service while remaining profitable, even as competition develops beyond the parcels and courier market into the letters market. This overall result is impressive and compelling. The case demonstrates the positive impact that a well considered statutory and regulatory regime can have on postal performance. The regime is reasonably simple and clear, and it has not been difficult or cumbersome to initiate and implement.

First, the postal regime is constructed within a broad policy framework or infrastructure designed for all state enterprises. This larger agenda has carried postal reform to a considerable extent. It established the basic structures, processes, and principles for all the state enterprises, including the Post. The most essential ingredient of this framework is that the state enterprise is to be treated, and expected to perform, like a private-sector business. This drove the corporatization of the Post and made it necessary for the board of the Post to focus on the Post's agenda, not the government's.

Second, the general legislative framework is complemented by legislative and framework agreements for each of the state enterprises, including the Post. This two-part framework created a well-designed postal regulatory regime. In the first instance, postal ownership was separated from postal regulation. The former was organized in a dual-ownership model, which itself balanced short-term financial prospects with long-term corporate development. The Treasury was supported by an institutional innovation, the CCMAU, which provided general and particular intelligence and expertise to the function. This is an innovation that should be considered in other regimes. The regulatory function was organized in a different ministry and manifests a light-handed regime. There is no independent third-party regulator that threatens to interfere in or obstruct postal activity and development.

Third, those responsible for the ownership and regulation functions articulate their expectations of the Post in public documents. These create an accountability framework for the Post that clarifies what the government expects it to do and lays a basis for evaluation. The documents also project to the public the balanced commercial and social roles to be pursued by the Post. On the one hand, the expectations of government as owner are articulated in the SCI, which lays out the state's commercial and financial expectations of the Post. The SCI was a mechanism for the state to raise the performance bar and insist on a performance level that emulated private firms in the market. On the other hand, the DOU lays out the Post's social obligations to maintain the universal system. The DOU mitigated public concerns about any negative implications to corporatization. It institutionalized past practice and required the Post to seek the government's approval for new departures.

Fourth, the ownership framework created by the SOE and postal acts provided the Post with a high degree of authority and business autonomy, allowing it to get on with the job of attaining the objectives set in the SCI. A top-notch board and an excellent management team head the Post. The strength and quality of each reflects the clarity and expectations of the postal acts. This gives confidence to board members and to management that they will actually be allowed – indeed expected – to run a good business and to look after the interests of the Post. Exceptionally strong boards and excellent management transformed the Post into a very well-run and successful company.

Fifth, the logic of the regime created a momentum for liberalizing the postal market. This evolved incrementally in a balanced fashion until the market was totally deregulated in 1998. By this time, the Post was eminently capable of performing competitively while continuing to provide the universal postal service. The deregulated and competitive market is not burdened by a high degree of regulation or government control. Indeed, there is no third-party regulator, and the Ministry of Commerce uses but a light touch in what is a very open market environment.

The New Zealand regulatory regime is an elegant, economical, and effective one that has stood the test of time for about fifteen years. During this period, there have been enormous developments, changes in government, and a number of tensions and crises over postal issues. While one can point to dubious decisions or flawed initiatives, it is difficult to avoid the conclusion that the model has been able to absorb changes and work to effect. Postal prices are low, service standards are high, the mechanical and retail networks are modern and strong, the Post is profitable, and a number of new markets, services, and product initiatives are being pursued.

There has been only a modest development of competition in the postal market, although the experience to date has been limited. On the one hand, the Post remains the overwhelmingly dominant player in the market and will remain so for the foreseeable future. On the other hand, the long ongoing threat of deregulation had led the Post to become price, service, and product competitive in anticipation of the new deregulated postal world. Both factors will make it difficult for domestic competition to flourish. This will require the ownership and regulatory ministries to remain on guard. There has been no public or business pressure to "create" competition, and no controversy over a major competitor complaining about unfair advantages enjoyed by the Post. The Ministry of Commerce has laid out rules for competition, and the Post must offer competitors fair and equitable access to its network. But competition has been moderate to date, and this has not yet placed any great strain on the system.

What will likely provide increasing competition to the Post in the future is international and product development. New Zealand has been protected from the former by its geographic isolation and the small size of its market. Nonetheless, given the emergence of global postal alliances, the Post will have to remain sharp to stay profitable in this new world. There are signs that product competition has affected the Post's bottom line. The growth of letter-mail volumes has slowed down if not stopped. This reflects actual competition as well as the advent of electronic communication. The Post will continue to face product and electronic competition in these expanding areas, which will also bring it into further contact with international realities and pressures. The key question that remains is what will happen when these pressures threaten to make the Post's operation unprofitable. This will place the state on the spot, and the temptation may be to change the universal-service obligation.

The Post is also likely to face increased pressure from its union. The Post benefited from the changed industrial-relations environment created in the late 1980s as well as from the anxiety created by the economic crises of that time. A generation later, the Post confronts a new industrial-relations agenda within a reconstructed labour environment. This will provide a real test to the Post in the deregulated environment. On the one hand, the Post will continue to devise ways to meet competitors in the market. On the other hand, some of these initiatives – such as contracting out, low-wage-cost subsidiaries, rationalization of the network – will have an obvious impact on a workforce that is less cowed by economic circumstances than in the past. The industrial-relations environment has worked over the last fifteen years for a number of reasons, including the promise that the government would stay out of these matters. It has been up to the Post's management and board to ensure a healthy industrial relations environment, and the same will be true in the future.

The New Zealand story has not lacked for drama and tension. As elsewhere, the early stages of corporatization were controversial, particularly in areas such as rural rationalization and retail-network adjustments. On the one hand, postal authorities benefited from a number of contingent circumstances: the absence of a concerted opposition, the anxiety created by the late 1980s economic crises, the weakness of the postal union, and the fact that the government was Labour. On the other hand, the postal regime grew and adapted to meet these pressures. The DOU established public benchmarks for universal service that, to a great extent, assuaged the political concerns that the universal system was unravelling.

The relationship between the state and the Post has generally been positive and consensual over the reform period. The regulatory framework inhibited the development of serious rifts, inasmuch as the main principles, structures, processes, and expectations are etched in legislative stone. As a result, the Post and the government have seen eye-to-eye on the big questions, and this has allowed postal development to move forward. Nonetheless, there is always a possibility that a crisis will emerge. The Freightways case was a wake-up reminder that the Post was still a state enterprise. Its shareholder – the government – retains real authority, including the authority to set financial targets, to appoint and fire the board, and to approve key initiatives. It will retain this authority until that time when the Post is privatized – a development that does not appear to be on the agenda at the moment (and unlikely to happen under the new Labour government). A Freightways type of case is unlikely to occur, as the government's recent support of the Post's banking initiative suggests. If it were to happen again, there would likely be a crisis at the board and management level, potentially an exodus of key people, and a drop in performance that would hurt the government's dividends. In these circumstances, the privatization issue would likely emerge front and centre.

The New Zealand experience is one of the most positive of the countries in this study. Its small market and isolated location may limit the overall significance of the case. But there is no denying the power and effectiveness of the postal regime that New Zealand has created, and the fact that this regime has contributed to the emergence of a well-run Post in a healthy and increasingly competitive postal market.

PART THREE

The National Model

A third category of response to the Posts' situation has been what can be characterized as the national or public model. The construction of each of the postal regimes examined in this book has been, to varying degrees, informed by national or political considerations. Moreover, the specific character of postal regimes – whether mercantile, market, or national – reflects a country's particular cultural, historic, and political inheritance. What distinguishes countries within the national or public postal regime from the mercantile and market ones is the continuing predominance of social and political considerations over economic ones in formulating and executing postal policy. Countries within this model include Denmark, France, and Canada.

The countries situated within this model have reformed their postal systems to a considerable extent. They are part of the present study, since these reforms qualify them for characterization as progressive postal regimes. Their Posts have been corporatized to a significant degree and are motivated in large part by commercial values and logic. Their postal markets have been partially liberalized, and their protected or reserved areas have been narrowed. Regulatory and operational matters have been separated to a certain extent, and their governments tend not to be as involved in the day-to-day life of the Posts as in the past. However, these reform processes have stopped at a point before total liberalization or complete corporatization. Their Posts continue to enjoy an exclusive privilege or protected area, which creates political obligations, dependency, and scrutiny. Continued state ownership has limited the process of corporatization in this

regime, where governments remain at the centre of postal-policy decision making. The result is that key decisions remain informed by
political as opposed to postal or economic considerations. National or
political factors and priorities have limited the reform process and
directed and shaped it to particular national ends and purposes.

There have always been both social and economic dimensions to
the Post's existence. Depending on circumstances, its twin duties
might not have been in conflict. The relationship between its social
and economic responsibilities became increasingly antagonistic over
the last two decades. As an over-generalization, the policy discourse
and practice of countries within the market model saw the predominance of economic objectives and the downplaying or elimination of
social ones. On the other hand, countries within the national or public
model have tended to maintain social objectives while bearing and
tolerating the economic costs of this choice.

Posts played a substantial historical role in national development,
economic expansion, and social modernization. For example, the
building up of the rural network connected far-flung towns and villages
to the centre of society, to both economic and political effect. The
marginal postal revenue generated by this expansion did not usually
cover the costs involved. The subsidization of the delivery of newspapers and magazines contributed to the education of the population
and the development of its civic sense – at considerable costs. The Post's
cheap (often under-priced) cost and accessibility offered an effective
communications subsidy to small- and medium-sized firms – often
resulting in postal deficits that had to be absorbed in the state budget.
For most of its history, the Post served both social and economic objectives in equal measure. The costs of the Post were typically hidden or
absorbed in the state budget. These costs were unchallenged or rationalized as a public investment in political and economic development.

This (oversimplified) picture changed in the 1970s and 1980s as a
result of technological change and the fiscal impact of the end of the
post-war boom. Indeed, this was the context in which the postal-reform
process unfolded. Technology provided communications alternatives
to the Post. Rising state budget deficits generated increased public
scrutiny of the value and costs of the services provided by the Post.
Governments were then forced to make difficult policy decisions. They
had to determine how important the postal option was relative to the
technological alternatives available. They had to rank which public
services should be allocated scarce public resources. These deliberations created tension between the social and economic objectives that
the Post had carried historically. For example, did the public value of
the rural postal service merit economic subsidy when there were

communications alternatives available and other pressing policy priorities? Should the Post be transformed into a more lean, focused, efficient, and self-financing operation – even if this meant a change or decline in postal services and/or the loss of thousands of jobs? Should postal products and services reflect real costs, even if this raised prices to users and potentially drove the Post out of a number of markets? What was the ultimate purpose of the Post: to contribute efficiently to economic progress or to contribute to the social fabric of the nation?

Countries within the national or public model have not been ignorant of the technological changes or economic realities that have threatened the survival of the Post over the last quarter century. In conceptualizing a strategic-policy response, though, political or national considerations have figured more prominently in decision making than in other countries. Postal policy in this type of regime is typically cast across a national backdrop. Employment, national unity, rural development, social solidarity, and many other public considerations are the key factors determining postal-policy choices. Proceeding in this fashion has strategic and operational consequences. Politics looms larger in this sort of postal regime than in others, in order that key postal decisions remain made by political authorities. While often corporatized, the Posts in this regime enjoy less commercial and market freedom, recruit less private-sector-oriented personnel, confront a more constrained set of policy options, see more public and bureaucratic figures on their boards, and remain under greater public, parliamentary, and media scrutiny. The economic performance of the Posts in this regime is important to the political authorities, but typically less important than the fundamental and wider political goals that ultimately drive postal policy. Indeed, the government typically directs the Post to absorb economic costs and attain a lesser rate of economic return, given that it has been obliged to pursue public-policy goals distinct from postal-policy goals.

Notwithstanding its political character, there is a policy rationale for this approach. The approach reflects a conscious evaluation of the best way to respond to the technological, international, and economic challenges facing the Post. The authorities within this model suggest that the best way for a country to meet these challenges is to control and manage them actively. The market approach, in contrast, accepts the logic of these changes and liberalizes the market to insist that postal operators build up the capacity to meet these challenges. The mercantile model, in contrast yet again, confronts the logic of these challenges by privatizing or corporatizing the monopoly Post so as to have it emerge as a stronger, dominant player in the new postal world. The national or public approach neither liberalizes nor privatizes, although it contains elements of both in an eclectic policy mix. This approach seeks to control or neutralize the challenges confronting the Post in order to ensure traditional postal objectives and government's control over the postal agenda. This has required some degree of protection of their Posts from these pressures, including the ongoing perpetuation of their monopoly status and their reserved area. The national or public approach comprises a mix of policy instruments, reflecting both postal-reform initiatives and politically motivated ones. At bottom, though, the approach is designed to protect the Post's capacity to serve social and political objectives on the domestic scene.

6 Denmark

The Danish postal regime remains in flux after a reform process that took place only recently (1994–95). A number of critical variables need to be addressed, including an uncertain and troubling labour situation. This has perpetuated the politically sensitive character of the postal system. The Danish postal regime was built upon a series of political compromises, which has made the regime unstable. With some exceptions, the Post has been corporatized and become a limited-liability company like other companies. Its reserved area has been narrowed to 250 grams, liberalizing the market to a degree. However, political authorities stand very much at the centre of the Danish postal regime.

The Danish postal system was founded on Christmas Eve, 1624, by King Christian IV. Postal operations were organized and operated until 1995 within the mechanics of a government department, accountable to a minister. The Post – or Postvaesenet – came into existence only in 1982. The Post Office Act was passed in 1989, after which it was managed by a general director, a kind of permanent secretary answerable to a minister. However, it continued to function basically as a department of government. Until quite recently, then, the Post enjoyed little to no corporate autonomy, faced little real market pressure (its reserved area was one kilogram), and the state managed its affairs quite directly. Every postal decision of note had to be approved by the Danish Parliament: any expenditures, change in service levels, introduction of new products, investment plans and decisions – all the basic ingredients of the postal operation needed political approval.[1] Investments had to be financed exclusively out of operational revenues because capital expenditures could not be depreciated. Long-term planning was not possible, since all decisions had to be approved politically. The Ministry of Finance used the Post as a cash cow. It withdrew revenue (that is, taxed the Post) without considering the Post's condition or needs.

The postal-reform process began in the 1980s, following a period when the Post had been struggling. It had endured serious financial and management difficulties, and the state was obliged to absorb a series of large postal deficits.[2] A new director general was appointed at the time, who turned the Post around so that it became profitable by the early 1990s. This modernization experience was complemented by further rumblings of change that were emanating from the EC as well as the competition threatened by the looming figures of international mail operators and new technological alternatives.[3] The Telecom – united with the Post in the mid-1980s – was separated from it in the late 1980s. The postal bank (Giro) system was also divorced from the Post, in a series of small steps. All of these changes and challenges – in conjunction with the Post's rocky financial state in the 1980s – caused considerable concern about the Post's viability. For example, the postal union was concerned that technology was undercutting the postal monopoly and mooted the scenario of the Post becoming the "postal operator of last resort."[4]

There was, therefore, broad-based agreement by the early 1990s on the need for postal change and reform. However, each of the major actors had a different view on what concrete shape this change should take. The conservative parties pushed to transform the Post into a limited-liability company within a shareholding model. The traditional postal union – Dansk Postforbund – was against the shareholding model, for it feared the loss of its members' civil-servant status as well as the eventual privatization of the Post. The minister did not give this option serious consideration as a result. The union instead favoured the transformation of the Post into a state enterprise but with its civil-service benefits and privileges intact. The Labour Party was comfortable with the status quo and was concerned not to upset the unions. There was no great public pressure for change, save for some business pressure to modernize the Post. Postal management itself pushed for more competitive and commercial freedom based on its experience in the turnaround of the late 1980s. Had it not pushed assertively for this, the reforms that followed might not have taken place.[5]

A political compromise was pieced together in the early 1990s and a new public-enterprise model was developed for the postal sector. As in many other countries, it was the Labour Party that brought this change into being in 1994 – although the reform path had been cleared by right-wing governments in the previous decade. The postal union played a key role in devising the new postal model. This "independent" public enterprise was set up apart from the state – with a separate organizational structure, a number of commercial and operational freedoms, and a budget outside the state budget. However, in deference to the postal unions – who felt betrayed over the earlier privatization of the Giro Bank – postal workers retained their civil-service status within the "independent" public enterprise.[6] This was a crucial feature of the new postal regime, which reflected political realities and generated serious policy consequences.

The political compromise surrounding postal reform was articulated in an all-party consensus document in November 1994.[7] The premise of the agreement – elaborated in the document – was that technological change, increased competition, and changing consumer and customer tastes had radically altered the environment in which the Post functioned. This new environment would in turn likely be altered further by postal policy emanating from the EC. At this time, only 60 per cent of the Post's revenues were generated in the reserved area, requiring the Post to be competitive in the market to maintain its overall revenues. The all-party agreement presented a new "model" for the Post to this end. It determined "to change the Post Office's competitive situation by reorganizing the state-owned business as an independent public business on special condition" (Section I). This would be done by "establish[ing] an up-to-date framework for the Post Office so that the business ... will be able to function in free market conditions in competition with private operators" (Concluding remarks).

The framework or model – to be reviewed in three years to evaluate its impact – comprised two broad elements: separating the Post from the state and allowing the Post to enjoy commercial freedom (Section III). The consensus document anticipated all of the ingredients that would subsequently be laid out in legislation to establish the new Danish postal regime. The Post would leave the embrace of government to become a business bound by the Companies Act. A government-appointed board would manage the Post, whose assets, budget, business plans, and capital initiatives would be separate from the state. The state would retain ownership functions, and the Post would pay it dividends and taxes. As will be seen below, the state would contract with the Post to provide the universal postal service, in return for monopoly privileges in a reserved area. Finally, the all-party agreement declared: "The proposed model does not include changes to the form of employment for the currently employed state tenure civil servants and employees employed on a union agreement basis" (Section Vg). This was a critical element of the agreement, whose impact is still unfolding.

THE STATUTORY AND REGULATORY REGIME

There are three statutory measures that created the new Danish postal regime: the Postal Service Act,[8] the Post Danmark Act,[9] and the "Concession"[10] granted by the state to Post Danmark. The first measure redefines the postal-policy regime, the second coporatizes the Post, and the third elaborates how the universal system will be maintained.

The Postal Services Act

The Postal Services Act is only four and a half pages long – testament to the Nordic trait of creating simple, straightforward legislation. However, there are fifteen pages of detailed comments on, and explanations of, the legislation that accompany the bill. This indicates the political sensitivity of the legislation.

The objective of the act is to ensure that Danish citizens continue to enjoy equal access to a high-quality national postal system with low and uniform prices. It declares the state's domestic and international obligations in this regard. The legislation defines the universal-service obligation, guaranteeing nationwide letter service up to one kilogram and parcels up to twenty kilograms. The legislation applies to all operators and businesses functioning in the postal market. But the state retains a "sole rights" area (exclusive privilege). The scope of the reserved area was reduced from the previous level (one kilogram) to 250 grams (or six times the letter price). This reserved area excludes courier, catalogues, express, and so on. The rationale for maintaining a reserved area was explained this way in the act's accompanying notes: "In the delimitation of the sole rights, emphasis has … been placed on the sole rights in the long term also being extensive enough to create the economic foundations for a universal postal service at uniform prices and of a high quality, as is traditional in Denmark, and which will ensure the maintenance of a suitably fine-meshed net of post offices."[11] This "fine-meshed" network is not defined in the act nor is it specified quantitatively. The act indicates that the minister of transport[12] has the authority to limit the extent of the rural network, but another note outlines the government's objective to maintain normal postal service in rural areas.[13]

The act, then, presents a delicate political balance between liberalization of the postal market and the political realities that inform the postal-policy area. The minister stands at the centre of the act, with the authority to change the extent of – or even eliminate – the reserved area. The minister can also alter the nature of the delivery and counters network and other features of the postal system. The act elaborates how the state's responsibility for the universal service is to be implemented (anticipating the corporatization of the Post Office in the Post Danmark Act). It determines that this responsibility will be transferred to the Post through a "Concession," which will lay out detailed service and quality goals, the extent of the network, accounting principles (to avoid cross-subsidization), pricing procedures, and other public expectations (Chapter 3). The accompanying notes spell out some of these politically sensitive details. The ministry of transport has the responsibility to ensure compliance; it will monitor public expectations regarding postal services and create an independent body to oversee the Post's performance (Chapter 3.2).

The Post Danmark Act

The second statutory ingredient of the new postal regime is the Post Danmark Act (8 February 1995). It is another short piece of legislation (three pages) but there are eighteen pages of accompanying notes, which comment on and explain the bill

The purpose of the act is to transform the Post Office into the Post Danmark, with greater flexibility, a commercial mandate, competitive capacity, and a customer orientation. The act lays out the rules and principles that will inform its operation. This new "independent public sector business," as the act characterized it, would operate in the market like any other limited-liability company. It would be subject to the Danish Act on Limited Companies and would compete on equal terms with other postal operators, with a few exceptions (to be noted below). Instead of being a government department under the surveillance of director general, it would function as an independent public company, directed by a board. The Minister assumed all the rights normally associated with shareholders, although there would be no shares and the Post could not be sold. An explanatory note explains, though, that the minister does not have the authority to issue instructions to the Post nor to insist on certain activities. This speaks to the principle of separating regulation from operations.

The legislation separated the Post from the normal operations of the state's budget, and the Post assumed its own liability. It was given authority to administer its capital and operational funds, to depreciate its assets, to take out loans using its own assets as security, to buy other companies or enter into joint ventures, and so on. This freedom from the state came at a "cost": the Post paid DKK2.6 billion to the state for "goodwill"; the remaining part of the assets was valued at DKK2.7 billion and was considered an investment by the state. These figures represent hard bargaining between the Post and the Department of Finance, which gained DKK2.6 billion and still retains the right to sell the company. The Post had to borrow DKK1.8 billion to finance its freedom (the rest was derived from liquid assets). This financial transfer was intended to put the Post on a level competitive playing field with other operators. The same principle informed the act's dividend and tax orientation. The Post was obliged to pay company tax and annual dividends, the latter at a level to be determined by the minister upon recommendation from the board and discussion with the minister of finance. An explanatory note to the bill suggests that the return on equity to the state should be 6 per cent or at least one-third of the profits before tax.

The act notes that the minister will issue a "Concession" to the Post to carry out the universal-service obligations. In return, the Post will be assigned the sole-rights area. Moreover, the act allows the Post to "carry out other business in order to support the nationwide post office network," including financial services (Section 1.3/2). The Post was assigned authority to set its own prices, save in the sole-rights and publications areas. The minister of transport would regulate these areas in collaboration with the minister of finance. An explanatory note outlined an RPI-X price-cap formula that would allow price increases in the sole-rights area at a rate 1 per cent below increases in the cost of living.

In all other areas but one, the Post would be free to act like an independent company. It would be free to negotiate and set working conditions for any employee that it hired after the act was passed. But existing employees would carry their civil-service status with them into the new corporation.

The Concession

The third ingredient in the new Danish postal regime was the concessionary agreement between the government and the Post. This agreement was based on an exchange: the Post was assigned the responsibility to carry out the government's universal postal obligations in return for the state's sole-rights area. There was no question that there could be any more than one Concession. There was also no question that this concessionary agreement would be executed with anyone other than the Post. In a note accompanying the Postal Service Act, the government commented that "the market is not large enough to bear the construction of a new competitive infrastructure necessary for the fulfillment of the obligation to convey associated with the sole rights."[14] At the same time, the Post insisted on being granted a sole-rights area in return for taking on the universal-service obligation.

The Concession takes the form of an executive order. In six brief pages, it lays out in clear and precise terms the social rights and obligations that it has assigned to the Post. On the one hand, the Post is obliged to provide a nationwide postal service: "The postal services covered by the universal service obligation must be provided in all parts of the country at uniform prices and high quality" (Part 2, Section 8(1)). In exchange, the Post takes over sole rights in the areas of addressed mail and incoming international mail up to 250 grams. This sole-rights area excludes courier and express, catalogues, unaddressed mail, and so on. This exchange in the concession is clearly articulated as a quid pro quo.

The scope of the universal service includes letters and addressed items up to 1 kilogram, publications up to 500 grams, parcels up to 20 kilograms, and literature for the blind up to 7 kilograms. The Concession detailed a service standard that the Post was obliged to meet: 97 per cent next-day delivery of letters. The Post was also obliged to do periodic surveys, at its expense, to demonstrate that it was meeting this target. The Concession obliges the Post to provide a national network. But it provides no specifics or details about this obligation, other than the requirement to provide an annual report on the issue. The Post is given price autonomy, which is limited in three ways. First, prices in the sole-rights area are to be set within the price-cap formula of consumer-price index minus 1 per cent. Second, any reduced or discount rates for volume mailings are to be offered in a non-discriminatory way. Third, the Concession expressly forbids cross-subsidization from the soles-rights area to competitive areas (save in those competitive areas that contribute to the universal-service obligation). This last point in turn was the basis for the Post's obligation to create an accounting system and to provide accounts that would allow the minister to make judgments.[15]

An annex to the Concession contains an "Executive Order on Postal Distribution of Newspapers and Magazines at Especially Low Rates." This annex lays out the terms and conditions for the state's compensation of the Post for the continuation of the postal policy of subsidized delivery rates for publications and materials for the blind. This compensation has subsequently been in the DKK500-million range.

In sum, the legislative measures created a particular Danish regulatory regime which maintained a considerable amount of political authority. A partial liberalization combined with a partial corporatization resulted in a postal regime that remained firmly situated in the political context. As will be seen in more concrete terms, the minister of transport retained considerable postal authority procedurally and in key policy areas.

REGULATION IN PRACTICE

The new Danish postal regime has existed only since 1995, so there has not been substantial opportunity for it to develop in practice. The presentation of the legislative framework has demonstrated that the model is a fairly simple and straightforward one, with few complexities or subtleties. This is because the postal monopoly continues to exist – and is commanded by the Post – and because the labour situation combines elements of the old and new postal regimes. These factors have had the effect of keeping postal matters on the political plane, with the ministers of transport and finance at the critical centre of postal life.

The Ministry

The Ministry of Transport is at the centre of the postal-regulatory regime and retains considerable authority and some operational control in postal matters. An explanatory note to the Postal Service Act declares that postal regulation and operation have been separated.[16] But the regulatory and ownership functions of postal policy remain housed in the same ministry.

The ministry has ultimate authority for postal matters in Denmark. It establishes the nature and scope of the universal postal system and has the authority, for example, to change or eliminate the sole-rights area. The ministry determines to whom the postal concession will be awarded and details the operational features of the universal system. The ministry determines the by-laws of Post Danmark, on recommendations from the board, and sets specific guidelines for its operation and behaviour. It offers the Post no financial guarantees and holds no liability for the Post's debt, but it has created a loan framework for the Post. The ministry assigns shareholder responsibility to the board, whose members are appointed by the ministry. These include two senior members of the Ministry of Transport and the Ministry of Finance. Thus, the relationship between the ministry and the Post combines elements of autonomy and control.

Nowhere is this more evident that in the area of financial returns that the ministry expects from the Post. There were clear and direct signals from the start that the ministry expected the Post to provide dividends to the shareholder (the government). This was laid out in the all-party agreement. The expected dividend in 1995 was set at 3 per cent of the Post's equity and at least one-third of the pre-tax profit; this would rise to 6 per cent in 1996 and 1997. This dividend target was ambitious, especially given the fact that the Post had had to pay the government DKK2.5 billion up front as a kind of purchase price for "good will" and its own existence. The target was subsequently reconsidered and recast at 5 per cent of equity and a minimum 50 per cent of profit after taxes.

The dividend issue has placed the Post and the ministry in an antagonistic position. On the one hand, the Post – which appears to have had no difficulty meeting the dividend target – maintains that the target is draining it of the resources that it requires to modernize the postal operation and to prepare itself for further European deregulation and competition. The postal unions appear to take the same point of view. On the other hand, by draining resources from the Post, the high-dividend policy maximizes the financial benefits accruing to the state budget. From the government's point of view, this is appropriate, since the Post is highly liquid financially. Moreover, the Post has not, from the government's perspective, proposed a compelling growth or investment model to justify a high level of retained earnings.[17] This tension and misalignment of perspectives will be discussed further below.

The Ministry of Finance looms large in the postal field. It sets profit and dividend targets in collaboration with the Ministry of Transport. Finance's presence in the postal regime is determined by the fact that pre-1995 postal employees retained their civil-service status in Post Danmark. This obliges Finance's presence for matters like contract settlements and is the basis for its representation on the board.

The Post thus finds itself in an uncomfortable context. The government benefits from the revenue it generates from the Post and is convinced that it can make better use of the surplus revenues than the Post can. Discussions with public officials and observers in Denmark suggest that this is more than just a financial grab – that it has a purpose. This purpose is to limit Post's access to financial surpluses to pursue a mercantile or growth strategy in the manner of the Germans or the Dutch, unless the Post presents a credible plan or strategy to this end that increases shareholder value. At the same time, though, it is unclear how the government wants the postal sector to develop or what it wants it to look like. It wants the Post to function well and to provide revenues. Beyond that, the government has not developed the kind of postal-policy awareness or ambition that exists in a number of other progressive postal regimes. Indeed, this financial orientation constrains the possibility of the postal-growth strategy that many feel is required.[18] A degree of policy anxiety and uncertainty thus informs the relationship between the Post and the government, whose views on the postal future are not well aligned. This reflects in part the highly institutionalized nature of the postal agenda, which constrains the development of a postal strategy or vision. The postal regime reflected an all-party consensus which was attained with a number of compromises – particularly regarding the Post's corporate status, the persistence of a sole-rights area, and the labour issue (see below). The unions negotiate with the Post, but their sense is that it is the government that ultimately says yes or no.[19] In sum, postal development does not head in either a mercantile or a market direction.

The ministry also retains some authority in the pricing of postal products. It approves price changes within a price-ceiling model in two areas – the sole-rights area and with respect to publications and magazines. The ministry retains the authority to approve any significant change in business strategy. It will be seen below that the Post has diversified, particularly at the retail level. But there has been little corporate diversification, partnering, or purchases, mainly because of the dividend policy discussed previously. In any event, any freedom enjoyed by the Post in this regard is conditional on board approval – and two government officials sit on the board.

The Ministry of Transport is authorized by the Postal Service Act to delegate its monitoring and compliance responsibilities to a third party. It has created a Postal Supervisory Authority, which is a subordinate but separate agency under the ministry. It has the responsibility to ensure the objectives of the Postal Service Act. It is consulted on issues like post-office closings. But, generally, it has played a passive role and does not have responsibilities in areas like licensing or pricing, which are retained by the minister.

The Post

The Board of Directors and Management Board have authority over the Post. The board enjoys the same competence as that of a board of a limited-liability company, approving the corporate plan and budget. The Ministry of Transport in turn exercises its powers of ownership at annual company meetings.

The board has nine members, including three members who are elected by postal employees. There are two government representatives on the board, at present the deputy permanent secretary in the Ministry of Finance and the deputy permanent secretary in the Ministry of Transport. With respect to the other four directors, an explanatory note to the all-party agreement indicates that the minister will

choose directors based on "social, user and commercial considerations, including persons with international and commercial qualifications." These four positions are currently held by directors, chairs
and board members from other corporations and organizations. The
board of Post Danmark is an "institutionalized" Board that does not
enjoy a high degree of independence. It essentially replicates the
political comprises and considerations that underlie the Danish postal
regime. It has an administrative orientation and does not provide the
basis for an independent corporate strategy.

The Board of Directors sets the budget (later approved by the
minister) and hires the CEO. The Post sets its own prices save in the
sole-rights area and with respect to magazines and publications. The
latter are set low deliberately as a matter of public policy, for which
the Post receives compensation in the area of DKK500 million.[20] The
Post carries its own liability, sets its budget, and can borrow (within a
loan framework determined by the ministry). It is expected to finance
its own operations, pay taxes, and provide dividends. This three-way
split of financial returns has been a source of tension, since the Post
feels that the arrangement has left it with insufficient resources for
modernization. The Post is allowed to provide other services and
products in order to support its network.

There has not been a substantial transformation of postal management since 1995. There have been some changes at the middle level,
but the top management has remained the same.[21] The senior managers – particularly on the operational side – are experienced managers of state enterprises. There has been little recruitment from the
private sector at this level. The present CEO has been at the Post since
1988 and was previously with the state railroads and with the Ministry
of Transportation before that. The deputy CEO also has a state-centred
background. The relationship between management and the board is
a good one, which reflects what might be called a similar administrative view. Some may think it ironic that the postal union feels that the
Post requires stronger management with new ideas.[22]

Postal Workers

In many ways, the union issue has overshadowed the postal scene in
Denmark since 1995. There are two elements to this issue. First, the
construction of the Danish postal regime reflected a compromise over
what kind of corporation the new Post Danmark would become, once
its days as a government department or bureaucracy ended. The
hybrid state enterprise that resulted saw postal workers retain their
civil-service status, notwithstanding the fact that they no longer worked

in a government department. Second, the Danish state decided in 1997 to end the practice of hiring civil servants, save in a narrow range of areas (for example, judges). All subsequent hirings by the state were of a "contract" character, without civil-service status. The upshot of this is that there are two different groupings of postal employees. On the one hand, there are the employees with civil-service status. They are represented by the Danish Postworkers Union (Dansk Postfor-bund). Its membership declines inexorably because, as each of its members resigns, that member is not replaced or replaced by an employee on contract.[23] That new member would be represented by a different union, the General Workers Union – SID (Specialarbejder-forbundet I Danmark).

The ongoing existence of two postal unions has created operational problems for the Post. It confronts situations in which two employees may be working side by side on the same task but belong to two different unions, with different terms and conditions of employment. The two unions have had different perspectives on operational and logistical changes proposed by management. Indeed, there was an extended period of time after 1997 when Postforbund refused to cooperate with the Post in introducing changes or experimenting with new distribution approaches. This had serious disruptive consequences for the introduction of the new letters system.

While the implications of this system fall on the Post, the situation is basically a creation of the state and requires a state solution as a result. The easiest solution would be for the state to eliminate the civil-service status of Postforbund employees. However, it is estimated that this would cost the government three years' pay and pension benefits, totalling DKK25 billion. This was a kind of poison pill that was built into the Postal Service Act in 1995, to persuade the union to agree to postal reform. The government appointed a lawyer to review the situation and to try to broker a deal between the two unions to create one organization. This appeared to be a highly unlikely prospect, since the two unions have different principles and objectives.[24] Nonetheless, an agreement-in-principle was reached in January 2000 to merge the unions some time in 2001, if members ratify the agreement and a deal is worked out to effect the merger.[25] The unions' interests are represented on the board, where three seats are allocated to the elected representatives of the employees. Recently, an election took place which saw a SID representative displaced by a Postforbund one. This has muddied the political waters since the government and management appear to favour SID, which has been more cooperative and supportive of new approaches.

The new Danish postal regime has perpetuated a close working relationship between the Post and the government. The Post's autonomy is limited by the powerful presence of two ministries, each of which has its own objectives for the Post. The government's presence on the Board of Directors limits the autonomy of the Post, which has not corporatized to any extent. It has not attracted, or been changed by, new management. As a result, it has not developed a compelling enough postal vision for the future to convince its shareholder that it should be allowed to retain its financial surpluses to expand the business. In key areas, the Ministry of Transport remains the dominant postal player. The long-term development of the Post remains deeply circumscribed by the government's policy towards the Post.

PERFORMANCE IMPLICATIONS

The postal-reform process in Denmark has been far less consequential than in other "progressive" regimes. This is because many of the characteristics of the previous regime were carried forward into the new one, in the absence of far-reaching liberalization and/or corporatization. It is thus not surprising that the implications of postal reform in Denmark have not been dramatic. The Post retains a reserved area or exclusive privilege of 250 grams. In traditional markets like the letter market, then, it confronts little direct competition in the domestic market. There are niche competitors like the "bike" companies that speed around major cities like Copenhagen, but they comprise a modest part of the market. As will be seen below, the Post purchased one of its only competitors in the courier market, Budstikken. The Post was turned around financially in the late 1980s and became profitable and competitive in the early 1990s.[26] The Post has subsequently maintained this fiscal and economic position. It maintains a capacity to carry out its universal-service obligations without much difficulty, although its quality achievements have not been as impressive as had been intended. This reflects, to a considerable degree, the ongoing tension and uncertainty on the labour front.

Revenues, Prices, and Profits

As indicated in Table 1 below, the Post's revenues expanded throughout the 1990s at a reasonable rate and hit the DKK10-billion level in 1998. Comparing the period pre- and post-1995, one sees a modest decline in the rate of growth of revenue. Turnover rose by 14.6 per cent between 1992 and 1995 and increased by 12.9 per cent between

Table 1
Postal performance in Denmark

	1992	1993	1995	1996	1997	1998
TURNOVER	7,800	8,100	8,938	9,364	9,722	10,092
letters				6,059	6,160	6,338
PROFIT						
pre tax			618	665	503	480
net			600	565	430	450
operating %			7	7	5	5
ROE %			13	12	8	9
Actual letters(m's*)				1,380	1,397	1,425
Employment	25,221		25,478	25,981	25,500	

* Millions.
Source: Post Danmark, *Annual Report*, 1998.

1995 and 1998. The Post reports that revenue growth is faster in the competitive than in the monopoly areas. Indeed, revenues from the monopoly area comprise only 45 per cent of turnover (and are declining by 2 per cent a year).[27] Labour uncertainty has had some impact on turnover. The revenue situation was not driven to any extent by price increases. The Post has the autonomy to set its own prices. But products in the reserved area are capped by a price formula – of consumer-price index minus 1 per cent. The letter price was increased by 7 per cent in January 1999, the first increase since April 1992.

As noted earlier, the profit picture has been positive. The Post is expected to be profitable (to a commercial-market standard) and to pay an after-tax dividend to the government. It has done so. This dividend is set (effectively) by the ministry, after a recommendation by the board. It has been set at around 6 per cent of equity. The Post's profits have enabled it to pay dividends regularly, but its overall rate of return has not reached commercial-market standards. In a number of ways, this is not surprising, given the large investments that it has made in technology, education, and reorganization and given also the degree of labour uncertainty that has persisted since 1995. For example, profits fell in 1997 upon completion of Distribution 96, the new letter service (see below). This program had the unintended consequence of raising labour costs, lowering labour morale, and harming productivity growth. Moreover, the Post makes a substantial pension contribution for those of its employees who are civil servants. Indeed, the ministry has required that this rate of contribution be increased from 15 to 22 per cent – at an annual cost of DKK190 million.[28] The decline in profits levelled off in 1998, but the fact is that the Post is not attaining the 10 per cent return that it would take to be self-sustaining. As the Post reported, "their level is not adequate for the longer term considering the increasing competition – especially internationally."[29]

Volumes

Post Danmark has had an extremely optimistic attitude with respect to mail volumes. The letters market was stagnant in the late 1980s and early 1990s. And, like other Posts, Post Danmark had expected a high degree of technological substitution and declining volumes. But all players on the postal scene report that the impact of electronic communications has not (yet) had the devastating impact on postal volumes that had been anticipated.[30] Indeed, the Post declared in 1998 that "the letter market is not likely to see any drastic fall in turnover over the next few years."[31] This is seen to reflect a number of factors, including the lively growth of turnover in the competitive sector, particularly the direct-mail sector. The Post is now able to introduce new products with less regulatory inhibition.[32]

The Post has worked to nurse its key customers. It set up Post Danmark Mailhouse (as an independent business unit) to strengthen sales and marketing in the letters area (an advertising campaign included the slogan "write a letter if you mean business"). It has entered partnerships to try and use e-commerce possibilities to expand postal business. For example, it delivers purchases of LEGO products that are warehoused by Dansk and ordered off of an IBM platform. Parcel turnover increased by 8 1/2 per cent in 1998.

The Post does not intended to be a direct player in the courier and express market. Instead, it has chosen to partner with TNT. It bought the largest courier in Denmark – Budstikken – which it owns directly only in the Copenhagen area (it is franchised elsewhere). One senses that the Post would like to get out of this area completely but that it has to move cautiously because of the implications for employment.

Indeed, the labour dimension looms large in this area as well. Lack of management-labour cooperation, illegal strikes, and bad morale (and turnover) have been bad for productivity and market image. Even more directly, when the new mail-delivery system was introduced (see below), this caused disruption and bad labour relations, which had a negative impact on postal volumes. It is difficult to catalogue and compare letter volumes in this period, because of changes in statistical reporting in the Post's reports. However, letter volumes appear to have increased by 5.4 per cent between 1990 and 1994. Volumes decreased by 2 per cent in 1995 to below 1.4 billion but bounced back to 1.425 billion in 1998.[33] The 2 per cent increase in letter volumes in 1998 was driven by growth in direct mail.

Mechanization

There have been a number of major initiatives undertaken by the Post to increase productivity and improve quality. Overall, about DKK1.4 billion has been spent on the Logistics Development Plan, which aimed to increase mechanical sorting of mail from the 40–50 per cent level to 85–90 per cent. This was designed to generate annual savings of DKK400 million, with a loss of 2,000 jobs (mainly in delivery).[34] Distribution 96 was a program to eliminate the piecework system that had previously underpinned the delivery system. The aim was to make the delivery system function more efficiently and at a higher level of quality, but it generated numerous labour problems and illegal strikes.[35] A new Parcel Centre was opened at Brondby in conjunction with the International Mail Centre at Copenhagen Airport. This plant has a capacity of 140,000 parcels a day. Generally speaking, the Post feels that it has had insufficient resources available to make needed capital investment, as a result of the state's financial demands. On the other hand, the government feels that the Post has not developed a substantial enough plan to warrant further investment and expansion. And the postal union worries about the long-term impact of technological change on the level of employment.

Employment

The labour scene has bedevilled the postal scene since 1995. This is a situation that the Post inherited after 1995, which needs to be resolved if the Post is to emerge as a self-sustaining commercial and competitive operation. The resolution of this issue rests with the state, not with the Post.

There are two inheritances that the Post has had to deal with. The first is the long-standing tradition of piecework payment for delivery. This was the situation until 1996, at which time the mechanization program required its termination and replacement by a hourly system and salary rate. The introduction of Distribution 96 was long overdue, but it created serious morale and operational problems in the transition period. This problems continued through 1998.

Second, as noted earlier, the new postal regime created a two-tier workforce. The state restricted civil-service status or hiring to all but a small selection of employees, particularly in the justice and law fields. When Post Danmark was created, the existing workers were allowed to retain their civil-service status in the new state enterprise. All employees hired afterwards, though, would be hired on contract, on terms and conditions set by the Post. Two different unions represented each group respectively. The absolute number of members in the former (the Danish Postworkers Union) will decline inexorably over time. For example, it declined by one thousand in 1998 (6.5 per cent).

These two factors have contributed to ongoing labour uncertainty, both with respect to the relationship between the two unions and with regard to the relationship between managers and the civil-service workers. For example, the Danish Postworkers Union (the civil-service workers) broke off relations with Post Danmark just before the end of 1997 and there were numerous illegal strikes in the distribution service in 1997. There was national labour unrest in 1998, which hurt postal business especially in the area of newspaper delivery and direct mail. Much of the disruption ended in 1998 and some cooperation is occurring. But the situation remains far from stable.

The upshot has been that productivity improvements at the Post have not been as high as had been anticipated by postal-policy makers, and, as a result, profits have been disappointing.[36] The postal union in turn feels that productivity targets have been too high, creating problems of labour stress and low morale. Indeed, the degree of turnover at the Post is striking – 23 per cent in 1997 and 27 per cent in 1998. Part of this can be attributed to the fact that the Post uses a high proportion of part-time workers. But it also reflects a serious morale problem among Post workers.

Mechanization and technological change will place downward pressure on the level of employment – which is expected to decline by 30 per cent in the sorting centres and delivery service in the immediate future. The level of employment is relatively stable at the moment. It fell from 28,235 positions in 1989 to 25,221 in 1993. It has remained in the 25,000 range since.

Quality and Innovation

The Post's quality standards have been acceptable but have not been as high as expected.[37] The letters standard is next-day delivery – which was attained 95 per cent of the time in 1994. It fell somewhat as a result of the introduction of new delivery systems but rebounded to 94.5 per cent in 1998. The EU standard is a modest 85 per cent rate, but the Post's target in the Concession is 97 per cent. An interesting and popular innovation was a system of evening delivery of parcels, at which time people are actually at home. This was complemented by an early morning parcel-delivery service for business.

Retail

Like networks around the world, the Danish counters network struggled in the 1990s as a result of changing consumer habits. Customers use the Giro (banking) services of the Post less and less, and annual transactions fell from nearly 110 million in 1991 to 63 million in 1998. The Post has been given considerable leeway to diversify its product mix to attract business, and it offers rail tickets, stationary items, video films and CDs, mobile phones, toys, and so on. Its BILLETnet (a ticket reservation/purchase system) was combined with the private foundation ARTE to create the publicly owned company BILLETnet A/S. It initiated a program of retail modernization in 1996 – called Tomorrow's Post Office.

The outlets are organized increasingly on a franchise basis. By 1997, there were 1,278 post offices, of which 636 were post-office outlets. There was a political controversy and battle over network rationalization between 1991 and 1994, when each closure was a political decision and event. Post Danmark's Concession does not require or set out a detailed target or minimum number of outlets. To close a large number now would require political approval, but as long as a national coverage is maintained the Post can open, close, and change particular sites.[38]

An amendment to the Postal Act allowed the Post to enter into an exclusive agreement with a financial institution to provide financial services through the post-office network. It struck an exclusive thirteen-year deal with BG Bank (Bikupen GiroBank A/S) in 1995, with the aim of setting up seventy-five outlets by the year 2000.[39]

Joint Ventures, Collaboration, and the Future

The Danish government has not made resources available to the Post to pursue an expansion and diversification plan, as in the mercantile model. While the Post's possibilities for diversification have not hit a limit, it does not have the capacity to be terribly expansive or ambitious in this regard. Moreover, any substantial or radical initiative would require board and later ministry approval.

As has been noted in earlier chapters, Post Danmark has become involved in a cross-border parcel-services venture, called Nordpack AB, with Sweden, Norway, and Finland. This collaborative Scandinavian effort will coordinate logistical and IT systems. The initiative has been slow to get off the ground, reflecting local union issues, domestic versus international considerations, and the usual array of national inhibitions. But it now appears that the Scandinavian Posts will be transferring their parcel operations into the collaborative organization.

In other activities, the Post purchased Belgavia Mailhouse B.V., a retail and letter-mail business in Brussels. It relaunched its courier product Jetpost, with a cooperative partner in Sweden (Posten Express). It bought the courier carrier Budstikken Transport A/S in February 1999.

The possibility of privatization is not far off the agenda, but it is unclear what the government's intentions are. At the moment, it is carrying out a review, in anticipation of new EC initiatives. What the government is likely to do depends substantially on what the Germans do. Liberalization and privatization in Germany would force the government's hand and give any qualitative policy change a political and defensible rationale. Within the general Nordic trend to privatization, the Danes are the farthest along this route, having sold $5.6 billion of state assets since 1993.[40]

HIGHLIGHTS OF THE DANISH CASE

What can one learn from the Danish case? What interest does its experience and the national or public approach hold for policy makers? The Danish regime has adopted a number of procedural innovations and initiatives. These include the introduction of third-party regulation and the specification of universal-service targets and expectations in a quantitative, contractual way, which can be monitored to ensure the Post's compliance with them. These are important developments that mirror similar developments across Europe and beyond. The consistency of these developments across models and nations suggests the extent to which they comprise the essential elements of a new postal-policy paradigm.

Yet such developments are not the most essential or compelling features that one can extract from examining the Danish case. At the most general level, the most obvious conclusion that one can draw is this: incremental change, as in the Danish case, is not likely to change economic performance and results nor to confront the fundamental problems facing the Post: international competition and technological change. The national or public model pursued in Denmark reflected but did not resolve or transcend those issues and pressures that led to the changes in the regime in the first place. The Danish postal regime continues to juggle political and economic goals, with political objectives or criteria being the determining factor. The result is that postal policy in Denmark lacks a strategic character or a clear sense of where the Post is going in the future.

This is not to suggest that the Danish postal situation is in crisis. Indeed, this case demonstrates that some sensible reforms and a modest degree of corporatization can result in solid performance and healthy profits. To this extent, the model adopted has been successful. The Post continues to attain the universal-service objectives – and at no cost to the government. There have been some ups and downs in service and quality, but overall there has not been a decline in the universal service. On this level, the Post is in tune with the authorities' political objectives, as laid out in the Concession. The political objective of maintaining postal service as in the past remains at the centre of postal policy. This dimension of postal policy has actually improved. The public's postal expectations are now detailed and quantified in a public, legal document, providing a standard against which the Post's performance can be evaluated.

On the other hand, this benign state of affairs may be resting on contingent circumstances. One cannot assume that the Post's capacity to pursue the universal-service obligations – at no cost to the state – can exist indefinitely without changes to the organization. The Post's present capacity and profitability rests on three conditions. First, it retains the sole-rights protection in the letter market, which underpins its market presence and economic performance. Second, the letters market remains relatively buoyant. Third, the impact of electronic and international mail has been only moderate to this point. The Post's capacity to maintain the universal system, and generate profits for the state, could change quickly if economic conditions deteriorate and/ or and technological and international competition increase. The Danish model does not offer the Post great incentive or capacity to modernize, to develop strategy, and to increase efficiency and capacity. This state of affairs could ultimately jeopardize the Post's ability to meet its universal-service obligations, an outcome that would in turn undermine the stability of this model or approach.

Politics and the state remain at the centre of the Danish postal regime, because neither corporatization nor liberalization has developed thoroughly or to its logical conclusion. The absence of a definitive liberalization or corporatization thrust has limited the extent to which the postal situation has been transformed. This stands in contrast to the national experiences in the other models. For example, the Dutch and German experience with, or anticipation of, privatization has transformed their Posts into organizations dominated by corporate values, personnel, and strategy. This transformation in turn generated an ambitious reconstruction of postal strategy. The elimination of the postal monopoly in Finland and Sweden has limited the political presence in postal matters and forces their Posts to increase their competitiveness. Post Danmark remains a political creature whose sole-rights and privileges continue to insulate it from market pressures. As a result, it has not developed a new corporate thrust, and the government looms large in postal decision making and the setting of the postal agenda. On the one hand, the state can insist on a quid pro quo for the sole-rights area, and its continuing monopoly character makes the Post an object of political scrutiny and public evaluation. On the other hand, the state's role as exclusive shareholder allows it to help set the corporate agenda, particularly through its presence on the board.

Indeed, the dividend policy pursued by the state is a metaphor for the centrality of political control of the postal agenda at this time. This political control places the state in a kind of conflict of interest, where it benefits from the policy inaction that exists on either the mercantile or market fronts. That is, such inaction allows the government to benefit from postal revenues. This also places it in conflict with public and postal interests. On the one hand, the Post's continued profitability suggests that the sole-rights area may be too large and unnecessary to maintain the existing universal-service obligations. But the government is not proposing or contemplating further liberalization. The result is that postal users are being taxed by the state. On the other hand, these "surplus" revenues are not being used for postal purposes, specifically, to increase the Post's future capacity to adapt to international and technological change. Over the long run, this may have serious public-policy consequences. The existing state of affairs reflects the fact that Danish postal policy lacks a strategic character. The objectives of postal policy are narrowly defined as the maintenance of postal service and the generation of revenues for the state.

Like other postal regimes, the Danish system reflects a consensus of sorts. From the late 1980s on, there has been a broad consensus that the changing postal environment requires a change in the organization of the postal sector. But, unlike the other regimes, a strategic *postal* consensus did not really emerge – either to strengthen the postal sector or to encourage efficiency and competitiveness through a market approach. Instead, the politics of the situation has dominated the postal logic of the situation. This has generated and perpetuated a political consensus rather than a postal one. The consensus translated into some changes in the form of the Post and the regime – like the transition from a department to an enterprise, the division of responsibilities between the state and the Post, and so on. But, fundamentally, postal policy and practice remained dominated by the state.

The labour situation has been a metaphor for all of this. A civil-service model was grafted on to a corporate or state-enterprise model, with predictable results. Moreover, the uncertain labour situation continues to demand a political solution and maintains politics at the

centre of the postal-policy regime. Similarly, the dominance of the
board by political and institutional interests has ensured that neither
the board nor management has the clout or authority to set the postal
agenda. Neither appears to have the authority or capacity to articulate
a new postal vision that can be assertively pursued. Notwithstanding
the formal changes that have taken place, postal policy in Denmark
has an administrative character that is not substantially different from
what existed before 1995.

7 France

The French Post Office – La Poste – has been a semi-independent government agency since 1991. It is *un exploitant autonome de droit public* – a public enterprise that exists within its own specific legislative and statutory framework.[1] Of all the Posts examined in this study, La Poste is the most self-consciously national and public. Government and postal leaders alike declare an open opposition to the liberal, market model, which is seen as an Anglo-American import into the countries of northern Europe. The French government has not supported postal liberalization and has acted to slow this process in Europe. Government and political leaders also reject the notion that a corporatization process should lead to privatization of the Post; this is an issue that is not even remotely on the public-policy agenda in France. Indeed, *vive la difference* is a phrase that could be applied to the French postal scene, whose authorities conceptualize the postal sector in a radically different way than is done in other progressive regimes. The French have situated themselves as leaders – particularly among a number of countries in southern Europe – of an alternative approach to postal development which emphasizes the Post's public character and mission. As a result, the Post has remained very much in the public consciousness and view in the 1990s.

The Post has had a long history in France, with royal and military origins in the fifteenth century. There has been a minister of post and telegraphs since 1879. Over and above the postal and telecom areas, it has played a substantial national role in providing banking and financial services (the National Savings Bank was established in 1881).

Its existence within this triumvirate of postal, telecommunications, and banking activities remained stable, dependent, and unchanged through to the 1990s. It was deeply embedded within the state as a department of government and part of the state's budget. Historically, the postal business was not profitable and the government was heavily involved in all postal decisions. The public-service dimension of the Post was paramount, and political objectives dominated economic ones in a policy paradigm where the Post was considered an important element in national development. Postal employees have civil-service status, a hard-earned accomplishment that was attained in 1946.

The postal-reform process in France began in the 1960s, at which time there were discussions about splitting the Post and the Telegraph into two separate organizations. This process was very much a state-driven one, with many government studies, reviews, and policy reports and recommendations. The process accelerated under the governments of Raymond Barre and Giscard d'Estaing. Later, the elections of neo-liberal governments saw market and liberalization issues emerge into public-policy discussions. The privatization of telecommunications was mooted. In 1989 a Socialist government was formed and a serious postal strike took place.[2] This set the stage for the postal reform that was initiated in 1990.

A government commissioned study[3] of the PTT's future set the wheels in motion for what turned out to be a restrained and modest postal reform. This reform reflected the tenor of the Prévot Report, which had followed extensive meetings, public hearings, and submissions across the country. Its analysis and conclusions were informed by five key themes:

- the PTT was caught up in an information and communications revolution which was unfolding in a diversified, competitive, and international way (14–19);
- there were widespread calls for increased PTT autonomy, in order to increase its capacity to deal with these changes (28, 71–4);
- notwithstanding these global and technological changes, there was a strong consensus that the state should remain central to the future of PTT, to ensure the maintenance of its public-service character (144);
- the PTT was nationally important for a number of reasons, including the fact that, with over 450,000 workers, it was the fifth-largest employer in France (16); and
- market realities and user groups suggested that PTT needed more autonomy to become commercial, but not at the cost of the abandonment of its public-service mission (28).

The report's conclusions were modest and framed by a tension between commercial and technical processes on the one hand and public goals and political realities on the other. Its major postal recommendation was to separate the Post from Telecom in a stand-alone organization. La Poste would have its own board, budget, and planning process distinct from the government. However, the report insisted on the ongoing centrality and authority of the state in the postal realm (144). It recommended the creation of a national council to oversee the operation of both the Post and the Telecom. The council would comprise representatives of important ministries, union delegates, and the territories, and the minister of posts and telecommunications would chair it (150). The report acknowledged the widespread call for postal autonomy. But its recommendations in this regard were modest. Its discussion comprised two small paragraphs about naming directors, organizing services, preparing a budget, and dealing with workers (147). On key issues – such as pricing, definition of service levels, setting of objectives, and planning – the Post would continue to work directly with the state. Moreover, postal employees would retain their civil-service status (155).

The Prévot report was a creature of its time and reflected the political culture surrounding it. All the key postal actors wanted modernization and change, but none of them pushed a particularly aggressive reform agenda. The state wanted change to modernize the PTT to adapt to the communications revolution. But the state did not particularly want to see its own authority diminished.[4] The Post was not anxious to eliminate its public-service orientation, nor were private users – notwithstanding some isolated calls for privatization. The postal unions wanted the Post to be strengthened, so as to increase its capacity to deal with competition and technological change. But the unions were intensely opposed to liberalization. They did not want to lose their civil-service status and they believed that only the state could provide an adequate public service.[5]

The French government introduced legislation in 1990 to transform the PTT. In the first instance, the Post was separated from Telecom and set up as a separate organization. This was agreed by all to be a necessary condition to put the Post on a modern footing. La Poste was given its own board with greater freedom to develop policy, to invest, and to act like a corporation subject to the market. It was given financial autonomy and expected to make a profit. Day-to-day ministerial involvement was cut back. But the minister retained a considerable degree of authority in postal matters. The state retained 100 per cent ownership of La Poste. It would elaborate its expectations of the Post in a contract with it (*contrat de plan*), which would frame the Post's existence as both a "corporation" and a "public service." The Post was given the state's exclusive privilege in a segment of the market (and some tax relief), in return for taking on the obligation to carry out the state's universal-service obligations. There was no question or suggestion that this could be done by anyone other than La Poste. What resulted, then, was a kind of hybrid state enterprise. It combined an increased amount of freedom for the Post with the maintenance of a considerable degree of state influence and authority.

Before presenting a more detailed elaboration of the Post's legal and statutory environment, it is worth pointing out a number of issues that this discussion might not capture adequately. First, two issues remained unresolved or uncertain after 1990 – the deficit and pension issues.[6] The postal legislation provided a two-edged sword for the Post. On the one hand, the Post acquired all assets; on the other, it was also required to inherit a debt of thirty-five billion francs – an enormous financial burden. The legislation also ensured the civil-service character of postal workers. But this meant that La Poste assumed the pension obligations of postal workers. The debt and the pension issue were central to the life and concerns of the Post after 1990 and have been serious impediments to its evolution and modernization.

Second, while the Post was "corporatized" to a degree, it was corporatized as a "social corporation." To illustrate this point, La Poste's 1997 report[7] includes interviews with the president (Claude Bourmand) and the director general (Martin Vial) which explain the social dimension of La Poste's existence. The former declares that "companies expect La Poste to act like a company and La Poste is adapting itself to its corporate customers' high level of demands. At the same time, La Poste proudly shoulders its mission of social solidarity and its role in social cohesion." Director General Vial then elaborates on the latter point: "Zones of social exclusion … genuinely imperil the social and republican pact underlying our country. As part of our fight against exclusion, we are developing our post office network to respond better to urban needs … We are also doing our part in the efforts favouring youth employment and the struggle against job insecurity. With its financial service activities our company … provid[es] even the destitute with basic means of payment." The Post's social mission and obligations – ranging from national and regional planning to youth employment and social support – are central to and frames its existence as a corporation. Indeed, the PTT minister defined this as a special French postal mission, differentiating France from other countries.[8] As a result, the 1990 changes were silent on the issue of postal liberalization or elimination of monopoly protection. In this framework, liberalization would undermine the capacity of the Post to execute its social responsibilities. These in turn go well beyond the universal-service obligations carried by other Posts.

Third, the most significant reform development in the French postal regime lies in the extensive and evolving network of subsidiaries to La Poste. A policy of *filialization* has been encouraged by the government and pursued by La Poste. This has been the primary mode of modernization and development and has taken place more or less outside the regulatory and political framework.

THE STATUTORY AND REGULATORY REGIME

The French postal regime is constructed on three levels. First, there is a general umbrella law for the organization of the public service for the post and telecommunication sector. Second, there are decrees that elaborate the specific organizational framework and activities of La Poste. Third, La Poste's relationship with the state, and the latter's expectation of it, are set out in a contract that is renewed periodically.

Law 90–568, 2 July 1990

This law reorganized the PTT and gave an independent identity to both the Post and the Telecom. The law transferred the state's postal rights and obligations to La Poste, including its exclusive privilege or monopoly powers as well as its universal-service obligations (V, 22). The exclusive privilege has been substantial in France until recently (letters and ad mail, nationally and internationally, up to one kilogram). This will change to the EC framework of 350 grams and five times the first-class price. Express mail, parcels, documents, and other competitive products are exempt. The legislation defined universal services (1, 8) as including letters, parcels (up to thirty kilograms), newspapers, banking activities, universal access, and participation in national and regional planning (*l'amenagement du territoire*). In return for its participation in town and country planning and its obligation to cover the entire national territory, La Poste was given an 85 per cent reduction in its local tax assessment. La Poste manages the National Savings Bank (the Giro System) on behalf of the state (the National Savings Bank). The legislation elaborated the principles of the universal service, including national coverage and presence, equal treatment of all citizens and groups, guarantee of quality of service, neutrality and confidentiality in carrying out activities, and a universal system of prices and service. Newspaper delivery was included as part of the universal-service obligation, with the government obliged to pay "fair financial compensation" to La Poste for carrying out this responsibility (around 1.9 billion francs annually).

The law established La Poste's commercial and economic freedom (V, 23) and defined its financial autonomy and its responsibility for financial balance. It set out La Poste's ownership of its assets and capital and placed it within the normal corporate tax regime (there were a number of transitional ingredients)[9](III, 14). The law also delineated how La Poste could partner with other firms and create subsidiaries in complementary activities (I, 7). The law declared the state's ongoing authority. It made the minister ultimately responsible for the postal sector and directed the minister to work with La Poste in preparing plans and working out a contract (VIII, 34). This contract – to be discussed below – would define the activities of La Poste by defining objectives, presenting the ways to realize the objectives, and specifying key issues like prices, investment activities, and performance (I, 9).

Finally, the law laid out the three ingredients of an administrative and organizational framework from within which La Poste would function:

- a national council for both Post and Telecom, comprising representatives of ministries, the state, users, unions, and so on, to advise the minister on post and telecommunication matters (VIII, 37);
- an administrative council (or board of directors), comprising seven representatives from each of the state, union, and expert communities, which would link the state's objectives to the postal management's activities and execute the contract and plans (II, 10–12); and
- a regulatory body – *commission supérieure du service public des postes et télécommunications* or CSSPPT – comprised of parliamentary representatives and experts, which would advise the minister on plans, contracts, and other important matters (VIII, 35).

Each of these administrative units will be examined in detail below.

Decrees 90–111, 90–1214, December 1990

Decree 90–111 elaborated the public organizational framework from within which La Poste would function. This will be discussed in detail in a section below. Here, we can note simply that the decree established the mechanism for ensuring the representation of the state's interest in the Post in two ways. First, an administrative council (or board), headed by a president, would transmit the objectives of the state to the Post and ensure the execution of public-policy objectives. Second, the minister appointed a *commissaire du gouvernement* to the council. He would have a consultative seat on the council, acting as the government's eyes and ears, to ensure that the Post's actions would be in tune with government policy and the Post's contract with the government.

Decree 90–1214 laid out the activities and responsibilities of La Poste. It defined the Post's universal-service obligations and principles, including responsibility for letters, parcels, financial services, and newspaper distribution, in a universal, equitable, and accessible manner. These obligations would be underpinned by the exclusive privilege that was given to the Post (Article 3). The decree allowed for exceptions for universal pricing, such as contracts with large users (Article 4), and it offered competitive opportunities for the Post to generate revenue (Article 7). The decree did not lay out specific expectations or goals, which would be elaborated in the *contrat de plan* (discussed below). This contract was the device by which the state and the Post would agree to a strategic orientation and a set of specific objectives and targets (quality, productivity, financial, employment, performance). The decree declared that the Post would have to be sufficiently autonomous and financially successful to carry out its universal-service obligations (Article 27). At the same time, though, the Post's prices would have to be approved by the minister (Article 33). The state created another check on the Post. It assigned a consultative presence on the administrative council to *une mission de contrôle économique et financier de l'État*. Headed by a *chef de mission*, this group would have the responsibility to oversee and regulate the economics and finances of the Post and its subsidiaries. The Post would prepare an annual plan and report on its network (Article 21). The principle of participation and consultation was established in the decree, in two ways. First, it provided for the creation of user councils at the local level (Article 25). Second, union participation in the preparation of the contract was required.

Contracts

As noted above, Decree 90–1214 established the contract as the mechanism for the state and the post to agree on the broad framework and objectives for the Post. These contracts would be for a minimum of three years and would set the management framework within which the Post would execute its business plan. The most recent contracts were in 1995–97 and 1998–2001, and are elaborated below. There is a broad, extensive institutional involvement in the preparation of a contract, which is looked at by CSSPPT, the ministers of Post and Telecommunications, Economics and Finance, and the Budget, as well as by the chair of the administrative council and representatives of the postal unions. The Post presents an annual report or plan to the three ministries (Post and Telecommunications, Economics and Finance, and Budget) on the execution of the contract.

The contracts are not particularly long or elaborate. They typically comprise about a dozen pages. Each contract contains a qualitative and a quantitative dimension. With respect to the former, the contract outlines a kind of mission statement and strategic orientation for the period it covers. For example, the 1995–97 contract set out a number of broad themes: the Post should become more competitive and market sensitive; it should accelerate modernization through the use of technology; it should focus its efforts on parcels and new products and services; and it should become more customer-oriented. Other qualitative commitments reflected the Post's social mission to provide youth employment and training, assist staff development, encourage public participation, and provide public access to the new technology. The 1998–2001 contract was particularly qualitative, focusing on five themes: growth, competitiveness, customer focus, productivity improvements, and the centrality of technology. Youth employment was also a central feature of the social mission that the Post is assigned.

On the quantitative dimension, the contract contains a forecast statement of revenues and expenses, which acts as a kind of reference document setting out the financial commitments of the Post. For example, the 1995–97 contract set a 6 per cent gross financial return as well as a number of business and accounting targets. The Post is directed to remain in financial equilibrium. The contract also contains quality-of-service targets (80 per cent next-day delivery, 96 per cent within two days). It lays down the objective of keeping postal-price changes within the framework of changes in the cost of living. The contract directs the Post to reduce the debt. The 1998–2001 contract set growth targets in the international area (10 per cent) and financial area (40 per cent), the rationale being the need for rising profits to allow the Post to maintain its universal-service obligations. Both contracts set out the state's financial assistance to the Post in delivering newspapers nationally. This support was 1.85 billion francs in 1998 and 1999 and 1.9 billion francs in 2000 and 2001. The Contract determines the Post's investment plan for the term of the contract (for example, nine billion francs in 1995–97).

ORGANIZATIONAL OVERVIEW

Relative to other postal regimes examined in this study, the French postal regime has a dense, elaborate institutional arrangement. This institutional network reflects two principles or objectives that cut across the idea of increased autonomy for the Post. First, regardless of the objective of corporatizing the Post, the state's objectives and presence should remain at the heart of the operation. Second, given the Post's character as a "social" corporation, its procedures and policy making should reflect a high degree of public participation. As these principles are applied, La Poste enjoys little policy or operational autonomy.

At the top of the institutional structure is the National Council for Posts and Telecommunications (Conseil National des postes et télécoms). Below the National Council is the minister for posts and telecommunications, who is advised by two commissions. One deals with social-policy matters (Commission Supérieure du personnel et des affaires sociales). The other has statutory responsibility to ensure that the Post carries out its public duties (Commission Supérieure du Service Public des postes et télécoms). Below the ministerial level is La Poste itself. It is headed by a board (Conseil d'Administration) comprised of ministerial representatives and appointees and union representatives. There are two other "consultative" state representatives on the board: an economic and financial adviser (contrôle économique et financier d'état) and a regulatory presence (commissaire du gouvernment). At the head of the board is a president (Chair of the board), appointed by the state, who in turn appoints a director general (CEO) of La Poste. At the lower level of La Poste, there is a series of consultative bodies that provide advice and share information.

This is a formidable array of organizations, which provides a considerable state or public presence in the affairs of La Poste. Each of the key institutions will be examined below.

Conseil National des postes et télécoms

The existence of this body reflects the fact that even the split of the Post from telecommunications was not totally complete. As noted earlier, the Prévot report had suggested that the essential unity of these two arms of national communication be linked in a national advisory council. The 2 July 1990 law created this body. The council comprises representatives from Parliament, the government, user groups, local authorities, and La Poste and France Télécom. It advises the minister of post and telecommunications about the role of La Poste in France's economic and social life. The National Council does not have formal decision-making authority, nor does it have statutory responsibilities. But it acts as a kind of formal "policy community," bringing together the main postal constituencies and interests to define and frame the postal agenda in global and universal terms.

The Minister of Posts and Telecommunications

There is a ministry with special responsibility for the Post, Telecommunications and Space. Within it, there is a department or Directorate General of Post and Telecommunications (DGPT), which reports to the minister. This minister is situated directly at the heart of the French postal regime. Short of privatizing the Post, this ongoing ministerial responsibility is inevitable, as French law disallows the delegation of regulatory powers. There has been an attempt to separate postal operation from regulation. But this exists more in theory than in practice. Corporatization and some liberalization have seen the La Poste and market given a role on matters dealing with competition and efficiency. But on allocative matters the state remains the final authority – for example, in setting postal prices.[10]

The DGPT is responsible for executing government postal policy. It sets out the Post's legal and technical framework and enforces regulation and legislation. This is particularly the case with respect to La Poste's public-service mission. It has responsibilities for monitoring prices, approving prices in the monopoly sector, monitoring quality of services, and drafting and monitoring contractual plans. It also has responsibility for personnel issues and social policy and represents the state internationally in postal bodies and activities.

The DGPT works in close concert with the economic and financial ministries of the government. Both the Ministry of Economics and Finance and the Ministry of the Budget have formal roles in drawing up plans and the contract with the Post. This creates an interministerial tension around postal policy, since each ministry has different objectives and agendas. For example, the economics and finance ministries are keen to maximize their returns from the Post while the DGPT has – or ought to have – the objective of ensuring that the Post has adequate financial capacity to modernize, develop, and provide public services. Similarly, the economics and finance ministries feel pressure from the private banking sector to open up the Post's predominance in certain banking and financial service areas, but the revenue from this source is important for La Poste's social mission.

Commission Supérieure du Service Publique des Postes
et Télécommunications (CSSPpt)

The CSSPpt was also created by the 2 July 1990 law. It is a hybrid organization. It is not really a third-party regulator, although it has some characteristics of such a body. It has a formal role in the postal-policy regime and policy process, although it does not really make decisions or have real authority. As noted above, this is necessary because French law does not allow the delegation of regulatory powers. Like the National Council, the CSSPPt reflects the reality that the political realm was anxious to retain input into and influence over postal affairs. The CSSPPt is essentially a political body, with some added expertise. It comprises seventeen members, fourteen of whom are parliamentarians. The other three members are "experts," named by the minister. Their respective party leaders appoint the parliamentarians, and their numerical composition reflects the weight of the political parties in the two parliamentary chambers. There is a president and two vice-presidents, again reflecting the political realities of the day.

The CSSPPt was an institutional innovation, designed to perpetuate some parliamentary input and control of postal affairs.[11] The minister has a statutory obligation to consult the commission on all major decisions related to the public dimensions of La Poste – including the state's contract with the Post, legislative and regulatory changes, or major changes in postal policy. The commission in turn issues regular responses to the minister on state postal initiatives and presents an annual report to the prime minister and Parliament. Any such advice or commentary is made public. Many of the parliamentarians appointed to the commission have a real interest in postal matters and carry out their responsibilities thoroughly and effectively. In order to provide reasonable and informed advice, the commission examines postal conditions, assisted by the three experts named by the minister and a permanent staff (some of whom are seconded from the ministry).

The CSSPPt has tended to function as a consensus body, trying to build up all-party agreement on important features of French postal policy. Until recently, the commission has managed to achieve consensus in most issues. This has seen parliamentarians not always following party lines. In this, the CSSPPt has tended to be more "progressive" than Parliament itself. That said, it has become increasingly difficult of late to find consensus on the commission, particularly over the difficult policy choices and decisions that postal modernization generates.[12]

The government and the CSSPPt disagree from time to time. For example, the government moved in 1999 to change the postal law to make it coincide with the December 1997 EC postal directive. It introduced a short and unambitious bill, to be passed quickly in order to avoid controversy (in areas such as postal closings, employment, pensions, and the Post's relationship with the banks). Its only substantive feature was the move to lower the exclusive privilege to 350 grams and five times the price of a first-class stamp. The CSSPPt encouraged the government to use this opportunity to redefine the postal legislation, to articulate a renewed and detailed sense of La

Poste's responsibility, and to draw up a vision for La Poste's future. A political stalemate of sorts ensued, which was eventually resolved by a government commitment to introduce a legislative review – at a date far in the future.[13]

Conseil d'Administration de la Poste

The administrative council is the Board of Directors of La Poste. Its role is to carry out the state's postal policy objectives and wishes. Notwithstanding its superficial resemblance to a corporate board, it is basically another state agency. It is a large and unwieldy body, comprising twenty-one members and three consultants. There are seven representatives of each of the state, unions, and experts (*personnalités qualifiées*), all appointed by the government. In the first group, there are two representatives of the minister of posts and telecommunications, and one each from the ministries of economy and finance, budget, transport, communications, and national and regional planning. The "expert" group comprises senior officials primarily from banks and communications companies with close ties to the state.[14] The union group comprises elected representatives from the various unions that represent postal workers. As noted above, a number of government officials act as consultants to the council. The contrôle d'état heads up a team that ensures financial and economic accountability, and the commissaire du gouvernment reviews postal activity from the perspective of the government's broader public-policy ambitions.

The council carries out the basic functions of a board, meeting six times a year and signing off on major policies like the contract and the annual plan. A president, who is named by the government and who is a high-profile personification of the state's presence in the Post, leads the council's work. The president names the director general (CEO), after consultation with the council. The president's responsibility is to execute the wishes of the government.

The council is the eyes and ears of the state in the postal area.[15] Notwithstanding La Poste's existence as a semi-independent state enterprise, the state still considers La Poste to be its property and it has created an institutional design to ensure its command of La Poste. The administrative council is a prime manifestation of this ambition. The council appears to reflect principles of "concertation" and participation, given the presence of representatives from the postal unions. However, the union influence on the council is negligible. Rather than deal with La Poste directly, the union continues to carry out its lobby and pressure activities in political locales – such as in Parliament, at the CSSPPt, and at the grass-roots level.[16] This demonstrates the extent to which La Poste itself is not an autonomous force or the site of postal authority.

La Poste

La Poste is a semi-independent government agency. It is *un exploitant autonome de droit public* – a public enterprise that exists within its own particular or specific legislative and statutory framework. This framework comprises a number of elements, including the institutional web outlined above. The 1990 change left much of the postal regime unchanged. A ministry still exists, run by a directorate that is substantial and active. Political influence and controls have taken new shape – but this has not diminished the political impact of the state in the functioning of the Post. Parliamentary influence plays out through the CSSPpt. The various departmental influences play out through the administrative council. The concrete objectives of the state are elaborated both in legislation and in periodic contracts with the Post. The operation of the Post is directed by a president and a director general, both of whose careers and roots typically lie within the traditional pre-1990 administrative Post. In late 2000, Martin Vial replaced Claude Bourmaud as president. Vial had previously been director general and had had a career in the public sector, in various finance and public-sector management positions, before coming to La Poste in 1997. Vial named Daniel Caille as the new director general; Caille had previously been assistant director general of Vivendi Universal and president of Compagnie générale de santé. There has been some outside recruiting at the middle-management level, but the senior levels of the Post remain very much oriented to the traditional statist involvement in the Post. There does not appear to be very much autonomy exercised by the senior executives of the Post, given the institutional network that exists.

La Poste is responsible for the universal postal service, and its universal service obligations are laid out in the 2 July 1990 legislation and the periodic contracts with the state. This includes an obligation to deliver newspapers, for which it is compensated by the state. It is obliged to collect mail from a set of accessible mailboxes every day and to provide daily delivery service to a specified quality target (80 per cent next-day delivery). It is required to inform the minister when it plans to introduce new services. Pricing policy is also set out in the contract in a schedule; the ministry controls the level and structure of price increases via a price-cap system. The pattern of monopoly prices is set in the plan over a number of years (to be set within the rate of change in the consumer-price index). Individual price changes have to be approved by the minister of posts and telecommunications and the minister of economy and finance. The Post can set prices in the competitive sector. One-off discounts with major users can be negotiated, but the terms must be open and approved by the ministry. The number of post offices and the character of the network are set out in a schedule of conditions in the contract. La Poste has to submit an annual plan to the minister in this regard. The contract with the state sets out a number of financial objectives, cost and productivity targets, a debt-reduction plan, and a series of management indicators. La Poste submits an annual implementation report to the minister and the financial supervisory bodies.

La Poste prepares an annual budget, which is subject to the approval of the minister for posts and telecommunications, the minister for economy and finance, and the minister for the budget, whose agents also approve the annual accounts. The administrative council constructs an investment plan, which is submitted for assessment to the governing body of the Economic and Social Development Fund (FDES), an interministerial body chaired by the Ministry for Economy and Finance. It evaluates the plan in light of the contract between the state and the Post. The approval of the minister of posts and telecommunications and the minister of economy and finance is required before the Post can establish a subsidiary or initiate a corporate takeover.

As noted above, La Poste is considered to be a "social corporation," with not only responsibilities for the universal postal service but also obligations in areas like employment and national and regional planning.

THE FRENCH POSTAL REGIME IN ACTION

The postal sector in France remains a politically sensitive area, with a high degree of state involvement. The Post's existence – even as a semi-independent state enterprise – intersects with a number of hot-button political issues – from youth and unskilled unemployment to pension issues, from the presence of the Post nationally to the delivery of newspapers, from the question of the state's role in the economy to France's place in Europe. All of these issues are confronted within a political framework and against the backdrop of a public or national agenda. For example, notwithstanding the objectives of making La Poste modern and competitive, there has been a moratorium on postal closings since 1993, for social and economic and not postal reasons. La Poste has not been insulated from politics, as in other types of postal regime. As a result, policy changes and initiatives are scrutinized

Table 1
Financial results (billions of francs)

	1992	1995	1996	1997	1998
Revenues	75.8	84.1	86.7	89.9	93.4
Subsidiaries	2.7		5.0		
Net profits		−1.1	−0.614	0.058	0.337

Source: La Poste, Annual Report, 1997 and 1998.

politically in a wide-ranging and thorough way. This is part of the reason why the legislation in response to the EC postal directive has been so fraught with controversy.

Economic and Business Performance

La Poste is obliged by law to make a profit, to be distributed in equal parts to the state, its clients, and its employees (as bonuses). As Table 1 indicates, La Poste has been at most a break-even operation. It has made a net profit of late, but at a very marginal level. Its best year was 1998 – 337 million francs in profit. Its profits in 2000 fell by half. Compared to France Telecom's 15-billion-francs profit, La Poste's is basically a balanced budget.

Why have its profits been so low? This is not the result of particularly poor mail volumes or bad postal business. Revenues at La Poste have grown by 23 per cent since 1992 and those of its subsidiaries have doubled. There has been a boom in direct marketing and the mail sector continues to grow steadily (4.4 per cent). Notwithstanding the introduction of on-line services, mail volumes have doubled in that period.[17] Its banking and financial business remains enviably healthy and has climbed to over twenty billion francs in revenue annually – about 23 per cent of La Poste's revenue. There were significant losses in 1995 (1.1 billion francs) and 1996 (614 million francs), primarily as a result of a large postal strike, which led to a considerable loss in mail business. But postal business has picked up subsequently and mail business reached 60 billion francs in 1997. The debt was cut for the sixth consecutive year in 1998. The 2000 results saw a revenue increase of 4.6 per cent, driven by an 8 per cent increase in financial services and a 16 per cent increase in parcel and logistics activity.

Clearly the bottom line would be stronger if there was stronger business and mail growth. But there are other structural factors at work. First, La Poste is obliged to make an annual contribution to paying down the mountainous debt that it inherited – 36 billion francs in total. It has managed to reduce its debt by a few hundred million

francs in this period. Second, La Poste has substantial pension obligations that were passed on to it by the state. The state pays only the
increase or growth in pension payments, not the total amount. In
1997, for example, La Poste reimbursed the government for pensions
paid to postal personnel to the tune of 12.8 billion francs.[18] Third,
there are numerous public-service obligations pursued by La Poste,
for which it may not be receiving adequate compensation. These
include the artificially low rates charged for distribution of newspapers, maintaining a number of unprofitable postal outlets, providing
bank accounts and financial services to all citizens including the
unemployed and welfare recipients, and the introduction of the thirty-
five-hour workweek.[19] Fourth, there is evidence that revenues from La
Poste are blended into the accounts of other state enterprises, to
create balanced accounts. The postal union's estimate of these expenses
is around 8 billion francs.

La Poste is compensated for a number of the service and social
activities that it carries out on the government's behalf. For example,
it is compensated for providing a subsidized newspaper-delivery service
and "uneconomic" services in socio-economic planning projects. The
exclusive protection is assigned to the Post for carrying out its universal-service obliations. It enjoys substantial business advantages from
being the dominant historical player in the postal market. But these
advantages may not neutralize the heavy financial burdens imposed
by its various obligations. It is difficult, if not impossible, to evaluate
La Poste's performance, given the intermingling of social and economic activities and finances.

Quality and Prices

The postal legislation and subsequent contracts set price and quality
objectives for La Poste. On the quality front, La Poste was set a target
of 80 per cent next-day delivery of letters. This target has not been met.
Indeed, recently there has been a modest decline in service, the next-
day rate of delivery falling from 77.2 per cent in 1997 to 76.3 per cent
in 1998. The two-day objective of 95 per cent has almost been met; the
record stood at 93.6 per cent in 1997 and 1998. Notwithstanding the
price-cap formula, the state remains involved in the setting of postal
prices – which remains very much a political issue in France. There was
a price increase in 1997, but the political "optics" of the change turned
out to be bad. The result has been that the state has subsequently been
reticent to approve price increases. The price issue is an area where
France characterizes itself as different from (and better than) the
market model – illustrating this difference by pointing to the 62 per
cent increase in prices in Sweden since its regime was liberalized.[20]

Network

La Poste is obliged by the state to provide an accessible national network of post offices, for both postal and banking purposes. This is not part of the universal-service obligation. The MAT – Mission d'aménagement du Territiore – is a government-created socio-economic objective. Neither the postal legislation nor contracts have specified or quantified the network. La Poste is obliged to provide the minister with an annual report on the state of the network. As in other postal regimes, there was some move after 1990 to rationalize the network – even the unions admit that most post offices are not profitable. Indeed, the counters operation comprises up to 20 per cent of total business costs.[21] However, postal closings were highly controversial, and the state quickly imposed a moratorium on postal closings in 1993.

The postal network is considered by the state to be an important instrument of national and social cohesion. Indeed, as a "model public service," La Poste is expected to do its part to this end – by ensuring a presence in volatile urban areas and depopulated rural zones. La Poste's annual reports suggest that it needs assistance from local authorities and other public-sector bodies (for which, for example, it distributes government information) to ensure its universal presence, which is an expensive proposition.[22] La Poste does get a tax reduction for this activity but it receives no direct subsidy.

La Poste signed an agreement with the state in September 1999 to increase the number of branches in disadvantaged areas over the next five years from the existing 400 outlets to 1,000 outlets. This initiative was foreshadowed in the 1998 contract. Among other things, it aims to maintain a state presence in disadvantaged areas, in order to distribute social-security payments and assure the population of its connection to the national government.

Press

Distribution of newspapers is considered to be part of La Poste's universal-service obligation. This reflects the state's consideration of the importance of citizens' access to information and public debate. The state has subsidized directly this element of the universal-service obligation – to the tune of around two billion francs annually.

This sector is competitive – La Poste does not have a monopoly on newspaper delivery. Moreover, the sector is not a growing one. As a result, there has been some tension between the press organizations and La Poste about this service, with respect both to the quality of delivery and to the prices that are charged. The state established a new roundtable process for discussions of these and related issues. A new framework has been established to deal with the quality of service, transparency in assigning costs, and mechanisms for sharing cost reductions.[23]

Labour

The labour context of the Post in France is different from that in most of the regimes examined in this study. While there is a political dimension to the labour situation in most countries, politics is at the heart of the labour issue in France. This is because of a number of factors. First, there is a long and intense tradition of unionization in France, where unions have made close alliances with political parties and legitimized their claims via internalization within the state. For example, postal workers won civil-service status in 1946 and have one-third of the seats on the administrative council. Second, the size of the postal labour force is intimidating, comprising over 300,000 workers throughout the 1990s. This makes labour a sensitive issue on the policy agenda, since there are so many jobs at stake at a time when the French economy has been struggling with high unemployment, particularly among the young and the unskilled. Conversely, the size of the postal labour force gives the postal union substantial political muscle. This was demonstrated in the bitter 1995 strike, which deeply radicalized the workers. That strike action had as much to do with changes in social policy as with postal initiatives. Third, the union's perspective on liberalization and the European postal directive place it on the same political wavelength as management and the government – neither of whom support deregulation and liberalization. All distrust the EC orientation and its likely implications for employment. Germany, which has eliminated 120,000 postal jobs since 1992, is characterized in a negative light in this regard.[24]

The labour issue in the French postal regime is thus framed within the notion of La Poste as a social corporation with social responsibilities. Since 1995, this has played out in two ways. First, La Poste has been encouraged by the state to give permanent as opposed to contract or temporary employment. As noted in its 1997 report, "our tradition and company culture are based on the principle of long-term recruitment." A social accord was struck between La Poste and the state in September 1999, the purpose of which was to decrease the proportion of workers on limited-term contracts and to increase to 96 per cent the proportion of workers on "indeterminate" or open-ended contracts.[25] Second, the state has reached accords with La Poste on providing employment for young people, particularly unskilled ones. La Poste gives priority to hiring high school graduates, providing them with open-ended contacts. It committed to providing 5,000 such jobs in 1997 and 1998.[26]

Overall, then, the level of employment at La Poste remains high. It is difficult to present this quantitatively, given that there is a two-track employment system (permanent versus contract) and a considerable amount of employment within the subsidiaries (see below). Figures in the annual reports show an overall decline in employment from 300,000 in 1991 to 280,000 in 1997. However, all statements and declarations by officials in reports and elsewhere suggest that La Poste employs between 300,000 and 310,000 people. It should be noted that about two-thirds of these have civil-service status, a proportion that is declining. Employees in subsidiaries are not civil servants.

Finance

There is a long tradition of the Post providing financial services and products. As noted earlier, La Poste runs the postal banking system for the state. The financial area has had a double purpose within the postal regime. On one level, providing universal access to financial services is part of La Poste's social obligation, particularly to ensure that the marginalized populations in rural areas and bad areas of cities have access to social services and payments. On another level, the financial area provides La Poste with revenues that allow it to maintain the universal service. Indeed, its success in this area has created tension with the private-sector banks, which resent La Poste's presence in and dominance over certain features of the financial market.

La Poste is France's third-largest financial operator, with 30 million clients, 44 million accounts, and a financial portfolio of over 1,000 billion francs (up from 567 billion in 1987). Revenues from this operation represent almost 25 per cent of La Poste's revenues (21 billion out of 86 billion francs in 1997). The financial sector has been given prominence in recent contracts, and it is expected to grow. Recent growth has been generated by expansion in areas such as life insurance and home-savings plans (it does not have the right to lend money). It increased its stake in La Caisse Nationale de Prevoyance from 17.5 per cent to 20 per cent in September 1998.

Parcels and Express

Both parcels and express are excluded from La Poste's exclusive privilege and so are competitive markets. Growth possibilities in these areas are enormous, but the competition is intense. Much of the initiative has been carried out through subsidiaries, but it is worth noting a few highlights.

With respect to parcels, La Poste has about 24 per cent of the market for parcels under thirty kilograms.[27] Its strategy is to build up a European network through partnerships and alliances, and it aims to have 10 per cent of the European parcel market by 2002. It recently purchased 100 per cent of Interspe and 50.1 per cent of DPD GmbH, two German parcel companies. It also purchased INSA in the United States, a distributor of European newspapers in North America. In a major initiative, it has also purchased Parceline and Interlink, the British and Irish express-freight units of Australia's Mayne Nickless Group. With respect to express, Chronopost has been a market leader and has enjoyed considerable success and profits. A new brand name was launched in 1997 for the intercorporate single-packet market – Dilipack. It recently purchased 100 per cent of Interspe and 85 per cent of Deutscher Paket Dienst (DPD), Germany's second-largest parcel company. This makes La Poste a major international rival to UPS and TNT in Europe.

Electronic

The postal legislation and recent contracts have highlighted La Poste's mission to engage in research and development and to make technology central to its future. The highlight of this agenda has been its commitment to providing universal access to electronic services in its post offices. It established 1,000 Internet terminals in its postal outlets and provided the public with access and accounts. It introduced a smart-card system in June 1998 for using these Internet outlets. In a related move, it purchased 66 per cent of the Seres corporation, a specialist in electronic-bill exchange.

Subsidiaries

La Poste has pursued its corporatization and market strategy and growth primarily through its subsidiaries, in a policy called *fililization*. This approach received government blessing in the July 1990 legislation and has been pursued with particular intensity since 1995. Postal strategy, then, appears to run on two tracks: public services through La Poste and competitive modernization through its subsidiaries.

The 1997 report lists nineteen subsidiaries of La Poste, of which eleven are partnerships with other firms. SOFIPOST was created as a holding operation for all of the subsidiaries. It has had responsibilities for strategy development in this area, for engaging and acquiring partners, and for the organization of subsidiaries' relationship with La Poste. The holding operation has been divided in two recently. A new holding operation – Société holding des filiales colis et logistiques – comprises a cluster of subsidiaries in the parcel and logistics areas (Chronopost, TAT, Denkhous, Publi-Trans). The major subsidiaries include:

Chronopost

Chronopost provides express transport and delivery of parcels up to thirty kilograms. It was the first company to stake a claim in this market in France and has attained over two billion francs in revenues. It has expanded across Europe through a network of alliances and purchases. It recently increased its stake in Jet Worldwide from 35 to 100 per cent. In 1997 it took a 34 per cent stake in Taxicolis, which provides urgent express service. It has subsidiaries in twelve other countries. As well, it has partners in Spain and alliances with Denkhouse in Germany and Belgium, APD in Holland, and Panic Link in the United Kingdom.

Tat Express

Tat Express specializes in intercorporate express transport. It has introduced the brand-name product Dilipack. It has a shareholding in the German transport company Denkhaus, which is the principal franchise of DPB Gmb, a parcels company in Germany and Belgium.

Data Post

Data Post is a joint company, in which La Poste has a 72 per cent stake (IBM is a 10 per cent partner). It specializes in the production of computer-generated documents.

Dynapost

Dynapost is a company that provides integrated mail processing for corporate customers of their own internal post.

Mediapost

Mediapost specializes in targeted direct mail.

IMC (Intra Muros Communication)

La Poste has a 51 per cent share in IMC, which specializes in direct-communications logistics and newspaper distribution.

STP (Société de Traitement de Presse)

STP specializes in the processing and routing of newspaper subscriptions.

Sogepost

This is a 50 per cent partnership arrangement with Caisse des dépôts et Consignations, for the management of mutual funds.

Somepost
Somepost is an information-technology and logistics company which operates in fifty-five countries.

Sofrepost
Sofrepost is a company that exports postal and technological know-how to other countries. It has entered arrangements with the postal services of a number of countries, including Poland, Burkina-Laso, Gabon, and the Ivory Coast.

Europe

One of the more sensitive and controversial issues has been the relationship between the French postal regime and the European one. France has not favoured a rapid movement toward liberalization in Europe. Its feeling is that liberalization should unfold incrementally and at a moderate pace. In no case should total liberalization be introduced as early as 2003 – the working target date for a number of countries.[28] In any event, France – with a number of southern European countries – continues to favour the protection of the postal monopoly as a way of underpinning the Post's social or national purpose. Moving to liberalization is seen to be an irreversible step with much uncertainty – so should not be taken lightly.[29] Notwithstanding the pervasive anxiety about the competitive and technological future, one's sense is that all the members of the postal-policy community in France will wait for the final possible moment in this regard – and then let the state settle matters. Indeed, there is a convergence of interests on not moving quickly, amongst the government, political parties, the Post, user groups, and the unions. The state does not have much political leverage in this area.[30]

This uneasy relationship with Europe has been informed by a number of challenges to French postal policy before the European Court. For example, the exclusive-privilege provision has been challenged (unsuccessfully) on a number of occasions. More recently, La Poste was taken to the European Court under a state-aid charge with respect to the Post's 85 per cent tax reduction. The Court ruled in France's favour, saying that the subsidy was warranted (under Article 90, paragraph 2 of the Treaty of Rome) given La Poste's public-service mission.

France's European strategy appears to focus on creating alliances with other national posts. For example, it has entered into an alliance with the Spanish Post which has three ingredients: the merging of their express operations; improvements in their international post; and the mutual development of hybrid products. It has also signed a letter of intent with the Italian Post to explore an alliance in the parcel and express-courier market.

CONCLUSION AND OBSERVATIONS

What can one learn from the French case? What interest does its experience and the national model hold for policy makers? To begin with, the French postal experience has three broad characteristics. First, postal reform has been incremental and moderate: there simply have not been changes of a qualitative or transformative character. Second, and related to the first, the French experience has solidified the Post's existence within a thoroughly political or public context, since the Post continues to be conceptualized primarily as a public service. Third, the French case explicitly rejects a market approach, which is seen to be unpredictable and potentially dangerous, creating higher prices and lower levels of employment while also weakening the Post's universal character. The French case, then, is of particular interest for countries that are seeking to reform and modernize their Posts within a public-service paradigm. For other countries, the overall strategy will be of little interest. But specific elements of the model may have interest in a tactical sense.

As in the Danish case, moderate institutional change has not resulted in enormous change in policy or postal performance. Indeed, changes must be tracked on two levels: public and economic. On the public level, the 1990 reforms have led to the extension of political initiatives to use the Post for public-policy purposes, particularly in the area of employment and regional planning. It is difficult to imagine, though, that these initiatives would not have taken place in the absence of the 1990 reforms. What has been tested is the state's will or capacity to use the Post for political ends – and this does not appear to have been weakened or undermined.

On the economic level, even the modest reform changes have led to some improvement in postal performance. La Poste seems to have achieved a relatively solid financial footing. Of course, postal conditions remain reasonably strong, the impact of electronic and other competition has not yet been deeply felt, and the liberalizing influences of the European postal directive have yet to manifest themselves. Moreover, it is unclear whether the Post will continue to enjoy the benefits of its financial and banking sector, given private-sector pressures on the government in this regard. Thus, La Poste's economic and strategic capacity to deal with technological and competitive changes has not yet been tested. On the other hand, it is extremely difficult to penetrate La Poste's business performance, given its mix of social and economic activities and the expensive obligations it carries that are associated with pensions and debt reduction.

The French, unlike the Dutch and the Germans, have not pursued the corporatization model. Nor they have pursued the liberalization model, as in Scandinavia and the Antipodes. La Poste has been given some autonomy, but in a quasi-corporatized fashion in a non-liberal market. As a result, the French reforms have essentially reproduced the politics of the Post in a new institutional arrangement. These institutional arrangements are formidable, with a multi-layered representation of state interests on strategic, financial, budget, and operational levels. These arrangements led to the generation of a parallel series of policies that are not inherently "postal" in nature but rather see the Post perform an instrumental role in the areas of employment, social cohesion, and nation-building. To these ends, the French model seems not inappropriate or ineffective. In another context, one could evaluate whether these postal policies are the most appropriate or effective ways of pursuing employment or regional objectives. But this sort of evaluation is outside the mandate and rationale of this study.

This French approach to postal matters appears to have reflected a broad consensus in the early 1990s that neither corporatization/ privatization nor liberalization was the appropriate approach to take in the postal realm. Unlike the experience, say, in Sweden or the Netherlands, the events of the 1980s in France did not neutralize or undermine the strong political cultural and public-service attitudes associated with the traditional Post. There may be fissures appearing in this consensus, though, now that the overwhelming realities of technological and international competition appear to be hitting home. For example, the union movement has been critical of postal strategy and is worried about the looming figures of the Dutch and German Posts. The unions do not see the present postal approach as one in which the French will be able to withstand the competition from the new postal behemoths in Europe. Indeed, they see pension, debt, regional, and other policies as a drag on increasing postal capacity. Similarly, many on the CSSPPT are also critical of what they see as a kind of lethargy in French postal policy, which does not seem to be moving in rhythm to the changes and dynamism in the international market. The approach to Europe is a metaphor for this. The French authorities – and many players in the postal-policy community – want to put postal liberalization off to the last possible moment. But there will likely be formidable chickens coming home to roost at that time. If La Poste is not sufficiently developed to meet the competition that this liberalization will unleash, the consequences could be far-reaching and dire – particularly for employment. In the absence of liberalization at the moment, there do not appear to be other French postal agents or operatives waiting to step in once the European market is liberalized.

There are a number of specific features of the French regime that are unique and worth highlighting. First, the French appear to be following a two-track postal policy. The public-service agenda continues to be pursued through La Poste, while the market or modernization agenda is being pursued through subsidiaries. The policy of *filialization* is an interesting approach to developing the "non-public" side of the postal equation. It may be that this approach has fewer built-in inhibitions – politically and otherwise – than an attempt by national Posts to build competitive products and services out of their traditional operations. Certainly the experience with express and parcels has been reasonably successful in the market and the approach allows a high degree of flexibility. Moreover, it differentiates public from market activity in a way that can neutralize the traditional concern about monopoly subsidy of competitive products and services.

Second, the contract model – between the state and the Post – is a further national example of the way in which governments set an open-accountability and performance regime for the Post. In the French case, this might appear to be a case of "overkill," given the degree of penetration of the Post by the state in other ways. Nonetheless, the contract provides a solid and useful mechanism for setting both a qualitative and a quantitative agenda for the Post, against which it can plan and be evaluated. Its fixed length is also an attractive device. This ensures that the postal sector is not taken for granted by the government, which has to reconsider the contract and its content when it expires.

Third, the public-institutional web surrounding the Post is unparalleled in its density, relative to the other countries examined in this study. At all levels – strategic, economic, financial, operational, service, and so on – the state has a number of mechanisms or avenues to express its objectives. Given the national approach, one could say that the institutional web fits the model well, and to effect. Whether this is a model to be emulated is quite another manner. The model allows for clarity of expression of the shareholder's view. But this has been done at the expense of limiting the autonomy of the Post itself.

Fourth, the French regime offers an alternative pattern of international behaviour to countries in the other models we have examined. In these models, the national Posts typically partner with private-sector competitors in each of the markets in which they wish to have a presence. In one particular example, one sees the French doing something different. In Spain, the French have made an arrangement or partnership with the Spanish Post – not one with the Spanish Post's competitors. This model of Post-Post cooperation is one that has been talked about in the abstract in postal-policy circles, and it will be discussed later in the concluding chapter on international developments. Given France's leadership role among the southern European countries (who have a stronger public-service tradition in this area), this initiative with Spain may be the leading edge of an alternative model in Europe and the world.

8 Canada

The reform of Canada's postal regime took place earlier than in most parts of the world. Canada Post Corporation was established in 1981 as a *crown corporation* – a state enterprise owned by the government but organized and operated on business terms outside the state's administrative structure. CPC was one of the world's first "progressive" postal organizations, after those in the United Kingdom and the United States. Countries that reformed their postal systems afterwards in the late 1980s and early 1990s often studied the Canadian experience and example. Two decades later, though, the countries that initiated their reforms at a much later date have overtaken the postal-reform process in Canada. The Post in Canada appears to be far less coherent and less strategically focused than these other Posts, whose rate of performance is also better. Indeed, one of the reasons why this study was undertaken was to explore this contrast and examine the possibility that it was due to a poor regulatory and governance design.

Postal reform had been on the Canadian policy agenda since the late 1960s. Two earlier attempts at reform (late 1960s, late 1970s) failed because the political agenda was too overwhelming and complex, foreshadowing the political character of the postal-reform experience in the 1980s and 1990s. By 1980, however, there was an overwhelming and far-reaching consensus that the Post simply had to be reformed. Ballooning deficits, perpetual strikes, technological challenges, and deteriorating service framed a postal agenda that seemed hopeless and futile. Any proposed change in postal format or approach appeared to offer an improvement over the status quo.

Postal reform in Canada was driven on its own terms – far more so than in the other countries examined in this study. First, postal reform was not propelled by some larger agenda, such as administrative or state-enterprise reforms or the microeconomic-reform response to international economic change, as in Scandinavia, Western Europe, and Australasia. Second, the Post in Canada had never been part of a PTT operation, so the telecommunications revolution of the 1980s and 1990s did not carry the Post along with it, as it did in many other countries. Third, the Post in Canada did not face the same degree of international competitive threat from bordering Posts that countries in Europe did. This was because the American postal regime prohibited the United States Postal Service from becoming an international postal actor. Canada's major competitive threats would come later from the private sector (UPS and FedEx). On all counts, then, postal reform in Canada developed within a purely postal context. This was enormously consequential. Postal reform in other countries was less open to political scrutiny and objection than in Canada, since their wider agendas insulated their Posts politically. Posts were simply state enterprises that had to be reformed. They were no better or worse off than any other state enterprise that had to adjust to international economic forces, administrative reform, or the reconstruction of the state-enterprise sector. These other Posts, then, were reformed within some sort of universal context that was always lacking in the Canadian experience. The Post in Canada was reformed in accordance with a specific and particular *postal* agenda. This in turn meant a basically *political* or national postal agenda, given Canada's history and culture.

The Post in Canada has had, and continues to have, enormous symbolic resonance. Canada is an extremely large country with a modest population and a harsh climate. It stretches 5,510 kilometres across six time zones comprising ten million square kilometres, eight million excluding the Arctic archipelago. Its postal density is 2.2 persons per square kilometre.[1] The Post played a significant historical role in facilitating national expansion, building social cohesion, and extending the Canadian market while allowing Canadians the capacity to keep in touch with each other and their governments in a timely, accessible, and inexpensive way. Canada's population is strung out in a long line along the Canadian-American border, with a substantial part of the population living in small towns and rural areas. The Post is still considered by most Canadians to be a vital universal service, notwithstanding the technological and communications alternatives to the letter. Indeed, there is remarkably little support for postal privatization in Canada. Public-opinion polls demonstrate a high degree of public support for the idea of the state-run Post. The business sector is not especially keen on the idea of privatization of a reasonably well run, inexpensive, and universal postal system.[2] The idea of the public Post, then, remains a powerful cultural, economic, and political force in Canada.

The Post's political existence and identity has been reinforced by two institutional inheritances in Canada. The first is the parliamentary system. The Westminster model of government is based on opposition, not consensus. Notwithstanding the fact that the Post has been studied perpetually in Canada, there is a remarkably low degree of political consensus about postal matters. Postal matters are not typically centre stage politically. But whenever they do come on to the agenda, the parliamentary process intensifies postal divisions, since government and opposition exploit this lack of postal consensus to their own political ends. The Post remains very much a football that political parties kick around when it is useful for them to do so. Second, Canada's electoral system generates the selection of a substantial number of MPs from rural areas and small towns. These representatives ensure the continued political resonance of the traditional rural issue on the postal agenda, which has by no means been eliminated from the postal equation. These traditional political impulses have not been mitigated by, or absorbed into, a wider policy agenda.

The absence of a wider agenda has had its most dramatic consequence in the area of industrial relations. When the Post was corporatized in 1981, there was no external force or event that neutralized or "scared" the postal unions or their members into lowering or muting their expectations or going along with a reform agenda. Indeed, their outlook was validated and their expectations were heightened by corporatization. The postal unions took with them into the new corporatized world the rights and privileges that they had bargained for and accumulated in the old regime. There has been some subsequent rationalization of the union situation, which has made the Canadian Union of Postal Workers the central, dominant postal union. It is a formidable and deeply radical organization, one of the most militant and intimidating of any of the postal unions examined in this study. Its postal ideas, discourse, and approach emanate from a pre-corporatization experience and agenda and are framed by a traditional socialist political and economic paradigm that is basically tangential to that of the reform agenda. There have been numerous consequences to this state of affairs, including periodic and deeply intense postal strikes. Most important, though, this has weakened the authority of Canada Post and perpetuated the basic political character of postal affairs. The Post has simply not had the capacity or the authority to resolve ongoing labour-management tension. Major disputes between the parties continue to require resolution by the government. This perpetuates the political character of the postal regime, particularly given that CPC is Canada's fourth-largest employer.

A fourth feature of Canada's inheritance is the absence of a strong ideological character or experience. Canada's politics have been essentially pragmatic and centrist, with some notable but infrequent exceptions. The upshot of this pragmatism has been that reform has tended to be of the "balanced" variety, which tries to keep the Post's social and economic obligations and objectives in approximate equilibrium. Indeed, this balance was built into the Canada Post Corporation Act itself, which articulates basic policy schizophrenia about the Post's objectives and responsibilities. This "middle way" appears benign in any particular snapshot. But it is difficult to maintain a perpetually balanced equilibrium, so that the Post's condition always seems to be uncertain and unstable. The perpetual tension between social and economic objectives has not been resolved. More important, events of the last two decades have not built up a postal culture, process, or experience capable of generating the mechanisms or formulae to maintain a working balance. Indeed, postal policy – with the exception of the period 1986–92 – has been politicized in an attempt to square the circle between social and economic objectives. As a result, postal policy has taken a myriad of forms, including deregulation and regulation, liberalization and protection, autonomy and control. None of this has produced a coherent strategic postal point of view.

This is particularly evident in the absence of an intelligent or reformed regulatory regime, which is perhaps the most striking lacuna in the two decades' experience of postal reform. The Canadian case provides an excellent case study of how a poorly designed regulatory and governance environment generates weaker than optimal performance and inhibits postal development. As will be seen below, the regulatory environment and process appears to be deliberately opaque and fragmented, to allow political control to be perpetuated in a surreptitious way. There was a period of policy coherence and accomplishment in the late 1980s and early 1990s, when the postal regime veered into a market direction. But the subsequent operational changes and successes were not matched by an equivalent reconsideration of or change to the regulatory regime. As a result, the Canadian regulatory regime is as informal and incoherent as it is inhibiting and political.[3]

This chapter will demonstrate how the Canadian postal regime remains within the national model. This is not to suggest that the Canadian authorities are unaware of the threatening environment that currently surrounds the postal sector. CPC is well aware of the competitive environment in which it functions, particularly the extent to which the future of the letter is threatened by the electronic alternatives open to its major business customers.[4] Newspapers and other distribution companies threaten direct mail. UPS and FedEx cast a long shadow over the small-packages market. As postal volumes stagnate or decline, the Post understands that its capacity to deliver the universal service is weakened.[5] The national or public model neither liberalizes nor privatizes in response to these conditions, although it contains elements of each in an eclectic and instrumental policy mix. This approach seeks to control or neutralize the postal environment in order to perpetuate traditional postal objectives and ensure the government's control over the postal agenda. Indeed, we will see that the Liberal government repoliticized the Post following a market-oriented period that it felt had given CPC too much autonomy. As a result, employment, national unity, rural development, social purposes, and other public considerations now loom as large as strictly postal objectives. On the one hand, this has required some ongoing degree of postal "protection," including monopoly status and exclusive privilege, for the Post to pursue these political objectives. On the other hand, it has necessitated the construction of a less onerous regulatory regime and the setting of lower government expectations of economic performance than in the other postal models. The upshot has been that the Post has not been given the strategic or commercial space, authority, or impetus to develop as in the other models.

It is not certain that the national model can persist indefinitely, given the delicate balances and calculations that maintain it. For example, the Canadian postal regime and its postal policies have been challenged legally. In April 2000 UPS sued the federal government for allegedly violating the terms of the North American Free Trade Agreement. Among other claims, UPS charged that, under articles 11 and 15 of NAFTA, the Canadian government favoured CPC and discriminated against its competitors.[6] If UPS wins the case, the government would be obliged to reimburse UPS for lost business and to change its postal framework and regime – which would be an extreme example of how internationalization is changing domestic postal policy. Indeed, UPS has successfully sued Deutsche Post under European law in a similar case, obliging the Germans to pay a fine of US$17 million and requiring them to segment their parcels and letters operations into different units.

HISTORY[7]

The following discussion provides a more elaborate historical treatment than that presented in other chapters. This is because of Canada's central position in the study, but also because our analysis of the Canadian regulatory regime – in the following sections – will focus on the period examined in most other countries, that is, since the early 1990s. The contrast between this latter period and the market-oriented experiences of the late 1980s and early 1990s is highly illustrative of the extent to which the Canadian postal regime fits the national model.

Early Days

The Post has roots in Canada's early settler days, with the *coureurs de bois* acting as the first letter carriers in the sixteenth century and ships' captains and tavern keepers providing early post offices. The French established the first postal system on a regular basis in 1734, basically for administrative purposes, connecting Montreal, Quebec City, and Trois-Rivières. Following the Conquest of 1760, the postal system was the first government institution to be put on a settled basis in British Canada. It was controlled by the British postmaster general until 1851, mainly for military and economic but also for fiscal ends (postal surpluses were sent back to the mother country). The British expanded the extensive French network in the late-eighteenth century, opening a postal route to Halifax and establishing post offices in all major communities. This expansion was uneven and service was poor, and postal reform comprised part of the agenda of the Rebellion of 1837–38. The Post Office also followed the opening of the west, and mail was sent to the Red River settlement (present-day Winnipeg) in the 1850s. There were fewer than two dozen post offices at the end of the eighteenth century, but there were six hundred when the Post Office came under domestic control in 1851. The Province of Canada Post Office Department (POD) was the second department, after Customs and Excise, to receive independence from Britain. The provinces operated the postal system until Confederation in 1867, at which time the Post became an exclusive federal responsibility and the POD was one of the first departments formed. It was then directed to assist Canada's social and economic development, which it did by extending the postal network across the country (there were almost ten thousand post offices by the end of the nineteenth century), introducing home delivery and free rural delivery, subsidizing publications mail, and providing a wide array of services at a low price.

The Post Office Department

The Post Office was organized as a unit or department of government, headed by a minister or postmaster general, although many of its important functions were in the domain of other departments (Public Works, Transportation, Labour, Finance, and so on). It had little policy or operational autonomy, save in the most narrowly defined postal areas, so there was an overall lack of accountability and control. Its internal organization was chaotic and it had a poor corporate culture. The POD was highly scrutinized politically, political forces set its agenda, and political interference was the rule not the exception. Postal policy was neither rational nor effective.[8] Postal prices were raised only four times between 1900 and 1967, so that the Post was always cash poor, seriously undercapitalized, and old-fashioned operationally. Its desperate fiscal situation was obscured by accounting practices that, until the mid-1960s, assigned many of its costs to other departments. When public-sector unionization arrived in the late 1960s and rising postal volumes necessitated capital investment for modernization, the POD's financial situation turned nightmarish. It ran deficits in every year from 1964 to 1981, ranging from 10–20 per cent of revenues until 1973 and 30–60 per cent thereafter. In the six years prior to corporatization, the POD generated $3 billion in deficits (all currency references in this chapter, unless otherwise indicated, are in Canadian dollars). Rising deficits paralleled growing labour unrest, particularly as overdue and accelerated postal mechanization exacerbated poor industrial relations. Postal strikes in 1965, 1968, 1974, 1975, 1978, and 1981 worsened what was an unreliable postal service and created the impression of a situation out of control.

Crowning the Post

After the disastrous 1970s, there was a broad consensus that the POD needed to act in a more commercial way to meet competitive pressures. It also needed a less political context if it were to improve labour-management relations, balance its finances, and provide better postal service. The government had become exasperated by postal issues and wanted to rid itself of political embarrassments and deficits. In 1978 Prime Minister Pierre Trudeau declared that the POD would become a crown corporation.[9] This idea had been floated since the early 1960s, but political complications, interests, and constraints had made it difficult to execute.[10] Indeed, it took another three years for the government to put Trudeau's declaration into action, marking the first time in Canadian history that a government department had become a crown corporation.

Canada had had a tradition of using the crown corporation as an instrument of national development, particularly in the areas of utilities, resources, transportation, and communications.[11] Its policy attraction had been its mixed logic: organized on a corporate rather than a departmental basis, adopting a commercial rather than a bureaucratic vision, and motivated by efficiency and rationality as well as by the public good. However, the corporatization of the Post took place after a series of spectacular crown corporation failures and misadventures, raising public suspicions as well as demands for greater government control. Canada Post Corporation was thus born under the twin and contradictory impulses of commercialization and control.

The Canada Post Corporation Act

Bill C-42 – the Canada Post Corporation Act – transformed the POD into Canada Post Corporation. This transformation aimed to improve postal finances, commercial performance, managerial decision making, and labour relations. Bill C-42 transferred to Canada Post postal power, authority, and responsibilities previously assigned to the POD. CPC was set up as a corporate organization outside of the daily processes of government, under the Financial Administration Act (FAA) (which applied to all crown corporations) and the Competition Act. The government introduced CPC as a "Schedule C" crown corporation, planning to reschedule it later under "Schedule D" – a corporation financially independent of government. The new postal regime combined elements of corporate autonomy and political control. A nine-member board (named by the government) would direct and manage CPC, appointing its senior-management team (approved by the government) and devising its strategies and plans (to be approved by the government). CPC was directed to establish and operate a "basic customary postal service" (Section 5.2), paying regard to "the desirability of improving and extending its products and services in the light of developments in the field of communications" (5(2)a). It was to

- "conduct its operations on a self-sustaining financial basis while providing a standard of service that will need the needs of the people of Canada and that is similar with respect to communities of the same size" (5(2)b);
- utilize "the human resources of the Corporation in a manner that will both attain the objects of the corporation and ensure the commitment and dedication of its employment to the attainment of those objects" (5(2)); and
- "maintain a corporate identity program approved by the Governor in council that reflects the role of the Corporation as an institution of the Government of Canada" (5(2)e).

These objectives – financial self-sufficiency, maintenance of the traditional universal postal service, improving labour-management relations, and keeping pace with technological change – created a policy juggling act for CPC. To assist it, CPC was assigned $1.67 billion in contributed capital and was granted a modest exclusive privilege or reserved area – at fifty grams and three times the regular letter rate, this was one of the lowest minimum price thresholds in the world. This comprised a fairly liberalized state of affairs. CPC's exclusive privilege over delivery of letters was also circumscribed; newspapers, magazines, books, catalogues, goods, and electronically or optically transmitted material were exempted from the monopoly. The government in turn retained considerable political authority over Canada Post. A government minister was given responsibility for Canada Post, as opposed to an independent regulator and/or a department. The regulatory environment that was created was highly informal and ad hoc. Basic postal initiatives – like price and regulatory changes – would be approved or disapproved directly by the government after a public "gazetting" process (the idea of third-party regulation was raised and dropped). CPC was obliged to present an annual report to Parliament, to be reviewed in committee; in 1986 CPC was directed to present annually five-year corporate and capital plans to be approved by the government.[12] The government retained a "directive" power over postal policy. CPC would not be allowed to borrow, take on debt, or sell property without government approval (Sections 21, 28). Government authority in postal matters thus continued to be substantial, reflecting public concerns about accountability at that time.

The Canada Post Corporation Act was a reasonably accurate reflection of Canadians' and Canadian governments' optimistic (if not indulgent) hope at the time that Canada Post could balance social objectives while acting in a commercial and businesslike fashion. During the Liberal administration that created CPC (1981–84), this balancing act was not terribly successful. CPC initiated a number of cost-cutting, revenue-increasing, and commercial moves to improve its financial, competitive, and service positions. But these initiatives almost invariably ran into negative reactions from labour unions, postal users, competitors, and political interests. The government typically sided with those "aggrieved." Not surprisingly, postal deficits remained in the $300–400 million range – despite a jump in the price of a first-class stamp from seventeen to thirty cents upon CPC's creation. The government was thus obliged to pick up $1.3 billion in postal deficits between 1981–82 and 1984–85.[13]

Corporatizing the Post, 1986–1992

Postal policy changed dramatically after the election of the Conservative government in 1984, which made deficit reduction and improved economic performance central to the policy agenda. The postal juggling act was abandoned deliberately and CPC's financial responsibilities became favoured over its social ones. Brian Mulroney's Conservative government forced this transformation and helped CPC to implement it. First, it reined in CPC's authority by rejecting CPC President Michael Warren's last corporate plan, which led to his resignation and the government's appointment of Don Lander, the hardnosed former auto executive. The government then created a private-sector committee (Marchment) to review CPC's mandate; it recommended that the government commercialize CPC and not try to balance the social and economic goals in perfect equilibrium. The government itself constructed the 1986 corporate plan, which it imposed on to CPC; this plan was a transforming moment as important as the passage of the Canada Post Corporation Act itself. The plan commercialized Canada Post through a range of cost-cutting measures, a severe rationalization of services, and a disciplined focus on business concerns. The government directed CPC to pursue the recommendations of the Marchment committee and the components of the 1986 corporate plan, in the process releasing CPC from many of its social responsibilities. It then insulated CPC from the inevitable political fallout to this approach.[14]

These major postal initiatives created a highly corporatized operation, heading towards privatization.[15] First, the government set increasingly demanding financial targets, insisting on budget balance by 1987–88, a surplus by 1989, and a 14–5 per cent return on equity and payment of $300 million in dividends by 1994. These targets were designed to force CPC to operate to private-sector performance standards. CPC reached a profitable position in 1988–89 ($96 million profit, a 6 per cent return on equity) and improved this to a $149 million profit in 1989–90 (11 per cent return on equity). Second, CPC contained mail-delivery costs by limiting the expansion of home delivery and introducing group or community mailboxes in suburbs and new neighborhoods and towns, which serviced over 700,000 addresses by 1992. Sorting and delivery of parcels were contracted out. Third, CPC rationalized the rural network, introducing a ten-year plan to privatize the 5,200 rural post offices. Many rural posts were closed or transformed into private retail operations. Thirty per cent of the rural network had been transformed by 1992. Fourth, much of the urban retail network was privatized, through franchising of counter services and new postal-service outlets (for example, Shoppers Drug Mart); the remainder was rationalized. Fifth, it contracted out non-core activities, including property and equipment maintenance, payroll functions, vehicle maintenance, and computer and electronic activity. Ground and air transport of mail was contracted out as well. Some sorting functions were devolved, by offering incentives for pre-sorting. Sixth, CPC attempted to reduce labour usage and costs to private-sector comparability, via mechanization, programs to reduce absenteeism, replacement of full-time positions by contract and part-time labour, and sustained use of disciplinary and legal action to alter and improve work practices. In all, 10,000 full-time jobs were cut and overall employment declined by 15 per cent. Aggressive negotiations in 1986, 1987, and 1991–92 resulted in postal strikes and stoppages. Yet these disruptions gained CPC some operational flexibility, particularly in contested areas such as contracting-out, franchising, employment cuts, and the use of part-time and casual labour. Seventh, it introduced user pay pricing. More and more of CPC's business was generated in the competitive, non-protected markets. Pricing of postal products came increasingly to be based on costs and cross-subsidization was lessened. Fiscal support to traditional public service areas – for example, second-class or publications mail – was cut. Eighth, it weakened its public-service functions. Responsibility for the rural network was decreased, subsidies for social mail were recategorized or cut, the centrality of home delivery was lessened, the importance of a community postal presence was diminished, and labour issues were not given special treatment. Ninth, the government presented an Employee Share Ownership Plan to allow employees to purchase up to 10 per cent of CPC's shares. Tenth, it projected a new corporate image and established a corporate culture, through balancing its budget, standing tough against postal unions, setting service standards, altering its product lines and exploring new markets, recruiting private-sector managers, making the board business-oriented, and increasing the emphasis on service and the customer.[16] CPC focused increasingly on its major business clients (who generated most of its revenues) and entered into alliances and partnerships with private-sector players. Finally, it purchased Purolator, a private-sector courier company, in 1993 to compete more effectively in the lucrative courier market. This in turn required CPC to devise more detailed product-costing systems, to prove that its competitive courier products were not cross-subsidized by activities in the reserved area.

There was relentless opposition to commercialization throughout the Mulroney years. Yet the Conservative government provided the political support and protection that allowed CPC to persist with these initiatives.[17] Harvie Andre was a senior and powerful minister (1986–93) who provided a stable and protected political environment, shielding CPC from political pressure and bureaucratic intervention while absorbing political complaints and attacks. Andre supported and reappointed the tough, determined, and business-focused Donald Lander as CPC president and made board appointments that ensured a commercial orientation and managerial dominance. The government transformed the chair's position into a part-time one and made the board's role largely symbolic. Lander himself was named chair in 1992. Neither political nor bureaucratic oversight was substantial or grew in a significant way. The Treasury Board review of corporate and capital plans evolved into a benign and sympathetic process. After a failed experiment with third-party postal regulation,[18] the status quo remained in the area of price and regulation setting (a gazetting process followed by ministerial approval). The government absorbed political criticism and stonewalled opposition about rural postal closings, community mailboxes, privatization, and contracting-out; by 1992 these issues had been rationalized and depoliticized and become matters of business routine. The government backed CPC's efforts to roll back wages and benefits, cut labour costs, increase productivity, and increase corporate postal authority. It sanctioned the use of replacement workers and the alternate-delivery system during strikes. It used back-to-work legislation to end strikes when required.

This period saw the Conservative government encourage and assist CPC in commercializing and corporatizing the Post. Canada Post's financial situation improved substantially. From 1982 to 1986, CPC had incurred cumulative losses of $1.4 billion. In contrast, during 1987–93 it made profits in four of seven years for a cumulative financial balance of $100 million.[19] Over 1,000 rural post offices were closed, and 300–50 post offices a year were privatized annually. Mail processed per hour increased by 47 per cent between 1984 and 1992 and mail delivery rose by 2 per cent. CPC met its new 2/3/4 delivery standard (two days within local areas, three days regionally, and four days nationally) 98 per cent of the time in 1991–92, up from 85 per cent in the mid-1980s.

The Conservative period, though, comprised a job only half done. The Post was corporatized and commercialized to a great extent. But this was carried out as an act of political will, in an informal and ad hoc manner without a formal process or regulatory pattern then or for the future. The Post was quasi-regulated, partially by competition and partially by the minister. The latter "looked the other way" to the extent that the Post continued to perform to the government's expectations and to improve financially. Thus, the Post as a "monopoly" was substantially unregulated. The CPC Act – particularly its social objectives – was more or less ignored. No formal regulatory environment tracked CPC's actions and performance. There were no operational criteria against which to judge CPC's performance – save for the minister's direct wishes. This was not a stable regulatory situation. It relied on particular political and personal circumstances, which were upset when the Conservatives lost the 1993 election.

1993 to the Present

A Liberal administration created Canada Post in 1981 and attempted to balance the social and economic goals that it had written into the CPC Act. This effort was unsuccessful, and CPC continued to generate substantial deficits. Moreover, the government insisted that CPC try to please all people and groups simultaneously, which made it difficult for CPC to forge a new identity or strategy. The Conservative government attempted to redress this situation by giving a focused direction to CPC and by creating a political environment that allowed CPC to implement this strategy. The return of the Liberals in 1993 thus raised a number of questions. Would the government maintain CPC's commercial focus or return to a more "balanced" public approach? Would it increase, maintain, or decrease CPC's autonomy? Would it revert to a pre-1986 posture and environment or extend the postal logic established by its predecessor?

The Liberals' postal position in opposition suggested that there would be substantial policy changes and reversals. First, the Liberals had criticized the political environment that had insulated CPC politically and that had allowed it to "run amok."[20] They bemoaned the trivial number of representations made in the price-gazetting process and the decline in MPs' influence over postal matters. Second, the Liberals had opposed the rationalization of the postal (rural) delivery network, which diminished the government's presence in the community. Third, the Liberals had criticized the hard-nosed approach to labour negotiations, blaming labour troubles on the 1986 corporate plan and the setting of profit and dividend targets that constrained the corporation's negotiating flexibility. Lastly, the Liberals attacked the government for setting financial, profits, and dividend targets and expectations which forced CPC to be overly commercial and not sufficiently conscious of its social role. The Liberals continued to characterize postal matters as an essential public service.[21]

When the Liberals returned to office, critics of postal policy lined up to pressure the new minister, David Dingwall, to see if they could get the satisfaction that they did not attain under the previous administration.

The courier companies complained about cpc's purchase of Purolator; newspaper and delivery companies complained about the Post's ad-mail initiatives; rural groups and mps complained about post-office closings; small business and backbenchers complained about postal prices. The minister took a number of immediate measures. He denied a postal-rate increase request from cpc and imposed a moratorium on closings of rural post offices. cpc was made a prescribed crown corporation in March 1994, which meant that it had to pay income taxes as if it were a private-sector corporation. Dingwall's most consequential decision was to launch a review of cpc's mandate, a decision that reflected a number of cross-pressures. A Mandate Review would assuage backbencher, rural, and small-business complaints about the Post. There had not been a serious Mandate Review since the Marchment report of 1985, and a periodic review was anticipated in the crown corporation legislation.[22] The bureaucracy thought it reasonable to extend the government's cost-cutting examination of the time to include the crown-corporation sector. The bureaucracy as well as the corporation saw the review as a potentially positive opportunity to get a clearer sense of the shareholder's expectation of cpc, particularly given the Liberals' past postal record and attitude.

We will examine the Mandate Review process and implications below. Suffice it to say here that the exercise turned into a procedural and policy fiasco and produced a report that was not useful to the government. Indeed, the results were a disaster for all parties involved – the Post, the government, the bureaucracy, and postal customers. The Mandate Review had the effect of creating a vacuum in postal-regulatory policy and uncertainty in governance for over three years, from its announcement on 6 November 1995 until the government finally issued a new framework agreement on 18 January 1999. In the interim, there was also a serious postal strike, the cpc president left office prematurely, the founding minister became chairman of the board, and the government clarified its postal intentions and embraced the national model.

There was no political fanfare when the new Framework Agreement emerged in early 1999; this reflected the government's embarrassment at how long it had taken to produce it as well as its sense that it was too "complicated" to explain to the public. Both sides, the government and the cpc, wanted it to be a low-key announcement.[23] There was palpable relief all around when it finally emerged. The agreement took many forms and drafts, each one apparently with less and less content and closer and closer approximation to the status quo. For example, it "formalized" the existing practice of price caps, at two-thirds the rate of growth in the consumer-price index (this would still require cabinet approval). If compared to the contract and service agreements between Posts and governments in Scandinavia and Australasia, it would pale in comparison. The Framework Agreement is not really a plan or a manifesto but a policy paper, although it does establish a kind of financial-management regime. It includes business indicators, such as operating income, return on equity, dividend policy, capital structure, and leverage, as well as financial-performance targets. The latter are modest and to be attained within the five-year framework (which needs renewal after this period). The agreement directs CPC to lever its network to generate increased revenues and confirms that CPC can continue to be active in competitive areas of the market. But it does so in the most implicit, understated way: "Canada Post will actively compete in the marketplace and manage its day-to-day operations according to sound business principles." The agreement also notes that evaluation of service performance will be extended to rural areas.[24]

The Mandate Review did not settle many postal policy issues definitively and generally missed the opportunity to connect the Canadian postal regime to the larger postal picture. The minister declared, though, that its presentation ended the debate on the future of CPC.[25] This certainly seemed to be the case with regard to privatization. A momentum for privatization seemed to have been building at the end of the Conservative period. "Does the government have to be in the business of delivering the mail," mused Minister Harvie Andre; "if you put the arguments for and against on the scale ... they will probably point towards privatization."[26] Prime Minister Kim Campbell – who replaced Brian Mulroney as Conservative party leader before the 1993 election – apparently favoured privatization of CPC.[27] However, submissions to the Mandate Review did not indicate much support for privatization.[28] After the report was issued, Minister Diane Marleau declared, "I want to set the record straight: Canada Post will not be privatized."[29] More recently, Minister Alfonso Gagliano announced that "Canada Post is not for sale; not today, not tomorrow and not in the foreseeable future." Gagliano explained: "This decision was not taken lightly. It was confirmed by the government ... after a complete review of the terms of reference of the Canada Post Corporation ... The conclusion was very clear. In a country such as Canada, whose land mass is so great and population so widely dispersed, no private system will ever be able to provide universal service for a reasonable price ... I believe Canada Post shouldn't be privatized. I believe it's an essential service."[30]

The postal-reform experience in Canada has comprised three stages over its two decades' history. A market-oriented middle period (1986–

93) has been sandwiched between two periods in which governments have attempted to balance social and economic objectives. The third period has not undone the market-oriented developments initiated in the second period, and the government remains interested that CPC be efficient and self-sufficient.[31] However, these developments have been slowed down and certainly not extended. The Post's exclusive privilege remains and further liberalization is not on the agenda. The question of privatization has been settled for the extended future. On the other hand, the Liberal government has recast the Post's existence within a more political context in which national, small-business, rural, social, and political objectives frame postal policy.

REGULATORY AND GOVERNANCE ENVIRONMENT

The Conservatives' commercialization and corporatization reforms were not paralleled by regulatory reforms of any significance. Generally, there has been far less experimentation and change in the governance and regulatory areas in Canada than there has been in the operations and corporate areas. As a result, the structures and processes of the regulatory process remain much as they were in 1981. The Canadian postal regime is a highly informal and unstructured one, relative to the other postal regimes that we have examined. The separation of ownership from regulation is less clear in the Canadian regime than elsewhere, where EC directives and informed debate and discussion have made a significant impact. The minister remains at the centre of the postal regime; other departments play a subsidiary, supporting, at times negligible, and usually invisible role. There is no third-party regulator, and any formal regulatory processes that exist have become highly ritualistic. There are few public documents or processes associated with governance and regulation, with the result that there is little by way of public accountability and visibility. CPC's annual report contains only the most basic information. There is little to no reporting on targets, accomplishments, and improvements. The Radwanski report of 1996 concluded: "The corporation is currently beyond any effective control by the government."[32] There is an element of truth in this characterization. Canada Post has a great deal of autonomy within a fragmented, loose, and informal regulatory environment. Traditional or formal controls are indeed lacking, and public-accountability mechanisms are all but non-existent. What this "system" allows, though, is a high degree of ad hoc political manipulation and control. The regulatory pattern at CPC resembles a tendency that has evolved recently in Canada, described theoretically by

Bruce Doern and his associates.[33] This pattern comprises incremental policy making, flexible policy implementation, and selective compliance. Regulation takes place in a non-coercive fashion, in a kind of bargaining process between the government and Canada Post. This pattern limits the possibility for public accountability and makes policy evaluation all but impossible to execute.

Statutory Context

There are two basic statutory instruments that determine the Post's legal existence. The first instrument is that part of the Financial Administration Act (1984) that applies to the "commercial" crown corporations (Part X). This statute reflects the political concern of the late 1970s and early 1980s that governments had lost control of crown corporations. The Part X provisions of the act assigned the government and Parliament new mechanisms and processes to assert their authority over crown corporations. The government was given the authority to issue directives and to approve the sale of crown corporations and the purchase of subsidiaries by them. The role of boards of directors was clarified. The act required crown corporations to provide increased information about their corporate plans and results. They were required to seek annual approval of their capital budgets by the Department of Finance and Treasury Board, which would also approve their annual submission of multi-year corporate plans and borrowing requirements. The auditor general was directed to carry out comprehensive audits. The legislation provided for improved reporting mechanisms to Parliament, including an automatic review of annual reports by standing committee. The act was amended again in 1995 (Bill C-263) to make commercial crown corporations still more accountable.

The second instrument is the Canada Post Corporation Act. This act brought CPC into existence and granted it the postal power, authority and responsibilities previously assigned to the POD. It sets out the corporation's goals and objectives and the procedures to be used in carrying them out. The Post was assigned the universal-service obligation to collect, move, and deliver the mail, while being mindful of complementary issues such as financial balance, technological change, rural service, and industrial relations. None of these goals was quantified in 1981, and their highly qualitative character has been a source of both flexibility and controversy. Canada Post was also given an exclusive privilege or monopoly area to assist in generating sufficient revenue to carry out the universal-service obligation. The government of Canada would be the regulator and the owner/shareholder. As the owner, it approves corporate plans, signs off on borrowing and acquisitions, makes appointments, and has a directive power (Section 22).[34] As the regulator, it approves price changes and evaluates the quality of service. A later amendment to the act allowed employees to purchase up to 10 per cent of total shares (this has never been implemented). Postal staff have their own status as employees of Canada Post and are not considered part of the public service.

The Minister

A minister responsible for CPC is at the centre of the Canadian postal regime. The minister was not assigned a staff or a department under the CPC Act, and the ministerial role was left implicit. The act is unspecific about the exercise of the shareholding and regulatory responsibilities. CPC has traditionally been assigned as a secondary, semi-related responsibility to a number of different ministries which have had wider policy responsibilities (for example, Labour, Public Works, Consumer and Corporate Affairs). This stands in contrast to the situation in other countries, where postal responsibilities have been assigned on an ongoing basis to more directly related ministerial areas (for example, Communications, Transportation). The result in those countries has been the possibility for policy continuity and for building up postal intelligence within the particular department that has had historical responsibility for the Post. This has not occurred in the Canadian regime, which has meant that there is no department with broad postal expertise. As a consequence, ministers responsible for CPC, particularly incoming ones, find themselves in an isolated position.

The present minister is Alfonso Gagliano, who heads Public Works and Government Services. He is the third minister responsible for Canada Post since the Liberals returned to power. This resurrects an earlier pattern, when there was a high turnover of ministers and a lack of policy continuity.[35] The previous two misters (Dingwall and Marleau) had short and not terribly effective stays. Ministers have brought different styles and approaches to their responsibilities, making it difficult to generalize about their behaviour. Harvie Andre asked explicitly to be given little bureaucratic support in carrying out his responsibilities, minimized bureaucratic interference, and tried to leave CPC on its own as much as possible. His office had one staff person with postal responsibilities. When Liberal ministers arrived on the scene, they had little postal support (and experience) and looked more to the bureaucracy. Different ministers have had different degrees of rapport with CPC. There is a sense that Dingwall and Marleau did not have good relations with CPC and so used the bureaucracy more and interacted directly with the corporation less. Gagliano appears to work more directly with CPC than previous Liberal ministers did. This reflects the fact that a previous minister and colleague, André Ouellet, has been chair and is now president of CPC.[36] In general, the absence of departmental continuity and support makes the minister's role open to ad hoc and informal actions.

The Corporate Implementation Group

There has been no particular bureaucratic branch that has had responsibility for the Post with respect to either the regulatory or the shareholder function, given the way that the Post has been assigned to ministers with different responsibilities. There was previously a unit within the bureaucracy that was assigned general responsibilities for crown corporations.[37] The Crown Corporations Directorate (CCD) of Treasury Board comprised individual analysts who were assigned responsibilities for particular crown corporations; this system has been disbanded. The CCD was a very hands-on unit, and its analysts often knew more about the crown corporations than the ministers. There was a sense, though, that the analysts and the corporations had became too close and dependent on each other. The government decided to replace the CCD with a unit that offered support that was more strategic than operational.[38]

A Corporate Implentation Group within PWGS now reports to the minister; PWGS has responsibility for a number of crown corporations. CIG came out of the Mandate Review and earlier government thinking that CPC (and other commercial crown corporations) required some sort of internal departmental support. CIG is a kind of secretariat for all of these crown corporations, providing support to the minister in his interaction with the government as he implements the FAA. CIG comprises a small, eighteen-person staff, with individual members who have particular crown-corporation responsibilities, including Canada Post. Parts of two staff positions are assigned to the Post. There has likely been a loss of knowledge in this approach, and the corporation may be less willing to share information in the horizontal as opposed to vertical way. How CIG works depends very much on the minister's style and approach, and some ministers do not use it much. Public Works uses CIG extensively, given that it has responsibility for a cluster of "commercial crowns," such as the Mint, Canada Lands, and CPC. CIG is a hybrid operation. It is not part of the bureaucracy per se and has no direct or decision-making authority. It is more politically sensitive and aware than the bureaucracy, and it acts as a kind of support network between the minister, CPC, and the government, getting CPC access to the cabinet quickly when necessary. Given the recent high turnover of staff related to the Post at Treasury Board and Finance, as well as recent executive turnover at CPC, CIG has perhaps the highest degree of postal intelligence within the regime. This gives it a high degree of informal postal authority. On one level, this is worrisome, inasmuch as CIG itself would admit that it lacks sufficient postal intelligence and does not have an adequate capacity to do policy study.[39] The bureaucratic support results in a kind of policy triangle, in which CPC officials, the minister, and CIG interact to devise corporate policy and the formal governance structure and process. This looks like a cumbersome arrangement since it involves more players than one typically sees. But there is a sense within the participant group that it works. Moreover, given the inherently political character of the regime, this process gives CPC greater access to the cabinet than it might ordinarily enjoy.

Regulatory and Shareholding Ministries and Processes

The ownership and regulatory functions intersect in the minister's office, although they are executed through the Department of Finance and Treasury Board respectively. Treasury Board focuses on the corporation's financial existence in the given year and carries out the regulatory function through the Financial Administration Act. CPC management prepares its draft corporate and capital plans, which are first approved by the board. The board presents the plans to the minister for signing off before they enter the Treasury Board process. There, Treasury Board approves the corporate and capital plans before they are passed on to cabinet. This takes place in a traditional iterative interchange with the budget and planning units of CPC, before and during the formal processes.[40] The highlights of the corporate plan are tabled with the annual report at the beginning of June. CIG works with Treasury Board to get the plan into political shape, but this relationship is fairly light-handed. Generally speaking, Treasury Board has only a modest involvement in postal affairs.[41] The Department of Finance becomes involved with respect to borrowing issues and the plan's impact on the budget. The staff at Treasury Board has been diminished as a result of cutbacks. They function on only the most aggregated and general issues, since they do not have the capacity to get involved in operational details. For example, the quality targets set for CPC are not tested or evaluated here but are done internally at CPC. The plan's highlights are published with the annual report, but the planning process is a highly closed one. The only accountability mechanism is via the minister to Parliament. The plan's targets and results are not presented in a manner that allows public evaluation of corporate performance or tests the extent to which the corporation is improving its service or financial performance. The planing, implementation, and evaluation processes are very much directed inwardly to the shareholder.

With respect to prices, the Canada Post Corporation Act states that postage rates should be fair, reasonable, and consistent so far as possible, so that the corporation's expenses are defrayed (Section 19.2). Regulation of prices in the exclusive-privilege area has been carried until recently via a public-gazetting process. After an internal process of deciding that a price increase is necessary, CPC management first presents the idea to the board and then to the minister. The minister publishes the proposed rate increases in the *Canada Gazette* and offers the public sixty days to comment and pressure. At the end of this sixty-day period, the minister has another sixty days to decide whether to accept the corporation's recommendation in light of public input. This allows the minister the opportunity to evaluate whether the public would tolerate a postal-price increase. Until recently, the rule of thumb was that the price of a letter would not be increased at a rate greater than the rise in the consumer-price index, plus a proportionate share of extraordinary expenses beyond the corporation's control. The new Framework Agreement now gives the corporation the formal "right" to increase the price of a stamp by a rate no greater than two-thirds the increase in the consumer-price index. Technically speaking, this will still require cabinet approval. The CPC Act allows variable rates for bulk and pre-processed mail (Section 21a) and experimental initiatives for a period up to three years (Section 21b).

The Department of Finance plays the ownership function and looks after shareholder value, although the PWGS minister has an interest in this as well. Finance provides the "challenge" function and is concerned more with long-term strategy than day-to-day or yearly operations. It focuses on borrowing plans, profits and dividends, and the corporation's impact on the government's budget. This process is structured to clarify the service versus financial-return tradeoff, but the dynamic is fairly passively expressed and has not yet been tested to any great extent. Again, Finance has only a modest involvement in postal affairs.[42]

The recent Framework Agreement has set financial return targets for CPC. The profit targets and dividend expectations are not well understood in Canada and have not been well articulated publicly or defended vigorously by governments. There are four basic rationales for setting profit goals and paying dividends. First, corporate profits will enable CPC to expand and improve its operations, and maintain and improve services, without being a drain on the government's budget. Second, these targets force CPC to behave efficiently and engender a corporate culture. Third, the obligation to make profits, pay taxes, and provide dividends creates a level and competitive playing field with private-sector operators in this sector. Fourth, dividends provide a financial return to the public for past and accumulated investments and commitments to the Post.[43]

The Board and Canada Post Corporation

The financial framework and corporate and capital plans are presented to the government for approval by a nine-person Board of Directors, which directs and manages the affairs of Canada Post Corporation. The Canada Post Corporation Act does not specify the composition of the board. No seats are reserved for or designated to postal unions, user groups, community representatives, or government officials, although there was an informal (but short-lived) practice in CPC's early years of assigning two seats to labour. The government appoints the chair, the directors, and the CPC president. The vice-presidents of the corporation are appointed by the board but approved by the government. The board's responsibility is to set the strategic orientation of the Post, as advised by senior management. Section 27.4 of the amended act refers to the practices of the Canada Business Corporations Act as the benchmark for its actions, as well as the FAA's expectations regarding dividends, which are to be determined by the board. It also presents the Post's five-year and capital plans to the government on behalf of the corporation. The board operates on a commercial basis and is obliged to make a profit, to be used to self-finance capital expansion and service improvements after taxes and dividends are paid to the government. Any deficits that are incurred are to be covered by banking transactions, although various sections of the act allow the board to borrow the money from the government (up to a maximum of $500 million – Sections 29, 30) and authorize the government to pay the Post's bills if it cannot (Section 31).

The CPC board has been an enigma. There were a number of significant appointments made to the board in the early 1980s, but this practice did not last long. Relative to boards in Europe and Australasia, the CPC board has been relatively insubstantial in character and unambitious in performance and impact. This is because the board has not been staffed by experienced representatives of the leading and complementary sectors in the communications, transportation, and related markets. Appointments to the board remain exclusively political ones;

governments name only party supporters to the board. The board does have a kind of "representative" quality – but not with respect to customers, employees, complementary sectors, and so on. Rather, the board has a "geographic" composition, with directors assigned by their regional origin for political balance. The board itself plays no role in recruiting its members. Board members have little relationship to the government once they are appointed. During the Conservative years, there was a deliberate government objective to decrease the board's already insubstantial role, in order to ensure a management-dominated company. Its role became purely symbolic and legitimizing.[44] Notwithstanding the good intentions and character of its members, the CPC board has not been as knowledgeable about postal affairs as boards in Europe and Australasia. It is not nearly as well connected to policy processes and thinking. For example, the board did not play much of a role in the Mandate Review and was not of significant assistance in the development of the new Framework Agreement. The board at CPC has not been nearly as central to postal development in Canada as boards have been elsewhere. Nor has it been nearly as assertive and aggressive in relations with the government, with respect to insisting on corporate autonomy and to aggressively asserting the needs of postal development.

The most recent chair has been André Ouellet, the past minister responsible for Canada Post Corporation. He has subsequently become president of the corporation, a development that will be scrutinized in the next section; an interim chair was named (Vivian Alpo, a benefits specialist from Great West Life Insurance). Ouellet initiated a number of organizational changes of the senior-management team, including the creation of a Strategic Priorities Committee, comprising Leo Blanchette as chief operating officer and executive vice-president and Phillippe Lemay as senior vice-president (with responsibility for electronic products and international affairs). He also reorganized board committees and processes, which now reflect his agenda. Indeed, one could argue that the organizational and governance situation has come full circle. The Canadian postal regime has reverted to something like that which existed prior to 1981. The board is fairly weak and dependent, and its membership and committees revolve around Ouellet. There has been a large bureaucratic turnover at Finance and Treasury Board, and the most important postal person at CIG, Jane Billing, has departed. As well, there has been turnover at the vice-presidential level at CPC, and the Strategic Priorities Committee comprises Ouellet loyalists. The regulatory environment is fragmented, informal, and ad hoc. In this context, André Ouellet functions much more like a minister of a department than as the president of a crown corporation.

The Government's Relationship to Canada Post

The government's relationship to Canada Post has been altered by the results of the Mandate Review process and the adoption of the new Framework Agreement in early 1999 (see below). This agreement was designed to emulate the service contracts and arrangements that have been devised in Australasia and many European countries, albeit in a far less ambitious, consequential, and public way. Once the framework is set, the idea is that the Post is then free to proceed in any way that it wishes in order to meet the objectives laid out in the agreement. The Canadian agreement comprises mainly financial targets and some principles. The government has set financial targets that the corporation is to meet within the five-year term of this agreement, that is, by 2003, although officials refer to a five- to seven-year framework. These targets include earnings before interest and taxes (EBIT) of $175 million, a return on equity (ROE) of 11 per cent, and a debt:capital ratio of 40 per cent. These targets are less onerous than had been anticipated or mooted by the TD Securities report that the government commissioned after the Mandate Review. The framework sets dividend rates at 40 per cent of ROE and, in terms of productivity and efficiency, a cost:revenue ratio of 97 per cent. This Framework Agreement is parallel to, but does not exclude, the normal annual corporate planning and approval process. As noted earlier, the agreement came out of the Mandate Review process after a protracted period of discussion between CPC and the government. Its presentation in 1999 was extremely low-key. It is a document that is barely public and certainly not highlighted as similar documents are in other countries that we have examined. It is very much a document geared to the inward-looking and intimate relationship between the Post and the government.

Other Players

There are a number of other formal and informal players in what might be termed the postal-policy community in Canada. Parliament has played an increasingly modest postal role since the early 1970s and especially since the mid-1980s. This reflects a general decline in Parliament's legislative and policy role and its transformation into a legitimizing institution. Within the postal world itself, Parliament's role was forever transformed when the POD was transformed into CPC, making its relationship to the Post a far more indirect one. There are no postal institutions or processes in which MPs are represented. Parliament rarely debates postal matters, save during crisis moments such as strikes. Members raise questions in the House of Commons and present petitions on behalf of their constituents, only to be reminded of CPC's status and independence from the government. Parliament receives the annual corporate report. This is discussed in periodic visits to a parliamentary committee by the chair of the board and CPC's president. These "hearings" are benign and fairly non-consequential events. CPC has an effective government-relations office, which tries to keep MPs happy and informed of postal developments through communications, explanations, and periodic mailings.[45]

There has been a postal ombudsman since 1997. This office developed out of the Mandate Review process, which concluded that there was a need for an impartial arbiter on behalf of postal users. The ombudsman's office is designed to be independent of CPC and to deal with customer issues and complaints that CPC was not able to resolve to customer satisfaction. In its original design, the ombudsman's office was to make a direct report to the minister. However, the ombudsman now reports to the chair and the board, which makes the operation appear to be "in-house." This image has been reinforced by the appointment of André Tessier as the first ombudsman. Tessier had been head of government relations and communications at CPC, and he had earlier worked as an executive assistant for various Liberal notables, including Prime Minister Jean Chrétien, postal critic Don Boudria, and minister responsible for the Post David Dingwall. The office produces a pamphlet "In All Fairness," which is widely distributed. The ombudsman received 5,609 enquiries in 1998–99 and 6,117 in 1999–2000. The ombudsman's annual report is presented in CPC's annual report. There is also a set of community Postal Service Councils that functions parallel to the ombudsman's operation, but this is a very low-key and not very visible operation.

The postal-policy community also comprises a set of interest or policy groups. There are two sorts: insiders and outsiders. The latter comprise groups that are basically critics of CPC in general or of a particular postal policy.[46] For example, a number of ad hoc groups were formed in reaction against commercialization, such as Rural Dignity, Citizens United for Equitable Postal Service, and Residents Against Mailboxes (RAM). They have had a limited lifespan and impact and have faded into the background or disappeared as the corporatized approach was regularized. The Coalition of Canada Post Competitors, the Canadian Couriers Association, the Canadian Community Newspaper Association, and the Canadian Federation of Independent Business are permanent groups, with professional staffs and budgets, who lobby for changes in postal policy. These groups typically focus their attention on the minister and backbench MPs, and they are successful only to the extent that cabinet concludes that postal policy is out of line with public opinion. They were influential in convincing David Dingwall to initiate the Mandate Review and also had a disproportionate impact on the Mandate Review process itself. Outsider groups have a limited effect, though, because they exist outside the normal policy process and outside the predominant postal-policy paradigm. Indeed, despite their "success" in getting the minister to initiate a Mandate Review – in which their concerns were highlighted – the government did not pursue the review's major recommendations.

Insider groups are permanent, professional organizations that deal with CPC and the postal-policy process on an ongoing basis. Foremost is the National Association of Major Mail Users (NAMMU), which has a close and almost permanent relationship with the Post on various committees and working groups that address operational issues and policy concerns. The Canadian Direct Marketing Association has had a similar relationship with the Post, but it became more high profile than NAMMU in the events surrounding the 1997 strike (see below). CPC has used both organizations as a way of expanding the postal business and ensuring that postal policy, services, technical needs, pricing, and so on are in tune with customers' needs. These groups do not always get what they want and seem to be perpetually frustrated about CPC's lack of understanding of their needs. But there is no doubt that they are pleased with the improvement in CPC's performance and orientation. By and large, they supported CPC during the Mandate Review and did not encourage the government to pursue the review's recommendations.

Generally speaking, the policy community has shifted towards business users, customers, and suppliers, as CPC has commercialized and shifted to a customer orientation. This is typified in the two Postal Conferences that CPC has organized – in 1995 and 1998. These were like enormous trade shows, with dozens of speakers, high-powered sponsors, and hundreds of corporate, government, and organizational participants from the financial and communications industries and a dozen foreign postal services.

THE POLITICS OF REGULATION AND GOVERNANCE

This section focuses on events since 1993 and the return of the Liberals to power. Earlier, we asked whether the Liberals' return to power accelerated or decelerated the corporatization process and increased or decreased CPC's autonomy. While there is a mixed array of activities to consider, there is a pattern of activities that suggests that the Liberals decided to harness Canada Post to political or broader public-policy purposes. This explains the Liberals' reluctance to formalize the regulatory and governance environment. An informal and ad hoc postal regime allows it to retain postal authority and gives it more flexibility to use CPC for political ends.

The Rural and National Issues

While in opposition, during the election campaign of 1993, and once in office, Prime Minister Chrétien stated that the practice of closing rural post offices would end. Indeed, within a month of the election, the minister responsible for Canada Post, David Dingwall, imposed a thirty-day moratorium on rural closings, which was extended into a permanent freeze in February 1994. This was an easy and benign action for the Liberals to take to signal a distancing from the previous government's postal policy. The massive and politically divisive rural postal closings had already been carried out by the Conservatives. Moreover, the Liberals made abundantly clear that their decision to stop rural closings did *not* suggest any possibility of the reopening of any closed rural offices.[47] Thus, the Liberals had the best of both worlds, playing the political high road while benefiting from the previous government's tough political decisions.

Canada Post accepted its shareholder's decision but could not have been happy with this intervention. The government's political decision limited the flexibility of corporate decision making. It also suggested to CPC that attaining financial targets and improving performance were less important than broad political objectives – like assuaging rural interests. Moreover, the decision was framed and executed in a non-businesslike and non-accountable fashion. In many other countries, governments calculate the financial cost of maintaining post offices that do not pay their way, as a basis for the government providing direct compensation to the Post to keep these post offices open. If the government decides to withdraw this compensation, then the post offices are closed. This places the decision on an economical and public-policy basis, which allows the possibility of determining political accountability. In the Canadian case, the decision was simply asserted in an ad hoc way with no connection to financial or postal-policy considerations. As in other postal-policy areas, the Canadian government has shown no inclination to expand the Framework Agreement into contract-type arrangements for CPC, as a way of specifying its expectations of CPC performance. The rural decision was a political one, which was tied more to the government's national-unity agenda than to postal objectives. The rural issue retains enormous political resonance and informs the government's predilection for a national

Post. It illustrates how public-service issues have been placed in the foreground of postal decision making.[48]

Parallel to the rural issue, the Post was also directed to serve the issue of national unity. The day after Dingwall was sworn in as minister, he directed CPC to start flying the flag over postal buildings again in all parts of Canada. The Canadian flag was posted on mailboxes in 1995. The word "Canadian" or "Canada" was gradually reintroduced into the Post's title and branding. It had been downplayed in the late 1980s and early 1990s because, by associating CPC in customers' minds with the government, bureaucracy, and inefficiency, it was considered to be bad for business. This change came to a head in January 1998 when CPC introduced a new branding and marketing image, which saw it change its name from "Mail/Poste" to "Canada Post/Postes Canada."[49] It was the third image change since 1981 (the other took place in 1989) but the only one that was motivated primarily by politics. The political intention was to create a closer identification among Canada Post, the federal government, and the Canadian state.[50]

Price Changes

As noted, the Canada Post Corporation Act established a "gazetting" system for price changes. Section 20 of the act provided the public with a sixty-day period to respond to CPC's announcement of a proposed price increase, and offered another sixty days for the minister to decide whether to accept the Post's recommendation for a price increase – given the public input that had been received. This system had deteriorated to a trivial ritual by the time the Liberals returned to office. There had been substantial public input regarding the price changes of January 1982, February 1983, and June 1985 (9,136, 2,467, and 4,000 submissions respectively). But once the public developed a sense that the results were preordained, it lost interest in the process. The seven price increases between 1988 and 1994 each generated fewer than 100 responses (the 1993 increase elicited nine responses). The regulatory practice of the gazetting of price increases had evolved, in effect, into a simple process of ministerial approval.

Before the introduction of the Framework Agreement, the Liberal government made three price decisions. All utilized the same gazetting process as under the Conservative government. These pricing actions have reflected financial, planning, or market considerations much less than they involved political calculations and trade-offs. When the Liberals entered office in 1993, the price of a stamp in Canada remained one of the lowest in the world. Moreover, one-cent increases had come to be a kind of formulaic annual ritual. In late September

1994, however, the cabinet unexpectedly refused CPC's request for a price increase. This proposed increase had been built into corporate planning (the stamps were printed and were sitting in a warehouse). The negative decision reflected pressure on the government from its rural caucus and from small business. The Canadian Federation of Independent Business crowed about its success when the negative announcement was made.[51] This decision would cost CPC $1 million a week and affect its bottom line substantially; it reported a $69-million loss in that fiscal year. In the event, the September 1994 decision merely had the effect of delaying a price increase. Cabinet approved a two-cent price increase in June 1995 (partially to pay for the labour contract[52]). On the eve of an election, though, CPC simultaneously announced a price freeze until 1997 – a freeze that continued into 2000.[53] Despite these corporate assurances, there was another quid pro quo to pay for the price increase of 1995 – the establishment of a Mandate Review (see below).[54]

These price actions were ad hoc, their motivations political, and their financial consequences uncertain. It was an awkward process for Canada Post, which saw an important policy instrument circumscribed by political actions and calculations. The experience signified a temporary reversion to pre-crown days, when proposed postal price changes were intensely debated and governments reacted according to the political climate. The subsequent price freeze neutralized the politics of postal pricing, as did the government's eventual imposition of a pricing formula at the end of the Mandate Review process. The Post will function within a price-cap formula for first-class mail and will be allowed to increase prices by no more than two-thirds the increase of the consumer-price index. This might have strengthened the Post's hand had it been constructed within the context of a more elaborate and detailed long-term strategy. But it was not. Such a strategy would not evolve for another three years.

Mandate Review

In an effort to cut its deficit, the government determined to review all program spending – and CPC and other crown corporations were included in the process. This initiative intersected with the politically driven impulse to review Canada Post's mandate. The resulting Mandate Review was eventful and complex, comprising six distinct stages.

The first stage was the setting of the terms of reference for the review. The bureaucracy and CPC officials anticipated that the review would be an inexpensive, internal, analytical, and basically financial process. Instead, Dingwall announced a Mandate Review on 6 November

1995 which would be an external, consultative, and non-analytical policy review, costing nearly $2 million. In the interim, the government responded to the pressures of its rural backbench MPs, small business, and the courier companies. They were upset about a number of postal issues, including the fact that the government had allowed price increases and had approved CPC's purchase of Purolator.[55] The CCA in particular had organized its members to pressure the government to "do something" about CPC. The result was an expanded review of Canada Post. This process would eventually generate benefits for each of these constituents: a price freeze, an end to rural postal closings, CPC withdrawal from certain parts of the ad-mail sector, and an evaluation of CPC's performance in rural areas. It had also been anticipated that a senior economist, bureaucrat, or policy analyst would head a review team. Instead, a surprise appointment emerged from the Prime Minister's Office (PMO), made by Chrétien's chief adviser, Eddie Goldenberg. George Radwanski would head a one-person review. This suggested the extent to which the process had taken a political turn, since Radwanski was a former Chrétien speechwriter, who was characterized in the press as a staunch nationalist with little business experience. The process had originally been designed to be enveloped in modest, inexpensive, and bureaucratic trappings, with a reasonably predictable result within given bounds. A small steering committee was established, comprised of people from the PMO, Treasury Board, Finance, Supply and Services, and Canada Post. However, Radwanski transformed it into an advisory committee, which he ignored, hiring and using his own staff instead.[56] With Chrétien's support, Radwanski out-manoeuvred the bureaucracy and received extremely wide terms of reference. He would eventually initiate cross-country public hearings (at the minister's prompting). CPC and the bureaucracy put a brave face on the situation, hoping that the process would produce a clearer idea of the new government's expectations of the Post. But this was a negative turn of events for CPC. A public Mandate Review would roll back the protected environment that had been constructed for it in the late 1980s and early 1990s. The review would allow and encourage a renewed politicization of postal matters while creating an extended period of policy uncertainty – which did not end until over three years later. As far as CPC and many postal observers were concerned, these turned out to be three lost years.

The second stage of the Mandate Review process comprised the public hearings that were held in six cities across Canada, from 21 March to 26 April 1996. The review received 440 formal submissions, 1,084 letters, 1,116 telephone calls, and 111 presentations. The hearings combined the good, the bad, and the ugly for Canada Post. The good news was that many firms and customers came forward and reported how Canada Post had developed into an efficient, reliable, customer-oriented service operation. The bad news was that there were many private communication and distribution firms and operations that saw Canada Post as a predator and an enemy. The ugly news was that a deterioration in the relationship between Radwanski and the leadership of Canada Post created an antagonistic mood that pervaded the hearings. Radwanski felt that CPC attempted to undermine the review process and limit its impact. Canada Post had had a study prepared for it by Coopers and Lybrand, which outlined various future scenarios and opted for one model.[57] Radwanski felt that this was an effort by CPC to limit the review by presenting a fait accompli. The tension between the two sides was palpable and was highlighted by an unbelievably awkward episode over a Canada Post photographer allegedly being instructed to take photos of the hearings to make it look like an insignificant event. The transcripts of the hearings make fascinating reading, particularly with regard to the way the chair aggressively cross-examined witnesses as if they were on trial. The hearings were basically a disaster for Canada Post. They exposed CPC to months of relentless scrutiny and criticism. When the hearings hit the heartland of Toronto, Ottawa, and Montreal, small business, courier companies, newspapers, and other competitors took centre stage and relentlessly assaulted CPC. The hearings publicized mainly the negative dimensions of CPC's operations and activities. To the extent that CPC then acted to redress these images and criticisms, it looked to be on the defensive and covering up, with no political shelter in which to hide.

The third stage in the process was the issuing of the report,[58] which the government received on 31 July 1996. Radwanski had negotiated a carte blanche arrangement with the government and he turned into a loose cannon. He wrote the report on his own. He did not take up the offers of advice made by senior executives of Australia and New Zealand Post and the International Postal Corporation. The report that he produced shocked most postal observers – including the government, Canada Post (which had not seen the report or any draft before it was issued), and the postal community abroad. His recommendations comprised a total rupture from past postal-policy development in Canada and from the evolving postal practice of the progressive postal regimes. His core recommendation was to limit CPC's scope of activity to processing and delivering the mail; CPC should exit non-mail functions and sell Purolator. It was evident, though, that letter mail would generate insufficient revenues to finance another core recommendation: the maintenance of the universal postal service at uniform price and service across the country.

Radwanski recommended two sources of revenue to finance the maintenance of the universal system: a huge letter-price increase to fifty cents and the introduction of a stamp (tax) on all mail not carried by CPC. The report was nothing short of a disaster and an embarrassment for both the government and CPC. An enormous price increase and a stamp tax were unpalatable politically, so the report was basically useless to the government. The business uncertainty that a report like this would create for CPC would be extremely destabilizing. Knowing that its core recommendations would not be adopted, the government held on to the report for over three months. During this time it prepared a detailed and strategic reaction to the report.

The fourth stage of the process unfolded when the government finally released the report on 8 October 1996. It took the unusual step of simultaneously issuing a tentative reaction to it, in order to calm the business waters and control the political fallout.[59] The new minister responsible for Canada Post, Diane Marleau, responded to but a few of Radwanski's recommendations. These were the ones that were politically attractive and palatable to CPC: taking CPC out of the unaddressed ad-mail business and maintaining the moratorium on rural postal closings.[60] For CPC, these were small costs to bear to allow the government to satisfy its backbenchers and to save political face. Nonetheless, once again, these political actions involved costs to the Post, for which it received no compensation. At the same time, the government initiated another study – by TD Securities – both to buy time and to cost out the implications of the Radwanski recommendations (the report had produced almost no financial or quantitative analysis, and Radwanski did not make use of CPC's private-sector accountants).

The fifth stage in the process was after the government received the TD Securities report on 17 April 1997. On 23 April 1997 – a year and half after the Mandate Review was announced – the government made its "final" or second response to the Radwanski report. On the eve of the May election, Marleau made a number of pronouncements. CPC would not be privatized; delivery standards would be established for rural areas; postal prices would be frozen for two years; Purolator would not be sold; the position of postal ombudsman would be created; and CPC would not be limited simply to its letter mail function.[61]

The sixth and final stage in the review process was the presentation of the government's Framework Agreement with Canada Post on 18 January 1999 (see below). This was three years and two months after Dingwall had announced the Mandate Review and two and a half years after the Radwanski report had been submitted.

The Mandate Review was ill conceived, a throwback to pre-1981 days, and a real setback for the evolution of postal policy in Canada.

First, it was a classic case of a government wanting to show the public that it was doing something. But the process got out of hand, because it was poorly constructed and managed, and damaged postal development. Second, the review was designed as a political quid pro quo for interests that felt disadvantaged by other postal decisions, again mixing political calculations with postal evaluation and consequences. Third, because of the review's open-endedness, a considerable amount of the corporation's time and energy in this period was expended inefficiently in participating in, tracking, and reacting to the process. Fourth, the process exposed CPC to considerable scrutiny and criticism – some of which was fair and useful but much of which was simply bad for morale, energy, and business. Fifth, after all the time and money expended, the report was not terribly useful in a policy sense. There had to be further efforts to contain the potential negative business fallout to the report. This extended the uncertainty in the postal environment. In sum, the government's intervention into the postal sector had serious unanticipated postal costs and consequences and few benefits.

That said, the Radwanski report did demonstrate that the universal service could not be maintained through a letter-mail monopoly alone. The Post needed higher prices and/or subsidies or other revenues generated outside the restricted area in competitive markets. In the event, the government rejected the former and accepted the latter, as being more politically acceptable. What was not considered was a change to the character (and cost) of the universal service. This was not raised because the report (and the government) accepted the importance of the universal postal system as a necessary public service. In this context, the report also created a legitimizing aura for the government's inclination to adopt the national postal model. It concluded that Canada Post had lost its sense of public purpose and needed to be reconnected to the political and national project: "Because Canada Post is present in virtually every community across the country, this corporation – probably more than any other institution – is the day-to-day face of the Government of Canada. Consequently it has an opportunity and a *responsibility* [emphasis added], in the opinion of the Review, to maximize the value of the presence by serving all Canadians in a manner that promotes national unity and makes the strongest possible contribution to quality of life" (51).

The report rejected the idea of privatization of CPC because of the "limit to our capacity to chip away at the presence and legitimacy of the Government of Canada without adversely affecting social cohesion and national unity" (76). The government was happy to oblige on this score. Finally, the report illustrated the glaring weaknesses in the postal regulatory and governance structures, which Radwanski urged the government to strengthen bureaucratically and through regulation. However, as we have seen and will see again, the government chose to ignore this suggestion, precisely because a loose governance and regulatory regime made it easier to direct Canada Post to the national and political project.

By the end of the Mandate Review process, the government had firmly adopted the national postal model. A number of operational changes or commitments had also been confirmed. These included:

- CPC would not privatized;
- CPC's primary focus would remain on affordable, universal service;
- CPC could remain in competitive fields, including electronic services, to support the universal service;
- CPC would not be obliged to sell Purolator;
- service levels and standards would be set for rural areas, with independent monitoring reports submitted to the minister;
- CPC would remain in the premium unaddressed ad-mail market but not in the economy market;
- there would no price increase in 1997 or 1998;
- a new office of the ombudsman would be introduced and report to the board chair;
- CPC's annual report would have to be accompanied by an audited statement declaring that the Post was not using monopoly profits from its protected areas to cross-subsidize its competitive products in the market;
- the government would develop a five-year policy and financial framework.

The "Liberalization" of the Board and Its Consequences

As discussed earlier, the government names members to the board of CPC, primarily for political party objectives. The board has been "Liberalized" since 1993, as all of the Conservative appointees have completed their terms and been replaced by Liberal ones. The board's composition reflects regional, gender, and other political considerations, not business, skill, or experience. Many of the Liberals are key party players, including Gilles Champagne, a major fund-raiser and Prime Minister Chrétien's long-time political agent. André Ouellet was appointed chair of the Board, directly from the cabinet after a political shuffle. This appointment increased the already substantial intimacy between the corporation and the government. Ouellet had also been the founding minister of Canada Post. He and the present minister

(Gagliano) are quite closely related both politically and geographically (both are from Quebec). Ouellet transformed the chair's position back into a full-time one (the Conservatives had made it a part-time position). This is untypical among the progressive postal regimes. Ouellet was an extremely hands-on chair, which likely contributed to the premature departure of CPC President Georges Clermont. In contrast to the previous administration, Ouellet (and the minister's office) have intervened more directly in customer- and citizen-relations issues. There is also a far greater interaction between the minister's office and the chair's office.

The "Liberalization" of the board has allowed the government to use the board against management when it desires (for example, in rejecting management's recommendation to eliminate Priority Post). This board can also more easily direct the Post towards the government's postal agenda. The board itself is not capable of resisting this development. Its capacity is slender and its inexperience in postal and related matters is obvious. It played little to no role in the Mandate Review process or its aftermath. It lacks substantive postal intelligence and experience as well as the business acumen and authority required to provide a strategic leadership role complementary to that of management. Indeed, with due respect to the individuals involved, the board of CPC is by far the weakest of those examined in this study. This has been consequential, as we will see in the following sections.

One interesting feature of this development is the manner in which Canada Post has become a kind of showpiece as a government organization with a substantial French-Canadian presence. This reflects the government's ambitions, particularly with regard to the national-unity agenda. The informal protocol of balancing a French or English president with an English or French chair was dropped when Ouellet became chair at the time when Clermont was still president. At the senior level, authority revolved around a core group of the then chairman and now president, Ouellet, the then chief operating officer, Leo Blanchette (since deceased), and the second executive vice-president, Phillippe Lemay. The operation projects a Gallic and patrician style – first set by Clermont – that does not seem to be in tune with the character of the business and the times and is not typical of the other postal regimes that we have studied.

The governmental domination of the Post has gone one step farther in the recent search for a replacement for CEO Georges Clermont, who departed prematurely. As noted earlier, the government appoints the president upon recommendation by the board. These appointments have been very political. For example, the appointment of Clermont as CEO was neither unusual nor unreasonable, since he had

had a long career at the Post in a senior and important area. But he did not have a particularly strong business background, nor did he seem to be a "natural" person to be running a mail company. He did, though, have strong political and lobbying skills and sensibilities and was well connected to the French power elite in Ottawa. After Clermont's exit, André Ouellet became acting president while he was still chairman of the board. A professional search for a new CEO was initiated, headed by Mandrake Management consultants. The search process did not go well or quickly and did not find a candidate with the requisite skills and experience at the salary level available. This was not surprising, given the state of affairs described above. It would be extremely difficult to make the CEO position look attractive to a talented and experienced individual, given the Liberals' political intervention in postal matters. Moreover, Ouellet's presence as chair flagged the government's own involvement in and dominance of the weak board. Ouellet had reshuffled the board, which had become very loyal to him. In the end, apparently unable to recruit a new CEO, Chairman Ouellet himself became CEO.

There is no similar situation in any postal regime that we have examined. The drift of the Canadian postal regime into the national model is symbolized and driven by Ouellet's appointment. Before their appointments, neither Ouellet nor Blanchette had business background or experience. All modern, progressive postal regimes that we have examined have CEOs and chairs with extensive and important business experience, typically in an area related to the Post. Governments attract these individuals to the job by promising and having strong boards, whose members are themselves well experienced and knowledgeable and capable of asserting the Post's authority and interests. There is a symbiotic relationship to this process. A strong, autonomous board can attract good management, who feels that they can get on with their job. Good management performing well on an autonomous postal agenda in turn makes a board appointment look to be a promising and satisfying assignment. André Ouellet is an able and interesting individual, whose affection for, and interest in, Canada Post are genuine and deep. But his is an agenda coloured by the political agenda. His position as CEO merges politics and management too closely. This augurs poorly for attracting good board members and postal management in the future.

The Labour Situation

The labour dimension of the Canadian postal regime is as complex and fraught with tension as that of any of the systems examined in this study. The Canada Post Corporation Act transferred labour's accomplishments, rights, and expectations into the new crown corporation framework. In a sense, the corporation has been struggling to deal with this labour regime ever since.[62] CPC appears to lack the authority and the capacity to sort this out on its own, without government or legislative assistance. On the other hand, the government itself continues to cast a shadow over industrial relations at the corporation. In good times, it maintains that CPC is an autonomous corporation that manages its own human resources. In times of trouble, though, both management and labour tend to anticipate an eventual government resolution of negotiations or other difficulties. The Liberal government has done little to contradict this perspective. The result is that the labour dimension of the Canadian postal regime remains as politicized as ever.

Given the history of labour negotiations at CPC, the 1994–95 settlement augured well for the future. This was the first time a contract had been signed before the previous had one ended. The positive negotiation process had been influenced by CPC's decision to use an outside professional negotiator, Jean Lafleur.[63] The settlement was also stimulated by CUPW's desire to reach a deal while it was still under threat of a raid by the letter carrier's union (LCUC), which had lost by only a narrow margin in the earlier one-union certification drive. This settlement also bought time for the new Clermont administration, but it did little or nothing to resolve ongoing labour and costs matters. The thirty-month deal maintained job guarantees, perpetuated the same number of postal outlets, increased vacation benefits, and guaranteed job opportunities for surplus workers. It provided a lump-sum payment of 2 per cent in each of the first two years and a 2 per cent wage increase in the last six months.[64] The deal contributed to the $66-million loss that CPC incurred that year and set the stage for the two-cent price increase the next year. This was a soft deal to help the new postal and political administrations. Finance Minister Paul Martin was unhappy about its cost. Negotiations in 1997 reverted to old "form" despite Lafleur's continued involvement; he remained on the scene until a shoving match between him and CUPW's chief negotiator, Philippe Arbour, led to his being relieved of his duties. The 1997 negotiations were animated by CPC's ambition to cut infrastructure costs by restructuring delivery routes. This was a red flag to the union, which saw a plan to eliminate jobs and increase workloads. CUPW was also keen to attain a real wage increase, after a period of restraint, and to increase the proportion of jobs that were full-time. Preliminary talks began in the spring but a fifteen-day strike started on 19 November 1997 – the first postal strike in six years. Given the proximity to Christmas, the government was under enormous public and business pressure to end the strike, which it did with back-to-work legislation in early December.

The negotiations had a distinctly political character. Overhanging their later stages was CUPW's revelation of a 6 August meeting between Minister Gagliano and Canadian Direct Marketing Association President John Gustafson. It was alleged that the minister guaranteed to the CDMA – representatives of CPC's enormous direct-mail market – that any strike would be legislatively nipped in the bud by the immediate introduction of back-to-work legislation. The government anticipated being tough and ending a futile strike. But its thinking was itself problematic. One purpose of the CPC Act was to distance the government from the Post in order to force the parties to negotiate as in any commercial operation. Instead, CUPW realized again that it was negotiating less with management than with the government and could wait for this moment to arrive. Similarly, this did state of affairs not provide much incentive for CPC to negotiate a deal.

The government used back-to-work legislation to end the strike – the same tool that it had criticized the Tories for using in the early 1990s. In this manner, it managed to generate the worst of both worlds – the country endured the agony of an extended strike and the normal processes of negotiation were disrupted. The strike and back-to-work legislation accomplished nothing in terms of the resolution of the ongoing labour-management, wage-comparability, and labour-costs problems at CPC. The government seemed to be simultaneously willing to be "tough" with CUPW while disinclined to confront the broader labour situation in any permanent or meaningful way. The government reverted to pre-1981 practice. By imposing a 5.15 per cent three-year contract, though, it did not leave the wage or financial settlement to the arbitrator. Indeed, the terms of the imposed settlement were related to Finance's objectives and had little relationship to the parameters of discussions within the postal environment. CPC's last tabled offer had actually been higher, and by imposing a lower settlement the government was deliberately penalizing CUPW for using the strike tactic (approximately $1,000 a worker over the three years). Crucially, the government did not create a wider policy context or framework in which CPC could negotiate effectively with CUPW on tough, far-reaching issues. These are issues that it is unlikely that Canada Post can resolve on its own.

The back-to-work legislation exposed the extent to which the government's postal orientation lacked concrete shape or strategic coherence. In the first draft of the legislation, the government included a clause that directed the arbitrator to take into account CPC's commercial and financial objectives and targets. The legislation directed the arbitrator to be conscious of the "need for terms and conditions of employment that are consistent with those in comparable industries in the private and public sectors and that will provide the necessary degree of flexibility to ensure the short- and long-term economic viability and competitiveness of the Canada Post Corporation." Critics claimed that this clause was surreptitiously altering the CPC Act. The clause was dropped under pressure from the New Democratic Party, as a condition of its acceptance of speedy approval of the legislation. The clause was replaced by a general reference to the CPC Act and to the viability and financial stability of the Post. The fact was, though, that the original clause could not have remained in the legislation, because it was an empty or meaningless one. The government had never specified what the targets or objectives were, and so the clause was inoperable. This eased the requirement on the corporation to hit the 11–12 per cent rate of return that had been mooted by earlier governments.[65]

The subsequent arbitration process took one and a half years to conclude and involved over 200 witnesses and more than 500 exhibits. During this time, CPC's planning and decision-making processes were circumscribed if not frozen. The arbitration process was itself fraught with controversy, as CUPW challenged the impartiality of the arbitrator.[66] As the process dragged on, André Ouellet and the new CUPW head, Dale Clark, kick-started direct negotiations between CPC and the union. A negotiated settlement was reached in late December 1999. This was over two years after the strike. The deal saw CUPW gain wage increases of 1.9 per cent in 2000, 2.5 per cent in 2001, and 3 per cent in 2002, as well as a lump-sum signing bonus. It also guaranteed full job security and consolidated some part-time positions to have the full-time portion of the labour force rise from 73 per cent to 78 per cent. In order for CPC to meet its financial targets, this settlement clearly requires further productivity improvements. This deal provided CPC with some stability over the next few years. It also seemed to demonstrate some willingness on both sides to forge a common approach to confronting the challenges faced by the Post.[67]

The deal may signal changed attitudes by both management and labour and offer the possibility of improved industrial relations in the future. If so, this will not be the result of efforts by the government, which has continued to frame industrial relations at CPC in political terms.

General Orientation

There are both similarities and contrasts between the Conservative and Liberal approaches to postal policy. On the one hand, the Liberals have not rolled back the Conservatives' commercialization and corporatization initiatives that they introduced between 1986 and 1993. On the other hand, these processes have not been extended, and the trend has been put on hold. Instead, the Liberals have recast the commercial environment within a more overtly political framework and agenda, and they have initiated a number of specific measures that weaken and inhibit commercialization and corporatization.

The Liberals accepted the Conservatives' postal commercialization as a kind of "done deal" that would be awkward and difficult to undo. It has maintained many politically controversial commercialization initiatives from the earlier period. A number of these actually benefit the government, which goes some way to explain why they have been retained:

- The government did not end or delegitimize the practice of setting financial targets and expecting to be paid dividends. Marleau tightened these targets for a time after the Mandate Review. As will be seen below, CPC has paid regular (albeit small) dividends to the government. The government also passed legislation in 1994 that obliged CPC to pay taxes, which it has done.
- The government maintained the results of the earlier rationalization of the postal network. It has not reopened any closed rural post offices, nor transformed privatized ones back to public status. Only 53 per cent of post offices in Canada belong to Canada Post. The government has not directed CPC to change the community mailbox program; there are currently nearly two million addresses serviced by community boxes, comprising 15 per cent of all addresses.
- The government continues to cut postal subsidies, the payments on behalf of postal users. The Conservative government halved these payments from $220 million to $110 million. The Liberals' fiscal-austerity cuts applied to this program beginning in 1993–94, after which the program was cut annually. By 1999–2000, support was $40 million.[68]
- The government did not stop the practices of franchising or contracting out of non-core activities. It allowed CPC to retain its purchase of Purolator. It did not accept the Radwanski recommendation to limit CPC's scope to the core letter-delivery business. It has allowed CPC to participate in competitive markets and to provide new commercial products and services.

In sum, the Liberals retained the broad contours of the Conservatives' commercial agenda. This suited its political and fiscal purposes of not having to invest anything in CPC. Indeed, it has made a modest financial gain of about \$100 million a year – \$20–25 million in taxes and dividends and \$70 million in reduced subsidies.

On the other hand, as noted earlier, the Liberals have initiated a number of particular postal moves that have limited or deflected this commercialization framework. These have included the moratorium on rural postal closings, the delay of price increases, the withdrawal of CPC from the low end of the ad-mail market, the rebranding of the Post as Canada Post, and the creation of the Mandate Review. These initiatives had political motives and were designed to recast the Post within a national strategic setting. They have had financial and strategic consequences for CPC. These ad hoc and incremental initiatives were introduced against the slow unfolding of a new mandate or Framework Agreement. In 1986 the Conservative government constructed a clear, focused postal strategy, which it directed CPC to carry out. It updated and clarified this strategy from time to time, particularly in specifying and raising its financial targets and by providing clear feedback of its happiness or unhappiness with corporate performance. In contrast, the Liberals took years to construct a framework or direction, which turned out to be a minor variation on the political status quo. The Mandate Review was poorly and politically motivated and evolved in topsy-turvy, out-of-control fashion. It created extended policy uncertainty for CPC, which was left floundering in a policy limbo, unclear about its future and facing uncertainty on the wage, labour, price, financial-target, and policy-objectives fronts. All the while, it confronted a shareholder that was apparently more politically than commercially sensitive. This led CPC to be decidedly short-term in its focus, unwilling and unable to plan into the future.

The new Framework Agreement that finally appeared in 1999 was the culmination of the extended Mandate Review process. From the government's perspective, this ended the question of Canada Post's future – particularly by rejecting privatization and by allowing Canada Post to retain Purolator and to remain in competitive markets. The Framework Agreement constructed a quasi-contractual relationship between CPC and the government, setting a five-year timetable to attain a number of financial goals and establishing a price-cap formula for first-class mail (two-thirds of the rise in the consumer-price index). The framework was an interesting and useful accomplishment in the evolution of Canada Post and the Canadian postal regime. However, what was most significant was what was not in the agreement.

First, the government set very modest financial targets for Canada Post over an extended time-frame, rejecting the TD Securities' guidelines as unreasonable and impractical.[69] In order for Canada Post to reach these more ambitious targets immediately or quicker, it would have required the introduction of policy and business decisions that the government would have found politically unpalatable. These modest financial and temporal targets essentially signalled an end to the deepening of the commercialization and corporatization process, and a commitment to, and validation of, the postal status quo. In the interim period, the government had resurrected the idea of the national Post and assigned some particular responsibilities and activities to CPC. These were neither costed nor accounted for and imposed financial burdens on CPC for which it was offered no public compensation. The responsibilities and activities in question included the array of issues associated with the national-unity agenda, from maintaining rural post offices to rebranding the Post as a Canadian institution. These two broad policy developments were interrelated. The government set modest financial expectations, in effect cutting CPC some financial slack. This was done to give CPC the space to deliver political goals. The result was increased CPC costs without a corresponding increase in revenues – and hence a lower potential rate of return. The lowered rate of return expected by the government was the quid pro quo for CPC's carrying out political tasks without requiring financial commitments from the government. This arrangement was executed outside any accountability process.[70]

Second, the government did not develop an accountability regime to accompany or implement the Framework Agreement. There had been an increasing sense that the Canadian postal regime lacked sufficient regulatory formality.[71] For example, both the Radwanski report (Chapter 6) and the TD Securities report had suggested the necessity of appointing some sort of governance or regulatory supervisor. This supervisor would evaluate and track Canada Post's activities against specific targets and expectations set by the government. The government instead determined to maintain the informal and opaque regulatory status quo. It did so precisely for political reasons. The introduction of regulatory formality would expose the political character of the government's relationship with Canada Post. It would require the political scrutiny of its postal goals as well as some sort of policy-accountability system. An informal, ad hoc regulatory relationship suited government purposes better. It allowed the government to maintain a bargaining and deal-making relationship with CPC, one that evolved in an invisible and stable fashion.

This in turn explains a third feature of the agreement: the absence of a service code or charter and customer-service accountability. The Framework Agreement is the least public-service or contractual agreement of any examined in this study. To begin with, the agreement is all but invisible. The document is difficult to find and has not been published or distributed in a public way. It has not been set out on any public platform. The agreement contains no mechanisms for regular follow-up or for public reporting regarding CPC's performance against the standards or expectations of the agreement. The document is sparsely written and has little substance, background, or explanation. Its array of targets and goals is limited and focused almost exclusively on financial targets. There is no elaboration of the components of the universal postal system or expectations about performance targets. There are few measures of productivity, service, and performance other than the most aggregated or general financial targets.

It took over three years of bargaining between the Post and the government for this agreement to finally emerge after the setting of the Mandate Review. This framework had been promised in the government's second response to the Radwanski report in April 1997. Yet it emerged only in January 1999 – twenty-one months later. Given this protracted period of time, one cannot suggest that the agreement was produced in a rush without paying attention to what had been left out or put in. First, the agreement represents the bare-minimum guidance provided by the government to project the impression of a regulatory framework. Second, the Framework Agreement is simply a spiced-up version of the status quo. It excludes the possibility of creating regulatory momentum to advance the framework between 1999 and 2004. There is no evidence that the government plans to move this process into any deeper waters. Further, the government has not mooted the possibility of furthering liberalization or broadening competition for CPC as a way of increasing performance (for example, there is no suggestion of reducing the exclusive privilege). Third, the framework fits the government's desire to maintain an informal regulatory and governance structure that will allow it to bargain with and use CPC for its political objectives. In sum, the Liberals have maintained but not deepened a commercial orientation to postal policy while increasing their political command of the area. But the government has done little to adjust the governance environment to assist CPC in meeting product, technological, and international competition.

PERFORMANCE

The Canadian Post Office was transformed in 1981 into a commercial crown corporation in order to allow it to become financially self sufficient, commercially viable, and technologically up to date while maintaining the universal postal service and establishing good industrial relations. In this section, we will review Canada Post's performance since 1991 with one eye poised on these objectives and the

Table 1
Financial performance (year ending)

	1994	1995	1996	1997	1998	1999	2000
Revenues (billions)	4.12	4.74	4.96	5.09	5.07	5.38	5.64
Operating Income (millions)	26	−38	63	134	53	59	76
(% Revenues)	0.6	−0.8	1.3	2.6	1.1	1.1	1.4
Net Income (millions)	−270	−69	28	112	36	50	75
ROE (%)	−22.5	−6.7	2.8	10.4	3.2	4.7	7.4

Source: Canada Post Corporation, *Annual Report,* various years.

other eye directed to evaluating CPC's performance within the national postal model. As an opening generalization, CPC has become a far more proficient, customer-oriented, and productive operation over the last two decades. As will be seen presently, it has stopped being a drain on the public purse. Its network is modern, efficient, and reliable. It has become a customer-oriented and commercially sensitive corporation and has improved its service record. All the while, it has maintained the universal system with low postal prices at approximately the same if not improved service level as compared to the situation before 1981. Public-opinion polls indicate a high level of support for Canada Post that is shared by the business community, which no longer encourages privatization of the Post and indeed wants it to be successful.[72]

Canada Post's overall performance record can be divided into three eras: the Liberal juggling act (1981–85), the Conservatives' commercialization and corporatization efforts (1986–93), and the Liberals' reestablishment of the national Post (1994 to the present). The overall financial performance of CPC in the first period was dismal: between the 1981–82 and 1985–86 fiscal years, it incurred $1.5 billion in deficits. In the second period, when corporatization really began, CPC ran modest surpluses in four of the seven fiscal years between 1986–87 and 1992–93, for an overall balance of $100 million. This was effectively a break-even performance but involved an enormous turnaround from the first period. During the third period, of Liberal national postal activity, CPC generated surpluses in five consecutive years (1996–2000). As Table 1 indicates, these surpluses were not terribly substantial in 1996–97, when CPC's operating profit was 2.6 per cent and its return on equity was 10 per cent. Its net income over the last five years has been $300 million – on revenues of $26 billion. This period has seen no significant increase in financial performance over the previous one.

Overall, in the period since 1986, then, Canada Post Corporation has essentially balanced its books. What is one to make of this performance? First, it should be recalled that the Canadian postal regime is a low-price one, arguably one of the lowest in the world (forty-six cents is the second-lowest price in the industrial world, according to CPC). In the period 1982–96, letter prices rose by only 69 per cent of the rise in the consumer-price index. Its increase to forty-six cents in January 1999 was the first price increase since August 1995 and was well below the rise in the consumer-price index. Second, the threshold for competition by courier and other private fast posts is relatively low. Canada Post has historically operated in a fairly liberalized postal environment, and the exclusive privilege has been undermined and trivialized by technological and product developments. Daily newspapers and distributors battle for market share in the ad-mail market and launch court actions to challenge any privileges that CPC enjoys in this area.[73] Retail outlets such as Mail Boxes Etc provide business alternatives and showcase CPC's courier and parcel competitors. Third, CPC's operation has basically been a postal one, with little contribution from other near- or non-postal sectors. It has no banking or financial arm and only a modest shipping and logistics presence, and its retail wing is underdeveloped relative to the Post in Australia or the United Kingdom. It is generally appreciated that CPC must lever its network in a varied way in order to generate sufficient revenue to maintain the universal service. This diversification remains a relatively foreign experience in Canada, where – unlike European countries – there is a weak traditional Post involvement in activities outside the core postal area.[74] As a result, the issue remains politically controversial. CPC has entered the electronic communications market (see below) but enjoys no privileges in this increasingly competitive sector. Fourth, the regulatory and governance environment has not contributed to rational or effective postal policy, including in the industrial-relations area. This has affected business performance particularly over the last three to four years, when there has been much policy uncertainty, substantial leadership turnover, and considerable incoherence in postal strategy.

These factors are not listed to excuse CPC's modest performance; rather, they are presented to give some preliminary context to its financial record. Canada Post's performance has been reasonable but not brilliant under the circumstances. It has not reached the expectations that it set for itself and its performance often falls short of its plans. For example, CPC predicted in 1996 that it would be generating net income of $300 million by 2001. Its subsequent financial returns have not been anywhere near that level. It generated sufficient revenues

Table 2
Employment (000s)

	1994	1995	1996	1997	1998	1999	2000
Full-time	49.9	50.2	50.9	51.2	50.6	51.7	52.7
Part-time (PT)	13	12.3	12.6	12,3	12.5	12.2	12.1
% PT	26	19.6	19.8	19.4	19,8	19.1	18.7
Total	62.9	62.6	63.5	63.5	63.1	63.9	64.9

Source: Canada Post Corporation, *Annual Report,* various years.

to repay an $80-million ten-year loan in 1998–99, it returned $200 million of contributed capital to the government in 1998–99, and it increased its stake in Purolator by $66 million. CPC has begun to hit its financial targets, but it has to be admitted that the targets themselves are modest and have been rolled back. CPC has provided indications of some financial accomplishment and capacity. Overall, though, its operating income has been low. It has paid only modest taxes ($34 million between 1995 and 2000) and dividends ($44 million for the same period). Its financial targets for the next five years are modest as well; they are expected to rise to an 11.5 per cent return on equity (or $175 million) by 2004, with dividends in the $12–18-million range.

Recent and prospective financial performance has been disappointing and worrisome in two areas. First, it is unlikely to provide sufficient revenue to modernize the postal operation and to maintain the universal service at a level in line with public standards and expectations. CPC has come to rely too much on long-term debt to finance its operations and investment. It has run down its equity holdings and used up its cash reserves; it has little financial self-sufficiency and has had to rely on a line of credit. Its net investment in assets has been greater than the cash that it has generated, which has contributed to its debt. But this investment in assets has exceeded depreciation only modestly. CPC simply has to generate more revenue out of its network and other activities if it is to have sufficient resources to modernize, keep up to date, and maintain the universal system.[75] Capital expenditures have declined recently – from $272 million in 1993–94 to $132 million in 1994–95 – and thereafter to $100 million or below annually, averaging $90 million a year. As Table 2 indicates, the employment level has remained fairly stable. However, it has increased over the last two years, notwithstanding the flat communications market (see below). This may be an ominous sign.

CPC's level of financial performance is worrisome for a second reason. The absence of improvement in performance suggests that CPC

Table 3
Postal activity (volume) (year ending, millions of units)

	1994	1995	1996	1997	1998	1999	2000
Communications	4,515	4,610	4,733	4,580	4,605	4,683	4,723
Ad mail: unaddressed	4,413	4,831	4,844	4,050	2,377	2,515	2,574
Ad mail: addressed	1,321	1,431	1,464	1,517	1,543	1,673	1,485
Ad mail: total	5,734	6,262	6,308	5,567	3,920	4,188	4,059
Physical	210	272	300	309	297	302	304
Total volumes (billions)	10.9	11.6	11.8	10.9	9.2	9.6	9.6

Source: Canada Post Corporation, *Annual Report*, various years.

is treading water. This is particularly the case given the solid foundations laid in the late 1980s and early 1990s for improved performance.

Postal Activity

Like Posts around the world, CPC faces an intensely competitive and
changing communications market. It also functions within a political
environment where policy decisions and political actions have business
consequences. For example, Table 3 indicates how overall volumes
have declined from a high of 11.8 billion units in 1996–97 to 9.2 billion
units in 1997–98 and rebounded slightly to 9.6 billion units in 1998–
99 and 1999–2000. There are a number of issues playing out here
simultaneously. On the political or policy front, the weakening in
postal volumes reflects, first, the government decision to remove CPC
from the low end of the ad-mail market, which led to a decline in
unaddressed ad mail by 1.5 billion units. As Table 3 indicates, though,
this has had some but only modest financial consequences. Second,
the overall decline in volumes in 1997–98 reflects the impact of the
December 1997 postal strike, which had political as much as business
origins. Third, these political factors exacerbated a flattening in postal-
volume growth caused by technological and product competition. The
letter-mail situation is flat and this market is a mature one. Personal
usage has been declining by 1 per cent a year over the last decade.
The decline in volumes in 1996–97 was the first time that there had
been an absolute decline in postal volumes, reflecting the rise of electronic competition and declining per-capita consumer use. Events like
the 1997 strike have accelerated this process. For example, more than
one million Canadians decided to switch to direct deposit for federal
government cheques, a permanent annual loss of $6–7 million in busi-
ness. CPC predicts stable volumes over the next two to three years
and then a decline thereafter, and a fall in revenues in the area of

Table 4
Postal revenues (year ending, millions)

	1994	1995	1996	1997	1998	1999	2000
Communications	2,151	2,217	2,286	2,273	2,262	2,322	2,467
Ad mail: unaddressed	227	246	250	245	174	188	190
Ad mail: Addressed	343	363	392	437	457	499	494
ADMAIL	570	609	642	682	631	687	684
Physical	871	1,381	1,492	1,566	1,598	1,777	1,873
Other	333	373	373	414	422	426	423
Total	4,115	4,743	4,956	5,085	5,066	5,380	5,637
Purolator	200	656	678	760	849	905	969

Source: Canada Post Corporation, *Annual Report,* various years.

$350 million over the next five years. The 1999–2000 results are "encouraging" to the extent that the letters market has held its own despite the acceleration of developments in electronic communications.

This suggests the increasing importance of near and non-postal activity for CPC if it is to generate the revenue required to maintain the universal service. Ad mail is seen as a potential saviour and CPC has made great efforts in this highly competitive area, including the hiring of an extensive staff of ad-mail specialists. As Table 4 indicates, revenue from this area has increased, despite CPC's being required to get out of the low-end, unaddressed ad-mail market. The results in 1999–2000 were flat, indicating the degree of competition in the market. Similarly, the courier market has become increasingly important generally and for CPC in particular. Revenues from Purolator rose from 14 per cent to 17 per cent of total revenues between 1994 and 1999, although 1999–2000 saw Purolator incur a $9-million loss. As in Europe and elsewhere, moving physical products (small packages) has become an increasingly important area, particularly in the world of e-commerce deliveries. CPC delivers for Chapters Online, La Senza, and Sears, among others, and has introduced eParcel shipping. It is also trying to extend its southbound package service, where it has but 5 per cent of this billion-dollar market; it has initiated some projects with Yves Rocher and Bombardier. Volumes have increased by 50 per cent in this sector in this period and revenues have doubled, to comprise 33 per cent of total revenues. Overall, revenue from the communications (letters) area declined from 52.2 per cent of total revenue in 1994 to 43–4 per cent in 1999–2000. Canada Post became a $5-billion company in 1997–98. The 1999–2000 five-year plan anticipates revenue growth of 6 per cent in 1999–2000 to $5.7 billion and 2–3 per cent growth in subsequent years, taking CPC into the $6-billion club in 2002 and to $6.3 billion in 2004.

Table 5
The postal network (year ending)

	1994	1995	1996	1997	1998	1999	2000
Retail Outlets (000s)	18.7	18.6	18.5	21	19.9	18.6	23.2*
Delivery Addresses (millions)	12.2	12.3	12.5	12.6	12.7	12.9	13.1

* Reflects introduction of National Stamp Retailer Program.
Source: Canada Post Corporation, Annual Report, various years.

The Network

Canada Post continues to maintain an enormous, complex, and expensive network to provide the universal postal system. It does not receive any compensation or support from the government to maintain the network, other than via the exclusive privilege. Unlike other countries, the costs of maintaining this system in Canada are not clear or well quantified, so policy discussions about the network are typically obscure. That said, the corporation initiated two radical departures in the 1980s that have brought the stratospheric costs of maintaining the network under some semblance of control. There have been some efforts, albeit modest and insufficient, to lever the networks to generate extra revenue to maintain the universal system

With respect to the retail network, the corporation closed many rural, small town, and urban post offices that were not generating sufficient business to warrant their continued operation. It complemented this initiative by setting up a franchise system in which retail outlets were opened in other business operations. The most visible of these was an arrangement with Shoppers Drug Mart, a large chain of retail, supermarket-style drugstores. There are currently three thousand private retail postal operators across the country. The corporation recently renegotiated financial arrangements with its franchisees, which led to some conflict with a newly created association of franchisees.[76] As Table 5 indicates, the size of retail network has levelled out in the 18,000–19,000 range; this is well over double the number of postal outlets in Canada in 1981, when there were only public post offices. There are 7,000 full-service postal outlets; this is about 1,000 less than the total number of post offices in 1981. CPC's retail outlets are not terribly diversified, compared to, say, retail outlets in Australia (where there are extensive financial and bill-paying services) or the United Kingdom (which provides hundreds of financial, insurance, and retail services). There are a modest number of complementary products offered in CPC outlets. This has always been a source of controversy in Canada, where the private sector protests vehemently whenever the Post enters retail trade. Canada has enjoyed a far more open and accessible banking system than in Europe, with the result that the Post has played only a minor role in the Canadian financial system. CPC has pursued a number of retail initiatives. For example, as the banks rationalize their networks, Canada Post has begun to offer banking services in areas where banks have closed their branches. For example, in a pilot project, CPC will provide banking services for Laurentian Bank in a select number of areas where the Bank has no branches or ATMs. CPC has also experimented with selling products like American Express cheques, is testing offering bill-paying facilities in a select number of communities,[77] and is placing bank machines in a number of its outlets. In order to proceed in such areas, the retail outlets would require far more sophisticated payment and recording facilities. To this end, CPC launched a Retail Outlet Automation Program, and it has introduced point-of-sale hardware and software at retail outlets. CPC would love to transform its outlets into a kind of "Service Centre" – offering access to postal, financial, government, and e-commerce services.[78] This requires successful negotiation with government departments, banks, and other business groups.

The second network departure was on the delivery side. Canada is a geographically large country that experiences perpetual sprawl. This is an expensive feature of the postal experience in Canada, since over 100,000 new addresses are added each year to CPC's delivery network. As the table above indicates, more than 700,000 new addresses were added over the last six years. CPC introduced the concept of the "community mailbox" in the 1980s. This involves a free-standing cluster of mailboxes and a drop-off, usually in an open area adjacent to a new suburban development. All new home addresses in Canada are serviced by community mailboxes, unless the new address lies within an established area that is already serviced by home delivery. This decision was an extremely controversial one in the 1980s, but the passage of time and a period of usage has regularized the issue and the service. It was also an important financial decision for CPC, given the divergent costs of servicing an address through home delivery (over $200 a year per address in the mid-1990s) versus a community mailbox ($120 a year).[79] This represents $8 million annually – forever – for every 100,000 new addresses. Canada Post has made considerable efforts to lever the delivery network, particularly through servicing and assisting the direct-marketing industry, which has created some conflict with newspaper associations and distribution and delivery companies in this highly competitive market. It clearly has some real comparative advantage in this area, and there are reasonable growth prospects.

With respect to the quality of delivery, CPC became the first Post in the world to measure its performance when it hired Ernst and Young in 1987 to subject its delivery performance to an independent audit (its external performance is measured by Price Waterhouse under contract to the International Postal Corporation). In a geographically sprawling country such as Canada, measuring performance is at best a rough-and-ready process. CPC introduced its 2/3/4 measuring standard to reflect the realities of the Canadian landscape. This standard was criticized originally for not being challenging enough. But it is a not unreasonable standard, given Canadian distances. These are greater than international distances across Europe, where standards are no higher than those within Canada. Moreover, the reality is that an inexpensive forty-six-cent stamp is buying reliability and a modest pace of delivery; faster service can be had for a higher price. The attainment of delivery standards peaked in 1992–94 at 98 per cent, and performance was around 95 per cent throughout the 1990s (the present target is 97 per cent). This is a substantial improvement over the situation in the late 1980s, when the achievement rate was in the 85–90 per cent range. There has been some criticism that the measurement system focuses exclusively on inter-urban mail. Service targets have now been set in ninety-six local areas and non-urban core areas. Measurement of large-volume deliveries has also been introduced. The government has mooted the idea of doing performance evaluation itself, rather than having the process carried out by CPC. This would require the government to build up its regulatory capacity.

Canada Post has also sought to control its overhead or infrastructural costs in other ways. For example, it has outsourced its computing and communication-utility services. In a $1-billion deal in 1993, it contracted SHC System House to manage its data-processing, telecom, and computer-system networks.[80] CPC also contracted out the management of its properties in 1994 to Profac (eastern Canada) and Royal Lepage Facilities Management (western Canada).[81]

New Products and the International Area

CPC has attempted to introduce new activities and products, for two reasons. First, it has to react to the hard reality that the letter market is a mature and uncertain one. Second, revenues from the exclusive-privilege area are simply insufficient to maintain the universal service at its existing level. Thus, Canada Post has had to discover and exploit new markets and products – all of which are competitive ones. As a generalization, one can easily observe that accomplishments in this regard – and in levering the network – are modest, relative to a number of other countries. However, Canada Post has been enveloped within a basically national postal regime, in which the government is highly sensitive to complaints from CPC's competitors. In the countries adhering to the mercantile model – Germany and the Netherlands – the national Posts have expanded into a bewildering array of areas through a dizzying set of investments and takeovers. These would be extremely difficult if not impossible to carry out in Canada. For example, the Dutch Post purchased two of the Netherlands' largest bookstore chains to expand its retail net – the equivalent of Canada Post purchasing SmithBooks and Coles. Both the German and Dutch Posts have purchased some of the largest shipping, distribution, and logistics companies in Europe. The Framework Agreement legitimated CPC moves in this direction, but without much policy thrust or encouragement. While Canada Post has initiated a number of new products and services, this section will focus on two key areas that are critical to its future: courier services and electronic products.

One exception to the scenario posed above is CPC's involvement in the courier market. It will be recalled that there is a time-sensitive exception to CPC's exclusive privilege: items that are fifty grams or less can be delivered by anyone as long as the price charged is at least three times the price of a letter-mail stamp. This feature of the Canada Post Act was controversial in 1981. Its inclusion more or less confirmed and extended the existence of the large private courier market, which had developed through the strike-filled and uncertain postal days of the 1970s. Canada Post was not well positioned to perform in this fast-growing and promising sector. Its first efforts in this area – Priority Post – developed slowly and expensively. In the early 1990s, CPC made what could be characterized as a typical and rational business decision: it decided to buy into the market to accelerate its presence. Fortuitously, Purolator Courier – the largest courier company in Canada – was for sale. CPC's desire to purchase Purolator put the Conservative government on the spot. On the one hand, given that it was vigorously pro-market, the government was not anxious to see a state enterprise expand. On the other hand, it had been encouraging CPC to act in a market-oriented commercial fashion and, from CPC's perspective, the takeover made good business sense. In the event, the government approved the takeover, in a relatively quiet fashion politically.[82]

The takeover made CPC a large (likely the largest) player in the Canadian courier market, although there was a dispute over whether it had 22 per cent or 45 per cent of the market. The deal was immediately controversial[83] and continues to be so. Competitors were alarmed that CPC would dominate the market and the CCA (which represented many of the 2,000 courier companies in Canada, including FedEx and UPS) challenged the takeover politically in Ottawa and legally before the National Transportation Agency and the Competition Bureau of the Department of Industry. The legal challenges were not successful.[84] The CCA continued to campaign politically and was successful to the extent that the government initiated the Mandate Review. [85] The Radwanski report, as we have seen, in turn recommended to the government that CPC sell Purolator.[86] The government did not accept this recommendation, and it continued to defend CPC's involvement in the competitive courier business as a way of generating revenue to support the universal service. André Ouellet has declared that "two successive governments have recognized that if Canada Post is to earn revenue and continue providing universal postal services to the Canadian public, it must be allowed to compete in sectors that generate profits."[87] CPC, then, will continue to operate and develop services and products in the competitive courier field. In a related initiative, CPC acquired a majority share of Progistix-Solutions, a wholly owned third-party logistics subsidiary of Bell Canada. In partnership with Intelcom Courier Canada, a same-day delivery and logistics-solutions company, CPC is entering the integrated business of third-party logistics and supply-chain management.

A second substantial area of CPC initiative is in electronic products and services. It will be recalled that the Canada Post Corporation Act directed CPC to remain aware of and respond to technological developments as it continued to provide customary postal service. In the intervening years, the electronic revolution has accelerated and its challenge to the future of the letter has intensified. CPC has introduced a number of electronic services over the years, such as Omni Post and other hybrid products, which have allowed electronic transmission of messages, bills, statements, and so on from a central site to regional centres, where they are printed, placed in envelopes, and delivered. CPC also plans to sell postal products over the Internet and its website receives tens of thousands of hits a week. One of its first "pure" electronic products was Post ECS, a global electronic courier service, which was developed under the leadership of the International Postal Corporation, in collaboration with La Poste and the USPS.

Its major and most daring initiative – and likely the most consequential one – is its introduction of the EPO, the electronic post office. This is an Internet mail-delivery system. Anyone can apply for a free electronic mailbox. This mailbox can receive electronic bills, statements, forms, catalogues, and information, and so on at this single site, as directed by the user. Bills can be paid as well. This initiative involves a certain amount of cannibalization of its own business, but CPC will receive revenues from the companies that use this service. In any case, if its electronic customers were not using its EPO, they would likely be using someone else's system. This system was developed in partnership with Cebra (a member of the Bank of Montreal Group) and in a technological alliance with SAP AG (the world's leading provider of inter-enterprise software solutions). The system was tested in 1998 and launched in 1999–2000. This is a major corporate initiative in a highly competitive sector. There have been other e-initiatives such as e-Parcel and PosteCS, which provides secure desktop-to-desktop file transfer via the Internet. This was developed with the USPS and La Poste.[88] In late 2000, CPC partnered with the Calgary-based company Cypersurf[89] to offer Internet access in selected postal outlets.

Some initiatives have not been successful, as often happens in business life. An early attempt at tapping into the home-shopping industry (a firm called UBI) anticipated but was surpassed by Internet shopping. In 1996–97 CPC sold its shares in GD Express Worldwide, the international courier venture, when the national Posts were unable to develop a coherent strategic consensus. However, CPC has been successful in marketing its expertise abroad through Canada Post International Limited (CPIL – formerly CPSML). CPIL is not allowed to invest externally, so these projects are always partnership arrangements. For example, CPC has combined its expertise with SNC Lavalin's $20-million equity investment in a twelve-year project to rebuild the postal system in Lebanon. CPC bid jointly for a five-year contract with the locally owned IPS (International Postal System) to overhaul the entire postal system of Guatemala.[90] All told, it has initiated over ninety projects in forty-five countries, including recent projects in Italy and Belgium. In a related domestic area, Canada Post has marketed its expertise to many of its major customers through Mailroom Management Services.

The international dimension of postal life has become increasingly clear and compelling. The major national Posts – TPG, DPAG, and Royal Mail – have all increased their activity in Canada recently.[91] The international dimension of postal life was confirmed in a harsh way when the Canadian government was sued by UPS under Chapters 11 and 15 of the North American Free Trade Agreement.[92] UPS has argued that the Canadian government failed to regulate CPC properly, allowing CPC to perform in a predatory and anti-competitive way by using its exclusive privilege to subsidize its courier products and by not allowing competitive courier products to be sold in its retail outlets. UPS has also maintained that the Canadian government has not treated it equitably as a domestic corporation, since CPC has been given privileges that it does not receive. CPC has dismissed the allegations, insisting that UPS has got things backwards: Canadian postal prices are low because of the contributions made by returns from its competitive activities.[93] Regardless, the UPS challenge will proceed. It looks for CPC to sell Purolator, to set it up as a separate company, or to get out of the courier area entirely.

OBSERVATIONS ON THE CANADIAN CASE

What can one learn from the Canadian case? What interest does it hold for postal policy makers? A number of issues will be set out in the Conclusion, where we will make several policy recommendations for the Canadian postal regime. The observations here will lay the foundation for these recommendations.

The Canadian postal regime is a mixed one. It lacks mercantile features – for reasons discussed below – but it contains elements of both the market and the national models. The latter's political elements intersect with and limit the further development of its market features. The postal regime is a muddy or opaque one. It is difficult to identify clearly how the regime works, who has responsibility, how decisions are made, how postal policy is evaluated, and so on. Unlike the French variant of the national model, the Canadian postal regime does not have formal political institutions and processes with public representation and input, via which postal-policy discussions, evaluations, and decisions take place. Rather, the Canadian regime is an informal and ad hoc one, which tends to close the policy process to scrutiny. Despite its political character, it offers negligible accountability mechanisms and processes. The political and market elements combine to make a confusing policy environment for Canada Post. It receives mixed signals and incentives. This is not a recipe for creating good postal policy or allowing CPC to develop a capacity to deal with technological and international changes.

The Canadian postal regime is framed by the Canada Post Corporation Act, which was passed in 1981. This was the first time in Canada that a department of government had been transformed into a crown corporation. The act thus had an experimental quality to it. The character of the act also reflected the mixed political temper of the times. The act presented Canada Post with an extensive and mixed bag of qualitative objectives and expectations. It also set up informal and generalized political-institutional mechanisms and processes for implementation and evaluation. CPC was simultaneously corporatized and put under strict political control. It was given public objectives and told to act like a private corporation. The act, then, constructed a complex web within which CPC was to function. The act could hardly have been expected to·establish a permanent or stable long-term regime all at once. Indeed, the postal environment itself has changed dramatically since 1981, under the influence of technological and international changes. However, the goals, expectations, and governance mechanisms of the Canadian postal regime remain essentially similar to those that existed in 1981. There was a period in which this web was simplified – in the intense commercialization and corporatization period of 1986–92. But governance changes did not match these corporate ones. The complex set of expectations and processes set in 1981 have been reconfirmed by the most recent government and the informal and ad hoc governance regime has been extended. There is a widespread sense in the Canadian postal community that the Canadian postal regime has fallen behind developments in the progressive postal regimes in other parts of the world. This reflects the absence of fundamental institutional and policy change since 1981.

The absence of policy and institutional change can be explained partially by the broader institutional context in which the Canadian postal regime has evolved and in which Canada Post functions. In the first instance, the postal regime is isolated institutionally and politically in Canada. The transformation of the POD into Canada Post was not connected to a wider state enterprise or economic-reform agenda. It did not benefit from the momentum, creativity, and policy insights associated with these sorts of reforms. At its origins and thereafter, postal policy has not been connected to wider government agendas such as communications or transportation policy. This would have placed different pressures on, and offered resources to, the formulation of postal policy. There have been some exceptions in areas such as rural and national-unity policy. But these have simply reinforced the Canadian bias to consider postal policy on narrow, traditional, and parochial postal terms. The Radwanski report was a classic example of this phenomenon in Canada. It was totally divorced from the productivity and competitiveness agendas of the time, and it ignored international postal developments that were themselves stimulated by these agendas.

An institutional metaphor for this state of affairs is the revolving-door assignment of Canada Post to a number of different government departments (the act specified that the Post report to a minister, not to a department). This practice has undermined policy continuity. It has also inhibited the building up of public postal capacity and intelligence. The latter is sorely lacking – at CPC, in the government, and among other players like the postal unions. There is a fundamental lack of understanding of what is going on in the wider postal and communications world. CPC has been settled most recently within the service-oriented Department of Public Works and Government Services. This makes it basically a policy orphan and places it low on the government's priority list. CPC is divorced from the mainstream and important policy issues and areas of the day: international competitiveness, communications, national infrastructure, international trade in services, and comparative advantage. These are the policy domains where the postal sector should be located and be making a contribution.

The absence of a strong institutional setting and policy context has resulted in the perpetuation of a traditional postal discourse, which is focused on small postal issues. This in turn has reinforced an unchanging set of postal expectations and pressures. Traditional discourse and expectations has undermined the possibility of building up a postal consensus on larger issues. This guarantees that postal-policy making will be of an incremental character. And an important result is that the mixed political and economic objectives formulated in the act in 1981 have not been resolved. They continue to coexist in a perpetually unstable fashion, requiring political intervention from time to time to redress any uncertainty. The hazy, qualitative expectations that were set out in the act have not been formalized, implemented, or quantified to any extent. A basic political consensus about postal matters is lacking, save for the generalized view that Canada Post should exist and that it should maintain the universal service. The Post has been studied and reviewed incessantly. But the postal-institutional process has been isolated from broader government concerns and issues. This has resulted in ad hoc postal decision making which has been divorced from the typical policy explanations and learning associated with a more integrated policy process. Instead, the Canadian postal regime offers infrequent bouts of intense postal debate at crisis moments, such as postal strikes and panic attacks about the future of rural Canada. This is exacerbated by the Westminster system of government, which ensures division and conflict. These processes do not lead to policy understanding and development. Rather, they tend to reinforce traditional concerns and biases about postal issues, which in turn require an imposed resolution politically from on high when disagreements arise.

Postal-policy changes in Canada have been incremental in nature. There has been little extension of the liberalization and corporatization processes, as experienced in the progressive postal regimes. The intense commercialization of the late 1980s and early 1990s was an exception. This reflected an act of ad hoc political will. It did not alter the basic contours of the postal-policy status quo, which has subsequently been perpetuated. The Mandate Review and the resulting Framework Agreement have not extended the corporatization or liberalization agendas into deeper waters. Indeed, the Framework Agreement – which took over three years of policy discussion and reflection – initiated few policy changes and essentially reconstructed the status quo. Policy processes have not led to a reflection on the basic meaning of the universal postal system, its character, and to possible change. Even the Mandate Review took as a given the traditional view of the universal postal service. This orientation to the policy status quo reflects the absence of ongoing institutional policy discussions of postal matters, the disconnectedness of postal from larger policy issues, and the lack of a real political consensus or understanding of the postal future. Indeed, this state of affairs betrays a kind of policy avoidance that was reflected in the Framework Agreement. The latter does not include targets, objectives, or evaluation processes whatsoever with respect to postal services, and it does not connect well to the larger postal picture.

There has been no change to the institutional processes and character of the postal regime initiated by the CPC Act in 1981. The act created an informal, ad hoc regulatory regime, centred in the office of the minister. Formal processes – such as the gazetting of price increases – became empty and ritualized; they have been replaced by a price-cap or formula approach. The setting of the corporate and capital plans is a closed, internal exercise directed inwardly in institutional fashion to the government. Only its barest and most general highlights are revealed to Parliament. The latter receives the annual report, but this is an insubstantial document that is not terribly useful. Neither process is set up as a public-accountability or evaluation exercise. It is not surprising that both are widely ignored in the media and by the public. The government's ownership and regulation functions are not well divided either conceptually or institutionally. This would not be allowed in the European context. Government leaders and most corporate executives continue to reject third-party regulation for being too cumbersome, inhibiting, and expensive. Formal regulation might provide the accountability and evaluation mechanisms that do not exist in the informal, ad hoc processes of the Canadian postal regime. Regulation forces a confrontation with these issues and the larger postal picture.

The informal and ad hoc approach "fits" the national model that characterizes the postal regime in Canada. The CPC Act placed the minister at the centre of the postal universe. It assigned considerable postal authority to the government, notwithstanding the postal corporatization that took place at the time. Nothing has subsequently occurred to roll back the government's postal authority or to limit its capacity to intervene in and/or determine postal policy and development. The "buckle" between the government and CPC is the board. As discussed earlier, it is dominated by government appointees and has been a weak instrument for corporate advancement and postal development. Senior postal managers in turn have come and gone.

The present group has closer political ties to the government than any previous administration had. Canada Post currently presents a more political face and image to the external world than it has since the early 1980s.

The postal-policy process has become a process of political mediation and negotiation. The government and Canada Post bargain over postal matters. This was reflected in the extended, protracted negotiations between the government and Canada Post in constructing the Framework Agreement. This should have been a straightforward matter. Instead, it dragged on for literally years, with consequential results. On the one hand, the agreement basically presented an incremental variation on the status quo. On the other hand, it did not set particularly high standards for Canada Post in terms of results or evaluation and accountability. With respect to the former, the financial targets that were set are modest and to be attained only by the end of a five-year period. This soft corporate target was an exchange for Canada Post's accepting the government's political objectives, with no compensation, in areas like rural and national policy. With respect to process and evaluation, the Framework Agreement contains no accountability mechanisms or process, no evaluation expectations (save at the end of five years), and little mention of service standards and expectations. Notwithstanding its political character, the Canadian postal regime is highly informal. There are no institutions or mechanisms for public input and accountability except for the presentation of material to the minister (who is responsible to Parliament) and for the presentation of the annual corporate report to Parliament and periodic hearings (which are benign and banal events). The French political regime is also a national or public one, but it offers a formal, representative dimension through institutions like the CSSPpt, which offers representation and input to parliamentarians. No such formal political representation exists in the Canadian postal regime.

The Canadian postal regime combines basic but limited elements of a market model, which in turn are framed within a national model. This regime does not offer CPC as much autonomy as it appears to do. Moreover, it does not allow Canada Post to develop nimble and effective responses to technological and competitive challenges. Indeed, its recent performance can be characterized as lethargic and as treading water. This reflects in a substantial way the awkward framework in which it performs. On the other hand, it is a model that allows for bargaining between the corporate and political dimensions of postal life. It is difficult to predict the results of such bargaining. But it is not likely to result in the kind of rational policy that would allow Canada's postal sector to adapt creatively and effectively to the changed technological and international environment in which it functions.

PART FOUR

The Hybrid Model

Not all countries have evolved "neatly" into one of the three models that we have examined to this point. Indeed, no country has had a "pure" experience; all postal regimes have some mercantile, market, and national elements within them. However, the countries that we have examined so far have one thing in common: one particular feature or element dominates the others, putting the country firmly within a particular model. Deregulation and the commitment to uninhibited postal growth place Germany and the Netherlands in the mercantile model. The elimination of the exclusive privilege places Sweden, New Zealand, and Finland in the market model. The predominantly political context of postal-policy making places France, Denmark, and Canada in the national model.

We have presented a fourth model called the hybrid or transitional model. It comprises countries whose postal regimes are in transition. They could evolve in a number of directions, to settle within one of the other models, but the ultimate destination remains unclear. Or they could remain as a kind of mixed or hybrid model for a time – although it is unclear whether such a position is sustainable over the long term. Countries in the hybrid model have pursued a number of corporatization, liberalization, and deregulation initiatives. But they have not yet resolved competing objectives and/or determined their ultimate policy paths. The United Kingdom and Australia were two of the first countries to initiate postal reforms and separate their postal operations from the machinery of government. They have long histories of postal reform and have recently been studied and scrutinized extensively. Both countries have recently introduced substantial legislative initiatives. Once passed and activated, these measures will certainly determine the direction of their postal evolution to a great extent. But neither set of measures by themselves will lead the United Kingdom or Australia firmly into any one of the three models.

As we will see presently, the legislative measures in the United Kingdom comprise what has euphemistically been termed a "politically balanced package." The state will retain considerable postal authority, to service public and union expectations. The Post will be pushed into deeper corporatized waters, but the government will retain considerable investment and strategic authority. The newly created Postal Services Commission – now called Postcomm – will study the future and extent of the exclusive privilege, which will be maintained. All in all, the reform initiative expresses mercantile, liberal, and national political concerns and sensibilities, with the result that the British postal regime will likely continue to be a hybrid one.

Similarly, the proposed postal reforms in Australia represented a political compromise. The National Competition Council made recommendations that would liberalize the entire postal market save for householder mail. The government was politically uneasy with this suggestion, particularly given the negative reaction from rural and "bush" areas and the postal union. It presented a policy compromise, proposing to roll back the exclusive privilege and to initiate an access regime to increase postal competition. This compromise and its aftermath unfolded over a three-year period – only to end with the government withdrawing the proposal in the face of sustained rural, union, and Labor Party opposition. Australia may develop in any number of directions. If the government pursues this and other initiatives, Australia may eventually enter the market model. If political concerns continue to inhibit change, then Australia will remain as a hybrid regime.

9 The United Kingdom

Any comparative study of national postal regimes should place the United Kingdom at its centre for a number of reasons. First, it is appropriate to give it a "pride of place" because the United Kingdom was the first country to modernize its Post.[1] That is, it was the first country to remove its Post from day-to-day public administration and make it a state corporation outside government. In this sense, the experience of the Post in Britain is a kind of benchmark against which all later postal developments can be sketched and evaluated. Second, precisely because of its longer "modern" history, the British case comprises a richer historical record than most countries that modernized only in the late 1980s or early 1990s. Third, the British case is superbly illustrative of the public-policy tensions involved in a nation deciding in what manner it wants its Post to respond to international pressures and technological change. Fourth, with the election of the Labour government of Tony Blair, the Post has lived through the neoconservative pressures of the Thatcher era and now emerges firmly into the "third way" politics of "New Labour" in the post-neoconservative era. The British postal scene demonstrates characteristics of all three models that we presented in the introductory chapter and that we have illustrated in the comparative chapters. A new Postal Services Bill was adopted by Parliament in the summer of 2000. The manner in which that legislation is implemented will determine to a great extent whether the British postal regime will emerge within the mercantile, market, or national model. At the moment, the British postal regime is a part of the hybrid model, reflecting competing claims and expectations that remain unresolved.

The British postal scene is informed by a number of particular features, pressures, and constraints. First, the postal situation has been studied, analysed, debated, and discussed incessantly for over two decades. The British were early out of the postal-modernization gate in 1969, when the Post Office Act established the Post as a publicly owned statutory corporation. Subsequently, there was an almost continuous process of evaluation and study of the Post following Margaret Thatcher's election in 1979. This perpetual process of postal reflection has had a number of consequences. It created a high degree of "intelligence" within the postal-policy community, and it perpetuated a great deal of uncertainty for postal management. Continuous public evaluation also contributed to a second important condition: the Post has remained a high-profile public issue long after it fell off the public agenda in many other European countries.[2] The political salience of the postal agenda in Britain reflects other factors, including the remarkable presence of the Post in the fabric of British life and the ongoing, unresolved industrial-relations issues in this sector. A steady stream of studies, reports, commissions, green papers, parliamentary hearings, ministerial announcements, and so on have kept the Post on the front pages of the papers and in the public consciousness up to the present. This nurturing of public awareness raises a third critical factor. Notwithstanding labour disputes, post-office closings, service changes, and political squabbling, the public remains remarkably supportive of and positive towards the Post. The Post delivers to twenty-five million addresses six days a week. Ninety per cent of the population get twice-daily delivery on working days and 80 per cent of the population live within half a mile of a post office. The Post handles seventy-five million pieces of mail a day and half the population visits a post office at least once a week. The Post's extensive network and presence, its twice-daily deliveries, and its increasing visibility as banks and others close down have made it highly valued by the public, which sees the Post as an important part of Britain's social fabric.[3] Indeed, there was little support demonstrated for privatization during the government's most recent review of the Post.[4] There was even substantial popular backlash when the Post introduced a new corporate name internationally – Consignia – to project an image of being more than simply a post office.[5]

This perpetual popularity explains to a great extent the fourth key component or reality of the British postal regime. The Margaret Thatcher and John Major governments pursued a privatization agenda through the 1980s whose results were not "undone" by the Blair government. Yet, by the late 1990s, it could be observed that "the only significant business to remain in 'public' ownership is the Post Office."[6] We will trace and explain the "failed" initiatives to privatize the Post below. For now, it is worth noting how this has created a public-policy dilemma and distraction for policy makers. Their attention and skills have been devoted to privatizing, organizing, and running the old public corporations and, more recently, to devising new regulatory regimes for them under the more muscular politics of the Blair regime.[7] The Post has been the "odd man out" in a double sense. On the one hand, it has not been privatized – an almost unique state-enterprise experience in the United Kingdom. On the other hand, policy making has been uncertain and tentative because of this. It was not clear how to pursue a more commercial, liberalized existence for the Post when the Post remained owned by the government. This tension was resolved, in a way, by adopting informal practices and devices in the Post's relationship with the government and by introducing some administrative reforms.[8] But this approach has had limits as the Post modernized and its commercial needs grew.[9] As will be seen below, the "constitutional" or legal question has informed postal discussions in Britain to a far greater extent than in other countries.

This constitutional issue can obscure what is a fifth key feature of the British postal scene. It is widely appreciated that the British Post has offered superior and reliable postal service and produced consistently high rates of return.[10] These surpluses were sucked up by the Treasury as a kind of hidden stamp tax and as such became a metaphor for two intersecting principles. On the one hand, the 1969 reforms had been directed to making the Post function in a commercial and corporate way, albeit as a state monopoly. On the other hand, the government instituted a set of financial-control mechanisms to ensure that the Post did not abuse its ongoing monopoly privileges. These financial controls – in particular the infamous EFL targets (External Financing Limit) – were designed to mimic market expectations and constraints on the Post and to make the Post subject to certain market and public disciplines. As time went on, though, these principles masked a less noble reality: the Post was being used as a cash cow for the insatiable financial demands of government. This was not an inconsiderable factor – the returns to government amounted to literally billions of pounds. The government's postal vision was predominantly financial, which biased it towards the perpetuation of a postal (financial) status quo.

One cannot underestimate the force of the financial consideration. It and the public's basic satisfaction with the Post cut deeply across the sixth feature of the British postal scene – the widespread understanding within the postal-policy community of the need to change the postal regime. This understanding has been fed by the same developments that inform postal policy making in other countries. As will be seen, the recent growth of mail volumes in Britain has been lower than expected and, notwithstanding the Post's successes, first-class mail growth has been modest. This reflects a number of factors, from technological and product substitution to international competition. There is growing awareness in Britain of the threat to the British Post from a number of quarters: increasing postal liberalization in Europe and in world markets, technological competition, globalization, and changing consumer demands.[11] There is a particular problem posed by the growth of large public postal competitors abroad – such as the German, the French, and particularly the Dutch. Indeed, eight overseas posts have offices and operations in London, along with the private companies like UPS and FedEx, all of whom compete with Royal Mail. This competition is highly visible and has made a real impact – even within the Post's protected or exclusive-privilege area. For example, Royal Mail took the Dutch Post to court recently for not respecting its domestic monopoly.[12] Participants within the postal-policy community recognize that, notwithstanding its early modernization, the Post has fallen behind developments in Europe and elsewhere. The Post itself would like to be able to compete with these large public posts. "Over the next few years," maintains Chairman of the Board Neville Bain, "we need to become one of a select group of truly global distribution companies."[13] But the British postal regime did not encourage this and placed the Post in policy shackles. There is substantial agreement that the Post needs increasing commercial freedom to be able to compete internationally and in various product markets, in particular with the Dutch TPG and the German DPWN. For good or bad, though, this has created tension with public expectations, which are focused on traditional letters and parcels and firmly planted in British soil.

Public "inward-lookingness" is a factor that cannot be attributed to the postal unions, which represent a seventh important variable in the British postal scene. British postal workers are represented in the Communication Workers Union. The CWU has a genuine postal intelligence, a sophisticated understanding of postal developments around the world, and an unrivalled research and documentation capacity. Its postal intelligence stands in a kind of schizophrenic contrast to industrial relations on the ground which, until recently, have been traditional, brutal, and unimaginative. This latter reality reflected a very old-fashioned work system which is only now being modernized. Yet the fact is that the CWU has been "onside" with postal reform, corporatization, and commercialization. This is reflected in its understanding of the key postal themes of the era:[14] that the postal monopoly is slowly slipping away, that liberalization of the European postal market is inevitable, that electronic products present a genuine competitive threat, that the Post exists in an increasingly globalized context, and that the Post has to become more sensitive to, and focused on, customer needs. The CWU has militated for postal reform – as long as the Post remains in public hands. This has reinforced the constitutional factor explored above. In sum, a highly sophisticated CWU has pressured for postal reform within a public-sector framework and has proposed new forms of public-enterprise existence and organization.[15]

The British postal scene, then, has been marked by a wide array of competing cross-currents. These have not synthesized into anything like a policy consensus or a coherent approach to postal reform. The absence of consensus and coherence about where the Post is going has extended policy discussion and review for over two decades. This extended period of reform stands in contrast to the experiences of many other countries that we have examined, and it reflects the reality that it is difficult to engineer reform when there is substantial disagreement among the major players in the postal-policy community. The views of postal management, postal unions, major customers, regulators, and the Treasury have not lined up together as has happened in Germany, the Netherlands, Scandinavia, or Australasia.

The reform process is still unfolding, in the form of the Postal Services Bill, which was adopted by Parliament in July 2000. This legislation itself reflects some of the crosscurrents, which in turn perpetuate mercantile, liberal, and political streams of postal existence. As will be seen, the legislation reveals some determination on the part of government to allow the Post to develop into an international behemoth like DPWN or TPG. But it retains real limits on how far the Post can develop and does not, at bottom, represent a substantially mercantile approach. There is an element of liberalization that informs the bill – but it reflects a "liberalization if necessary but not necessarily liberalization" tactic. This is not like the experience in Finland and Sweden, each of which took a "big bang" approach. The Postal Services Act does not propose to end the postal monopoly. Also, the government retains considerable postal influence and has put the universal-service obligation and other service expectations into legislative form. But this is not a national agenda like that of the French. At bottom, the British model continues to be a hybrid one, with elements of mercantile, market, and national strategies.

HISTORY

The British Post is the world's oldest, having been established in 1635. The idea of a public, universal postal service was given concrete expression and form in the nineteenth century, when Rowland Hill introduced the idea of a one-price universal service. The Post has had a statutory monopoly since the introduction of the penny post in 1840.

The postal-reform process in Britain began in the 1960s. This reform unfolded on two levels: operations and policy. With respect to the former, the Post underwent a ten-year modernization program, which saw the introduction of the national postal code and the introduction of mechanized sorting.[16] The government also decided at the time that the Post should introduce profit-and-loss accounting.[17] This latter decision generated a momentum for policy reform, which culminated in 1969 with the passing of the Post Office Act. This established the Post as a publicly owned corporation, separate from the government, with its own statutory powers. The minister appointed a chair and board for the Post. It was given a separate financial status and a defined set of obligations, but it would function independently of government on a day-to-day basis. The act – in conjunction with Section 66(1) of the British Telecommunications Act – set out the responsibilities of government towards postal services.

The British were the first in the world to separate their Post from the government to make it a postal state enterprise. Similarly, the British were the first to consider seriously privatizing their Post – in the late 1970s, when most Posts around the world were still departments of government. The 1979 election saw the formation of the Thatcher government, which unleashed the neoconservative revolution in Britain and across the industrialized world. Privatization of state enterprises was a central feature of the Thatcher revolution. The Post's monopoly was studied and reviewed on two occasions during this period (1979 and 1984) by the Monopolies and Mergers Commission (MMC). On both occasions, the MMC defended the Post's exclusive privilege (monopoly powers over letters). Its conclusion was based on the argument that the elimination of the postal monopoly would see the end of the universal service, the development of the practice of "cream skimming," and the deterioration in services in outlying and regional areas.

While the Post was not privatized during the Thatcher years, numerous reforms were introduced. After the first review, telecommunications was completely divorced from the postal operation and was itself privatized, and a separate Post board was created. The Girobank was restructured at this time and was managed separately until its sale in

1989. This move foreshadowed the 1986 reorganization of the Post into five businesses: Royal Mail (letters), Parcelforce, Post Office Counters, Girobank, and TV licensing. The Post's monopoly powers were rolled back, its exclusive privilege reduced to one pound sterling. The Post was directed by the government to make a financial return. Notwithstanding its declared ambition to improve postal services and to liberalize the postal market, the government retained considerable authority over the Post. The Post was still not allowed to borrow funds on the capital market; tight financial controls were imposed by the EFL; and the government approved any significant initiatives and new products or ventures as well as the five-year plan.[18]

Two substantial postal strikes fed into the reform process. A seven-week strike in the winter of 1971 saw the suspension of the postal monopoly, and over fifty companies were given approval to get into the mail business. This experience did not, though, legitimize the idea of privatizing the mail. The postal strike in 1988 triggered some further reorganization and decentralization of the Post's operations into strategic business units, each with responsibility for its operations. Parcelforce became a completely independent business at this time and Girobank was privatized. The headquarters of the Post was cut to less than 100 persons and middle management was downsized by 3,500 jobs.[19]

The two decades after the 1969 reform were turbulent times for the Post, then, marked by two major strikes and ongoing government review and organizational restructuring. However, two fundamental issues had not been addressed or altered in the process: the government dominance of the Post and the Post's future in the market economy. These universal themes were addressed substantially, relentlessly, but haltingly from 1992 until the introduction of the Postal Services Bill in January 2000. This process unfolded in two stages: one Conservative and one Labour. With respect to the former, Michael Heseltine announced a postal-review process in the summer of 1993, with the ultimate intention of privatizing the Post. A Green Paper was introduced and various select committee reports were made – but nothing substantial changed. After the election of the Labour government, the Department of Trade and Industry (DTI) minister, Ian McCartney, introduced another review in the spring of 1997, which led to a White Paper, more committee reports, and, ultimately, the introduction of the Postal Services Bill in January 2000.

Both stages were informed by the two fundamental issues confronting the Post at the time. On the one hand, there was widespread agreement that the commercial and competitive challenges confronting the Post were intense and of a character that required fundamental reform. On the other hand, the government's authority over the Post constrained the Post's capacity to meet these new challenges. Symbolic of the government's authority over, and constraints on, the Post was the infamous EFL requirement. It was a mechanism by which the government controlled public-sector debt and financial requirements. The government set EFL limits on state enterprises, which limited their borrowing. In the case of the Post, the government actually established a negative EFL – that is, a positive target or rate of return that it expected (in effect, a dividend). This EFL was absorbed by the Treasury and not reinvested into the Post.

The Conservative stage of this process generated no significant policy changes. But it had the unintended implications of weakening the case for privatization and strengthening the government's hold over the Post. The process began with the government preparing itself for privatization of all parts of the Post save for the Counters operation, which was seen to be too politically sensitive to touch. The government appointed Kleinwort Benson and KPMG to advise it on the postal review and Price Waterhouse was hired to prepare for the privatization of Parcelforce. Parliamentary committee hearings were held, and a coalition of forces began lobbying against privatization with, ironically, a particular focus on the privatization of Counters.[20] The Trade and Industry Select Committee (TISC) issued its first report in March 1994, which was much in line with Heseltine's ambitions. Responding to the commercial and competitive pressures facing the Post, TISC insisted that the Post could not be maintained in its present form and that the government should stop using the Post as a revenue generator. It proposed that the government sell 51 per cent of its equity in Royal Mail and Parcelforce – in effect, it recommended the privatization of letters and parcels. The committee envisioned the construction of a three-way partnership among the public, employees, and the government.[21]

The first TISC report was followed by the government's green paper on the Post, "The Future of Postal Services."[22] The green paper presented three options: assigning the Post greater commercial freedom, a 100 per cent share sale, or a joint partnership. The government favoured the last (as well as the maintenance of a degree of postal monopoly), signalling the public's desire to maintain a link between the government and the mail service.[23] The green paper process intersected with an intense anti-privatization campaign ("Protecting Postal Services"), which saw 15,400 responses to the consultative document (typically, such a process would generate 100–200 replies).[24] Combined with a Conservative backbencher revolt (the rural MPs), the government abandoned its plans to privatize the Post.[25]

While Heseltine promised that there would be no privatization in the lifetime of the Conservative government, he did introduce some incremental measures to increase postal autonomy. These included relaxation of the government's scrutiny of the Post's investment projects, opening the door to joint ventures outside the United Kingdom up to ten million pounds, and granting access to private capital through the Private Finance Initiative. The Counters operation was diversified, from travel insurance to currency exchange. But it continued to be constrained by the government's unwillingness to allow it to take commercial risks and by its fear that the Post would be a predator in the market.[26] Heseltine promised to cap the government's levy on the Post to half the Post's forecast after-tax level of profits. In the event, the government actually *increased* its EFL expectation from ten billion pounds over five years to ten billion pounds over three years. The incremental policy and organizational changes amounted to little. While committed to commercializing the Post in a privatized setting, the government did not support real commercialization of the Post once it was clear that it was to stay in the public sector.[27] And, when the government did not generate revenue through a share sale, it kept on raising funds through the EFL tactic for non-Post public expenditures.

The subsequent Labour government review of the Post went through a similar juggling act. It struggled with the idea of how to commercialize a public-sector operation while maintaining the integrity of traditional public-sector financial requirements. In his second public appearance after being elected Labour party leader, Tony Blair appeared at a press conference with the secretary general of the CWU to declare that he was against postal privatization.[28] The Labour Party's subsequent election manifesto insisted that there would be no postal share sale. On the other hand, the election manifesto promised to give more commercial freedom to self-financing state enterprises like the Post. In May 1997 Labour DTI Minister McCartney announced a comprehensive review of options for the Post. The most "extreme" option that was posed was a minority share sale. The other options were the status quo (with increased flexibility), a public-sector trust (a non-starter), and the creation of an independent publicly owned corporation (the option eventually chosen).[29]

Labour's review took place in two stages, split organizationally and by politics. Carried out by a special postal-review team in the DTI, the first stage was widely consultative and was dominated politically by what might be termed "old" Labour. The secretary of state with responsibility for the Post was part of the politics of "old" Labour, and so the privatization option was driven completely off the agenda. TISC issued a report during this period, in which it recommended the creation of an independent, publicly owned company. This was an idea now widely described in an acronym – IPOC. The committee also recommended the continuation of the postal monopoly and increased flexibility for the Post to raise capital privately, to participate in overseas ventures, and to pay the government a predictable and reasonable dividend.[30] This first stage ended in April 1998 with a government assurance that the Post would continue to provide a universal service and would remain in the public sector, although the Post would be given more commercial freedoms. The government extended the Post's authority to enter into joint ventures. Previously, it had been allowed to enter into arrangements abroad and the government would now allow domestic ventures, subject to guidelines (such as the need for the activity to be self-financed and in core services).[31]

The second stage was internally driven by an interdepartmental group, which reviewed options and policy from the government perspective, in particular for a new minister. Peter Mandelson was more "new" Labour and looked for less traditional options and solutions. However, the kinds of options favoured by Blairites – such as a 40/40/20 diffusion of ownership among the government (40 per cent), the private sector (40 per cent), and employees (20 per cent) – had been pushed off the agenda in the first stage.[32] The formal review process ended with Mandelson's December 1998 presentation of a reform package that was designed to increase the Post's commercial freedom to deal with the new international competitive environment. This package was characterized as "the most radical set of reforms since the modern Post Office was created in 1969." The package proposed the creation of a new form of public enterprise, operating at arm's length from the government within a strategic plan and overseen by an independent regulator with responsibility to ensure the maintenance of competition and universal service.[33] The details of the package were to be fleshed out in a white paper[34], which finally appeared seven months later, in July 1998.

The white paper foreshadowed the legislation that the government would introduce in January 2000, which will be examined in the next section. The main features of the White Paper were:

- the transformation of the Post Office into a public limited company (plc) under the Companies Act (1985), with the government as the sole shareholder;
- a separation of ownership and regulation, with the government limited to a strategic role and the Post's board accountable to the company;

- greater commercial autonomy and flexibility for the Post, including a profit target set in a strategic plan, greater retained earnings for investment (only 40 per cent of profits as dividends), greater freedom to invest without government approval or with faster government response, and greater freedom to borrow commercially;
- putting universal-service obligations, universal price, service expectations, and network access into law;
- reduction of the exclusive privilege to 150 grams and 50 pence by April 2000; and
- creation of an independent regulator to guarantee competition and the universal service.

The introduction of the white paper came two decades after the Thatcher government first began the process of re-evaluating the form and purpose of the Post in Britain. Twenty years later, the most fundamental questions appear to have been answered. But some detail remained to be specified in the legislative process. The first and most fundamental issue was that the Post would not be privatized. The move to plc status did not rule out the possibility of selling shares. But any process surrounding it would be difficult politically and strong elements of the Labour Party, and the cwu, stood ready to block moves in this direction. For the indefinite future, then, the Post will remain in public hands. Second, it appears that the government will lessen its day-to-day grip and its financial stranglehold over the Post, which will enjoy more commercial freedom. But the government will continue to exercise strategic influence over the Post – which will not have a free hand in investment decisions. A £75-million independent investment limit is very small when one talks of joint ventures or takeovers worth millions of pounds.[35] Third, the universal system would remain in place on all levels – access, price, and service – underpinned by the perpetuation of some level of exclusive privilege or postal monopoly.

THE POSTAL SERVICES BILL, 2000[36]

After more than two decades of discussion, analysis, consultation, and review, the British government adopted a new statutory and regulatory regime in the year 2000. The Postal Services Bill was given first reading in Parliament on 27 January and passed on 28 July 2000. The bill was a longer and more elaborate piece of legislation than many of the acts that we have encountered (particularly in the Scandinavian countries). This demonstrated the ongoing salience of the constitutional or legal dimension of the Post. There were few surprises in the bill, inasmuch as the major postal themes and issues had already been debated thoroughly. The Labour government's position on most of them had been worked out through the review processes, internal party debates, and the previous summer's white paper. In some ways, what was *not* in the bill was as important as what was. For example, the government rejected the option of privatization or a joint-share option – both of which had fallen off the agenda in the earlier stage of the review process. The bill left open the possibility of selling shares, but in a very circumscribed process. Similarly, after months of being hammered politically,[37] the Labour government withdrew its proposal to reduce the exclusive-privilege protection to 50 pence or 150 grams from one pound or 350 grams. The possibility of further market liberalization was left open. The government created a regulator – the Postal Services Commission – which was asked to study the issue and to make a recommendation to the government. On two key themes – corporatization and liberalization – the bill did not extend the postal regime into much deeper waters than where it was already positioned. The legislation did present real reforms and changes to allow the Post more commercial freedom to deal with the new postal realities of the twenty-first century. But these changes do not comprise a liberalization strategy as in Scandinavia, or a mercantile strategy as in Germany and the Netherlands, or a national strategy as in France. Rather, the British postal regime has the ongoing characteristic of a hybrid model, with touches of market, national, and mercantile approaches. This reflects the political nature of the compromises represented in the legislation.

The Postal Services Bill created a new kind of state postal corporation in a restructured regulatory environment. The postal regime fulfils the expectations set by the EC postal directive, particularly with regard to the separation of ownership and regulation. The first half of the bill – Clauses 1–50 – deals with the new regulatory regime. The second half focuses on ownership issues and expectations. This represents what the government characterizes as a politically "balanced package" between the business needs of increased commercial autonomy and the political requirements of regulatory discipline.

With respect to ownership, the bill transforms the Post from a statutory corporation to a plc – a public-limited company. This reforms the Post and registers it under the Companies Act, subject to normal company law. The purpose of this transformation is to give the Post greater commercial freedom to compete in the new technological and international postal environment. The government still owns the new Post. But its relationship with the Post is rolled back to a strategic relationship, expressed in a rolling five-year strategic plan presented by the Post to the government annually for its approval. This approach was designed to minimize day-to-day contact, direction, and control. Details of its financial relationship will be outlined below. The main change in this area is the proposal to end the traditional EFL relationship and replace it with a dividend expectation that typifies normal shareholder-company relationships. The state's universal-service obligations are, for the first time, given legislative expression.

Second, the bill determines that the postal sector will operate within a new licensing and regulatory system. A new Postal Services Commission – now called Postcomm – has been given wide-ranging regulatory authority to implement and monitor the government's expectations about the postal sector – in the areas of postal pricing, the universal-service obligation (including access to the network), quality of service, and market competition. The Postcomm will issue licences to operators participating in the postal-reserve area, including the Post. A strengthened and restructured POUNC – renamed the Consumer Council for Postal Services, and now called Postwatch – will work with the PSC and focus on consumer protection.

Commercial Freedom

The ultimate purpose of the act is to allow the Post to react commercially to international and technological competition while maintaining the universal system at a high level of quality and profitability. There had been widespread agreement that the state's control over the Post's finances and financial decisions had made this impossible. On the other hand, there had been a constitutional inhibition to allow the Post too much freedom, given its public-sector and monopoly status. The regulatory regime – detailed below – will deal with the latter issue. A new financial framework will deal with the former. The extension of more commercial autonomy to the Post had been pursued through administrative measures over the previous years. The Post had been given greater commercial and borrowing freedom, had seen its retained earnings increased to allow higher levels of investment, and had been allowed to enter into joint ventures abroad under certain conditions. These incremental changes were put together in a more strategic and elaborate framework in the bill.

First, as a plc, the Post will no longer be bound by the traditional EFL obligations imposed on state enterprises. In its place, the Post is directed to provide the shareholder (the state) with an annual dividend, calculated as a percentage (40 per cent) of profits.[38] This will allow the Post more predictable financial elbow room for investments, acquisitions, and joint ventures domestically and abroad, for which it was also given increased authority. The legislation gives the Post freedom in these areas as well as the authority to borrow money and to price commercially, to introduce new products and services, to move into new market areas, and to initiate commercial bulk discounting with larger mail users.

However, this commercial freedom remains circumscribed in a number of ways. For example, the Post's borrowing and investment authority is limited to £75 million; any amount above that will require government approval. The new regime proposes a government "fast tracking" system for consideration of larger Post proposals (no longer than twenty-eight days). But no legislation can guarantee that such a system will work. The Post is also limited to borrowing from the National Loans Fund.

Perhaps the most controversial or contentious issue in this context concerns a possible full or partial privatization in the future. This issue was addressed in Clause 56. The legislation did not anticipate privatization or make a future privatization easy. Indeed, the act makes clear that any sale of shares would require new legislation save in the case of a share swap or sale that was part of a commercial venture or partnership. This sort of initiative would require an extremely open and accountable process. The clause elaborated a series of steps that would have to be executed before the Post could pursue a partial share sale as an instrument of a joint venture or a partnership:

- the Post would have to make the case that this was in its "commercial interests";
- the minister would have to be satisfied with this case;
- the treasury would have to approve the measure; and
- both Houses of Parliament would have to approve the share issue, with respect to its size, nature, purpose, and ownership results.

There was no limit put on the size of the potential share issue.

The government trumpeted that the Post will have up to £600 million more over the next three years for investment and modernization. This was calculated as the difference between the old EFL requirement (which consumed 80–90 per cent of profits) and the 40 per cent dividend expectation, plus the £75 million a year in borrowing that the Post was authorized to undertake without government approval. However, what the government gave with one hand it (or the market) took back with the other. First, the Post will no longer receive the interest that it normally gained on its accumulated EFL surpluses (a loss of £100 million annually). Second, the government had decided not to proceed with the Horizon project, which would see social-security payments transferred electronically through the

Counters network. This loss of government business to the banks would diminish the revenues received by the Counters operation (another £100 million annually). Finally, the likely decrease in the exclusive privilege will inevitably have effects on the Post's revenues.[39]

Regulatory Environment

The Postal Services Commission had been set up as an advisory body in 1999. The recent legislation established it as a traditional independent regulatory authority, paralleling those agencies in the United Kingdom that regulate the privatized utilities industries. Postcomm has a wide array of powers and responsibilities:

- to regulate prices, likely according to a price-cap formula of its choosing, within a uniform tariff regime;
- to set service levels to be met and to ensure quality of service;
- to promote postal competition;
- to maintain the universal service;
- to protect the postal monopoly;
- to review the case for the postal monopoly, ensuring proportionality between the exclusive privilege and the costs of providing the universal-service obligation;
- to issue licences in the reserved area – not just to the Post and possibly in geographic and niche areas – with an eye to furthering the interests of users and to maintaining a competitive environment; and
- to provide information and advice to the government about the retail network.

The PSC – or Postcomm – comprises a part-time chair, a CEO, and a five-person board of independent commissioners. Two directors and a staff of a dozen or so provides technical and intelligence support. It has considerable powers to gather information and to impose decisions and to enforce them (and to penalize licence holders for noncompliance). None of the Postcomm or senior staff have postal experience and most have a civil-service background (representing areas such as labour, charity, industry, and so on).[40] Early indications are that the commission plans to "shake things up" and has a pro-competition agenda and orientation.[41]

There were a number of particularly compelling developments in this area. First, the government withdrew its plan to roll back the protected or monopoly area to 50 pence or 150 grams from one pound or 350 grams. Instead, it asked the Postcomm to review this issue and to make a recommendation to it within a year. This relieved the government of political pressure for the short term, but it left uncertain the government's plans for liberalization of the postal market.[42]

Second, a licensing system will, in a way, replace the postal monopoly. The Post – like any other potential operator – will have to apply for a licence to operate in the reserved area. Moreover, Postcomm can issue licences to operators other than the Post, if it feels that this is in the interests of postal users and competition. Postcomm issued its first licence to Consignia on 26 March 2001. The fifteen-year licence was designed to ensure that Consignia continued to provide postal services across the entire United Kingdom at a uniform rate. Its major conditions require Consignia to freeze its core prices for two years; improve the quality of its service (to 92.5 per cent next-day delivery of first-class mail); and allow potential competitors access to its network on fair terms. At the same time, Postcomm is entertaining three licence applications from private firms – two from TNT (UK) for niche-market licences and one from G3 Worldwide Mail (UK) for an outbound cross-border licence.[43]

Third, for the first time, the universal-service requirements are to be put into legislative form (Clause 4), and Postcomm is obliged to enforce the Post's attainment of them. This includes daily delivery, to all addresses, at a uniform and affordable price, of letters up to two kilograms and parcels up to twenty kilograms. The act also laid out minimum criteria for public access to the network and a government commitment to maintain the postal network (not part of the universal-service obligation) (Clause 32). The specification and criteria of this objective will be made public to Parliament, monitored by Postcomm, and set out in the licence issued to the Post.[44]

Ongoing Government Authority

The Postal Services Act aims to create an environment in which the Post can act commercially, respond to technological and international forces, and take on the challenges provided by the large public competitors like the German and the Dutch Posts. The Post can now form joint ventures, make acquisitions, and move into international waters more easily to forge alliances and to construct a more integrated international network. The legislation goes some way to this purpose, in creating increased autonomy and financial independence for the Post. At the same time, the likely further liberalization of the market, Postcomm's mandate to promote competition, and the creation of a licensing system will open the postal market to considerable competitive pressures. Yet the government will continue to enjoy a considerable amount of postal authority. This reflects the reality that the Post remains owned by the state and the state itself feels the need to keep its hands on the Post, to protect itself politically in the context of public and union expectations.

The government retains considerable authority inasmuch as it names the key players in the new postal regime. It appoints the members of Postcomm, Postwatch, and the Consignia board. It sets guidelines for Postcomm with respect to access to the network, it retains reserve powers, and it can give directions to Postcomm. The government approves the Post's five-year strategic plan and has a say in all Post loans and investments over £75 million.

Reaction to the legislation was generally positive. The CWU was pleased that the government extended autonomy to the Post and that the Post remains a public enterprise. However, it remains cautious about the prospects for future privatization and/or rolling back of the reserved area. The Post was positive about the construction of a predictable regulatory regime and about the commercial autonomy that it had been granted. However, it expressed some concern about how the regulatory regime will work in practice, particularly how regulatory and shareholder goals will be made consistent or harmonized. The Post had long accepted that formal regulation would be the policy quid pro quo for gaining increased commercial autonomy.[45] However, the legislation cannot anticipate the combined impact of Postcomm and the government's ongoing authority and presence on postal operations. "It is somewhat unusual for a company to be directed by two such powerful separate bodies," stated CEO John Roberts, "and it is therefore vitally important for us to have clarity and consistency in the way the relationships will work."[46] The Post and the CWU have expressed concern that Postcomm has been a more assertive regulator than had been anticipated and may in fact limit rather than expand the Post's business flexibility.

STATUTORY AND REGULATORY ENVIRONMENT

The statutory and regulatory environment in Britain is in transition, given the recent introduction of new postal legislation. The recent practice in this area may or may not be a harbinger of how the new postal regime will work in practice. This section, then, will review the major players and ingredients in the system as it has unfolded, with an eye on the future that the Postal Services Act appears to promise.

The Universal Service

The universal-service obligation has a deep tradition in Britain, likely stronger than in many other countries examined in this study. This goes to the heart of the British postal experience, which has been integrated intimately into the social fabric of the nation. The issue is connected to other factors such as the presence of the queen's image on stamps, the title of the *Royal* Mail, and so on. Tampering with the Post thus borders on the sacrilegious. This is an important reason why Prime Minister Thatcher backed away from privatization of the Post.

There has been a clear sense of the Post's wider role in society. The British Telecommunications Act required the Post to serve the social, industrial, and commercial needs of the nation. The universal-service obligation has always been clear and well articulated. It was set by the Post, after consultation with the government. The universal-service obligation has included the obligation to deliver mail and parcels up to defined weights, the obligation to offer quality universal service regularly at a uniform price, and the guarantee of access to a universal network. These expectations are deeply ingrained in British society, where a system of twice-daily delivery – including early first-class delivery – is assumed to be a normal condition of life, and they have been transferred to the proposed new postal regime. In this regime, they are carved in legislative stone and will be set out as obligations in the postal licences that are issued by the regulator. They are widely advertised in the Post's publications – such as the "Customer Charter and Code of Practice" published by each of Counters, Parcelforce, and Royal Mail divisions.[47] In sum, the Post's universal-service obligations have been widely understood and are substantial.

Reserved Area

The Post has had an exclusive privilege or reserved area since the mid-nineteenth century, within which it enjoys a postal monopoly. The rationale for this privilege has been the traditional one, that the reserved area ensures a revenue stream that affords the Post the financial capacity to maintain the universal service. The present level was set under the Postal Privilege (Suspension) Order of 1981. The Post has the exclusive right to deliver mail up to 350 grams and/or a charge of one pound (four times the then first-class rate of 26 pence), which is within the area defined by the EC postal directive. The Post has not enjoyed a monopoly in the parcels market, which is a competitive one, and there have been some other specialized or "niche" exemptions to the exclusive privilege. Over time, the impact of the one-pound limit has lessened as a result of inflation. The exclusive privilege has not been a particularly large one relative to, say, the German or the Dutch system. Moreover, the Post itself was placed in the position of protecting its own monopoly, which became a difficult challenge in the context of the internationalization of the postal system.

The responsibility for protecting the exclusive privilege has passed over to Postcomm in the new regime. The regulator will also recommend to the government whether there is a reasonable proportionality between the extent of the Post's reserve area and its universal-service obligation. This has not been an area historically where there has been much quantified study, particularly given the informality of the regulatory system. The government has been keen to reduce the reserved area, even in advance of developments in the rest of Europe, in order to prepare the Post for what may be a completely open, liberal European postal market in the future. The Post itself has been cautious about liberalizing ahead of the pack, given the financial implications of its ongoing social obligations. The CWU has not favoured this approach.

Financial Regime

The Post has been expected to make a profit since the earlier postal reform in 1969. A target was set by the minister and this money was paid to the Treasury, within the context of the government's public-sector lending and financial system. The EFL had traditionally been set as a negative target (that is, a negative of borrowing = positive saving). This target – which typically amounted to 80–90 per cent of the Post's profits – was used to buy Treasury gilt-edged bonds, which financed other operations and activities of government. The system was justified by the government on the grounds that it imposed financial discipline and a set of surrogate market pressures and incentives on the Post. The government set targets on the return on capital employed and reduction in real-unit costs. This practice was increasingly criticized over time for various reasons.[48] First, the targets were set three years in advance and had no relationship to the Post's needs. Second, the EFL drained the Post of much-needed capital investment, particularly in the context of the Post's not being allowed to borrow on capital markets (which would count as public sector borrowing). Indeed, this financial orthodoxy acted as a huge constitutional constraint on reform, for there was no principle or formula available that would avoid or neutralize the accounting reality that its capital borrowings would count as public-sector borrowing. Third, the Post's focus on these targets had unintended consequences on price and quality. Prices were often raised or the quality of service cut to reach financial targets. Nonetheless, the system continued to be used as a kind of hidden stamp tax to finance the Treasury. This system has been replaced by a standard corporate dividend policy, set at 40 per cent of profits. It is curious, though, that a minimum or a minimum formula independent of profit has not framed the target. This may encourage the government to maintain a large reserved area, which suggests that the ongoing contradiction between the Post's needs (to develop competitive capacity) and the government's needs (for revenue) may not have been resolved in the proposed postal regime.

The Ministerial Setting

The 1969 postal reforms set the Post outside of the governmental or departmental framework, but the state retained ownership of the Post. The Department of Trade and Industry is the government's lead agency on postal matters. The postal part of the DTI comprises a small group of about eight permanent staff, which was supplemented by five people for the recent review of the Post. Given the size and presence of the Post, this is a fairly small operation which focuses mainly on the Post and not on the postal market.[49] This is because the DTI has limited capacity and resources to develop postal intelligence. The interface between the Post and the government is mainly and directly through the DTI, but there is a third policy player. The Treasury has been a dominant, presence in postal affairs over the years. This is because the EFL targets have been central to the strategic and regulatory framework established by the government. Each year the Post has presented annually a five-year strategic plan, which is generated through informal consultations among these three players. In theory, the minister approved the plan once it was developed. Central to the plan were the three basic targets: the EFL, the rate of return on capital, and the reduction in real-unit costs. Once these were set, there was little interest in the actual content of the plan itself. Over the last decade or so, there were only two ministerial responses to the plan,[50] precisely because the government's primary concern was the attainment of the remarkably high EFL targets. This macro concern inhibited the development of much interest in the micro details of the operation. Scrutiny of the postal plan itself was also obscured by the fact that the Post was not a problem and hit its targets. In any case, there was little policy capacity on the government side to be attentive to these details.[51] In sum, the planning process has been a fairly informal affair, dominated by the broad macro targets associated with the EFL. No real public strategic or industrial plan was ever developed.

The ministerial context was a three-way relationship, in which the Post had only an indirect relationship with the Treasury. The DTI has been obliged by law to consult with the Treasury about anything that had financial implications. The tensions among the three players were real and inevitable.[52] For example, the Post would include a capital-expenditure plan (as part of its five-year plan) but this would cut directly across the Treasury's EFL expectation. The regulator – the DTI

– in turn would focus on competition, low prices, and a moderate rate of return, all of which conflicted with the interests of Treasury. The Post might consider new postal services and corporate initiatives, but the ministry would be loath to experiment lest this affect the bottom line.[53] The DTI had to approve everything of any substance or importance, such as investment plans, capital expenditures, new ventures, pricing.[54] This three-way tension might have been useful to ensure accountability, in what was an unusual situation: there were no precedents as to how to regulate such a hybrid corporate entity. In this way, Treasury orthodoxy was the only sure parliamentary or constitutional weapon, and it emerged as the primary regulatory approach in the absence of any other viable one. But the application of this approach has not been propitious for postal development, since the Treasury was not particularly informed about the technological and international threats confronting the Post.[55]

The Post

Once removed from the operations of government in 1969, the Post was placed on a corporate footing and organized like a private-sector corporation. It has been led by a Board of Directors and senior executives, who are appointed by the government. The board is relatively small for an operation of the Post's size and its structure is typical of the corporate sector. It comprises nine members: a chair, three executive members, four non-executive members, and a secretary. The chair's position is considered a two-day-a-week job while the other non-executive positions are part-time. The current chair – Dr Neville Bain – has a strong and substantial corporate background, having spent twenty-seven years at Cadbury Schweppes and being a group chief, chair, and non-executive director of firms such as Viyella, Hogg Robinson, Scottish and Newcastle, and Safeway. He is a no-nonsense type of businessman, with little interest in politics. Of the four non-executive directors, one is from the union side (Dr John Lloyd from the Amalgamated Engineering and Electrical Union), although this union representation is neither required nor a convention. Nor is the person from a postal union. The other non-executive members have a corporate background (Sainsbury, Whitbread and Beefeater, Stagecoach Holdings). The most recent non-executive appointment was Allan Leighton, chairman of British Home Stores. The non-executive group is competent and non-aligned politically.

The board appears to be a management-oriented one, which takes seriously its responsibility to run the business well. But the government limited its strategic authority. This may change under the new postal legislation that puts the Post under the Companies Act, thus making it possible that the board will be more able to represent the best interests of the company. The three executives on the board – the CEO, the finance director, and the strategy and personnel director – have long associations with the Post (since 1967, 1987, and 1973 respectively). This reflects the fact that a position at the Post has generally been a career appointment. Postal staff have their own status as employees of the Post, which has its own pay and personnel policy. The Post has been organized on fairly traditional lines over its history, with little recruiting of people from the private sector. More recently, the "Shaping for Success" initiative has seen the traditional business divisions replaced by an organization of the company around nine key markets.[56] There has been a morale challenge at the Post, particularly after it was not privatized in the 1980s. There has also been frustration that it was not able (or allowed) to compete directly with the Germans and the Dutch. The government has controlled the behaviour of the Post to a great extent, so that the Post has willingly accepted the reality of regulation by a third party as the price to pay for increased commercial autonomy.[57]

Other Players

The Post Office Users National Council – now called Postwatch – was the independent statutory body established under the 1969 Post Office Act to represent postal users' interests. It comprises up to sixteen members, who apply to join Postwatch and perform on a voluntary basis. It has no regulatory powers but relies on persuasion and publicity in its dealings with the Post. It has the statutory right to be consulted about price and service changes and makes representation to the government and to the Post on behalf of users. It replaced the ministry as the political agency that deals with complaints raised by individuals and businesses about the Post, in an effort to insulate the Post from political intrusions. Postwatch has been staffed by a small number of employees on loan from the DTI. It has been relentless in defending the universal service and universal tariff in its annual reports, criticizing the government's EFL policy (for its impact on the quality of postal service) and scrutinizing the Post's service and quality record – sometimes to embarrassing effect.[58]

The Communication Workers Union represents the postal workers. It is a substantial union with an enormous research and intelligence capacity – indeed, it has the greatest such capacity of all the unions examined in this study. It has a sophisticated understanding of the emerging international postal market which, perhaps, belies its image

Table 1
Postal performance (millions of pounds)

	93–4	94–5	95–6	96–7	97–8	98–9	99–00
$ Turnover	5,568	5,878	6,210	6,370	6,759	7,010	7,522
Pre-tax Profit	306	472	422	577	651	608	(171)
PROFIT	195	341	270	365	447	496	(264)

Source: The Post Office, Annual Report, assorted years.

as a tough representative of workers' interests in industrial relations. The latter have been tense and have included periodic strikes. These strikes – and the tension between postal understanding and action – reflect the fact that the organization of the postal system and its pay system have been very traditional. It has been difficult to undo the past, as will be seen in the next section.

PERFORMANCE

The Post has been financially successful in recent years while maintaining the universal service at a reasonably satisfactory level. Through 1998–99, the Post had had twenty-three consecutive years of subsidy-free profit. It is basically a debt-free operation. The Post has contributed £2.5 billion to the government since 1981. Its 1999–2000 results were negative, showing a post-tax loss of £264 million (to be met from the Post's reserves, not by the taxpayer). This reflected the fact that the Post was obliged to absorb an exceptional charge of £571 million associated with the Horizon project[59] (see below). Profit before tax and exceptional items was £474 million (down 13 per cent from the previous year).[60] As Table 1 indicates, the Post's revenues have expanded steadily in recent years, by 35 per cent between 1994 and 2000. After-tax profits in the same period totalled over £2 billion. As seen in Table 2, this growth and profitability was driven mainly by Royal Mail. The Counters operation remains profitable, but only marginally so. As in most public Posts, the parcels operation struggles to get into balance.

The Post has consistently made the strategic targets set for it by the government. For example, it reached its EFL targets of £310 million in 1998–99 and outstripped its 1997–98 target of £313 million by £25 million. In 1998–99, it hit its unit-cost reduction target of 6.2 per cent and its return on capital target of 22.6 per cent. By division, Royal Mail has been outperforming its EFL target, Parcelforce has been underperforming, and Counters has been meeting its EFL target. These targets are not terribly "rational," inasmuch as they were set according to government's needs rather than the Post's.

Table 2
Performance by division (millions of pounds)

	96–7	97–8	97–8	98–9
ROYAL MAIL				
Turnover	5,019	5,411	5,570	
Profit	518	547	560	485
PARCELFORCE				
Turnover	457	465	474	
Profit	−21	−14	−14	−25
COUNTERS				
Turnover	1,161	1,130	1,148	
Profits	34	33	33	32

Source: Post Office, *Annual Report,* assorted years.

Letters, Parcels, and Mechanization

The mail division is organized in Royal Mail, a large operation that employs nearly 170,000 people. It utilizes 30,000 vehicles, making it one of Britain's largest fleets. It processes seventy-seven million units a day, using the new integrated mail processors that have cut a letter's sorting time from ninety to two minutes. The Post aims to sort 90 per cent of the mail in an automated fashion. The Post has provided excellent mail service, although its product line and electronic presence is underdeveloped (see below). Its share in the wider communications market is 15 per cent and falling. This is because fax and electronic-document exchange have been growing recently at a 20–30 per cent annual rate while the mail has been growing about 3 per cent a year. There is increasing competition in the delivery of mail even in the protected areas; there has been a Dutch presence in this market since 1991. The growth and performance of the mail sector has been affected by industrial relations, most recently by problems in 1996 and 1997, which had an impact on business and on performance. As Table 2 above indicates, Royal Mail has been consistently profitable. It provides 75 per cent of the revenues, and 90 per cent of the profits of the Post.

As Table 3 indicates, postal volumes are increasingly driven by second-class mail. The latter grew by 36 per cent between 1995 and 2000, while first-class mail grew by a little over 7 per cent. The result was that first-class mail's share of total volumes fell from 34 per cent to 29 per cent. Overall, 44 per cent of mail volumes comprise financial mail. While the overall impact of technological competition has been

Table 3
Postal volumes

	94–5	95–6	96–7	97–8	98–9	99–00
1st class	5,149	5,329	5,372	5,489	5,475	5,516
2nd class	9,871	10,967	10,970	12,064	12,615	13,410
Total	15,020	16,296	16,342	17,553	18,090	18,926
International	717	793	805	836	852	861

Source: Post Office, *Annual Report*, assorted years

less than expected, there is a sense of disappointment in recent first-class mail volumes, which have also been squeezed by international competition.[61]

By European standards, the price of the mail is towards the low end of the scale. In an effort to keep the Post competitive, prices had been frozen at twenty-six pence in July 1996 until late 1999, at which time the government approved a one-pence increase to twenty-seven pence (to be implemented in April 2000). Overall, the cost of a first-class stamp has fallen by 16 per cent in real terms over the last fifteen years. The price of a second-class stamp was cut recently from twenty to nineteen pence and it was not increased in April 2000. Consignia applied to Postcomm for a one-pence increase in the price of first- and second-class stamps days after it was issued a licence which indicated that its prices must be frozen for two years. This will provide a test-case for how the postal regulatory system will function.

By its own high standards, the quality of mail service has been somewhat shaky recently. As Table 4 indicates, Royal Mail had typically delivered from 90 to 92 per cent of its mail the next working day, but this has fallen below 90 per cent recently. This is well above the EC expectation or standard of 85 per cent. The industrial action in 1996 upset this performance, however, and there has been a struggle to get back up to or above the 92.5 per cent standard that Royal Mail and the government have set as the working standard. POUNC had been extremely critical of Royal Mail's failure to reach service standards. Its 1998–99 annual report was submitted with a press release entitled "First Class Failures," which maintained that this was the fifth consecutive year that first-class delivery targets had not been met. POUNC questioned why these targets had been rolled over year-to-year since 1994–95, even as the standards were not attained. Indeed, it did not endorse the targets recently for this reason. On the other hand, POUNC attributed the problem partially to the government's previous financial targets, such as the EFL and the real-unit costs (RUC). The EFL payments drained profits and resources from the Post that could

Table 4
Service results

	94–5	95–6	96–7	97–8	98–9	99–00
All 1st mail	92	92.3	85.9	91.5	91.1	91.0
All 2nd mail	98.1	97.9	96.2	98.3	98.6	98.8

Source: Post Office, Annual Report, assorted years

have been used to increase capacity. The reduction in unit costs has an unintended irrational relationship to quality: cutting unit cuts could be attained at the cost of reducing quality (for example, volume increases without employment increases).[62] Overall, productivity gains appear not to have negated or balanced all of the volume increases of recent years. There was 190,000 staff in 1993–94, a level that grew to 200,000 in 1998–99.[63]

The parcels operation is organized within Parcelforce, which has commercialized its operation to a great and fairly successful extent in a very competitive market. It offers a range of services, including two-day, next-day, and premium delivery, both domestically and internationally. There is no quality data available for time-guaranteed services (for competitive reasons). The domestic service sets a target of 88 per cent delivery within three working days. This target was met in 1998–99 after performance in the 85-88 per cent range in recent years.[64] Parcelforce Worldwide is in the process of developing an advanced parcel-tracking system. It has invested £100 million creating Europe's largest and arguably most advanced parcel-distribution centres. This has been the single largest investment in its history. The distribution centre in Coventry is capable of handling more than 100 million items a year. The national hub will have the capacity to process 50,000 items an hour. This sector is expanding into the growing area of supply-chain management. A logistics-distribution centre has been established at Swindon, making 6,000 shipments to 20,000 destinations daily. Evening deliveries have been attempted on a trial basis and will soon be widely available.

The Post has built the biggest train station in Britain this century, the Princess Royal station in Willesden, north London. This is a "passengerless" station, which transports 100 million letters a week, organized around a fleet of sixteen new mail trains. Three new rail terminals were opened in 1998 – at Warrington, Doncaster, and Wishaw. All told, this represented a £150-million investment in rail facilities.

As noted above, the Post's presence in the electronic-communications area has not been pronounced. It has made some initiatives, such as the arrangement with Microsoft that allows users to send large, multiple-page documents via the Internet, for printing, enveloping, and eventual delivery. A third electronic mail centre opened in Leicester in 1997–98, increasing the Post's capacity to over 200 million items a year. Royal Mail is now the preferred supplier for Amazon.co.uk. The Post provides hybrid services, like Relay One, and has introduced Via-Code, the United Kingdom's first e-commerce service. Secure Messaging provides verification of the origins of e-mail and their attachments. The Post has entered the telephone marketing and merchandising business, with arrangements with firms like the clothing company JD Williams, Amerada Gas, and so on. It has opened call centres in Plymouth, Sunderland, and Bristol, which handle 500,000 calls a week. Its Subscription Services Limited (SSL) provides customer-management services in over forty different contracts, with insurance companies, banks, and the BBC. With respect to the latter, it recently bid successfully for the BBC licensing business in a seven-year contract with Bull computers and WPP (the Environ consortium).

Counters

The Post's retail network has been organized as a separate division called Counters (Post Office Counters Limited, or POCL). It is a wholly owned subsidiary of the Post and has 15,000 staff. Its network comprises the largest retail chain in Britain (indeed, in Europe), larger than the major banks and the building societies combined. It handles over two billion transactions a year, seeing more than twenty-eight million customers a week. The value of its transactions was £154 billion in 1998–99. Over half of this comprised girobank services, and over one-third was pensions and allowances. More than £500 million of bills were paid at Counters and £400 million worth of currency transactions were carried out. In sum, over 75 per cent of its revenues is derived from non-mail services. It has been consistently profitable since 1986.

As Table 5 indicates, the network comprises both traditional post offices and commercial franchises and outlets. There has been a rationalization of the traditional Post-owned retail network, which now comprises only 600 outlets (about 3 per cent of total of outlets). The retail network is now primarily a franchise operation.[65] The "Crown Post Office Conversion Programme" was suspended during the recent postal review but was lifted in December 1997. There has been some concern expressed by groups like POUNC[66] about the decline in the extent of the network, since there were almost 2,000 fewer outlets at the end of the 1990s than at the beginning (a decline of 9 per cent).

Table 5
Number of counters outlets

	89–90	91–2	93–4	94–5	95–6	96–7	97–8	98–9	99–00
POS	1,339	1,019	800	699	653	606	601	600	598
Agencies	19,276	19,067	18,922	18,908	18,761	18,645	18,407	18,175	17,795
TOTAL	20,615	20,160	19,782	19,607	19,414	19,251	19,008	18,775	18,393

Source: Post Office, Annual Report, assorted years

Counters has expanded its range of businesses and services into a variety of postal and non-postal activities. Some government agencies use it as an outlet (for example, Benefits Agency, Driving and Vehicle License Agency). Its outlets provide 170 core services across a broad range of activities. These include banking and insurance services, benefits collection, passport applications, vehicle, television and game and fishing licences, foreign currency exchange and travel insurance, lottery tickets, and bill-paying services (utilities, phone, council tax, mail order, and so on). As the private banks rationalized their networks, Counters has developed partnerships with a number of them to provide services to their customers. Its principal banking partner is Alliance and Leicester, through which it offers a full range of personal and business banking services, including personal loans. It recently signed a deal with Lloyds TSB, which will allows Lloyds customers to deposit and withdraw money at most post offices. It also provides banking services for customers of the Co-operative Bank. POCL is an agent of Royal and Sun Alliance for the sale of life insurance. It sells premium bonds and savings certificates and provides personal pension-management services. In February 2000 Barclays Bank announced that it would provide personal customer service at 270 post offices in a pilot program (focusing originally on Cornwall).[67] Link, the cash-machine group, will partner with the Post to connect its 18,000 branches to almost all the United Kingdom's banks and building societies. This will allow customers of all basic bank accounts to use Post Office branches to carry out basic transactions over the postal counter.

The Post's retail operations represent one of the great postal retail success stories of the Posts examined in our study. Like Posts elsewhere, however, there is some sense of anxiety about the future that hangs over the operation. This is because of the difficulties associated with the Horizons project. In May 1996 the Post granted an automation contract to Pathway, a consortium comprising ICL, Girobank, De La Rue and the Irish Post. This billion-pound project will see 40,000 personal computers placed at 19,500 counters to create an automated counter-transaction capacity at each of the Counters' outlets. However, it has been plagued with technical problems and delays. There has also been uncertainty regarding how the government would distribute social-security payments in the future. The Benefits Agency announced recently that it is going to shift its payments process to the banking system beginning in 2003. This represents a potentially enormous loss of revenue for Counters – up to one-third of its revenues. The economic rationale of the Horizons scheme was thereby undermined and the assets of Horizon have been written down substantially. There is widespread concern that this development will undermine the Post's capacity to retain a retail presence in rural areas. Nonetheless, the government has committed itself to the Horizon project and more than 40,000 interlinked computer terminals have been installed throughout the country, which will enable people to pay bills and access services.[68] The Post itself understands the need to expand retail activities to underwrite the cost of maintaining the retail network.

Labour and Employment

Industrial relations within the old British postal regime were neither progressive nor effective. This was symbolized by the serious industrial action taken by the postal union in 1996, a stoppage that focused on many traditional issues that should have been sorted out years earlier. There were "modern" issues associated with corporatization – such as post-office closures and the balance between full- and part-time employment. But at the heart of the matter were traditional concerns like security, pay, the length of the work week, and delivery issues. The Post was perhaps the last labour-intensive industry to be modernized. Historically, postal workers were never paid as well as those in comparable industries, based on the traditional notion that they enjoyed job security. The result was that, for workers, the pay system focused increasingly on getting overtime. This old-fashioned pay and organization structure was markedly out of line with new management approaches and the need to modernize the Post to keep it internationally competitive.[69]

After the 1996 dispute, management and labour constructed an agenda for the future called "The Way Forward."[70] This package of issues had been discussed since the early 1990s. The Post struck a deal with CWU in late 1999 which was ratified by CWU members in a record 100,000-person vote in early 2000. This deal comprised both a pay settlement and a "New Way of Working" agreement. The former included a 2 per cent pay increase, an increase in pensionable earnings, better overtime rates and pay protection, and a reduction in the work week. A new Working Time Directive was agreed to, which would phase in a forty-hour and five-day work week over the next few years. The ambition is to eliminate outdated work cultures and practices and to relieve the pressure on overtime.[71]

There has been an increase in wildcat strike activity since the introduction of the recent postal reforms. There were 22,000 working days lost mainly to unofficial industrial action in 1991–2000. In 2000–01 this figure is likely to rise to over 60,000 working days as Consignia sheds jobs in the face of increased competition.

Mergers, Acquisitions, and International Developments

One of the most serious implications of the old postal regime was the manner in which the Post was not able to act as an autonomous company in pursuing business investment opportunities, joint ventures, and acquisitions, as any normal company would do. On the one hand, the EFL system drained profits out of the Post, which was then not available to pursue business opportunities. On the other hand, the Post was not allowed to borrow capital privately or to make serious investments or partnerships without government approval. The latter was only infrequently forthcoming, since the government's interest was more traditionally and fiscally focused. Symbolic of the constraints on the Post was the case of GD Express Worldwide, which represented the public Posts' collective attempt to compete with the private express market. But the government's prohibition on joint ventures meant that the British Post was not allowed to participate in this initiative.[72] The postal-review process highlighted the ongoing problems with the system and the competitive disadvantage that these created for the Post – at a time when its major competitors were acquiring foreign partners and complementary businesses in Europe and across the world. This was particularly true with respect to the mercantile initiatives of the Posts in Germany and the Netherlands.

The Post was given some investment and commercial freedoms prior to the introduction of the Postal Services Bill in January 2000. It took advantage of the increasing amount of autonomy offered to it by the government to pursue a number of business ventures and acquisitions abroad. Indeed, the Post sees itself in a global-development battle and in a race for purchases of key companies and business partners. There were twenty purchases in Europe in 1998–99 alone. "If anyone had said even ten years ago that major international companies like German Parcel, TNT, DHL and Securicor would be either taken over or bought up in great chunks by post offices, they would not have been believed," declared CEO John Roberts; "but that is precisely what is happening and the gloves are coming off as competitive pressures get tougher." Roberts predicted the creation of a "superleague" of three or four post offices dominating the European market and a few more across the world.[73] The following is a summary of these actions, as the British Post tries to catch up to and position itself against the Dutch and the Germans in particular.[74]

German Parcel

The Post's first major initiative was the £256-million takeover in January 1999 of German Parcel, the third-largest private carrier in Germany (£250 million annual sales, 100 million parcels a year, 4,500 employees, 4,000 vehicles). German Parcel also owns a 23 per cent stake in General Parcel, which services thirty European companies. The takeover included, twenty-four franchise operations that provide parcel services in Germany, as well as to and from the rest of the world. German Parcel has reputedly the most modern parcels-distribution centre in the world, handling two million parcels each week for next-day delivery. In July 2000 German Parcel purchased Domberger Paket Dienst and Deutscher Paket Dienst, two parcel companies operating in southern Germany. In May 1999 the Post bought one of Germany's leading express carriers – Der Kurrier. It comprises a network of 80 depot and 2,500 employees, with £40 million in revenue. This acquisition was carried out by German Parcel. The Post recently purchased the courier company Dascher and is now challenging the French for the number-two position in Germany.

Williames Group

The Post bought the Williames group of companies in October 1999, an Irish parcel and logistics-service company, for £10 million. The group offers a number of services including parcels and logistics, airfreight, and distribution services. The acquisition was executed by German Parcel.

Citipost Group

The Post strengthened its presence in the North American market by purchasing 100 per cent of Citipost Group in November 1999 for £25 million. Citipost is a New York-based document-delivery company, with operations in North America, Europe, and the Pacific rim. Citipost specializes in providing express next-day document-delivery services in the central business districts of major U.S. cities. The Post first established a presence in the North American market with an office in New York in 1994. By the end of the century, it had a dozen sales offices around the United States and distributed products for McGraw Hill and Time Warner. Royal Mail is the fourth-largest carrier of international mail in North America.[75]

Crie Group
In February 2000 the Post purchased the Paris-based Crie group of postal companies, for £6 million. The group comprises Crie s.a., a French domestic and international express-mail operation; Redmail s.a., a delivery service for addressed mail and postal items in the Paris area; Systeme c.s.a., a facilities-management and mailroom-services firm; and Crie Multi Services s.a., an international mail service provider. Later in May, it purchased Extand, one of France's leading operators for express delivery of parcels and small packets.

Pakke-Trans a/s
In March 2000 the Post purchased Pakke-Trans a/s, one of Denmark's leading parcel-distributor companies, with 13 per cent of the domestic market. It is part of the General Parcel network that accesses all of Europe.

City Mail
In an earlier initiative (May 1998), Royal Mail acquired a 10 per cent stake in the Swedish mail delivery company City Mail. Since then, it has increased its investment stake, so that it owns two-thirds of City Mail's delivery system.

Selektvraacht
In another earlier initiative (May 1998), the Post entered a joint venture with Selektvraacht, a Dutch letters- and parcels-delivery company that is a wholly owned subsidiary of the Royal Nedlloyd Group. It operates a next-day, nationwide delivery service and does twice-weekly delivery in the pre-sorted direct-mail market. Together, they operated a mail-sorting and processing hub in Utrecht. This joint venture ceased in the fall of 1999, when Deutsche Post purchased Selektvraacht. In March 2000 the Post purchased Nederlandse Pakket Dienst (NPD), the third-largest parcel company in the Netherlands.

General Parcel Austria, General Parcel Slovenia
These acquisitions were made in March 2000.

Szybka Paczka Spolka
The Post purchased 25 per cent of this Polish delivery company from Thereab, a Dutch logistics firm, allowing it to penetrate the East European market.

TPG and Singapore Post
In March 2000 the Post Office signed an agreement with TPG and Singapore Post to establish a global joint venture in cross-border mail. This will create the world's largest business mailing partnership, with headquarters in Belgium. TPG will have a 51 per cent stake and the other partners 24.5 per cent each. All cross-border mailings for European and North American clients will be managed through this new company.[76]

Bull
The Post and Bull Information Systems entered a partnership in July 1998. The objective of this partnership is to integrate Bull's systems and technology expertise with the Post's customer-management and market strengths.

British Postal Consultancy Service
Like many major Posts, the British Post has been selling and marketing its expertise abroad, in consulting arrangements or partnerships with other public Posts. In 1998–99, 200 consultants worked on sixty projects in more than forty countries. It is part of the consortium that is transforming the Argentinean Post. It is involved in the Air Mail Centre project in Hong Kong and is managing the EU project to assist the Greek postal service to attain European standards. It also designed the new high-tech sorting operation in Singapore and devised a home-delivery service in Kuwait.

Following this extensive array of international initiatives – amounting to £500 million and twenty international companies – the Post decided to project a new image globally by changing its corporate name to Consignia. This was designed to signal that it was more than a Post, and to create a distinctive and identifiable identity to support its various brands and activities that will stand out from the competition. While the domestic brand names will not be affected (for example, Royal Mail, Post Office, Parcelforce), the new name will be presented to corporate customers in the financial-services, telecommunications, home-shopping, utilities, and advertising and marketing sectors.[77]

OBSERVATIONS ON AND HIGHLIGHTS OF THE BRITISH CASE

What can one learn from the British case? What interest does its experience hold for policy makers? The British postal regime is in transition, so it is difficult to draw substantive or far-reaching conclusions at a time of some policy uncertainty. Nonetheless, we can offer some observations at this time.

First, the British Post was the first to be detached from day-to-day departmental existence within the government. But the postal model or regime established in 1969 was not one that was viable over the long term or one that should be emulated. The government simply retained too much authority over postal matters. On the financial level, the Treasury seriously circumscribed the Post's existence. On the commercial level, the DTI controlled its strategic and capital decisions. The Post performed admirably well under the circumstances. Yet, as international and technological competition intensified, the postal regime was unable to respond quickly, given the vested interests of the Treasury and the DTI. This led to the long-extended review process and an agonizingly slow process of incremental reform.

Second, the Thatcher government's decision not to privatize the Post in the early 1980s has had tremendous policy and practical consequences. In the first instance, it separated the Post from the experiences and processes surrounding the other British state enterprises – most of whom were privatized and/or entered different and predictable regulatory regimes. In contrast, the Post has led an isolated existence over the last two decades. It is one of the few remaining state-owned enterprises of substance and its regulatory and statutory environment is unique and seriously outdated. This has resulted in the scrutiny and evaluation of the Post not being deflected to, or refracted by, a wider state-enterprise agenda or regulatory environment. In other countries, postal reform was carried along by this wider agenda and implemented in a regulatory environment that was applied across many sectors and enterprises. This was not the case in Britain.

Third, and as a consequence, it has been far more difficult to build up a postal consensus in Britain than in a number of other countries. There has been agreement that international and technological competition threaten the Post's future. But this shared analysis has not translated into a policy consensus on where the Post should be headed and/or how it should be organized. This absence of a consensus was exacerbated by the fact that the Post exists within the Westminster parliamentary system, which emphasizes division and conflict rather than consensus building. The political system also forced a more legal consideration of the Post's status and its relationship to the government than has been the case in other countries, particularly with regard to questions of public-sector financing. As a result, postal issues and discussion unfolded in a conflictual, divisive, and tentative way, which made building a policy consensus difficult. Hence, it took over twenty years to see through the postal-reform process, during which time many opportunities were lost and competitors grew stronger.

Fourth, as a result, postal reform in Britain has taken the form of extended, incremental change. As suggested, the recent Postal Services Act itself is not a radical departure from the past. This can be illustrated by focusing on the two key elements of any serious reform agenda: corporatization and liberalization. With respect to the latter, the act leaves to future consultation the thorny issue of the exclusive privilege. It directs Postcomm to encourage competition, but time will tell whether Postcomm will do so once Consignia and the CWU begin to lodge the inevitable complaints with the government. The Act does not alter the Post's exclusive privilege. With regard to corporatization, the Post's legal structure and status is altered and the board has more strategic authority and a more focused responsibility to the company. Nonetheless, the array of government authority over the Post remains substantial, particularly with regard to major investments and activities. Moreover, the Post now faces the prospect of a dual-authority model, with the introduction of Postcomm.

Fifth, for good or for bad, the incremental pattern of change has not led postal discussions to confront the character and substance of the universal-service obligation. The British public's sense of the universal-service obligation has likely been stronger than that in most other postal regimes, and it has not been challenged or weakened by the process of incremental postal reform. As a result, the Post's position within British society remains as political and national as it is economic and commercial – notwithstanding the widespread understanding within the postal-policy community of the international and technological challenges facing the Post. Indeed, the universal-service obligation has been given legislative form, an approach that most countries have avoided. The latter opted for a more contractual type of approach between the state and the Post or licence holders (with such contracts being periodically altered and/or renewed). Placing the universal-service obligation within legislation makes it difficult to adapt the obligation to changing circumstances.

Sixth, the British postal regime will now comprise two core elements: a Post with plc status functioning within a third-party regulatory system. This so-called "balanced" approach has one feature that appears to be the wave of the postal future in Europe: an independent third-party postal regulator. The development of a third-party regulatory authority reflects the EC's postal directive to separate ownership and regulation. In the British case, it also symbolizes a move from the informal regulatory norms of the old postal regime to the increasingly formal processes of the new regime. Postcomm will regulate the Post in a legal way – with respect to the array of universal-service obligations (political expectations) – as well as in an economic manner, with respect to competitive issues. The former will limit the degree of corporatization while the latter may or may not have an impact on liberalization. The move from the previous informal norms and planning procedures to a more formal, legalistic approach will likely increase the degree of conflict within the postal regime. There are already indications that this will politicize postal issues in a manner that has been avoided in the new regulatory regimes in the market and mercantile models.

Seventh, the real extent of the Post's increased autonomy to deal with international and technological competition is unclear and uncertain. In the first instance, the Post confronts a double-barreled regulatory threat – from Postcomm and from the government. Indeed, it is unclear how the government and the regulator will interact and what their combined impact on the Post's autonomy will be. In particular, it is not obvious how financial and regulatory objectives will be made consistent or harmonized with each other. At the moment, this appears to be a formidable regulatory constraint, since Postcomm is somewhat more assertive than had been anticipated. On the one hand, the government's relationship with the Post may turn out to be a benign one, if the Post performs well, delivers its dividends, maintains its universal-service obligation, and keeps out of trouble with Postcomm. On the other hand, the government has retained some key financial levers over the Post which could bias or limit the Post's initiatives and developments. The Post has been remarkably active in acquisitions and business ventures over the last year, so it may be that the government will not use its postal authority to block the Post's ambitions. The big question is what will happen if international and technological competition undermines the Post's financial performance. How will the state respond if the Post cannot meet both its regulatory and its financial objectives simultaneously?

In sum, the British postal regime continues to have elements of all three models – mercantile, market, and national. This reflects the incremental steps that have been taken over the last twenty years. First, the Post continues to be presented by the government with a set of national or political objectives, which are now enshrined in legislation. This legislative expression validates and socializes the public's expectations of the Post. Second, the Post has been granted some increased corporate and commercial autonomy to deal with the changed postal environment. But this has been limited by the state's retention of considerable postal authority and by the initiation of formal third-party regulation. Third, the Post will likely face a more liberalized environment domestically, but for the time being the national and political constraints on liberalization remain considerable. This "mixed" approach may be attractive to countries that do not feel that they have the economic capacity to pursue a mercantile approach, that do not want to risk the "big bang," or all-at-once, approach, or that believe that the public's postal expectations and ambitions are modest. Indeed, given the Post's attractive record of performance – both financially and in terms of service – this incremental and mixed approach may have real public-policy attractions. However, given the intensity of pressures that the postal regime faces, it is unclear whether the hybrid model is sustainable over the long term. It may be that the Post and the government will have to decide whether to embrace a "purer" model, such as the mercantile or market one.

10 Australia

Australia has not fully liberalized its postal market, but there is substantial anticipation that this will happen in the next few years. Furthermore, while the government has retreated from its latest initiative in deregulating the postal market, Australia already offers one of the most liberalized postal environments in the world outside the market model. Thus, it is fair to group Australia with those countries that have taken a "market" approach to the technological and international challenges posed by recent changes in the postal market. There are some striking similarities between the New Zealand and Australia cases, which is not surprising given their geographic proximity and their shared history and traditions. Indeed, New Zealand has itself provided an example for Australian policy makers to respond to and even to emulate. However, the two cases unfolded on fairly different paths and with some substantially different results – including the different degrees and pace of liberalization. We categorize Australia within the hybrid or transitional model, because it retains a monopoly or restricted postal element. This reflects the continuing influence of political factors in formulating postal policy, as illustrated in the successful effort˙of the postal union, the rural areas and the Labor opposition to construct a political coalition to block further deregulation. The government may try again in the future and Australia may embrace the market model. But if political concerns continue to limit policy change, Australia may revert to the national model.

The postal-reform process in Australia has unfolded for over a quarter of a century, but its most vital experience has been since corporatization in 1988. The Post was removed from the direct operation of government in 1975 and has not received a government subsidy since. It was reorganized as the Australian Postal Commission from 1975 until 1988. It was then reformed as Australia Post and "corporatized" (along with other crown corporations) as a Government Business Enterprise (GBE). Since that time, the Post has been expected to perform commercially, to pay taxes, and to provide the shareholder (the government) with dividends.

The Post has been one of the most studied institutions in Australia society. There were postal inquiries in 1915, 1919, 1954, 1959, 1974, and 1982 and four major reviews after corporatization in the late 1980s. As a result, there is an unrivalled degree of postal knowledge within Australia. The country has seen an extensive quantification of postal issues, such as the costs of the universal service, which has made policy discussions well informed, thorough, precise, and almost "academic." A high degree of quality analysis and a series of related policy initiatives have made Australia, according to Jim Campbell, a "leader in reform and modernization."[1] This is partially but substantially the result of the development of an intelligent, balanced, and light-handed regulatory regime. Australia Post has become one of Australia's biggest companies in terms of revenue, profit, and employment. It is one of the most financially successful and well-run public postal operations in the world. It maintains a high-quality universal service while providing high rates of financial return to its shareholder.

Australia's postal-reform process has been informed by a number of crucial themes. First, as in Scandinavia and New Zealand, the postal-reform project was carried along by a wider public-policy agenda. For over a decade, the economic-policy discourse in Australia was framed by the micro-economic reform agenda.[2] This agenda aimed to rid the Australian economy of barriers to efficiency and competitiveness in order to allow markets to work effectively. It produced initiatives such as the reduction of tariffs, the reform of industrial relations, the abolition of exchange controls, deregulation, industrial free trade, and micro-economic reform of the national infrastructure and industry. Within this micro-economic reform agenda, state enterprises were transformed into GBEs. They were expected to perform commercially and to contribute to the health of the national economy. This was the strategy and rationale informing postal reform: "Postal services are used by every business in Australia. There are only a few essential services which affect the cost of so many industries. Therefore, the cost of postal services is not only important from the perspective of the postal industry, but also its impact on all industries in Australia. Lower prices from this essential service will flow through into lower costs across the whole economy."[3] A subsequent national competition-policy initiative has seen all governments agree to review and reform legislation that contains restrictions on competition. A recent deregulation impulse has in turn developed from these exercises.

This wider economic agenda drove postal reform, which was rarely first or in front of the pack.[4] As a result, postal reform was shielded from intense political scrutiny. The general policy approach – as in other cases like telecommunications – took the political heat, not the Post. Postal reform thus unfolded in a less intense and politically charged manner than it did in Canada. Moreover, the overall reform approach was highly visible and well articulated, with the consequence that there could be no uncertainty about the government's intention. This clarity of purpose and design generated real policy momentum. But it also framed a reform process in which, for the most part, the Post and the government saw eye-to-eye. Indeed, such identity of purpose and focus allowed the government to let the GBEs be regulated in a light-handed manner. This contributed substantially to the success of postal commercialization and AP's financial success, which in turn validated and encouraged the light-handed regulatory approach.

The micro-economic reform agenda developed out of the economic crisis that enveloped Australia and other industrial economies in the early part of the 1980s, when the post-war Keynesian system began to unravel. This economic crisis led to a decline in confidence in the Australian economic model, which had comprised a protected domestic market, an intensely focused external market, and the welfare state.[5] The Australian model produced a high-wage, high-exchange-rate economy that was battered as the international economy changed. The domestic fallout in Australia was extensive. The government confronted an enormous fiscal problem, and the combination of an over-priced dollar and an inflationary wage spiral undermined Australia's exports, which slowed economic grow and heightened unemployment. A sense of urgency was intensified by the dollar crisis in 1983 (and 1986), and the dollar was floated in 1983. The fear of economic decline to third-world status was heightened by the then Federal Treasurer Paul Keating's infamous "banana republic" warning. There was general anxiety that Australia could be overtaken economically by the rising economies of Malaysia, Singapore, and so on.[6] As Australian government and business struggled to make adjustments, industrial relations became strained and over four million working days were lost to industrial action in 1981. These economic conditions and events led to the introduction and acceptance of a different economic policy mix, one that emphasized market themes such as efficiency and competitiveness as well as the reform of state enterprises.

The economic-reform package was introduced and implemented by a new Labor government, which enjoyed its longest run in office in this period. This had two effects. First, the "reform" government was in office long enough to stay the policy course. Second, the fact that it was a Labor government limited the amount and intensity of opposition to the reform agenda, including the postal-reform process, for the unions – the strongest potential source of opposition – had no political alternative to Labor. This in turn was crucial, for two reasons. First, unlike the "pure" Westminster model in New Zealand, the Australian political process is far more consensually based, particularly given the fact that Australia is a political federation and there is an upper house which can and does often block government initiatives. Second, organized labour had attained a central role in the policy-making process and had long helped to determine the policy agenda in Australia. The existence of a long-term Labor government strengthened the hand of moderate elements in the labour movement, who worked with the government to get the best possible deal for workers within the reform agenda. The government in turn was obliged to deal creatively with the unions, given the consensual nature of the policy process. The positive working relationship between the government and the unions was partially the result of the flow of union leadership into politics (for example, Prime Minister Bob Hawke had been head of the Australian Council of Trade Unions, or ACTU). It was also based upon the close personal relations of political leaders like Treasurer (and later Prime Minister) Paul Keating and Bill Kelty, the head of ACTU. They struck a "Joint Statement of Understanding" that facilitated industrial relations and policy making during this period. They were also able to construct a series of "Accords" that saw the unions and the government agree on the broad outlines of the economic-policy framework. The implementation of the economic-reform agenda was not destabilizing politically, since the unions participated in the process. They made shrewd policy trade-offs made between wage increases, on the one hand, and tax decreases and certain social guarantees, on the other. These initiatives and actions comprised a kind of cultural transformation in industrial relations, which set the conditions for real policy reforms through the 1990s. This in turn transformed labour relations and economic expectations at the postal level.

The transformation of the Post into a GBE, the economic-reform package, and the transformation of industrial relations contributed to postal commercialization and corporatization. But it did not result in a call for postal privatization. There has been little recent support for postal privatization in Australia. It has not been an issue on the postal agenda in any serious fashion since the Industry Commission last mooted it in 1990.[7] Various postal studies reported the deep support by Australians for the maintenance of a public post that provided a universal postal service. Major postal users supported it in the 1998 review, since they did not want to see a fragmentation of the postal system. Small business supports it as well.[8] Polls indicate that 90 per cent of Australians support the social-equity principles that inform the existing organization of the postal market.[9] Most recently, the National Competition Council's recommendations took into account Australians' support of the universal postal system.[10] This deep support for the universal system, and indifference to privatization, is related to the political salience of the rural issue in Australia. Notwithstanding the fact that most Australians live in large cities, 98–99 per cent of Australia's terrain is considered rural and remote, and this area comprises over a quarter of the population. Australia is an enormous country, and service to the rural and remote areas is a highly sensitive issue. As a result, Australian politicians have supported the maintenance of the universal service and the maintenance of a public postal system.

Thus, two strong forces have intersected in the Australian postal-reform process. On the one hand, postal reform was encouraged by the larger economic agenda, and it was carried out with a minimum amount of disruption within the context of a stable government-labour framework. On the other hand, postal reform was contained within the boundaries set by the expectation that the universal service would be maintained to ensure service to rural and remote areas. The process of postal deregulation in Australia has at each stage been informed by the question of how far postal liberalization could proceed without undermining the Post's capacity to maintain the universal system.

HISTORY

The origins of the Australian postal system lie in the nineteenth century. The first postman was appointed in Sydney in 1809, overland service between Melbourne and Sydney began in 1837, and the first official post office was constructed in Melbourne in 1841. There have been uniform postal rates in Australia since 1849. The federated governments created the Postmaster General's Department in 1901, and the Post operated as a department of government for the next seventy-five years. From that point on, the postal-reform process unfolded, in four stages.

The Australian Postal Commission, 1975–88

As noted earlier, the Post was the object of government inquiry and scrutiny for much of these seventy-five years. This culminated in the

Vernon inquiry and report in the mid-1970s, by which time the postal situation had deteriorated in a quite serious fashion. The economic performance of the Post in the 1960s and 1970s was poor and its management was weak. It incurred losses in every year, ranging from 5 per cent to 20 per cent of revenues. In the mid-1970s, the losses ranged between $50 and $75 million. These losses undermined the Post's capacity to finance its much-needed capital expenditure and modernization. The government refused to raise postal prices to this end, for fear of the electoral consequence of public disapproval.[11] The harsh reality of the Post's weak financial situation was mitigated somewhat by the cross-subsidy that it received from the telecom side of the operation.[12] But the situation was fundamentally a "catastrophe."[13] Postal service was very bad and the public complained incessantly.[14] The industrial-relations situation was chaotic and strikes took place constantly. The Redfern plant at Sydney was notorious, and there was a siege-like military environment in the sorting plants. Feather-bedding was widespread.[15]

After the Vernon report was submitted, the government initiated the first step in a quarter-century process of postal reform. It transformed the Postmaster General's Department into separate postal and telecommunications arms. The resulting Australian Postal Commission (APC) was a stand-alone institution, separate from the day-to-day activities of government. The government directed the APC to cover its costs and to balance its budget. This would have to happen without any subsidy or transfer from the telecom side, which was now a separate operation. The government also directed the APC to finance at least half of its investment and capital expenditure programs from its own revenues. The APC was helped to this end by the government's long overdue increase in postal rates (the letter rate increased from ten cents to eighteen cents). The Post was given a number of traditional social obligations, but these were articulated very broadly.[16]

The Australian Postal Corporation Act, 1988

The creation and development of the APC required a painful reorganization of the postal operation. The APC period had some successes but a number of fundamental problems were not resolved. The APC itself remained a bureaucratic organization, with a hierarchical, top-down management style. Management was able to place the APC on a "profitable" footing. But profits were low and flat, and it is fair to characterize the APC as a break-even operation. Government meddling and interference frustrated management.[17] The Post's share of the communications market was falling, so its economic prospects were not bright. The APC had not been able to sort out the industrial-relations situation, which was at a constant breaking point. This situation was exacerbated by the mechanization process, which resulted in kind of perpetual guerilla warfare within the Post.[18]

The postal situation was addressed as part of the government's wider economic-reform agenda in the mid- and late 1980s. The Labor government aimed to improve the micro-economic foundations of the Australian economy so as to increase its efficiency and capacity to compete internationally. Within the public sector, the government reformed its state enterprises, with the aim of having them contribute to improving the economy's efficiency and competitiveness. It transformed state companies into GBEs. This corporatization of state firms required that they operate viably in a sound business and commercial manner. They were directed to generate a sufficient return on assets, pay taxes like any corporation, and provide a reasonable rate of return (dividends) to the shareholder (the government).

This was the broad context in which Australia Post was formed. The Australian Postal Corporation Act of 1988 established the Post as a GBE. The act separated ownership and regulation from the actual operation of AP. The act also clarified and distinguished AP's corporate objectives from its social ones. Each of these will be examined in turn.

Australia Post would continue to be owned by the government, which would appoint a Board of Directors to operate the company. The board would be recruited from the private sector, and it would appoint a CEO and senior-management team with private commercial experience. Staff would be employees of AP and not part of the public service. The Department of Communication and the Arts (DOCA) – later the Department of Communications, Information Technology and the Arts (DCITA) – would provide government oversight and have regulatory responsibility for AP. The Department of Finance (DOFA) would oversee the shareholder's interest in maintaining and expanding the value of its assets and investments. The basic purpose of the act was to limit government and bureaucratic interference in postal operations. The Board of Directors was directed to initiate a corporate-planning process, which would culminate in the presentation of a three- to five-year plan to DOCA for approval. This plan would set financial and performance targets that AP was expected to attain. Once this broad framework was established, AP was free to perform and act like any private company. The government would no longer be involved in contract negotiations, land purchases, major construction, pensions, introduction of products, and so on. AP would be allowed to borrow on the open market and would fully fund its pension plan. It would determine and set its prices, which would be regulated by the

Australian Competition and Consumer Commission (ACCC) under the Prices Surveillance Act.[19]

The act separated AP's corporate objectives from its social responsibilities. These latter responsibilities – termed Community Service Obligations (CSOs) – were set out in the statute. They comprised the traditional requirements of providing a universal and equitable service at a uniform price. The CSOs would be specified and quantified in the corporate plan. The costs of the CSOs would also be specified, by an agreed upon formula (the defined cost-avoidance method). The CSOs would be "financed" by AP's ongoing exclusivity in the letters market (which included ad mail and letterboxes).

Parallel to the corporatization process was the reform of Australia's industrial-relations system. This reform evolved via a series of "accords" between the government and the unions, which set out a new manner in which collective bargaining was to take place. A major breakthrough occurred in 1989, when the Labor government and ACTU signed a Joint Statement of Understanding which provided a detailed, progressive approach to future labour relations. In broad terms, collective bargaining was shifted downwards from a centralized, sector-wide process to enterprise bargaining at the level of the individual firm. New guidelines were established by the Australian Industrial Relations Commission that required all large companies – like AP – to construct "joint-enterprise agreements." Enterprise bargaining weakened the centralized authority and power of the central union organizations. Indeed, under the subsequent Conservative government, enterprise bargaining could work without a union. This process was designed to attain cooperative and collaborative labour relations, flexibility in work rules, and fairer and more rational pay rates, as well as policy experimentation and innovation.[20]

1994 Amendment to the Postal Act

We will explore the statutory and regulatory environment created by the 1988 act in the next section and track the performance of AP in the section after that. For now, we will continue to track the trajectory of the postal-reform process. The Post's corporatization did not end scrutiny of it. Indeed, there have been four major studies of AP since corporatization. These studies continued to push the micro-economic agenda and analysed the impact of corporatization on the universal system.

The 1989 act required AP to be examined once it was in operation, in order to evaluate the extent to which there were any institutional or regulatory inhibitions on postal efficiency. This study was carried out by the Industry Commission, which issued a report in October 1992.[21]

This report is admirably thorough and professional, and it provides a tremendous introduction to, and overview of, postal themes, issues, and activities. The commission's central recommendation was to abolish AP's monopoly and establish a deregulated postal market, in which AP should make a minimum 16 per cent rate of return. It also proposed that the uniform postal rate should be reconceptualized as a maximum rate, to allow price flexibility below that. The commission encouraged a number of operational changes, including increased contracting out (including in the area of mail sorting), a greater degree of interconnectivity, and increased AP authority in the areas of purchasing, employment, and borrowing.

The Labor government did not act on the commission's recommendations, which it found to be too far-reaching at this time.[22] Its view was that there was insufficient community or industry support for deregulation, and inadequate documentation of the impact of deregulation. Indeed, a parliamentary study recommended against deregulation at this time as well. The Vaile report[23] was stimulated by the political concern that the corporatization and commercialization process was leading to a diminution of postal service in the rural areas. The minister asked the parliamentary committee to review the CSO situation and to focus on the quality of service in rural and remote areas. The report found that the quality of rural service remained acceptable. It rejected deregulation for a number of reasons. It concluded that, for AP to maintain its CSOs in a deregulated environment, it would require a direct government subsidy. The report rejected this approach in favour of maintaining the traditional internal cross-subsidy financed through the reserved area.

While the government rejected total postal deregulation, it moved to extend its micro-economic efficiency agenda and increase competitiveness while maintaining AP as a public corporation. The government amended the act in 1994, initiating the following changes:

- the exclusive privilege was reduced from ten times to four times the price of a stamp, and the weight limit was reduced from 500 grams to 250 grams;
- outbound international mail was exempted from protection;
- document exchange and internal company mail were exempted from the reserved area;
- more opportunity was provided for private-sector niches in the postal market, such as bulk mail, time-sensitive mail, and express;
- the terms of private companies' access to the Post's network and discounts for pre-sorted mail and drop shipments were set out; bulk

mail lodged at specified mail centres would receive a discount that reflected the costs avoided by AP;

- a price-cap system was introduced for letter mail, and formerly protected markets would be subject to the scrutiny of the Prices Surveillance Authority; and
- AP's accountability for the quality of its services was increased.

The effect of the amendment was to expose a further 16 per cent of AP's domestic and international letter traffic to competition. This amendment did not guarantee that competition would be forthcoming. Indeed, in the event, AP lost some outward-bound international mail and little else. The purpose of the amendment was to make AP act in a more businesslike and commercial fashion by increasing the competitive pressures it faced while obliging it to maintain its financial and social obligations. The Industry Commission process and the 1994 legislation put AP on notice that further liberalization was inevitable and that it had to prepare for it.

The NCC Process and Increased Deregulation in 2000

The micro-economic reform agenda was extended into deeper waters in 1995, again by a Labor government. The Council of Australian Governments (COAG) initiated a joint process to promote competition. Australian governments, at both federal and state levels, signed a Competition Principles Agreement (CPA), which committed them to reviewing their legislation with an eye on eliminating features that were anti-competitive. This process extended the Trade Practices Act to apply to states, territories, partnerships, and small businesses. It was an enormous process, which involved reviewing around 2,000 statutes that contained anti-competitive measures. All sectors of the economy were to be studied. With respect to state enterprises, the principle underlying this process was "competitive neutrality" – the idea that GBEs should not enjoy competitive advantage as a result of their being publicly owned. Two organizations were established to implement this initiative. ACCC was established to manage and enforce the Trade Practices Act. The National Competition Council was established to oversee and implement various features of the legislative and competition review. The NCC comprises a twenty-person unit, led by a five-person board headed by Graeme Samuel – an ex-president of the Chamber of Commerce and a strong proponent of the market. Among its other activities, it pursues issues that were placed on the policy agenda by governments.

In June 1997 the new Conservative government's minister of communications and the arts asked the NCC to carry out a study of the postal sector. This was the first legislative review that the NCC was requested to undertake and it was a high-profile request politically. Thus, the AP review and its aftermath would go a considerable extent to establishing whether the process would have any credibility or not. The issue of the ownership of AP was *not* placed on the agenda. Rather, the NCC was asked to advise the government on ways in which efficiency and competition could be increased while ensuring that public-service commitments were respected.[24] The ensuing process did not include public hearings, which was a cause of some discontent.[25] Rather, the NCC drew up a list of interested parties, to which it sent invitations to meet or make submissions. These submissions were made public. It released an options paper in October 1997 to stimulate discussion, it visited various interested groups, and it held a number of workshops on key themes. The process generated a modest amount of media and public interest before the NCC issued its report in February 1998.[26]

The NCC's recommendations were framed by two large themes. The first was that there was enormous public and business support for the universal postal service. The NCC concluded that the government should take this public support into account when it considered how to continue to guarantee universal service. Second, there was considerable business support for the idea of increasing the competitiveness and efficiency of AP, from which business would benefit economically. The trick for the NCC, then, was how to increase and maximize competitiveness while ensuring the universal-service principles. Andersen Consulting was directed to undertake detailed financial analysis of the impact on AP of reducing protection, based on data provided by AP. The NCC's core recommendations rested on the conclusion reached in the Andersen study, namely, that observers had generally underestimated AP's capacity to finance the CSOs.[27] The NCC looked at the moderate costs of the CSOs ($67 million) in light of AP's financial successes, and it concluded that AP did not require much protection or help to maintain the universal system. In this context, it made the following key recommendations:

- the reserved area should be narrowed to one segment of the letter market – household or individual mail – at two times the standard letter price;
- all business mail should be open to competition, and all carriers should be licensed;

- all international mail should be open to competition (outgoing was already liberalized);
- the rates for business mail could be discounted, to the degree that business rates would not be greater than the standard letter rate;
- AP's service standards should be placed in legislation, to be monitored by ACCC; and
- AP's CSOs could be financed by a combination of cross-subsidy and direct government support, or an industry levy (the last was second-best option).

Australia Post was not enthused by the NCC's recommendations and responded on 11 March 1998. Interestingly, Linda Nicholls, the board chair, issued the response, and not the management of AP.[28] This indicated a substantial degree of solidarity between AP management and the board. AP reiterated the argument that it made to the NCC in its August 1997 submission.[29] It warned against deregulating too quickly, without some sort of transitional arrangement and/or fallback safety net. Its analysis was that the NCC recommendations would increase the AP revenue open to competition to 93 per cent (from 49 per cent). The limited protection offered by householder mail would offer negligible assistance, if any at all, to the Post's efforts to meet the CSOs. It suggested that the actual savings for business would be only marginal, given that AP was planning to introduce a bar-coding system that would result in discounts averaging nearly 9 per cent. It criticized the idea of direct subsidizing of the CSOs and expressed concern about the difficulty in distinguishing between household and business mail. Finally, it offered an alternative approach for planned deregulation:

- reduction in the reserved area to two times the letter price and 125 grams in 1999 and one times the letter price and 125 grams in 2001;
- a price freeze until 2003;
- interconnectivity arrangements; and
- a further review in 2003.

AP estimated that its proposal would open up 70 per cent of the business to competition.

The postal unions rejected the government's position and backed AP's, and it launched a "Save Aussie Post" campaign.[30] The public reaction was muted, given that it had seen dozens of such reports and knew that the real moment of interest would be when the government made a decision.[31] The government did not have a lot of room to manoeuvre, given its commitment to the public post and to the universal service on the one hand and to the competitiveness agenda on the other. It had to react positively in some way to the NCC recommendations, lest it undermine the credibility of the process that it had initiated, particularly in the eyes of the state governments. Distancing itself too far from the board of AP, however, would create another credibility problem and potentially damage AP's operations and its own relationship with the board.

The government responded to the NCC recommendations in July with a political compromise. It did not go as far as the NCC recommended, but it went farther than AP's proposal. It announced its intention to:

- limit the reserved area to forty-five cents (the standard letter rate) and 50 grams;
- deregulate all international mail, making the reserved area domestic only;
- allow AP to negotiate contract rates with major mailers, with discounts for major mailers using barcodes and a reduction in the volume threshold (from 2,500 to 300) for bulk-mail discounts (only AP would be allowed to offer bulk-mail discounts below forty-five cents on letters fifty grams or less);
- provide an access regime to allow competitors access to AP's network on a similar basis and on terms and conditions no less favourable than those AP offers its own customers;
- set an aggregation minimum at 10,000 items (this would allow competitors such as mailshops to mix mailings from a number of different sources);
- freeze prices at forty-five cents until 2003;
- legislate minimum-performance standards, clarifying the definition and scope of the universal service (AP to produce a "Code of Practice" for its relationship with its major users and a "Service Charter" outlining its CSO obligations); and
- fund the CSOs by the cross-subsidy from the remaining reserved area.

The government walked a fine political line in this response. It was feeling some pressure from the rural constituencies and the postal union, and an election loomed. Legislative measures would be required to enact these proposals, which would generate an open parliamentary debate. Indeed, the government delayed and, notwithstanding its July 1998 announcement, its legislative proposals would not be forthcoming for almost two years until well after the October 1999 election. The minister promised that these proposals would not result in any post-office closures and the Service Charter was designed to give public confidence that the universal service would be maintained.[32] On the other hand, the government followed the NCC's recommendation to increase competition in business mail, in two ways. First, it created competition by getting more large letters (that is, greater than fifty grams) out of the reserved area. Second, it insisted that AP increase and improve the accessibility it offered to business, including its competitors. For its part, AP reminded Australians that the government's measures would open competition up to 88 per cent of the market, doubling the amount of AP's revenues that came from competitive sources, from $1.5 billion to $3.1 billion (all currency references in this chapter are in Australian dollars). AP's CSOs would have to be financed from only $450 million in the protected market. It reiterated its commitment to a price freeze in 2003 and gave the assurance that there would be no post-office closures or reductions in service in bush areas.[33]

The government subsequently introduced an amendment to the Postal Services Bill in early 2000. In large measure, the "Postal Services Legislation Amendment Bill" made concrete the government's July 1998 response to the NCC report. It proposed to reduce the scope of reserved services (forty-five cents and fifty grams domestically) with the objective of increasing postal competition; and it extended this competitive thrust by providing a regulated postal-services access regime, to oblige AP to provide access to its competitors on terms set by ACCC. The bill also proposed to convert AP from a statutory corporation under the Australian Postal Corporation Act to a public company under the Corporations Law, with the objective of ensuring competitive neutrality.[34] If this legislation had been passed, postal competition would likely have increased considerably and AP would have been corporatized to a further extent than it is at present. AP would have continued to be the dominant provider with a number of market advantages, including a reserved area that protected a substantial part of the business-mail market.

But none of this happened. The postal union persisted with its "Hands Off Aussie Post" campaign, and the John Howard government, faced with a Labor/rural coalition steadfastly opposed to further deregulation, and anticipating resistance in the Labor-dominated Senate, withdrew the postal bill in late March 2001. This ended a three-year effort to continue the deregulation of the Australian postal market.

STATUTORY AND LEGAL ENVIRONMENT

The Australian postal-regulatory regime was shaped primarily by the micro-economic reform agenda, which in turn emanated from the early 1980s economic crisis. The reform agenda comprised a number of ingredients, including the transformation of the state-enterprise sector. The key element in this transformation was the decision to shift basic decision-making processes away from the government and departments to agencies, statutory bodies, or corporatized state enterprises. This decision resulted in a new conceptualization of state enterprises as Government Business Enterprises. The basic principle behind the GBES was the axiom, "let the managers manage." The government would back off and distance itself from the GBES, exercising oversight at the general, strategic, and long-term level. The government would appoint boards of directors to manage and operate the firms, according to commercial objectives and practices. The boards would be held accountable to the government for their performance, to be evaluated against targets and expectations set in corporate plans. The regulatory regime would be light-handed, in order to allow and encourage the commercialization of GBES, without state inhibition. The sense was that the best way to increase the efficiency and the competitiveness of the GBES was to increase the competitive environment in which they operated. At the postal level, the objective of reform was to have Australia Post make a contribution to the efficiency and competitiveness of the overall Australian economy. In order for it to have this impact, it would itself have to become more efficient, decrease its costs, and improve its services.[35] A minimum of regulation in a deregulated environment would provide the spur to these developments.

Ownership

Australia Post is a Government Business Enterprise, which is owned by the state but independent of government funding. The APC Act directs it to attain a reasonable rate of return, to pay the full range of government taxes and charges, and to provide its shareholder with an annual dividend. The Australian postal regime has recently adopted the two-shareholder model that was first developed in New Zealand. Until 1997, the Department of Communication and the Arts was the central player in the postal regulatory regime. This changed somewhat in 1997, after the Humphrey report. The Department of Finance and Administration was directed to increase its oversight of GBES, for two reasons.[36] First, there was concern that regulatory authorities were in a conflict-of-interest situation, because they regulated a sector in which a GBE was only one of a number of participants. For example, DOCA regulated the postal sector, in which there was both AP and private competitors such as Streetfile and Mayne Nickless. Second, the government raised its expectations with regard to increasing the asset value of the GBEs. The result was that DOFA was assigned increased authority to maximize shareholder value in the state-enterprise sector. A complementary development was the creation of CSAU – the Commonwealth Share-holder Advisory Unit. It has responsibility for the fifteen GBEs. This unit comprises ten staff, who call on consultants when required.

The adoption of the dual-shareholder model is a new development which should clarify and distinguish ownership and regulatory functions. Nothing substantial has changed in a legal sense, since DOCA remains the principal administrator. It is too early to determine how the relationship between DOCA and DOFA has worked out in practice. There is a protocol between the two departments on how they will interact and the level of consultation that each expects.[37] Generally, this duality should enable a balanced consideration of potentially competing interests.[38]

DOFA's primary focus is on shareholder value, AP's financial performance, and the rates of return AP provides to the government. DOFA oversees the government's investment in AP and seeks to increase the value of its assets. Prior to 1997, DOFA simply looked at reports and issued a few comments or observations to the DOCA minister. After 1997, it adopted a more defined and high-profile role, and it now has ultimate financial responsibility for AP. As a result, it has increased its interest in AP and has required a higher degree of basic information, particularly financial, than in the past. This has caused some mild apprehension in AP, which has tended to be possessive about information. DOFA has a general power to issue policy directives, but this power has never been used. Its bottom-line focus is on dividend policy, which it expresses through the corporate plan (typically 60 per cent of after-tax profits). The planning process – to be discussed below – is led by AP's board. DOFA reacts to rather than sets the plan. Some tension may emerge here as DOFA's authority and interest increases. Given DOFA's financial objectives, it has been lukewarm to cool about postal diversification and risk. It has the authority to veto new initiatives outside the postal core, although there has been no high-profile incident such as Freightways in New Zealand. AP has recognized DOFA's point of view and adjusted its ambitions and strategy accordingly.[39] This has raised some concern that AP will be starved for funds, if it cannot expand its business horizons to mitigate likely weakness in letter-mail revenues.[40]

The Treasury had greater involvement in postal affairs before 1997, when it was consulted on all major issues. The Treasury would also comment on the corporate plan to the treasurer, who would communicate with the DOCA minister. Its role has diminished since 1997. It continues to comment on broad issues like the consistency of policy in the GBE area, pricing, the soundness of investment plans, and how productivity gains are being shared. The Treasury has no direct contact with AP's board. It intervenes only when it thinks that it is vitally important to do so.[41]

Regulation

The Department of Communication, the Information Economy and the Arts, formerly the Department of Communication and the Arts, is the primary authority in the postal-regulatory regime. It performs the formal regulatory function, since there is no third-party regulator in the Australian regime. The postal act was its creation, and it takes the legislative lead hand at times when amendments are required or mooted, such as after the NCC process. It is the government's main specialist in postal matters, and it has a small unit of four people dedicated to this end. It is an omnibus department, with origins in 1987 when a number of common functions and activity were grouped together. The very size of the department, and its diffused interests and foci, results in a tendency to interfere minimally and modestly. Its general impulse has been to leave AP alone, as far as possible. DCITA has responsibility for the entire postal industry, not just for AP. It is concerned with the efficiency and service of the industry and has encouraged increasing competition to these ends.

The regulatory regime is a light-handed one, as has been noted. The minister has only informal involvement in postal matters, and there is no ministerial executive assistant on postal matters. There is a modest amount of formal interaction between the department and the board and postal management. In earlier times, there was a departmental representative on the Board of Directors, but this tradition has passed. The relations with AP are informal and continuing but not particularly substantial, detailed, or involved. The operating principle is to let the company run itself, while DCITA will look after the public interest. Given AP's financial and service record, there has not been much pressure for DCITA to get involved. Indeed, the department appears to be actually protective of the board's autonomy and has only modest reporting expectations (the rolling three-year plan and quarterly reports).[42] Price regulation also displays a light touch. AP sets its own prices. Its reserved prices are subject to oversight by the Prices Surveillance Act via the Australian Competition and Consumer Council. ACCC has to be notified of proposed price increases in the reserved area, and it makes a recommendation to the government. The Prices Surveillance Act is the court of last resort, if the minister asks ACCC to conduct a public enquiry. ACCC can arbitrate cases regarding changes in bulk charges and access to other reserved services provided by the

Post. But, given the price freeze in letters since 1992, there has not been much action or concern on the pricing front.

DCITA's relationship with DOFA is still unfolding. It is clearly the lead department in the dual-shareholding model and a positive protocol has been established between the two departments. Clearly, though, tension could develop between the two if, for example, DOFA ratcheted up its financial expectations to a level that affected AP's performance and service accomplishments.

AP's service requirements are termed community-service obligations. These are a legal requirement under the act for AP to provide a universal and accessible postal service at a uniform price. AP's service obligations are highlighted in the corporate plan, and it has a statutory obligation to report on this in its annual report. Indeed, the financial and statutory section in AP's annual report is over thirty pages long. On the service level, it includes three elements. First, there is a basic statement of AP's CSOs under the act. Second, it presents detailed and precise statistical summaries on the retail and delivery network, access to the network, prices, frequency of service, and letter-delivery performance. Third, it presents the service targets that had been included in the corporate plan and a report on AP's performance against these targets. Parallel to the service requirements are AP's financial requirements, which are also set out in the annual report. These include statistical summaries of financial and industrial performance, a statement of objectives and strategies, and a report of performance against targets. Generally speaking, this is the most detailed and thorough accounting of a Post's service responsibilities and performance of any country in this study. Moreover, the reporting is highly quantified, a hallmark of the Australian postal-policy experience.

The accountability regime has been ratcheted up to a more formal and public level in two documents that have emerged from the NCC exercise. The Code of Practice (21 October 1999)[43] is a service document between AP and its major mail users. Its purpose is to facilitate better commercial relations between AP and its customers and to improve the quality of postal service. The document focuses mainly on bulk-mail practices and sets delivery standards and performance expectations. It also outlines a process for the commercial dealings between AP and its clients, which includes a problem-resolution mechanism should disagreements arise.

The Service Charter[44] elaborates AP's CSOs in a widely distributed public document. Three principles inform the CSOs:

- AP will provide all Australians with a letter service that reasonably meets social, industrial, and commercial needs;

- the letter service will be reasonably accessible to all Australians on an equitable basis; and
- there will be a uniform price for letters.

These principles are in turn detailed and quantified in a series of commitments:

- letters will be delivered anywhere in Australia for forty-five cents (this price has been frozen since 1992);
- any future price increases will be less than the increase in the consumer-price index;
- a minimum of 98 per cent of delivery points will get at least five-day delivery, and the remaining 2 per cent will get no less than one delivery a week;
- at least 94 per cent of mail will be delivered on time;
- there will be a minimum retail presence of 4,000 outlets, of which at least 2,500 will be in rural or remote areas; and
- there will be a minimum 10,000 mail boxes.

AP estimates that its CSO obligations cost it $65–70 million a year. There has been a substantial and lively debate in Australia about how this cost should be borne. The NCC recommended a more direct government payment or an industrial charge, but AP – as well as the public – prefers the internal cross-subsidy method financed through a reserved area.[45] If there were to be a direct subsidy approach, DOFA would be obliged to pay, presumably out of the dividends and/or taxes that the government receives from AP.

The postal area continues to create some political pressure and public interest. DCITA receives some public complaints but redirects them to AP. Since 1991, there has been a Postal Services Consultative Council, which serves as a public advisory body to AP. Chaired by a member of the board, it meets three times a year. The council is a stakeholders' group with representatives of major users (for example, Hallmark Cards, Readers Digest), householders, and rural residents. AP tables its annual report in Parliament, where a legislative committee reviews it from time to time. AP also appears before the Senate Estimates Committee, but this is a quick and benign event.

Australia Post

All the head of AP is a Board of Directors which determines the objectives and strategies of the corporation and develops the supporting policies to realize these objectives. Under contract law, the board is responsible to the shareholder. It sets a business framework for the Post and is accountable to the government for AP's financial performance. It works with the shareholder to produce annually a multiyear corporate plan which includes forecasts of costs and revenues and financial and performance targets. By design, the regulatory regime allows the board and management to run postal operations. The board is distanced from the government but accountable to it. There is little direct relationship between the minister and the board. The chair meets the minister perhaps two or three times a year and board reports to the minister have changed from monthly to quarterly submissions. The main contact is between management and the shareholding departments. In practice, the board has become fiercely loyal to the Post and has worked to increase AP's autonomy. DCITA itself has worked to protect the role of the board and to shield its functioning from government.[46] Overall, the government has taken a "hands off" approach to the board.[47] The low level of intervention and interference has been due as much to AP's tremendous financial performance as to the nature of the regime framework itself.[48] The board appears to be oriented more to management than to the shareholder. For example, it was the board chair who made AP's reply to the NCC recommendations. This projected a close, shared perspective between the board and management on AP's future.[49] The chair of the board and the managing director present AP's annual results together.

The board is comprised of up to nine members, who are appointed by the government. Given its commercial responsibilities, board members have been drawn mainly from the world of business and commerce. There was a government representative (from DOCA) on the board in earlier times; however, this tradition ended after it became clear that the result was tension and a conflict of interest for the government representative.[50] There has also been a tradition of reserving a place for labour on the board. This has been a generic appointment, rather than a direct representative of the postal or central trade union. Board appointments are highly scrutinized[51] and targeted to weaknesses or priorities on the board. The board has become an increasingly "hands-on" and working body.

Board chairs and members have been extremely experienced and capable. For example, Chair Maurice Williams had been a director of the Bank of Australia and the former CEO of Australian Gaslight. The present chair is Linda Nicholls, an excellent and highly respected businessperson. She has had an extended involvement with the Post, starting with the APC, and has been on the board since 1989.[52] Her background is in investment management and international and domestic finance and banking. She is a corporate adviser (for example,

Price Waterhouse Coopers) and company director (Sigma Pharmaceutical, Perpetual Trustees). She is an energetic, active, and effective chair and works very hard and closely with AP management. The deputy chair is Alan Rydge, who is chair of Amalgamated Holdings, Carlton Investments, Rydges Hotels, and the Greater Union Organization. Other members have extensive backgrounds in banking (Ken Allen, senior director of Macquarie Bank); information technology (Megan Cornelius, chair and managing director of Expertise Australia Technology Group); business (Katie Lahey, CEO of New South Wales Chamber of Commerce); government (Michael Keating, various high-level-civil service positions); media and popular opinion (Rod Cameron, former director of the Australian Broadcasting Corporation and managing director of ANOP Research Services); and industrial relations (Peter McLaughlin, managing director of World Competitive Practices, past executive director of the Business Council, and a senior federal bureaucrat).

The AP board is a substantial, experienced, and generally active group which has developed an excellent, intimate, and hands-on working relationship with management. Prior to 1989, postal management dominated the boards, but this has not been the case recently. The board appreciates the technological and financial challenges facing AP and has set an ambitious agenda for AP's survival and development. The chair has organized corporate-planning strategy sessions for management and the board and has had board members develop working specializations.[53]

The managing director (CEO) of AP is appointed by the board. AP executives are employed under contracts similar to those of private-sector employees. Senior management was recruited actively from the private sector after corporatization; about three-quarters of the top managers have been from private enterprise. AP management was in tune with the objective of commercialization. There have been three managing directors, whose appointments have tracked the commercial evolution of AP. Don Eltringham was from the Department of Defence and interacted only episodically with the board. Ray Taylor had a government background but was not from the Post and brought a different perspective to its operations (particularly on the industrial-relations front). At this time, a number of executives were recruited from the private sector. Some came from competitors (such as TNT and Maine Nickless) while others were recruited for their functional expertise. One of these eventually became the third managing director. Graeme John joined AP in 1990 as chief manager, National Operations. With a commercial background and extensive experience in the transport business, he was appointed managing director in 1993.

AP (through the board) and the government have confronted issues that have generated tension – or could have generated tension – between them. In each case, the government had to decide whether to back up AP or to veto its initiative. For example, news agencies complained to the government that AP was selling non-statutorily defined products in its shops. The ministry defended this initiative, maintaining that AP paid taxes and charged fair taxes and was not cross-subsidized, and so it had every right to sell these products. In any case, the government was keen to see retail post offices remain open in rural areas. On the other hand, the government vetoed AP's plans to move into the financial-services area. Its rationale was that this sector had just recently been deregulated.[54] Generally, the government has been "hands off" for much of AP's history, although there is a sense that the Howard government is getting more directly involved. Overall, the government has been pleased with AP's performance, which it sees as a success story and an example of first-class corporate practice.[55]

The major interaction between AP and the government is during the construction and approval of the corporate plan. The corporate plan is effectively the contract between the shareholding ministries and the board. It is a rolling three-year document, produced annually. It is for internal eyes only; the public sees last year's targets and results in AP's annual report. The corporate plan follows a bottom-up process. Each of the states is a self-contained centre, and information is aggregated upward through geography, business, and functions. AP's internal corporate plan is extremely detailed, but it takes the form of a broad and general scheme before it reaches the two shareholding departments. AP is jealous both of this process and of the information that feeds it. No draft is presented to the minister before it has been reviewed by the board, which insists on being the lead hand and central to the process. Then, a parallel iterative process unfolds, with various draft versions working their way back and forth between the departments and AP. Consultation tends to deal with broad directions rather than with details. The board approves the plan in May, and the government has six weeks to review it. The minister is not involved until the actual submission. The shareholder's imprint on the plan has been quite light, if not benign. This reflects the past performance of AP, which has not given cause to the shareholder to intervene strongly in the process. This light touch also reflects the challenge that the process entails for the government. It receives a huge pile of GBE plans simultaneously, and the departments have a limited time and staff to process them. Prior to 1997, the minister could comment on only two areas: the CSOs and financial targets. In practice, this was never actually done. After 1997, the minister has had a broad, general power to ask the board to reconsider certain elements of the plan or to provide more detail or rationale. This power is limited to changes or variations in strategies and policies carrying out the CSOs and the financial target under the plan. The government can respond to the plan, note areas of concern, or express disquiet.[56] If the minister were very unhappy with the plan, or with results against the plan, he could dismiss the board.[57] But so far there have been no negative or critical ministerial reactions to the corporate plan.

The corporate plan presented to the shareholder is very much a broad, brush-stroke document.[58] It is not long (seventy-five to eighty pages) and comprises qualitative and quantitative analysis and targets. The plan reviews the business and financial environment, delineates the corporate strategy and major projects for the period, reviews the Post's CSOs, and outlines the supporting policy strategies. There are sections on the human-resource situation and subsidiary companies, and there are appendices containing assumptions, past performance results, performance indicators, and projections. The plan objectives and targets are made public in the following year's annual report, at which time AP accounts for its performance against the objectives and targets agreed to in the plan.

The Labour Situation

The last ingredient to review in the postal regulatory regime is the labour situation. This is an important ingredient to consider, inasmuch as the Australian economic model had seen labour participating in national policy making and the industrial-relations scene was based on national bargaining across sectors. This was not a situation in which the Post had much control over its human-resource situation and, indeed, the postal labour scene was difficult if not impossible prior to 1989.

The economic-reform agenda aimed to transform industrial relations. A series of legislative and policy initiatives resulted in a decentralization of industrial relations and a diffusion of collective bargaining away from the industry to the enterprise level. Enterprise Bargaining Agreements (EBAs) forced the reorganization of the structure of unions to the work place level, while the Workplace Relations Act lessened the role of union membership and encouraged more direct relations between the employees and management. Thereafter, union density in Australia declined to 35 per cent. A Joint Statement of Understanding between ACTU and the government in 1989 set a broad framework for this transformation. Among other principles, the unions accepted the reality of technological change and the

importance of profit and productivity improvements, in return for a
guaranteed participation and consultation in the process of change.
A type of social contract developed between the government and
labour, and a series of Accords were signed (starting in 1983) whereby
wage demands were moderated (and focused on real wages) in return
for tax cuts and pension and social-welfare guarantees.[59]

This was the broad national framework in which industrial relations
at AP changed. As a GBE, AP is not part of the Australian public service.
Its staff has its own status as employees of AP. There is not a closed
shop, and postal-union density is around 70 per cent. The national
reforms devolved and decentralized authority, weakening broad union
control over AP. Postal workers pursue their own industrial-relations
policies, collective bargaining taking place at the enterprise level. AP
negotiates an EBA with its workforce. There were a number of obvious
procedural changes that resulted, including the consolidation of
twenty-three bargaining units into four (of which only two are significant.) This has simplified the postal labour scene and processes
enormously.[60] AP and the postal union CEPU (Communications, Electrical, Plumbing Union) embraced the principles of the Joint Statement, which informed the collective agreement in 1989.

The postal union went along with the reformed industrial-relations
situation for a number of reasons. First, there was a broad appreciation
that the postal situation was a mess, that previous industrial relations
were horrible, and that there had to be a better way. Second, the union
eventually accepted the proposition that technological change would
ensure postal viability over the long run. Third, there was anxiety that,
if postal performance did not improve, the Post would be sold off.
There was considerable privatization taking place at this time. Fourth,
the union was sobered by the loss of the courier business, which demonstrated the competitive uncertainty that the Post confronted. Fifth,
the unions concluded that it was better to have a public postal corporation making profits and paying dividends, which could be used to
maintain the social safety net. Sixth, the new approach had some advantages for the union, in exchanging industrial peace for influence.[61]

The general result has been that industrial relations have unfolded
in a far more stable fashion since 1989, which has allowed the postal-
reform process to unfold without enormous clashes or crises. Industrial action has been minimal and days lost have been less than the
national average. In 1989 there were 1.5 days lost a year per each full-
time employee. This declined by half in 1990 and to a tiny fraction
by 1994 (.08). The union has developed reasonably good relations
with AP, and it has been willing to make deals to make things work.
For example, it allowed the introduction of permanent part-time

workers, and it has at least allowed experimentation with productivity and piece-rate pay (in Queensland.) AP has signed four EBAS since corporatization, the most recent in 1999. The second EBA in 1995 was reinforced by a Participative Relations Statement, which confirmed the principle of cooperation and worker participation. The fourth EBA (1999) comprised an 8.5 per cent pay raise (over twenty-six months) and laid the basis for technological change and job restructuring. The EBAS have provided reasonably good real-wage increases, as well as decent conditions and tenure of work. This would not have been possible without the sustained productivity gains made by AP since 1990 – which in turn reflect the more stable and cooperative industrial-relations scene in this period.[62]

Through CEPU, postal workers have exerted pressure on the government to slow down the recent deregulation process (through its "Hands Off Aussie Post" campaign). This has seen postal workers as an ally of AP in its negotiations with government.

PERFORMANCE

Australia Post has been one of the most successful public postal operations in the world. As indicated in Table 2, it has failed to make a profit only once since 1976 and has been profitable every year since corporatization in 1989. During the 1990s, AP attained $2.663 billion in profits, and it recorded record profits in the late 1990s and 2000. It also paid more than $2.5 billion in taxes and payments to the government and provided over $1 billion in dividends. AP's return on assets has been persistently above 10 per cent since 1991. It was awarded a Standard and Poors "AAA" credit rating in 1994. All the while, it fulfilled its statutory obligations to carry out its CSOs.

AP has consistently attained the targets set in its corporate plans. For example, the 1998–99 annual report indicated that AP had met its plan targets, shown in Table 1. Rapid productivity gains have been at the heart of AP's success. In the early 1990s, these amounted to but 1 per cent or so a year. But after 1992, annual productivity gains were consistently in the 4–6 per cent range. These productivity gains were shared with all of its stakeholders: service standards were maintained, a customer focus was pursued, prices were kept low, wage and benefit gains were provided, and dividends were substantial. These activities and results in turn helped to maintain and increase postal volumes, maintain labour peace, and keep politics and the government out of the postal arena. At the same time, this performance unfolded in an increasingly competitive business environment for AP. Over half of its revenue and two-thirds of its profits are now earned in competitive

Table 1
AP targets and results, 1997–98

	Target	Result
Profit (before interest, tax)	$331 million	$385 million
Dividends	$137 million	$149 million
Return on Assets	12.1%	13.8%
Quality of Service	94% on time	94.4% on time
Price	Freeze	Freeze
Productivity Increase	4%	5.1%

Source: Australia Post, Annual Report, 1998-9.

Table 2
AP's financial performance (millions of dollars)

	91	92	93	94	95	96	97	98	99	00
Revenue	2,184	2,310	2,421	2,568	2,754	2,890	3,110	3,300	3,449	3,743
Profit (pre-tax)	146	179	249	287	332	344	347	335	373	392
ROA* (%)	9.7	11.1	11.1	12.3	14.8	15.5	14.6	12.8	13.8	14
CSO cost	60	52	46	62	65	72	67	71	70	79
Taxes	187	242	273	227	254	306	308	295	328	327
Dividends	25	50	62	90	120	143	220	215	149	158

* Return on assets.
Source: Australia Post, Annual Report, various years.

markets. This situation is likely to develop even further, once the latest round of deregulation in implemented in 2000, particularly with respect to improved access for bulk mailing.[63] AP faces increasing competition, of both a direct and indirect character, albeit not in the same range or size as in the telecom industry. Substitute products like e-mail and e-commerce continue to expand, although AP will likely benefit from the parcel-delivery business associated with Internet commerce. There are keen competitors in the Australian market, waiting for a more liberalized environment to unfold. It is unlikely that deregulation will result in no competition developing (as has been the case in Finland, which has not resolved its licensing problem).[64] Mailing houses, pre-sorting operations, bulk mailers, and others have few (albeit high) barriers to entry – such as the forty-five-cent barrier in the proposed regime (that is, they will not be allowed to offer bulk discounts below forty-five cents). The proposed regime will, though, give competitors greater access to the network. A firm like Streetfile claims to have coverage for 95 per cent of the catalogue-delivery and magazine market.[65]

As deregulation increased, AP intensified its strategy to maintain productivity increases and keep prices low and service levels high, in order to maintain its core business-mail market. It has introduced the latest OCR (optical scanner readers) technology and bar-coding, increased the use of part-time and casual labour, reconfigured the delivery network, maintained the letters-price freeze, and offered deep discounts to volume mailers.

Volume and Price

Forty years ago, the Post carried two billion of Australia's four billion messages. By the year 2001, AP's volumes will have more than doubled to 4.5 billion units. But this represents only 17 per cent of the enlarged communications market of twenty-seven billion messages. Notwithstanding the growth in electronic communications, AP still holds one-fifth of the communications market.

AP's volumes grew by 40 per cent in the 1990s, as indicated in Table 3. It anticipates that mail will grow by another 40 per cent by the year 2004, assisted by the growth in e-commerce (deliveries and bill confirmation). The volume growth in 1999–2000 was the highest in nine years. Prior to 1998, about 60 per cent of AP's postal activity was open to competition. This will increase substantially once the latest round of liberalization takes hold. The growth of the letters market is slowing, and there has been a continuing decline in the profitability of letters. Revenue growth fell below GDP growth in 1998–99 for the second time in the 1990s.[66] This is the competitive future faced by AP, which requires it to diversify its business. For example, it has developed a national network of EDIPost bulk-mail handling sites, and it has become a world leader in high-speed electronic-letter and document transmission, printing, and delivery.

There are four basic postal markets: household to household (H-H), business to business (B-B), and household to business mail and vice versa (B-H, H-B). H-H mail has been basically stable, but it represents a small proportion of volumes (and is expensive to process). B-B mail is regressing, since this is the sector that is the most susceptible to electronic substitution. H-B is basically healthy. But B-H mail is growing substantially. It is a market that grew by over 250 per cent in the 1990s.[67] There is an enormous business in targetted business mail and the associated activities of producing data and mail lists and providing reply and confirmation feedback. Indeed, postal volumes have been pulled up by the growth in addressed ad mail, which grew by 14 per cent in 1997–98 and 19 per cent in 1998–99. It will top 500 million units in 2000. AP has introduced DPID – Delivery Point Identifier

Table 3
AP performance

	91	92	93	94	95	96	97	98	99	00
Volume (billions)	3.2	3.3	3.4	3.6	3.8	4.1	4.2	4.4	4.5	4.8
% On-delivery (%)	94	96	92	93	94	93	94	94	94	94

Source: Australia Post, *Annual Report*, various years.

System – to supply address-validated mail. This promises to reduce the rate of incorrectly addressed ad mail, reducing costs to mailers and increasing the accuracy of targetting.

AP has been reasonably price-sensitive, since it has worked to maintain and grow its volumes. It has functioned under a price-cap regime since 1992, and the forty-five-cent price of a letter has been frozen since then. Given growth in the consumer-price index, the price of a stamp fell by 14 per cent in real terms between 1992 and 1999. AP is committed to the forty-five-cent price until at least 2003, which entails another price cut in real terms. Moreover, AP has absorbed the advent of the goods and services tax (GST) on stamps. A business applying for a rebate received an effective price reduction of 4.1 cents, or 9 per cent. This development cost AP $50 million in one-time start-up expenses and $100 million a year in 2000–01. The cost of mailing a letter in Australia is the fourth-lowest in the world. In the late 1990s, only Spain, New Zealand, and the United States provided a cheaper stamp. All this said, AP has not cut its standard price, which may very well have been possible given the productivity increases and high rates of financial return that it experienced in this period.

Other Activity

AP has attempted to mitigate developing weaknesses in mail volumes by expanding its business in mail- and near-mail-related products and activities.

For example, AP introduced its answer to courier service in 1991, and Express Post became a leading next-day deliverer. AP has also developed into the leader in home-market and small-parcel delivery. It is attempting new services on a trial basis, including Internet fulfillment (Post eDeliver) and home delivery of supermarket products ordered on line (in conjunction with Coles Myer). It has entered the logistics field and doubled its customer base in the last few years. AP is offering an Internet bill-payment service, with trials starting in April 2000. A U.S. company, Transpoint, in a joint venture between Microsoft and

First Data Corporation, will provide the technology. This will allow customers to pay their bills through AP's website.

Service and the Network

Australia comprises an enormous land mass, with a peculiar distribution of population. While most Australians live on the coast in large cities, a substantial number are scattered about the 98–99 per cent of the terrain that is considered to be rural or remote (although many of them live in regional centres within rural or remote areas). Australians are extremely sensitive to the rural issue, which has deep political salience. This sensitivity is the foundation upon which rests Australians' commitment to the universal service.[68] As a result, AP's service and its network policy and commitments have been very much alive to the needs of rural and remote Australia.

These concerns are articulated clearly and quantitatively in AP's Service Charter, which is the public statement of AP's community-service obligations, as outlined above. In 1999, 98.1 per cent of Australians received five or more letter deliveries a week (94.1 per cent of the rural population and 93.9 per cent of the remote population received this five-day delivery service). AP sets delivery standard targets, which are geared to distance travelled and the complexity entailed.[69] As Table 3 indicates, on-time delivery has consistently been in the 94 per cent range.

AP has been obliged since 1998 to maintain a retail network of 4,000 outlets, of which 2,500 must be in rural and remote areas. Table 4 indicates that this commitment has been realized via an altered mix of types of postal outlets. Many traditional post offices or agency offices have been replaced by franchises and licensed outlets operated by small businesses. This conversion plan was negotiated successfully with the unions, and kept out of the courts, in the context of a strong Australian tradition of unofficial post offices.[70] The retail-conversion plan is basically complete. Small business operators now account for about three-quarters of AP's retail presence.

Most public posts have unprofitable retail networks, which has been the reason for rationalizing and privatizing the network. The Australian experience is compelling, because AP has transformed a losing retail operation into a profitable one. The retail operation was out of the red by 1996–97, at which time it turned an $18-million profit. Profits currently are above $30 million a year. This transformation into profitability represents the results of a huge retail reform and modernization initiative that began in 1994–95.

In the first instance, the retail situation was clarified by separating the retail operation from the delivery operation. A five-year, $73-million

Table 4
AP network

	90	91	92	93	94	95	96	97	98	99
Corporate Outlets	1,356	1,352	1,348	1,299	1,203	1,132	1,084	1,009	957	905
Licensed POS	3,045	3,009	2,977	2,928	2,789	2,822	2,873	2,925	2,965	2,998
Post Points			120	630	779	803	888	899	843	881
Delivery Points (millions)	6.95	7.1	7.15	7.28	7.47	7.67	7.92	8.21	8.17	8.51

Source: Australia Post, *Annual Report*, various years.

upgrade was initiated, including an enormous investment in the latest retail counter technology. Not only is the retail network Australia's largest – over 800,000 people a day visit a retail postal outlet – it also comprises the largest electronic-line counter network. AP invested $135 million to update its EPOS system (electronic point of sale) to a RIPOSTE – Retail Integrated Point of Sale Transaction – environment. Of its retail outlets, 2,600 are electronically linked. This allows AP to be a major player in a number of markets. For example, AP is now the leader in the third-party bill-payment network. It acts as a bill-payment transaction agent for over 350 companies and agencies, handling everything from electricity and gas bills to tax payments. Over 170 million bills are paid at AP outlets, representing 28 per cent of the over-the-counter bill-payment market and 13 per cent of all bills paid.

AP provides the largest personal-banking network in Australia, through its giropost and its banking arrangements with forty-one private financial institutions. Personal banking services are provided at 3,800 AP outlets, about half in rural areas. AP has made a joint initiative with the Commonwealth Bank that allows businesses to do their daily banking business at seventy select postal outlets (the target is 200). AP outlets also provide a number of non-postal products and services, including fax services, packing containers, financial services, books, and passports. AP has launched a successful line of house-brand stationary, whose sales increased by 28 per cent in 1997–98 and 35 per cent in 1998–99. Its retail merchandising more than doubled between 1995 and 1999. In sum, over $85 billion passes over AP's retail counters in a year.

Mechanization and Employment

Australia has traditionally been a leader in postal mechanization and modernization. The world's first mechanical handling was carried out in Sydney in 1930. Australia introduced a postal-code system in 1967.

Table 5
AP productivity

	91	92	93	94	95	96	97	98	99	00
FT* Employees	34,843	33,605	31,934	31,130	31,621	32,040	31,111	29,564	28,205	26,915
Productivity (%)		1.6	4.2	5.1	6.1	6.4	4.0	5.7	6.0	5.0	6.5

* Full-time.
Source: Australia Post, Annual Report, various years.

The Melbourne Mail Exchange was opened in 1972, with machines capable of handling 25,000 letters an hour.

AP invested over $600 million in the period 1994–99 to modernize its sorting and handling systems. By 1996, over three-quarters of its mail was being sorted by OCRs. Major capital initiatives have been made to redesign the mail-processing network and upgrade information technology. The massive Future Post undertaking was the latest stage in mechanization, which has upgraded the OCRs and made the operation more computer-driven from a bar-code platform. This will reduce the need for most labour in sorting while increasing the accuracy of addressing. Mechanization has contributed enormously to AP's annual productivity improvements, which have only twice been less than 4 per cent in the last decade (see Table 5). Indeed, the cumulative increase in productivity over the decade was 58.4 per cent, double the productivity growth of the national economy. Mechanization has made an impact on AP's overall level of employment and the mix of its composition. While AP remains Australia's seventh-largest employer, employment has been cut by over 20 per cent over the decade, from 35,000 to 27,000 full-time employees. On the other hand, the number of permanent part-time employees has grown to over 8,000.

Joint Ventures and International Initiatives

Like many public posts, AP has been pursuing alliance partnerships and acquisitions, but it does not yet have much to show for these efforts. AP seems to be more focused on the internal efficiency of its core business, and the shareholder has not appeared to be keen about diversification beyond this core. AP recently introduced a joint initiative with TELSTRA (the telecommunications company). Each firm will provide services to the other, in a multi-million series of contracts.

AP has a number of subsidiaries worth noting. It purchased 12 per cent of International Data Post in 1994–95, a bulk electronic-mail system. In December 1995 it and Chase Manhattan Australian formed Austrapay, a venture in the area of electronic payment and processing. AP has also formed a strategic alliance with Unisys Australia to sell its retail counter technology in the Asia-Pacific region, and it has carried out some postal consultancy work in Thailand, Papua New Guinea, Kiribati, and the Philippines.

CONCLUSION

What can one learn from the Australian case? What interest does its experience and its approach hold for policy makers? The first and most compelling observation to make is the one that has been made previously with respect to Finland, Sweden, and New Zealand. The Australian case demonstrates again that a postal regime can combine a high degree of liberalization and deregulation while maintaining the universal postal system. Indeed, the Australian case provides a more ambitious setting for "testing" this possibility, since its enormous land mass and relatively modest population pose more intense logistical and financial challenges than those in other countries. This may explain the more moderate, twenty-five-year period of postal reform in Australia, which sees Australia still retaining an area of exclusive privilege for AP, albeit a declining one. AP has been as financially successful as any modern, progressive Post. It has provided billions of dollars to the government in taxes and dividends while self-financing far-reaching modernization programs on both the operational and retail levels. Its basic letter price has been frozen for a decade and is one of the lowest in the industrial world. At the same time, the universal postal system has more or less the same contours that it had before 1989 – a universally accessible network that provides high-quality service to all Australians in equitable fashion at a uniform price. The politics of this transformation has been more complex than in a number of other postal regimes. This contributed as well to the more protracted period of reform and the less than fully deregulated result. The salience of the rural issue, the particular place of organized labour in the Australian policy system, and the federal, consensual political system and processes in Australia made postal policy making more highly charged and complex than in countries with a unitary system, a weaker labour movement, and a less intense public-service inheritance. These factors have maintained a political dimension to the regime that limits the market thrust, thereby maintaining Australia in the hybrid or transitional model.

The postal-reform process in Australia has unfolded in a linear and fairly stable way. This was basically because the postal agenda rode the momentum of economic reform and the wider economic-policy agenda. The result was a clear and non-negotiable context for the reform of the state-enterprise sector. Once AP became a GBE, there was no uncertainty about the commercial purposes of state enterprises and the option of turning back was eliminated. This cleared the political track, and potential political disagreements on the postal front took place only within this context. Similarly and crucially, the wider transformation of the industrial-relations system allowed AP to get some semblance of control over its labour situation. The postal union eventually accepted the rationale and implications of this wider agenda. As the focus shifted to the enterprise level, AP and its unions interacted within a context that set finite boundaries and determined the broad terrain of outcomes. This wider agenda contributed to another development that was uniquely Australian. The process generated a series of in-depth, almost scholarly studies of the postal sector. The Industry Commission and the NCC studies were intelligent, theoretically informed, and highly quantified analyses, which raised the level of postal intelligence in policy debates. The analysis, data, and insights generated from these studies and their discussion provided a firm and useful foundation for postal policy making and debates. This is well illustrated in the explanatory notes to the recent postal legislation, which provides concrete, quantitative, and well-informed analysis of the various options considered and the potential impact of each.

The Australian postal-regulatory regime is a clear and straightforward one, which combines a firm accountability regime with a high degree of postal autonomy. While these may appear to be contradictory impulses, they do not work out in this manner in practice. The postal-regulatory structure is a dual-track model, now following the New Zealand example. In the first instance, postal ownership and regulation are clearly separated from postal operation. Then, ownership and regulation are separated, with oversight provided by DOFA and DCITA respectively. There is no independent third-party regulation. Both DOFA and DCITA set precise, quantified, and public targets and expectations for AP. The Service Charter is a public declaration of AP's CSOs, against which its performance is tracked and evaluated in the annual report. The CSOs are set in statutes and their basic elements are non-negotiable. The corporate plan outlines the shareholder's financial and performance expectations, which are laid out in the following year's report and against which that year's performance is evaluated. Two other dimensions of this accountability regime are worth noting. First, the targets and expectations are quantified, which clarifies the shareholder's expectation for AP and makes evaluation a straightforward task. Second, the shareholder's targets and expectations are made public, even if they lag behind by a year. The financial targets emerge from a corporate-planning process that is not public, for obvious commercial and competitive reasons. Moreover, this process allows AP and the shareholder – as well as the two shareholder departments – to work out any disagreements that they might have.

On the operations side, the guiding GBE principle was to allow the postal managers to get on with their job of running and operating the postal corporation. The GBE principles and other legislation, including the APC Act, signalled this policy intention clearly. The primary policy implication was the development of strong, effective, and committed boards of directors. The board has exercised its authority fully and attempted to protect and increase AP's autonomy from the government while maximizing AP's growth. On the most general level, the shareholder and AP have seen eye-to-eye, which has allowed the corporatization and commercialization process to unfold without many political inhibitions. The shareholder made it clear that it did not want AP to diversify much beyond its postal core, and this has been a source of tension in government-Post relations. But it has not inhibited AP from, for example, developing a complex, varied, and profitable retail network. The shareholder granted AP a high degree of autonomy at the start of the process, and this autonomy has been validated and expanded as a result of AP's financial and operational success – which has neutralized any impulse for political intervention. Indeed, until recently, the operating hypothesis seemed to have been that granting autonomy would guarantee operational success. Thus we have the light regulatory touch that is a particular characteristic of the Australian postal regime. There appears to be some evidence, though, that the Howard government aims to increase its presence in postal deliberations.

This light regulatory touch has been complemented by a regulatory discipline of a different sort: increased competition. Indeed, the creation of the Australian postal regime created a momentum for liberalization that took on increasing steam in the late 1990s. It should be noted that deregulation or liberalization was also a new, overarching theme placed on the policy agenda by the government, emanating from the micro-economic and competitiveness agenda. Deregulation has unfolded in a balanced and extended way in Australia, for the reasons noted above (rural, labour, and political). And it is highly likely that the Australian postal market will be deregulated further, when political circumstances are more propitious. What will be interesting to see is whether AP will receive a quid pro quo for supporting greater deregulation. At the moment, it retains a small reserved area to finance the csos. If the government decides to eliminate the reserved area, it may have to offer a direct subsidy to AP in its place. On the other hand, AP could conceivably ask the government for less regulatory inhibition on diversification and commercialization into wider markets – arguing that it would use the increased income to finance the csos on its own. This is a central issue that has been resolved in the market model, which provides the trade-off. The character of the Australian regime in the future will be determined to a great extent by how policy makers determine this issue.

There has been a limited amount of competition to this point, which is not surprising given AP's historical role and competitive advantages (good service, low price). Additional proposals to extend and regulate bulk-mailing deals and access to AP's network would likely generate more competition and keep AP on its competitive toes. Similarly, product competition (for example, e-mail) as well as international postal competition will likely increase, and this will accelerate the already declining letters market. Increased competition could potentially be a threat to AP's bottom line and its annual productivity gains.

The Australian postal regime is a pragmatic, well-designed, and effective system which has encouraged the development of an effective and successful AP in an increasingly competitive postal market. The character of the system has not been established completely. The basic and evolving market-orientation of the system remains limited or inhibited by ongoing political considerations, which maintain a protected area and some limits on AP's corporate autonomy. The operation of the Australian regime will be tested in the decision to liberalize and corporatize totally or not to do so. If the latter option is pursued, then the regime will continue to be affected by both market and political considerations. If the regime is fully liberalized, then the Australian system will face another test. If full competition lowers AP's rate of return – which it will likely do – this may undercut AP's capacity to maintain its csos and to provide ongoing benefits to each of the stakeholders – customers, workers, shareholder. This in turn will force choices and place a strain on Australia's dual-shareholder model and its industrial relations.

Conclusion

This book has tracked the changes in postal-regulatory and governance structures and processes against the backdrop of the three trends and conditions that have dramatically affected the postal sector – technological change, internationalization, and neoconservatism. The execution of the study has been based on the premise that the postal world will retain considerable economic and social importance in the future. Thus, the postal sector will remain – or should remain – a matter of policy interest for governments.

This book has examined the unfolding postal world from the perspective of the policy makers who devise public policy for the postal sector. Governments confront a postal world that is not of their own making. There is little to nothing that they can do about the realities of technological change and internationalization. As a result, all governments have found themselves experiencing the same pressures and reacting in similar ways to these relentless pressures. As shareholders of the Posts, though, they retain genuine power and authority and have real opportunities to shape the postal experiences in their countries to politically determined objectives. Indeed, as this study has illustrated, the pattern of postal policy has not been consistent from country to country, which has reflected differences in decisions made by governments. Governments establish particular institutional and governance arrangements for their postal sectors, and these arrangements launch postal-policy processes and activities of different sorts. We have identified four different patterns or models of public postal activity that have emerged as a result of political decisions in the countries that were examined in this study. These models have emerged from the intersection of two forces: a universal trend to policy convergence around shared experiences, and particular political decisions and choices that reflect different national experiences, pressures, and institutions. These models in turn have shaped the broad contours of postal activities and results, which have varied from country to country.

The models themselves reflect national values, history, institutions, and past policy choices, which comprise the nations' political inheritance. There is no "right" or "wrong" postal policy in either a normative or a comparative sense – although, in a technical sense, some policies are more efficient or have more positive economic results than others do. The model that any nation embraces reflects the choices made by its government, and these choices in turn reflect broad issues like the national economy's place in the world economy, domestic political pressures and expectations, the ambitions and skills of their postal management, and so on. For policy makers and observers, however, it is important to recognize how the decisions that governments make are consequential. Particular decisions "aggregate" into a particular paradigm or model, which has enormous implications with respect to policy opportunities and constraints.

This chapter will be organized in three parts. First, it will present a number of overview observations about the experiences of the progressive postal regimes over the last decade. Second, it will offer some specific policy recommendations with respect to reforming the Canadian postal regime. Third, it will conclude by considering the postal future from the perspective of a fifth postal model which is evolving in the international context of postal development.[1]

POSTAL-POLICY CONVERGENCE

This study has been framed by two political frameworks that reflect the broad contexts in which postal policy is made. First, postal policy is made within a political-economic context that has seen the accelerating impact of technological change and globalization. From the perspective of postal-policy makers, the challenge has been how to shape, direct, or transform the domestic postal sector in the context of these external pressures. As a preliminary generalization, the most effective postal regimes are those that are most sensitive and alive to international and technological changes and move nimbly to make creative policy adjustments to these changes. Second, while postal-policy makers confront similar political economic pressures, they do so in particular domestic contexts. Their policy choices reflect domestic political pressures as well as their own interests and ambitions. For good or bad, politics matters – and it matters tremendously. The intense and deep domestic postal expectations in the United Kingdom, the strong public-service tradition and suspicion of the market in France, the sensitivity to rural or employment issues in Canada, the parliamentary tradition in unitary New Zealand versus the more consensual approaches of federal Australia – these and other political matters create constraints on and opportunities for the way in which policy makers adjust to or even conceptualize the technological and international changes that are taking place in the postal world. The interaction of internal domestic expectations and external pressures has produced four broad patterns of decisions, or the models that we have examined.

Yet there are a number of policy tendencies or themes that can be identified across the national experiences. These common tendencies suggest that a kind of policy convergence is emerging around a number of approaches, attitudes, or tactics within the different strategic models. These tactics or themes represent a kind of *policy reality* or *best practice* around postal policy in the twenty-first century. There are five interrelated issues worth noting here: corporatization, liberalization, deregulation, re-regulation, and internationalization.

Corporatization

In an operational sense, the most successful Posts are the ones that are able to distance themselves from governments as far as possible, within their particular domestic circumstances. This is achieved in a number of ways, but there are two issues of particular importance if postal corporatization is to take place in a genuine or authentic fashion. First, effective Posts are granted a high degree of corporate autonomy from the government. This autonomy can be established in a number of ways. The legal framework for the Posts should be little different from that of any private corporation. The political framework for the Post should specify the boundary between postal and political autonomy and authority, and specify as concretely and specifically as possible those areas where political authority persists. One of the most important dimensions of this autonomy is the government's willingness to create a strong and assertive Board of Directors. The most successful Posts are those whose boards are made up of top people from the business, public, and international worlds. However, these sorts of people can be recruited to the board only to the extent that the assignment looks interesting and satisfying to them – that is, if the board has real autonomy and authority to act. Once established, a strong and assertive board will carve out an ambitious agenda for its Post to pursue, and then a strong and experienced postal management will be required to execute this agenda. Good managers will be attracted to the Post only if they sense that they will have the opportunity to pursue an interesting and ambitious agenda. A strong board and strong management ensure the construction of a postal agenda and course of action that has integrity and makes corporate sense, within the boundaries of whatever public policy framework may be established.

A second critical factor in corporatization must see the government ground this commitment to corporate autonomy by constructing a financial- and corporate-accountability regime that requires corporate performance to a market standard – including corporate sufficient levels of profitability. Owners and management have a shared interest in this requirement. For the shareholder, profitability is an important test that the Post is using its capital investment and opportunities to good and proper effect, to maximize shareholder value over the long term. For management and the board, a profitability target demonstrates that the government expects the Post to act like a corporation.

Liberalization

There is a relentless trend internationally to the limitation, if not elimination, of any exclusive privilege or reserved postal area. International competition, technological advances, new communications products and innovations, and changing customer demands and habits are weakening and trivializing the remaining monopoly elements in the postal sector. A number of countries have already eliminated their exclusive privilege (Sweden, Finland, New Zealand), many others are lowering their level of protection (Australia, the Netherlands, likely the United Kingdom), and the European Commission is working to reduce the exclusive privilege to 150 grams.

Over and above these tendencies, formal liberalization of the postal market is important from a postal-policy perspective for two reasons. First, it represents a commitment by both the shareholder and management to be more sensitive to price, market, and customer issues. This projects well to the market, expressing the position that customers are central to the postal enterprise. Liberalization contributes to the efficient use of resources and to the creation of price and market sensitivity, which helps the Post to remain competitive. Second, liberalization of the postal market mitigates if not neutralizes the charge that the Post has unfair competitive advantages in the market. Countries have long struggled with this issue. How much of a restricted area is required to defray the costs of maintaining the universal service? A commitment to postal liberalization will require that that issue is articulated and scrutinized properly, as a matter of public policy. This process will raise the principle or criterion of proportionality, which tests precisely how much protection is needed to finance a particular type of universal service. This test also requires precise quantification of the costs of universal service, by way of establishing the proper proportionality between the universal service and any exclusive privilege. In some countries, the cost of the universal-service obligation has been found to be far less than had been previously assumed. Moreover, the historical position of the Post in a particular domestic market may be sufficient to generate the revenues needed to defray the universal-service costs. Regardless of the particular domestic circumstance, the important issue is the commitment to extend liberalization as far as possible. This should be done according to some public schedule.

Deregulation

Deregulation complements the trend to liberalization. Posts around the world are diversifying their products and services to a remarkable extent. The more ambitious Posts are transforming themselves into broad-based communications organizations in which mail and the letter play but a minor part. Posts are using their networks to provide new products and services. Many successful Posts have been given increased commercial freedom to diversify and maximize their opportunities for growth. The more mercantile Posts have been purchasing companies in many countries and building partnerships across sectors and regions around the world. This deregulation thrust complements liberalization and corporatization in a number of ways. First, the traditional concern that new areas of activity would be subsidized by the exclusive privilege can be neutralized to the extent that the exclusive privilege is eliminated. If the Post is simply another economic actor in the postal market, why should it not be allowed to act like its private competitors? Second, deregulation and diversification assuage concerns that the loss of monopoly revenue will weaken the Post's capacity to maintain the universal system. To the extent that the Post successfully levers its networks, it can generate new sources of revenue to be used to maintain the universal system. Third, deregulation is a natural extension of corporatization. Strong boards and experienced management will naturally seek to set an ambitious market agenda that will include diversification. The government's commitment to deregulation is another test that will attract good people to the board, who will in turn ensure that diversification is not executed in a cavalier manner.

Re-regulation

Corporatization, liberalization, and deregulation have accentuated the need for a kind of re-regulation of the Posts. There is an international trend to use third-party regulation, albeit of a certain sort (for example, Britain, Scandinavia, the Netherlands, Germany). This trend has tracked and responded to the corporatization, deregulation, and liberalization effects noted above. Such regulation also reflects the sharpening legal and policy distinction between regulation and ownership of the Posts. This has seen the elaboration of these two public functions, via their location in different spots within the government apparatus.

Re-regulation has been required for a number of reasons. First, the financial or corporate performance of the Post has to be tracked by the government in some way once the public corporation is given increased autonomy. A number of postal regimes have developed public or contract-type arrangements, in which an array of corporate performance goals is set publicly. The boards are then held accountable for the attainment of these goals. To the extent that commercial autonomy is allowed and encouraged, these public targets act as a check on corporate indulgence. Second, re-regulation is required to ensure and make effective the public-service dimensions of the public Post. Re-regulation addresses public concerns about the maintenance of the universal service, in the face of the government's heightened corporate and financial expectations. There is an international trend to creating public contracts or documents that set out and quantify performance and service standards for the universal system. The Post is then evaluated by the regulator against these performance expectations.

These new regulatory regimes have increased postal accountability to the public. One part of the government – the shareholder department such as a Department of Finance or Treasury Board – sets corporate performance standards, which are jointly negotiated and set with the Board. Another department of government – such as a Department of Communications or Transportation – sets service performance standards and expectations, which are agreed to by the board. Both agreements are set out and articulated in public documents. Financial and service performance goals can stand in conflict with each other. It is the responsibility of the two departments of government to sort out the relationship between longer-term financial goals and more immediate service objectives before laying them out in contractual arrangements with the Post. Finally, a hands-off, third-party regulator is often established to "apply" the service standards or document against the actual performance of the Post. Generally speaking, this regulation has been of a light-handed sort, involving primarily a passive application of service- and corporate-performance contracts to the activities of the Posts. Indeed, a common refrain from officials in the most successful postal regimes suggests that the secret to regulatory success is to keep the process simple, sensible, pragmatic, and light-handed.

Internationalization

Successful Posts have developed within postal regimes that are highly sensitive to developments on the international stage. This has played out in two ways. First, domestic postal-policy discussion and development has been framed by a wider international framework of analysis and policy that are in turn informed by issues such as comparative advantage, contributions to national productivity and efficiency, and international trade. An internationalized framework has bolstered the liberalization and deregulation themes, underpinning as well the need for strong corporatization and boards with international experience. Second, customer demand and globalization have expanded the international horizons of Posts. The most successful ones have been given the green light by their shareholders to think and expand internationally, within some sort of corporate-autonomy framework. This has been implemented through partnership arrangements with public and private corporations abroad or by the purchase of private companies to help their international strategies.

These five tendencies or themes frame the basic requirements of effective postal policy in the twenty-first century. In some ways, they are independent of the particular model that is chosen politically for the postal sector. Each model assigns different relative emphasis to each of these elements, which determines the character of each of the models. For example, liberalization features centrally in the market model, but this model need not accentuate deregulation and diversification (for example, neither is a strong feature of the Finnish or New Zealand experience). Diversification has been an important feature of the growth strategies of the countries in the mercantile model, neither of which liberalized terribly quickly. International strategic purchases are a key feature of the mercantile model but less important in the market and national models.

There are three compelling questions that remain unanswered, notwithstanding this trend to policy convergence. How these issues are resolved will be the primary determinant of policy tendencies in the future. First, to the extent that countries limit or eliminate their protected areas, corporatize their increasingly diversified operations, and initiate a regulatory performance formula, what will compel governments to retain their ownership of their Posts? Second, policy makers in different countries will become increasingly aware of and concerned about postal policy in other countries. As we will discuss in the concluding section, postal liberalization and deregulation have generated increased internationalization of the postal sector. National Posts come into contact with each other with increasing frequency and with greater consequence. How will governments make policy adjustments or take important policy decisions in this new environment? Lastly, this discussion rests on the premise that Posts will continue to generate sufficient revenue from postal and other activities to maintain the universal service. How will governments react if their Posts do not attain their corporate-performance targets, as a result of the decline in postal volumes? What will governments do if Posts miss or lower their service targets in order to meet their financial targets?

THE CANADIAN EXPERIENCE AND POLICY RECOMMENDATIONS

In a concluding section in my earlier study on Canada Post (1994), I wrote that the "postal experience since 1981 has demonstrated that a Crown corporation can embrace commercial values and behave like a private sector corporation ... What remains unclear ... is whether a balance can be struck between the postal Crown's commercial values and broader public or social goals."[2] This present study has demonstrated that a number of countries have established balanced postal regimes which maintain quality universal postal service within a competitive, liberalized, and commercialized postal market. There is no good reason why Canada cannot do the same.

The commercialization and corporatization of the Canadian postal system from 1986 to 1993 was a one-sided process and accomplishment. The Conservative government directed Canada Post to corporatize and commercialize its operation, and CPC carried out this mission to real effect. But two important ingredients were missing in this experience. First, the experience was an act of political will, imposed from the top. It did not emerge from institutional or governance process that guided or formalized the experience. Rather, it was basically an ad hoc initiative. And it did not establish a framework or guidelines to maintain and guide this experience in the future. Once the Conservatives were voted out of office, there was – in effect – no postal governance environment or process to fall back on that would oversee the functioning of a commercialized, corporatized Post. There was simply political will. The failed experiment with third-party regulation in the early 1990s left a lacuna in postal governance. The Conservatives themselves were aware of the dilemma of how to regulate a commercialized Post without inhibiting it. But they did not know what to do. They were ideologically predisposed to privatization, but they did not push this option for a combination of political and emotional reasons at the time. The bottom line was that they did not develop a formula or framework for overseeing a commercialized public Post.

Second, the Conservative postal experience between 1986 and 1993 emphasized commercial objectives to the considerable exclusion of social ones. The government proceeded as if the former could be attained only to the diminution or neglect of the latter. CPC's commercial and financial performance improved, to be sure. But this state of affairs could not endure for long, since a backlash from the public as well as from CPC's competitors was inevitable. Indeed, upon the Liberals' return to office, the "public" dimension was injected back into the postal regime. Thus began an extended period of policy uncertainty. Would the commercialized Post be maintained or would there be a return to the pre-1986 era? If the latter, how would commercial and social values be balanced or traded off? And what of CPC's relationship to its competitors? The Mandate Review was initiated in this uncertain context, in order to determine the future of the postal sector. But the review process and its political aftermath were policy fiascos, and the Canadian postal regime continued to be in a confused state.

The government's recent postal-policy thinking has been muddled as policy leaders struggle to decide what precisely to do about the Post. This struggle resulted in the 1999 Framework Agreement, which is a tentative, incomplete, and insubstantial document. At its heart, it implicitly poses an antagonistic relationship between commercial and public objectives. It pitches financial objectives at a deliberately modest level by way of allowing the Post the financial space to pursue a number of non-commercial public activities, which are determined by the government. This presents a confused postal environment, and its mixed policy messages have resulted in lethargic postal performance. Here is another example – albeit a negative one – of how the regulatory framework affects postal outcomes.

Against the backdrop of postal experiences from Finland to New Zealand, Canada's postal-policy approach appears to be irrational and uneconomic. In the first instance, many countries have managed to create a competitive postal environment and set and attain ambitious financial and performance targets for their Posts while still maintaining the character and accomplishments of their universal system. Indeed, clear-headed postal thinking suggests that the universal postal system will be maintained only to the extent that the Post performs at a high performance level. This will provide it with the financial capacity to maintain and adapt the universal system in a changing and uncertain communications environment. Protecting the Post, or limiting its ambitions, is a recipe for lowering its long-term capacity to maintain the universal system. Moreover, political subsidies to the Post for these ends are unpopular and not viable politically. Second, the relationship between social and commercial goals in Canada has played out as an either/or scenario. This zero-sum political game has led governments to deal with the issue behind the scenes, as a non-debatable subject. Governments fear the political controversy and embarrassment of choosing one approach over the other. Successful Posts around the world have not "resolved" this question, which will always be a difficult one. Rather, their governments have worked with their Posts to articulate social and commercial expectations and targets and to set them out in writing in a public way. Then, they have let their Posts go out and try to attain them. The extent to which their Posts have met these objectives and expectations is evaluated before a new or renewed set of targets is constructed.

Recent Canadian policy makers appear to have backed into the national model, albeit without a great deal of public discussion or debate. The resulting governance or regulatory system in Canada is, as we saw earlier, a sloppy and confusing one. Moreover, it is one in which there is not a great deal of public accountability. This eclectic arrangement reflects an ongoing Canadian political predilection for trying to make policy that is all things to all people. The unintentional result of this approach is that Canada is stuck in what might be termed the small or traditional political world. This is one in which postal issues are discussed conceptually as they were in the 1970s and 1980s. Such a world may be politically satisfying to some policy makers and government officials. And it may provide sufficient satisfaction for boards and management of a certain sort. However, the approach is guaranteed to produce a small, parochial, financially declining postal world. It will be difficult for the Canadian postal regime to survive over the long term, save as a postal deliverer of last resort in an increasingly subsidized delivery system. Canadian policy makers have to decide whether they want Canada to join the larger postal world, as exemplified by many of the countries that we have examined in this study. What follows is a series of policy reflections and ten recommendations for the Canadian postal regime in the twenty-first century.

Recommendation One: Highlight the Postal Sector

In the first instance, the postal sector should be taken out of the political shadows and placed in the policy spotlight. The government – on behalf of the Canadian people – owns an expensive and important asset. Yet this asset is treated and managed as a policy afterthought. The traditional political defensiveness about the Post should be shaken off and its policy importance should be asserted firmly and regularly. There is no need for the government to be defensive about the Post or to be overly cautious or anxious about its future. Notwithstanding international and technological changes, there is no evidence in any serious postal regime of a government abandoning this sector or planning to do so. There are isolated cases of postal privatization. But these have taken place in one of two contexts. First, where the postal system is archaic and underdeveloped, it may make sense to privatize in order to attract the capital and technology to develop a non-existent system. Second, if a country determines that its postal system can become a world leader, it may make sense to privatize the Post. This will attract capital and talent, intensify its performance capacity and results, and simplify the Post's ability to make its way in the wider world. The Canadian postal system fits neither of these situations. Canada Post could use an injection of new capital and talent, but it basically provides a well-developed system. On the other hand, the Canadian postal regime is light years away from being a world powerhouse or leader (like DPWN or TPG) in a mercantile strategy. This strategy would not fit with political-cultural traditions or market realities.

The remarkable popularity of the universal postal system in Canada – and around the world – demonstrates its ongoing importance and policy attraction. Notwithstanding changes in technology and competitive alternatives, the postal system remains well used, offers many comparative advantages, and enjoys a high degree of recognition and trust. How people use it now, and how they will use it in the future, is changing. The Post will have to work to adapt to changing demands and expectations. But it is absolutely clear that business – big and small – as well as organizations, groups, citizens, consumers, and so on want to maintain a universal postal system.

Recommendation Two: Conceptualize the Postal Sector within a Broader Economic Framework

In maintaining and promoting its postal asset, the government must decide how it wants to conceptualize or frame the Post's existence. This is necessary to ensure consistent and appropriate postal policies and to create an appropriate regulatory and governance process and environment. There are three broad options: a market approach, a mercantile approach, and a national approach. As illustrated earlier, the Canadian government has adopted the last approach, although it has done so in an implicit and understated way. Its actions suggest that it wants to eat its postal cake and have it too. That is, it wants to reinject political and public objectives into the postal process while leaving the Conservatives' market-oriented achievements in place. It will be difficult if not impossible to sustain this approach over the long term, for it assumes that the former will have no impact on the latter. Moreover, the government has not provided a regulatory or governance framework that is appropriate to this mix of expectations. The government has simply allowed the mixed policy scenario to play itself out.

The government seems to have placed the cart before the horse. There is no questioning its authority to "use" the Post as it sees fit; after all, it is the shareholder. If it wants the Post, first and foremost, to serve national and public goals, then it can make this decision and be held accountable for its results at election time. However, given the nature of the postal environment, the government's current approach is shortsighted and is being executed in a clumsy and unaccountable fashion. On the one hand, the Post's capacity to serve national and public goals will be a function of its financial and performance capacity. This hard reality should be elevated to the top of postal-policy considerations – before any talk or discussion of the use of this capacity for public goals. On the other hand, if the shareholder – acting on behalf of the Canadian people who are the real owners of the Post – is going to use the Post for alternative public purposes and ends, it should do so in a way that is democratically clear and accountable.

This discussion has two consequences, both of which will be elaborated in subsequent recommendations. First, the postal-policy discourse and context should be widened to connect with government thinking on international trade, comparative advantage, national productivity and efficiency, and so on. The postal sector makes an integral infrastructural and service contribution to Canadian economic performance in the broadest sense – not just with regard to specific political objectives like rural development or being a national presence in the community. The Post's future capacity and performance should be discussed and pursued in no different terms and process than any similar sector in the transportation and communications markets. The Post's capacity will develop positively only to the extent that it is scrutinized, tested, managed, treated, and pushed to these high standards and expectations. Second, the Post requires a different institutional and regulatory environment for two important reasons. First, it must be motivated and evaluated within this broader economic context. Second, if its capacity is to be used for broader public and national ends, then the shareholder's representative – the government – must be held accountable for using the Post in this manner. If a national approach is to frame postal policy, then the postal regime requires a far higher degree of public input and evaluation, and a far greater discussion of the relationship between maximizing postal performance and delivering public policy goals.

*Recommendation Three: Strengthen the Postal Board
and Clarify the Autonomy of the Post*

These considerations have a number of governance and institutional implications. The first is the need to reconsider how the board of Canada Post fits into and operates in the Canadian postal regime. This book has demonstrated how postal boards in most progressive postal regimes are comprised of accomplished and experienced corporate, institutional, and international leaders of considerable experience. The boards of the Posts in Australia, New Zealand, the Netherlands, and Germany are particularly noteworthy in this regard. Many countries, such as the Netherlands, specify the characteristics and experiences required for appointment to the postal board, emphasizing international qualifications. Other countries – such as New Zealand – select their board members in a formal and politically detached manner, to ensure excellent appointments that are appropriate to the board's needs at any particular time. These boards have then pursued an assertive and ambitious corporate agenda, insisted on corporate autonomy and postal growth, and attracted high-quality executives and managers. This was especially apparent in New Zealand and Australia, where the Posts have had lively and effective battles with their governments whereby they asserted their corporate autonomy. This has not been the tradition or experience in Canada. Appointments to the CPC board have been political ones, directed to regional and party-political considerations and balance. Board members have not been selected via criteria that reflect the Post's needs as a corporation in a changing technological and international environment. The composition and character of the board changes along with electoral results. The upshot of this has been that the board of Canada Post has not played as substantial, leading, effective, or positive a role as the boards in other countries. It has not added much value to the Post, because it has not brought corporate, international, and technological experiences to CPC's strategic thinking. It has not asserted a corporate or postal agenda with as much thrust or effect as in other countries. It has not insisted on corporate autonomy and postal growth, and it has had difficulty attracting quality management at the highest levels.

The activities of the Post should be considered within a wider economic context, and the economic expectations of the Post should be pitched at a higher level than at present. In order to attain these objectives, CPC needs a more substantial board to work with the government and management to set a modern corporate and postal strategy for the changed international and technological context. In ideal circumstances, primary responsibility for appointments to *all*

418 The Politics of Postal Transformation

commercial crown corporations should be assigned to a unit of government with broad oversight responsibilities for the state's assets – something akin to the CCMAU in New Zealand. This unit would make appointment recommendations to the responsible minister, after reviewing the board's particular needs and the availability of potential appointees. Second, the minister and the board should draw up a list of objective qualifications for potential board members, as well as a list of areas of expertise that should be covered by the board, as is done in the Netherlands. If the government desires to continue having regional or other political "representation," it should pursue this objective outside of the board environment. It should consider adopting a users' watchdog like the United Kingdom's Postwatch.

There is further compelling reason for ensuring that there are strong boards with strong management. This study has suggested that governments and postal management have switched roles or positions with regard to maintaining and accelerating the postal-reform process. At its start, governments pushed a reform agenda onto an often-reluctant postal management. Governments were animated by their experience of rising deficits and the pressures that they felt from business and customers for improved postal service. To the extent that the Posts have successfully pursued this agenda, and have attracted strong management and boards, it is they who now push an aggressive postal agenda or should. Governments have become increasingly reticent to follow an ambitious path. For them, the postal situation has improved and, as the neoconservative era winds down, postal-policy change looks dangerously consequential for politically sensitive issues like jobs and service. The postal agenda in successful regimes will be pushed increasingly by postal management and boards, who have an inherent interest in and responsibility for postal development and growth. That is why it is important to have a lively, committed board and ambitious management, without which the postal-reform process will stagnate or regress. That said, this study has also demonstrated that the postal-policy process and agenda evolves positively to the extent that the government and the Post see eye-to-eye.

In order to ensure that competent people are attracted to the board, the government should review the CPC Act and the FAA and issue a statement or policy guideline clarifying the responsibilities and authority of the boards of commercial crown corporations in particular and that of CPC in particular. This statement should clarify the legal responsibilities of the board, champion and reassert its autonomy, and delineate the extent and limit of its authority. As noted in the country discussions in earlier chapters, successful Post operations have tended to be led by strong and assertive boards, which are loyal to the Posts and which aggressively promote and defend the Posts' interests.

Recommendation Four: Liberalize and Deregulate

There are many reasons to recommend liberalization and deregulation. In the first instance, in order to attract strong board members (and management), the government should clarify the prospects in Canada for future liberalization and deregulation. Strong board members and sharp managers are not especially keen to be working for a corporation that is "protected" by the exclusive privilege or otherwise seen to be a government agency or monopoly. They want to work for aggressive, assertive firms with opportunities for growth, development, and high performance. They understand as well that, if the shareholder insists on the pursuit of non-postal or political goals, then there has to be some sort of quid pro quo for the corporation – whether in the form of some exclusive privilege, subsidy, or formula.

We recommend that the government assert the principle that the Canadian postal market will be liberalized in a sequence of planned steps over time, with the ultimate objective of eliminating the exclusive privilege altogether. Any remaining exclusive privilege should be justified and demonstrated through precise quantitative studies of the non-economic cost of maintaining the universal service in specific areas. This, of course, raises the question of the standards or objectives of the universal service, an issue that will be addressed below. A further commitment to liberalization will demonstrate the government's seriousness of purpose, that it desires that the Post increase its competitive and operational capacity to perform in the wider technological and international markets. This progressive liberalization is a process that is unfolding inexorably around the world, for multiple policy objectives. Generally speaking, a liberalized postal environment raises postal standards, expectations, and performance, and it will attract board members and managers who prefer to work in this kind of environment.

A government commitment to deregulation should complement the government plan to liberalize the postal market. This policy initiative has been a kind of quid pro quo in postal regimes around the world. Liberalization forces Posts to improve their capacity, productivity, and efficiency. However, in a competitive market environment, even the most efficient Post may lose market share – particularly as the market changes. The Post requires a level of financial capacity to maintain the universal system. To the extent that liberalization weakens financial performance and/or changing conditions increases the costs of the universal service, the government should allow the Post to seek alternative sources of revenue and growth. There is no general reason why this commitment should be limited. There could be a limit placed on the size of any investment or limits on the involvement of the Post in an area of the economy that is totally non-complementary to its core activities. Generally speaking, though, if the government wants the Post to act like an efficient corporation, then the Post should be given the autonomy to participate fully in the economy and to develop as any private corporation would do in similar circumstances.

Increased postal autonomy touches on two traditional issues. The first is the question of how to "compensate" the Post for pursuing public-policy objectives that may not be economic. The country studies presented here have demonstrated that the idea of offering direct subsidies to the Post to carry out these tasks is not a popular one. It has been rejected deliberately in many countries, such as Australia and Sweden. Generally speaking, countries that have not been able to liberalize their markets completely have opted for the maintenance of some level of exclusive privilege that is quantitatively proportional to the costs of the non-economic tasks. Countries that have liberalized completely have often demonstrated that the Post's historically dominant position in the market provides it with advantages sufficient to carry out the public-policy objectives. If this is not the case, then the emphasis has been on creating an autonomous Post that can commercialize and diversify in an uninhibited way, in order to generate the necessary revenues. Traditionally, postal competitors have expressed concern that the Post will use its earnings from the monopoly sector to cross-subsidize and gain a competitive advantage in the non-postal sectors. This concern should be assuaged, if not dispelled, by the elimination of the exclusive privilege or restricted area. If any restricted area is retained, then the quantitative studies alluded to above become an even more important element of this approach. That is, the Post will then be obliged to demonstrate that there is a financial firewall between its activities in the market environment and those in its protected areas. As a general proposition, this will require the Post to become more quantitatively precise about the costs and revenues associated with its activities. Indeed, as this study has illustrated, quantification of postal issues and activities has led to improved postal discussions and policy. This has particularly been the case in Australia, where the studies by the Industry Commission and the NCC have framed policy discussions in a precise and effective way. The quantification of postal targets and objectives is also an important development. By setting accessible and comprehensible criteria for evaluation, this process will increase the degree of postal knowledge and intelligence within the postal regime.

In short, the government should declare as a matter of policy principle that it is committed to the maximization of postal liberalization and postal autonomy. This will have the double effect of projecting a seriousness of purpose to potential board members and managers while creating a working environment for the development of postal competitiveness, efficiency, and growth. The government can point to the experiences of Australia, New Zealand, Finland, and Sweden as examples of liberalized postal regimes performing to high standards of financial and service performance. The anticipation of liberalization was quite effective in forcing their Posts to prepare for it, such that their adaptation to a more liberalized and eventually open market was not as difficult as had been feared.

Recommendation Five: Separate Ownership from Regulation

One of the clearest developments in the modern postal world is the formal separation of postal ownership from postal regulation. For example, we will see in the concluding section that the EC postal directive insisted that member countries separate these two functions in a formal way. The principle informing this rule is both simple and compelling. The owners of the Post are in a conflict-of-interest position if the same people, departments, or sectors regulate the Post's activities and determine the Post's level of financial performance. The conflict is clear: to the extent that the Post is directed to increase its service performance or exist in a more competitive market, this regulatory decision can negatively affect the Post's financial performance. Conversely, the state can insist on a higher level of financial performance, requiring a diminution of the universal service. As long as the Posts remain owned by the state, governments will be in this potential public-policy conflict of interest, between its objectives as a shareholder and its responsibilities as a regulator of the Post's performance to public ends.

States have separated the ownership from the regulation function in one of two ways. First, countries like New Zealand and Australia have followed a twin-ministerial model, in which one department of government is assigned regulatory responsibilities and a different one is assigned shareholder responsibilities. Each of the departments pursues its responsibilities in the various policy processes associated with the setting of the corporate plan and the creation of service and performance documents. A second approach sees the ownership and regulatory functions housed within different sectors of the same department (for example, Sweden, Finland, Germany, and the Netherlands), with an independent third-party regulator assigned the task of overseeing the state's regulatory responsibilities. This is the model that the United Kingdom is in the process of adopting. The regulatory body typically reports to one division of the ministry that has responsibilities for monitoring the application of postal legislation and regulation. The degree of independence exercised by the regulators reflects the regulatory traditions in individual countries. In both models, the respective responsibilities are spelled out in legislation or regulatory directives, as are the criteria of evaluation.

The separation of ownership and regulation is a bit muddied in the Canadian case, for a number of reasons. First, the principle is not spelled out clearly so that the two functions tend to overlap or merge into each other in policy discussions. Second, the Post has been assigned to different departments over time and its ownership and regulatory relationship tends to be with a minister rather than with permanent units of government. Third, the regulatory process in the Canadian postal regime has been relatively thin, insubstantial, and hidden from public view. Fourth, the normal shareholding functions and responsibilities have been fragmented and exercised through a kind of gauntlet process – from board, to minister, to Treasury Board, to cabinet – and the lines of responsibility and accountability have not been clear. This has been exacerbated by the absence of a permanent postal "bureaucracy" or support, which has developed under ministerial prodding in a kind of ad hoc way.

We recommend that this situation be reconsidered and simplified. There are a number of simple options. For other reasons to be discussed below, responsibility for the Post should be removed from Public Works and Government Services Canada. The Post should be assigned to a department that has a wider economic outlook and that has economic responsibilities more than service ones. This department would have regulatory responsibility for the Post. Shareholding responsibility should be assigned directly to Treasury Board and the Department of Finance. Shareholding and regulatory responsibilities should unfold and be discussed in two different processes, intersecting in the discussions regarding the corporate and other plans and in cabinet. This will ensure that the different dimensions of the postal world are articulated thoroughly and in a balanced and fair manner.

Recommendation Six: Reassign the Post to
an Economics Department

Following the discussion of the separation of ownership from regulation, the Post should be assigned to a separate department with a wider economic orientation. The Post's location within the government's apparatus determines to a great extent the government's attitude towards to the Post. The Canadian tradition has been to assign CPC to a service-oriented department – such as Consumer and Corporate Affairs or PWGSC. With no disrespect to these organizations, their orientation is simply not in line with the new realities of the technologically changing, globalized postal world. Indeed, there is no evidence that the government has considered the manner in which the Post can contribute to the national infrastructure or its comparative advantage, as has been the case, for example, in New Zealand and Australia.[3] Embedded within the concerns of a service department, CPC is conceptualized very much like the old Post Office, with a tendency to serve the government's interests rather than broader economic interests. No national Post examined in this study has been assigned to a service department. Typically, they are assigned to a department such Industry, Commerce, Communications, Economics, or Transportation. These departments have different policy sensibilities, responsibilities, and experiences. They are geared towards broader issues of economic development, communications in the modern economy, and the contribution of state infrastructure to a nation's productivity and efficiency.

The shareholder should be interested in how the Post fits into the modern worlds of communications, transportation, and technology. It should understand how the Post supports business. It should be thinking about the likelihood that postal services will be part of the next round of international trade talks. For these and other reasons, the government should assign responsibility for CPC to a department or unit of government that is thinking about and making policy in areas dealing with the modernization of the economy and its adaptation to globalization. Once within such a department, the Post would have a stronger champion for the development of postal policies to strengthen its capacity to compete and perform in the new economy. This department would, over time, build up a useful degree of postal understanding and intelligence. And this in turn would combine with a stronger CPC board to develop a more inspiring and rational policy framework for the Post. Another option would be for the government to group its commercial crown corporations together in one ministry, as has been done in a number of countries with a Ministry for State Enterprises. In either case, this department would have the responsibility for establishing, articulating, and defending the postal-regulatory framework. This will be discussed more fully below. The regulatory framework would focus on service standards, competition, and other non-financial objectives. Financial objectives would be the responsibility of a separate shareholding department of government, whose responsibilities would be to maintain and expand shareholder value.

Recommendation Seven: Prepare More Elaborate Contracts
between the Government and the Post

This study has demonstrated another clear pattern of postal-policy development: the construction of open "contracts" or "agreements" between Posts and their governments. These agreements set quantitative and qualitative targets or expectations agreed to by both the Post and the government. The documents then become the standard against which the Post plans and performs and by which the shareholder evaluates postal performance. These agreements take different form and cover varying areas in different countries. In Australia, the Post and the government construct a Service Charter (regarding regulatory matters and service goals) and a Corporate Plan (with regard to financial and performance objectives.) The equivalent documents in New Zealand are the Deed of Understanding and the Statement of Corporate Intent. These shared objectives are spelled out in Denmark's Concession, France's contract, the Dutch General Directive, the licensing agreement in Sweden, and Finland's Decrees. This approach has a number of compelling features that commend it. First, and most obviously, the contract or agreement sets defined, quantified policy objectives. These go a long way to defining the nature and character of the country's universal system which, of course, can be discussed and/or altered in the process. Second, the contract or agreement demonstrates the government's ultimate responsibility for the postal sector, in the sense that it is party to these service or contract targets. If the public or customers feel that these targets are over or understated, they can articulate this point of view to the government. Similarly, the government and/or the public cannot anticipate or insist on performance or activity by the Post that is not part of the agreement. Third, the board or management of the Post can be held accountable for non-performance. The government can remove the board if it does not take the arrangement seriously, or management can be released or changed for non-performance. Similarly, rewards can be issued for performance above and beyond expectations.

At the end of the Mandate Review process, the government and Canada Post adopted a Framework Agreement that appears to have been constructed in the sprit of the above discussion. However, the Framework Agreement – which took years to produce – is a slender, tentative, and incomplete document that is more akin to a policy framework or set of financial expectations then anything else. It combines qualitative statements and wishes with quantitative financial goals, soft targets, and statements of service intent. Compared to documents such as New Zealand's Statement of Corporate Intent and Deed of Understanding, Canada's Framework Agreement looks like a set of preliminary or rough notes. Indeed, we recommend that the New Zealand pattern be adopted. First, the shareholding department should work with CPC to produce a detailed declaration of corporate objectives. This could be a variant on the existing corporate plan, but more elaborate, quantitative, accessible, and meaningful. It would include various anticipated rates of return, the amount of capital and labour to be employed, and so on. It should be issued annually and publicly. The regulatory department should work with Canada Post to construct a Service Charter. This charter could be produced for a longer time-frame and include a range of targets, including delivery speed and rates of performance, delivery times, the extent of the network, conditions for subsidy of service activity (if any), retail outlets (total number and composition), formulas for closing retail outlets and changing universal-service obligations, and so on. The departments involved should carry out the evaluation of the Post's performance annually, after submission of information by the Post. The results of this evaluation should be made public.

Recommendation Eight: Third-party Regulation

A number of countries have used or have adopted third-party regulation of their postal sectors. In some cases, this simply represents an inheritance from the past. In other cases – such as in the United Kingdom recently – this reflects a conscious policy decision to remove the direct exercise of the regulatory function from the day-to-day operation of the bureaucracy. There seemed to be a division between consensual and parliamentary governments with respect to regulation. The consensual democracies tended to use third-party regulation (OPTA in the Netherlands, TAC in Finland, PTS in Sweden, Reg TP in Germany). Parliamentary democracies tend to use the dual-authority departmental model (DOFA and DCITA in Australia, Finance and Commerce in New Zealand). However, the newly devised postal regime in the United Kingdom will include an independent third-party regulator. We anticipate that this will become the prevalent model in the future.

We recommend that this approach be given serious consideration and introduced in Canada, for a number of reasons. First, Canada has adopted the national postal model. For this reason, it is imperative that extra precaution be exercised in distancing the government (as shareholder) from regulatory practice. Second, we anticipate that the exclusive privilege will be maintained in Canada for some time, given the perpetuation of the national model. If so, third-party regulation is needed to set a framework that will assure postal competitors and customers that the restricted area is not being abused. Third, there is a serious deficiency of postal expertise and intelligence in Canada. A third-party regulatory model will force members of the postal-policy community to be more professional and to articulate and defend their interests more precisely and concretely.[4]

There have been three traditional Canadian arguments against regulation of Canada Post. The first is that regulation would be a backward step, since it would inhibit Canada Post's autonomy. However, the government currently regulates CPC in a manner that may be informal but is no less inhibiting than formal regulation. Moreover, there are no boundaries to government interference in this informal non-regulatory model. The second argument focuses on the time and expense of regulation, particularly as exemplified in the long and costly regulatory process of setting prices in the United States. However, there is no need to follow the detailed and elaborate American approach to regulation. Its precise form reflects American conditions, where there is little to no legislative or executive scrutiny of the USPS. In other countries, the regulatory process is modest and indeed almost "passive." The regulator is asked to evaluate postal activity and performance against the guidelines and criteria set out in the contract or agreement between the government and the Post, in a specified range of areas that does not include financial or corporate performance. The latter remains the responsibility of the shareholding minister. This need not be an elaborate process nor should it be. After all, the main goals and objectives will have been set in the agreement – not by the regulator. For example, postal prices can be altered automatically without regulatory scrutiny according to a formula agreed to by the Post and the government. Similarly, the opening and closing of postal outlets can be a matter of targets and formulas established in these agreements. The third Canadian argument against regulation is less an argument than a practical concern. Where would this regulation be located – within the Canadian Radio, Television and Telecommunications Commission or the Canadian Transportation Commission? This argument was always a red herring. More important, the answer is easier now that we have seen the example of Post regulation under the terms of service agreements and contracts. We recommend following the British example of setting up a small, stand-alone regulatory operation, with a small staff and a limited budget, to exercise what we have called a "passive" regulation.

There is another reason for considering third-party regulation at this time, again inspired by developments abroad. As postal markets are liberalized, the public Posts take on the character of being just another entity in the market. Private competitors enter and exit the postal market, as in other sectors. In this situation, a number of countries abroad have adopted licensing systems, whereby postal operators apply to the government to participate in the postal market. This is the system adopted recently in New Zealand and a more elaborate variation of it is developing in Germany. The licensing system can be as straightforward as the process of applying to become an ice-cream vendor, or it can be an elaborate system of getting a license for specific parts or areas of the market under particular terms and conditions. In Finland, there has been some attempt – unsuccessful so far – to use the licensing system as a mechanism for ensuring the maintenance of the universal system. One can anticipate a situation developing in a number of years in which Canada Post is but one of a number of postal operators in the market, applying with others to perform certain functions under particular conditions. It would be extremely useful to have had a third-party regulatory process up and running for a while, in order to build up the experience and knowledge to make a licensing system operate smoothly. The regulatory processes in Germany and Sweden have been more elaborate, as those countries struggle to make a liberalized model work. As was noted in the country discussions, liberalization does not guarantee competition, and the regulatory process has been used in these countries to nurture competition. It is anticipated that, once the transition to a competitive market is attained, the regulatory processes in Sweden and Germany will become more passive.

In sum, third-party regulation in the Canadian regime would distance regulation further from the shareholding function, assure citizens and customers of the fairness of the postal regime, give assurance of good postal performance, and increase postal professionalism and understanding. The regulator would report annually to Parliament and to the minister. This would form the basis for reconsideration and/or reconfirmation of various elements of the contract agreement. There is no need, then, for regulation to be elaborate, assertive, or heavy-handed. The regulatory regime should be designed to ensure a passive approach and a light-handed touch.

Recommendation Nine: Clarify the Division of Responsibilities

Most progressive postal regimes abroad have developed a clear division of responsibilities within their postal regimes – far clearer than in Canada. For example, in conjunction with the board, the shareholding ministry devises financial performance plans, targets, and evaluation. In conjunction with the Post, the regulatory ministry sets service and public targets and objectives. These are executed and evaluated increasingly by a separate regulator. There are separate organizations, separate personnel, and separate processes for each of these activities. The ministers' and board's roles and responsibilities are also well articulated and delineated. Similarly, complaints about service or operational questions are handled clearly. First, they are addressed internally by the Post itself. But if a resolution cannot be achieved internally, some sort of agency external to the Post is available to pursue the issue. This agency exists outside the direct machinery of government and outside the Post. The recent development of a postal ombudsman in Canada speaks to this need. But the operation of this office leaves something to be desired, as it is currently constituted. The ombudsman's role is located too close to the Post. The reporting relationship should not be internally to the board of the Post. Rather, it should operate independently and provide an annual report and recommendations to the regulatory minister. We recommend, then, that the government increase the independence of the ombudsman. His/her role could also be brought into the orbit of the array of users' councils that operate at the local and regional levels. A model to examine in this regard is POUNC in the United Kingdom (now renamed Postwatch). A more formally aggregated network of postal councils, backed by a small ministerial staff, could become a high-profile and effective defender of the interests of postal users.

Recommendation Ten: Create a Public-Accountability Regime

A further feature of postal developments abroad has been an increased emphasis on postal accountability to the public. This tendency reflects the increased contemporary demand for public accountability and scrutiny of the remaining state enterprises, particularly if they enjoy any kind of exclusive privilege or restricted area.

This is especially important for postal regimes within the national model, given the political goals of their postal sector. However, a "representative" model of accountability has not gathered much favour abroad. The exception to this is in France, where there is parliamentary representation on the regulatory board (CSSPPT) and public and union representation on the Board of Directors of the Post. This makes some sense, given the deeply political or public nature of the French postal regime. The accountability and planning processes guarantee that political and public goals remain at the centre of postal experience.

In other countries, the accountability regime is far more functional. The service and contract arrangements between governments and

Posts are public documents which are widely distributed and openly viewed and discussed. These documents typically form part of the Post's annual review and the Post's report to Parliament. They contain a statement of future intent as well as a report on present accomplishments against the expectations and promises made in the previous year. The development of the service charters and performance contracts, and their articulation and execution publicly, has been critical to the performance of the postal sector and to the integrity of the postal regime. The development of an open-accountability regime has gone to considerable lengths to reassure the public that the commercialization of the Posts has not been at the cost of good service. Moreover, it has placed into the open issues such as the Post's place in the market and the maximization of shareholder value.

The Canadian postal regime has accountability mechanisms, but they are opaque and indirect. As a general characterization, they tend to be directed inwardly to government and postal authorities and the corporation itself rather than outwardly to the public at large. For example, the Post itself (in conjunction with a consultant) carries out the evaluation of service and delivery performance. The results are directed to government authorities (they are reported in a few lines in the annual report, which is the extent of their public articulation). The setting of service-performance targets should be established within a public-service document and evaluated by an independent regulator. The results of the evaluation should be presented to the regulatory minister and made public. Similarly, highlights of the five-year plan are released. But there are few details, which are presented in such a low-key way that the event is not reported in most media. The shareholding minister should devise a public statement of corporate performance and expectations, which should be released publicly and advertised at regular intervals. The recent Framework Agreement was delivered in a hushed and almost secretive and furtive way. Moreover, the agreement has no mechanisms for public reporting or follow-up until its conclusion five years later. There is a short ombudsman's report in the annual review, but the ombudsman himself reports inwardly to the chair of the board and not outwardly to the public save through a page in the Post's annual report.

Postal accountability in Canada is strangely and well out of tune with the times. This experience speaks to an ongoing and traditional political sense that talking too openly about postal matters is dangerous, since it might generate undesirable and unattainable expectations and public scrutiny. The Canadian government should adopt a far more open and elaborate accountability regime for the Post. This would complement a number of our earlier recommendations: moving the postal sector into the policy spotlight, strengthening the board, separating ownership from regulation, setting contract and service agreements, and introducing third-party regulation. This regime will give assurance to the public and customers about the Post's service performance. It will also assure Canadians that the Post's assets – which the public owns – are being used well and to maximum effect. An improved accountability regime will also provide a fillip to Post performance. In countries with such a regime, the successful attainment of targets and their presentation to the public has provided a real boost to morale and productivity.

The best model to follow would be the Australian one. The Post has had its reporting requirements spelled out in statutory fashion. The government's and customers' expectation of the APC are well articulated and advertised in documents such as the Service Charter, the Code of Practice, and the Corporate Plan. Corporate and service expectations are detailed and clearly spelled out, and their performance against expectations and commitments is documented in the annual report. This ensures public scrutiny. The Canadian government should prepare, with the Post, a list of performance indicators and objectives that include, at a minimum, the expectations and objectives contained in the service or contract arrangements. These should be elaborated annually in the annual report and the Post's performance against them should also be reported in the annual report.

To sum up, our recommendations for an improved regulatory and governance for the postal sector are:

1) highlight and assert postal policy;
2) pursue postal policy in a broader economic framework;
3) strengthen the Board of Directors and clarify the autonomy of the Post;
4) liberalize the postal market and deregulate the Post;
5) separate formally the government's ownership and regulatory responsibilities;
6) assign postal responsibility to an economics department;
7) set elaborate service contracts between the government and the Post;
8) establish a third-party regulatory model;
9) clarify the division of postal-regulatory responsibilities; and
10) create a public-accountability regime.

INTERNATIONALIZATION AND THE POSTAL FUTURE

The postal market remains a substantial one, and it has increasingly and rapidly become international in scope. There are over one-billion letters posted daily around the world, totalling over 400 billion a year. Of this, nearly nine-billion letters a year cross international borders.[5] This figure is likely understated, given how technological change has blurred the distinction between domestic and international mail. Bulk mail and remail is an enormous business. Companies and Posts around the world exploit national-price differentials, shipping and remailing mail to lower their costs. Computer technology allows bills, invoices, and statements to be sent across borders electronically, to be printed and mailed in another country as "domestic" mail. Generally speaking, international mail is growing faster than domestic mail, and the express, parcels and direct-mail (ad-mail) markets look particularly strong. The value of international mail and express mail in 1998 was over us$40 billion. The international mail market is complemented by two other international developments: postal financial networks (like Eurogiro[6]) and international postal consultancy, which has developed into an enormous and lucrative area.

The internationalization of the postal market has been influenced by two broad developments. On the one hand, we have seen how states have liberalized their domestic markets in order to increase efficiency and competitiveness. Starting with Finland in 1991, Sweden in 1993, and New Zealand in 1998, there is a trend to create open and competitive postal markets. A substantial part of the Australian market is deregulated, and even mercantile countries like Germany and the Netherlands are liberalizing their domestic markets at a pace faster than that mandated by the EC. Domestic postal liberalization has allowed and encouraged internationalization. Indeed, domestic governments encouraged their Posts to commercialize and diversify in order to compensate for any revenues lost by the elimination of the restricted market, and this inevitably took Posts abroad.

On the other hand, the postal liberalization process has tracked economic globalization. Postal customers have demanded more and better international service, and they have insisted on end-to-end service and quality. Postal customers are not obliged to use their national Post to get postal service in another country. Indeed, they are able to shop for the best price and the highest quality in the market. This created a dilemma for national Posts. Traditionally, they used the services of the corresponding national Post in other countries. But they could not control or guarantee the standards, quality, and service that they would get for their customers from the facilities of a national Post in another country. The pressure on national Posts to deliver end-to-end quality for their customers led them to make partnership arrangements with, or even purchase, delivery and communications companies abroad. Serving customer requirements in an increasingly competitive environment required Posts to internationalize their perspective, organization, and activity.

This has had enormous consequences for the Posts and for postal policy. First, the Posts found themselves in foreign markets in a double sense: operating in other countries but also in markets in which they were but minor players. Postal customers' international demands were most substantial in the express-mail and parcels markets. The international express market is a huge and growing field, having more than doubled in the last five years. It is worth over $US30 billion and will grow to over $US50 billion by 2001.[7] The growth of domestic and international e-commerce will lead to vibrant growth in the parcels market. Traditionally, neither market had been in the restricted areas of most countries. Thus, internationalization saw national Posts having to adjust their business strategies, but as minority players in contested markets. For example, while the Posts enjoyed 80 per cent or more of the letters market in Europe, their share of the express market was in the 7–10 per cent area and their share of the parcels market was in the 20 per cent range. The public Posts command only 30 per cent of the international mail and express market.[8] This placed huge pressures on the Posts to increase their productivity and competitiveness to participate in these markets, and provided the Posts with the rational business case to "buy into" these markets.

Second, the domestic Posts have looked to increase their corporate autonomy in order to increase their international market presence. To this end, they have organized themselves outside the reach of their domestic governments and expanded their contacts with national Posts and private players abroad.[9] This has undermined or weakened the logic of domestic postal organization and regulation. But, as we will see below, it has also undermined the logic of international organizations like the Universal Postal Union, which has had the historic role of regulating international postal activity. This is because the national Posts have moved broadly from a cooperative relationship with each other into a competitive one. And national Posts have entered into alliances, partnerships, and ownership arrangements with the important private-sector international players, who lie outside the regulatory and governance ambit of the UPU.

As Tim Walsh has written, the traditional international postal world was one of inter-state cooperation. The new globalized world sees increasing market divergence, the replacement of the postal "flag" by the postal "brand," and the intensification of international postal competition. This competition has taken two forms. The first is the traditional and ongoing competition between national Posts and private express companies in various parts of the market. At the top end, the competition is with enormous and ambitious firms like UPS and FedEx (with 1999 sales in the area of $US25 billion and $US17 billion respectively).

The other and newer form of competition is among the national Posts themselves, the larger of which are positioning themselves to become world leaders. In the first instance, the Posts worked to secure the mail of other national Posts. For example, ten or so national Posts have offices in London, looking for international business. Royal Mail in turn has international communications offices that market its services in other countries. Remail is an enormous and competitive business, which sees national Posts in intense battles with each other, often leading to legal disputes.[10] The Dutch are a world player in this regard, acting as a hub for international mail in Europe; the proportion of its mail that is international is enormously high (20 per cent). The national Posts also compete with each other as a result of the strategic alliances that they have created with private companies in each other's markets. Indeed, the general ambition of the mercantile and larger Posts is to become the number-two performer in any foreign market. As we have seen in our country studies, this impulse has also led to a number of purchases by national Posts of private postal operators abroad. For example, the Post in the United Kingdom has purchased German Parcel and Der Kurrier in Germany, part of City Mail in Sweden, the Crie Group in France, the Citipost Group in the United States, and the Williamcs Group in Ireland. DPWN has purchased firms in Austria, Belgium, Poland, and other countries in Europe and North America, as well as a majority share in DHL, which has the best network in the world for express mail, documents, and parcels. The Dutch Post purchased TNT, an acquisition that immediately made it a player in most every postal market in the world.

The internationalization of the postal sector may intensify if the postal sector becomes a subject of interest at the next round of trade talks through the General Agreement on Tariffs and Services. This framework was used to liberalize trade in insurance, securities, and financial services in 1995 and telecommunications in 1997. At a speech celebrating the fiftieth anniversary of the World Trade Organization (WTO), President Bill Clinton called for liberalization in several key service areas, including express delivery, and the WTO itself has encouraged open trade in the postal sector.[11] For various reasons, internationalization of trade in postal services may be more difficult to accomplish than in telecommunications.[12] However, there may be a momentum for liberalization if a sufficient number of countries conclude that it is in their interest – particularly countries that lack the adequate capital and technology to develop the capacity to establish or maintain their universal postal system.[13]

The internationalization of the postal sector is real, substantial, and evolving rapidly. Two issues remain unclear. The first is whether this internationalization will continue to be characterized by competition, as opposed to cooperation. The second issue is how this internationalization will be shaped or governed politically – if at all. These issues can be grouped together into three scenarios: bilateral cooperation, multilateral cooperation, and Darwinian competition. Each of these scenarios will be reviewed below.

Bilateral Arrangements

National Posts have entered into bilateral agreements with one or two other Posts in particular areas. This is done for reasons of efficiency and rationalization or to contend with a larger competitive threat. For example, national Posts have engineered cross-border cooperative deals to increase the speed of their courier service; Canada Post and the USPS have such an arrangement. Canada Post has developed an international document-exchange technology and protocol with La Poste and the USPS. Denmark, Sweden, Finland and Norway have executed a joint-parcel initiative in Europe (Vasagatan). Nine Posts are shareholders in International Data Post, a cooperative effort based in Copenhagen which is developing a range of hybrid mail and electronic services for the postal sector. Twenty per cent of the world's Posts have some sort of working arrangement with TNT.

This is a scenario that will likely proceed indefinitely in a wide variety of areas and among a large number of countries. But it is unlikely to be the predominant mode of international activity for a number of reasons. First, bilateral agreements typically have a limited scope and are time-consuming to create and execute. Second, broader regional arrangements and alliances with (and purchases of) private-sector players are more useful and consequential.

Multilateral Cooperative Arrangements

A second international cooperative scenario sees national Posts and countries cooperating with each other to create more coherent and integrated postal networks through increased cooperation and/or capital consolidation. This scenario tends to be favoured by mid-size states and emerging Posts. This section will present and examine three institutional arrangements and processes that have unfolded, albeit at different levels of inclusion and universalism – the Universal Postal Union, the International Postal Corporation, and the European Community.

The Universal Postal Union is the world's second-oldest international organization.[14] It was created in 1874 by the Treaty of Berne and became a specialized agency of the United Nations in 1948. It is currently headed by an energetic American director, Tom Leavy – formerly of the USPS – who was elected for a second term at the UPU's recent congress in Beijing. The UPU's constitution and regulations are binding on its 189 members, as a diplomatic act. The UPU is located in Berne, where a small staff of 150 people runs the organization. It organizes international postal arrangements, sets some standards and protocols, provides facilities for liaison, information, and consultation, promotes technical cooperation, and acts as a clearing house for the settlement of accounts. More recently, it has promoted the development of new products, provided programs on improving postal administration, and encouraged technological cooperation. In conjunction with the World Bank, it has initiated a number of pilot projects and loans in developing countries.[15] The UPU has orchestrated an international postal intervention in the international express market. EMS (Express Mail Service) was introduced in Switzerland in 1979, gained full operation in 1981, and expanded through 1987, only to stagnate in the early 1990s. The UPU has an EMS cooperative group and the initiative was relaunched in 1996.

The UPU holds a congress every five years, at which time policy is set and a direction given to postal developments for the next five years. Since the 1989 congress in Washington and the 1994 congress in Seoul, the UPU has promoted postal modernization in line with the predominant themes and tendencies that have emerged amongst the progressive postal regimes. Its strategy has included managerial autonomy and financial independence for Posts from governments, a greater focus on customers and the market, and an increased emphasis on the quality of service.[16] The 1999 Beijing congress saw the UPU declare the right of all citizens to quality postal service at an affordable price, and made the universal postal service part of the UPU convention. The congress approved an improved system of terminal dues (discussed below) and encouraged the expansion of postal financial services.[17] The congress also encouraged postal reform to aid the transition of developing postal systems into modernized ones; the Germans helped to establish a Technical Cooperation Fund to this end with a DM1-million donation for the next two years.

Critics of the UPU suggest that its organizational structure and vision preclude its likely policy effectiveness. It faces a governance and organizational crisis, partially as a result of the trend to separate ownership of the Post from it regulation and operation. The UPU is a government body, with government-based representation. Yet the postal world comprises a host of players, from regulators to independent state enterprises to large private postal operators. To the extent that these players – and their views and interests – are not represented within the UPU, it is difficult to imagine that the UPU can retain credibility or forge effective postal policy. Moreover, the UPU is a large and cumbersome body representing nearly two hundred countries. The majority of these countries have not attained a high level of modernization and development. Their interests and needs are exceedingly different from those of the major world postal players. Indeed, many of these latter countries have set up a separate organization – the International Postal Corporation – to articulate and pursue their shared interests. This development was looked upon as an act of treason by the UPU. It is all but inevitable that the UPU will seem out of step with the activities and ambitions of the leading sectors of the postal world. This is particularly the case with respect to issues like setting and enforcing postal standards. Its unwillingness (and incapacity) to set international standards of performance and to impose sanctions for poor postal service have undermined the UPU's relevance.[18]

At the Beijing congress in the fall of 1999, the UPU tried again to address criticisms that it is an institution that is out of step with the times. It created a high-level group of twenty-five countries to propose structural changes to the UPU and created an advisory group of representatives from postal unions, NGOs, and private operators as a kind of stakeholder forum.[19] However, the tactic of creating a high-level group is another example of the decade-long and fairly unproductive process of internal discussion and consultation that has produced little policy initiative or advance.[20]

What are the prospects for multilateral international postal cooperation through the UPU? The UPU is caught between the twin impulses of liberalization and deregulation on the one hand and the social goals of extending and maintaining the universal postal system on the other. This is a perpetual challenge within any given nation. It is an enormous challenge in balancing the interests of many countries – the vast majority of whom are struggling to establish a modern, universal postal system. While nominally in tune with modern progressive themes, the UPU will likely remain the site for the articulation of a traditional social view of postal circumstances and objectives, given the composition of its membership. Its large and varied members are sharply divided on key postal issues. It has been impossible to differentiate and distinguish ownership from commercial functions. The UPU is suspicious of the intentions and activities of the larger postal players who, in turn, do not take the actions of the UPU seriously enough. The UPU's capacity is partially a function of the assistance that it receives from member states. With only 150 staff, its potential organizational and policy thrust is limited, and it relies on member states for information, expertise, and implementation of policy positions. Individual staff are nominated by the home countries and elected and approved by member states, which limits the talent and skill pool of the organization.

In sum, the UPU is an organization that is struggling to find its feet in the new globalized, high-tech postal world. Its existence is, in some ways, a throwback to the earlier days of international postal cooperation and bureaucratic oversight of the postal regime. The recently established high-level organizational discussions may generate a formula for a more progressive decision-making and policy-making regime, with some authority and sanctions. However, this is unlikely, since the internal processes of the UPU limit its capacity to make fundamental organizational changes. Until then, it appears that the UPU has limited capacity to generate international postal cooperation, notwithstanding its many fine initiatives and motives.

The International Postal Corporation was founded in 1988 as the cooperative and private initiative of the CEOs of the world's major Posts, including those in the OECD countries, North America, Australia, New Zealand, and Japan. Its composition has subsequently changed to include mainly the bigger countries in Europe and North America. The IPC is a private holding company registered under Dutch law and headquartered in Brussels. Its $US40-million budget is financed by contributions from its members, prorated to their size. Its first director was Yves Cousquer, the former head of La Poste; its present director is Georges Clermont, former president of Canada Post. The UPU saw the formation of the IPC as a case of the big postal players going off to run the world on their own.[21]

There was a twin motivation for its creation. On the one hand, these Posts felt threatened by the new market dynamics and the competition provided by the private international express companies. On the other hand, they felt inhibited by the traditional attitudes and limited capacity of the UPU to devise an effective response to this situation. In the first instance, these national Posts resolved to establish a joint company to operate an international cargo airline for express shipments and to provide marketing and management services for international mail. For some, this seemed to be an insufficient initiative to take on the international express companies, so the group flirted with more ambitious initiatives like GD-net. It nearly purchased DHL when it was for sale in 1990. In 1991 a number of its members gave up on this shared initiative as too difficult to coordinate, and France, Germany, the Netherlands, Sweden, and Canada purchased 50 per cent of TNT. This initiative saw Australia and New Zealand exit from the IPC, since they felt it was too European-oriented and, in any event, TNT was a major competitor in their areas. The other members eventually sold their share of TNT to the Dutch Post. Thus ended the experiment to devise a collaborative international response to the private competitors. It foundered as a result of the Achilles heel of any international initiative: national self-interest and the absence of authority to impose decisions on national members. Many national Posts were unwilling to submerge their identities to the joint international brand.

The IPC has subsequently evolved into an organization that promotes quality, aims to raise and coordinate service levels, and provides and tests technical support. For example, it collects and distributes postal market intelligence to IPC members. It carries out sophisticated diagnostic testing to identify bottlenecks in the delivery system. Its CAPE system provides computer-aided post through electronic-document exchange. As a private company, it has less "official" connection with public organizations (such as the UPU) that are based on inter-governmental relations. Nonetheless, it has observer status at the UPU and helps the UPU in preparing standards and testing, providing a kind of laboratory for modernization and a means to avoid duplication. The IPC also tracks the EC's directives and minimum-service standards. UNEX – Unipost External Monitoring – tests delivery performance on international routes. Its members attained a performance level of 82.4 per cent in 1997, outstripping the EC target of 80 per cent; this was an increase of 12.9 per cent since 1994 (of three-day delivery service anywhere in Europe).

One of IPC's more interesting initiatives has been in the area of terminal dues. Terminal dues are the payments that Posts make to each other for the delivery of mail in the receiving country.[22] Before 1984, there was no system for balancing international accounts. This state of affairs was based on the presumption that different countries generated and received basically the same amount of international mail. A system for balancing international postal accounts was introduced only in 1984, managed by the UPU. It was based on the weight of mail that was received in each country. Again, this system rested on the assumption that the sacks of mail received by countries contained roughly the same volumes of articles. However, a number of countries exploited this assumption as the basis for the international remail system. Countries tried to steal mail from each other and export postal-delivery costs to the receiving country. The European countries subsequently attempted to devise a more cost-based system of terminal dues on their own. Self-interest, the EC green paper, and a 1993 EU court case stimulated this orientation. Thus, the REIMS system was born and developed – Remuneration of the Exchange of International Mails. There have been two versions of REIMS. It aims to fix remuneration by the sending country to the receiving country of a payment that approximates costs (to around 80 per cent of the costs in the receiving country). It also aims to provide remuneration corresponding to the quality of service against a benchmark. Countries are divided into three groups, on demographic and geographic grounds. If a country hits 100 per cent of its quality-service target, it gets 100 per cent of its payment; at 95 per cent it gets 95 per cent, and so on down to 80 per cent and 80 per cent. The system will likely standardize quality over the long term, but it will increase prices in low-price countries as prices converge. The IPC acts as the secretariat for the REIMS system and monitors and implements the system in action. It tests the system through monitoring of selected mail that is wired by antennae. The REIMS system has reflected an extremely complex set of negotiations and difficulties in building up consensus about issues like quality and price. It may eventually eliminate a substantial part of the remail business. While there has been a certain amount of innovation and consensus, a number of countries have been unwilling to agree to the wishes of the majority.

What prospects does the IPC offer for engineering international postal cooperation? The IPC represents an interesting institutional development for building up postal consensus, implementing policy, and testing this policy in a limited number of areas. The IPC does not take independent policy opinions and decisions, since it does not enjoy any authority. It does not have the authority or the capacity to neutralize issues of national concern. The experience with EMS and recent struggles over REIMS has demonstrated the possibilities for collaboration as well as the limits to cooperation. The case of the IPC indicates that countries want to cooperate *and* compete with each other.[23] Its existence may constrain the capacity of the UPU to create international consensus, thereby undermining its relevance. However, its own members are divided on key issues, which makes it unlikely that it can be the lead forum in building a system of international cooperation.

A third example of international postal cooperation is unfolding at the regional level in Europe through the European Union. The postal sector was one of the last sectors to experience economic liberalization in Europe, where there has been considerable national division and resistance to change. Nonetheless, a postal-policy framework is developing in Europe that may include a degree of postal cooperation or international management. European postal policy centres institutionally around DG XIII – the General Directorate on Telecommunications, Information Market and Exploitation of Research. The postal area is linked with the telecom group under one commissioner. It is a small group, comprised of less than ten people. So its bureaucratic infrastructure does not by itself provide much thrust to the process. The only European-level rule that applies to the Posts is the Treaty of Rome itself, which articulates a set of competition rules. The treaty provides for the general principle of free trade between members while deferring to members in local matters of local or national interest.

The liberalization of the postal market in Europe has been driven by the application of competition law to the postal sector. The law has made Posts sensitive to their legal obligations under the Treaty of Rome, and a series of court cases has also stimulated policy development. This reinforced a number of domestic governmental impulses to initiate postal reform, including the desire to reduce state deficits, to limit disruptive postal strikes, to improve the quality of service, and to respond to increasing competition and product substitution. The professionalization of the Posts has also encouraged change.[24] Governments considered the Posts to be important, particularly given that they employed close to two million workers and their revenues represented 3 per cent of the GDP of the EU countries. However, it was evident to them that the Posts were functioning in a basically inefficient market, marked by poor service, lack of harmonization, and trade distortions. These considerations led the European Posts and governments to ask the EC to initiate a comprehensive review of the postal sector. A review process began in 1988, whose aim was to generate policy to liberalize cross-border mail and to establish limits to Europe's postal monopolies.

Four years later in 1992, a green paper finally emerged, after extensive and complicated consultations that included over two hundred written submissions. The green paper then entered the internal consultation process within the EC, where it was discussed and followed up in an involved and complex way. It took another five years for a postal directive to be issued, in December 1997. The directive was adopted under the legal basis of a "single market" harmonized regulatory structure. This first and decidedly tentative step in the postal-reform process had taken ten years to unfold, demonstrating the political delicacy and complexity of postal-policy collaboration and reform in Europe.

The substance of the postal directive that finally emerged represented a success for those countries that wanted to maintain national postal control and see the process of postal liberalization take place at a slow and steady pace. It was a serious disappointment for countries that had deregulated their domestic markets and supported quick liberalization. The postal directive pulled back from the expectations created by the green paper about postal liberalization. For example, the green paper had proposed the liberalization of cross-border and direct-mail services, a recommendation that was not pursued in the directive.[25] Generally, user groups and private delivery firms supported the green paper, while many Posts and postal unions were opposed to it. A post-green paper process saw two hundred more written submissions and a division of opinion among member states (for example, France saying to go slow, the Netherlands urging liberalization). The ensuing postal directive, born after an elaborate process of EC summaries, reports, resolutions, and statements, harmonized a set of principles regarding the creation and maintenance of the universal service, the maximum scope of the reserved area required to maintain the universal service, and the regulatory measures that needed to be adopted by member states. They were directed to meet these harmonized minimum obligations by February 1999. However, following the principle of subsidiarity, they were given the freedom to determine the means to attain these ends. The major principles included in the directive were: minimum five-day delivery, a maximum reserved area of 350 grams, and five times the letter price (apparently 97–98 per cent of the existing letter market, including direct and cross-border mail), and minimum-quality standards (three-day delivery 85 per cent of the time; five-day delivery 97 per cent of the time). No mention was made of a universal price, although the principle was adopted that prices should reflect costs. Member states were also required to separate the regulation of their Posts from their ownership and operation. The directive anticipated that further discussions about extending liberalization would take place beginning in 1998–99, but it was not anticipated that any further liberalization would take place before 2003.

This first stage in the European process of postal reform illustrated the traditional tensions faced between long-run principles (of competition, liberalization, and the market) and short-run pressures (the politics of employment, monopoly, and national government versus market control). There is a general division in these areas between the northern countries, which support liberalization and modernization of the postal sector through market competition, and the southern countries, which support a public-sector orientation to state-run Posts. Since the directive was issued, countries have moved to alter their postal regulations and initiate institutional reform, where necessary, as seen in the country studies. Some tentative steps or statements were made regarding further liberalization by EC Commissioner Martin Bangemann, who promoted liberalization of the postal sector along the same lines as the successful liberalization of telecommunications. But individual countries made agreements among themselves to keep the agenda from moving forward in this direction. New draft legislation was supposed to have been introduced in 1999, but this was put off by the mass resignation of the EC executive associated with a corruption scandal.

A new plan finally emerged from the EC in the spring of 2000.[26] It included three ingredients. First, it proposed to reduce the reserved area to 50 grams, below which competitors would have to charge at least 2.5 times the standard-letter price. Second, all outgoing international mail would be liberalized. Third, all weight and price limits on express mail would be eliminated. This was a compromise proposal, which would have liberalized only 20 per cent more of the European mail market than is open at present (the 350-gram limit liberalized only 3 per cent of the market). The EC estimated that this proposal would still protect at least 50 per cent of the Posts' activities as reserved areas (70 per cent at present). Nonetheless, many countries criticized the proposal, and the initiative failed to generate sufficient political support. Indeed, a compromise proposal to lower the limit to 150 grams has also stalled. Further liberalization of the European postal market is likely to take place, but it will do so slowly and incrementally.

What prospects does the EC case hold for international postal cooperation? The green paper, the postal directive, and recent events demonstrate the extent to which postal matters in Europe remain highly political. On the policy level, the EC thinking reflects the spirit of the times, and a concern for "over-regulation" of the postal area frames much policy thinking and action.[27] A small EC staff has limited authority to press the process along among nations, many of whom remain interested in retaining domestic authority over the postal sector for political and policy purposes. This tendency is reinforced by the principle of subsidiarity, which allocates considerable national-level authority in applying broad, general objectives. As a result, the capacity to develop policy consensus and rules is seriously undermined. These divisions have been expressed institutionally through the fragmented EC political process, in which the interests of postal operators and governments are played out via the tensions between the commission and the council. In any case, it is unclear whether a consensus can be reached, given the serious philosophical differences in attitude towards the postal sector. France has gathered a set of southern allies who are all committed to a more traditional public conception of postal affairs and who are suspicious about and antipathetic towards market liberalization. Many of these countries have not endured the often-painful measures associated with market liberalization. This stands in stark contrast to the more market-oriented attitudes of the northern European countries, many of whom have invested considerably in, and made adjustments to, liberalization and reform. The European reform process has been slow and painful to this point, and its experience does not offer much optimism for the prospects of easy international cooperation in the future. National and ideological interests remain alive and substantial. There is likely to be some narrowing of the reserve area in a small series of steps over time. But these actions will be seriously insufficient and out of proportion to the accelerating developments and realities in the wider postal marketplace. This will then encourage individual nations and posts that feel inhibited by the EC to take actions on their own – which will intensify the increasingly Darwinian character of the postal market.

Darwinian Competition

The evidence to date suggests that Posts would like to cooperate with each other when necessary and opportune, but they do not necessarily want to cooperate in all situations and circumstances. Indeed, many of them want the opportunity to compete and grow in the international marketplace and find cooperative arrangements or institutions to be inhibiting. Moreover, even within the cooperative or legal arrangements to which they are party, there is no guarantee that individual Posts will "behave." Indeed, there are numerous examples of Posts taking each other to court, for allegedly breaking the rules. For example, the British Post and five other operators have recently complained that Deutsche Post has abused EU anti-trust law and the European Court is examining whether the German state provided unfair state aid to its Post.[28]

The prospects for international cooperation at this moment are not high. International institutions are weak and lack the authority or capacity to lead a cooperative movement. The international postal market is in the early days of liberalization and deregulation. It is highly fragmented and the start-up competitive dust has yet to settle. First, as noted at the start of the chapter, postal liberalization and deregulation has encouraged competition not cooperation. To the extent that cross-border postal exchange is liberalized, then each national Post seeks to secure the best possible competitive and quality advantage in each national market. This may or may not lead to a domestic alliance with a national Post; indeed, it will likely lead to the opposite, an arrangement with a local competitor to the national Post. This tendency will be encouraged to the extent that the domestic letter-mail market is liberalized as well. Each national Post will vie to become the *number-two* domestic player in the local market of other national Posts. Clearly, though, there can be only one *number-two* – indeed, only one *number-one* – in each domestic market. So the stakes are high and the competition in each local market is intense. The mercantile Posts – those of the Netherlands, Germany, and, increasingly, the United Kingdom – look to become predominant players in all the major markets. They each set up an international network to rival the service of their competitors. The Germans joke about having yellow flags all around the world and the Dutch are committed to becoming the world leader. There is a fierce battle for market pre-dominance in Europe, which will then extend to the rest of the world. These are not the conditions in which one can anticipate a significant amount of international postal cooperation. Indeed, the difficulties in building up a consensus for REIMS II, the battle over remail, the international buying spree, and the various court battles at the EC all speak to the seriousness of the competitive struggle. This competitive-ness is intensified by the parallel battle with the large private interna-tional express companies – UPS and FedEx. Each of these companies is poised to take advantage of the new competitive possibilities and each of them is likely to take legal action to assert their rights in the international market (for example, UPS against DPWN in Europe and against Canada in North America.) Moreover, each of them is diver-sifying and setting up its own retail network – FedEx in conjunction with USPS and UPS via its purchase of Mail Boxes Etc.

Second, it should be recalled that there are substantial national, political interests at stake which pose limits to postal cooperation. The Posts in Europe are extremely labour-intensive, and the employment issue frames postal-policy discussions and decisions. Moreover, the postal unions have retained some authority and presence in postal-policy discussions at both the corporate and governmental levels. Further, governments themselves are not disinterested in how the postal issue plays out. Given their continued position as shareholder, they anticipate and enjoy receiving dividends and taxes from profit-able Posts. Their popularity can be enhanced to the extent that they can maintain the popular universal postal service at no cost to their budgets. Despite internationalization, the Posts remain matters of deep national concern and attention.

Third, neither the objective conditions nor the philosophical basis for cooperation are strong at the moment. There is no postal vision or agreement about how large, commercial, and growth-oriented national Posts are going to deal with each other – and with large private operators – in an increasingly competitive and threatening international market. On the one hand, there are deep philosophical divisions in the postal community that parallel the underpinning of the market, mercantile, and national models. On the other hand, these models themselves reflect the reality that the conditions of the Posts and domestic postal markets differ enormously, and these differ-ences frame different philosophical outlooks. There is tremendous unevenness among the Posts in terms of modernity, capacity, techno-logical sophistication, capitalization, growth prospects, managerial tal-ent, and so on. While there is a degree of postal rationalization and convergence that has taken place, these differences remain considerable

– even among the countries of the advanced industrial world. There are even greater differences between those countries and the rest. These differences limit the possibility of building international postal consensus and cooperation.

Unevenness and division may actually become the basis for the emergence of a different sort of international model – an alliance one. This model would mimic the alliance arrangements that have evolved in the airline industry, such as Oneworld, Star Alliance, Wings and, most recently, SkyTeam.[29] In this model, national airlines group around one or two central dominant airlines, in order to access brand recognition, economies of scale, improved end-to-end customer service, shared technology, and system integration and rationalization.[30] In the postal world, a number of predominant players are emerging, which are highly diversified, ubiquitous, integrated, and underpinned by enormous pools of capital that allow them to access technology. They are developing international brand identities and absorbing domestic postal operators at the national level (both private and public) through purchases and alliances. Most other postal operators will simply not be able to compete against them. They will continue to exist in local or niche areas (particularly if geographically isolated or demographically small) or in domestic mail areas that the large operators are not interested in. This will create a "dual model," of large international operators and domestic Posts.[31] As TPG's CEO put it, "the advent of liberalization will forge a series of alliances in mail around the four major European operators – Deutsche Post, La Poste, Royal Mail and TPG."[32] The international alliance struck in 2000 among the Posts of the United Kingdom, the Netherlands, and Singapore is likely a foreshadowing of things to come. Posts (and their governments) will then confront two options: they can enter an alliance with one of the large operators, or they can pursue an independent national postal existence. The latter choice would see their national Posts marginalized and limited to narrow, domestic activities. Their universal systems would be maintained either through high charges or direct government subsidies. Many of the smaller Posts in Europe – those of Italy, Greece, Switzerland, Austria, Luxembourg – have entered into strategic or direct alliances with one of the major national players.

The recent spate of corporate acquisitions, conglomerations, takeovers, and international alliances and networks is both the cause and consequence of postal internationalization. Where this will end is unclear. Much will depend on how legal authorities determine the propriety of conglomeration, how the private operators interact with the public ones, how international rules and trade law unfold, and so on. What is clear is that the big postal players – TPG, DPWN, Consignia, and La Poste on the public side, and FedEx and the UPS on the private side – will drive the process, not governments. National governments no longer seem to be in control of this process, which they have abdicated to the major players and the market. Many governments have become increasingly defensive, timid, and reactive. They will, of course, be obliged to make decisions and to set public policy within a narrowing set of policy alternatives. But one thing is certain. Most governments will not have the option of setting postal policy to an exclusively national agenda. If they try to do so, their policy will likely be terribly inappropriate and doom their postal sector to also-ran status and eventual takeover by one of the large postal operators.

Notes

INTRODUCTION

1 The term "Posts" will be used as a short form to indicate a country's national Post Office or public postal system.

2 For an overview discussion of this issue, see Leslie A. Pal, ed., *How Ottawa Spends 1999–2000: Shape Shifting: Canadian Governance Toward the 21ˢᵗ Century* (Don Mills, Ont.: Oxford University Press 1999). In particular, see my article "The Fourth Fiscal Era: Can There Be a "Post-Neo-Conservative' Fiscal Policy?" 113–50.

3 "Progressive" is a term used in the postal world to refer to Posts that have initiated postal reform and that have adjusted to technological and international change. See John M. Dowson, Edward E. Horgan, Jr., and T. Wood Parker, *Postal Performance: The Transformation of a Global Industry* (Arlington, Va.: Coopers and Lybrand 1997).

4 Christopher Pollitt, Stephen Hanney, Tim Packwood, Sandra Rothwell, and Simon Roberts, *Trajectories and Options: An International Perspective on the Implementation of Finnish Management Reforms* (Helsinki: Ministry of Finance 1997), 30.

5 See G. Bruce Doern et al., *Changing the Rules: Canadian Regulatory Regimes and Institutions* (Toronto: University of Toronto Press 1999), and G. Bruce Doern and Stephen Wilks, ed., *Changing Regulatory Institutions in Britain and North America* (Toronto: University of Toronto Press 1998).

6 The Rutgers' Center for Regulated Industries has organized regular conferences on Postal and Delivery Economics. Michael A. Crew and

Paul R. Kleindorfer have edited papers from these conferences in
a series of books.

7 See Universal Postal Union, *125 Years 1874–1999* (London and Berne:
ISCL [International Systems and Communications Ltd] and UPU 1999),
and K. Ranganathan, *Redirecting Mail* (Washington, D.C.: Private Sector
Development Department, The World Bank 1996).

8 See Dowson, *Postal Performance*, and Price Waterhouse, "A Strategic
Review of Progressive Postal Administrations" (February 1995 and
February 1996 update).

9 The Rowland site: www.jcampbell.com/rowland/. The site is named after
Rowland Hill, the nineteenth-century British postmaster widely credited
with introducing the universal postal system. Alas, Jim Campbell has
retreated from the postal scene, at least in this public way.

10 For example, see Vivienne Smith, *Reining in the Dinosaur: The Story Behind
the Remarkable Turnaround of New Zealand Post* (Wellington: New Zealand
Post 1997). The British union CWU is the best example of a postal
union using its resources and capacity to do postal analysis. See its
website at: www.cwu.org/.

11 There has been no significant scholarly or academic studies on the Post
in Canada since my last book, *The Politics of the Post: Canada's Postal
System from Public Service to Privatization* (Peterborough, Ont.: Broadview
Press 1994). There were earlier works, however, including David Stewart-
Patterson, *Post-Mortem: Why Canada's Mail Won't Move* (Toronto: Macmillan 1987); Julie White, *Mail and Female: Women and the Canadian
Union of Postal Workers* (Toronto: Thompson Educational Publishing
1990); Douglas Adie, *The Mail Monopoly: Analysing Canadian Postal Service* (Vancouver: The Fraser Institute 1990). See also two doctoral disser-
tations: I. Lee, "The Canadian Postal System: Origins, Growth and Decay
of the State Postal Function, 1765–1982" (Carleton University, 1989),
and T. Langford, "Workers' Attitudes and Bourgeois Hegemony:
Investigation of the Political Consciousness of Workers in the 1980s"
(McMaster University, 1989).

12 The Universal Postal Union produces various documents that present a
statistical profile of the mail market. For example, see the "fact sheet"
that it produced for the Beijing Conference at www.upu.int (Beijing
1999 – 22nd UPU Congress).

13 Ibid.

14 United Parcel Service (UPS) – a private competitor – carried the equivalent of 6 per cent of American GNP in 1998.

15 See its website at www.postexpo.com.

16 Universal Postal Union, *125 Years*, 240–1.

17 Interview with John Dowson, 17 November 1998.

18 See Campbell, *The Politics of the Post*, 276–7, for a discussion of this development in Canada.

19 OECD, Working Party No. 2 on Competition and Regulation, *Promoting Competition in Postal Services: Background Notes by the Secretariat (Paris: 27 January 1999)*.

20 Institute for the Future, *The Coming Transformation of Mail: Competition, Technology and the New Consumer* (Menlo Park, California, 1996), 20–3, and *Post Serving Business and New Consumers: Tomorrow's Purchasing Cycle* (Menlo Park, 1997), 23. Universal Postal Union, *Post 2005* (Berne, April 1997), 152.

21 Institute for the Future, *The Coming Transformation of Mail*, vii. See also Natalie Southworth, "Delivery woes batter on-line retailers," *Globe and Mail*, 5 August 1999, B24, 26.

22 Dowson, *Postal Performance*, 37–8, 210.

23 See Tim Burt, "Sweden plans state company overhaul" and "Nordic governments on path to privatization," *Financial Times*, 29 January 1999, 3.

24 For the Canadian case, see Campbell, *The Politics of the Post*, 366–7.

25 Dowson, *Postal Performance*, 167.

26 Interview with Yves Cousquer, president of International Postal Corporation. See also Tim Walsh, "Globalization and Implications for Governance," paper presented to the Conference on Postal and Delivery Economics, Sintra, Portugal, June 1999, 11.

27 See Phillip Hastings, "Facing a Changing Environment," in Universal Postal Union, *125 Years*, 130.

28 James I. Campbell, Jr, "Overview of the International Postal Reform Movement," 1, Rowland's web site.

29 See Campbell, *The Politics of the Post*, chapter 9; H.N. Janitsch and R. Schultz, *Exploring the Information Revolution: Telecommunications Issues and Options for Canada* (Toronto: Royal Bank 1989). Universal Postal Union, *Post 2005*, 31–5. UPU *Geneva Strategy Conference*, 1997, 145.

30 OECD, *Promoting Competition in Postal Services*, 9.

31 GAO Testimony before the Subcommittee on the Postal Service, Committee on Government Reform, House of Representatives, "U.S. Postal Service: Challenges to Sustaining Performance Improvements Remain Formidable on the Brink of the 21st Century," 21 October 1999, 3.

32 OECD, *Promoting Competition in Postal Services*, 5; Walsh, "Globalization," 7.

33 Universal Postal Union, *Post 2005*.

34 OECD, *Promoting Competition in Postal Services*, 7–8.

35 Institute for the Future, *The Coming Transformation of Mail*, 9.

36 FedEx will place its drop boxes in 10,000 post offices and will carry express, priority, and first-class USPS mail in its jets.

37 Interview and discussions with K. Ranganathan.

38 See the papers by Bradley and Colvin ("Measuring the Costs of Universal Service for Posts"), Cremer, Grimaud, and Laffont ("The Cost of
Universal Service in the Postal Sector"), Cohen, Ferguson, Waller, and
Xenakis ("Universal Service without a Monopoly"), and Robinson and
Rodriguez ("Liberalization of the Postal Market and the Cost of the Universal Service Obligation") in Michael A. Crew and Paul R. Kleindorfer,
eds., *Current Directions in Postal Reform* (Boston: Kluwer Academic Publishers 2000).

39 PriceWaterhouse Coopers, *Postal Market Review* (London, July 1998).
This study was prepared for the Dutch ministry with responsibility for
the post.

40 See G. Bruce Doern, *Changing the Rules* and *Changing Regulatory Institutions in Britain and North America.*

41 See "The Universal Service Obligation: Myth and Reality," paper presented at Eighth Conference on Postal and Delivery Economics, Rutgers
University Center for Research in Regulated Industries, Vancouver,
Canada June 2000, 7. The cost-structure of postal service is as follows:
collection – 10 per cent; outward sorting – 18 per cent; transportation –
2 per cent; inward sorting – 5 per cent; final delivery – 65 per cent.
OECD, "Promoting Competition in Postal Services," 10.

42 PriceWaterhouse Coopers, *Postal Market Review,* 21.

43 The United States Postal Service (USPS) was one of the first Posts to be
corporatized. But its evolution has been stalled within a political environment that has made postal reform difficult if not impossible to
accomplish. The American system of separation of powers undermines
postal accountability. It is difficult to establish who in the United States
actually acts as the "owner" of the Post. There is strong and highly
focused third-party regulation, through the Postal Rates Commission.
But the shareholder function is all but abdicated to congressional pressures. There, the regional, rural, and sectoral interests of congressmen
make it difficult to construct a coalition for postal reform, in the context of the traditional attitude that "if it ain't broke, don't fix it." There
was a heroic five-year effort to bring modest reforms to the postal sector
(Bill HR–22) led by Congressman John McHugh. But this effort foundered at the committee stage, where it faced a powerful political alliance that checked reform. On the one hand, regional and rural
interests (particularly areas west of the Mississippi) reacted negatively to
postal reform. They feared the decline in universal service that reform
might bring, in a country where there are tens of thousands of uneconomical post offices, postal routes, and services employing and/or servicing tens of thousands of voters. On the other hand, the private express
companies and newspaper associations were also against postal reform.
This surprising position can be explained by the fact that the USPS is

highly regulated and constrained to act like an old-fashioned public enterprise. This limits its participation in the postal market to narrow, traditional functions. Reform would create a commercially oriented USPS that could become a formidable competitive threat to the newspaper and express industries. The lack of a strong executive (shareholder) champion, the dominance of reactionary congressional interests, and the self-interest of private postal players combined to halt postal reform in the United States. The consensus view is that postal reform will not take place in the United States until a postal crisis emerges to force change. The crisis may emerge even faster than has been anticipated, given that the USPS attained a multi-billion deficit in 2000–01.

44 Institute for the Future, *The Coming Transformation of Mail,* 9.
45 Under political pressure from the unions and its own party, the government withdrew its proposal to reduce the exclusive privilege from one pound and 350 grams to 50 pence or 150 grams.
46 See *Union Postale,* the Universal Postal Union Review, summer 2000 (3).
47 Pollitt et al., *Trajectories and Options,* 9.

PART ONE   THE MERCANTILE MODEL

1 See *Economist,* 17 July 1999, 57–8. See also Dirk Palder, "European Post: An Industry in Transition," *Post-Express,* 16 December 1998, 16–19.

CHAPTER ONE   THE NETHERLANDS

1 See J. Campbell, "Overview of the International Postal Reform Movement."
2 Dowson, *Postal Transformation,* 178ff.
3 See Rudy B. Andeweg and Galen A. Irwin, *Dutch Government and Politics* (London: Macmillan 1993), 187–211.
4 Ibid, 200. Interviews with Dutch postal and political authorities confirmed this.
5 Interview with Meinder Van Den Berg, ABVAKABO, 28 October 1998.
6 "The Standpoint of the Government of the Netherlands with Regard to the Report of the Steenbergen Committee Entitled 'Signals for the Future – A New course for the PTT.'" E/c195/86, 7–8, 14. No publishing details were listed, but this document was obviously produced in 1986.
7 Ibid, 7.
8 Ibid., 9–11, 40–3.
9 Interview with Petra de Roover, Socio-Economic Affairs Division, Policy Affairs Directorate, Telecommunications and Post Department, Ministry of Transport, Public Works and Water Management. As will be seen

below, the Post was not keen to roll back the exclusive privilege below the 350-grams target set in the European postal directive. The government proposed a 100-grams exclusive privilege.

10 PTT Post, *Annual Report*, 1996, 18.
11 "The Standpoint of the Government," 4, 15, 18, 21, 24, 33.
12 Interview with Petra de Roover.
13 Ranganathan, *Redirecting Mail*, 73.
14 Raymond van Doorn, "Ten Years privatisation of PTT Post in the Netherlands and challenges for the future." Paper presented to the Conference on Postal and Delivery Economics, 24 June 1999, Sintra, Portugal, 4. Interview with Petra de Roover, ministry. On the special or "golden" share, see TPG, *Annual Report*, 1999, 99–100.
15 J. Campbell, "Overview of the International Postal Reform Movement," 9.
16 Dowson, *Postal Transformation*, 6.
17 Interview with Petra de Roover.
18 The Netherlands, the Postal Act of 1988, as amended, preamble, 1.
19 These exceptions include time-sensitive mail, mail with added features (for example, security, tracking, and tracing), family and non-commercial mail, bills accompanying parcels, and so on.
20 Much of what follows in the discussion of OPTA is derived from an interview at OPTA on 26 October 1998.
21 Interview at OPTA.
22 See TPG, *Annual Report*, 1997, 11.
23 Interview with Meinder van den Berg, 28 October 1998.
24 Interview at Public Affairs.
25 Inteview at Public Affairs.
26 Ibid.
27 Interview with Petra de Roover.
28 Ibid.
29 Ibid.
30 See, "Amendment to the Postal Act and certain other Acts in connection with Directive 97/67/EC of The European Parliament."
31 TPG, *Annual Report*, 1998. "In my opinion the advent of liberalization will force a series of alliances in mail around the four main European operators: Deutsche Post, La Poste, Royal Mail and TPG." Ad Sheepbouwer, chair and CEO, TPG, 1999 Report, 7.
32 For a good overview, see Paul Overdijk, "Postal Services: Competition in the Netherlands," a paper delivered to the Fourth Bi-Annual Conference on Postal and Delivery Economics, 22–25 May 1996, Monterey, California, and PricewaterhouseCoopers UK, "Postal Market Review," July 1998, a report to the Telecommunications and Posts Department of the Ministry of Transport, Public Works and Water Management of the Netherlands.

33 TPG, *Annual Report* 1997, 3

34 TPG, *Annual Report* 1999, 5.

35 All data in this and following sections are taken from TPG annual reports, 1997 and 1998. It is difficult to present a statistical overview of Dutch postal developments, because the purchase of TNT and the de-merger have upset statistical sequences.

36 See TPG, *Annual Report*, 10–11.

37 Interview with de Roover.

38 Interview with van den Berg.

39 Overdijk, "Postal Services," 6.

40 Van Doorn, "Ten Years Privatisation," 5–6.

41 See press release, "TPG Announces Record Results for First Half of 2000," 4 September 2000.

42 One cannot do year-over-year comparisons before 1996, as a result of the purchase of TNT.

43 TPG, *Annual Report*, 3.

44 See note 41.

CHAPTER TWO   GERMANY

1 J. Campbell, Jr., "Overview of the International Postal Reform Movement," 10.

2 Interview with Dr J. Lohmeyer, Department of Strategy and Alliances, Deutsche Post, 27 April 1999. Interview with Dr Hans Engelke, Reg TP, and Mr Gerald Reichle and Mr Axel Kirmess, Ministry of Economics and Technology, 26 April 1999. There are many books that have been written on the telecom experience, but none on the posts.

3 Ibid.

4 See the Deutsche Post website: www.deutschepost.de/postagen.

5 Deutsche Post, *Annual Report*, 1997, 37.

6 DPAG President Zumwinkel at press conference introducing 1997 *Report*, as listed on DPAG website.

7 Interview with John Dowson.

8 See Deutsche Post, *Annual Report*, 1998.

9 Part of the rationale for the growth strategy was the objective of building up a financial capacity to support the pension plan. I would like to thank Paul Kleindorfer for drawing this to my attention. The proceeds of the IPO will go to the state, not to the Post.

10 Interview with Lohmeyer. See also press conference at release of 1998 *Report*, 19 April 1999: "The reconstruction phase is over; now, a growth strategy and a policy of internationalization are being pursued."

11 See Peter Knauth and Friedhelm Dommermuth, "Reorganization of the Postal Sector in Germany," paper presented at the Conference on Postal and Delivery Economics, Helsingor, Denmark, June 1997.

12 See Deutsche Post, *Annual Report,* 1997. Interview with Eugen Pink, Regulation Management, Deutsche Post, 27 April 1999.
13 Deutsche Post, *Annual Report,* 1997, 2
14 See New York *Times,* "Shares rise 2.4% on debut day for Deutsche Post," 21 November 2000, and Deutsche Post press release, 18 November 2000, "Deutsche Post AG shares priced at Euro 21."
15 Interview with Andrea Van Arkel, International Department, Deutsche Post, 27 April 1999. The EC commissioner for telecommunication and posts at that time was a German, Martin Bangeman, who was pushing very hard for liberalization. At the time, Germany compromised to avoid a pitched battle between the Dutch and the French.
16 "The purpose of this Act is, through regulation of the postal sector, to promote competition and adequate services throughout the Federal Republic of Germany." Chapter 1, Section 1, Postal Act, 22 December 1997.
17 Interview with Engelke et al.
18 "Ordinance Concerning Universal Services for the Postal Sector."
19 These outlets must be staffed with DPAG personnel until at least 31 December 2002.
20 Chapter 10, Section 45, Postal Act.
21 Competitors can use DPAG's network, but none has applied to do so at this time.
22 Chapter 2, Section 6, the Postal Act.
23 Interview with Engelke et al.
24 Chapter 5, Section 19. A dominant position is defined under the Law against Restraints of Competition, Section 22.
25 See C. Schwarz-Schilling, "Regulation of Postal Markets in Germany: Main Issues," paper delivered at the Rutgers Conference on Postal Economics, June 2000, Vancouver, Canada.
26 As outlined in Chapter 12, "Transitional Provisions," Postal Act.
27 Chapter 2, Section 10, Postal Act.
28 This is elaborated in Chapter 3 of the Postal Act.
29 Interview with Pink.
30 Brian Parkin, "Deutsche Post Forced to Open Segment of Mail Delivery to UPS," bloomberg.com, 18 September 2000. Deutsche Post argued that the UPS should use its own network, but it minimized the impact of the ruling since it affects but 1 per cent of its revenue.
31 Deutsche Post, *Annual Report,* 1998, Statement by group management, 2.
32 Interview with Engelke, Reichle, and Kirmess.
33 Interview with Lohmeyer.
34 DPAG press release, 19 April 1999, on DPAG website.
35 DPAG, *Annual Report,* assorted years.
36 Interview with John Dowson.

37 See *Globe and Mail*, 18 January 1999.
38 Interview with Pink. See DPAG's statement on its website, 21 July 1999.
39 Deutsche Post, *Annual Report*, 1998.
40 The election of the Social Democratic government may put the employment issue back on the agenda in Germany. Similarly, eleven of fifteen EC countries currently have Social Democratic governments, and this may inject the employment issue into postal-policy discussions at the European level.
41 See *Economist*, 18 November 2000.
42 Deutsche Post, *Annual Report*, 1998.
43 Interview with Lohmeyer.
44 *Globe and Mail*, 18 January 1999.
45 Interview with Thomas Baldry, Manager, Strategic Marketing Letter Post, Deutsche Post, 27 April 1999.
46 To be found at www.evita.de.
47 Deutsche Post, *Annual Reports*, 1997, 1998.
48 See President Zumwinkel, press conference at release of 1998 *Annual Report*, on DPAG website.
49 Interview with Lohmeyer.
50 The case revolves around the status of mail send by German firms abroad back to Germany. The Germans claim that this mail should be considered to be domestic German mail.
51 See Royal Mail press release, "AEI Takeover by DPAG," 15 November 1999. See also *Globe and Mail*, 16 November 1999.
52 Interview with Lohmeyer.

PART TWO   THE MARKET MODEL

1 PriceWaterhouse Coopers UK, "Postal Market Review," July 1998, a report to the Telecommunications and Post Department , Ministry of Transport, Public Works and Water Management, 11.

CHAPTER THREE   FINLAND

1 Interview with Liisa Ero, director of the Mass Media Unit, Ministry of Transportation and Communication.
2 Interview with Pekka Leskinen, chief legal counsel, Finland Post.
3 Interview with Tero Alen, Public Affairs, Finland Post; interview with Samuli Haapasalo, director of the Ownership and Privatization Policy Unit, Ministry of Transportation and Communication.
4 See Tim Burt, "Nordic governments set out on path to privatization," *Financial Times*, 29 January 1999, 3. See also Ministry of Trade and Industry, "State Shareholdings in Finland 1997," Helsinki, 1998.

5 Interview with professors Markku Temmes and Pertti Ahonen.

6 Interview with Antti Palkinen, Union of Post Office Employees, and Matti Nissinen, Finnish Post Workers' Union. Interview with Haapasalo.

7 See Heikki Nikali, "The Substitution of Letter Mail in Targeted Communication, " Finland Post, Quality and Business Development Studies 27, Helsinki 1998.

8 Finland Post, *Report*, 1998, 4.

9 Interview with Haapasalo.

10 Interviews with Temmes and Ahonen, Ero, Haapasalo.

11 For example, see Finland Post, *Annual Report*, 1998, 7, where the CEO declares that the Post should focus on its core competencies.

12 Interview with Alen.

13 Miliza Vasiljeff, "The Reform of State Enterprise Leads to Better Service and Productivity," Ministry of Finance, typescript, 8 pages, n.d.

14 Interviews with Alen and Haapasalo.

15 Interview with Alen.

16 Interviews with Temmes and Ahonen, Haapasalo.

17 Interview with Alen.

18 Interview with Ero.

19 Ibid. A new postal services law is being prepared in 2001.

20 Interview with Ero.

21 This subsidy amounted to FIM98 million in 1994 and 1995 but was eliminated in 1996.

22 Interview with Lasse Autio, a director of the SSM.

23 Interview with Jorma Koivunmaa (director) and Matti Linnoskivi (legal counsel), Telecommunications Administration Centre (TAC); interview with Palkinen and Nissinen.

24 Interview with Haapasalo.

25 Ministry of Transport and Communications, Elina Normo and Timo E. Toivonen, "Opening up of the postal market to more competition," 29 March 1996, 138 pages. The report is available only in Finnish.

26 Interview with Autio.

27 Interview with Leskinen.

28 Interview with Autio.

29 Interview with Ero.

30 Interview with Haapasalo.

31 Interview with Temmes and Ahonen.

32 Interview with Haapasalo.

33 Ibid.

34 Interview with Alen.

35 TAC, *Report*, 1998.

36 Interview with Leskinen, interview with Koivunmaa and Linnoskivi.

37 TAC, *Report*, 1998, interview with Koivunmaa and Linnoskivi.

38 Interview with Koivunmaa and Linnoskivi.

39 Ibid.

40 Ibid.

41 Interview with Temmes and Ahonen.

42 There is a case surrounding the closing of a post office in central Helsinki that threatens to become a political issue.

43 Interview with Temmes and Ahonen.

44 Interviews with Palkinen and Nissinen.

45 Interview with Riita Hyhanen (deputy director) and Petajaniemi-Bjorklund (senior research officer), Finnish Competition Authority. See OECD, Directorate for Financial, Fiscal and Enterprise Affairs, Committee on Competition Law and Policy, Working Party No. 2 on Competition and Regulation, "Promoting Competition in Postal Services: Finland," February 1999.

46 Postal volumes declined from 2.159 billion in 1990 to 1.931 billion in 1992.

47 This decision reflected less a Post decision than the newspapers' unwillingness to pay for the costs associated with inside delivery. As noted, the Finns take reading their papers very seriously. Until recently, newspapers and mail were delivered to the door even in apartment buildings, up through three floors.

48 Turnover doubled from 1980 to 1985 to FIM3 billion and reached FIM4 billion in 1988.

49 This was the explanation provided by the Board of Directors in Finland Post, *Report*, 1998, 39.

50 Interview with Sinikka Turunen (secretary general), Consumers Association.

51 Finland Post, *Report*, 1998, 33.

52 Interview with Turunen.

53 The story is outlined in Finland Post, *Report*, 1998, 9.

54 For a good overview, see Finland Post, *Report*, 1997, 3.

55 Finland Post, *Report*, 1998, 12.

CHAPTER FOUR   SWEDEN

1 Post and Telestyrelsen (PTS), "The Deregulated Swedish Postal Market," February 1999, 1; J. Campbell, Jr, "Overview of the International Postal Reform Movement"; Dowson, *Postal Performance*, 19–20. See also OECD, Directorate for Financial, Fiscal and Enterprise Affairs, Committee on Competition Law and Policy, "Promoting Competition in Postal Services – Sweden," Working Party No. 2 on Competition and Regulation,

9 February 1999. Two recent overviews are Peter Andersson and Mats Bladh, "Experiences from Liberalizing the Postal Market in Sweden," and Anna Lundgren and Sten Selander, "Uniform Tariffs and Prices Geared to Costs? – Swedish Experiences of the Incompatible Demands Article 12 of the EC Postal Directive," papers presented to the Conference on Postal and Delivery Economics, June 2000, Vancouver, Canada.

2 Tim Burt, "Sweden Plans State Company Overhaul," *Financial Times,* 29 January 1999, 3. See "Annual Report: Government Owned Companies, Summary 1999," Regeringskansliet, 2000, 2,4.

3 Interview with Sten Selander, PTS.

4 See National Economic Research Associates (NERA), "Overseas Postal Reform: Final Report for the National Competition Council, London, October 1997, 7, 73.

5 See Sweden Post reports in late 1980s and early 1990s. Interview with Sture Wallander, Sweden Post. Torsten Zillen, director, International Relations Secretariat, Sweden Post International, "Sweden Post – Public Operator on [sic] a Deregulated Market," paper delivered at the Euroforum Conference on the Liberalization of the European Postal Services, Amsterdam, 8 December 1994, 3.

6 Andersson and Bladh, "Experiences from Liberalizing the Postal Market," 3–5.

7 Interview with Goran Olsson, SEKO. SEKO is the umbrella union that represents postal workers. It also represents City Mail workers.

8 Ibid.

9 Interviews with Sture Wallander, Sten Selander, Goran Olsson.

10 Interview with Wallander, Olsson.

11 Zillen, 3.

12 Desiree Veschetti Holmgren, Ministry of Transport and Communications, "Postal Services in Sweden," February 1997, 1.

13 Zillen, 5.

14 Interview with Wallander.

15 See Report to the Ranking Minority Member, Subcommittee on Post Office and Civil Service, Committee on Governmental Affairs, US Senate, Postal Service Reform, "Issues Relevant to Changing Restrictions on Private Letter Delivery Service," September 1996.

16 Interviews with Selander, Wallander. Zillen, 3.

17 Interview with Hakkan Ohlsson, City Mail.

18 Zillen, 3.

19 Zillen, 6.

20 See Ranganathan, *Redirecting Mail,* 59.

21 ibid, 37–8.

22 Government-Owned Companies, *Annual Report,* 1999, 4.

23 Interview with Jonas Iversen, Division of State-Owned Enterprises, MIEC.

24 Interview with Selander.
25 Interview with Olsson.
26 Interview with Selander.
27 Ibid.
28 Interview with Wallander. K. Ranganathan, *Redirecting Mail,* 103–6.
29 Burt, 3.
30 Interview with Iversen.
31 Interview with Olsson.
32 Interview with Post and government officials.
33 PTS, "The Deregulated Swedish Postal Market."
34 Interview with Selander and Rygaard.
35 For example, see Sweden Post, *Report,* 1997, 3.
36 Interview with Selander.
37 Interview with Rygaard.
38 Ministry of Transport and Communications, "Summary of Government Bill 1997/98:127, Responsibility of the State in the Postal Sector," June 1998.
39 On the postal market in Sweden, see Catherine Gallett, "Authorization Procedures in the Postal Sector: Possible Lessons from Other Sectors for Entry Regulation," paper presented at Conference on Postal and Delivery Economics, Montreux, Switzerland, June 1998. See also Andersson and Bladh, "Experiences from Liberalizing the Postal Market," and Peter Andersson, "Entry on Deregulated Postal Markets."
40 Interview with Olsson.
41 Andersson and Bladh, "Experiences from Liberalizing the Postal Market."
42 It services half of the postal codes each day, so that each household is serviced twice a week. It does no delivery on Wednesday.
43 Interview with Selander.
44 Interview with Goran Ohlsson. See also Sweden Post, *Report,* 1996.
45 City Mail, *Report,* 1998.
46 J. Campbell , "Overview of International Postal Reform Movement," 8.
47 For a review of a number of these cases, see OECD, Directorate for Financial, Fiscal and Enterprise Affairs, Committee on Competition Law and Policy, Working Party No. 2 on Competition and Regulation, "Promoting Competition in Postal Services – Sweden," Paris, February 1999. See also Erik Nerep, "Current Competition Law Issues in Regard to the De-(re-)regulation of the Swedish Postal Services Market – Especially the Problems of Defining the Relevant Market, and Establishing Price Discrimination and Predatory Pricing," Stockholm School of Economics, October 1996. See also Andersson and Bladh, "Experiences from Liberalizing the Postal Market," and Lundgren and Selander, "Uniform Tariffs."

48 Sten Selander, "Postal Liberalization," IEA Conference on the Future of European Postal Services, 10 March 1999, 2–3.

49 Interview with Selander.

50 Sweden Post, *Report*, 1997, 3. Interview with Wallander.

51 See Lundgren and Selander, "Uniform Tariffs," 4.

52 PTS, "The Deregulated Swedish Postal Market," 3.

53 See Selander, "Postal Liberalization."

54 Correspondence with Selander and Rygaard.

55 Interview with Wallander, Selander, and Rygaard.

56 Interview with Wallander.

57 Correspondence with Rygaard, interview with Selander.

58 See Sweden Post, *Report*, 1996, 1997, and 1998.

59 Sweden Post, *Report*, 1998.

60 Interview with Olsson.

61 Interviews with Wallander and Olsson. See Andersson and Bladh, "Experiences from Liberalizing the Postal Market," 10.

62 International Postal Corporation, *Report*, 1998.

63 Sweden Post, *Report*, 1997, 1998.

64 Sweden Post, *Report*, 1998, 45, and 1996, 43.

65 Sweden Post, *Report*, 1997, 5, 8.

66 Sweden Post, *Report*, 1996, 1997, 3.

67 Sweden Post, *Report*, 1998, 93.

68 Sweden Post, *Report*, 1997, 5.

69 Ibid.

70 Sweden and Norway tried unsuccessfully to merge their telephone companies. See Linda Andersson, "Sweden, Norway hang up on merger," *Globe and Mail*, 17 December 1999.

71 Sweden Post, *Report*, 1996, 22.

CHAPTER FIVE   NEW ZEALAND

1 See James I. Campbell Jr., "Overview of the International Postal Reform Movement," 2–4.

2 Interview with John Dowson.

3 Dowson, *Postal Performance*, 83.

4 Frances Castles et al., *The Great Experiment: Labour Parties and Public Transformation in Australia and New Zealand* (Auckland: Auckland University Press 1996), 7–8.

5 Brian Easton, *The Commercialization of New Zealand* (Auckland: Auckland University Press 1997), 6–7.

6 Barry Spicer et al., *Transforming Government Enterprises* (Auckland: Centre for Independent Studies, Policy Monograph 35, 1996), 2.

461   Notes to pages 184–90

7 David Mayes, "The New Zealand 'Experiment': Using Economic Theory
to Drive Policy," *Policy Options*, September 1997, 18, 7: 34–6.

8 Jane Kelsey, *The New Zealand Experiment. A World Model for Structural
Adjustment?* (Auckland: Auckland University Press 1997).

9 Ibid., 24–7, 33; Easton, *The Commercialization of New Zealand,* 79–81;
Castles, *The Great Experiment,* 36–40. Interview with Louise Affleck, company secretary, New Zealand Post. This approach is less likely to occur
since the introduction of MMP and the resulting coalition government.

10 See Dowson, *Postal Performance,* 76–8; Ranganathan, *Redirecting Mail,* 67;
Smith, *Reining in the Dinosaur,* 12–25, 35–7. Interview with Warren Kyd,
MP, who chaired a parliamentary committee study of the Post.

11 See R.N. Mason and M.S. Morris, "Post Office Review," Wellington,
21 February 1986.

12 See Spicer, *Transforming Government Enterprises.*

13 See New Zealand Post, "The Corporatization Experience," October
1996.

14 Report of Officials Committee to Cabinet State Agencies Committee,
Summary Paper, October 1988.

15 It argued that it was premature, that it would lead to further rural
closures, and that the universal system would suffer as a result of cream-
skimming.

16 See Smith, *Reining in the Dinosaur,* 85–98.

17 Interview with John Allen, New Zealand Post, group leader, Letters.

18 The National Party would have preferred to sell the Post, while the Post
was surprised at the speed of the government's announcement. The
explanation seems to have been that the government did not have a deep
legislative agenda; the postal deregulation measures were, in effect, ready
from previous flirtations with the issue. In a parallel development that
increased political tensions at the time, the Post raised the issue of who
would sponsor postal services for the blind. This development was greeted
by public outrage. The Post hastily put together a new arrangement until
March 2003. Interviews with Affleck; Labour MPs Marion Hobbs and Paul
Swain; Greg Harford and David Galt, Resources and Networks Branch,
Ministry of Commerce; Rex Jones, national secretary, NZ Engineering
Printing and Manufacturing Union; Elmar Toime, CEO of NZ Post.

19 The nine original SOEs were: NZ Post, Airways Corporation, Coal Corporation, Electricity Corporation, Government Property Services, Land Corporation, Forestry Corporation, Post Bank, and Telecom. Most of these
have been privatized. Through August 1999, thirty-four state assets had
been sold for $19 billion. The SOE model was developed at the time as
an alternative to privatization. Smith, *Reining in the Dinosaur,* 204. There
are currently nineteen SOEs.

20 There was an initial share capital of $120 million along with $53 million for asset disposal, $60 million of personnel liabilities, and $8 million of net current assets, for a total valuation of $241 million. The setting of this figure was itself a political battle, between the government and the first board of the Post. It took a year to resolve, requiring the Post to operate under a licence for the first year. See Smith, *Reining in the Dinosaur*, 55.

21 Spicer, *Transforming Government Enterprises*, 58.

22 Interview with Jean Pierre Andre, Asset and Liability Branch, Treasury.

23 Spicer, *Transforming Government Enterprises*, 52.

24 See Minister of Communications, news release, "New Deed of Understanding Guarantees Universal Service," 17 February 1998.

25 There appear to be few letters of complaints or interventions by MPs.

26 Interview with Garry Whale, executive assistant to the chief executive, New Zealand Post.

27 Ibid.

28 Interview with Galt and Harford.

29 Interview with various government and postal officials.

30 See www.med.govt.nz/pbt/post_pol/register/index.

31 John Cooper, the previous principal adviser, was from Phillips; John Wardrop had a commercial background before coming to Treasury.

32 Interview with John Cooper, principal adviser, and John Wardrop, senior adviser, State Owned Enterprises, Crown Company Monitoring Advisory Unit.

33 Interview with Cooper and Wardrop.

34 Smith, *Reining in the Dinosaur*, 60–1.

35 Interviews with postal and government officials.

36 Interview with Andre and Toime.

37 Spicer, *Transforming Government Enterprises*, 54–5. Interview with Andre.

38 Ibid.

39 Ranganathan, *Redirecting Mail*, 123; interview with Affleck; interview with Armstrong.

40 Interview with Cooper and Wardrop.

41 Other than Ross Armstrong, Bryan Reeves used to be a National MP.

42 Interview with Allen.

43 Ibid.

44 Smith, *Reining in the Dinosaur*, 63.

45 Mayes, "The New Zealand Experiment."

46 Ranganathan, *Redirecting the Mail*, 67.

47 Elmar Toime, "Unlocking the Potential: The Future of the Post," Universal Postal Union Strategy Conference, Geneva, 13–14 October 1997.

48 Interview with Allen.

49 Smith, *Reining in the Dinosaur*, 55.

50 Interview with Armstrong. See also Smith, *Reining in the Dinosaur,* 117ff.
51 Interview with Allen.
52 Interview with Affleck.
53 Interview with Armstrong.
54 Interviews with Armstrong, Affleck, Allen, and Whale. The government slapped the wrist of Contact Energy over this, a minor punishment.
55 Interviews with Whale, Andre, Armstrong.
56 Interview with Armstrong.
57 Interview with Whale.
58 Interview with Andre.
59 Ibid.
60 Interview with Allen.
61 Interview with Ron Burgess, past director of the postal union. See Smith, *Reining in the Dinosaur,* 56–9.
62 Interviews with Jones and Allen; interview with Robert Lake, operations leader, NZ Post.
63 Interview with Allen.
64 Interview with Sarah McRae, Engineers Union.
65 Smith, *Reining in the Dinosaur,* 69–83.
66 Ibid., 117ff.
67 See Ministry of Commerce, "Postal Services in New Zealand," 7 March 1997, for an overview of the Post's performance in the reform period.
68 See Toime, "Unlocking the Potential." See also NZ Post, *Annual Report,* 1997, 8, 10; 1996 (5): "The letters business environment remains buoyant despite advances in electronic media." In the post-deregulation pamphlet "Delivering for New Zealand," NZ Post argued that "while recognizing the strong international growth in the use of electronic communications, we are confident that there is a strong future for letters."
69 Smith, *Reining in the Dinosaur,* 66.
70 Interview with Dowson. Comparing postal prices across nations can be misleading, since different countries offer varying degrees of speed of delivery and service.
71 Interview with Allen.
72 It should be noted that residential delivery is usually to the lot line, not to the front door, as in Canada. This would increase delivery costs threefold. Interviews with Allen, Lake.
73 Interview with Suzanne Morton, research manager, NZ Post.
74 Historically, DX ran a closed private-box network that was sorted and delivered by DX. Before deregulation, it delivered mail only to its own boxes. It has now started street deliveries in the central business districts of most major cities. It also has an access agreement with the Post so that mail that it cannot deliver can be passed to the Post for delivery.

75 There is an updated registry available on the Ministry of Commerce WebPage, cited in n. 30 above.
76 See www.fastwaypost.com and www.nationalmail.co/nz.
77 It can be found at www.ebil.co.nz.
78 Smith, *Reining in the Dinosaur,* 136–40.
79 NZ Post, *Annual Report,* 1996, 6.
80 The government provided NZ$78.2 million start-up funds. The Post's and the government's view is that the New Bank will be successful for a number of reasons, including the fact that it will be the only New Zealand bank (all others are foreign-owned). The New Bank will have the largest network in the country and will enjoy a strong brand image.
81 Interview with Sarah McRae.
82 See the long section on internationalization in NZ Post, *Annual Report,* 1997.
83 See press release, "NZPIL Signs Memorandum of Agreement with Nigerian Government," 30 June 2000.

PART THREE   THE NATIONAL MODEL

CHAPTER SIX   DENMARK

1 Interviews with Troels Thomsen, head of International Relations, Post Danmark, and Carsten Marckstrøm Olesen and Carl Thaarup-Hansen, Ministry of Transport, Postal Affairs Division.
2 Interview with Thomsen.
3 Interview with Olesen and Thaarup-Hansen.
4 Interview with Jan Svendsen and Lars Lyngse, Dansk Postforbund.
5 Interviews with Thomsen, Olesen, Thaarup-Hansen, Lyngse.
6 Interview with Thaarup-Hansen and Olesen. See also "Report from the Danish Postworkers Union, Development of the Danish Postoffice," typescript, n.d.
7 Ministry of Traffic, "Agreement on the Modernization of the Post Office," 21 November 1994.
8 Minister of Traffic, "Bill on Postal Business," 24 November 1994.
9 Minister of Traffic, "Post Danmark (the Danish Post Office)," 24 November 1994.
10 "Executive Order on the Concession Granted to Post Danmark," 23 February 1995.
11 Notes on Chapter 2, Subsection 5, Postal Services Act.
12 The Ministry of Transport is often referred to as the Ministry of Traffic. They are the same body.
13 Notes on Chapter 2, Postal Services Act.
14 Ibid., Chapter 3.

15 The Ministry of Transport produced a document for this purpose, "Accounting Regulations for Post Danmark," August 1997. The ministry provides competition-law guidelines for the Post, to prevent distortion of competition by way of cross-subsidization, and insists on the full-costs method of allocation. It also provides accounting regulations for the Post, insisting on three sets of accounts: one for the sole-rights area, one for the universal-service obligations subject to competition, and one for the pure competitive area.

16 "The Minister does not have the authority to issue instructions to the board of directors, and thus does not have the authority to impose the performance or non-performance of certain activities." Explanatory notes to the Postal Act, Section 6, Subsection 4.

17 Interviews with Post, union, and ministry officials.

18 Interview with Lyngse.

19 Interview with Mutty Rotenberg, SID.

20 The compensation was DKK482 million in 1995 and 503 million in 1996.

21 Interview with Thaarup-Hansen and Olesen.

22 Interview with Lyngse.

23 About 300–400 members resign a year.

24 Interviews with Lyngse and Rotenberg.

25 Correspondence with postal union.

26 See the Cooper and Lybrants study for the Radwanski report.

27 Post Danmark, *Annual Report*, 1998, 4.

28 Ibid., 8.

29 Ibid., 5.

30 Interviews with Thomsen, Olesen, Thaarup-Hansen. See Post Danmark, *Annual Report*, 1997, 5, and 1998, 8.

31 Post Danmark, *Annual Report*, 1998, 8.

32 Interview with Thomsen.

33 See Post Danmark, *Annual Report*, 1995, 8, on the 1995 decline.

34 See Post Danmark, *Annual Report*, 1996, 12. See also 1998 report.

35 Post Danmark, *Annual Report*, 1996, 4, and 1997, 4.

36 Interview with Thaarup-Hansen and Olesen. See Post Danmark, *Annual Report*, 1997, 1998, 5.

37 Interview with Thaarup-Hansen and Olesen.

38 Interview with Thomsen.

39 Post Danmark, *Annual Report*, 1995, 5

40 See Tim Burt, *Financial Post*, 29 January 1999, 3.

CHAPTER SEVEN   FRANCE

1 See United States Postal Service, "A Strategic Review of Progressive Postal Administrations: Competition, Commercialization and Deregulation,"

prepared by Price Waterhouse, February 1996, 17–19. See also Dowson, *Postal Performance*, 61.

2 Roundtable interview with Force Ouvrière des Travailleurs des Postes et des Télécommunications (FO), including Jacky Arches and Michel Pesnel.

3 Hubert Prévot, "L'avenir du service public de la poste et des télécommunications," study prepared for Paul Quiles, Minister of La Poste and Telecommunications, 31 July 1989.

4 Roundtable interview with Commission Supérieure du Service Public des Postes et Télécommunications (CSSPpt), hosted by Marie-Josée Varloot (secretary-general) and Marie-Claude Brun (head of the secretariat), and including a number of political and expert members.

5 FO interview.

6 CSSPpt interview.

7 La Poste, *Report*, 1997, 2–3.

8 François Fillon speech to the National Assembly, 26 November 1998, 3.

9 In the period 1991–93, La Poste paid a transitional flat-rate levy to the government. La Poste entered the common tax system in 1994, at which time it paid 328 million francs in corporate tax.

10 Interview CSSPpt.

11 Ibid.

12 Ibid.

13 Ibid.

14 Three recent appointments may signal a strategic sea-change – the appointment of board members who are directors of private-sector firms. These were Thierry Breton, president and director general of Thomson SA and Thomson Multimdeia; Jean-René Fourtou, vice-president and director general of Aventis, and Philippe Lagayette, president and director general of J.P. Morgan.

15 Interview CSSPpt.

16 Interview with FO.

17 La Poste, *Report*, 1997.

18 This represented 42 per cent of its payroll. The comparable proportion for its competitors was 36 per cent. See La Poste, *Report*, 1997, 4.

19 According to FO, half of the postal network is unprofitable, the press subsidy is only a third of what it should be (at a cost of three billion francs to the Post), and the cost of servicing accounts is two billion francs.

20 Interview with Édouard Dayan, director of European and International Affairs.

21 See Bernard Roy, David Storer, and Joelle Toledano, "Economic Costs in Postal Sector – From Theory to Practice." Paper presented to the Conference on Postal and Delivery Economics, Vancouver, Canada, June 2000.

22 La Poste, *Report*, 1997.

23 See La Poste, press releases 15 November 1995 and 15 January 1997.
24 Interview with Dayan.
25 See La Poste, press release, 23 September 1999: "Bilan Social: La Poste renforce sa politique en faveur de l'emploi stable."
26 See La Poste, *Report*, 1997, 13.
27 See La Poste, *Report*, 1997, 31.
28 CSSPpt interview.
29 Interview with Dayan.
30 CSSPpt interview.

CHAPTER EIGHT   CANADA

1 There are 12 times more points of call per square kilometre in the United States and 120 times more in the United Kingdom.
2 For example, an Angus Reid poll reported that 91 per cent of Canadians declared that their ability to send mail anywhere is one of the great things about life in Canada. See *Globe and Mail*, 11 March 1996. The Radwanski report stated that privatization "was not an option that received strong support in submissions made to the review ... very few companies have expressed any enthusiasm for full privatization of the corporation." See Canada Post Mandate Review, *The Future of Canada Post Corporation* (Ottawa: Minister of Public Works and Government Services Canada 1996), 72, 75. Hereafter referred to as the Radwanski report.
3 See Ranganathan, *Redirecting Mail*, 266–7, 252, 280. The chapter on Canada contrasts its operational and modernization accomplishments with the absence of regulatory reforms, a state of affairs that could lead to a decline in CPC autonomy.
4 See Canada Post, *Report*, 1999–2000, 24.
5 For a good overview, see the chairman's remarks in Canada Post Corporation, *Annual Report*, 1998–99, 3.
6 The UPS suit contains a wide-ranging array of claims under Chapters 11 and 15 of Section A of NAFTA – which more or less surveys all of the criticisms and challenges made by postal critics and competitors over the last two decades. UPS is seeking $230 million in damages.
7 For a more extensive treatment, see Robert M. Campbell, *The Politics of the Post*, Part I.
8 For a more elaborate explanation, see Campbell, *The Politics of the Post*, chapter 2. For a similar perspective, see Ranganathan, *Redirecting Mail*, 257.
9 "The situation in the Post Office is intolerable and has been for some time. Canadians are losing their patience. They are increasingly fed up. So am I." *Globe and Mail*, 2 August 1978.
10 See Campbell, *The Politics of the Post*, 171, 178, and 180.
11 Ibid., 396n.19, and 172–8.

12 The Financial Administration Act was amended in 1984 to require crown corporations to submit annually a five-year plan and capital budget for government approval.

13 See Campbell, *The Politics of the Post*, chapter 7.

14 Ibid., chapter 8.

15 Ibid., chapter 9.

16 Former CPC vice-president Keith Joliffe reported at a Fraser Institute conference on privatization that privatization had already taken place internally, since CPC's attitudes gave it a privatized view of the world. See his paper "Canada Post Privatization: A Postal Reform Option" in the proceedings of that conference, 23 June 1989.

17 Campbell, *The Politics of the Post*, chapter 10.

18 See Robert M. Campbell, "Symbolic Regulation: The Case of Third Party Regulation of Canada Post," *Canadian Public Policy*, 19, 3 (September 1993): 325–9.

19 See CPC's annual reports. The losses incurred in 1987 and 1991 were related to the strikes in those years.

20 As reported by Doug Moffatt, executive director, Canadian Couriers Association, in an interview.

21 House of Commons, *Debates*, 1986, 13571, 13583, 14213.

22 There was a minute attached to the Treasury Board/cabinet minute approving the 1993 corporate plan. Interview with Jane Billings, Corporate Implementation Group, Public Works and Government Services Canada.

23 Interviews with government and postal officials.

24 See Canada Post Corporation, *Annual Report*, 1997–98, 5.

25 See Minutes of the Standing Committee on Natural Resources and Government Operations, 22 April 1999.

26 See *Globe and Mail*, 9 September 1989; *Toronto Star*, 25 April 1990.

27 Interviews with postal and government officials.

28 See Radwanski report, 75: "Very few companies have expressed any enthusiasm for full privatization of the corporation." For a general overview of the topic, see 73–7.

29 See various statements in the House of Commons, *Debates*, 20 March 1997, 9289; 10 April 1997, 9554; 14 April 1997, 9653; 8 October 1996, 5244 and 5246.

30 Minutes of the Standing Committee on Natural Resources and Government Operations, 17 February 1998. See also his statement in the House of Commons, 2 December 1997.

31 Interview with Billings.

32 Radwanski report, 64.

33 See G. Bruce Doern et al., *Changing the Rules: Canadian Regulatory Regimes and Institutions*, 396, 402.

34 This directive power has never been used.

35 See Campbell, *The Politics of the Post*, 54–5.

36 Interviews with government and postal officials.

37 For the period to the early 1990s, see Campbell, *The Politics of the Post*, 176–7, 237, 248, 251,

38 Interview with Billings.

39 CIG appears to resemble an old idea that had been mooted (but rejected) in the first draft of the CPC Act in 1978. The plan was to have a secretariat comprising senior bureaucratic officials to oversee the Post. This was rejected on the grounds that it would have perpetuated too much bureaucratic influence in the ostensibly autonomous crown corporation.

40 See Campbell, *The Politics of the Post*, 302.

41 See Radwanski report, 64.

42 Ibid.

43 See Canada Post, *Ensuring Universal Service at Affordable Rates*, 15 February 1996, its submission to the Mandate Review. See also Gagliano at Standing Committee on Natural Resources and Government Operations, 17 February 1998.

44 See Campbell, *The Politics of the Post*, 300–1.

45 Interview with Tim Burke, Government Relations, Canada Post. For an overview of the decline in Parliament's role, see Campbell, *The Politics of the Post*, 307–8.

46 For a detailed overview, see Campbell, *The Politics of the Post*, 308–12.

47 See House of Commons, *Debates*, 21 January 1993, 644; 17 February 1994, 1505; 18 February 1994, 1559.

48 See Gagliano at Standing Committee on Natural Resources and Government Operations.

49 See CPC press release, "Canada Post Introduces New Look," 6 January 1998. See Gagliano at Standing Committee on Natural Resources and Government Operations.

50 For the expression of pride associated with the reintroduction of the use of the word "Canadian" in the name: interview with Gagliano. See also Radwanski report, 103–4, which encouraged this.

51 See *Globe and Mail*, 4 October 1994.

52 Ibid., 1 July 1995, B2.

53 Ibid, 27, 28 June, 1 July 1995. Minister Marleau extended this price freeze after the Mandate Review, as part of the government's response to that report.

54 *Globe and Mail*, 7 July 1995.

55 See *Globe and Mail*, 7 November 1995; *Financial Post*, 17 August 1995. Interview with CCA President Doug Moffatt. Interviews with various CPC officials. For a good overview of the origins and process of the Mandate Review, see Mary Bundy, "An Examination of the Canada Post Mandate Review," paper presented to the Rutgers University Fifth Conference on Postal and Delivery Economics, Helsingor, Denmark, 11–14 June 1997.

56 Interview with Hank Klassen, past executive vice-president, Canada Post.

57 Coopers and Lybrands Consulting, *Choices for a Self-Sustaining Canada Post,* prepared for Canada Post Corporation, November 1995. Canada Post's submission itself was *Ensuring Universal Service at Affordable Rates,* 15 February 1996. The Coopers and Lybrand study tested four "models" for Canada Post's future, including ones that eliminated the exclusive privilege and/or limited CPC's commercial autonomy. It recommended that, like postal regimes abroad, Canada Post be allowed to maximize its revenue possibilities through increased commercial autonomy – the exact opposite of what Radwanski recommended.

58 Radwanski report.

59 *Globe and Mail,* 8 October 1996.

60 See *Maclean's,* 21 October 1996; *Globe and Mail,* 8 October 1996, B10; 14, 15 November 1996. The ad-mail decision led to large labour protests about the loss of jobs that this generated. See House of Commons, *Debates,* 22 October 1996, 5563; 3 December 1996, 7041; 9 December 1996, 7240–1; 21 November 1996, 6563–4. The government also directed CPC to respect environmental stickers at addresses that did not want to receive admail.

61 See *Globe and Mail,* 4, 18, 19 April, 18 May, 4 June 1996; *Maclean's,* 1 April 1996, 43.

62 This is the perspective of most senior CPC executives that I have interviewed over the years.

63 Interview with André Villeneuve, vice-president, Human Resources, Canada Post Corporation.

64 *Globe and Mail,* 2, 3 February 1998. See also *Globe and Mail,* 6 December 1997, B2. Interview with Villeneuve.

65 The first draft of Bill C-24 included the following: "The mediator-arbitrator shall be guided by the need for terms and conditions of employment that are consistent with those in comparable industries in the private and public sectors and that will provide the necessary degree of flexibility to ensure the short- and long-term economic viability and competitiveness of Canada Post Corporation, taking into account (a) that the Canada Post Corporation must ... (I) Perform financially in a commercially acceptable range." The final draft dropped the contentious references to commercial viability and comparability and read, "The mediator-arbitrator shall be guided by the need for terms and conditions of employment that are consistent with the Canada Post Corporation Act and the viability and financial stability of Canada Post."

66 Judge Guy A. Richard was overheard by a postal employee on a plane making statements and observations which ostensibly demonstrated a pro-management orientation.

67 Interview with officials.

68 See Canada Post, *Report*, 1999–2000, 44. Even as late as 1999–2000, the subsidy was cut from $58 million to $40 million.

69 "[These targets] were no longer realistic in the current context, so we are pleased that the government has agreed to more realistic targets and has given us the time to achieve them" André Ouellet, CPC press release, "Multiyear Policy Framework Established for Canada Post," 18 January 1999.

70 This conclusion was reached through piecing together the logic of statements in interviews with various officials.

71 See Ranganathan, *Redirecting Mail*, 252, 280.

72 See the results of an Angus Reid poll in *Globe and Mail*, 11 March 1996. Eighty-two per cent of those polled had a favorable impression of Canada Post and 79 per cent were satisfied with its service. As indicated earlier, there was little business support given to privatization at the Mandate Review hearings. For an external evaluation of CPC, see Ranganathan, *Redirecting Mail*, 252, 276–7, 280.

73 See *Montreal Gazette*, 26 August 1993, F1.

74 For example, see Canada Post, *Annual Report*, 1995–96, 3, and 1999–2000, 24–5.

75 See Ranganathan, *Redirecting Mail*, 277; Coopers and Lybrands, *Choices for a Self-Sustaining Canada Post.*

76 For the new arrangement, see the Canada Post Release "Improved Payment Structure for Private Postal Outlets Takes Effect Today," 1 December 1998. With respect to the controversy this generated, see *Maclean's*, 8 June 1998, 49; Heather Scoffield, "Canada Post cuts franchisees' stamp sale commissions," *Globe and Mail*, 2 December 1998, B4, and "Canada Post plan could force franchises into bankruptcy," *Globe and Mail*, 28 November 1998, A5.

77 For example, the Bank of Nova Scotia and CPC are testing in ten remote communities in Newfoundland. See Paul Brent and Sinclair Stewart, "Post offices to be tested as banking providers," *National Post*, 7 July 2000, C3. CPC has had a similar arrangement with the Bank of Montreal.

78 See Canada Post, *Corporate Plan*, 1999–2000 to 2003–4. Canada Post, *Report*, 1997–98, 8.

79 See Canada Post, *Annual Report*, 1996–97. As noted in chapter 5, n. 72, home delivery in Canada involves delivery right to the front door, which is part of the reason for its high-unit cost compared to mail service in, say, New Zealand, where delivery is to the lot line.

80 See *Globe and Mail*, 7 April 1993 and 26 October 1993, B2.

81 See *Globe and Mail*, 31 March 1994 and 8 December 1994, and *Financial Post* 3 December 1994. CPC's host department – Public Works and Government Services Canada – lost out in the bidding.

82 Purolator had been one of Gerry Schwartz's Onex Corporation's few business fumbles. The Liberal opposition did not raise a fuss that might have embarrassed Schwartz, who was a party backer and fund-raiser.

83 See the editorials and business section in the *Globe and Mail*, 5, 8, 29 (C1) June 1993; *Maclean's*, 14 June 1993.

84 See *Globe and Mail*, 8 September 1993, B18, 30 September 1993, B6, 27 November 1993, B6, 25 May 1995, B4.

85 Interview with Doug Moffatt. See *Financial Post*, 12 March 1994, S13–14, Montreal Gazette, 24 August 1994, D4.

86 Radwanski report, 84.

87 See André Ouellet and Alfonso Gagliano at Standing Committee on Natural Resources and Government Operations.

88 See Jim Carroll, "Canada Post delivers innovation," *Globe and Mail*, 10 July 2000, B7. A Bain survey placed Canada Post's E-post service in the number-nine position in its ranking of Canada's hottest dot-coms.

89 It offers a CD-ROM that allows customers to get connected and receive free e-mail service on the 3web network, which was Canada's first and largest free Internet and e-mail service.

90 See Carl Neustawdter, "Canada Post leads Latin revolution." *Globe and Mail*, 9 November 1998, B13.

91 Canada Post, *Report*, 1999–2000, 24.

92 See Ian Jack, "UPS suing Ottawa for $230 million," *National Post*, 22 April 2000, and Heather Scoffield, "UPS jeopardizing rural mail: CUPW," *Globe and Mail*, 10 May 2000, B7.

93 See Canada Post press release, 22 April 2000, "Canada Post Dismisses Latest Courier Allegations."

PART FOUR   THE HYBRID MODEL

CHAPTER NINE   THE UNITED KINGDOM

1 See National Economic Research Associates (NERA), "Overseas Postal Reform." Final Report, prepared for the National Competition Council (Australia), London, October 1997. The Post is perhaps best known as the "Royal Mail," which, however, is actually but one part of the larger postal operation that includes separate organizations for retail, parcels, and other activities. As will be seen presently, the Post has adopted the name "Consignia" for international marketing and branding purposes. The Royal Mail, the Post Office, and Parcel Force retain their corporate identities. For ease of presentation, this book will refer to the "Post."

2 Interview with Alan Johnson. Johnson had been the general secretary of the CWU and was elected as an MP in the Blair victory. He was named

parliamentary secretary of state at the Department of Trade and Industry, with responsibility for employment relations, the Post Office, and Industry. He is now minister for Competitiveness, Department of Trade and Industry.

3 Ibid. See also *Economist*, 13 February 1993, 10. A Mori poll indicated that 64 per cent of the population opposed privatization of what is seen as a non-negotiable public service.

4 Interview with Mike Whitehead and Nigel Reese of the postal-review team at the Department of Trade and Industry. See *Economist*, 13 February 1993, 10.

5 This was introduced in January 2001. The Post's domestic brand names – the Post Office and so on – would continue to be used. The name "Consignia" was derived from the verb "consign," meaning "to entreat to the care of." See Post Office press release, "Consignia – The New Name for the Post Office Group," 9 January 2001.

6 Peter Vass, "Regulatory Reform and Relations among Multiple Authorities in the United Kingdom," in Doern and Wilks, eds., *Changing Regulatory Institutions in British and North America*, 237. The anecdotal view is that Thatcher considered it inappropriate to privatize something called the *Royal* Mail. See *Economist*, 16 January 1993, 53–4, and 13 February 1993, 10. Michael Heseltine was committed to privatizing the Post in 1994, but his plan was derailed politically by a coalition of rural Tories, Labour MPs, and the unions. See *Economist*, 21 May 1994, 65, and 5 November 1994, 56.

7 Brian W. Hogwood, "Regulatory Institutions in the United Kingdom: Increasing Regulation in the "Shrinking State,'" in Doern and Wilks, *Changing Regulatory Institutions*, 92.

8 Interview with Whitehead and Reese. Interview with Ian Reay, head of competition and regulation policy at the Post. See Stephen Wilks, "Utility Regulation," in Doern and Wilks, *Changing Regulatory Institutions*, 157.

9 Ranganathan, *Redirecting Mail*, 243.

10 Ibid. The author should declare a modest personal bias. I have lived in England, and was always impressed by the speed and reliability of the first-class mail. In a recent research visit, I was struck by how modest, indeed spartan, were the Post's headquarters.

11 For a good overview, see the recent white paper produced by the secretary of state for trade and industry, "Post Office Reform: A World Class Service for the 21st Century," July 1999, chapters 1 and 2. See also CWU papers, "Why the Post Office Needs Commercial Freedom," July 1998; "Freedom to Deliver: Posting the Way to Greater Success," February 1997; "Why the British Post Office Should Not be Privatized," November 1996.

12 This case was dropped in favour of an out-of-court settlement once the British made a strategic alliance with the TPG and Singapore Post. See

the following section on mergers and acquisitions. The British – and others – are also suing Deutsche Post for not delivering their international mail in the German market, since the Germans act to protect their domestic territory.

13 Post, *Report*, 1997–98, 4.

14 See "The Communication Workers Union Submission to the DTI on the Review of the Crown Office Network 1997" and CWU's "Further Submission to the Government Review of the Post Office," June 1998.

15 See London Economics, "An Evaluation of the Independent Publicly Owned Corporation and its Applicability to the Post Office," October 1998. This study made the case that the IPOC approach was superior to privatization.

16 See Dowson, *Postal Performance*, 98ff.

17 Ranganathan, *Redirecting Mail*, 243.

18 See Dowson, *Postal Performance*, 104; Ranganathan, *Redirecting Mail*, 243ff.

19 Dowson, *Postal Performance*, 111; Coopers and Lybrand, study prepared for Canada Post, Radwanski postal review.

20 The group was called Protecting Postal Services.

21 "The Government's provisional conclusion is that the best way of meeting all its objectives is to allow Royal Mail and Parcelforce to operate as a private company owned by the public and employees, with the Government retaining 49% of the shares. The public services would not be put at risk by such proposals. The Government's commitment to the universal service and uniform tariff would be written into legislation, and a strong and independent regulator would be appointed to enforce standards of service under the Citizen's Charter." Trade and Industry Select Committee, First Report into the Future of the Post Office, London, March 1994.

22 Department of Trade and Industry, "The Future of Postal Services," A Consultative Document, London, June 1994 (the green paper).

23 "The Government recognizes ... that many people would prefer a closer link [than 100 per cent share sale]. The desire to see such a link reflects the important role which Royal Mail plays in our national life." Similarly, the government declared that a degree of monopoly would still be required "to support the maintenance of the universal service and uniform tariff structure." Ibid., 16.

24 Interview with Johnson.

25 See *Economist*, 21 May 1994, 65, and 5 November 1994, 56.

26 Dowson, *Postal Performance*, 106–8; interview with Whitehead and Reese, DTI.

27 Interview with Whitehead and Reese.

28 Interview with Johnson.

29 See DTI press release, "Ian McCartney Announces Immediate and Comprehensive Review of Options for the Post Office," 16 May 1997.

30 See Select Committee on Trade and Industry, *Third Report*, 22 January 1998.

31 See DTI press release, "Beckett Announces Commitment to Public Sector Post Office," 6 April 1998. See also Select Committee on Trade and Industry, *Fifth Special Report*, appendix, which contains the government's formal response to TISC's 22 January 1998 Third Report.

32 Interview with Johnson. Interview with Richard Adams, secretary to the Post Board. The model would be 40 per cent government, 40 per cent private shares, 20 per cent postal workers.

33 See Department of Trade and Industry, "Mandelson Announces Radical Proposals for Post Office," 7 December 1998.

34 Secretary of State for Trade and Industry, "Post Office Reform: A World Class Service for the 21st century," July 1999.

35 For a critical assessment of the white paper, see *The Economist*, 10 July 1999, 51.

36 For an overview of the bill, see Stephen Agar and Catherine Churchard, "Postal Reform in the UK – The Postal Services Bill 2000," paper presented at the Conference on Postal and Delivery Economics, Vancouver, Canada, June 2000.

37 The CWU, the Trade and Industry Select Committee (TISC), and the Trades and Union Congress (TUC) recommended strongly that the government withdraw the proposed recommendation to narrow the exclusive privilege. For example, see the CWU press release, "Parliamentary Support for Union Position on Post Office Monopoly," 21 September 1999, and "Government Re-Think on Post Office Monopoly," 1 October 1999.

38 The profit target would no longer comprise separate profit targets for each of letters, parcels, and counters but would be an integrated target.

39 The CWU estimated that 8.5 per cent of the market would be "freed" in halving the restricted area to fifty pence. Of course, not all of this market would be automatically lost to the Post's competitors.

40 The chair is Graham Corbett, deputy chair of the Competitions Commission and former CEO of Eurotunnel. The CEO is Martin Stanley, former DTI principal private secretary and former director general of the Regulatory Impact Unit of the Cabinet Office. The part-time commissioners are Robin Aaronson (an economist and business consultant, previously at the Treasury and the Monopolies and Mergers Commission); Tony Cooper (General Secretary of the Engineers and Managers Association and member of the TUC General Council); Janet Lewis-Jones (formerly of the Board of Film Classification, British Waterways Board); Julia

Kaufmann (director of Children in Need Appeal); and Ken Olisa, chair and CEO of Interregnum, an IT firm).

41 See Post Services Commission Business Plan, 10 November 2000, and Martin Stanley's speech to the CWU, 7 June 2000, both located on the commission's website, www.psc.gov.uk.

42 If the PSC recommended a narrowing of the protected area, this change would have to be approved by both houses of Parliament. Similarly, if the PSC recommended the change but the minister rejected it, the government would have to table its explanation in both houses. See Clause 8.

43 The details of the licence, as well as a consultation document associated with the issuing of the licence, are available on Postcomm's website. With respect to larger and more expensive postal items, Consignia would be allowed to increase its prices no faster than the rate of inflation. The market would set prices in competitive products like express-courier services.

44 The PSC has opened up a consultation process about these major issues, issuing two consultation documents in September 2000: "Licensing Postal Services" and "Promoting Effective Competition between Postal Operators." They are both available on its website.

45 Interviews with Adams and Reay.

46 See the Post's press release, "Post Office Welcomes Bill – A Springboard to Beat the Competition," 28 January 2000.

47 For example, Royal Mail's business practices and service standards are articulated clearly in this pamphlet.

48 For example, see Ranganathan, *Redirecting Mail,* 247–8; green paper ("The Future of Postal Services"); various TISC reports; various POUNC reports; interviews with Reay, Adams, Johnson.

49 Interview with Whitehead and Reese, DTI.

50 Interview with Adams.

51 Interviews with Reay and Adams.

52 Interview with Johnson.

53 C. Pollitt and S. Haney, *Public Management Reforms: Three Anglo-Finnish Case Studies,* Ministry of Finance, Helsinki, 1997, 81–2.

54 Interview with Whitehead and Reese, DTI.

55 Interview with Johnson.

56 See Post, *Report,* 1998–99, 7.

57 Interviews with Adams, Reay.

58 See POUNC, *Annual Report,* various years. On quality and the EFL, see especially 1996–97, 4, 6, 11.

59 This was the result of the collapse of the Public Finance Initiative in Counters, which meant that the Post would have to absorb the costs of the Horizon venture between the Post, ICL, and the DSS Benefits Agency.

60 The Post attributed the decline in the level of profits to increased technological competition and the freeze and/or reduction on various postal
   charges. See Post's press release, "Underlying Profits Fall 13% as Post
   Office Faces up to Tough Transition,"19 June 2000, and *Report*, 1999–
   2000, 2.

61 See the CEO's comments in the Post's *Report*, 1998–99, 11 and 4.

62 Interview with John Hackney, Chair of POUNC. See *Annual Report*, 1996–
   97, 14–16; 1998–99, 20–1.

63 See Post's *Report*, assorted years.

64 POUNC, *Report*, 1998–99, 29.

65 It is estimated that these franchises brought £1 billion in investment to
   the operation. See Ranganathan, *Redirecting Mail*, 244.

66 See POUNC, annual report, various years.

67 This initiative complements Barclays branch-rationalization scheme. It
   closed 171 of its branches in April 2000. See David Ibison and Chris
   Tighe, "Barclays PLC pilloried for bank closures," *Financial Post*, 8 April
   2000, D3.

68 See POUNC, *Report*, 1998–99. See CWU submission to the postal review.
   "Allan Johnson confirms Post Office package on track," Department of
   Trade and Industry press release, 26 March 2001.

69 Interview with Johnson. Interview with Derek Bright, CWU.

70 See Derek Bright, "Challenges Currently Facing our Postal Members,"
   CWU Research Paper, 23 March 1998.

71 See CWU press release, "'Way Forward" for Royal Mail Workers and the
   Industry," 10 February 2000.

72 See Ranganathan, *Redirecting Mail*, 249.

73 See Post's press release, 19 January 1999, "Britain Post Office Pledges to
   be a Top Player in New 'Superleague.'" See also Post's *Report*, 1997–98,
   4, and 1998–99, 12.

74 See Alan Pike, "Post Office arms itself for global market battle," *Financial Post*, 7 April 1999, 12.

75 See Post's press release, "Post Office Unveils Dramatic Growth in North
   America," 10 May 1999.

76 See Post's *Annual Report*, 1999–2000, 7.

77 See Post's press release, "Consignia – The New Name for the Post Office
   Group," 9 January 2001.

CHAPTER TEN   AUSTRALIA

1 See Jim Campbell, "Oveview of the International Postal Reform Movement."

2 See Ranganathan, *Redirecting Mail*, 227.

3 National Competition Council, *Review of the Australian Postal Corporation
  Act, Final Report*, vol. 1, Melbourne, 1998, 15.

4 Interview with Linda Nicholls, board chairman, Australia Post.

5 See Castles, *The Great Experiment*, 8–10.

6 John Edwards, *Keating: The Inside Story* (Penguin Australia, 1996), 296–7.

7 Interview with Gerry Ryan, board secretary, Australia Post. See also the United States Postal Service, "A Strategic Review of Progressive Postal Administrations: Competition, Commercialization and Deregulation," Price Waterhouse, February 1996, 13–4.

8 Interview with Senator Chris Schacht, recounting his time as minister of small business.

9 See Graeme John, speech to Universal Postal Union, Beijing congress.

10 National Competition Council, *Final Report*.

11 Ranganathan, *Redirecting Mail*, 223–6.

12 Dowson, *Postal Performance*, 10.

13 Interview with Maurice Castro, group manager, Strategic Planning, Australia Post.

14 Senator Chris Schacht recalled his days as private secretary to the PMG, when the office received 300 complaints a day.

15 Interview with Schacht. The right to strike had always existed in the public sector in Australia, and industrial action was never outlawed. The result was that industrial action did not follow the cycle of negotiations but rather took place continuously, particularly over workplace-related issues. Interview with David Barker, group manager, Human Resources, Australia Post.

16 Ranganathan, *Redirecting Mail*, 226.

17 Ibid., 228ff.

18 Dowson, *Postal Performance*, 13. See Towers Perrin Study, "Connections," 1995.

19 When AP was first corporatized, the Prices Surveillance Authority (PSA) administered the Prices Surveillance Act. The PSA merged with the Trade Practices Commission in 1995 to become the ACCC. The scope and mix of its regulatory coverage changed over time. Currently, this scope comprises all the reserved services.

20 See Castles, *The Great Experiment*, 11–12, 31. See also Tom Sheridan, "Labour Relations in Australia 1940–90," in Jim Hagan and Andrew Wells, eds., *Industrial Relations in Australia and Japan* (St Leonard's, Australia: Allen and Unwin 1994).

21 Industry Commission, *Mail, Courier and Postal Services*, 30 October 1992.

22 AP and government officials did agree to the targeting of a 16 per cent rate of return.

23 House of Representatives, Standing Committee on Communications, Transport and Microeconomic Reform, *Keeping Rural Australia Posted*, August 1996.

24 See joint press release by the treasurer, Peter Costello, and the DOCA minister, Senator Richard Alston, "Australia Post Review," 2 June 1997.

25 Interview with Jim Claven, industrial research officer, and Brian Baulk, divisional assistant secretary, CEPU (Communications Electrical Plumbing Union).

26 National Competition Council, *Final Report.*

27 Interview with Deborah Cope, deputy executive director, National Competition Council.

28 See press release, "Australia Post Confirms Reform Proposal," 11 March 1998.

29 See Australia Post, "Response to the National Competition Council's Options Paper on its Inquiry into Australian Postal Corporation Act 1989 and Associated Regulatory and Institutional Arrangements," December 1997, 3–4, 31–7.

30 Interview with Claven and Baulk.

31 Interview with Jim Livermore, assistant secretary, Market Competition Branch, Treasury.

32 See Senator Richard Alston, 16 July 1998 press release, "Government Delivers Better Postal Performance."

33 See Graeme John, press release, "Reform Will Cause No 'Bush' Closures," 16 July 1998. See speech by Linda Nicholls to the Australian Major Maul Users Union, 15 October 1998.

34 See Postal Services Legislation Amendment Bill 2000, "A Bill for an Act to amend legislation relating to postal services and for related purposes." There is an excellent explanatory memorandum that accompanies the bill. It includes a regulation-impact statement and an extended discussion of options.

35 Interview with John Neil, assistant secretary, Enterprise Policy and Radiocommunications Branch, Telecommunications Industry Division, Department of Communication and the Arts. Interviews also with Livermore and Nicholls.

36 Interview with Livermore.

37 Interview with Robert Gray, group manager, Business Strategy, Australia Post. Interviews also with Livermore and Neil.

38 Interview with Ryan.

39 Interview with Castro.

40 Interview with Claven and Baulk.

41 Interview with Livermore.

42 Interview with Neil.

43 Australia Post and Major Mail Users of Australia Limited, *Code of Practice,* Melbourne, 21 October 1999

44 Australia Post, *Service Charter,* Melbourne, June 1998.

45 See Graeme John, speech to the Universal Postal Union, Beijing congress.

46 Interview with Neil.

47 Interview with Ryan.

48 Interview with David Ingham, DOFA, and Genevieve Bessell, adviser, Office of the Minister of Finance.

49 Interview with Nicholls.

50 Ibid. The last time an "appointed government director" appeared on the board was in 1994 – Mike Hutchinson, DOCA deputy secretary.

51 Interview with Neil.

52 Linda Nicholls is an American who did her MBA at Harvard. She has had banking experience in New Zealand and in Australia. A Labor government appointed her.

53 Interview with Ryan, Gray.

54 Interview with Neil.

55 Interview with Ingham, Bessell.

56 This description has been distilled from discussions with Neil, Ingham, Gray, and Ryan.

57 This happened on one occasion, but not with regard to AP.

58 I was able to look at a draft copy of a plan in preparation, under confidence.

59 See Scott Prasser and Graeme Starr, *Policy and Change: The Howard Mandate*, Hale and Iremonger, Sydney, 1997. Interviews with Schacht, Barker, and Claven and Baulk.

60 Interview with Claven and Baulk and Barker.

61 Ibid.

62 Interview with Barker, Castro, and Claven and Baulk. See Michael Easson, "'Good While it Lasted': The Position and Prospects of Australian Unions in 1993," in Hagan and Wells, *Industrial Relations in Australia and Japan.*

63 For example, aggregation will be allowed (minimum 10,000 articles), so that mailshops will be allowed to mix mailings from a number of different original mailers.

64 Interview with Cope.

65 Interview with John Power, group manager, Letters, Australia Post.

66 Australia Post, *Annual Report*, 1998–99, 6.

67 Interview with Power.

68 See Graeme John, speech to the Universal Postal Union, Beijing congress.

69 For details, see any Australia Post annual report. Intrastate delivery targets are either next day or second day after posting. Interstate range from two- to four-day delivery, depending on locations. For example, next-day delivery is the standard for mail within the metropolitan areas of capital cities, two-day delivery is the standard for mail between metropolitan areas of capital cities in different states, and four-day delivery is the standard for mail between country locations in different states.

70 Interview with Castro.

CONCLUSION

1 This is the subject of the author's next research project, which will focus on international market and institutional developments.

2 Robert M. Campbell, *The Politics of the Post,* 370.

3 Interviews with officials.

4 Interview with Georges Clermont.

5 Universal Postal Union. Beijing congress, Fact Sheet.

6 Eurogiro is the world's largest branch network, comprising 80 million accounts and 50,000 offices. See "EUROGIRO – a cost efficient international payment system," in Universal Postal Union, *125 Years 1874–1999,* 240–1.

7 See Anik Lambert, "UPU Drive to Boost Express Mail Services," in ibid., 222.

8 See James I. Campbell Jr, "Reforming the Universal Postal Union," in Michael A. Crew and Paul R. Kleindorfer, eds., *Future Directions in Postal Reform* (Boston: Kluwer Academic Publishers 2001).

9 See Tim Walsh, "Globalization, Posts and the Universal Postal Union," in Michael A. Crew and Paul R. Kleindorfer, eds., *Current Directions in Postal Reform* (Boston: Kluwer Academic Publishers 2000).

10 Michael Mann, "Deutsche Post probe launched," *Globe and Mail,* 30 May 2000, B9.

11 See Phillip Hastings, "Facing a Changing Environment," in UPU, *125 Years,* 134.

12 See James Campbell, Jr, "GATS and Physical Delivery Networks," in Michael A. Crew and Paul R. Kleindorfer, eds., *Emerging Competition in Postal and Delivery Services* (Boston: Kluwer Academic Publishers 1999), 6–7.

13 See Mary S. Elcano and Anthony Alverno, "Postal Reform in the Universal Postal Union and the World Trade Organization," in Crew and Kleindorfer, *Future Directions in Postal Reform,* 293–308.

14 The oldest is the International Telegraphic Union. For a fuller review of the origins and evolution of the UPU, see UPU, *125 Years,* 17–27.

15 The World Bank has recently begun to use its lending program to assist the postal sector in developing countries. In a major study published in 1996, the Bank urged countries to pursue the corporatization and liberalization path and a greater role for the private sector. This was premised on its view that governments were no longer willing to subsidize postal loses or pay for needed capital investment. It encouraged private-sector partnerships and the trading off of monopoly rights in return for access to capital and expertise. See Ranganathan, *Redirecting Mail.*

16 For example, see Universal Postal Union, *The UPU Looks to the Future: Seoul Postal Strategy,* 1994, and *Geneva Strategy Conference,* Geneva 1997.

17 The congress adopted country-specific rates in developed countries, moving to a system based on cost and market factors. The system will differentiate between developed and developing countries until 2005, with developing countries continuing to pay present rates. The rates are to be set at 60 per cent of domestic costs, rising over time, and provision was made for a quality-of-service fund to assist postal improvements in developing countries. See Universal Postal Union Review, *Union Postale*, October, November, and December 1999 (24–9).

18 See Walsh, "Globalization, Posts and the Universal Postal Union."

19 See *Union Postale*, the UPU review report on the Beijing congress, fall 1999. See also UPU press release, "Blueprint for Action by the Postal World," 27 September 1999. On the last issue, see the British Post's press release, "British Post Office Warns UPU: 'Change or Become Out of Date,'" 8 November 1999. For an update on these developments, see *Union Postale*, summer 2000.

20 For an overview of UPU discussions, see J. Campbell Jr, "Reforming the Universal Postal Union," in Crew and Kleindorfer, *Future Directions in Postal Reform*.

21 Interview with Yves Cousquer.

22 See Royal Mail document by Ken Pearson, "International Pricing," n.d.

23 Interview with Cousquer.

24 Interview with Fernando Toledano, head of division, Directorate General XIII of the European Commission.

25 See "Green Paper on the Development of the Single Market for Postal Services," COM [European commission], 1991, 476 (11 June 1992).

26 See europa.eu.int/comm/internal_market/en/postal/posten/html.

27 Interview with Toledano.

28 Michael Mann, "Deutsche Post probe launched," *Globe and Mail*, 30 May 2000, B9. The British Post had also launched a case against the Dutch Post, which was settled once it entered into the alliance with the Dutch and Singapore Posts (see below).

29 Star Alliance centres on United Airlines, Air Canada, and Lufthansa. One World includes American Airlines and British Airways. Wings contains Northwest and KLM. SkyTeam joined Air France, Delta, Aero-Mexico, and Korean Air Lines.

30 See *Economist*, 17 July 1999, 57–8. Dirk Palder, *Post-Express*, 16 December 1998, 16–19.

31 Interview with John Dowson.

32 TPG, *Annual Report*, 1999, 7.

Bibliography

Adie, Douglas. *The Mail Monopoly: Analysing Canadian Postal Service.* Vancouver: Fraser Institute 1990.

Agar, Stephen, and Catherine Churchard. "Postal Reform in the UK – The Postal Services Bill 2000." Paper presented at the Conference on Regulatory Economics, Vancouver, June 2000.

Andersson, Peter. "Entry on Deregulated Postal Markets: Lessons from Sweden." Paper presented at Rutgers Conference on Postal and Delivery Economics, Sintra, Portugal, June 1999.

Andersson, Peter, and Mats Bladh. "Experiences from Liberalizing the Postal Market in Sweden." Paper presented to the Conference on Postal and Delivery Economics, Vancouver, June 2000.

Andeweg, Rudy B., and Galen A. Irwin. *Dutch Government and Politics.* London: Macmillan 1993.

Bundy, Mary. "An Examination of the Canada Post Mandate Review." Paper presented to the Conference on Postal and Delivery Economics, Helsingor, Denmark, June 1997.

Campbell Jr, James. "Overview of the International Postal Reform Movement," 4 December 1998, Rowland website (www.jcampbell.com/rowland), unpaginated.

Campbell, Robert M. "Symbolic Regulation: The Case of Third Party Regulation of Canada Post," *Canadian Public Policy,* 19, 3 (September 1993): 325–39.

– *The Politics of the Post: Canada's Postal System from Public Service to Privatization.* Peterborough, Ont.: Broadview Press 1994.

– "The Fourth Fiscal Era: Can There be a 'Post-neo-conservative' Fiscal Policy?" Leslie A. Pal, ed., *How Ottawa Spends 1999–2000: Shape Shifting:*

Canadian Governance Toward the 21st Century. Don Mills, Ont.: Oxford University Press 1999, 113–50.

Canada Post. *Ensuring Universal Service at Affordable Rates.* Ottawa: 5 February 1996.

Canada Post Mandate Review. *The Future of Canada Post Corporation.* Ottawa: Minister of Public Works and Government Services Canada 1996.

Castles, Frances, et al. *The Great Experiment: Labour Parties and Public Transformation in Australia and New Zealand.* Auckland, NZ: Auckland University Press 1996.

Communications Workers Union. "Why the British Post Office Should Not be Privatized." London: November 1996.

– "Freedom to Deliver: Posting the Way to Greater Success." London: February 1997.

– "Why the Post Office Needs Commercial Freedom." London: July 1998.

Coopers and Lybrands Consulting. *Choices for a Self-Sustaining Canada Post.* Prepared for Canada Post Corporation, November 1995.

Crew, Michael A., and Paul R. Kleindorfer, eds. *Emerging Competition in Postal and Delivery Services.* Boston: Kluwer Academic Publishers 1999.

– *Current Directions in Postal Reform.* Boston: Kluwer Academic Publishers 2000.

– *Future Directions in Postal Reform.* Boston: Kluwer Academic Publishers 2001.

Doern, G. Bruce, and Stephen Wilks, eds. *Changing Regulatory Institutions in Britain and North America.* Toronto: University of Toronto Press 1998.

Doern, G. Bruce, et al. *Changing the Rules: Canadian Regulatory Regimes and Institutions.* Toronto: University of Toronto Press 1999.

Dowson, John. M., Edward E. Horgan Jr. and T. Wood Parker. *Postal Performance: The Transformation of a Global Industry.* Arlington, Va.: Coopers and Lybrand 1997.

Easton, Brian. *The Commercialization of New Zealand.* Auckland, NZ: Auckland University Press 1997.

Edwards, John. *Keating: The Inside Story.* Penguin Australia 1996.

Gallett, Catherine. "Authorization Procedures in the Postal Sector: Possible Lessons from Other Sectors for Entry Regulation." Paper presented at the Conference on Postal and Delivery Economics, Montreux, Switzerland, June 1998.

Hagan, J., and A. Wells, eds. *Industrial Relations in Australia and Japan.* St. Leonard's, Australia: Allen and Unwin 1994.

House of Representatives, Standing Committee on Communications, Transport and Microeconomic Reform. *Keeping Rural Australia Posted.* Canberra: August 1996.

Industry Commission. *Mail, Courier and Postal Services,* Canberra: 30 October 1992.

Institute for the Future. *The Coming Transformation of Mail: Competition, Technology and the New Consumer.* Menlo Park, California, 1996.

– *Post Serving Business and New Consumers: Tomorrow's Purchasing Cycle.* Menlo Park, California, 1997.

Janitsch, H.R., and Richard Schultz. *Exploring the Information Revolution: Tele communications Issues and Options for Canada.* Toronto: Royal Bank 1989.

Joliffe, Keith. "Canada Post Privatization: A Postal Reform Option." In Proceedings of Fraser Institute Conference on Privatization, 23 June 1989.

Kelsey, Jane. *The New Zealand Experiment: A World Model for Structural Adjustment?* Auckland, NZ: Auckland University Press 1997.

Knauth, Peter, and Friedhelm Dommermuth. "Reorganization of the Postal Sector in Germany." Paper presented at the Conference on Postal and Delivery Economics, Helsingor, Denmark, June 1997.

Langford, Thomas. *Workers' Attitudes and Bourgeois Hegemony: Investigation of the Political Consciousness of Workers in the 1980s.* Hamilton, Ont.: McMaster University 1989.

Lee, Ian, *The Canadian Postal System: Origins, Growth and Decay of the State Postal Function, 1765–1982.* Ottawa: Carleton University 1989.

London Economics. *An Evaluation of the Independent Publicly Owned Corporation and Its Applicability to the Post Office.* London: October 1998.

Lundgren, Anna, and Sten Selander. "Uniform Tariffs and Prices Geared to Costs? – Swedish Experiences of the Incompatible Demands Article 12 of the EC Postal Directive." Paper presented to the Conference on Postal and Delivery Economics, Vancouver, June 2000.

Mayes, David. "The New Zealand 'Experiment': Using Economic Theory to Drive Policy." *Policy Options*, 18, 7 (September 1997), 34–6.

National Competition Council. *Review of the Australian Postal Corporation Act, Final Report.* Volume 1. Melbourne: 1998.

National Economic Research Associates (NERA). "Overseas Postal Reform." Final Report, prepared for the National Competition Council. London: October 1997.

Nerep, Erik. "Current Competition Law Issues in regard to the De-(re-)regulation of the Swedish Postal Services Market – Especially the Problems of Defining the Relevant Market, and Establishing Price Discrimination and Predatory Pricing." Stockholm School of Economics: October 1996.

Normo, Elina, and Timo E. Toivonen. "Opening up of the postal market to more competition." Ministry of Transport and Communications, 29 March 1996.

OECD, Working Party No. 2 on Competition and Regulation. *Promoting Competition in Postal Services: Background Notes by the Secretariat.* Paris: 27 January 1999.

OECD, Directorate for Financial, Fiscal and Enterprise Affairs, Committee on Competition Law and Policy, Working Party No. 2 on Competition and Regulation. "Promoting Competition in Postal Services: Finland." Paris: February 1999.

– "Promoting Competition in Postal Services – Sweden." Paris: February 1999.

Overdijk, Paul. "Postal Services: Competition in the Netherlands." Paper delivered to the Conference on Postal and Delivery Economics, Monterey, California, May 1996.

Pollitt, Christopher, and Stephen Haney. *Public Management Reforms: Three Anglo-Finnish Case Studies.* Helsinki: Ministry of Finance 1997.

Pollitt, Christopher, Stephen Hanney, Tim Packwood, Sandra Rothwell, and Simon Roberts. *Trajectories and Options: An International Perspective on the Implementation of Finnish Management Reforms.* Helsinki: Ministry of Finance 1997.

Post and Telestyrelsen (PTS). "The Deregulated Swedish Postal Market." Stockholm: February 1999.

Prasser, Scott and Graeme Starr. *Policy and Change: The Howard Mandate.* Sydney: Hale and Iremonger 1997.

Prévot, Hubert. "L'avenir du service public de la poste et des télécommunications." Study prepared for Paul Quiles, minister of posts, telecommunications and space, 31 July 1989.

Price Waterhouse. "A Strategic Review of Progressive Postal Administrations." February 1995 and February 1996 update.

PriceWaterhouse Coopers UK. "Postal Market Review," July 1998.

Ranganathan, K. *Redirecting Mail.* Washington, D.C.: Private Sector Development Department, World Bank 1996.

Roy, Bernard, David Storer, and Joelle Toledano. "Economic Costs in Postal Sector – from Theory to Practice." Paper presented to the Conference on Postal and Delivery Economics, Vancouver, June 2000.

Schwarz-Schilling, Cara. "Regulation of Postal Markets in Germany: Main Issues." Paper delivered at the Conference on Postal and Delivery Economics, Vancouver, June 2000.

Selander, Sten. "Postal Liberalization." IEA Conference on the Future of European Postal Services, 10 March 1999, 2–3.

Smith, Vivienne. *Reining in the Dinosaur: Behind the Remarkable Turnaround of New Zealand Post.* Wellington, NZ: New Zealand Post 1997.

Spicer, Barry, et al. *Transforming Government Enterprises.* Auckland, NZ: Centre for Independent Studies, Policy Monograph 35, 1996.

Stewart-Patterson, David. *Post-mortem: Why Canada's Mail Won't Move.* Toronto: Macmillan 1987.

Toime, Elmar. "Unlocking the Potential: The Future of the Post." Universal Postal Union Strategy Conference, Geneva, 13–14 October 1997.

Universal Postal Union. *The UPU Looks to the Future: Seoul Postal Strategy,* 1994, and *Geneva Strategy Conference,* Geneva 1997.

– *125 Years 1874–1999.* London and Berne: ISCL [International Systems and Communications Ltd] and UPU 1999.

van Doorn, Raymond. "Postal Services: Competition in the Netherlands." Paper presented to the Conference on Postal and Delivery Economics, 24 June 1999, Sintra, Portugal.

Veschetti Holmgren, Desiree. "Postal Services in Sweden." Stockholm: Ministry of Transport and Communications February 1997.

Walsh, Tim. "Globalization and Implications for Governance." Paper presented to the Conference on Postal and Delivery Economics, Sintra, Portugal, June 1999.

White, Julie. *Mail and Female: Women and the Canadian Union of Postal Workers.* Toronto: Thompson Educational Publishing 1990.

Zillen, Torsten. "Sweden Post – Public Operator on [sic] a Deregulated Market." Paper delivered at the Euroforum Conference on the Liberalization of the European Postal Services, Amsterdam, 8 December 1994.

Index